The Penguin Dictionary of

JUDAISM

Nicholas de Lange

PENGUIN BOOKS

PENGUIN BOOKS

Published by the Penguin Group
Penguin Books Ltd, 80 Strand, London WC2R 0RL, England
Penguin Group (USA) Inc., 375 Hudson Street, New York, New York 10014, USA
Penguin Group (Canada), 90 Eglinton Avenue East, Suite 700, Toronto, Ontario, Canada M4P 2Y3
(a division of Pearson Penguin Canada Inc.)
Penguin Ireland, 25 St Stephen's Green, Dublin 2, Ireland (a division of Penguin Books Ltd)
Penguin Group (Australia), 250 Camberwell Road, Camberwell, Victoria 3124, Australia
(a division of Pearson Australia Group Pty Ltd)
Penguin Books India Pvt Ltd, 11 Community Centre, Panchsheel Park, New Delhi – 110 017, India
Penguin Group (NZ), 67 Apollo Drive, Rosedale, North Shore 0632, New Zealand
(a division of Pearson New Zealand Ltd)
Penguin Books (South Africa) (Pty) Ltd, 24 Sturdee Avenue, Rosebank, Johannesburg 2196, South Africa

Penguin Books Ltd, Registered Offices: 80 Strand, London WC2R 0RL, England

www.penguin.com

First published 2008
1

Copyright © Nicholas de Lange, 2008
All rights reserved

The moral right of the author has been asserted

Set in ITC Stone Sans and ITC Stone Serif
Typeset by Data Standards Ltd, Frome, Somerset
Printed in England by Clays Ltd, St Ives plc

Except in the United States of America, this book is sold subject
to the condition that it shall not, by way of trade or otherwise, be lent,
re-sold, hired out, or otherwise circulated without the publisher's
prior consent in any form of binding or cover other than that in
which it is published and without a similar condition including this
condition being imposed on the subsequent purchaser

ISBN: 978-0-141-01847-8

www.greenpenguin.co.uk

Penguin Books is committed to a sustainable future
for our business, our readers and our planet.
The book in your hands is made from paper
certified by the Forest Stewardship Council.

To YHD
Yedid nafshi

Contents

List of Tables

List of Maps

Preface

In the course of the 20th century Judaism gradually became an English-speaking religion. More than half the Jews in the world today speak English as their mother tongue or use it in their everyday lives, and English is the language in which most books on the Jewish religion are published. (Before 1914 it was German, together with its offshoot Yiddish, that occupied this role.) But understanding what is said or written, by Jews and non-Jews, about Judaism in English is not always plain sailing, partly because there is a lot of technical terminology, such as one finds in any religion, and partly because foreign languages keep getting in the way – not just ancient languages like Hebrew and Aramaic, which are still used everywhere in Jewish worship, but a bewildering mass of modern languages, since many Jews are immigrants who remain attached to long-familiar expressions. And even quite ordinary English words are sometimes used in Jewish contexts in a sense that may not be obvious to an outsider.

My aim in this book is to provide a handy guide to the distinctive vocabulary of Judaism, for specialists, students and general readers. In preparing it I have read a large number of books, keeping a close eye on the technical terms and special usages. I have also tried to answer many of the questions I have been asked in the course of a long career spent teaching about Judaism.

The main focus of the dictionary is on the beliefs and practices of Judaism, and closely related topics. Some topics from general history and religious studies have been included (e.g. Aristotelianism, Enlightenment, Zionism), but I have addressed only the aspects of these that are directly relevant to Judaism. I did not feel it appropriate here to address such subjects as the Crusades, the Spanish Inquisition or antisemitism, the Dead Sea Scrolls, Apocrypha and Pseudepigrapha, or Christian and Muslim attitudes to Judaism, even though they are sometimes considered to belong to the story of Judaism. Once one starts straying further afield it is hard to know where to draw the line, and I wanted this book above all to have the coherence that results from clearly drawn boundaries. I have not sought to usurp the task of the many dictionaries of the Bible. There is no denying the importance of the Bible in Judaism, and I have tried to give the kind of information about biblical books and characters that students of contemporary Judaism are likely to need. As a general rule, I have directed the beam of my searchlight primarily at Judaism as it exists today: earlier layers are introduced as background, and I have tried to eschew mere antiquarianism.

I have generally tried to keep the entries short and factual, particularly where straightforward technical expressions are concerned. I did not hesitate, though, to add more information where I thought it would assist understanding. For example, in glossing words such as 'minyan' or 'Passover', I have provided both a brief definition and what I hope is useful information that may help a puzzled reader to understand the context in which the word is used in a book or article. I have also made free use of cross-referencing, to avoid unnecessary repetition and also to provide a gateway into those paper-chases that make dictionaries such fun to use. In some cases, where the subject-matter seemed to justify it, I have given myself more freedom, and provided survey essays on specific topics. These are mainly large subjects that I did not feel I could do justice to in a few words, and that are essential for a fuller understanding of the history or the teachings of Judaism. Most are subjects that I do not feel are adequately covered in other reference books about Judaism. I have also inserted some short essays on subjects as varied as books, honey and humility on which I felt readers might find a Jewish perspective interesting.

There are many different Jewish communities, and each has its own words and phrases. I have tried to be inclusive, and I have not assumed that one form of Judaism is the norm and the rest are aberrations. I apologize in advance for any omissions or misrepresentations.

Spelling is always a problem when transliterating from languages that use a non-Roman alphabet. The scholarly systems of Hebrew transcription often yield forms that are far removed from those actually in current use. Instead I have aimed to follow as closely as possible the forms I found in my reading, and the usual pronunciation of the words. More information about this can be found in the Introduction.

Translations are my own unless otherwise indicated.

In writing any book one inevitably runs up debts of gratitude. I cannot thank by name all those who have helped me with specific enquiries: they know who they are and that I am grateful to them. Andrew Berns, of the University of Pennsylvania, generously read through a draft of the entire alphabetical section and made invaluable comments and corrections. Eva Maria Lassen, of the Danish Institute for Human Rights, kindly drafted an article on human rights which forms the basis of the present entry. The original suggestion of compiling such a dictionary was put to me by Nigel Wilcockson in the autumn of 2002: I hope he is pleased with the outcome of his initiative. I must also thank all those at Penguin Press who have had a hand in the book, particularly Kristen Harrison, as well as an anonymous reader who made some very helpful suggestions.

Last but not least I am grateful to my parents, for instilling in me an enduring love for Judaism, and to my children, for asking challenging questions.

Nicholas de Lange
Cambridge
September 2007

How to use this book

The dictionary has been planned to be simple and straightforward to use, but there are some ground rules that will make your visit more enjoyable and fruitful.

What you can expect to find in this dictionary

This is a dictionary of the Jewish religion, as it is practised around the world today. The topics covered include issues of identity and different groupings of Jews, Jewish community life and its institutions, the synagogue and its furniture, prayers and blessings, and practices in the home.

We cannot fully understand the present without knowing something about the past, and so there are brief entries about the great teachers and thinkers whose work continues to influence contemporary Judaism, and longer entries about some of the important intellectual movements that guided them. Some outstanding later personalities are also listed, but living people have been excluded.

Types of entry

There are four main types of entry, depending on the nature of the subject.

In most cases, particularly in the case of technical terms, I have limited myself to giving a definition, plus an indication of the word's origin and any further information that is necessary for understanding its use. In the case of persons I have given the dates of birth and death (where known) and a very brief account of their life and works.

Sometimes, however, what was needed seemed to be not so much to define an unfamiliar term as to explain how the Jewish religion works in practice. For example the observance of the major festivals is described in some detail, and the same is true of other basic rites such as marriage or mourning. Characteristic beliefs such as covenant, exile and return, or rewards and punishments, are also dealt with in this way. And I have included short articles on everyday things such as bread, candles and hair, which, while not at all remarkable in themselves, constitute matters of concern within Judaism.

I have included some headwords that are not in themselves unfamiliar, or even obviously distinctively Jewish, but which I thought worth exploring briefly from a

Jewish point of view. Many of these are –isms (Aristotelianism, atheism, dualism, feminism), but there are also topics of general concern, such as art, ecology, homosexuality and human rights. In each case the entries were selected not because I imagined readers wondering what the word meant but rather wondering how Judaism has dealt with the issues raised.

Some particularly large or complex issues are treated at greater length in the form of longer survey essays. These are intended to give greater depth and coherence to the dictionary, and to anchor the shorter entries by offering detailed information, historical surveys and general discussions. It is my hope that they will be read as essays in their own right, and not just quarried for information. A list of these entries can be found on page xiv.

Cross-references and signposts

Some entries consist simply of a cross-reference (that is *See* followed by another headword). This is partly because of variations in spelling (see below) and partly because there are often different ways of referring to the same thing, for example by a Hebrew or English name. Cross-references may also appear in the course of an entry, or at the end. The purpose of these is to point to places where you will find more information about this or a related topic, or to suggest further lines of enquiry. All cross-references are in SMALL CAPITALS.

Spelling

There is no 'standard' way of transcribing the Hebrew alphabet into English. The system I have adopted in this book is intended to be simple and straightforward, close to the forms you are most likely to come across in your reading, and the most helpful in saying the words correctly aloud. (What it will not let you do is transcribe the words back into the original alphabet; those who know the foreign language should, however, have no trouble in doing this.) I know that I have not been entirely consistent, mainly because I have tried to respect some conventional spellings. In particular, biblical names and place names, as well as some common terms like Torah, Mishnah and Shavuot, have been spelt in the way they usually appear in English books, not according to the rules given below.

The basic rules are as follows:

Letters and combinations of letters generally have the same sound as in English, but note that ch is always pronounced as in loch or Bach.
The apostrophe (') is inserted between vowels to show they are to be pronounced separately, not run together.
The stress is indicated by an accent if it *cannot* fall on the last syllable of the word.
An accent on the last syllable means that the stress *must* fall on this syllable. In other cases it is acceptable to stress *either* the last-but-one *or* the last syllable.
In Yiddish words, the letter combination ei is pronounced as in eiderdown.

List of Survey Essays

BCE

Rule of King David, c. 1010–970
Building of the Temple in Jerusalem, 10th century
Babylonian exile begins, 597
Destruction of Jerusalem Temple by Nebuchadnezzar, 586
Cyrus of Persia captures Babylon, 539
Cyrus allows exiles to return to Jerusalem, 538
Rebuilding of the Temple, c. 520
Alexander of Macedon conquers the Persian empire, 331
Temple desecrated by Seleucids, 167
Hasmonean revolt, 166
Death of Judah the Maccabee, 161
Roman conquest of Jerusalem by Pompey, 63

CE

Hillel (late 1st century BCE–early 1st century CE)
Shammai (late 1st century BCE–early 1st century CE)
Philo of Alexandria (d. after 40)
Josephus (c. 38–c. 100)
Jewish revolt against Roman rule in Judaea, 66
Destruction of the Temple by the Romans, 70
Fall of Massada, 73
Yochanan ben Zakkai (1st century)
Bar Kochba revolt, 132–5
Akiba (d. 135)
Simeon bar Yochai (late 1st–early 2nd century)
Mishnah completed, c. 220
Judah the Nasi (d. c. 229)
Rav (3rd century)
Palestinian Talmud completed, 5th century
Babylonian Talmud completed, 6th–7th century
Conquest of the Middle East and North Africa by Arabs, 7th century

Muslim conquest of Spain, 8th century
Anan ben David (8th century)
Yehuda'i Ga'on (8th century)
Rise of Karaism, 9th century
Benjamin Nahawendi (9th century)
Daniel al-Kumisi (fl. c. 900)
David Mukammis (9th–10th century)
Sa'adya Ga'on (Sa'adya ben Joseph) (882–942)
Ya'akub al-Kirkisani (fl. c. 930)
Masoretic text of Bible completed, 10th century
Yefet ben Eli (late 10th century)
Rabbenu Gershom (c. 960–1028)
Isaac Alfasi (1013–1103)
Solomon Ibn Gabirol (1021/1022–c. 1070)
Bachya Ibn Pakuda (late 11th century)
Rashi (Rabbi Solomon Yitschaki) (1040–1105)
Moses Ibn Ezra (c. 1055–after 1138)
Judah ha-Levi (c. 1075–c. 1141)
Abraham Ibn Ezra (c. 1090–1164/1167)
Crusaders capture Jerusalem, 1099
Abraham Ibn Daud (c. 1110–80)
Abraham bar Chiyya (12th century)
Judah Ibn Tibbon (12th century)
Judah Hadassi (12th century)
Moses Maimonides (d. 1204)
Samuel Ibn Tibbon (c. 1150–1230)
David Kimchi (c. 1160–1235)
Judah the Chasid (d. 1217)
Eleazar of Worms (c. 1165–1230)
Moses Nachmanides (1194–1270)
Meir of Rothenburg (d. 1293)
Menachem Meiri (1249–c. 1316)
Asher ben Yechiel (c. 1250–1327)
Abraham Abulafia (13th century)
Zohar (late 13th century)
Isaac Ibn Sahula (late 13th century)
Jacob ben Asher (c. 1270–1340)
Gersonides (1288–1344)
Expulsion of Jews from England, 1290
Chasdai Crescas (c. 1340–1410/1412)
Joseph Albo (c. 1380–1444)
Attacks on Jews in Spain, 1391
Tortosa Disputation, 1413–14
- Elijah Bashyachi (c. 1420–90)
Isaac Abravanel (1437–1508)

Obadia Yare di Bertinoro (c. 1450–1509)
Expulsion of Jews from Spain, 1492
Obadiah Sforno (c. 1475–1550)
Joseph Caro (1488–1575)
Forced baptism of Jews in Portugal, 1497
Moses Isserles (c. 1525–72)
Solomon Molcho (d. 1532)
Isaac Luria, the 'Holy Lion' (1534–72)
Maharal of Prague (d. 1609)
Chayyim Vital (1542–1620)
Yom Tov Lipmann Heller (1579–1654)
Manasseh Ben Israel (1604–57)
Baruch Spinoza (1632–77)
Shabbetai Tseví proclaims himself Messiah, 1665
Chayyim Ibn Attar (1696–1743)
Baal Shem Tov (c. 1700–60)
Moses Chayyim Luzzatto (1707–47)
Ezekiel Landau (1713–93)
Vilna Ga'on (1720–97)
Dov Ber of Mezhirich (d. 1772)
Rise of Polish Chasidism, late 18th century
Jacob Frank (1726–91)
Moses Mendelssohn (1729–86)
Levi Yitzhak of Berdichev (d. 1810)
Shneur Zalman of Lyady (1745–1813)
Chayyim of Volozhin (1749–1821)
Moses Sofer (1762–1839)
First partition of Poland, 1772
Nachman of Bratslav (1772–1810)
Mendelssohn's *Jerusalem* published, 1783
Nachman Krochmal (1785–1840)
Salomon Ludwig Steinheim (1789–1866)
French Revolution: emancipation of Jews in France, 1789
Solomon Judah Rapoport (1790–1867)
Leopold Zunz (1794–1886)
Zvi Hirsch Kalischer (1795–1874)
Samuel David Luzzatto (1800–65)
Zacharias Frankel (1801–75)
Solomon Ganzfried (1804–86)
Samuel Holdheim (1806–60)
Great Sanhedrin in Paris, 1807
Samson Raphael Hirsch (1808–88)
Salomon Formstecher (1808–89)
Abraham Geiger (1810–74)
Israel Salanter (1810–83)

Moses Hess (1812–75)
Samuel Hirsch (1815–89)
First Reform congregation founded in Germany, 1817
Verein für Kultur und Wissenschaft der Juden founded, 1819
Isaac Mayer Wise (1819–1900)
Ezriel Hildesheimer (1820–99)
Collegio Rabbinico Italiano founded, 1821
Elia Benamozegh (1822–1900)
Moritz Lazarus (1824–1903)
First Reform congregation founded in USA, 1825
Yosef Chayyim (1832–1909)
Chafets Chayyim (Israel Meir Kagan) (1838–1933)
First Reform congregation founded in England, 1840
Hermann Cohen (1842–1918)
David Zvi Hoffmann (1843–1921)
Kaufmann Kohler (1843–1926)
Brunswick rabbinic conference, 1844
Frankfurt rabbinic conference, 1845
Breslau rabbinic conference, 1846
Solomon Schechter (1847–1915)
Yichya Kafach (1850–1932)
Monatsschrift für Geschichte und Wissenschaft des Judenthums founded, 1851
Emil Gustav Hirsch (1851–1923)
Breslau Rabbinical Seminary founded, 1854
Achad Ha-am (Asher Ginsberg) (1856–1927)
Alliance Israélite Universelle founded, 1860
Theodor Herzl (1860–1904)
Simon Dubnow (1860–1941)
Abraham Isaac Kook (1865–1935)
Emancipation of Jews in Austria-Hungary, 1868
United Synagogue established in London, 1870
Union for Reform Judaism founded, 1873
Leo Baeck (1873–1956)
Hebrew Union College founded, 1875
Martin Buber (1878–1965)
Chazon Ish (Abraham Isaiah Karelitz) (1878–1953)
Rise of political antisemitism, 1880s
First pogroms in Russia, 1881
Great migration, 1881–1914
Mordecai M. Kaplan (1881–1983)
Pittsburgh Platform, 1885
Ernst Bloch (1885–1977)
Jewish Theological Seminary of America founded, 1886
Yeshiva University founded, 1886
Franz Rosenzweig (1886–1929)

Moshe Feinstein (1895–1986)
First Zionist Congress, Basle, 1897
Ignaz Maybaum (1897–1976)
Gershom (Gerhard) Scholem (1897–1982)
Union of Orthodox Jewish Congregations of America created, 1898
Central Conference of American Rabbis founded, 1889
Mizrachi organization established, 1902
First Liberal congregation founded in England, 1902
Menachem Mendel Schneerson (1902–94)
Milton Steinberg (1903–50)
Joseph Dov Soloveitchik (1903–93)
Hans Jonas (1903–93)
Yeshayahu Leibowitz (1903–94)
Emmanuel Levinas (1905/6–95)
Hannah Arendt (1906–75)
First Liberal congregation founded in France, 1907
Abraham Joshua Heschel (1907–72)
Eliezer Berkovits (1908–92)
United Synagogue of America founded, 1913
Emil Fackenheim (1916–2003)
Russian Revolution: emancipation of Jews in Russia, 1917
Balfour Declaration, 1917
Louis Jacobs (1920–2006)
Jewish Institute of Religion founded, 1922
British Mandate for Palestine begins, 1923
World Union for Progressive Judaism founded, 1926
Arthur A. Cohen (1928–86)
First Liberal congregation founded in Netherlands, 1931
Nazi persecution of Jews, 1935–45
World Jewish Congress established, 1936
Columbus Platform, 1937
End of Mandate: State of Israel declared, 1948
Six-Day War, 1967
Reconstructionist Rabbinical College founded, 1968
Yom Kippur War, 1973
Centenary Perspective, 1976
International Federation of Secular Humanistic Jews founded, 1985
Union for Traditional Judaism founded, 1990
Miami Platform issued, 1997
Pittsburgh Statement issued, 1999
Dabru Emet issued, 2000

THE PENGUIN
DICTIONARY OF
JUDAISM

Aaron (Aharon) In the Bible, the brother of Moses and Miriam, consecrated as the first priest (kohen), and thought of as the ancestor of all priests. In rabbinic teaching, a type of the peace-maker: 'Hillel said: Be a disciple of Aaron, loving peace, pursuing peace, loving humankind and bringing them to the Torah' (Mishnah, Avot 1.12).

ablution *See* BATHING; MIKVE; WASHING.

abortion Killing of a foetus. The Bible does not forbid abortion, and the Mishnah explicitly prescribes it in certain circumstances: 'If a woman has a difficult labour, the foetus must be cut up in the womb and brought out limb by limb, since the life of the mother takes precedence over that of the child; once the greater part of the child has emerged, however, it may not be touched, since the claim of one life cannot override that of another' (Oholot 7.6). Such legal sources, while tending to license abortion in cases where the mother's health is endangered, do not provide much basis for engagement in modern debates about non-therapeutic abortion, and a wide range of rabbinic views can be found today, some relatively permissive and others very restrictive. All authorities would agree, however, that foeticide is not to be undertaken lightly, and would rule it out as a method of family planning.

Abraham (Avraham) First of the three biblical PATRIARCHS, commonly referred to in rabbinic writings with the epithet 'our father' (avínu). The salient details of Abraham's life are presented in Genesis chapters 11 to 25. According to the biblical story he was originally called Avram, but his name was changed by God to Avraham, 'for I have made you a father of many nations' (av-hamon-goyim) (Genesis 17.5). This refers to the promise that Abraham would become the ancestor of a vast progeny, who would bring blessing to the other nations and inherit the land of Canaan for ever. (The true etymology of the name is unknown.) Abraham is represented as a seminomadic tent-dweller, a kind of prosperous and powerful bedouin sheikh, pitching his tents mainly in the hill-country of Palestine and the Negev (in what is now southern Israel), although his origin is in Ur of the Chaldeans (in modern Iraq). Abraham is 100 years old when ISAAC is born, the only son of his wife Sarah, who is 90 at the time. Abraham enjoys a special relationship with God, but one day God orders him to sacrifice his son Isaac, as a test of the relationship (Genesis 22, *see* AKEDA). Abraham passes the test, and is promised again that his descendants will be numerous and a blessing to all the nations of the world. He dies at the age of 175 and is buried in a double cave named Machpela at HEBRON. Later tradition makes Abraham the first worshipper of a single, incorporeal god (he is described in the Midrash as smashing the idols manufactured by his father, Terah), and a model of trust in God (see FAITH). Philo explains his name as 'chosen father of sound', and makes him the first philosopher and a type of the virtuous man. 'A good (i.e. generous) eye, a humble spirit and a lowly soul' are the marks of a disciple of Abraham, according to the Mishnah (Avot 5.19). As the first and greatest of the patriarchs, who is said to have brought many to a knowledge and love of God, he is the father of all proselytes, and they carry his name instead of that of their natural father. This underlines that the fatherhood of Abraham is not considered a matter of genetic descent.

Abraham is also considered the father of the Arabs, through his elder son Ishmael, and the supposed family tomb of Abraham in Hebron is a sacred shrine for Jews and Muslims. Abraham occupies an outstanding position as one of the founding figures of Judaism (although it is hard to consider him as a Jew himself), and as a man so intimate with God that some have considered him a prophet. For Maimonides, he achieved the highest degree of prophecy after Moses. He is also of powerful symbolic value today because of his significance for Christians and Muslims, who both look to him as a kind of early founder, so that it is possible to refer to Judaism, Christianity and Islam as the 'Abrahamic faiths'. No one else in the Bible bears his name, but since the Middle Ages it has been very popular as a name among Jews.

See also COVENANT; ISHMAEL; MAGEN AVRAHAM; PROSELYTES.

Abraham bar Chiyya (12th century) Philosopher. His best-known work is the ethical treatise *The Meditation of the Sad Soul*. He also wrote books of mathematics and astronomy, and an influential eschatological work, *The Scroll of the Revealer*, in which he predicted the coming of the Messiah between 1136 and 1448. Abraham, who lived in Christian Spain, was the first philosopher to write in Hebrew (other medieval Jewish philosophers wrote in Arabic), and he may be considered a pioneer of Hebrew literature as it developed later. He was an original thinker who achieved a creative synthesis of NEOPLATONIST, ARISTOTELIAN and RABBINIC ideas.

Abravanel, Isaac (1437–1508) Statesman, philosopher and biblical commentator. Abravanel lived in a time of great upheavals, some of which touched his life personally. Born in Lisbon, he was 16 when Constantinople fell to the Ottomans; he succeeded his father as treasurer to King Alfonso V of Portugal, and used his high position at Court on several occasions to intervene on behalf of the local Jews when they were attacked or threatened with repressive measures. In 1483, fleeing court intrigues under Alfonso's successor João II, he moved to Toledo, where he entered the service of the Spanish king, but was unable to prevent the decree of expulsion of 1492, of which he was one of the most distinguished victims. He subsequently served the king of Naples, but was exiled again when Naples fell to the French in 1494. He died in Venice and was buried in Padua. He was a prolific author, penning commentaries not only on the biblical books but on the Mishnah tractate Avot, the Passover Haggada and Maimonides' *Guide*, as well as philosophical and apologetic works. In all of these he reveals his considerable learning, not only in the Jewish sources but in wider literature as well. His experience of public life and the upheavals his own life underwent occasionally mark his biblical commentaries, which are rich in reflection on social and political matters; his measured rationalism and the breadth of his learning help to account for the respect in which he was held by Christian as well as Jewish readers.

Abulafia, Abraham (13th century) An original (not to say eccentric) mystic, whose main contribution was a theory that illumination could be achieved through the contemplation of the various combinations of the letters of the Hebrew alphabet. He went to Rome to convert the Pope to Judaism, and narrowly escaped being burnt at the stake.

Achad Ha-am ('one of the people', pen-name of Asher Ginsberg, 1856–1927) Hebrew essayist and a founder of the Zionist movement. Achad Ha-am became involved in the Hebrew enlightenment (*see* HASKALA) and the fledgling Zionist movement (*see* CHIBBAT ZION) in Odessa. He moved to London in 1907 and settled in Palestine in 1922. He never held any official position in the Zionist movement but had an enormous influence in it through his writings (particularly his pithy essays). He opposed the 'political' Zionism associated with HERZL in the name of a cultural Zionism that called for a moral and cultural regeneration of the Jewish people. As an adherent of Haskala he dismissed traditional Judaism as obsolete, but he insisted that a secular modern Jewish culture must be based on the best of Jewish values from the past. The aim of Zionism should be to establish a 'Jewish state', not just a 'state of Jews' (the original title of Herzl's famous pamphlet), and this should serve as a cultural powerhouse for the many Jews who would inevitably remain in the Diaspora.

acharonim ('later [authorities]') Term applied in halachic discussion to more recent authorities, as opposed to RISHONIM (earlier authorities). The dating of the acharonim is not fixed. The term was first used by Ashkenazim in the early 15th century to refer to scholars of the previous century. Nowadays it is applied loosely to halachists since the compilation of the SHULCHAN ARUCH (late 16th century). Generally, the rishonim are invested with greater authority than the acharonim; however, *see* Moses ISSERLES.

acronym Word made up of the initial letters of a name or phrase. Many of the great Jewish rabbis and scholars of the past are commonly known by acronyms, e.g. MAHARAL, Radak (David KIMCHI), Ralbag (GERSONIDES), Rambam (MAIMONIDES), Ramban (NACHMANIDES), RASHI, Rosh (ASHER BEN YECHIEL). Other common acronyms include Shas (Shisha sidrei mishna, 'six orders of the Mishnah', for the Talmud) and Tanach (Torah, Nevi'im, Ketuvim, for the Bible).

acrostic Text, often a poem, arranged so that the initial letters of the lines or other key letters follow alphabetical order or spell out a message. Alphabetical acrostics are found in the Bible (e.g. Psalms 111, 112, 119, 145, Lamentations 1–4). The device was an essential element in the poetics of medieval Hebrew verse: alphabetical acrostics, sometimes of great complexity, are common in liturgical poems, and poets often signed their names by incorporating them as acrostics in their verses. *See also* ÉSHET CHÁYIL.

Adam and Eve (Adam ve-Chava) The first human couple, according to the Bible. The narrative in Genesis 2 portrays Adam as being created directly by God, whereas Eve is derived from Adam and described as his helper. Successive generations of Jews, consciously or not, have been influenced by this androcentric model of the sexes. According to Genesis 1.26 and 5.2, however, God created Adam both male and female. In Hebrew, from the Bible on, human beings are termed 'sons of Adam'. The name Adam evokes the earth or clay (adamá) from which he was supposedly formed, while that of Eve evokes life; she is called 'the mother of all living' in Genesis 3.20.

Adam Kadmon ('primordial man') Term used in kabbala to conjure an image of the divine macrocosm of the SEFIROT in quasi-human form. In the LURIANIC KABBALA Adam Kadmon represents an intermediate stage in the unfolding of the Godhead, between the unknowable EIN SOF and the Sefirot, which come into being as divine light bursts from its eyes, ears, nose and mouth.

Adar Sixth month of the year counting from New Year; twelfth counting from Passover. The celebration of Purim falls on the 14th, and imparts a joyful flavour to the whole month. As the Talmud says, 'When Adar arrives, joy increases'. In leap years a second month of Adar is intercalated, as according to the Bible this is the end of the year (*see* NISAN).

Adath Yisroel or **Adass Jisroel** ('congregation of Israel') Hebrew phrase chosen as a name by separatist German Orthodox congregations (*see* AUSTRITTSGEMEINDE), following the lead of S. R. HIRSCH in Frankfurt (1851). Later similar congregations were established outside Germany. Some, like Hirsch himself, preferred the title Adath (or Adass) Jeschurun (*see* YESHURUN for the origin of the name), a title originally adopted (rather confusingly) by a strongly modernist and universalist secessionist community in French-ruled Amsterdam in 1797.

Admor Title adopted by Hasidic rabbis. It is an abbreviation of the Hebrew phrase Adonenu Morenu ve-Rabbenu, 'Our Lord, Teacher and Master'.

Adon Olam ('Eternal Lord' or 'Lord of the Universe') Hymn, so named from its opening words: 'Lord of the universe, who reigned/ Ere earth and heaven's fashioning,/ When to create the world he deigned,/ Then was his name proclaimed king.' Of unknown authorship, it is one of the most popular of the synagogue hymns, and is generally sung at the end of the musaf (additional) service. Its closing words make it appropriate also for private devotion before falling asleep or on the deathbed: 'My soul into his hand divine/ Do I commend: I will not fear./ My body with it I resign,/ I dread no evil: God is near.'

Adonai Name of God. The Hebrew word adon means 'lord' or 'master', and is often applied to God, particularly in prayers and poems. It occurs a few times in the Bible. Adonai literally means 'my lords', but when used as a divine name it always has a singular verb. It is the most usual way to name God in Hebrew, and is the way that the Tetragrammaton (INEFFABLE NAME) in the Bible is read aloud. The rabbis considered that this name represented God's attribute of mercy, as against Elohim, which represented his attribute of strict justice. For the kabbalists it corresponds to the sefira Malchut (*see* SEFIROT).

adultery Sexual relations between a married woman and a man who is not her husband. Such relations are strictly forbidden in the Bible, which lays down the death penalty for both parties (Leviticus 20.10). The prohibition is the seventh of the TEN COMMANDMENTS. The wife's adultery is grounds for divorce; in such a case the woman is forbidden to marry her partner in adultery, nor, if she has been married to someone else in the meantime, may she remarry her original husband. No particular penalty attaches in law to relations between a married man and an unmarried woman, but the HALACHA now considers this an example of loose living that can allow the court to compel him to grant his wife a divorce. Special rituals surrounded the treatment of a wife suspected of adultery in the Bible and the Mishnah; these are no longer practised (*see* SOTA).

afikoman Name given to a half of the middle MATSA of three used in the Séder ritual at Passover. By tradition the officiant breaks the middle matsa in half at the beginning of the Séder, and one half becomes the afikoman, which is then hidden, perhaps as a way (among several others applied during the Séder) of arousing the curiosity of the children present. A custom has arisen for the children to hunt for it after the meal, and to refuse to hand it over until it has been 'ransomed' by a gift. It is then broken and distributed to all present, who eat it. (Some superstitious Jews keep it throughout the year as a protection against the evil eye.) The afikoman is considered to symbolize the sacrificial lamb of Passover, which in antiquity was the last food to be eaten at the festive meal; hence nothing is supposed to be eaten after it. Some authorities even forbid the drinking of anything except water, and the ritual glasses of wine. Various suggestions have been put forward about the origin of the term, none of them entirely convincing.

afterlife

Many different beliefs have been, and are, held by Jews on the subject of what, if anything, happens to the individual after death. The Bible is not very explicit on the subject, but some passages seem to envisage the personality of the individual somehow surviving in a shadowy existence in Sheol, the underworld. Elsewhere death brings cessation: 'The dead praise not the Lord, neither any that go down into silence' (Psalm 115.17). The idea that people are compounded of material bodies and immaterial souls probably entered Judaism under Greek influence, from the 2nd century BCE on, but found some warrant in the biblical account of the creation of Adam. The soul is created, attached to the body at birth, and separated from it at death, but according to one understanding will be reunited with it at the RESURRECTION. Hence the wording of a morning prayer: 'My God, the soul you have given me is pure; you created it, formed it and breathed it into me; you preserve it within me; and you will take it from me and restore it to me at a future time.' Resurrection was a belief of the Pharisees that was rejected by the Sadducees. It was embodied in the second benediction of the AMIDA, where God is described as keeping faith with those who sleep in the dust, and addressed by the title 'the Reviver of the Dead'. The idea of survival is commonly linked to that of REWARDS AND PUNISHMENTS. As the Mishnah puts it (Avot 4.22): 'Let not your [evil] tendency assure you that Sheol will be your place of refuge [from judgment], because just as whether you wish it or not you were formed and born, you live and you die, so whether you wish it or not you will hereafter be called to account before the Emperor of emperors, the Holy One, blessed be He.' Another related idea is that of the Coming Age or OLAM HA-BA. A view that reconciled various elements maintained that after death the soul is judged provisionally, and after a temporary stay in hell, to expiate sins, it goes to heaven, from where it will eventually be summoned to resurrection and final judgment. In the Middle Ages Maimonides complains that observant Jews in his day hold widely differing and totally confused ideas on the subject. He distinguishes five different groups. The first maintains that the good are rewarded in the Garden of Eden and the bad are punished in Gehinnom. The Garden of Eden is 'a place where people eat and drink without effort, where houses are built of precious stones and beds are spread with silk, where rivers flow with wine and aromatic oils, and so forth', while Gehinnom is 'a place of blazing fire, where bodies are burnt and people suffer various pains and torments which would take too long to describe'. The second group believes that the reward of the virtuous is to live to see the days of the Messiah, when 'ready-made clothes and ready-baked bread will spring from the earth, and suchlike impossibilities'. The third group believes that the virtuous will be rewarded by being brought back to life after their death, 'to rejoin their family, eat and drink, and never die again'. The fourth group maintains that the reward for virtue is 'physical peace and fulfilment of worldly desires in this world, such as good harvests, wealth, large families, physical health, peace, confidence, a sovereign Jewish king and dominion over our enemies'. The fifth group combines all these various beliefs, and looks forward to the coming of the Messiah and the resurrection of the dead who will enter the Garden of Eden and live for ever. Maimonides quite obviously has a low regard for all these opinions, which he ascribes in the main to an over-literal interpretation of the words of the Bible and the rabbis. He himself insists that the biblical and rabbinic teachings have to be understood figuratively, and that the ultimate reward, which he identifies with the Coming Age, is the purely spiritual reunion of the immortal soul with God, while the ultimate punishment for evil-doing is the annihilation of the soul. The resurrection of the dead Maimonides describes as a fundamental and essential principle of Judaism, but it will only apply to the righteous. The way to achieve the eternal life of the Coming Age is to observe all the commandments of the Torah out of perfect love and for no ulterior purpose. Since Maimonides' time belief in bodily resurrection has become even weaker, although the idea of an immortal soul has held its ground well. The American Reform PITTSBURGH PLATFORM declared in 1885: 'We reassert the doctrine of Judaism, that the soul of man is immortal, grounding this belief on the divine nature of the human spirit, which forever finds bliss in righteousness and misery in wickedness. We reject as ideas not rooted in Judaism the belief both in bodily resurrection and in Gehenna and Eden (hell and paradise), as abodes for everlasting punishment or reward.' Progressive liturgies tend to omit any mention of resurrection, sometimes replacing them by allusions to 'renewal' or 'eternal life'. *See also* GILGUL.

aggada Derived from a Hebrew root meaning 'to tell' or 'narrate', the term commonly refers to non-legal teachings derived from the Bible and embodied in the Talmud and the various Midrashic works. Aggada is naturally paired with its opposite, HALACHA. It embraces a huge range of subjects, including elaborations of the biblical narrative, ethical teachings, folklore and theology – anything, in fact, that does not result in a command or prohibition. There is a great deal of aggada in the Talmud, which was collected together in the early 16th century in Salonica by Jacob Ibn Chabib in his work EIN YA'AKOV; the richest rabbinic source of aggada, however, is in the various Midrashim, and in the medieval compilations derived from them. The word is etymologically identical to HAGGADA.

agnosticism Sceptical or open-minded stance concerning the existence of a deity. *See* ATHEISM.

Agudas Harabbonim *See* UNION OF ORTHODOX RABBIS OF THE UNITED STATES AND CANADA.

Agudat Israel or **Agúdas Yisróel** ('union of Israel', also known as the Aguda) World organization of traditionalist Ashkenazim united by their hostility to modernism, secularism, and particularly Zionism, Established in 1912 in Kattowitz (Katowice), the organization declared its aim as being: 'to solve in the spirit of Torah and the commandments the various everyday issues that will rise in the life of the people of Israel'. The ultimate and indisputable authorities on all affairs are Gedolei Hatora (Torah Sages). A 'Council of Torah Sages' supervises and guides the decisions of the movement, and through a new doctrine known as dá'as tóra ('Torah knowledge') the Sages are invested with almost unchallengeable authority to determine not only religious but political and even economic questions. Despite its principled opposition to Zionism, the Aguda has co-operated with the state of Israel since the latter's inception, standing for election to the Knesset (the Israeli parliament) and even participating in government coalitions. (Contrast NETÚREI KÁRTA.) This position represents a historic compromise between various very different groups making up the Aguda, which has remained a very unstable alliance.

Most of its non-Chasidic supporters seceded from the party before the 1988 elections to form a new CHAREDI party known as Dégel Hatora ('banner of Torah'). The immediate cause of the split was a controversy between MITNAGGEDIM and CHABAD CHASIDIM regarding the messianic claims advanced by the latter in favour of their venerated leader, Rabbi Menachem Mendel SCHNEERSON of Lubavitch. The two Ashkenazi charedi parties have tended to form a strategic alliance by the name of United Torah Judaism to contest Israeli elections.

aguna ('chained woman') In HALACHA, a woman who is tied by marriage to a husband whose death cannot be definitely certified or who refuses to grant her a GET (divorce document). Since there is traditionally no presumption of death and since a woman cannot initiate a divorce, such a woman is trapped in a predicament that is repugnant to modern ethical sensibilities, all the more so since it involves a blatant discrimination between the sexes (because in theory a man may have more than one wife). Various legal remedies have been proposed, including notably a prenuptial agreement committing the man to grant a get in the case of break-up of the marriage, or a conditional form of marriage. However these remedies have proved difficult to establish. Consequently, when all efforts fail, the Conservative movement will retrospectively annul the marriage. In the Reform movement a civil divorce is generally considered to dissolve the marriage. *See also* MAMZER.

akdamut (Aramaic, 'introduction') Liturgical poem recited in Ashkenazi synagogues at the beginning of the Torah reading at SHAVUOT. It speaks of the glory of God and the splendid destiny reserved for the oppressed people of Israel, and was composed in Aramaic by Meir ben Isaac of Worms in the 11th century.

akeda ('binding') The biblical account of Abraham's response to God's call to sacrifice his son Isaac on Mount MORIAH (Genesis 22). (The word is also a technical term for the binding of a sacrificial animal.) The episode is represented as a test or trial of Abraham and it ends with the divine recognition that Abraham is a God-fearer. The story has raised many problems for commentators down the ages, but it has also exerted a great power on the Jewish religious imagination. Abraham is a model of EMUNA, trust or faith in God (cf. Genesis 15.6). The presence in the story of a ram's horn (*see* SHOFAR) probably explains why the passage was selected as the scriptural reading for the second day of New Year, a time of penitence in preparation for the divine judgment; when the shofar is blown on the festival the following words are included in the prayers: 'Remember to us, Lord our God, the covenant, and the loving kindness, and the oath that you swore to Abraham our father on Mount Moriah; may the image of the binding of Isaac by Abraham our father upon the altar appear before you, and just as he overcame his compassion to do your will wholeheartedly, so let your compassion overcome your anger at us ...' Another prayer associated with the blowing of the shofar says: 'Gaze upon the ashes of Isaac our father heaped on the altar, and deal with your people Israel according to your attribute of mercy'. This reminds us of a tradition that Isaac really was killed and immolated by Abraham (he was supposedly resurrected, as he appears later in the biblical narrative). At times of persecution and massacres, particularly those committed in the Rhineland during the First and Second Crusades, the image of the akeda appears recurrently, evoking not only the steadfast faith of the father but also the idea of the martyrdom of the son, who is seen as willingly giving up his life in response to the divine command.

'Akeda' is also a technical term for a kind of PIYYUT (liturgical hymn) telling the story with poetic embellishments. This genre was pioneered in ASHKENAZ by Meir ben Isaac of Worms, a poet who died shortly before his wife and son, also Isaac, were killed in the Rhineland massacres of 1096; the most famous example is by Ephra'im of Bonn, a chronicler of the attacks during the Second Crusade: '[Abraham] hastened to pin [Isaac] down with his knees;/ he made strong his two arms;/ with a steady hand he slaughtered him as required;/ a complete sacrifice prepared.'

Akiba (d. 135) One of the leading TANNA'IM, who, according to rabbinic legend, was martyred in the Roman suppression of the revolt of BAR KOCHBA. Some 370 statements by him are preserved in the Talmudic literature, and he is said to have trained large numbers of students. He favoured a method of interpretation that sees every detail of the Torah, including apparently trivial repetitions, as significant; any repetition implies an additional teaching. Some of his teachings have a mystical flavour, and he is remembered as a champion of the sacred status of the SONG OF SONGS, which he understood as an allegory of the love relationship of God and Israel. He is also said to have supported the messianic claims of Bar Kochba. Historical research has been unable, however, to find any confirmation of the rabbinic legends about Rabbi Akiba.

Al Chet ('for the sin') Also known as the Great Confession, this alphabetical prayer, repeated several times during the KIPPUR services, enumerates a sequence of sins for which God's forgiveness is sought. Some modern liturgies have rewritten the prayer, introducing more 'relevant' contemporary sins. *See also* ASHÁMNU.

al-Fayyumi *See* SA'ADYA GA'ON.

al-Kirkisani, Ya'akub (fl. c. 930) Karaite scholar. He lived in Iraq, and reveals the influence of KALAM as well as other rationalist trends. His best-known work is *Kitab al-Anwar wa'l-Maraqib* (*The Book of Lights and Watchtowers*), a compendium of Karaite law containing excursuses on a number of non-legal subjects.

al-Kumisi, Daniel (fl. c. 900) Karaite scholar. Born in the Qumis district of northern Iran, near the Caspian Sea, he settled in Jerusalem around the year 880 and became a leader of the 'Mourners of Zion', a group that practised ASCETICISM and looked forward to the redemption. He established the main characteristics of Karaism: rejection of the Rabbanite belief in the oral Torah, promotion of immigration to the Land of Israel, and the practice of asceticism and mourning for Jerusalem and the Temple. He wrote a number of commentaries and other works, of which relatively little survives. His innovative biblical commentaries gave Karaite exegesis a voice of its own for the first time. An epistle or sermon attributed to him is the earliest work of KALAM in Hebrew; it is also the earliest Jewish attempt to formulate a set of dogmas or articles of faith.

al-Mukammas, Daud *See* MUKAMMIS, DAVID.

Albo, Joseph (c. 1380–1444) Philosopher. A pupil of Chasdai CRESCAS, Albo lived in Spain in the final century leading up to the expulsion or forcible baptism of the Jewish population. He was one of the leading participants in the Tortosa Disputation of 1413–14, the last of the great show disputations in which Catholic theologians attempted to demonstrate the truth of their faith against the claims of Judaism. It was during the disputation that he conceived the idea of setting out plainly the principles on which Jewish faith rests, and he did this in his *Séfer ha-Ikkarim* (*Book of*

Principles). Albo reduced the basic principles to just three (as against the thirteen of Maimonides: *see* THIRTEEN PRINCIPLES): the existence of God, the divine origin of Torah, and REWARDS AND PUNISHMENTS. He adds to these three eight other 'root beliefs', such as God's unity and incorporeality, though he considers these to be secondary beliefs. As for articles of faith such as creation from nothing, resurrection of the dead and the coming of a Messiah, these are relegated to the third and even lower category of 'branches': they are not essential, since Judaism can be conceived of without them. It has been suggested that in demoting the messianic hope in this way, as in other particulars of his system, Albo is reflecting the debate with Christianity, in which it is a central and indispensable belief. In a remarkable expression of tolerance and of freedom of thought, Albo declares that only someone who wilfully rejects a principle that he knows to be taught in the Torah can be considered an unbeliever; one who conscientiously upholds the Torah but is misled in his theological reasoning may still be considered a wise and pious man, although his error is a sin that requires ATONEMENT.

alcohol *See* DRUNKENNESS.

álef The first letter of the Hebrew alphabet. In Greece, an álef was a form of birth certificate placed over the bed of a woman who had just borne a son, and kept there until after the circumcision. It served as an amulet to protect the mother and her uncircumcised son, and was adorned with garlic to avert the evil eye.

ALEPH Alliance for Jewish Renewal. *See* RENEWAL.

Aléynu ('it is [incumbent] upon us') Prayer recited towards the end of all services, named for its opening words: 'It is incumbent upon us to praise the Lord of all, to proclaim the greatness of the Creator ...' The theme of this ancient prayer is firm loyalty to the worship of the God who made the world. In Ashkenazi congregations a second paragraph is added, which prays for the establishment of God's rule in the world (*see* KINGDOM OF GOD). The prayer offers an interesting example of self-censorship, relating to the description of the worship of other nations: 'for they prostrate themselves to vanity and emptiness, and pray to a god who cannot save them'. Deleted at first by Christian censors, these words were voluntarily omitted from printed Ashkenazi prayer books, on the grounds that they might cause offence and attract hostility. Progressive and, indeed, Orthodox prayer books in the Diaspora continue to omit them, as not being conducive to good community relations.

Alfasi, Isaac (1013–1103) Talmudic codifier. Also known as Rif (from his initials, Rabbi Isaac of Fez). Born in Algeria, he lived for a while in Fez, and later moved to Lucena in Spain. His influential work *Séfer ha-Halachot* (*Book of Laws*) is one of the earliest authoritative attempts to codify the Talmudic HALACHA. Following the layout of the Talmud and using its language, Alfasi eliminates discursive discussions and focuses on the actual laws. A witness of the end of the Babylonian ge'onim (*see* GA'ON), Alfasi presents a digest of their legal thought, while concentrating on the text of the Talmud, which by his time had fallen into a certain neglect. He was largely responsible for introducing Talmudic study into Spain, and for many of those who came after him it was his book, rather than the Talmud itself, that was studied.

aliyya ('ascent') In current parlance this term has two separate uses. **1** In synagogue, ascent to the reading of the TORAH. A fixed number of people (adult males in traditional and Orthodox synagogues; elsewhere men or women) are 'called up' by name, using their Hebrew patronymic (*see* NAMES AND NAMING). The Torah is normally read from a raised dais (*see* ALMÉMAR), hence they 'go up'. **2** Travel to the Land of Israel, nowadays usually for purposes of immigration. It has become customary in Zionist circles to speak of 'making aliyya'. The idea of 'ascent' is normally explained with reference to the sanctity of the Land.

When the TEMPLE in Jerusalem existed, 'aliyya la-régel' (ascent for the festival) referred to 'ascent' to Jerusalem on the occasion of the three pilgrim festivals (*see* PILGRIMAGE).

Alliance Israélite Universelle International organization founded in 1860. Its declared objectives are to work for the emancipation and moral progress of the Jews, to give support to those suffering persecution as Jews, and to encourage publications to further these ends. It has been particularly active in educational work, particularly through founding Jewish schools in Muslim countries.

almémar (from Arabic al-minbar, 'the pulpit') Raised platform in synagogue from which the TORAH is read. Synonym of bima, teba.

alphabet, Hebrew The Hebrew alphabet has twenty-two letters, which are all considered to be consonants (i.e. they can all start a Hebrew syllable). Five letters have special forms when they end a word. Vowels may be indicated by marks added above or, more usually, below the letters, but the use of these is optional, and in some contexts, e.g. in Torah scrolls, mezuzot and legal documents, they are consistently omitted. The square-shaped letters currently used in printed texts such as Bibles and prayer books and the main text in the Talmud were originally an Aramaic alphabet that was chosen to replace the old Hebrew ('palaeo-Hebrew') alphabet. The old alphabet can be seen on ancient coins, and is very similar to the alphabet still used by the Samaritans. Besides the square letters other forms of the alphabet are in use today: the semi-cursive (often called 'Rashi script' because it was used for the first printed edition of RASHI's commentary), and various forms of cursive, the commonest being an Ashkenazi script that has been spread to other communities largely thanks to its widespread use in Israel. Each letter of the alphabet has a numerical value, and numbers that cannot be represented by a single letter (such as 11 or 500) are made up by combining letters. This is the basis of CHRONOGRAMS (*see also* GEMATRIA; NUMEROLOGY).

See table at p. 364.

AM Abbreviation of Anno Mundi, Latin for 'In the year of the world'. AM years are designated according to the so-called era of the creation. This is now the usual way of dating Jewish documents, replacing older formulas such as the era of the destruction (dating from 68 CE) or the era of the documents or Seleucid era (dating from 312/311

BCE). As the Jewish year begins in the autumn, AM years do not correspond exactly to CE years. For example the year 5770 AM runs from September 2009 to September 2010 CE.

am ha-árets ('people of the land') An ignoramus, particularly one ignorant of the rules and rituals of Judaism. This expression has changed its meaning several times. In the Bible it refers to natives of a land in general; after the return from BABYLON it is applied to inhabitants of the Land of Israel who were hostile to the returning exiles, and who were lax in their religious observance. In rabbinic usage it curiously shifts from identifying a group to designating an individual ('an "am ha-árets" '): it refers to a person who was ignorant, particularly of the rules of IMPURITY and of TITHES (as opposed to a CHAVER). According to the Mishnah, an am ha-árets cannot be truly pious (Avot 2.6). Nowadays its connotations are entirely pejorative. (*See also* DEMAI.)

Amalek In the Bible, a nomadic people (also known as Amalekites) who attacked the Israelites during their journey from Egypt to the Promised Land (Exodus 17.8–16). The Israelites are paradoxically commanded to 'remember what Amalek did to you on your journey' and 'blot out the memory of Amalek from under heaven' (Deuteronomy 25.17–19). Several later raids on Israel are recorded in the Bible, and 'the wicked Haman', the villain of the book of ESTHER, is said to be a descendant of an Amalekite king (*see also* PURIM). Amalek has become a symbol of cruelty and enmity. The moralists speak of the need to eradicate the Amalek (that is, the aggressive tendency) residing within each human heart.

amen ('so be it') The word is used several times in the Bible to signify assent to an oath or to praise of God. The rabbis stated that it should be said on hearing a BENEDICTION. Amen comes from the same Hebrew root as emet ('truth') and emuna ('faith').

American Sephardi Federation Zionist organization created in 1973 to represent the interests of SEFARDIM nationally and internationally. It originally developed out of an American branch of the WORLD SEPHARDI FEDERATION, and is in sympathy with the aims of the world organization. It encourages the emigration of American Sefardim to Israel. Since 2002 it has been closely associated with Sephardic House, a cultural centre in New York founded in 1978.

Amida ('standing [prayer]') The main statutory prayer, consisting of a series of BENEDICTIONS. In rabbinic usage it is often referred to simply as the Prayer (Tefilla), or as the Eighteen (Shemone Esre), referring to the original number of benedictions. It is prescribed for recitation three times daily, in the evening, morning and afternoon, whether one is praying with a congregation or in private. The structure is more or less fixed, the main variations depending on the occasion: weekday, Sabbath or festival. In traditional and Orthodox prayer books the wording is now basically fixed (although considerable divergences are recorded well into the Middle Ages); however, the wording is varied slightly at different times of the year and in certain special circumstances. The other modernist movements, while retaining the traditional structure, have revised the wording to a greater or lesser extent, primarily to make the language more gender-inclusive and to accommodate some changes in current theological beliefs (such as bodily RESURRECTION). In private devotion the prayer is said silently; in congregational worship it is said silently and then, in the morning and afternoon services, it is traditionally repeated aloud by the reader. The weekday Amida now contains nineteen benedictions; their basic structure is as follows (the name of the benediction is given first, with its Hebrew form in brackets; the closing words (CHATIMA), which function as titles of God and sum up the message of the benediction, follow): 1. Patriarchs (avot): Shield of Abraham. 2. Mighty deeds (gevurot): Reviver of the dead. 3. Holiness of the Name (kedushat ha-Shem): The holy God. 4. Knowledge (dá'at): Gracious giver of knowledge. 5. Repentance (teshuva): He who desires repentance. 6. Forgiveness (selicha): Gracious one who abundantly pardons. 7. Redemption (geulla): Redeemer of Israel. 8. Healing (refu'a): Healer of the sick of his people Israel. 9. Blessing of the years (Birkat ha-shanim): He who blesses the years. 10. Ingathering of exiles (kibbuts galuyot): He who gathers in the scattered ones of his people Israel. 11. Restoration of justice (hashavat ha-mishpat): King who loves righteousness and justice. 12. Blessing of the heretics (birkat ha-minim): He who breaks foes and humbles the arrogant. 13. For the pious (al ha-tsaddikim): Trusted support of the righteous. 14. Rebuilding of Jerusalem (binyan Yerushaláim): Rebuilder of Jerusalem. 15. Messiah (Mashíach ben David): Who makes the horn of salvation to sprout. 16. Hearkening to prayer (shomé'a tefilla): Hearkening to prayer. 17. Worship (avoda): Who restores his presence to Zion. 18. Thanksgiving (hoda'a): You whose name is Goodness, and to whom it is fitting to give thanks. 19. Peace (shalom): He who blesses his people Israel with peace. On Sabbath benedictions 4–16 are replaced by a single benediction that speaks of the sanctity of the Sabbath day, and concludes with the chatima 'Who sanctifies the Sabbath'. *See also* KEDUSHA.

Amora'im (Hebrew plural of Aramaic amora, 'lecturer', 'interpreter') The rabbis of Palestine and Babylon whose opinions are cited in the Talmuds (contrast TANNA'IM). Palestinian Amora'im have the title Rabbi; Babylonian Amora'im have the title Rav. The age of the Amora'im begins with the completion of the Mishnah in the early 3rd century, and continues to the completion of the two Talmuds (early 5th century in Palestine, late 6th in Babylon).

Amos Biblical book, first of the Twelve Minor Prophets. It presents the outpourings of a prophet supposed to have lived before the destruction of the northern kingdom of Israel (8th century BCE), which he predicts. With rhetorical skill he rebuts comfortable assumptions: Israel's status as 'chosen people' does not guarantee divine protection – on the contrary, if Israel sins it will be all the more vulnerable to divine punishment. The 'day of the Lord' is not a day of light and joy but of darkness and judgment. Morality is more important than religious forms.

Anan ben David (8th century) Considered by Karaites as the founder of their movement. The details of his life are obscure. He is considered to be the author of a legal compilation, the *Séfer ha-Mitsvot* (*Book of Commandments*), that is one of the earliest surviving Jewish CODES OF LAW.

androgyny The rabbinic Hebrew word androgynos is of Greek origin and means 'man-woman'; it denotes a person having the outward organs of both sexes. 'The androgynos resembles men in some respects and women in others, and in some respects is like neither' (Mishnah, Bikkurim 4.1). Some rabbis agreed with Plato that the original human condition was androgyny, quoting the verse 'male and female created he them' (Genesis 1.27). *See also* GENDER.

angels The word angel is derived from a Greek word meaning 'messenger', and this is also the meaning of the Hebrew word malach. In the Bible angels are messengers of God; for the most part they lack individual names or personalities, and do not have a hierarchical structure. Gabriel and Michael are mentioned in the book of Daniel, and the theophanies (visions of God) in Isaiah and Ezekiel mention classes of heavenly beings: seraphim (Isaiah 6), cherubim, 'living creatures' (chayyot) and 'wheels' (ofanim). The post-biblical literature abounds with references to angels, and clearly derives from a society with a highly developed sense of the presence of angels as active forces in the world and as intermediaries between the celestial and terrestrial spheres. Interestingly, they are never mentioned in the Mishnah, but are frequently referred to in the Talmud and Midrashic writings, as well as the TARGUMIM. God is envisaged as a monarch served by angelic ministers (malachei ha-sharet), and each nation is thought of as having its own guardian angel. Angels are servants of God and are not to be worshipped or even supplicated, according to the Talmud, but in the theurgical tradition, which has left a powerful legacy in the KABBALA, they were invested with supernatural powers of their own and appealed to in amulets and incantations. In the AGGADA, on the other hand, they are sometimes represented as entering into dialogue with God, even criticizing him or being rebuked by him. For example they are represented debating with God whether the creation of humankind is a good or bad idea, and when the angelic choirs begin to sing praises to God after the drowning of the Egyptian army in the Red Sea God silences them with the protest, 'How can you sing when my children [the Egyptians] are drowning?'

The medieval philosophers generally consider angels from a rational perspective as purely spiritual beings with no matter or form. Angelology has never been developed into a central theological system in Judaism, and so belief in angels, while implicitly or explicitly abandoned under the influence of the ENLIGHTENMENT and religious MODERNISM, did not become a subject of controversy. Orthodox prayer books still retain traces of the belief in angels. For example the KEDUSHA, a central prayer, begins by comparing the worshippers to the seraphim who proclaimed God's sanctity in the theophany of Isaiah 6. A popular hymn sung by Ashkenazim on Sabbath eve begins 'Greetings [Shalom aleichem], O ministering angels, angels of the Most High, of the emperor of emperors, the Holy One, blessed be He'.

Anim zmirot *See* HYMN OF GLORY.

animals, treatment of Jewish law (HALACHA) has an ambiguous attitude to animals. On the one hand it is permitted to kill and eat them, and indeed to use them for other purposes; on the other hand it is forbidden to cause them unnecessary suffering. These ambivalent attitudes are enshrined in the Bible: for instance it is forbidden to take eggs or chicks from a nest in the presence of the mother hen (Deuteronomy 22.6–7), or to slaughter an animal and its young on the same day (Leviticus 22.28); and while it is even forbidden to muzzle an ox that is treading grain (Deuteronomy 25.4) there are laws regulating the killing of animals for food and as sacrifices to God, who is portrayed as taking pleasure in the smell of roasting meat. This ambivalence pervades modern discussions of such issues as hunting, vivisection and the use of animals in laboratories.

anthropomorphism The attribution of human characteristics to spiritual beings, such as God or his angels. Anthropomorphism can take various forms. The Bible applies terms derived from the human body to God, speaking for example of his 'strong arm' (might) or 'long nostrils' (patience); it describes God as experiencing human emotions such as pleasure, regret or compassion; and it also portrays him in human terms, for example as walking in the garden of Eden, or sitting in the sky and resting his feet on the earth. Much of this language can be explained as harmless poetic licence or metaphor, and the rabbinic AGGADA takes it up and considerably extends its range; purists, however, have objected to it as grossly misrepresenting the nature of the Divine and erecting a barrier between humankind and the true perception of God. Some of the TARGUMIM, for example, render the common biblical expression 'God spoke' by 'the word of God spoke'. Philo, Maimonides and other philosophers systematically transposed biblical anthropomorphisms into abstract, spiritual language. At the other extreme, the KABBALA makes very free use of human language in speaking of the Godhead, and Jewish liturgies have traditionally adopted a relaxed attitude to anthropomorphic language, neither taking pains to avoid it nor deliberately exploiting it.

anusim ('forced [converts]') Term applied by some historians, especially in Israel, to Jews forcibly converted to Christianity, particularly in Spain and Portugal in the 15th century.

apikóros (Greek epikoureios, 'Epicurean') Unlike the English association of the philosophy of Epicurus with the pursuit of luxury and sensuality, in Judaism it is associated with the denial of divine providence. The term is applied in the Mishnah (Avot 2.14) to a foe whose criticisms one must be prepared to rebut, and it is even denied that such a Jew has a share in the Coming Age (OLAM HA-BA) (Sanhedrin 10.1). In modern usage it is sometimes applied to a freethinker, a Jew who denies the tenets of the religion.

apostasy The abandonment of Judaism for another religion, commonly regarded as a grave act of betrayal. In the Middle Ages it was relatively rare, and when it did occur was often attributable to coercion. In such cases it was sometimes viewed with a measure of understanding. Since the Enlightenment large numbers of Jews have abandoned Judaism without necessarily adopting another religion (*see* ASSIMILATION), and the atavistic repugnance has been to some extent attenuated. (*See* CHÉREM; CONVERSION; MESHUMMAD; MUMAR.)

Arabic Semitic language akin to Hebrew, but speakers of the two languages cannot easily understand each other. Arabic was a local Jewish vernacular in the Arabian peninsula before the rise of Islam; in fact we know of some Jewish poets who wrote in it. With the spread of Arab power and influence throughout the Middle East and north Africa and into southern Europe beginning in the 7th century many Jews came to speak the language, instead of Greek, Aramaic, Berber and various Romance languages. Beginning in the 10th century Jews wrote in Arabic too, using the Hebrew alphabet when addressing a Jewish readership. With very few exceptions, all the Jewish thinkers (such as SA'ADYA GA'ON, JUDAH HA-LEVI and MAIMONIDES) who lived in Arabic-speaking countries wrote their philosophical works in Arabic. The term Judaeo-Arabic is applied to Arabic used by Jews. Today Arabic is the mother tongue of many Jews, and some literature is still written by Jews in Arabic. (*See also* TAFSIR.)

Arachin ('vows for valuation') Tractate of Mishnah, Tosefta and both Talmuds, in order Kodashim, dealing with vows to the temple concerning persons or immovable property (Leviticus 27). Since these cannot be handed over to the temple, they must be valued for purposes of monetary payment.

Aramaic Semitic language, closely related to Hebrew. In antiquity Aramaic was an administrative language of the Persian empire and was used over a vast area of the Near East. It is the language of some parts of the Bible, notably parts of Ezra and Daniel. The Hebrew Bible was translated into Aramaic at various times (*see* TARGU-MIM), indicating its widespread use as a vernacular among Jews who could not easily understand Hebrew. The rabbinic movement, while encouraging Hebrew study, also made use of Aramaic, and it is the main language in which both TALMUDS are written. Rabbinic Hebrew is heavily influenced by Aramaic, and many rabbinic Hebrew writings (such as the Midrash) assume a knowledge of Aramaic. The primary language of the two Talmuds is Aramaic, although they use Hebrew too, mainly for the quotations from the Mishnah and the baraitot (*see* BARAITA). It was also used for composing prayers, some of which are still said in Aramaic today (e.g. KADDISH; KOL NIDREI; HA LACHMA); the marriage deed (KETUBBA) is also still written in Aramaic. It is the language in which the ZOHAR was written in 13th-century Spain, a fact that encouraged its use by kabbalists. Aramaic was spoken in living memory by some Jews from northern Iraq, but it is rapidly dying out.

arayat (Arabic, from Hebrew keriyot, 'readings') Among Syrian Jews, reading of the Psalms in memory of the dead, held at the end of the week, month and year of MOURNING. It is customary to deliver eulogies of the departed.

arba kanfot *See* TSITSIT.

arba'a minim *See* FOUR SPECIES.

Arba'a Turim ('four rows') Halachic code, compiled in the early 14th century by JACOB BEN ASHER of Toledo. The laws contained in the two Talmuds (omitting those no longer observed since the destruction of the Temple) are organized thematically in four parts (whence the title): 1. Órach Chayyim (Path of Life, Psalm 16.11), dealing with everyday duties, including daily, Sabbath and festival prayers; 2. Yore De'a (Teaching Knowledge, Isaiah 28.9), concerned with ritual laws; 3. Éven ha-Ézer

(Stone of Help, 1 Samuel 7.12), on family law; and 4. Chóshen Mishpat (Breastplate of Judgment, Exodus 28.15), on civil law. This original arrangement was followed in later halachic works, most notably in the SHULCHAN ARUCH.

Arendt, Hannah (1906–75) Philosopher. Born in Germany, she moved to Paris after the rise of Hitler to power, and in 1940 moved again to the United States. Her book *Eichmann in Jerusalem* (1963), based on reports of the trial of the Nazi Adolf Eichmann that she wrote for the *New Yorker* magazine, introduced the concept of the 'banality of evil', and also suggested that Jews had co-operated in the Nazi programme of genocide.

Aristotelianism Ancient philosophy that entered Jewish thought in Arab lands from the 10th century, through Arabic translations of Aristotle's works, and later through Hebrew translations made from the Arabic. However, it should be noted that the 'Aristotle' of the Middle Ages is different from the ancient Aristotle, because he reached the Arab philosophers accompanied by Greek commentaries; Jewish thinkers read him through the lens of Greek and Arabic commentaries. Medieval Aristotelianism accepted a number of ideas from NEOPLATONISM. The first important Jewish Aristotelian was Abraham IBN DAUD. The greatest of the Jewish Aristotelians was without doubt Moses MAIMONIDES, in the 12th century, who achieved a remarkable synthesis of Aristotle and biblical thought. Maimonides tended to give priority to Aristotle except on a small number of issues where he was unable to follow him. For instance he could not agree with Aristotle that the world was eternal and had no beginning, a view that is clearly incompatible with the biblical doctrine of creation; on the other hand Maimonides showed that eternity was not an essential component of the Aristotelian system, and so the synthesis was sustained. GERSONIDES disagreed with this approach, and tended to give priority to Aristotle; thus he maintained that the world was created from formless matter and not from nothing. In the early 15th century Chasdai CRESCAS mounted a ferocious attack on Maimonides and the Aristotelian roots of his thought, but later in the century Aristotelianism underwent a short-lived revival in Spain.

ark Receptacle for TORAH scrolls, the most prominent and distinctive feature of a synagogue. The English term ark is derived from the biblical account of the 'ark of the COVENANT' (Exodus 37), in which the tablets of the covenant were kept, and which had the form of a chest or ark. The synagogue ark is generally located in such a way that a worshipper looking towards it is facing east or towards Jerusalem (in Jerusalem, towards the site of the Temple), which is the canonical direction for saying the AMIDA. The ark commonly has the appearance of a wardrobe, with hinged doors, and may be an elaborate, ornate structure, with a Hebrew inscription above. However, there is no prescribed form, and much ingenuity has been lavished on the construction of the ark. Other associated features may be a curtain in front of the ark (*see* PARÓCHET) or inside the doors, and a lamp above (*see* NER TAMID). The ark is generally on a platform approached by steps; in many synagogues the reading desk and pulpit have been moved to this platform (*see* BIMA; SYNAGOGUE). One or more Torah scrolls are kept inside the ark, and the opening of the ark is a solemn moment in services at which the scroll is read. At certain other moments in the services the ark is opened even if the scrolls are not removed, or removed and not read. The congregation rises whenever the ark is opened, and remains standing as long as the ark stays open. *See also* ARON HAKÓDESH; DUCHAN; ECHAL.

aron hakódesh ('holy ark') Name given to the ARK, particularly by Ashkenazim.

art While recognizing the dangers of IDOLATRY and ANTHROPOMORPHISM, Jews have tended to adopt a positive attitude towards art and pressed it into the service of religion, following the biblical precedent of the construction of the tabernacle by Bezalel (Exodus 31 and 35), who is described as endowed with artistic skill by God. In late antiquity synagogues were lavishly decorated with mosaic floors, frescoes and carved reliefs, and while many modern synagogues are designed in a spirit of artistic austerity others are embellished with stained-glass windows and other artistic devices. Manuscript illumination makes its appearance from the late 10th century, and we have some richly illustrated bibles and prayer books as well as secular manuscripts from the later Middle Ages and the early modern period. The finest artistry in gold, silver, wood and other materials has been applied to ceremonial objects for use in synagogue and home. At the same time it is impossible not to detect a strong current of disapproval, ranging at different times and in different places from ambivalence or suspicion to (rarely) outright condemnation of all artistic expression. The most persistent criticism has concerned the representation of God and the ministers of his power. This attitude is attested in the Bible (notably Exodus 20.4 and 23) and developed by the rabbis (particularly in the Talmudic tractate Avoda Zara). In late antique synagogue art pagan divinities (such as the sun god in his chariot) are prominently displayed, but God is mostly represented only by a hand descending from heaven. In general, pictorial representations of God are extremely rare. As for images of human beings, while these are often present in late antique synagogues and in medieval manuscripts from Christian countries, at other times they tend to be avoided, particularly in the context of prayer. Some illuminated prayer books show human figures but not their faces (sometimes these are replaced by the heads of animals or birds). There has also been a tendency to avoid three-dimensional representations, particularly in the synagogue. Animals are generally shown without restraint (indeed lions figure very commonly in synagogue art), but this practice too has been opposed at times. We have portraits, including images of famous rabbis, from the 17th century on, and photography has attracted very little objection.

arvit Alternative name for MA'ARIV, the evening service.

ascamot In Western Sefardi usage, congregational regulations or bye-laws.

asceticism Abstinence has generally been frowned on in Judaism, along with any attitude that sees the body as inherently evil or impure, that glorifies self-denial, or that advocates individual self-righteousness. FASTING is prescribed as an act of contrition on certain (relatively rare) occasions, but other forms of self-denial, such as abstinence from alcohol or sexual relations, have generally been discouraged. That said, there have been examples of ascetic movements among Jews, beginning perhaps with the ancient Essenes. After the destruction of the Temple some Jews abstained from meat and wine as a sign of mourning, but this was opposed by some rabbinic authorities; this form of asceticism was particularly associated in the Middle Ages with a community of Karaites who lived in Jerusalem before the Seljuk and Crusader conquests of the 11th century. Karaites in general avoid sexual activity and the preparation of hot food on the Sabbath, and they used to prohibit lights and fires on this day. Under the influence of Sufism, BACHYA IBN PAKUDA recommends asceticism as a necessary preliminary to the religious life. NACHMANIDES, in commenting on Leviticus 19.2, observes that while the Torah forbids certain things it permits others, such as sexual acts within marriage or eating and drinking, without specifying a legitimate degree. Anyone who indulges in them to excess is 'a villain with the full sanction of Torah'. In commanding holiness, the Torah is advising us to separate ourselves from what is unnecessary. Nachmanides' commendation of a life of self-restraint, denying oneself legitimate pleasures, has found some followers, particularly among kabbalists and Chasidim, some of whom have conceived of holiness as an ideal available only to a select few. It must be stressed, however, that asceticism is not characteristic of Judaism, and a Talmudic dictum warns that 'in times to come we shall be called to account not only for the sins we committed but for the legitimate pleasures we denied ourselves' (Yerushalmi, Kiddushin 4.12). *See also* CHASIDEI ASHKENAZ; NAZIR.

ashámnu ('we are guilty') Also known as the Lesser Confession, this alphabetical litany of twenty-four sins is recited in each of the synagogue services on the Day of ATONEMENT. Worshippers often beat their breasts while reciting it, as an outward mark of contrition. *See also* AL CHET.

Asher ben Yechiel (c. 1250–1327). Also known as the Rosh or Asheri. Halachic authority. A bridge between the worlds of the ASHKENAZIM and SEFARDIM, Asher was the leading pupil of MEIR OF ROTHENBURG in the Rhineland, but settled in Spain and became the head of the rabbinical academy of Toledo in 1305. More than a thousand of his RESPONSA have been collected and published, and his lucid and straightforward annotations to the Babylonian Talmud are traditionally printed in all editions of that work. In many ways he combines the best features of Ashkenazi and Sefardi scholarship, and his authority was recognized by both communities. His major halachic work, the Piskei ha-Rosh, had a great influence on the Arba'a Turim of his son JACOB BEN ASHER, and through it on subsequent attempts to codify the HALACHA.

ashkabá ('laying to rest'; also ashkavá, hashkabá) Sequence of prayers recited by Sefardim in memory of the dead. It is recited by those called up to the Torah reading on the anniversary of the death.

Ashkenazim Jews who trace their remote origins to the Rhineland communities of the early Middle Ages. The name Ashkenaz, found in a genealogy in the Bible (Genesis 10.3), came to be applied to these communities, who developed a distinctive prayer rite as well as distinctive laws and customs. In time Ashkenazi Judaism spread westwards into northern France and England and eastwards into central and eastern

Europe. Here their main spoken language was YIDDISH, and they had a distinctive tradition of pronouncing Hebrew (differentiated from other traditions notably by a recessive stress, and by pronouncing as o and s written characters that are usually pronounced by other Jews respectively as a and t or th). In the 19th century a population explosion coupled with difficult economic and political conditions led to a mass movement of Ashkenazim from the Russian empire westward to western Europe and on to the Americas, South Africa, Palestine and other parts of the world, and they became the largest and most widespread group of Jews. They suffered far greater losses in Europe than other groups in the HOLOCAUST, and, particularly in Israel, their Yiddish language and pronunciation of Hebrew have all but disappeared. Nevertheless, they tend to retain a strong sense of their own identity. In Israel, where they assumed a dominant role in political life even before the establishment of the state in 1948, they have sometimes been accused of deliberately marginalizing non-Ashkenazi Jews. *See also* AGUDAT ISRAEL; ASHER BEN YECHIEL; ISSERLES, MOSES; RASHI; ZIONISM.

assimilation Absorption of an individual or a minority group into the surrounding culture, or the adoption of the lifestyle and values of the environment by an individual or group. 'Assimilated Jews' are Jews whose norms of behaviour differ little or not at all from those of people around them. Jewish communities have generally been open to influences from the surrounding societies, while remaining distinct (by choice or compulsion or a combination of the two) in what have been regarded as key domains, such as religion and family life. As a consequence of political EMANCIPATION, with the attendant social integration, Jews in modern nation states have felt a pressure towards a more far-reaching assimilation, extending to intermarriage and to the abandonment of Jewish religion and perhaps conversion to the majority faith. It was to combat this trend and find a new compromise that the various forms of Jewish religious MODERNISM were developed in the 19th and early 20th centuries.

astrology Study of the influence of heavenly bodies on earthly affairs and human destinies. The popular belief in such influence has been very widespread among Jews down the ages, even though it is expressly disparaged (at least so far as Jews are concerned) by some of the rabbis cited in the Talmud. Several strong Talmudic statements affirm the power of the heavenly bodies, and excavated synagogues in Israel from the late antique period feature a representation of the zodiac prominently in their mosaic floors. In the Middle Ages, when astrology was still viewed as an exact science, several Jewish authors, including some of the best-known scholars (such as ABRAHAM BAR CHIYYA and Abraham IBN EZRA), endorsed astrology and wrote treatises about it. Only MAIMONIDES roundly condemned it.

atheism Denial of the existence of a god. The Bible takes the existence of a single supreme being as axiomatic. Paradoxically, Jews were sometimes accused of atheism by hostile Greek and Roman critics in antiquity, meaning that they denied the gods of the pagan pantheon. The Jewish Epicureans (*see* APIKÓROS) were extreme rationalists who could not accept that there was a personal god who governed human affairs. The belief in a god, however defined, remained axiomatic in Judaism until modern times, and denial of God generally entailed departure from the community. Modern Jewish atheism has its roots in the HASKALA, which shared the anti-religious and anti-clerical sentiments of the European Enlightenment in general, and in the Jewish socialism that emerged in the second half of the 19th century. Both these movements nourished early Zionism, and a majority of the Jewish settlers in Palestine before World War II were militantly or implicitly atheist, while identifying strongly as Jews. Nowadays, thanks to these developments, it is regarded as perfectly acceptable for a Jew to be an affirmed atheist or agnostic (a weaker position maintaining an open mind about the existence or non-existence of a god). *See also* GOD; HUMANISTIC JUDAISM; SECULAR JUDAISM.

atonement At-one-ment, i.e. reconciliation between humans and God. SIN is thought to distance people from God, and atonement requires that they return to him (*see* TESHUVA). Sin must be first acknowledged, and then expiated; God's FORGIVENESS follows. The ancient sources mention various ways to expiate sin: monetary payment (in the case of sins against other people), SACRIFICE and other rituals, suffering and, ultimately, death. All, however, are only considered effective if accompanied by sincere repentance. Since the destruction of the Temple sacrifice is no longer available, and is replaced by prayer, a development apparently anticipated in the Bible: 'Now we shall render instead of bullocks the sacrifice of our lips' (Hosea 14.3); 'Should I come before him with burnt offerings, with one-year calves? He has shown you, O man, what is good: what does the Lord require of you but to act justly, love mercy, and walk humbly with your God' (Micah 6.6–8). The Day of Atonement (*see* next entry) is offered to Jews as an annual opportunity to atone for sins against God. The idea of 'vicarious atonement' (atonement on behalf of others), which from the biblical practice of animal sacrifice has been developed in Christianity into a key doctrine, is largely absent from Judaism, but there is a rabbinic teaching that the death of the young or of particularly righteous or saintly individuals atones for the sins of others. This attempt to vindicate the suffering of the innocent has been used by some to find some positive element in the killing of numerous very young, pious or learned Jews in the pogroms and the Holocaust.

Atonement, Day of (also known as Kippur or Yom Kippur or Yom ha-Kippurim) Solemn fast day, celebrated annually on the 10th of Tishri, nine days after the first day of the new year. (For the intermediate days *see* TEN DAYS OF PENITENCE.) It is one of the major festivals of the Jewish year, and unlike the others is celebrated exclusively in the synagogue. There are five distinct services, one in the evening (*see* KOL NIDREI) and the other four the following day. Many worshippers remain in synagogue throughout the day (or even for the entire twenty-five hours, although this practice is rarely observed nowadays). In the morning service (SHACHARIT) the traditional Torah readings (Leviticus 16 and Numbers 29.7–11) recount the original institution of the festival and its rituals, including these key words: 'It [the day] is a Sabbath of Sabbaths for you, and you shall afflict yourselves, an eternal ordinance. The priest duly anointed and installed in succession to his father shall make atonement; he shall put on the sacred linen vestments and make atonement for the sacred sanctuary, the tent of meeting and the altar, and also for the priests and all the assembled people. This shall be an eternal ordinance for you, to make atonement for all the Israelites because of all their sins, once each year' (Leviticus 16.31–4). The haftara, Isaiah 57.14–58.14, castigates the false religiosity of those who adopt only the outward forms of contrition: 'Is the fast I prefer not rather this: to loosen the fetters of injustice, to untie the heavy burdens, to set the oppressed free and to smash every yoke? To share your bread with the hungry, to take the homeless poor into your home, to clothe anyone you see naked and not hide yourself from your own kin?' The additional service (MUSAF) includes a formal re-enactment of the rituals performed on this day by the High Priest in the Temple (see AVODA (2)). In the afternoon service (MINCHA) the biblical prohibitions on illicit sexual acts (Leviticus 18) are read, followed by the book of Jonah, with its lesson that God is always ready to grant pardon for sins in return for true repentance. As evening approaches the concluding service (NE'ILA) is read. The mood becomes more confident, almost joyous, as the fast reaches its end; the service concludes with a single long blast on the SHOFAR. Throughout all five services confessions and penitential prayers predominate (see AL CHET; ASHÁMNU; AVÍNU MALKEÍNU). In addition to the prohibition of all kinds of work forbidden on the Sabbath, five special restrictions mark this fast day: abstention from food, drink, sexual intercourse, anointing, and the wearing of leather shoes. (For most people it is the ban on eating and drinking that is particularly associated with the day.) Among Ashkenazim there is a custom (by no means universally observed) of wearing the KÍTTEL on this day, and also of prostrating oneself at certain points in the service (see KNEELING). The predominant colour in the synagogue is white; hence the day has sometimes been called 'the white fast'.

See also KAPPAROT; YOMA.

atsei chayyim See ETS CHAYYIM.

atsilut See EMANATIONISM.

Attributes, Thirteen See THIRTEEN ATTRIBUTES.

Auschwitz German name of one of the Nazi slave labour and extermination camps in Poland during the HOLOCAUST. (Polish name, Oświęcim.) It has come to be used symbolically by theologians to designate the Nazi programme of genocide of the Jews as a whole.

Austrittsgemeinde (German, 'secession community') Name given to Orthodox congregations set up outside the established community framework (see EINHEITSGE-MEINDE), following a change in Prussian law in 1876 permitting such secession. The movement for secession was led by S. R. HIRSCH; it remained relatively small in its impact, most Orthodox congregations preferring to remain within the communal structure. See also ADATH YISROEL; NEO-ORTHODOXY.

autonomism See DUBNOW, SIMON.

Av Eleventh month of the year counting from new year; fifth counting from Passover, corresponding roughly to August. According to an old tradition, the Jerusalem Temple was destroyed in this month (see TISH'A BE-AV), and consequently the month itself is sometimes referred to as Menahem Av (Av the Comforter), and its first nine days are traditionally marked by a sombre mood.

avel *See* MOURNING.

avínu malkeínu ('our Father and King') Litany of supplication sung at New Year and on the Day of Atonement and certain other days. God is addressed as both a stern king and a loving father. While the prayer itself is moving and much loved, the form of address has been criticized by feminists as irredeemably sexist, and in some Reform liturgies has been replaced by more acceptable wording.

avoda ('service') **1** Originally the word meant work or service in general (this is the meaning it has in modern Hebrew). Often in the Bible, however, it is used in the specialized sense of service of God, i.e. worship. (The Greek word 'liturgy' has a similar development.) A rabbinic saying states that the world stands on three things: study, avoda (worship), and charitable deeds (Mishnah, Avot 1.2). The underlying idea here is 'service of the Creator'; it is not merely the fulfilment of an obligation, but expresses an attitude of gratitude, devotion, and loyalty. It is a service which is offered gladly and willingly, and which brings a sense of fulfilment and joy. Prayer, on the basis of another rabbinic dictum, is sometimes referred to as service of the heart (or mind).

    2 Avoda has a specific sense, denoting the service of the High Priest in the Temple, and the liturgy commemorating this, that is included in the additional service for the Day of Atonement. This liturgy is based on the account preserved in the Mishnah tractate Yoma, and incorporates liturgical poems (piyyutim).

    3 Avoda is also a technical term used by specialists to denote a PIYYUT on this subject. The genre began in the earliest phase of the piyyut, and some of the early creations are still chanted today. Notable examples were also composed by SA'ADYA GA'ON and the Spanish poets. While dwelling on the theme of ATONEMENT, these poems also look back on a period of national independence that contrasted with the conditions of subjugation under which the poets lived.

Avoda Zara ('idolatry') Tractate of the Mishnah, in the order Nezikin, with corresponding tractates in the Tosefta and both Talmuds. Its subject matter is idolatrous worship (*see* IDOLATRY), and ways for Jews to avoid coming into contact with it. It is a rich source of rabbinic reflection on relations between Jews and other peoples, and is also much used by historians interested in the daily life of Jews in the Roman period.

Avot ('fathers') **1** Hebrew term referring to the biblical PATRIARCHS.

    2 Tractate of the Mishnah ('sayings of the Fathers'), placed in the order Nezikin, although it has nothing to do with the main subjects of that order, namely laws of damages and other monetary issues. Indeed it is unique among the tractates of the Mishnah in not being concerned with HALACHA at all. Beginning with a chain of tradition that established the continuity of rabbinic Torah from SINAI to the TANNA'IM, it contains a collection of sayings attributed to various rabbis, mainly of the 2nd century, offering moral, religious and practical advice. Also known as Pirkei Avot (chapters of the Fathers, or chapters of Avot). On account of its edifying character and because it constitutes an introduction to rabbinic thought on a range of subjects, the custom arose of reciting a chapter of the work each Sabbath afternoon in the summer months. Hence it is transmitted in prayer books as well as in copies of the Mishnah.

3 Name given to the first benediction of the AMIDA, which praises God as the God of the patriarchs.

4 Talmudic term meaning 'fundamental principles'. Some scholars maintain that the title of the tractate Avot carries this meaning, rather than referring to the founding fathers of rabbinic Judaism.

awe *See* CHAREDI; FEAR OF GOD; HESCHEL, ABRAHAM JOSHUA.

áyin hara *See* EVIL EYE.

azhara ('admonitions'; plural azharot) Type of liturgical poem, enumerating and expounding the 613 COMMANDMENTS and designed to be recited at Pentecost. SA'ADYA GA'ON'S azharot were widely influential, but the best-known example is by IBN GABIROL; it is widely used among Sefardi congregations. The term is also applied to poetic compositions detailing the regulations for Passover or other festivals.

bá'al keri'a ('master of the reading') Title given to the individual in a community who performs the public Torah reading.

Baal Shem Tov ('master of the good name', or 'possessor of a good reputation') Title under which Israel ben Eliezer (c. 1700–60), the founder of CHASIDISM, is usually known. (The shorter form Baal Shem and the acronym Besht are also widely used.) 'Ba'al Shem', Master of the Name, is an old title given to wonder-workers who achieve magical results by their mastery of divine and angelic names, typically associated with amulets, spells and mystery cures. The Baal Shem Tov seems first to have acquired a reputation as such a wonder-worker in his native district of Podolia and in the neighbouring regions of Volhynia and Galicia. Little is known for certain about his life, however; much that was written about him in his time and later belongs to the genre of hagiography (saints' lives), and invests him with supernatural powers. In 1740 he opened a school and attracted many followers to his teaching of a Judaism that distanced itself from the stultifying dryness (as he saw it) that characterized the Talmud study of the contemporary YESHIVA and instead embraced joy, ecstatic prayer and KAVVANA. His theology is based in large part on that of Isaac LURIA, which it reinterprets in significant ways. It is panentheistic; in other words God is present in all things. The Baal Shem Tov is said to have described how he once ascended to the hall of the Messiah, and asked him when he would come. The reply was that when the Baal Shem Tov's teachings were thoroughly spread in the world, then all the 'shells' (KELIPPOT) trapping the divine sparks would be ended and the era of salvation would begin.

bá'al teki'a ('master of the shofar blowing') Title given to the individual in a community who performs the public SHOFAR blowing at Rosh ha-Shana.

bá'al teshuva ('possessor of TESHUVA') A person who repents of a transgression. Nowadays this traditional term is often applied to a person who 'returns' from a secular or indifferent lifestyle to observance of the COMMANDMENTS. Special YESHIVOT have sprung up to cater to such individuals.

Baba Sali (Arabic, 'Praying Father') Popular name of Rabbi Israel Abu-Chatsera (1889–1984), a rabbi venerated as a saint by Moroccan Jews in Israel. His grave near his home in Netivot in the Negev has become a place of pilgrimage, particularly at the time of his HILLULA (4th of Shevát).

Babylonia Region of southern Mesopotamia named after the city of Babylon. It is remembered particularly as the home of the oldest Diaspora community and for the Talmud that was composed there. The Hebrew name of Babylon, Bavel (often written Babel), was explained in antiquity as meaning 'confusion'; in the Bible (Genesis 11) God confuses the speech of the builders of the Tower of Babel, which is the origin of the different languages of humankind. Later in the Bible the Judaeans come under the domination of the powerful empire of Babylonia, ruled by king Nebuchadnezzar, who puts down a rebellion (597 BCE) and exiles king Jehoiachin, his nobles and officials, and 10,000 men to Babylon (2 Kings 24). This is the beginning of the Babylonian exile. A second revolt a few years later leads Nebuchadnezzar to besiege the city of Jerusalem; the city is taken, the Temple is destroyed (586) and more Judaeans are led into exile (587). A further rebellion results in the departure of a further group of exiles (582). The period of exile marks a watershed in biblical history and religion, and in particular a time when the conception of God became more universal. Babylon was captured by King Cyrus of Persia in 539, and the following year he promulgated an edict allowing the exiles to return to Jerusalem and rebuild the sanctuary. Many, however, chose to remain, and from the early 3rd century CE Babylonia became the home of a rich Jewish cultural and scholarly life that continued for some 800 years. The academies (yeshivot) of Babylonia rivalled those of the Land of Israel, particularly once the latter centre came under Christian rule in the 4th century, which marked the beginning of a period of relative decline. The main Babylonian academies at Sura, Pumbedita and Machoza became the outstanding centres of rabbinical study; the discussions of the AMORA'IM that took place here are embodied in the Babylonian Talmud. Babylonian Jewry at this time was ruled by an exilarch, a counterpart of the patriarch who ruled the Jews of Israel and the Roman empire. From the time of the Arab conquest in the 630s CE the land was known as Iraq, but Jews continued to refer to it as Bavel. The SAVORA'IM and ge'onim (see GA'ON) continued the work of the Amora'im until the line of the ge'onim came to an end in the early 11th century.

bachur ('young man') In the Bible the term is applied to a young man in his prime. In the Talmud it can simply mean a bachelor, and this sense has persisted, for example in calling such a person up to the reading of the Torah. It is particularly used of an unmarried YESHIVA student (in Yiddish, yeshíva bócher).

Bachya Ibn Pakuda (late 11th century) Spanish philosopher and moralist. His *Book of Directions to the Duties of the Heart* (*Séfer Chovot ha-Levavot*) has come to be seen as a classic of Jewish thought. The title of the work is derived from the contrast between the outward observance of the various practical commandments, the 'duties of the limbs', and the inward, spiritual 'duties of the heart'. Bachya warns against attending to the former to the neglect of the latter. 'The duties of the limbs', he writes in his introduction, 'are of no use to us unless our hearts choose to do them and our souls desire their performance.' His book is thus intended to complement the halachic literature, and it sets out to be no less systematic. The duties of the heart are classified and expounded in turn, and the whole scheme constitutes a kind of spiritual ladder leading up to the highest rung, which is true love of God. This scheme is not original

– it is derived from the works of Muslim mystics and Bachya's ideas are deeply indebted to Arab Neoplatonism – but it represents a new departure in the Jewish tradition, and the book achieved enormous popularity, being translated from Arabic into Hebrew in the 12th century and into many other languages subsequently.

Baeck, Leo (1873–1956) One of the outstanding German Jewish religious thinkers of his time. Like Martin BUBER and Franz ROSENZWEIG, Baeck was much influenced by Hermann COHEN. He developed a theology in which God is known particularly through the commandments and the moral code. He is also remembered for his striking distinction between classical religion (Judaism) and romantic religion (Christianity). His best known works are *The Essence of Judaism* and *This People Israel*. A Liberal rabbi, Baeck became the spiritual leader of German Jewry during the Nazi period. He survived incarceration in the 'model' concentration camp of Theresien-stadt (Terezín).

There is a strong apologetic tendency in Baeck. The title of his book *The Essence of Judaism* echoes that of an earlier book by the well-known Christian theologian Adolf von Harnack, and is intended as a Jewish response to Harnack, although he does not mention him by name. Baeck begins with the distinction made explicit by Moses MENDELSSOHN: 'Judaism has no dogmas and therefore no orthodoxy, as religious orthodoxy is usually understood'. In Judaism, 'man's function is described by the commandments: to do what is good; that is the beginning of wisdom'. We glimpse the lapse of time that separates the Liberal Jew Baeck from his 18th-century prede-cessor in the next sentence: 'Man's duty toward man comes before his knowledge of God, and the knowledge of him is a process of seeking and enquiring rather than an act of possession.' It is through understanding one's own spiritual needs and those of other people that one comes to understand and have faith in God. This approach places Baeck firmly in his own century. In keeping with the tenets of LIBERAL JUDAISM, Baeck interprets the COMMANDMENTS as basically the moral law. Following the philo-sophical tradition to which he was heir, he sees God as being that which gives continuing meaning and value to man's moral behaviour. In this respect he was close to Hermann Cohen. Baeck seems to strive to go further than Cohen when he speaks, as he often does, of God as 'mystery': he was, after all, a rabbi and preacher, whereas Cohen was a professor of philosophy. The characteristic feature of Judaism, Baeck says, is the relation of man to God, and specifically the uniquely Jewish sense of being created. 'Though he is unfathomable and inscrutable, yet we emanate from him'. The stress, in the midst of encounter, on the unknowability of God is char-acteristic of Baeck. The centrality of encounter links him to Rosenzweig, Buber and later to HESCHEL. But Baeck's theology remains always tentative and provisional, in keeping with his original insistence on the absence of dogma in Judaism. Baeck settled in London after the war. The Progressive rabbinical seminary (*see* PROGRESSIVE JUDAISM), founded in London by German refugee scholars and partly intended to train rabbis for the ravaged European communities, carries his name, as does a research institute dedicated to the study of German Jewry.

bakkasha ('petition, supplication') Technical term for a type of selicha (*see* SELI-CHOT), composed either in rhymed prose (e.g. KÉTER MALCHUT) or in formal verse. The plural, bakkashot, is the name given to a cycle of hymns sung in some, particularly Sefardi, congregations before the commencement of the Sabbath morning service. In congregations of Syrian or Moroccan origin, this activity has developed into a separate service, conducted at dawn on the Sabbath.

bal tashchit ('do not destroy') Biblical prohibition on cutting down fruit trees, even when besieging an enemy city (Deuteronomy 20.19–20). The Talmud and commentators extend the prohibition to cover any senseless destruction or waste, thus providing a basis for some halachic arguments in the ecological sphere. *See* ECOLOGY.

Bar Kochba, Simeon (d. 135) Nom de guerre of the leader of a revolt against Roman rule in Judaea: the revolt began in 132 and ended with Bar Kochba's death. The name means 'Son of the Star', apparently an allusion to Numbers 24.17, understood as a messianic prophecy. Our knowledge of his life and campaigns has been greatly increased in recent decades by archaeological discoveries, and particularly by the discovery of a cache of letters from and to him in a cave in the Judaean desert. From these we can see that his real name was Simeon bar Kosiba. It seems that his Jewish enemies nicknamed him Bar Koziba, 'Son of the Lie'. At the height of the revolt he controlled a large territory and even issued coins, featuring the Jerusalem Temple that he presumably planned to rebuild. However, the Romans gradually gained the upper hand. He was killed at Beitar, a name that has consequently become heavy with symbolism to Jewish nationalists today.

bar mitsva (Aramaic/Hebrew, 'son of the commandment') In Talmudic usage, an adult Jewish male, who is subject to the full rigour of the COMMANDMENTS. Nowadays commonly used of the ceremony marking the attainment of legal majority. According to Talmudic HALACHA, the legal age of majority is 13 years; from this age a male Jew is responsible for his own actions, whereas previously his father bore responsibility for him. It has become customary to mark the occasion by calling him up to the reading of the Torah; he may also read the HAFTARA, and nowadays he sometimes does much more, for example leading the congregation in prayer or giving an address. The coming of age, which in the common Jewish mind has become notional and far removed from any concrete or detailed sense of legal liability, has also come to be marked by a joyous family celebration, and this too is often referred to as a bar mitsva. So central has the ceremony become in family and social life that it is even observed today by Karaites, although it has no scriptural basis. *See also* BAT MITSVA.

baraita (Aramaic, 'external [teaching]'; Hebrew plural baraitot) Technical term used by Babylonian Amora'im to denote a Tannaitic teaching that is 'external', i.e. that was not included in the MISHNAH. There are many such teachings in both Talmuds; they are cast in Hebrew, unlike most of the Talmudic text which is in Aramaic, and are introduced by the Aramaic formula tno rabbanan, 'our rabbis have taught'. These teachings resemble the extra-Mishnaic teachings collected together in the TOSEFTA.

Baron, Salo Wittmayer (1895–1989) Historian. Born in Tarnow (Galicia), he studied at the University of Vienna and also graduated as a rabbi from the Jewish Theological Seminary in Vienna in 1920. After emigrating to the United States and teaching for a while at the Jewish Institute of Religion in New York, Baron was offered a newly created Chair of Jewish History, Literature, and Institutions in 1930 by Columbia University, where he remained for the rest of his career. His great work was *A Social and Religious History of the Jews* (18 volumes, 1937–83). Focusing on the social history and cultural accomplishments of the Jews, rather than on what he termed the 'lachrymose conception of Jewish history', Baron also sought to reintegrate religious experience into the historical fabric of Jewish life.

Bashyachi, Elijah (c. 1420–90) Karaite scholar. Born in Adrianople, he moved to Constantinople soon after the Ottoman conquest of the Byzantine capital, and quickly established his authority over Karaite communities in different countries. He is particularly remembered for his legal code, Adderet Eliyyahu. He was an advocate of rapprochement between Karaites and Rabbanites.

bat *See* NAMES AND NAMING.

bat kol ('daughter of a voice') In the rabbinic literature, a supernatural voice, purporting to give the divine view of an event or decision.

bat mitsva ('daughter of the commandment') An adult Jewish woman, subject to the COMMANDMENTS, particularly on the occasion of attaining her majority, or the occasion itself. Women are traditionally considered to achieve legal majority a year earlier than men, on their twelfth birthday. Because of the restrictions traditionally governing women's participation in synagogue services, the introduction of a public bat mitsva ceremony, analogous to the BAR MITSVA for men, proved a contentious issue, particularly in Orthodoxy. In the other modernist denominations, however, it has now become accepted as a normal part of the life of the congregation. In Reform and Liberal congregations it is usually celebrated at the age of 13.

bathing Prescribed in the Torah as a ritual of cleansing from various kinds of pollution or impurity, or before participating in certain religious rituals. In the Roman period some Jewish groups (such as the Essenes) practised daily immersion as a matter of course. Bathing was also prescribed by the rabbis for PROSELYTES, as a prerequisite to admission into the Jewish community. Today it is considered mandatory only for women after menstrual impurity and after childbirth, and for proselytes of both sexes. Such bathing is performed in a MIKVE or in natural running water. Some particularly pious Jewish men also bathe before the Sabbath and festivals. Cleanliness is a great virtue, and Jews are generally enjoined to bath and wash thoroughly, particularly in readiness for the Sabbath and festivals. Before the widespread availability of private baths the communal bathhouse was one of the natural focuses of Jewish social and religious life. *See also* IMMERSION; WASHING.

Bava Batra (Aramaic, 'last gate') Tractate of the Mishnah, Tosefta and both Talmuds, located in the order Nezikin. The tractate deals with one's rights and obligations in respect of others, and includes such issues as purchases and inheritance. Also included are such topics as the right to privacy, protection of the environment and honesty in business dealings.

Bava Kamma (Aramaic, 'first gate') Tractate of the Mishnah, Tosefta and both Talmuds, located in the order Nezikin. The tractate deals with torts. It begins by distinguishing the main categories (AVOT) of damage to property, and goes on to consider theft and bodily injury.

Bava Metsi'a (Aramaic, 'middle gate') Tractate of the Mishnah, Tosefta and both Talmuds, located in the order Nezikin. The subject matter includes, among others, found property, purchases, usury and rentals.

Bavli ('Babylonian') Term applied particularly to the Babylonian TALMUD.

BCE Abbreviation for 'Before the Common Era' or 'Before the Current Era'. Alternative designation for years of the pre-Christian era, avoiding the Christian designation BC ('before Christ'). *See also* CE; AM.

beard The Talmud calls the beard 'an adornment of the face', and in ancient times it was generally the practice for men to wear beards. The Torah forbids the shaving of the 'corners of the beard' (Leviticus 19.27, 21.5), and the rabbis interpret this to mean that facial hair must not be shaved at all. Other methods of removing hair are not forbidden. Thus the SHULCHAN ARUCH (Yore De'a 181.10) permits cutting the beard with scissors, even if it is cut so closely as to look as if it were shaved. Many Orthodox Jews consider this permission to extend to electric razors. Depilatory creams are permitted, too, provided they are not scraped off with a metal blade. Traditionalist men, both Sefardi and Ashkenazi, have a strong preference for letting the beard grow. It is customary for men not to shave during the period of the ÓMER, or while mourning.

Bechorot ('firstborns') Tractate of the Mishnah, Tosefta and both Talmuds, located in the order Kodashim. The tractate deals with laws concerning firstborn male offspring of animals and humans, which according to the Bible (e.g. Exodus 13.2, 12) have to be dedicated to God.

bedéken (Yiddish) Ashkenazi veiling ceremony, immediately before a wedding, at which the bridegroom places the veil on the bride.

beit din ('place of judgment'; plural battei din) A rabbinic law court. The Mishnah distinguishes three kinds of court. The lowest, presided over by three judges, was empowered to hear civil cases. The next court, also termed lesser Sanhedrin, had twenty-three judges and heard criminal cases. The 'great beit din' or Sanhedrin had seventy or seventy-one judges, and tried the most serious cases: for example an entire tribe, a false prophet or a high priest could supposedly only be tried by such a court. Today in most countries the beit din only deals with matters of personal status (such as divorce, conversion, or the determination of Jewish status); it can also act, by agreement of the parties, as a court of arbitration. The technical term for the president of a court is av beit din ('father of the court').

Beit Hillel *See* HILLEL.

beit kenéset ('place of assembly') Hebrew term for a SYNAGOGUE.

beit midrash ('place of teaching') A place dedicated to the study and teaching of Torah (in the wider sense, including Talmud and halacha). In practice the meaning of the term is little different from that of YESHIVA.

Beitar *See* BAR KOCHBA, SIMEON.

bells Jews do not use bells as Christians do, to summon the faithful to prayer or to mark high points in the liturgy. However, they attach tiny bells to the silver adornments of the Torah scroll, particularly the FINIALS, which for this reason are often referred to as 'bells', especially among English-speaking Sefardim. Their use recalls the little bells sewn on the hems of the priests' robes in the Torah (Exodus 28.33-5).

Bemidbar ('in the desert [of]') Hebrew name of the biblical book of Numbers, of which it is among the opening words.

ben *See* NAMES AND NAMING.

Ben Ish Chai *See* YOSEF CHAYYIM.

Ben Israel, Manasseh (1604-57) Dutch theologian. Born in Madeira of crypto-Jewish parentage (*see* CONVERSION), he served for many years as spiritual head of the Sefardi congregation in Amsterdam, and devoted himself to helping other refugees from the Inquisition like himself. Thanks to his extensive knowledge of theology he came to be regarded as a spokesman for Judaism. His theological writings aimed at a Jewish and general readership led to friendships with leading men of his time, such as the Christian theologian Hugo Grotius and the painter Rembrandt, who painted and engraved his portrait. His study of the messianic ideas of Judaism, *The Hope of Israel*, led to involvement in the campaign for the readmission of the Jews to England; in 1655 he travelled to London and presented a petition to this effect to Oliver Cromwell. He set up Amsterdam's first Hebrew printing press in 1626.

Ben Sira, Wisdom of Ancient Hebrew work included in some Christian Bibles under the name Ecclesiasticus, but absent from Jewish Bibles. The author lived and wrote in Jerusalem in the early 2nd century BCE, and his book was translated into Greek later in the century by his grandson. The Hebrew original, which is quoted in the Talmud, was lost until parts of it were recovered from the Cairo GENIZA at the end of the 19th century and from Qumran and Masada in the 20th. The book consists largely of moral maxims and exhortations, as well as praise of famous men. A much later Hebrew work, the Alphabet of Ben Sira, contains sayings attributed to Ben Sira as well as other material, largely frivolous in character.

Benamozegh, Elia (1822-1900) Italian philosopher and kabbalist. Benamozegh was unusual for a Jewish religious thinker of his time in having a positive attitude to KABBALA, and in fact he saw it as the true speculative and rational tradition of Judaism. In a series of works written in Hebrew, French and Italian he confronted this tradition with European thought, particularly with the idealism of Hegel. In *Morale* *juive et morale chrétienne* (1867) he questions the ethical superiority of Christianity. In *Israël et humanité* (1885) he insists that all religion is 'revealed legislation' (a term that Moses MENDELSSOHN had famously applied to Judaism as contrasted with Christianity); taking up a Talmudic distinction between the 613 COMMANDMENTS binding on Jews and the seven NOACHIAN COMMANDMENTS given to the rest of humankind he shows that Jews and Gentiles are bound up in a single humanity regulated by divine laws.

benching *See* BENTSHN.

Bendigamos (Spanish, 'Let us bless') A grace after meals in the form of a song in Spanish. It begins: 'Bendigamos al Altísimo,/ Al Señor que nos crió,/ Démosle agradecimiento/ Por los bienes que nos dió' (Let us bless the Most High, The Lord who raised us,/ Let us give him thanks/ For the good things which he has given us).

Bene Israel ('children of Israel') Biblical expression (denoting all descendants of JACOB) specifically applied to a community of Jews originally from the villages of the Konkan coast in Maharashtra (north-west India). In the 19th and 20th centuries they gradually left their villages and began to settle in Bombay and other Indian cities, in Aden, and eventually in Israel, where for a long time they were not recognized as Jews by the chief rabbinate, because of doubts about their origin.

benediction (in Hebrew, beracha; plural berachot) Characteristic unit of Jewish worship, typically expressed in the form 'Blessed (baruch) are you, O Lord...', followed by a description of some aspect of God's activity. Benedictions play a large part in private devotional life as well as in the worship of the synagogue. Many of them were composed by the rabbis of the Talmud. They may be long or short, the short ones often consisting of only a few words. Blessings begin in one of two ways, 'Blessed are you, Lord, our God, King of the universe' (perhaps better translated 'eternal King') or simply 'Blessed are you, Lord'. What follows this opening may be anything from a long paean of praise to a short formula, often consisting of only two words, identifying an aspect of God's character or activity. A curiosity of these formulae is that they are frequently worded in the third person, even though the introduction is in the second person. (For example: 'Blessed are you, Lord, who blesses His people Israel with peace'.) The formulae are best understood as being in effect titles of God, 'resurrecter of the dead', 'clother of the naked', 'blesser of his people', and so forth. If the benediction is a long one it will often conclude with a short benediction, summing up the message of the longer one. This short benediction is known as a 'seal' (CHATIMA). A seal is frequently found at the end of a prayer which does not begin as a benediction; in this case the whole prayer is considered to be a benediction. The AMIDA is made up of benedictions, and another sequence is included in the morning prayers, but in fact a large part of all Jewish worship is made up of benedictions, and specific benedictions are prescribed to be said on various occasions. These may be divided into three categories: 1. those said on fulfilling a religious obligation, such as lighting Sabbath lamps or putting on the TALLIT (these contain an acknowledgement that the religious obligation in question is of divine origin); 2. those expressing gratitude for sensual pleasures and bodily sustenance, such as food and drink, and sweet smells; 3. those acknowledging that all the out-standing moments of our lives, whether joyful or sombre, are of divine origin.

Benei Akiva *See* MIZRACHI.

Benei Mikra *See* KARAISM.

beneí tóra ('sons of Torah') Term applied to themselves by CHAREDIM in Israel who place Torah study, in the YESHIVA, at the centre of their lives. They endeavour to make the text, as interpreted by their experts, the sole criterion for choices in everyday life (*see* DÁ'AS TÓRA; FUNDAMENTALISM), and to distance themselves from the pollution of modern life, the demands of the state, and gainful employment.

bentshn Yiddish term, derived ultimately from Latin benedicere, to bless, and applied to the pronouncing of a BENEDICTION. Its commonest application is to the grace after meals. English-speakers often corrupt it into 'benching', with a corres-ponding verb, 'to bench'.

beracha (plural berachot) A BENEDICTION.

Berachot ('benedictions') Tractate of the Mishnah, Tosefta and both Talmuds, located in the order Zera'im. The tractate deals with worship of God, and covers the rules for reciting the SHEMÁ, the AMIDA, GRACE AFTER MEALS and miscellaneous BENEDICTIONS.

Bereshit ('in the beginning') Hebrew name of the biblical book of GENESIS, of which it is the first word. *See also* MA'ASE BERESHIT.

Berkovits, Eliezer (1908–92) Theologian. Born in Transylvania and ordained an Orthodox rabbi in Berlin in 1934, Berkovits lived in the United States from 1950 until 1967, when he settled in Israel. He wrote nineteen books, the best-known being *Faith After the Holocaust* (1973), *Crisis and Faith* (1976), *With God in Hell: Judaism in the Ghettos and Death Camps* (1979), and *Not in Heaven: The Nature and Function of Halakha* (1983). Two major concerns are HALACHA and how to accommodate it to modernity, and theodicy in the light of the Holocaust (*see* HESTER PANIM).

Bertinoro, Obadia Yare di (c. 1450–1509) Halachist. Born and brought up in Italy, he settled in Jerusalem. Of his many writings the one that has achieved enduring fame is his commentary on the Mishnah, which has accompanied the text in most Mishnah editions since its first publication in 1558–9. It is a lucid distillation of earlier comments, and states the definitive HALACHA in the innumerable places where the Mishnah records an open-ended discussion.

Besht *See* BAAL SHEM TOV.

Beta Israel Community originating in Ethiopia, and now mainly living in Israel, as a result of mass emigration between 1977 and 1993. Formerly often known by the pejorative name of Falasha, the Beta Israel had a strongly biblical religion resembling the dominant form of Ethiopian Christianity but lacking distinctively Christian features. As a result of efforts by Jewish missionaries, and more recently by contact with Jews in Israel, their religion has moved closer to familiar forms of Judaism. Customs such as animal sacrifices and monasticism have been abandoned and Hebrew has replaced Ethiopic as the language of Bible readings. One religious custom that has been maintained in Israel is Sigd (from Ethiopic sagada, 'to prostrate oneself'), a pilgrimage and fast observed forty-nine days after the Day of Atonement, and commemorating the renewal of the COVENANT in the time of Ezra and Nehemiah. Worshippers climb a hill carrying rocks on their heads to symbolize submission, and read the TEN COMMANDMENTS and passages from Ezra and Nehemiah.

beth din *See* BEIT DIN.

Betsa ('egg') Tractate of the Mishnah and Talmud, located in the order Mo'ed. The tractate deals with work forbidden or permitted on festivals. Also called Yom Tov ('festival days').

Bible

The term 'Bible' is borrowed from Christian usage, and the Jewish Bible contains substantially the same texts as the Christian Old Testament, although they are arranged differently. In earlier Hebrew sources we find such designations as 'the books' or 'sacred books', reminding us that the Bible is not a single work but a library composed of many individual volumes. We also find the expression 'reading' (mikra), a term that points to public reading. The title that figures on modern editions is TANACH, an acronym made up of the initial letters of the three sections, Torah, Nevi'im and Ketuvim. This abbreviation has been in use since the middle ages. The Hebrew text used by Jews, as indeed by Christian scholars, is the so-called Masoretic text, which reached its present form in the 10th century.

Originally the sacred books were written (like other texts) on parchment scrolls, and this ancient form of book is still retained for the copies of the Torah used in the synagogue. The scroll of Esther read at Purim is handwritten on parchment, as are mezuzot and tefillin. In time, however, for other purposes the scroll gave way to the codex, and the manuscript codex was eventually replaced by the printed book. The Hebrew Bible was first printed in its entirety at Soncino, near Mantua in northern Italy, in 1488, and other editions soon followed. In 1516/17 the 'rabbinic Bible', a Hebrew Bible accompanied by an Aramaic TARGUM and rabbinic commentaries, was printed in Venice by a Christian printer, Daniel Bomberg. The Bible has been printed in Hebrew many times since, by Jews and Christians, in various editions. However, there is hardly any variation in the text contained in the different editions, because they are all based ultimately on the Masoretic text. Jews freely use Hebrew texts edited and printed by Christians, and have adopted the Christian chapter divisions.

BOOKS OF THE BIBLE

	English name	Hebrew name
Torah	Genesis	Bereshit
	Exodus	Shemót
	Leviticus	Vayikra
	Numbers	Bemidbar
	Deuteronomy	Devarim
Nevi'im (Prophets)		
Nevi'im Rishonim (Former Prophets)	Joshua	Yehoshú'a
	Judges	Shoftim
	Samuel	Shemu'el (two books)
	Kings	Melachim (two books)
Nevi'im Acharonim (Latter Prophets)	Isaiah	Yesháya
	Jeremiah	Yirmíya
	Ezekiel	Yehezkel
Tresar (Twelve Minor Prophets)	Hosea	Hoshé'a
	Joel	Yo'el
	Amos	Amos
	Obadiah	Ovadia
	Jonah	Yona
	Micah	Micha
	Nahum	Nachum
	Habakkuk	Chavakkuk
	Zephaniah	Tsefania
	Haggai	Chaggai
	Zechariah	Zecharia
	Malachi	Malachi
Ketuvim (Writings)	Psalms	Tehillim
	Proverbs	Mishle
	Job	Iyov

Song of Songs	Shir ha-Shirim
Ruth	Rut
Lamentations	Eicha
Ecclesiastes	Kohélet
Esther	Ester
Daniel	Daniel
Ezra	Ezra
Nehemiah	Nechemia
Chronicles	Divrei ha-Yamim (two books)

The authority of these various books, the most ancient works to have come down to us in the Jewish tradition, is enormous. However, the different books enjoy different kinds and levels of authority, and various sectors of Jewry have different understandings of the claims the books exert on Jews today. At the heart of the matter is a theological question: whether the books are believed to emanate directly from the 'mouth of God'. For more or less the whole of the Jewish tradition down to the beginning of the 19th century and for all traditionalist and Orthodox authorities today, the five books of the Torah at least are a direct REVELATION from God given to Moses and the people of Israel at Mount Sinai. This tenet has been challenged in the past two centuries from a number of angles, historical, philosophical and theological, but despite all the challenges the authority of the Torah has remained very strong, and is invoked even by Jews who reject any supernatural belief. Also in the modern period the appeal to the prophets has become stronger, notably among Reform Jews and Jewish socialists (particularly in Israel), who admire the loud and confident cry for justice and compassion for the less privileged members of society.

The reading of the biblical books is inseparable from their interpretation, and the Jewish tradition of interpretation is embodied in a large mass of writings going back to antiquity. We have a vast literature, mainly written down in Hebrew or Aramaic, of which the earliest layers are found within the biblical books themselves, as later books rewrite or expound material from earlier books. The Masoretic notes also embody a large amount of interpretation, and much more interpretation can be found in the pages of the Mishnah and Talmud. However, the classical rabbinic sources for the interpretation of the biblical books are found mainly in the bodies of writings known as TARGUMIM, MIDRASH, and COMMENTARY (perush), each of which comprises an enormous mass of written materials. Selections from these three categories of writing accompany the Hebrew text in the rabbinic Bible, which is the foundation of serious biblical study among Jews, and in the annotated texts that are used by congregants in synagogues for following the public reading.

Since the rise of critical biblical study in the 19th century the Bible is no longer read either as a sufficient and reliable guide to ancient history or as an infallible account of God's character and activity. Research may have confirmed some of the details, but it has disproved so much else that the authority of the whole has been fatally undermined for all but those who choose to put their trust in the Bible and suppose that it is the scholars who are in error.

That is not to say that Jews have cast off the Bible as a worn-out vessel that has served its purpose. It still has the power to fascinate and even compel new generations, and modern scholarship has served to enrich understanding. In Israel even godless Jews read it and bandy quotations in support of their views. Nevertheless it is fair to say that the power of the Bible has declined, for a number of reasons besides the abandonment of the old doctrine of divine revelation. For all the immediacy and poetry of its language (and the revival of Hebrew has made this language accessible to a much wider audience), the Bible speaks of very remote times. The way of life it advocates has noble elements, some of which may have been in advance of their times, but in other ways it strikes many readers as archaic and even primitive. Even Orthodox Jews have expressed perplexity at the complex regulations for animal sacrifices, for example, and one does not have to be a feminist to feel that the biblical assumptions about the respective roles of men and women can no longer serve as the basis for Jewish society. Many of the Bible's teachings are too vague or inconsistent to be put into practice, and a great deal is simply irrelevant to contemporary life.

See also TORAH.

biblical commentary *See* COMMENTARY, BIBLICAL.

bikkur cholim Visiting the sick. This is a highly valued social and religious obligation in Jewish ethics. According to the Talmud, it is a commandment to which no limit has been prescribed, and which is rewarded in both this world and the next.

Bikkurim ('first fruits') Tractate of the Mishnah, Tosefta and Palestinian Talmud, located in the order Zera'im. The tractate deals with the offering of first fruits of harvests in the Land of Israel (Exodus 23.19, Deuteronomy 26.1–11).

bima (Greek, 'platform') Raised platform in synagogue from which the TORAH is read. Synonym of almémar, teba.

Bina ('understanding') In kabbala, one of the SEFIROT. *See also* CHABAD CHASIDISM.

bioethics A branch of applied ethics addressing ethical questions raised for society and individuals by medical science, including particularly, but not limited to, questions related to the beginning and the end of life. As with all ethical issues, Jewish approaches take account of halachic sources but also take non-halachic (e.g. philosophical and theological) arguments into consideration. Questions concerning the beginning of life include such issues as fertility and infertility treatments, use of donated genetic material, stem-cell research and cloning; questions related to the end of life concern issues around terminal illness and the approach of death, the process of dying, and disposal of the corpse and body parts after death. Jewish ethics, which is generally based more on obligations than on rights, and which asserts very strongly the respect for life and for the human person (including respect for dead bodies), sometimes tends towards solutions to these questions that differ to a greater or lesser extent from those put forward by non-Jewish ethicists. While many of these issues have a long history of discussion, recent rapid scientific advances mean that often there is little or no directly relevant material in the traditional sources, and general principles have to be applied in areas where very different alternative solutions are possible.

birkat ha-mazón *See* GRACE AFTER MEALS.

birkat kohanim ('blessing of priests') Blessing of the people by the hereditary priests. Sefardim also call it nesi'at kappáyim (raising of the hands). This relic of Temple ritual is preserved in most synagogues to this day; it has been abolished along with other priestly prerogatives in Reform synagogues, and some Conservative congregations have abandoned it too. The wording of the threefold blessing is given in Numbers 6.24–6: 'May the Lord bless and protect you. May the Lord let his face shine upon you and be gracious to you. May the Lord look kindly on you and grant you peace.' The words of the blessing have been included in the public recitation of the AMIDA in the morning and additional services, as an introduction to the benediction of peace. On certain specified occasions (generally on festivals unless they fall on the Sabbath; in Israel daily) the kohanim ascend to the DUCHAN and bless the rest of the congregation. Before beginning the ceremony they remove their shoes and have their hands washed by the LEVITES present. Once on the platform they turn to face the congregation, their heads and faces covered by the TALLIT, hands extended in front of them in a special form (thumbs touching, pairs of fingers making a V shape), and repeat the words of the blessing individually following prompting by the reader. The worshippers traditionally refrain from looking at the priests as they pronounce the words of the blessing.

Birnbaum, Nathan *See* ZIONISM.

birth control *See* CONTRACEPTION.

bitachon *See* FAITH.

bittul chamets ('cancellation of leaven') Legal act, performed on the eve of Passover, of disowning any leaven (CHAMETS) that may remain in one's possession after examination and destruction. The act is accomplished by pronouncing an Aramaic formula.

bittul ha-yesh ('annihilation of being [i.e. of the self]') Also called simply bittul. In CHASIDISM, the ultimate goal of the chasid. The concerns of the individual are left behind as the soul soars aloft in contemplation of the all-encompassing Godhead. The concept of bittul plays an important part in the approach to contemplative prayer developed by the early CHABAD masters.

Bi'ur ('explanation') Commentary on the Torah by a team of scholars working under the guidance of Moses MENDELSSOHN, written in Hebrew and published in the early 1780s. The commentary, published alongside Mendelssohn's own German translation of the biblical text printed in Hebrew characters, combines comments on the plain meaning of the text derived from classic medieval Hebrew commentaries with contemporary observations. It opened a new era in Jewish Bible study, introducing many Jews to the ideas of the ENLIGHTENMENT.

bi'ur chamets ('destruction of leaven') Destruction of leaven (CHAMETS) on the morning of the day before PASSOVER.

See also BITTUL CHAMETS.

blasphemy *See* CAPITAL PUNISHMENT; HOLINESS; NOACHIAN COMMANDMENTS.

blessing *See* BENEDICTION.

Bloch, Ernst (1885–1977) Marxist philosopher. Born in Germany, he moved to the United States in 1938; in 1948 he accepted an invitation to teach philosophy at Leipzig, in East Germany, then in 1961 left for West Germany. In *Geist der Utopie* (*Spirit of Utopia*, 1918) Bloch looks forward to a renewal of Judaism in messianic terms, and the messianic heritage (specifically the messianism of Isaac LURIA and the idea of TIKKUN) reappears in his subsequent writings, notably *Das Prinzip Hoffnung* (*The Hope Principle*, 1954–9). He adopts a kabbalistic interpretation of EHYE ASHER EHYE: God shares the exile of his people; the translation 'I shall be who I shall be' indicates the presence of futurity at the very core of God's being.

blood *See* DIETARY REGULATIONS; NIDDA.

Bonastruc ça Porta *See* NACHMANIDES, MOSES.

books Judaism has always been a text-based religion. Literacy has traditionally been highly valued, and the written word has enjoyed a status that is all the stronger for want of a well-developed continuous tradition of musical or visual art. In the past the book was accorded a status little short of magical. At the heart of Jewish worship is the display, reading, and exposition of a written text, the Torah. Public education has been accorded a high priority in Jewish society down the ages, and the possession of books has been a feature of Jewish homes even when it was rare in the surrounding culture. Scholarship has been valued as a profession, and those who earned their livelihood by other means have made time in their lives to pursue it, often to a high standard. Respect for the book as an object is enjoined in the codes of Jewish practice, and this applies not only to sacred texts but to books of all kinds, which must not be used for inappropriate purposes, or defaced, or even left lying open or fallen on the ground. When a religious book is no longer fit for use it is not thrown out but buried with due honours in the cemetery. A great rabbi of the 15th century banned from attending his lectures a student who had refused to lend another student a book. With the invention of printing, Jewish books were among the first to be printed in large numbers, and in many places the first printing presses to be set up were Hebrew ones. Even today, when the publishing and reading of books is widespread, Jews are prominent among writers, publishers, and readers.

bread Considered in Jewish tradition the staple food, and an essential element in a meal. A special benediction is said on eating it (*see* HA-MOTSI), and once this benediction has been pronounced at the beginning of a meal there is no need to recite further benedictions over other foods that are eaten. The full GRACE AFTER MEALS is only said after a meal at which bread has been consumed. In the ritual of the tabernacle and the temple bread played a special role. In addition to offerings of flour mixed with oil, which were offered up raw, baked, grilled or fried (Leviticus 2), twelve loaves of bread were displayed on a table 'before the Lord as a gift from the Israelites' (Leviticus 24.5–9). Each Sabbath they were replaced with new ones. Nowadays the Sabbath is welcomed with two challot, plaited loaves baked from a rich dough (*see* CHALLA). These two loaves are often said to symbolize the manna, the 'bread from heaven', of which a double portion was given in readiness for the Sabbath (Exodus 16.22–6). Bread comes in two forms, leavened (raised with the addition of yeast or by means of natural airborne yeasts) and unleavened. All the offerings mentioned above were unleavened, as is all bread eaten at Passover (*see* MATSA). Matsa is described as the bread of affliction, or poverty (*see* HA-LACHMA).

See also MENACHOT.

breaking of the vessels *See* SHEVIRA.

brit *See* COVENANT.

brit mila *See* CIRCUMCISION.

Buber, Martin (1878–1965) Religious philosopher. Born in Vienna, he spent part of his childhood in the home of his grandfather Solomon (*see* next entry). He taught Jewish thought in Frankfurt and from 1938 in Jerusalem. Buber was a friend and close associate of Franz ROSENZWEIG (with whom he undertook a new German translation of the Bible), and his well-known philosophy of dialogue, set out notably in his most famous book *Ich und Du* (1925; *I and Thou*, 1937 - a better translation of the title would be *I and You*), is based on personal experience and relationship. This is undoubtedly one of the most original and influential Jewish books of the 20th century. The term 'Ich und Du' can be traced back to Hermann COHEN, who wrote in a study published in 1908: 'The ethical self must be engaged in action. For this self, there exists no I without a You.' The argument of Buber's *Ich und Du* is by now well known. So far as God is concerned what it boils down to is that God is not to be studied, but only encountered. Buber uses the analogy of a close relationship between two people (who may but need not be lovers). The speaker who says 'You' is also an 'I'; within the I–You relationship the two terms, although they do not merge to the point of losing their identity, do not have an independent existence. The relationship is reciprocal. Behind each 'You' whom we address, we catch a glimpse of the unique everlasting You, whom we call God.

Buber's God, characterized as the 'Eternal You', is known not through doctrinal formulation or metaphysical speculation but through personal encounter. It is the encounter with the Eternal You that constitutes revelation, and this revelation, which has no objective content, is open to anyone who is prepared to relate fully to the surrounding world. Buber's ideas represent an extreme reaction against the traditional quest for a rational understanding of God, and give voice to a newer search for a more personally fulfilling explanation. Although in a formal sense it is no doubt true to say that they have so far had a more marked impact on Christian than on Jewish thinkers, they have also answered the unformulated need of many Jews either disillusioned with institutional religion or bewildered and repelled by the traditional teachings about God.

Buber is also remembered for his books on Chasidism, notably his *Tales of the Chasidim*, in which he presented and interpreted the religious ideas and folk tales of the movement for Western readers, and for his staunch commitment to ZIONISM coupled with an equally staunch refusal to allow its political dynamics to outweigh humane Jewish social and cultural values. He was a passionate believer in Jewish and Arab co-operation in the development of a single, bi-national state, and to this end he joined in founding a political movement (Ichud) in 1942.

Buber, Solomon (1827–1906) Editor of rabbinic literature. Born in Lemberg (Lviv), Buber was a successful banker, and was thus able to finance his scholarly activities. He pioneered the critical edition of rabbinic Midrashim, and between 1868 and 1902 he published an astonishing number of editions, most of which remain the best or only editions of the works in question, notably *Pesikta de-Rav Kahana* (1868), a version of *Midrash Tanchuma* (1885) and the *Midrash on Psalms* (1891). He also published historical works, particularly on the history of the Jews in Poland.

Bund, the (Yiddish) Abbreviation of Algemeyner Arbeter Bund in Polyn un Rusland, General Jewish Workers' Union in Poland and Russia, a political association founded in 1897. The Bund sought full civil rights for the Jews in Russia coupled with recognition of their 'national-cultural autonomy', similar to other national groups. At first the question of securing national rights for the Jews was hotly debated, but eventually it was agreed as an aim. At the same time the Bund was resolutely opposed to the out-and-out nationalism of the Zionists. The Fourth Party Convention, in May 1901, declared that 'Zionist propaganda inflames nationalist feelings and hinders the development of class consciousness among the Jewish proletariat'. Despite the hostility of the Zionists and of both Jewish and non-Jewish socialists, the Bund attracted a large following, and continued to be active politically in Poland until the Nazi occupation.

burial Jewish tradition teaches that the dead must be buried as soon as possible, usually within twenty-four hours, unless death has taken place on the eve of Sabbath or a festival, or if there is a particular reason to postpone the burial, for example to wait for relatives and friends to arrive from far away, or if suitable shrouds or a coffin are not available. Before the body is placed in the coffin it is cleaned and ritually washed. This is often done by members of a special society, the CHEVRA KADISHA. Same-sex teams attend to male and female corpses, out of respect for the deceased, and throughout the washing great care is taken to maintain due respect. The body remains covered at all times. After the body has been carefully washed the 'purification' (tahara) is performed, by pouring a quantity of water over it. The body is then dried and dressed in a special set of clothes (tachrichim), which are the same for everybody, without distinction of wealth, status or learning. They are of white muslin, cotton or linen, and are made and put on without any knots. If a man has his own KÍTTEL, it forms part of the tachrichim, and he is also wrapped in his TALLIT, which has had the tassels (tsitsit) removed. A little earth from the Holy Land is sprinkled on the body, and it is placed in a plain coffin which is then sealed; it is not customary to display the body to view, nor is the application of cosmetics allowed. The funeral is known as levaya, 'accompanying'. It is considered a duty to accompany the dead, and a mark of respect which is all the more commendable as the recipient is unable to reciprocate. Prayers are said at home before proceeding to the cemetery, where further prayers are said in a hall or chapel, and a eulogy praising the deceased's virtues and accomplishments may be delivered. Nowadays a rabbi often officiates at a funeral, but there is no requirement to have a rabbi present. Pallbearers, or relatives and friends, carry the coffin from the chapel to the grave, pausing seven times on the way. The coffin is lowered into the grave, and immediate relatives, followed by the rest of those present, shovel some earth onto it. Worn-out bibles, prayer books and other texts containing the divine name may be buried in the grave, or they may be placed in a grave of their own, since they too are to be disposed of respectfully and not simply jettisoned. After burial the mourners recite the KADDISH. Before the mourners leave the cemetery, they are greeted with these words of condolence: 'May God comfort you together with all those who mourn for Zion and Jerusalem.'

Cairo Geniza *See* GENIZA.

calendar The Jewish year is essentially lunar. The month is a lunar month of twenty-nine or thirty days. Ideally the long and short months alternate, but occasional adjustments are made to prevent certain festivals from falling on particular days of the week. In biblical times the day of the new moon was a festival; today it is marked only by some minor variations in the liturgy, and by a public announcement on the preceding Sabbath. Originally the occurrence of the new moon (*see* ROSH CHÓDESH) was determined by observation; the calendar was fixed by calculation in the 4th century, and still corresponds to the observable phases of the moon. The calendar is not purely lunar, however, for if it were the festivals would move round the cycle of the seasons, whereas PASSOVER must fall in the spring, the season at which the exodus from Egypt took place. This adjustment is achieved by 'intercalating' an additional month seven times in every nineteen years. The additional month is inserted before the month in which Passover falls (*see* ADAR). All Jews today share this calendar (with the exception of the few remaining KARAITES, whose calendar is a little different). There is, however, a discrepancy with regard to the so-called 'second days' of festivals. Jews in Israel follow the biblical rules with regard to the three 'pilgrim festivals', Passover (the first and seventh days are full festivals), SHAVUOT (one day) and Tabernacles or SUKKOT (the first and eighth days are full festivals). According to ancient custom, outside Israel Jews added an extra day to each of these, probably because of uncertainty about the precise date before the calendar was fixed. Today Reform Jews in the Diaspora have reverted to the biblical dates, and some Conservative rabbis are in favour of doing likewise. New Year, however, which was a one-day festival in the Bible, is celebrated for two days both within and outside Israel, except among some Reform Jews, who prefer to follow the biblical practice.

The passage of the seasons is marked in the regular prayers by subtle variations, but in a larger sense the rhythm of the year as a whole is set by the cycle of the major festivals. The year has two focal points, one in the autumn and the other in the summer, corresponding to the ancient harvest festivals which were celebrated in the Temple period by pilgrimage to Jerusalem. The week-long autumn festival of Tabernacles is preceded by the solemnity of the TEN DAYS OF PENITENCE, framed by the NEW YEAR (Rosh ha-Shana) and the major fast of the Day of ATONEMENT (Yom Kippur). Together these constitute a festive period lasting just over three weeks; a month of penitential prayers leads up to it, and it ends with an explosion of joy at SIMCHAT TORA, marking the end of the annual cycle of Torah readings. The summer festivals are the week of Passover (Pésach) and the feast of Weeks (SHAVUOT). The seven intervening weeks, known as the 'Counting of the ÓMER', were probably a period of joyful celebration in ancient times, but they have come to be marked by a mood of muted sadness. Outside these two periods of major celebrations there are some lesser observances, such as the eight days of CHANUKKA in midwinter or PURIM in the early spring.

See table at p. 366. *See also* SABBATH.

candles Wax candles are associated today with joyful occasions such as the Sabbath and festivals, and also with remembrance of the dead; they have largely superseded the oil lamps that were used for lighting in the ancient Mediterranean region. A special benediction accompanies the lighting of candles or lamps at the inauguration of the Sabbath and each of the festivals, the wording being varied to suit the occasion. (Basic formula: '… who has sanctified us by his commandments and commanded us to light the lamp for …') These lights are traditionally lit by a woman, and it is customary to light two of them, but this number is not mandatory, and some Sabbath candelabra allow for seven lights, symbolizing the seven days of the creation story. A candle is used for the HAVDALA ceremony marking the end of the Sabbath or festival, and for this a different benediction is said ('… creator of lamps of fire'). Ashkenazim, taking punctilious note of the plural form 'lamps', use a braided candle with several wicks for this purpose. CHANUKKA is a veritable festival of lights, with forty-four candles or lamps being lit in the course of eight successive evenings (including the SHAMMASH).

The lighting of lamps for the Sabbath is considered to contribute to the joyful mood of the day (*see* ÓNEG SHABBAT). However, despite the wording of the benediction it is not a biblical command, and is traditionally ignored by Karaites, who, on the contrary, extinguish lamps and fires at the onset of Sabbath.

Proverbs 20.27, 'the spirit of man is the lamp of the Lord', is sometimes cited to explain the association of lamps and candles with the dead. A lit candle is traditionally placed at the head of the corpse, and is kept burning until after the burial; memorial lights are also lit by Ashkenazim during the week of mourning, on the anniversary of the death, and on the eve of the Day of Atonement. Electric lights are also permitted for this purpose, and in some synagogues one may see a board with many electric lights burning to commemorate the departed.

The same verse of Proverbs, interpreted differently, is also used to explain why the search for leaven before Passover is traditionally conducted by the light of a candle: as one removes leaven by the light of a candle so should one remove evil from one's heart by the light of one's conscience.

See also MENORA.

cantillation Form of chant used for the public reading of the Torah, the HAFTARA and the FIVE SCROLLS. Different branches of Judaism such as Ashkenazim and Sefardim have their own distinctive traditions of cantillation, but the written signs, which were devised by the MASORETES, are standard for all; they are marked in manuscripts and printed books, but not in Torah scrolls. Thus those reading the Torah in public must learn them by heart. In German Liberal Judaism the practice of cantillation was abandoned, on the grounds that it obscured the meaning of the text; however the pendulum has now swung back, and many congregations practice the chant.

cantor *See* CHAZZAN.

capital punishment Biblical law prescribes the death penalty for certain particularly serious offences (murder, forbidden sexual relations, blasphemy, idolatry, desecration of the Sabbath, witchcraft, kidnapping, and delinquent behaviour towards parents). These laws are discussed in the Mishnah and Talmud, but the force of the laws is attenuated by all kinds of additional requirements, and some rabbis expressed their opposition to the whole practice of capital punishment (Mishnah, Makkot 1.10). It is doubtful in any case that Jewish courts at the time had the power to condemn offenders to death. Today there is no characteristic Jewish view on the use of the death penalty.

Carlebach, Shlomo *See* NEO-CHASIDISM.

Caro, Joseph (1488–1575) Halachist. The compiler of the SHULCHAN ARUCH was born in Spain. After being twice exiled owing to Christian intolerance (from Spain in 1492 and Portugal in 1497) he settled in the Ottoman empire and became one of the leading figures of the new centre in SAFED. His great halachic work the Beit Yosef (House of Joseph) was intended as a commentary on Jacob ben Asher's ARBA'A TURIM; the Shulchan Aruch is a concise summary of this work, designed for the needs of students and as a handy reference book. It achieved enormous respect and authority as a codification of halacha, and has never been superseded. Caro is the author of a number of other halachic works. In addition to his work as a halachist, he had a rich inner spiritual life, and claimed that he was visited by a MAGGID, a heavenly mentor whom he identified as the Messiah or as the SHECHINA. He recorded these revelations in a diary. Caro played a central part in a circle of kabbalists that combined fervent messianic yearning with extreme ASCETICISM. He was influenced by the martyr Solomon MOLCHO, whom he may have met.

Catholic Israel A theological conception of the essential unity of the Jewish people, developed by Solomon SCHECHTER and based partly on the old idea of KLAL YISRA'EL and partly on the Christian concept of Catholicity. Judaism is not based simply on the Bible as revealed scripture but on a continuous tradition of interpretation and on a consensus that accepts some traditions and discards others, accepting innovations in accordance with the spirit of the tradition in general and the ethos of the times. This consensus is to be distinguished alike from the IJMA' of the Karaites, which is fundamentally sectarian and associated with a rejection of tradition, and from the 'folkways' of Mordecai KAPLAN.

CE Abbreviation for 'Common Era' or 'Current Era'. Alternative designation for years of the Christian era, avoiding the Christian designation AD (annus or anno domini, Latin for 'Year of the Lord'). *See also* AM; BCE.

celibacy is generally frowned on in Judaism, and celibates are traditionally barred from certain religious and judicial functions, in keeping with the command to 'be fruitful and multiply' (Genesis 1.28), commonly described as the first command in the Bible (although Abraham IBN EZRA points out rather scathingly that it was first given to fish, not humans). The SHULCHAN ARUCH sums up the dominant traditional view: 'Every man is obliged to marry in order to fulfil the duty of procreation; whoever does not contribute to the propagation of humankind is considered as a shedder of blood, who diminishes the divine image and causes God's presence to depart from Israel' (Éven ha-Ézer 1.1). An exception is made in the case of homosexuals by some modern Orthodox halachists, who recognize the difficulties raised by subjecting such individuals to the duty of procreation, and recommend that they should abstain from sexual activity entirely.

cemeteries It is considered obligatory for a Jewish community, however small, to own a cemetery, since the burial of the dead is considered a solemn obligation that rests upon the entire community. Jewish cemeteries are set apart by a wall or hedge, and are treated with great respect. Eating, drinking and frivolous behaviour are forbidden, and walking on graves is avoided. The presence of corpses is technically a source of pollution, and it is customary to wash the hands on leaving a cemetery. (On account of pollution, priests are not supposed to enter cemeteries.) Normally only Jews are buried in Jewish cemeteries, but some permit the burial of non-Jewish family members. By old tradition, suicides, apostates and notorious sinners are buried away from other graves, near the wall; however, this practice has been relaxed in recent times. Graves are usually marked with a tombstone: Ashkenazi graves have a standing headstone while Sefardi graves are covered with a stone lying flat. All stones carry an inscription in Hebrew or the vernacular, or both. Occasionally a grave is marked 'GENIZA': this is where discarded holy books are buried. Jewish gravestones are normally simple, without elaborate carvings. Pictures of the deceased are not allowed. Flowers are not placed on the coffin or on graves; people who visit a grave will often place a small stone on it to mark their visit.

Centenary Perspective A summary of the views of American REFORM JUDAISM adopted by the Central Conference of American Rabbis at San Francisco in 1976 on the occasion of the centennials of the Union of American Hebrew Congregations and the Hebrew Union College-Jewish Institute of Religion. The statement begins by expressing satisfaction at the adoption by Jews generally of much of the Reform conception of Judaism, while singling out a number of areas in which modification has become necessary: for example the Holocaust 'shattered our easy optimism about humanity and its inevitable progress'; 'the State of Israel, through its many accomplishments, raised our sense of the Jews as a people to new heights of aspiration and devotion'; and 'the survival of the Jewish people is of highest priority'. The document continues with a strong statement about diversity of opinion: 'Reform Judaism does more than tolerate diversity; it engenders it'. Six topics are then singled out on which Reform Jews are said to be united: (1) the existence of God; (2) the uniqueness of the Jewish people, 'because of its involvement with God and its resulting perception of the human condition'; (3) the Torah as 'a heritage whose study is a religious imperative and whose practice is our chief means to holiness'; (4) commitment to Jewish practice, including creating a Jewish home centred on family devotion, lifelong study, private prayer and public worship, daily religious obser- vance, keeping the Sabbath and the holy days, celebrating the major events of life, involvement with the synagogues and community, and other activities which pro- mote the survival of the Jewish people and enhance its existence; (5) commitment to the state of Israel and to Jewish life in the Diaspora; (6) the maintenance of a twin commitment to humanity and to the Jewish people, however these two imperatives may seem to conflict. The Perspective concludes with a message of hope: 'We remain God's witness that history is not meaningless. We affirm that with God's help people are not powerless to affect their destiny. We dedicate ourselves, as did the gener- ations of Jews who went before us, to work and wait for that day when "They shall not hurt or destroy in all My holy mountain for the earth shall be full of the know- ledge of the Lord as the waters cover the sea."' The Central Conference of American Rabbis subsequently adopted the MIAMI PLATFORM in 1997 and a Statement of Prin- ciples for Reform Judaism in Pittsburgh in 1999 (*see* PITTSBURGH STATEMENT).

Central Conference of American Rabbis The CCAR is the principal organiza- tion of Reform Jewish rabbis in the United States, founded in 1889 by Rabbi Isaac Mayer WISE. The Conference issues responsa, resolutions, and platforms, but, in keeping with the principles of Reform Judaism, its positions are not binding on individual rabbis or congregations. It is the publisher of the quarterly *CCAR Journal*, and runs the CCAR Press, which produces Reform prayer books.

Chabad Chasidism A branch of CHASIDISM also known as LUBAVITCH. Chabad is an acronym formed from the initials of three Hebrew words, chochma (wisdom), bina (understanding) and dá'at (knowledge). Founded by SHNEUR ZALMAN OF LYADY in the late 18th century, it has had seven spiritual leaders or rebbes who have provided the movement with outstanding spiritual and intellectual leadership. Many of the beliefs of Chabad are shared with other branches of Chasidism. What really distin- guishes it is the emphasis on the intellect rather than the emotions. Other distinct- ive beliefs of the movement include a belief in direct divine revelation (gilui mi- shamáyim) vouchsafed to its rebbes, and a controversial faith, not maintained by all adherents, in the messianic identity of the last rebbe, Rabbi Menachem Mendel Schneerson (1902–94), who succeeded his father-in-law, Rabbi Joseph Isaac Schneer- sohn (1880–1950) to become the seventh leader of the movement. On his death many of his followers refused to accept that he had truly died, and so declined to designate a successor, but continue to await his return. Chabad is very active in the former Soviet Union, providing many rabbis to lead congregations. However, their activities have given rise to considerable conflict. In 1994 they withdrew from the main organization of Russian Jewish congregations and formed their own Feder- ation of Jewish Communities of Russia, which has adopted a militant policy, for example designating their own chief rabbi in 2000 when there was already a serving Chief Rabbi of Russia. A similar action was taken in Ukraine in 2003. The movement is strong in the USA and Israel, and maintains a presence throughout the Jewish world. It is a strongly missionary organization, which pursues its messianic aims by reaching out to secularized and assimilated young Jews and attempting to win them over to their values; to this end they engage with modernity, and particularly with modern techniques of communication. *See also* TANYA.

chabra ('meeting place') In the Ottoman empire, an elementary school, also known in some places as meldar (a Judezmo word of Greek origin meaning 'to study'). It commonly consisted of a single room; the teacher usually lived on the premises.

chacham ('sage') In the Talmud the term is sometimes applied very broadly to a wise and learned person, whether Jewish or not; however, it also has a technical use (particularly in the plural, chachamim), to refer to the rabbis. The acronym Chazal (chachameínu zichronam livracha, 'our sages of blessed memory') is sometimes applied generically to the rabbis of the Talmudic period. In later times Sefardim have tended to prefer the title Chacham (in Turkish, Haham) in preference to Rabbi. In the Ottoman empire the hahamim exercised communal leadership within the millet (nationality) system regulating minorities, and the title Haham Bashı (Chief Rabbi) was granted to the leading rabbi of the empire, based in Constantinople, as well as to the main rabbinical authorities in Egypt and the Holy Land. In England the title Haham is reserved for the chief Sefardi rabbi.

Chad Gadya (Aramaic, 'One Kid') Much-loved song sung in Aramaic by Ashkenazim at the close of the Passover SÉDER. Resembling a nursery rhyme, it is structured cumulatively, beginning with 'one kid that my father bought for two zuzim' (a zuz is a small coin), and culminating in the arrival of 'the Holy One, blessed be He, who slew the angel of death, who slew the slaughterer who slaughtered the ox that lapped up the water that extinguished the fire that burnt the stick that beat the dog that bit the cat that ate the kid that my father bought for two zuzim'. It is thought to have been composed in central Europe in the 15th century and inserted at the end of the Séder to entertain tired children. Various allegorical explanations have been put forward. Its popularity is such that a Judezmo imitation ('Un Kavretiko') has circulated among Sefardim, particularly in Salonica.

Chafets Chayyim ('who desires life') Popular name of Rabbi Israel Meir Kagan (1838–1933). The name is derived from the title of his first book, which itself is taken from Psalm 34.12. The work, published in Vilna in 1873, is devoted to the centrality of the prohibition of SLANDER in Jewish life, a topic to which he returned repeatedly in later work. The Chafets Chayyim lived in Radin, Lithuania, where he founded and maintained a YESHIVA that achieved wide renown. He became one of the most respected and influential Orthodox figures of his time, and was a founder and strong supporter of the AGUDAT ISRAEL. Among his other writings the most celebrated is the MISHNA BERURA, a commentary on the laws of everyday Jewish life in the SHULCHAN ARUCH.

chag ('festival'; plural chaggim) In the Torah the term is used for five FESTIVALS, the three pilgrim festivals, SUKKOT, PASSOVER (Pésach) and SHAVUOT, and the festivals now known as NEW YEAR (Rosh ha-Shana) and the Day of ATONEMENT (Yom Kippur). The term 'chag' is particularly reserved in the rabbinic writings for the autumn festival of Sukkot. *See also* ÍSRU CHAG.

chag saméach ('happy festival') Greeting used during the FESTIVALS.

Chaggai Hebrew name of the biblical book of HAGGAI.

Chagiga ('festival offering') Tractate of the Mishnah, Tosefta and both Talmuds, found in the order Mo'ed. The title is derived from the term for a sacrificial offering made in the Temple by pilgrims on each of the three main FESTIVALS (chaggim) (Deuteronomy 16.16). The tractate deals with laws relating to the pilgrimage and its sacrifices.

chalitsa ('removal') Ceremony of removing the shoe, performed by a childless widow to her dead husband's brother (*see* LEVIRATE MARRIAGE).

challa 1 Originally, in the preparation of bread, dough separated as a gift for priests (Numbers 15.7–21). After the fall of the Temple it was no longer given to the priest but symbolically burnt. Originally binding only in the Land of Israel, the practice was extended by the rabbis to the Diaspora as well. They considered it a commandment binding particularly on women (Mishnah, Shabbat 2.6). During bread-making, a tiny piece of dough is symbolically burnt and a benediction is recited. It is customary at the same time to set aside a donation to charity. The term is also applied, by extension, by Ashkenazim (who traditionally pronounce it chólle) to the special loaves baked for the Sabbath and festivals. It is customary to prepare two loaves for the Sabbath eve meal, supposedly in memory of the double portion of manna collected by the Israelites ahead of the Sabbath in the biblical story (Exodus 16.22). They are traditionally plaited, generally made of a rich dough and often sprinkled with poppy or sesame seeds. At New Year, however, their form is round, perhaps to signify that the year has no real beginning or end.
　2 (**Challa**) Tractate of the Mishnah, Tosefta and Palestinian Talmud, found in the order Zera'im. The tractate deals with the biblical requirement to separate some of the new dough and offer it up (Numbers 15.17–21).

chalukka ('distribution') A relief system by which Jews in the Holy Land (particularly poor scholars, but also widows and orphans) were sustained by charitable contributions from Jews in other countries. The system goes back to the Middle Ages, and originally it was considered meritorious to send money to support the academies and scholars in Jerusalem and the other holy cities (HEBRON, SAFED and TIBERIAS). It was recognized that they devoted themselves unselfishly to the Torah and had no other means of supporting themselves. In the course of the 19th century, however, many Jews came to look upon the institution as parasitic and degrading.

chaluts ('pioneer'; plural chalutsim) Name given to the early Zionist settlers in the Land of Israel, typically young men from eastern Europe who put the religious values of Judaism behind them and devoted themselves to hard labour on the land in harsh conditions, 'to build the Land and to be built by it'. They created a type of 'new Jew', a counter-image to that of the yeshiva students of the SHTETL, who were seen by them as stunted both physically and mentally, in thrall alike to their rabbis and to Gentile powers.

chamets ('leaven') Technical term in HALACHA for grain that has become wet and begun to ferment or sprout. Five species of grain are involved: wheat, oats, barley, rye and spelt. According to biblical law, no chamets is permitted in Jewish homes during the festival of Passover, nor is it permitted to eat chamets outside the home during this period (Exodus 12), in commemoration of the exodus from Egypt, when the departing Israelites did not have time to wait for their dough to rise. In the Temple, the grain offerings also had to be free of chamets (Leviticus 2.11). Today a veritable industry is devoted to certifying that food to be consumed during Passover is free from chamets. A complicating factor is that Ashkenazim have a stricter definition of chamets than other Jews, and forbid, in addition to the five species of grain already mentioned, rice, maize, millet, dried beans and peas, and various other foods. Whisky and other alcoholic drinks made from sprouted grain are forbidden. (Wine is permitted, although it is made by fermentation, because it does not normally contain grain. Kosher wine is certified free from chamets and fit for Passover use.) Theoretically, all chamets must be destroyed or nullified (see BITTUL CHAMETS; BI'UR CHAMETS), but a legal fiction has been devised to help owners of large quantities of chamets, such as shopkeepers: they may sell it to a non-Jew for a nominal sum and then buy it back after the festival.

chanukiyya See CHANUKKA.

Chanukka ('dedication') Festival commemorating the rededication of the Jerusalem Temple by the Maccabees on the 25th of Kislev 165 BCE after it had been desecrated by the Seleucid army three years earlier. Chanukka is celebrated for eight days, beginning on that date. It is a minor festival: there is no feasting, and it is not a holiday from work. The main way it is observed is by lighting oil lamps or candles, one on the first evening, two on the second, and so on, until on the eighth evening eight lights are lit. On each evening an additional 'servant' light (shammash) is used to light the main lights. Special lamps or candle-holders (known by the name of menora or chanukiyya) are used, sometimes devised in fanciful styles, and they are placed in a window so as to shine out into the darkness. The lighting of the lamps is accompanied by special prayers, and the singing of a much-loved hymn, 'MA'OZ TSUR'. A special blessing praises God for 'performing miracles on those days at this season'. Among the ancillary customs that have grown up, children are given gifts of cash, and play gambling games with little spinning tops inscribed with four Hebrew letters, called dreidls in Yiddish. Fried foods, such as látkes (potato pancakes), doughnuts or fritters, are traditionally eaten. Karaites do not traditionally observe this post-biblical festival, although where they live in proximity to Rabbanites some have begun to celebrate it.

chanukkat ha-báyit ('dedication of the house', from Psalm 30.1) Ceremony of dedicating a new home, including the fixing of the MEZUZA and the recitation of some psalms, including Psalm 30 ('A Psalm of Dedication of the House'). The ritual grew up first among Sefardim; Ashkenazim imitated it from the 19th century, beginning probably in Britain.

charedi ('fearful'; plural charedim) Designation of Traditionalist Judaism (*see* TRADITIONALISM), particularly in Israel. The Hebrew epithet means 'fearful' in the sense of maintaining an attitude of awe or veneration (an expression borrowed from Isaiah 66.5). The Charedi movement unites CHASIDIM and MITNAGGEDIM, despite their historic divisions. Charedim affect a distinctive style of dress: the men wear beards and sidelocks and black coats and hats, while married women have shaven heads, covered by a wig or headscarf, and wear modest clothing that hides most of their bodies. Charedim in Israel are increasingly violent in their hostility to modernizing trends, and particularly to secular Zionism. *See also* AGUDAT ISRAEL.

charity Kindness to others, particularly of a material kind. It is considered to be a binding obligation to help those less well-off. The Talmud distinguishes between tsedaka (almsgiving) and gemilut chasadim (charitable actions in general). 'In three respects gemilut chasadim is superior to tsedaka: tsedaka can be performed only with one's material possessions, gemilut chasadim either in kind or by service; tsedaka can be given only to the poor, gemilut chasadim to poor and rich alike; tsedaka can be given only to the living, gemilut chasadim to the living and the dead' (Bavli, Sukka 49b). MAIMONIDES, in his code, insists that anyone who can afford to do so must give to the poor according to their needs, beginning with members of one's own family, then to one's townspeople, and finally to those from other towns. Charity should be given cheerfully and willingly; anyone who gives grudgingly, with a surly face, nullifies the merit of his giving. He distinguishes eight degrees of charitable giving, the highest being that aimed at making the recipients self-supporting, so that they are no longer reliant on charity. Charitable activities that have been particularly singled out include the provision of soup kitchens, hospitals, hostels for travellers, dowries for brides and homes for the care of the elderly, ransoming captives, helping couples to marry and set up home, covering funeral expenses and distributing MATSA at Passover.

charóset Sweet reddish paste placed on the SÉDER dish and used as a dip for MAROR. The precise recipe varies around the world. Ashkenazim make it from grated apples, chopped walnuts or ground almonds, cinnamon and sweet wine, which they mix together without cooking. Elsewhere various dried fruits are often added, and the charóset is stewed. It is said that the reddish colour and consistency are a reminder of the mortar used by the Israelite slaves in Egypt.

Chasidei Ashkenaz A term applied to various pietistic circles that existed in the Rhineland and northern France in the later 12th and 13th centuries, and particularly that associated with the family of JUDAH THE CHASID and ELEAZAR OF WORMS. They developed distinctive forms of esoteric theology, ASCETICISM and meticulous devotion to ethical rules of behaviour. They insisted on the utter transcendence of God, attributing the divine immanence in the created world to various intermediary powers, and particularly the created GLORY. They have left a significant legacy of written works, including some of the earliest commentaries on the prayers and hymns, as well as the SÉFER CHASIDIM.

Chasidism Revivalist religious movement that began in Poland in the mid-18th century. Critical of the remoteness and elitism of both the Talmudists and the kabbalists of their day, their leaders, beginning with the BAAL SHEM TOV, reached out to ordinary Jews and offered them a religiosity that was within their reach. After the death of the Baal Shem Tov in 1760 his disciple Dov Ber of Mezhirech ('the Maggid') assumed leadership of the nascent movement, and disseminated it very effectively throughout Poland. The most telling resistance came in Lithuania, where the VILNA GA'ON and his disciples pronounced bans on it, and even invoked the state authorities to suppress it. The opponents came to be known as MITNAGGEDIM. They charged the Chasidim with being innovators, destroyers of tradition, and dangerous revolutionaries. However, the opposition eventually ran out of steam, and by the early 19th century Chadisim reigned supreme throughout the Jewish communities of eastern Europe. This was the heyday of the movement. As the HASKALA gathered strength its proponents renewed the rationalist onslaught, depicting the Chasidim as backward and superstitious. The movement was also severely damaged by economic and social changes, by the pogroms, the two world wars and the Holocaust, and by the banning of religious activity in the Soviet Union. Chasidism is now divided into a number of separate and often conflicting groups, based mainly in the United States (Satmar, Lubavitch, Bobov) and Israel (Belz, Bratslav, Ger, Vizhnitz).

The Chasidim stressed the attitude of sincerity and selfless devotion which is within the reach of everybody. The intellectual contemplation of the kabbalists was replaced by a highly charged emotional enthusiasm which was especially manifested in prayer. The Chasidim prayed with an intensity which aimed to detach them from the trammels of the corporeal world and sought a complete union with the divine nothingness. Kavvana (intention), devekut (cleaving), and hitlahavut (enthusiasm) are key terms in Chasidism, and some of the Hasidic masters go so far as to seek the complete annihilation of the self in union with the Divine. A development which is particularly associated with SHNEUR ZALMAN OF LYADY, the founder of the Chabad school of Chasidism, reinterprets the Lurianic doctrine of TSIMTSUM so as to restore the essential unity of God and the world. According to this view, only the Godhead really exists; everything else is contained within it, and there is no place empty of God. The universe is kept in being by the unfailing power which emanates constantly from the EIN SOF; without this it would vanish in an instant. In CHABAD CHASIDISM the stress is removed from emotion and placed once again on intellectual contemplation. Worshippers, for example, rather than submitting blindly to the inner upsurge of joyful ecstasy, are to direct their minds to the way in which the Ein Sof keeps the whole universe in being, tracing the path of the divine light from world to world down to this material world and back up again to the Ein Sof, until they achieve the ecstatic union with the Divine.

See also BUBER, MARTIN; NEO-CHASIDISM.

Chatam Sofer *See* SOFER, MOSES.

chatan ('bridegroom') *See* MARRIAGE.

chatan Bereshit ('bridegroom of Genesis') Person honoured by the congregation to be called to the Torah when the first section of Genesis is read at SIMCHAT TORA.

chatan tora ('bridegroom of the Torah') Person honoured by the congregation to be called to the Torah when the last section of Deuteronomy is read at SIMCHAT TORA.

chatima ('sealing') Short form of BENEDICTION, beginning with the words 'Blessed are you, Lord', and continuing with a phrase which is essentially an attribute or activity of God. This may conclude a longer benediction, or stand as a benediction on its own. The term is also used for another kind of sealing, the sealing of the 'Book of Life' on the Day of Atonement: *see* GEMÁR CHATIMA TOVA.

Chavakkuk Hebrew name of the biblical book of HABAKKUK.

chaver ('associate', 'comrade', 'friend'; plural chaverim) In its most general sense chaver means a friend or a colleague: 'Get yourself a teacher [rav] and acquire a colleague [chaver]' (Mishnah, Avot 1.6). In the ancient rabbinic system of education it meant a fellow student who shared one's outlook (Mishnah, Eruvin 2.6, Yevamot 16.7; the saying from Avot just quoted could be interpreted in this sense too). The word also had a technical meaning: a person who was very scrupulous about observing the rules of tithing and ritual purity; in this sense it can be the opposite of AM HA-ÁRETS. In time it came to mean a pious or learned man. Thus a disciple who reached a high standard of scholarship is called in the Talmud a talmid chaver, and chaver became a synonym of TALMID CHACHAM. Chaver has been used as a title of honour, with different meanings in different times and places. In Babylonia it was accorded to three leading rabbis who sat in the front row in the academy; the use was gradually extended, and by the end of the geonic period it could be applied to sages outside the academy. In early modern central Europe it was applied to young scholars who were not ordained rabbis. In eastern Europe the custom arose of giving the title to particularly distinguished scholars. This custom was current in Germany before the Second World War, and is still found among Jews of German origin in the United States and elsewhere today.

chavura ('group'; plural chavurot) The Pharisees used this term of associations that scrupulously observed the rules of tithing and ritual purity, sharing their meals in a state of purity (cf. CHAVER). In recent times the term has been applied in the United States and elsewhere to associations for religious renewal, formed for the purpose of prayer, study and fellowship. The chavura movement emerged in the late 1960s in response to the alienation felt by young Jews from what was perceived as the soulless formalism of synagogue worship and a preoccupation with institutional organization rather than genuine religious life. Chavurot spread at first in university campuses, but they were also formed within synagogues (particularly Conservative ones). They fostered experimentation and full, egalitarian participation in worship. *See also* RENEWAL.

Chayyim of Volozhin (1749–1821) Rabbinic leader. A disciple of the VILNA GA'ON, in

1773 he was appointed rabbi of Volozhin, Lithuania, where he founded in 1803 a celebrated YESHIVA whose syllabus laid stress on the plain meaning of the Talmud, rather than the prevalent method of PILPUL, and incorporated secular subjects. Strongly opposed, like his master, to CHASIDISM, he became the leader of the MIT-NAGGEDIM in eastern Europe.

chazak ('strong') Exclamation traditionally uttered to congratulate someone on the successful completion of a task; also commonly added by medieval Hebrew poets to their names in ACROSTICS. Sefardim congratulate one who has been called up to the Torah reading with the words chazak u-varuch ('[may you be] strong and blessed'). On the completion of the public reading of any of the five books of the Torah it is customary for the congregation to rise and chant 'Chazak, chazak, ve-nitchazek' ('be strong, be strong, and let us be strengthened [in our resolve]'), a phrase based on a biblical expression in 2 Samuel 10.12 and 1 Chronicles 19.13. The meaning is understood to be 'May we be strengthened in our resolve to live according to the precepts contained in the Torah'.

chazal *See* CHACHAM.

Chazon Ish ('vision of a man') Name popularly given to the Talmud scholar Abraham Isaiah Karelitz (1878–1953), after the title of his first work, published anonymously in 1911. Born and brought up in eastern Europe, he settled in Palestine in 1933 where he soon became recognized as the religious leader of the CHAREDI community. After the establishment of the state of Israel in 1948 he guided the community in its relationship with the state. Although he was unrelenting in his hostility to Zionism he argued that charedim should grant the state de facto recognition and participate in elections so as to further their own communal interests. He laid stress in his writings on the centrality of law in Judaism: he advocated exclusive devotion to the study of HALACHA and its meticulous observance as the only path for the Jew to spiritual and ethical self-perfection.

chazzan ('cantor'; plural chazzanim) Derived from an Akkadian term meaning overseer or governor, the Hebrew word originally refers to a communal functionary whose duties included teaching young children, looking after the synagogue, and blowing the SHOFAR from the roof of the synagogue to announce the beginning and end of the Sabbaths and festivals. In time the meaning became virtually limited to the precentor who intoned the prayers (*see* SHELÍACH TSIBBUR). In the Middle Ages the chazzanim were often learned men who composed and performed PIYYUTIM. As they led the congregational worship their office acquired dignity and status, and various conditions for the task were listed; already in the Talmud (Bavli, Ta'anit 16a), when his tasks were more varied, we read that a chazzan should be of mature age, prefer-ably married and a father, with a good knowledge of the Torah and prayers, respected by the community and religiously observant, and with a pleasant voice and appearance. In later times complaints were voiced against chazzanim who had other qualities but lacked a good singing voice, or who were more devoted to their music than to the other requirements of the office.

In Europe as Jews became acquainted with the music of the world around them the chazzanim became more self-conscious and ambitious, and some combined synagogal with operatic careers. Meyer Leoni (1740–96), cantor at the Great Synagogue in London, for example, was fired when he sang in a performance of Handel's *Messiah*. More recently the Polish cantor Gershon Sirota (1877–1943), 'the Jewish Caruso', was a popular performer in the concert hall, as was Yossele Rosenblatt (1882–1933), who emigrated to the United States in 1912 and commanded huge fees. The Chasidim inveighed against this abuse of the office, as they saw it. To be fair, the new role of the chazzanim and the changing character of their music corresponded to what many congregants required in the post-emancipation era, and they often focused on choral direction and composition rather than simply leading the prayers. Nowadays many congregations have dispensed with the chazzan altogether; others have once again broadened the chazzan's remit to include various pastoral and educational roles. *See also* MUSIC.

chéder ('room') The elementary school of the SHTETL. It was often located in a single room in the teacher's home, whence the name. Boys attended from an early age (often as young as three) until they reached the age of 13, when the more intellectually able ones moved on to YESHIVA. The hours were long, and there was an emphasis on learning by rote, particularly for the younger pupils who were learning to read Hebrew, to recite the prayers and to follow the Torah reading. More advanced students would read the Torah with RASHI's commentary; some might be introduced to the Mishnah and Babylonian Talmud.

chen ('grace') **1** The graceful appearance and demeanour of a woman (said to be a delusion in Proverbs 31.30; *see* ÉSHET CHÁYIL). **2** A gift of grace from God, often coupled in supplications with CHÉSED.

chérem ('ban') Term originally designating property consecrated to God, and thus either set apart for Temple use or, in extreme cases, designated for destruction. In the Middle Ages and early modern period it referred to the exclusion of an individual or a group from the community, all contact with them being forbidden (*see* EXCOMMUNICATION). In the medieval conditions of isolation in which Jewish communities existed, it was a very effective form of deterrence or punishment; however it was open to abuse, and with the emancipation it has become all but ineffective and has more or less died out.

chésed ('love', 'kindness') **1** An attribute of humans and of God. People show chésed by means of acts of charity and service to those less fortunate than themselves (*see* GEMILUT CHASADIM). Analogously, God is entreated to show kindness to mortals in many prayers. **2** (Chésed) In kabbala, one of the SEFIROT.

Cheshvan Second month of the year counting from New Year; eighth counting from Passover, roughly corresponding to November. It is also known as Marcheshvan.

chevra kadisha (Aramaic, 'holy society') Society devoted to the burial of the dead according to Jewish law. To assist in the burial of the dead is a valuable service and a sacred duty, and it is considered an honour to belong to a chevra kadisha. Separate teams of men and women attend to the washing and preparation of male and female bodies. Formerly they supervised all aspects of the burial and performed the functions now fulfilled by funeral directors. Rabbi Judah Löw (MAHARAL OF PRAGUE) is credited with the foundation of the first such association in Prague in 1593. It was customary for members to hold an annual banquet, usually on the 7th of Adar, the traditional anniversary of the death of Moses.

Chevron *See* HEBRON.

chevruta (Aramaic, 'fellowship') A small group of students studying texts together.

Chibbat Zion ('love of Zion') Proto-Zionist movement that started in eastern Europe in the 19th century. Its members were called Chovevei Tsiyon ('lovers of Zion'), and their avowed aim was to settle Jews in the Land of Israel. A pioneering agricultural school, Mikveh Israel, founded near Jaffa by the French ALLIANCE ISRAÉ-LITE UNIVERSELLE in 1870, can be reckoned the first concrete outcome of the movement, but little else was achieved before the beginning of the Russian pogroms in 1881 boosted its impetus, and societies for the colonization of Palestine were founded in various Russian cities. In 1882 the colony of Rishon le-Tsiyon was settled by a group calling themselves BILU (Hebrew acronym of a biblical rallying-cry, 'House of Jacob, come, let us go!' (Isaiah 2.5)). At a conference held in Kattowitz in 1884 the headquarters of the movement were established in Odessa, and soon branches had been set up in Berlin, Paris, London and even the United States. By 1897 nineteen Jewish colonies had been founded; in that year the Chovevei Tsiyon merged with the newly formed Zionist Organization. The movement was disbanded in 1920.

chiddush ('innovation'; plural chiddushim) Innovation, particularly but not exclusively in Talmud study. The Talmud itself states that there is no house of study without a chiddush; in the Middle Ages scholars devoted great ingenuity to raising and solving problems in the text, and these came to be known as chiddushim or by the analogous Latin term novellae. Such study was not restricted to Talmudic HALACHA, but covered the AGGADA contained in the Talmud and also other works, such as the MISHNE TORAH of Maimonides and the SHULCHAN ARUCH. *See also* RENEWAL.

chief rabbi An office that has no basis in Jewish law, and varies in character from country to country. In some countries (for example the United States and Canada) it is completely unknown. In the British Commonwealth the Chief Rabbi of the United Hebrew Congregations is appointed by the main centrist Ashkenazi Orthodox synagogue body in London and, while his authority is formally acknowledged only by this body, he enjoys respect in the wider community, particularly in England. The first formal election to the office was made in 1845. The English Sefardim have their own chief rabbi, known as the Haham (*see* CHACHAM). In Israel, where the rabbis are state functionaries, the two chief rabbis (Sefardi and Ashkenazi) are elected to serve for ten years, non-renewable, and enjoy considerable power. The office was created formally under the British Mandate in 1920, but has older roots in the Ottoman empire. (The Sefardi chief rabbi, known today as the RISHON LE-TSIYON, still wears the formal robes of his Ottoman predecessors.) In addition to the two national chief rabbis, each city in Israel has two chief rabbis, and smaller communities have a single chief rabbi. Many European countries have a system of chief rabbis, generally appointed by the Jewish communities but enjoying some recognition and authority in the country at large.

chilloni (modern Hebrew, 'secular'; plural chillonim) Israeli term for a secular Jew (as opposed to DATI).

chillul ha-Shem ('desecration of the Name') An unworthy action which reflects discredit upon Judaism, and thus indirectly upon God (*see* HA-SHEM). The origin of the term is found in Leviticus 22.32, 'You shall not profane my holy name'. It is particularly applied to wrongdoings committed against non-Jews, as these are particularly likely to bring the reputation (another meaning of the word shem) of Judaism and the Jewish people into disrepute. According to the Mishnah (Avot 5.11) 'wild beasts come into the world on account of perjury and chillul ha-Shem'; some commentators explain 'wild beasts' here as referring to savage human beings driven by irrational hatred of Jews. The term is a natural opposite of KIDDUSH HA-SHEM.

chochma ('wisdom') **1** A positive human attribute; also an attribute of God. There are many references to wisdom in the Bible, particularly in the writings known to modern scholars as the 'wisdom literature' (including such books as Proverbs, Job and Kohélet, as well as some psalms, notably Psalm 119). They praise wisdom as a gift from God or even as a personified embodiment of the divine wisdom, and they offer advice, particularly to the young, on how to conduct one's life. This tradition was continued in some post-biblical writings, including the rabbinic collection of sayings AVOT. This body of wisdom is distinct from revealed Torah and from divinely inspired prophecy. It is rooted in rational investigation with a view to practical outcomes, and is open to insights originating outside Judaism. At the same time it is explicitly linked to reverence for God, which is described as 'the beginning of wisdom' (Psalm 111.10, Proverbs 9.10, cf. Kohélet 12.13). The benediction prescribed on seeing a Gentile sage, or a man who is wise in secular studies, is 'Blessed be he who has imparted of his wisdom to flesh and blood', thus insisting that even secular wisdom is a gift from God. An analogous benediction on seeing one wise in Jewish learning is '... who has granted of his wisdom to those who fear him'. In medieval thought wisdom is considered one of the divine attributes.

2 (Chochma) In kabbala, one of the SEFIROT. *See also* CHABAD CHASIDISM; CHACHAM; TALMID CHACHAM.

chol General term denoting whatever is not specifically holy (*see* HOLINESS). The word is from the same Hebrew root as chilloni, chillul and chullin. It is particularly applied to the working days of the week, as opposed to the Sabbath and festivals, which are holy days.

chol ha-mo'ed ('weekday of the festival') Term designating the middle days of the two long festivals Passover and Tabernacles. Only the first and last days are festival days on which work is forbidden; the intermediate days are joyful days on which work is generally permitted, but not encouraged. Mourning is prohibited, and marriages are not performed, because 'one joy should not be mingled with another'. Sefardim (and nowadays many Ashkenazim) do not put on TEFILLIN; special prayers are said. At Tabernacles one eats in the SUKKA (1), and at Passover CHAMETS is forbidden.

See also MO'ED KATAN.

choral music Choral singing played a prominent part in the worship of the Temple, but was discontinued after the destruction. So far as we know the practice was not resumed until the 17th century, in Italy, where the composer Salamone Rossi (c. 1570–1628) of Modena published settings of 33 psalms and other liturgical texts in 1622–3. Choral music in the synagogue, however, really came into its own with the German reforms of the 19th century. Membership of synagogue choirs was now no longer limited to men and boys: female, and indeed non-Jewish, singers were also admitted. Salomon Sulzer (1804–90) published settings of the entire liturgy for cantor and choir, with congregational responses. His pupil Louis Lewandowski (1821–94), who was the first professional Jewish choral director, also published many choral settings. Their work is still performed, together with that of many subsequent composers. Orthodox synagogues have been reluctant to admit mixed choirs, and some which previously had them have replaced them with all-male choirs. Traditional Judaism, and the more traditional wing of Orthodoxy, reject choirs altogether, preferring the CHAZZAN and unregulated congregational singing.

Chorin, Aaron (1766–1844) Pioneering religious reformer. As rabbi in Arad (Transylvania) from 1789 he introduced various liturgical reforms and adopted a liberal interpretation of many religious laws, permitting bareheaded worship, travelling and writing on Sabbath, and even marriage between Jews and non-Jews.

chosenness *See* ELECTION.

Chovevei Zion *See* CHIBBAT ZION.

Christianity and Judaism Christianity has generally considered itself to have grown out of and superseded Judaism, and has maintained a sense of rivalry with its 'parent religion' that has occasionally broken out into open hostility and even violence. For their part, Jewish communities living under Christian political domination and subjected to discriminatory legislation, deliberately offensive behaviour, pressure to convert to the dominant faith and fear of violent attacks naturally responded by cultivating a negative image of Christianity. Particularly in the Byzantine empire, where the forcible baptism of all Jews was decreed several times from the early 7th century on, synagogue hymns looked forward to the ending of Christian rule and a prayer for the eradication of Christianity was inserted into the twelfth benediction of the AMIDA. Jewish religious thinkers both in Muslim and in Christian lands applied their minds to issues raised by Christianity and to constructing defences of Judaism against Christian polemic. MAIMONIDES, for example, classifies Christianity as a form of IDOLATRY and rules that Christians are subject to all the disabilities placed on idolaters by the HALACHA. On the other hand, in reply to a question, he permits teaching the COMMANDMENTS of the Torah to a Christian, since Jews and Christians share the same holy scriptures, and teaching them the correct interpretation may bring them to an appreciation of the true faith. A prolific apologetic literature was written with Christianity in view: we know of some 140 works of this kind written between the 8th and the 18th century in Hebrew alone (from the 16th century on they were also composed in Latin and other European languages).

Since the ENLIGHTENMENT and political EMANCIPATION a different kind of response has emerged, in which the aim is to discuss the differences between Judaism and Christianity in a more detached way, with the apologetic element being less pronounced. Moses MENDELSSOHN's *Jerusalem*, published in 1783, is an early prototype of this approach, which also includes Hermann COHEN's *Religion of Reason*, Franz ROSENZWEIG's *The Star of Redemption* and Leo BAECK's *The Essence of Judaism*. The Nazi Holocaust marked a watershed in Jewish–Christian relations: afterwards for the first time Jews and Christians came together to seek common ground and genuine understanding, in the hope of putting an end to the antagonisms and violence of the past. Soon after the War a meeting of Jews and Christians in Switzerland formulated guidelines for the presentation of Judaism in Christian preaching and teaching (the 'Ten Points of Seelisberg'), and these were developed further in the document 'Nostra Aetate' ratified by the Second Vatican Council. *See also* DABRU EMET.

Chronicles (Divrei ha-Yamim) The last book of the Hebrew Bible. Originally it was one book, but it is now divided into two. It begins with genealogies, starting with Adam and ending with the inhabitants of Jerusalem at the time of the return from the Babylonian exile. It then describes the reign of King David and his son Solomon, and the remaining history of the kingdom of Judah, with an emphasis on priests and Levites and the Temple worship. According to tradition the author was EZRA the scribe.

chronogram A written text that yields a date when the numerical values of some or all of the letters are added together. Chronograms are found commonly on old inscriptions and on title pages of old books. Often they take the form of a biblical quotation, which may have some special relevance to the occasion.

Chuetas *See* XUETAS.

Chullin ('profane things') Tractate of the Mishnah, in the order Kodashim, with corresponding tractates in the Tosefta and Babylonian Talmud. Its subject matter is the laws concerned with the butchering of animals for everyday use, as opposed to the sacrifices of the Temple.

chummash A volume containing the five books of the Torah. The word is derived from the Hebrew chamésh, five, and originally it applied to any one of the five books, or a printed volume containing it.

chumra (Aramaic, 'severity') In HALACHA, the stricter of two possible rulings (the other is kulla). Originally, while it was agreed that in the case of doubt concerning a biblical law the stricter interpretation should be applied, in the case of rabbinic laws it was considered wrong to apply the stricter solution indiscriminately. In the course of time, however, particularly among Ashkenazim, there was a tendency to regard chumra as the default position in case of doubt. The term also came to be applied to self-denying rules applied by particularly pious individuals to themselves, while acknowledging that they need not be imposed on others.

chuppa ('canopy') The MARRIAGE canopy, or the ceremony of marriage itself. The canopy symbolizes the bridal chamber in which marriages were consummated in ancient times. It is often a richly decorated structure supported on four poles; however, its place may be taken by a TALLIT held aloft by four people.

churban ('destruction') Term applied to the destruction of the First and Second Temples, sometimes in the form 'the First Churban' 'the Second Churban'. 'The Third Churban' is an expression applied, by analogy, to the Nazi Holocaust, particularly by Ignaz MAYBAUM.

chuva (from Hebrew chova, 'obligation') ROMANIOT name for the Passover SÉDER.

circumcision A minor surgical operation involving the removal of the prepuce or foreskin. Circumcision of a male child is a religious obligation devolving upon the father (though he is usually only too happy to delegate it to a specialist circumciser, termed a mohel). It is customary to assemble a gathering of family and friends, and to serve a festive meal afterwards. Circumcision is a visible sign of the covenant between God and the Jewish people (although it should be noted that a son of a Jewish mother who for whatever reason is not circumcised is still Jewish). It is consequently known in Hebrew as berít mila, 'covenant of circumcision', or more commonly simply as berít, 'covenant'. It is therefore the first stage of a process that is completed at the age of 13, when the child comes of age in halachic law and takes upon himself the obligations laid down in the Torah (*see* BAR MITSVA). The occasion is marked by festivity and joyfulness. It used to be a custom to embroider the baby's swaddling band with his name and the date of the circumcision, and the hope that he may achieve bar mitsva, marriage and good deeds (a form of words taken from the blessings recited on this occasion). The band was donated to the synagogue, where it was used to bind the scroll of the Torah.

The proper age for circumcision is the eighth day, that is the same day as the birth a week later (see Genesis 17.12, Leviticus 12.3). However, this is understood as a minimum age, and the circumcision may be deferred for reasons of health.

Circumcision may be performed at home, at synagogue, or in any other place. (If the eighth day falls on Yom Kippur it is performed in synagogue, since that is where the congregation is assembled.) A couple, sometimes an engaged or childless couple, are designated as godparents, and they hand the baby to the sandek, the person who will hold the child during the proceedings. Before the circumcision the mohel recites a blessing, and afterwards the father and the mohel both recite special blessings. The child is then given a Hebrew name, in the form of a patronymic – N son of N. This is the name by which he will be known all through his life in synagogue, and which will be inscribed on his KETUBBA and his tombstone. The baby is given a drop or two of wine, and the father and mother also drink some wine (in traditional circles the mother is not present in the room, and the goblet of wine is taken out to her). After the festive meal which follows there is a special form of grace, invoking blessings on the parents, the child, the mohel and the sandek.

Circumcision is aesthetically repugnant to some people, and carries with it a small but real risk to the health of the child; it is also a visible mark of difference. For these reasons it came under outspoken attack in the Reform movement. And yet it is maintained by the vast majority of Jewish families today (even if they often resort in the West to the services of a surgeon rather than a mohel). It may be that in an age when other visible signs of Jewish identity have progressively disappeared it has become all the more important to hang on to this one. Even so critical a Jew as Baruch Spinoza could say: 'Such great importance do I attach to the sign of the covenant that I am persuaded that it is sufficient by itself to maintain the separate existence of the nation for ever.'

clothing *See* DRESS.

codes of law

A systematic collection of legislation. The Torah contains a good deal of law, but it is not presented systematically, although scholars have detected certain sections that have the form of a code (e.g. the 'Holiness Code' of Leviticus 17–26). Nor can the Mishnah and Talmud, in both of which halachic materials predominate, be considered to be law codes in the proper sense of the term, even though, again, both contain sections that begin to codify the law on specific topics. The Mishnah, having stated a law, frequently proceeds to cite dissenting opinions, so that it has more of the appearance of a textbook than a code. This tendency is accentuated in both Talmuds, which seem to revel in disagreement rather than consensus. In rabbinic Judaism, codification of the HALACHA takes off tentatively with attempts at summarizing topics in the Talmud, undertaken during the geonic period (*see* GA'ON) probably for teaching purposes rather than as an authoritative tool for jurists. An early landmark is the Halachot Pesukot attributed to YEHUDA'I GA'ON (8th century), which attempts to resolve numerous issues that remained unclear in the Babylonian Talmud. Parts of this work are quoted verbatim in the slightly later Halachot Gedolot. The peak of this early phase of activity is the code of Isaac ALFASI, produced in the middle of the 11th century. Like its predecessors it follows the order of the Talmudic tractates, and deals only with topics still of practical application, omitting those areas of the halacha which only apply in the Land of Israel or in the existence of the Temple.

The next great code, the Mishne Torah of MAIMONIDES, is based on different principles. Maimonides aimed to include all the topics of the halacha, including those not of current application, and he arranged his material not in Talmudic order but on the basis of a new classification of the subject matter. He also deliberately omitted all reference to Talmudic sources, names of authorities and dissenting opinions, in the interests of producing a simple, straightforward code which could be readily used by anybody, and not only by halachic specialists. He even devised a special, simple form of Hebrew for his code, as opposed to the Arabic in which he wrote his other works or the complex, formulaic Aramaic of the Talmud itself. While Maimonides' work was greatly admired in some quarters, in others he was sharply attacked for daring to sever the laws themselves from their background in the tradition. As a result his code never achieved its aim of superseding the detailed study of the tradition for practical purposes, even though it exerted a considerable influence on subsequent compilations.

Although the Ashkenazim did not compose codes as such, they did compile annotated lists of the COMMANDMENTS. Two such lists made in the 13th century that achieved great popularity were the Séfer Mitsvot Gadol (Greater Book of the Commandments) of Moses of Coucy and the Séfer Mitsvot Katan (Lesser Book of the Commandments) of Isaac of Corbeil. The latter was heavily exploited in an ambitious early 14th-century compendium by Aaron of Lunel, entitled *Orchot Chayyim* (*Paths of Life*).

JACOB BEN ASHER, in the 14th century, devised a new division of the subject matter of the halacha under four headings or 'rows' (whence the title of his code, ARBA'A TURIM, which means 'The Four Rows'). The first deals with daily life and the rituals connected with the Sabbath and the festivals; the second includes the DIETARY REGULATIONS and various other topics; the third row is concerned with the relations between the sexes; the fourth is devoted to the civil and criminal law. Jacob's general approach is similar to that of Maimonides, although he lacks his interest in philosophical questions. Unlike Maimonides, however, he mentions various conflicting opinions before offering his own conclusion, which often concurs with that of his father, ASHER BEN YECHIEL, who was himself the author of an important halachic code.

Jacob ben Asher's really lasting contribution was his fourfold classification of the halacha, since it was adopted in the 16th century by Joseph Caro in his SHUL-CHAN ARUCH or 'Laid Table', which has remained the most widely consulted halachic code to this day. Caro, who had settled in Safed in Galilee after the expulsion from Spain, began by compiling an extensive critical commentary on the Arba'a Turim, in which he attempted to synthesize the existing diverse traditions by following, wherever possible, the majority opinion of his three outstanding predecessors, Alfasi, Maimonides and Asher ben Yechiel. From this larger work he extracted the final decisions, which he embodied in the Shulchan Aruch, which is a remarkably concise and orderly reference work, making an authoritative summary of the halacha available to a very wide public.

The Shulchan Aruch was quickly disseminated through printing (it was first published in 1565), and it achieved enormous popularity, which was augmented when a Polish scholar, Moses ISSERLES, added notes (known as the MAPPA or 'Table-cloth') on Ashkenazi practice to complement the work of the Sefardi Caro. The Shulchan Aruch was the last great codification of halacha. Although it has given rise to numerous commentaries it has never been supplanted.

The Karaites have their own codifications of the law, starting with the Séfer ha-

Mitsvot (Book of The Commandments) attributed to ANAN BEN DAVID (8th century). Another influential work of the same name is a Hebrew translation of a code originally compiled in Arabic by Levi ben Yefet in the early 11th century. In the 14th century Aaron ben Elijah in Constantinople composed a code entitled Gan Eden (Garden of Eden), which enjoyed considerable success until it was superseded in the 15th century by the Addéret Eliyyáhu (Elijah's Mantle) of Elijah BASHYACHI, which has remained the authoritative code for Karaites to this day.

Cohen, Arthur A. (1928–86) American theologian. Born in New York, Cohen held no rabbinic or permanent academic position. He worked as a publisher and as a bookseller, and he wrote on a wide range of subjects. Theology was an enduring concern, and he was anxious to counter the prevailing distrust of or disdain for theology that he considered characteristic of American Jews in his day. As a theologian he is remembered primarily for two books. In *The Natural and the Supernatural Jew* (1962), reacting against the naturalism of Mordecai KAPLAN, Cohen contrasts the 'natural Jew', rooted in nature and history, and the 'supernatural Jew', who is a 'messianic being', transcending history and conscious of being summoned by God to the work of redemption. These are not so much two different types of people as two potential stances which need to be united within each individual. In *The Tremendum*, a theological interpretation of the Holocaust (1981), he challenges theodicy that begins from the axiom of the goodness and omnipotence of God, and suggests instead that the Holocaust compels us to entertain the possibility that God is limited by the existence of radical evil.

Cohen, Hermann (1842–1918) German philosopher, Professor of Philosophy at Marburg 1876–1912. He achieved a great reputation as founder and leader of the neo-Kantian school. After his retirement he moved to Berlin and taught at a Liberal rabbinical seminary there. He now turned his attention from Kant to religion, and specifically Judaism. Cohen can be considered the last of the 'classical' Jewish philosophers, who grafted Jewish thought artificially onto the trunk of universal philosophy. The effort to identify Judaism with the religion of reason, initiated by Moses MENDELSSOHN, found its last and fullest expression in his work, and especially in his last book, *The Religion of Reason Drawn from the Sources of Judaism*, published posthumously in 1919. Here Cohen moves beyond the ethical idealism of his earlier work, in which God is conceived as an impersonal idea, towards a thoroughgoing account of Judaism in which God once again becomes a personal being, existing apart from humankind and involved in a relationship with them which can be expressed as a relationship of love, or 'correlation': they are 'co-workers in the work of creation'. The Kantian moral law does not help me to cope as an individual with my sense of personal moral failure, of sinfulness, and without religion I could easily fall into despair. The concept of a forgiving God enables me to become reintegrated into an ethically committed humanity, by an act of self-rededication. The relation with God has an impact on my relations with other people: in seeking God I will find my fellow humans, and learn to treat them with compassion, and through finding my fellow human beings I may eventually find God. Cohen's religious philosophy clearly prepares the ground for his disciples Martin BUBER and Franz ROSENZWEIG, and for other leading 20th-century Jewish thinkers.

Columbus Platform A declaration issued by a conference of US Reform rabbis meeting in Columbus, Ohio, in 1937. It replaced the PITTSBURGH PLATFORM, that had served as the basic statement of Reform principles for more than half a century, during which many changes had taken place. Retaining the stress on Judaism's compatibility with science, on the centrality of the moral law, and on the progressive nature of revelation, it supported the use of traditional ceremonies and Hebrew in the liturgy and re-emphasized the idea of the Jewish people. The Platform is arranged under nine headings: Nature of Judaism, God, Man, Torah, Israel, Ethics & Religion, Social Justice, Peace, and The Religious Life. Key statements include the following:

> Judaism is the historical religious experience of the Jewish people ... its message is universal, aiming at the union and perfection of mankind under the sovereignty of God.

> The Torah, both written and oral, enshrines Israel's ever-growing consciousness of God and of the moral law. It preserves the historical precedents, sanctions and norms of Jewish life, and seeks to mould it in the patterns of goodness and of holiness. Being products of historical processes, certain of its laws have lost their binding force with the passing of the conditions that called them forth. But as a depository of permanent spiritual ideals, the Torah remains the dynamic source of the life of Israel. Each age has the obligation to adapt the teachings of the Torah to its basic needs in consonance with the genius of Judaism.

> Though we recognize in the group loyalty of Jews who have become estranged from our religious tradition a bond which still unites them with us, we maintain that it is by its religion and for its religion that the Jewish people has lived.

> In the rehabilitation of Palestine, the land hallowed by memories and hopes, we behold the promise of renewed life for many of our brethren. We affirm the obligation of all Jewry to aid in its upbuilding as a Jewish homeland by endeavoring to make it not only a haven of refuge for the oppressed but also a center of Jewish culture and spiritual life.

> Judaism as a way of life requires, in addition to its moral and spiritual demands, the preservation of the Sabbath, festivals and Holy Days, the retention and development of such customs, symbols and ceremonies as possess inspirational value, the cultivation of distinctive forms of religious art and music and the use of Hebrew, together with the vernacular, in our worship and instruction.

See also CENTENARY PERSPECTIVE.

Coming Age *See* OLAM HA-BA.

commandments

(in Hebrew, mitsvot) Practical precepts considered traditionally to have been ordained by divine revelation. The total number of the commandments of the Torah (*see* MIDDE'ORAYETA) was agreed to be 613, made up of 248 positive commandments and 365 prohibitions. (These figures are said to correspond to the number, respectively, of bones and muscles in the human body.) The number of 613, which goes back at least to the time of the AMORA'IM, cannot be reached by actually counting the laws mentioned in the Torah, and while various medieval scholars produced lists of all 613, these lists do not agree among themselves. The most famous of these lists is MAIMONIDES' Séfer ha-Mitsvot (Book of the Commandments). A later list is found in the anonymous 13th-century Catalan work Séfer ha-Chinnuch (Book of Education). Two important Ashkenazi compilations from the same period are the Séfer Mitsvot Gadol (Greater Book of the Commandments) of Moses of Coucy and the Séfer Mitsvot Katan (Lesser Book of the Commandments) of Isaac of Corbeil.

A topic discussed both in the Talmud and by medieval thinkers is the reason for the commandments: are they the arbitrary decrees of an absolute ruler who has no need to justify himself, or are they open to rational explanation? SA'ADYA GA'ON distinguishes systematically between two sorts of commandments, the ceremonial commandments, which rely on the authority of revelation alone, and the ethical commandments, which are rational and would be observed even without revelation. For Maimonides, all the commandments are rational, but some are beyond our current limited understanding. This idea was widely accepted by subsequent theologians, as recently as the 19th-century Orthodox rabbi S. R. HIRSCH, who offered a reason for each of the commandments.

For Liberal and Reform theologians the issues raised by the commandments were different. Once belief in the divine authority of the Talmud, and then of the Torah, was undermined by historical research and Enlightenment philosophy, the binding force of the commandments was naturally questioned. Sa'adya's distinction took on renewed importance: the ethical commandments, which on the whole are shared by Jews and non-Jews, were affirmed as being central to the universal message of Judaism, while the ceremonial commandments were, with a few exceptions, jettisoned. Thus the 1885 PITTSBURGH PLATFORM declared: 'We accept as binding only the moral laws and maintain only such ceremonies as elevate and sanctify our lives, but reject all such as are not adapted to the views and habits of modern civilization.' With the 20th-century theology of relation a new role was found for the commandments, as a form of unique communication between God and humanity. Leo BAECK, true to the Liberal tradition, more or less identifies the commandments with the moral law; this understanding places them at the centre of the relation with God. For Franz ROSENZWEIG the command to love God (Deuteronomy 6.5) is at the heart of the relation. How can love be commanded? In human terms it is a paradox, but in the unique relation between God and humanity the command to love is heard in the depth of our soul: it is immediate and always in the present, and once it is heard we find our life transformed. Rosenzweig, far from accepting the commandments as something given, a body of law to be accepted and obeyed without question, argued his way back to them one by one.

In kabbala the commandments have a dual aspect. In the outward ('exoteric') understanding, they are seen as a guide to the service of God and an essential tool in the struggle against the forces of evil (*see* SITRA ACHRA) and to obtain merit and gain the life of the Coming Age (OLAM HA-BA). On the esoteric level, the commandments are a reflection of the realm of the SEFIROT: each individual commandment has its place within this complex system and plays its part in the promotion of the union of the Godhead. The LURIANIC KABBALA relates this to the 'raising of the sparks': the purpose of observing a commandment is not to obtain personal salvation but to bring about the restitution of the cosmos (*see* TIKKUN).

As expressed in CHABAD CHASIDISM, the commandments are seen as 'links' or 'connections'. As the Torah, which is perceived as literally a part and extension of the Creator's wisdom, descends into the physical world of action, it takes the outward form of laws, commandments and restrictions; however in their inward essence these are connections that allow the Creator and the creation to be bridged through Torah. Therefore, according to Chabad thinking, when Jews perform a commandment, they unite the world and themselves with the ultimate source of all existence.

See also AZHARA; NOACHIAN COMMANDMENTS.

commentary, biblical Biblical commentary in Hebrew arose in the course of the 10th and 11th centuries, replacing and at first building on the tradition of MIDRASH and no doubt echoing trends in contemporary Arabic study of the Qur'an and Greek study of the classics. The work of the MASORETES fed an interest in the 'plain' meaning of scripture (PESHÁT) as opposed to the flights of fancy that are characteristic of Midrash. The impact of the Greek philosophical tradition is apparent in commentaries written in Arabic in the Middle East in the 10th century, notably by the Rabbanite SA'ADYA GA'ON and the Karaites Ya'akub AL-KIRKISANI, Salmon ben Yeruchim and Japhet ben Eli. Of the commentators whose writings are still widely known and used the earliest is RASHI, who lived and wrote during the 11th century in Troyes in Champagne. Rashi's work is characterized by brevity and clarity, and he avoids being drawn into technical arguments. His commentary is thus remarkably accessible to anyone who can read Hebrew (although he often explains difficult words in French), and it is often the first port of call even today for serious Jewish readers in search of guidance on the meaning of a biblical obscurity. It is printed alongside the biblical text in rabbinic bibles and drawn on freely in annotated editions, side by side with the commentaries of Abraham IBN EZRA and David KIMCHI, who represent the Spanish tradition characterized by an interest in the study of grammar and a rationalist philosophical orientation. Another Spanish commentator, Moses NACHMA-NIDES, while aiming to expound the peshát, rejects Maimonidean rationalism and is rooted instead in KABBALA: 'We possess an authentic tradition' (he writes) 'that the entire Torah consists of the names of God, and that the words we read can be divided in a very different way so as to form (esoteric) names.' Many other commentaries survive from the Middle Ages, written both by Rabbanites and by Karaites. Those written in Christian lands increasingly show the influence of Christian exegesis and thought, which their authors sometimes polemicize against and often imitate. One of these was GERSONIDES, who wrote extensive commentaries with a strongly philosophical bent. Philosophical interests are also to the fore in the 16th-century commentaries of Isaac ABRAVANEL and Obadiah SFORNO. A new era in Jewish Bible commentary was inaugurated by Moses MENDELSSOHN, the towering figure of the German Jewish Enlightenment movement of the 18th century. Mendelssohn published in the 1780s his own translation of the Torah into German, accompanied by a commentary in Hebrew (known as the BI'UR) composed by a group of scholars under his direction, and combining traditional comments with the ideas of the Enlightenment. Subsequent Hebrew commentaries have tended to follow in Mendelssohn's footsteps in combining traditional and modern insights.

communion Intimate encounter with God. *See* DEVEKUT.

compassion Sympathy for the suffering of others; a divine attribute and human virtue. The Hebrew equivalent, rachamim, is related to the word for womb, réchem. God is addressed as 'Father of Compassion', Av ha-Rachamim, and referred to as 'Merciful and Compassionate', Rachum ve-Chanun (e.g. Psalm 145.8), or as the 'Compassionate One', ha-Rachaman. In rabbinic Judaism God's two key attributes, compassion and JUSTICE, are held in balanced tension. The Midrash imagines his inner monologue: 'If I create the world with compassion alone, sin will prevail; but if I create it with justice alone, how can it endure? Therefore I shall create it with both.' The name Adonay is held to represent the former attribute, the name Elohim the latter. Worship of God is said in the Talmud to mean becoming compassionate like God, and so human compassion is enjoined on the principle of IMITATIO DEI. Jews are sometimes called 'the compassionate children of compassionate parents'.

confirmation Ceremony of rededication of the individual to Judaism on reaching maturity. This innovative alternative to the BAR MITSVA ceremony is first recorded at Cassel, Germany, in 1810. By the beginning of the 19th century 13 had begun to seem a very early age for a boy to become formally a man, and indeed many boys at this age hardly seem mature enough to appreciate the responsibilities they are supposed to be undertaking. At the confirmation ceremony the rabbi asked the boy to give well-rehearsed answers to questions about such subjects as belief in God, and then to recite Maimonides' THIRTEEN PRINCIPLES. Large numbers of Jewish catechisms were published, both in Hebrew and in German, and the emphasis was on general rather than specifically Jewish principles. The influence of the Christian environment is obvious, and the new ceremony was objected to by some who felt it went too far towards imitating the Church, and pointed out that Judaism does not have a creed, so that catechizing is not strictly appropriate. Nevertheless, confirmation became an established feature of Reform Judaism, being made available to girls as well as boys, and spreading to America, where it gradually replaced the bar mitsva. The age of confirmation also rose, from 13 to 15 or 16. This was connected to a notable emphasis on Jewish education in American Reform Judaism in the years between the two world wars. Confirmation at a later age meant that young people were better prepared, in terms both of knowledge and of religious and moral maturity. Confirmation is now practised in the Reform, Reconstructionist and, in a more limited way, Conservative movements in America, and in the Liberal movement in Britain.

consensus Agreement. In the Torah, the laws are dictated by God and receive the people's assent; scope for disagreement is severely limited, and the agreement of the many is perceived as a threat to justice: 'You shall not follow the many to do evil, nor shall you speak up in a dispute so as to incline after the many' (Exodus 23.2). Rabbinic Judaism developed a different approach in the discussion of legal matters: while the views of individual authorities are frequently cited, the decision of the majority (often preceded in the Mishnah by the formula 'the Sages say') is decisive. The procedure is summed up in the tag 'An individual versus the many, the halacha follows the many', and the rabbis even go so far as to cite the final words of the verse of Exodus quoted above detached from their context, and interpreted to mean 'You shall incline after the many'. The same principle of majority decision is applied in the law court. The smallest permissible number of judges is three, to ensure a majority decision, and however many judges there are their total must always be an odd number, for the same reason (Mishnah, Sanhedrin 1.6). Judgment must be given by majority vote, however long it takes to reach a decision. In Karaite jurisprudence, the CONSENSUS (in Arabic, ijma') of scholars on the interpretation of a biblical law is a fundamental guiding principle. The medieval Rabbanite CODES OF LAW give primary weight to the Talmud and other earlier authorities, but it is worth noting that Joseph CARO applied a principle of consensus in formulating the law in his great codes. The principle of MARA DE-ATRA invested individual rabbis with great authority as interpreters of halacha, and discouraged attempts to seek consensus. The clash between these two principles broke out into outspoken public controversy in the late 1830s around the so-called GEIGER–TIKTIN AFFAIR. A central issue in this controversy was precisely the authority of the rabbi; the reforming party went on to convene a series of rabbinic conferences in Brunswick (1844), Frankfurt (1845) and Breslau (1846). These synods were in themselves the embodiment of the principle of consensus, which has remained very influential in Reform Judaism.

Conservative Judaism

Religious movement based mainly in the United States. In Israel and some other countries it is known as Masorti ('traditional'). Among the three main modernist movements Conservative Judaism occupies a centrist position, being more open to change than Orthodoxy and more wedded to tradition than REFORM JUDAISM.

The acknowledged roots of the movement are in the so-called HISTORICAL SCHOOL in Europe. Conservative Judaism in America similarly began as a reaction to Reform Judaism's rejection of traditional Jewish law and practice.

In 1886 the Jewish Theological Seminary (JTS) was founded in New York City as a more traditional alternative to the Reform seminary. In 1902, Solomon SCHECH-TER accepted the invitation to become president of JTS. The aim of the founders was to embrace the liberalism and pluralism of American Reform while safeguarding traditional practice.

The leaders of Conservative Judaism have always resisted the temptation to embody the ideals and principles of the movement in an authoritative statement. Certain strongly held beliefs, however, can be seen to be characteristic of the movement. In the first place, there is a firm commitment to the people of Israel and its religious values, coupled with a certain open-mindedness concerning the way these values should be interpreted. The intellectual founder of the movement, Solomon Schechter, declared that iconoclasm has always been a sacred mission of Judaism, and, while he insisted that it is mistaken to say that Judaism has no dogmas, felt that it had to be open to the demands of changing times. He coined the term CATHOLIC ISRAEL to indicate a non-denominational approach which put the developing character of the Jewish people at the centre of the religion. Schechter presided over the establishment in 1913 of the United Synagogue of America (later named the United Synagogue of Conservative Judaism), 'a union of congregations for the promotion of traditional Judaism'.

Conservative Judaism views Jewish law as normative and binding, but takes the position that it should evolve to meet the changing reality of Jewish life. The movement maintains a Committee on Jewish Law and Standards that offers guidance on specific issues; it has issued many RESPONSA, few of which, however, have been published.

Conservative Judaism enjoyed rapid growth in the first half of the 20th century, and became for a while the largest American Jewish denomination. Its centrist ethos, coupled with a refusal to issue dogmatic statements about belief (but *see* EMETVE-EMUNA), contributed to its success. However, it was too resistant to change for some, and in 1963 advocates of the philosophy of Mordecai KAPLAN seceded from the movement to form Reconstructionist Judaism (*see* RECONSTRUCTIONISM); subsequently, after JTS voted in 1983 to admit women for ordination as Conservative rabbis, opponents of this decision left the Conservative movement to form the UNION FOR TRADITIONAL JUDAISM.

The 1990s were a period of numerical decline. In 1990 a survey showed Conservative Judaism as still the largest Jewish denomination in America, with 43 per cent of Jewish households belonging to Conservative synagogues (compared to 35 per cent for Reform Judaism and 16 per cent for Orthodoxy). Ten years later only 33 per cent of synagogue-affiliated American Jews belonged to Conservative synagogues. At the same time, certain Conservative institutions, such as day schools, had shown significant growth.

The United Synagogue now has well over 800 member congregations in the United States and Canada, and is itself a constituent of the World Council of Synagogues, established in 1957, and embracing synagogues in South America, Europe, South Africa and Israel.

consistoire (French, 'consistory') Governing body of national and local communities in France, Belgium and Luxembourg. The system of consistories was established by a Napoleonic decree of 1808, following the deliberations of the SANHEDRIN. It was a part of Napoleon's reorganization of relations between the religious minorities and the state. The central consistoire in Paris later became responsible for administering the chief rabbinate and the rabbinical seminary. Today the consistoire is associated with modern Orthodoxy, and many synagogues, both Liberal and traditionalist, choose to remain outside its control.

contraception Halachic discussions of contraception begin from two COMMANDMENTS, a positive command to 'be fruitful and multiply' and a negative command prohibiting 'destruction of seed'. Both commandments are considered to be binding on men, and consequently it has been easier for halachists to permit female contraception. The Talmud (Bavli, Yevamot 65b) allows women to use an oral contraceptive where there is a history of painful births and provided the husband has already fulfilled the commandment to procreate. Orthodox authorities today follow the principles laid down in the Talmud. A key consideration is danger to life or health, although some authorities would allow economic considerations to be taken into account.

conversion Change of religion by an individual or group. In pre-modern times conversion from Judaism to another religion was strongly discouraged and occurred surprisingly rarely, usually under duress (*see* APOSTASY). Those who merely converted formally to save their lives were not treated as apostates, and those who subsequently returned to Judaism were welcomed and not punished or reminded of their lapse. MAIMONIDES, who lived in Muslim countries in a time of religious fanaticism, permitted outward conversion to Islam if it was a matter of life and death. Forcible conversions to Christianity in Spain and Portugal resulted in large numbers of insincere converts who were contemptuously termed 'Marranos' (swine) by Old Christians. Many of these 'New Christians' kept up some Jewish practices in secret; some small communities of this kind survived until modern times. Conversions to Judaism were much rarer in the Middle Ages, but even though both Christian and Muslim authorities forbade it under pain of death some isolated cases are recorded. More significant are the mass conversions of whole populations, such as the Edomites in antiquity, and the Khazars in southern Russia in the early Middle Ages. Since the Enlightenment the constraints on both sides have become much weaker, and religious conversion in general has become accepted as a fact of life. Many Jews have converted to other faiths; broadly speaking the halacha regards them as 'sinful Jews' rather than as non-Jews. Smaller but significant numbers of non-Jews have converted to Judaism (*see* PROSELYTES). Such conversions, in line with tradition, are not encouraged, but many rabbis and congregations (particularly the more liberal wing) have adopted a welcoming attitude.

See also PITTSBURGH STATEMENT.

corporal punishment Flogging as a judicial punishment is envisaged in the Torah, with a maximum of 40 strokes (Deuteronomy 25.1–3). The rabbis interpreted this maximum as thirty-nine (*see* MAKKOT). Beating of children and slaves was entirely acceptable in antiquity. Modern sensibility is opposed to both practices.

correlation *See* COHEN, HERMANN; THEOLOGY.

Council of the Four Lands The governing body of Polish Jewry from 1580 to 1764. The 'Four Lands' were Great Poland, Little Poland, Podolia and Galicia. (Lithuania had its own separate council from 1623.) The important communities in these territories sent delegates (up to 30 in all) to a synod that met regularly once a year, and later twice a year at the fairs of Lublin and Jaroslaw. Most of the delegates were laymen, but the religious committee was under the authority of a rabbi. The Council's work had two aspects: relations with the government and regulation of the Jewish community. The latter included taxation, overseeing education, and resolving internal conflicts. The Council famously outlawed SABBATEANISM in 1676. The power and authority of the Council gradually declined, and it was wound up following the first partition of Poland.

covenant (in Hebrew, berít) A formal agreement, specifically one between God and the Jewish people. Covenant is a key element in biblical theology: at several points in the Torah God agrees to protect the people and to give them the Land of Canaan in exchange for their commitment to him as their one god and observance of his commandments. The first covenant is made with Abraham; it is subsequently confirmed with Isaac and Jacob, and renewed at SINAI (see Exodus 24, where it is embodied in a written document, the Book of the Covenant, and symbolized by the blood of sacrificial bulls, the Blood of the Covenant). The two Tablets of the Covenant, recording the obligations accepted by the Israelites (the TEN COMMANDMENTS), are stored in the Ark of the Covenant. It is renewed again under Ezra (Nehemiah 8). In keeping with a prophetic promotion of inward righteousness of the heart rather than outward forms, in Jeremiah (31.30–33, 31–4 in English Bibles) God speaks of a coming new covenant: 'I shall set my Torah within them and upon their hearts shall I inscribe it'. Circumcision is a concrete symbol of the covenant (Genesis 17.9–14), and the Sabbath is described as an 'eternal covenant' (Exodus 31.16). The Bible also speaks of other covenants, notably a covenant of priesthood with the descendants of Aaron and a covenant of kingship with the family of David. The biblical prophets and the rabbis after them explained the successive national catastrophes that overtook the people (notably the destruction of the Jerusalem Temple by the Babylonians and again by the Romans) as caused by the unfaithfulness of the Jews rather than that of God. The covenant itself continued to be seen as everlasting. Since the Enlightenment, however, the idea of a particular covenant between God and the Jews has come under attack (*see* PARTICULARISM), and the emancipation implicitly did away with the special relationship, while traditionalists have tended to reassert the covenant in a strong form, rejecting modernity and the breaking down of the ghetto walls that it brought about. The Holocaust posed a further challenge to the concept of covenant: if God is really bound into a pact with Israel how could he have permitted the catastrophe (*see* HOLOCAUST THEOLOGY)? Since the Holocaust several leading theologians have endeavoured to reinterpret the idea of the covenant. ZIONISM, although a largely secular ideology, can be seen as an attempt to reinterpret and reassert the idea of covenant for the modern age.

covering of the head *See* HEAD-COVERING.

creation In theology, the notion that the universe was brought into being by the free act of God. While not entirely incompatible with DUALISM or EMANATIONISM, it is clearly not compatible with PANTHEISM. It rests ultimately on the belief in a personal, supernatural god. Both the rabbis and the medieval philosophers maintained the strong form of the doctrine, creation out of nothing, often called by its Latin name, creatio ex nihilo (in Hebrew, yesh me'áyin), against the idea of creation out of pre-existing matter. The first chapter of the Bible asserts very firmly and dramatically the idea of God as creator, which consequently became very deeply rooted in Jewish thought and worship. A prayer said every morning (known as YOTSER) addresses God as the one 'who forms light and creates darkness, who makes peace and creates all things', and the first of the THIRTEEN PRINCIPLES states that 'the Creator, blessed be his name, is the creator and guide of all created things, and he alone made, makes and will make all that is made'. Medieval thinkers admit that the scriptural doctrine cannot be proved rationally, but also tend to insist that it is not in conflict with reason.

creed A concise and authoritative formulation of important points of doctrine. Such statements, while characteristic of Christianity, are not as prominent in Judaism, lacking as it does a central religious authority and at the same time generally refusing to assign a central role to DOGMA. The SHEMÁ, with its strong statement of the unity of God, is sometimes characterized as 'the Jewish creed', but it is doubtful whether the term is appropriate here. The term is also applied to Maimonides' THIRTEEN PRINCIPLES, but despite their inclusion in prayer books and their embodiment in a popular hymn (the YIGDAL) they are not generally recognized as binding, and indeed it is doubtful if any statement of beliefs could be used, as the Christian creeds have, as a key test to establish a formal body of true believers.

cremation Burning of corpses. Traditionally, Jews buried their dead, and did not countenance cremation. Cremation became popular in the late 19th century, and REFORM JUDAISM has no strong objection to it, but it is frowned on in CONSERVATIVE JUDAISM and forbidden in ORTHODOXY. In Britain the Orthodox authorities permit the ashes of someone who has been cremated to be buried in a Jewish cemetery, provided the ashes are placed in a normal coffin. Elsewhere some Orthodox rabbis do not even permit this.

Crescas, Chasdai (c. 1340–1410 or 1412) Aragonese rabbi and philosopher. His best-known work is a critique of the influence on Jewish thought of ARISTOTELIANISM, which he saw as a harmful alien system, entitled *Or Adonai* (*The Light of the Lord*). His main target in this work was MAIMONIDES, and he particularly objected to the latter's negative formulation of the attributes of God. He proposed six positive essential Jewish beliefs, apart from the fundamental belief in a single, incorporeal and unique god: (1) God's omniscience; (2) God's omnipotence; (3) God's providence; (4)

prophecy; (5) the beneficial purpose of Torah; (6) the purpose of humankind (which is to love God). He mentions other beliefs, too, such as creation from nothing, the immortality of the soul, rewards and punishments, resurrection and the Messiah, but these, while obligatory, are in a separate and inferior category to the six. Love of God plays a key part in his thought: this is what religion is all about, rather than the abstract beliefs of the Aristotelian philosophers. Crescas explained the dispersion of the Jews as intended to advance their own moral standards and through them the salvation of all humankind. A vernacular work, surviving in Hebrew translation, attacks the doctrines of Christianity. Joseph ALBO was his most distinguished disciple; he also had an influence on Baruch SPINOZA.

cross-dressing *See* DRESS.

crown Used metaphorically as a symbol of power and respect. 'There are three crowns, the crown of Torah (i.e. learning), the crown of priesthood and the crown of kingship, but the crown of a good name excels them all' (Mishnah, Avot 4.15). The phrase 'crown of kingship' (KÉTER MALCHUT, Esther 2.17) was borrowed by IBN GABIROL as the title of his great philosophical poem. The rabbis liked to imagine the ministering ANGELS weaving crowns for God from their own praises and those offered up on earth by Israel. *See also* KÉTER.

custom (in Hebrew, minhag) Practice sanctioned by usage. In the sense of established practice not ordained in biblical or rabbinic legislation, custom has a special place in HALACHA. Formally less binding than law, established customs have considerable force, and can even take precedence over law. Moses ISSERLES, in his commentary on the ARBA'A TURIM, declared that 'minhag is law'. Isserles was concerned to incorporate Ashkenazi practice into codes compiled by Sefardim. Many practices that have become part of the fabric of Judaism originated in the Middle Ages. They include the festivities of SIMCHAT TORA, the practices associated with becoming BAR MITZVA, and the custom of covering the head during prayer, as well as the commemoration of the dead by special prayers on the anniversary of their death each year and in the synagogue worship of the three pilgrim FESTIVALS. Through the halachic literature and especially the CODES OF LAW such customs gradually acquired the force of law, and their observance was spread far beyond the locality where they were first adopted. The founder of Modern Orthodoxy, S. R. HIRSCH, expressed the place of custom very forcefully in the face of the reforming tendencies of his day, asserting that its force was tantamount to that of law, and it has remained a very strong element in Orthodox practice ever since. In Reconstructionism, as expounded by Mordecai KAPLAN, the opposite tendency comes to the fore: all religious practice is assigned a status tantamount to that of custom, which he terms 'folkways'.

D

dá'as tóra (Ashkenazi Hebrew, 'knowledge of Torah') A basic concept in present-day CHAREDI society, attributing to outstanding rabbinic authorities direct insight into the divine will on the basis of their knowledge of Torah. Of recent origin in this sense, dá'as tóra is rooted in the traditional belief that through the diligent study of Torah, the observance of the COMMANDMENTS and the effort to perfect one's character one can achieve a greater understanding of God's will. Chasidim have for a long time ascribed extraordinary spiritual powers to their REBBES, and have turned to them for practical guidance not just on matters of halacha but on all aspects of their lives on that basis. Similar views are now held by all charedim, including non-Chasidim. Their great scholars, known as gedolim ('great ones'), offer practical guidance on the conduct of one's life or indeed on matters of public policy. Many believe that the gedolim receive divine guidance in their leadership role.

dá'at ('knowledge') Knowledge, seen as a gift from God. Thus a benediction of the daily AMIDA begins: 'You favour mortals with knowledge [dá'at] and teach humankind understanding [bina].' In some kabbalistic systems, dá'at is one of the ten SEFIROT, mediating between CHOCHMA and bina. The term is also applied in Chasidism to a mystical state in which all ten sefirot are united as one.

Dabru Emet ('speak the truth', from Zechariah 8.16) A statement signed by some 160 rabbis and academic specialists in Judaism that first appeared in the *New York Times* in 2000. Taking note of the radical changes that have affected Christian approaches to Judaism since World War II, it contains eight brief statements about how Jews and Christians may relate to one another: (1) Jews and Christians worship the same God; (2) Jews and Christians seek authority from the same book – the Bible; (3) Christians can respect the claim of the Jewish people upon the Land of Israel; (4) Jews and Christians accept the moral principles of Torah; (5) Nazism was not a Christian phenomenon; (6) The humanly irreconcilable difference between Jews and Christians will not be settled until God redeems the entire world as promised in Scripture; (7) A new relationship between Jews and Christians will not weaken Jewish practice; (8) Jews and Christians must work together for justice and peace. The statement aroused considerable controversy when it first appeared, but is generally considered to have made a positive contribution to Jewish–Christian relations.

Daniel Biblical book, found in the Ketuvim. The book, couched partly in Hebrew and partly in Aramaic, is in two parts. The first (chapters 1–6) contains a series of stories about Daniel, a God-fearing Jew in the Babylonian exile, and his three companions; they include the famous episodes of the fiery furnace, the writing on the wall at Belshazzar's feast and the lions' den; the second (chapters 7–12) contains a series of symbolic visions and prophecies. These include a vision of four beasts emerging from the sea, interpreted as a sequence of empires, and an image of God as 'the Ancient of Days', an old man with white hair. Thought to reflect political conditions during the time of the HASMONEAN REVOLT, they contain the seeds of much subsequent speculation about the ending of history and the coming of the Messiah.

darda (shortened from dor de'a, 'generation of knowledge') Yemeni enlightenment movement, formed around the halachic scholar Yichya Kafach (1850–1932). The movement tried to counter the pervasive influence of kabbala, and encouraged secular studies.

dati (modern Hebrew, 'religious'; plural dati'im) Israeli term for a religious Jew (as opposed to CHILLONI).

dáven (Yiddish) To say prayers.

David Biblical king of Israel, thought to have reigned c. 1010 to 970 BCE. The youngest son of Jesse (Yishai), whose story is told in the Bible from 1 Samuel 16 to 1 Kings 2 and 1 Chronicles 11–29; many of the Psalms bear his name. He is remembered as the greatest king of Israel and the ideal type of king, despite his all too human shortcomings. The future Messiah, it is said, will be 'a son of David', i.e. descended from him, or possibly even David himself: according to the Talmud (Bavli, Rosh ha-Shana 25a), 'David, king of Israel, lives for ever'. The supposed tomb of David on Mount Zion in Jerusalem is a place of pilgrimage. The citadel of Jerusalem, next to the Jaffa Gate, has come to be known as the 'Tower of David'. He has also given his name to the six-pointed star or 'shield of David' (MAGEN DAVID).

day The Jewish day begins technically at sunset, which is why the Sabbaths and festivals are inaugurated by lighting candles or oil lamps in the home a little before sunset. It ends at the following nightfall (marked by the appearance of stars). The rhythm of the day is marked for observant Jews by the succession of prayers. There are actually two different cycles: the SHEMÁ is recited twice daily, in the evening and in the morning, while the statutory prayer or AMIDA is recited three times each day, evening, morning and afternoon.

Days of Awe Alternative name for the TEN DAYS OF PENITENCE.

dayyan ('judge') A judge in a rabbinic court (BEIT DIN). The word comes from the same root as DIN.

dayyenu ('[it would have been] enough for us') Song sung during the Passover SÉDER, recounting the manifold acts performed by God for the Israelites, beginning with the exodus from Egypt and concluding with the building of the Temple in

Jerusalem. At the end of each phrase those present respond 'dayyenu'. The author is unknown; it is first attested in the 10th-century prayer book of SA'ADYA GA'ON.

death Death is accepted in Judaism as an inevitable aspect of the human condition. Everything possible must be done to promote health and save life, and killing is viewed with abhorrence, but Jewish teachers have insisted that one should not be afraid to die or be angry about it, but should accept one's death, whatever the circumstances. On hearing news of a death one is supposed to respond with the words 'Blessed be the true judge', affirming one's confidence in the justice of God's decrees, however hard it may be to accept the individual verdict.

A Jew who senses the approach of death and is able to do so recites a confession. The following form of words is found in prayer books, and NACHMANIDES says that it was already old in his day: 'I acknowledge before you, Lord my God and God of my ancestors, that both my cure and my death are in your hands. May it be your will to send me a perfect healing. Yet if my death is fully determined by you, I will lovingly accept it from your hand. May my death be an atonement for all the sins, iniquities and transgressions that I have committed before you. Grant me some of the great happiness that is stored up for the righteous. Make known to me the path of life. In your presence is fullness of joy; at your right hand bliss for evermore.'

Other prayers may be said, and as the end approaches those present recite the following verses aloud, concluding with the opening words of the SHEMÁ:

The Lord reigns, the Lord reigned, the Lord shall reign for ever and ever.
Blessed be the name of his glorious reign for ever and ever.
The Lord, he is God.
Hear, Israel, the Lord our God, the Lord is One.

A dying person should never be left alone, and those present have an obligation to treat a dying person with consideration and respect, and to avoid doing anything that might hasten death.

According to classical halachic sources, the cessation of breathing marks the moment of death. Since the concept of 'brain death' emerged in the late 1960s there has been some rabbinic discussion of the possible need to revise the old definition, particularly in relation to the vexed question of organ transplantation.

Once death has been established the eyes of the corpse are closed, preferably by a son, and the body is carefully placed on the floor. A dead body must be handled with the same respect as is due to a living person. It is not stripped naked, but is always decently covered, and it is not disturbed more than is necessary. It is not left alone, but traditionally 'watchers' (SHOMERIM), who may be relatives or friends, stay with it until the burial, reciting psalms.

Dégel Hatora *See* AGUDAT ISRAEL.

Demaí (Hebrew/Aramaic, 'produce not certainly tithed') Tractate of the Mishnah, Tosefta and Palestinian Talmud, in order Zera'im. The subject of the tractate is agricultural produce from which it is not known for certain that tithes have been separated. A CHAVER, who was scrupulous about tithing, had to take special precautions in his dealings with an AM HA-ÁRETS, who must be suspected of not having tithed his produce. This tractate explains these precautions.

derásh ('exposition') Biblical interpretation, especially homiletical exposition. The word is related to DERASHA and MIDRASH. *See also* PARDES.

derasha A sermon. The term derúsh is also used.

dérech érets ('the way of the world') Expression used by the rabbis in a number of senses: 1. sexual intercourse; 2. etiquette, courtesy; 3. employment. In modern times it has acquired the further meaning of general culture or university studies: *see* TORA IM DÉRECH ÉRETS.

Deuteronomy (Devarim; Greek, 'second law') Fifth book of the Torah, containing the last address by Moses to the Israelites, including exhortation to obedience to God and a recapitulation of the laws. It ends with a final blessing and song, and the account of Moses' death. It includes a number of well-known passages, such as one of the versions of the TEN COMMANDMENTS, and two of the three passages that make up the SHEMÁ. Many traditional commentators have accepted the idea that the whole book was written by Moses, including the account of his death, although the Talmud also puts forward the view that the last eight verses were added after his death by Joshua (Bavli, Bava Batra 15a). Abraham IBN EZRA is a lone voice among medieval commentators in stating that the final twelve verses, from Moses' ascent to the mountain on which he would die, must have been added later.

Devarim ('words') Hebrew name of the biblical book of DEUTERONOMY.

devekut ('state of adhering') Ecstatic communion with God. Devekut is an abstract noun derived from a verb meaning to adhere or hold fast, in the sense of Deuteronomy 11.22, 'to love the Lord your God, to walk in all his ways, and to hold fast to him'. It is the goal of the mystics' endeavour, in which all other thoughts are banished and they experience nothing but the contemplation of God. MAIMONIDES (*Guide*, 3.51) says of the greatest saints that they can have God always present in their minds, to the extent that they are immune to any harm, and can even walk through fire and water. According to NACHMANIDES, people who achieve this state share in the eternal life in this world, because they have made the SHECHINA their dwelling. The kabbalists speak rapturously about this intimate communion, but they are generally careful not to describe it as an actual union of the soul with God, in which the individuality of the soul is dissolved. Devekut is particularly important in Chasidism: Chasidim endeavour to serve God by having him in their mind whatever they are doing. Torah study, for Chasidim, becomes a devotional rather than a merely intellectual activity.

Diaspora (Greek, 'scattering through') Dispersion, specifically a collective term for Jews living outside the Land of Israel. The root meaning of 'diaspora' is to scatter seed (the English words 'spore' and 'sperm' come from the same root), so it can be understood in a positive sense: just as a farmer scatters seed to bring in a richer harvest, so God scattered the people so as to win proselytes. This attitude is meant to counter the view that dispersion means exile and punishment, which has been more prevalent, both in the Bible and in subsequent Jewish tradition. Another motive for the praise of dispersion in the rabbinic literature is the harshness of Roman rule. 'God knew that Israel would be unable to bear the cruelty of Edom (Rome), and so he exiled them to Babylon.' In Babylon there is peace and prosperity, and the Jews are able to devote themselves to the study of Torah. Furthermore, dispersion makes it less likely that the people will be destroyed by persecution: if they disappear in one place they will survive in another.

A positive evaluation of diasporic existence can be found throughout the ages, though it is outweighed by the far more numerous texts that protest against exile and look forward in hope and prayer to the end of the dispersion. The idea of the Jewish people as a 'light to the nations', which was prominent in Jewish theology of the emancipation period, implies a positive evaluation of diaspora. The Jews, it was argued, are ordered to be a 'a kingdom of priests and a holy nation' (Exodus 19.6): just as the priests had no territory of their own but were scattered among the tribes to minister to God, so the Jews too had no land of their own but were scattered among the peoples to witness to God and his teachings. The anti-Zionism of Liberal and Orthodox Judaism has become more muted since the creation of the state of Israel, but the theologian Ignaz MAYBAUM, who was a strong supporter of the idea of a sacred Jewish mission to be a 'light to the nations', declared in a sermon delivered in 1956: 'The state of Israel is not the successor of the Diaspora, but it is part and parcel of it. As a people of the Diaspora we can only exist as a priestly nation, not as a political nation. The state of Israel is a dearly loved but very vulnerable part of the Diaspora.' In modern times the positive attitude to the Diaspora is associated particularly with Simon DUBNOW, who refused to see the Diaspora in a negative light, but chose to interpret it instead as a natural and organic development in Jewish history. Even when they ruled the Land of Israel, he observed, the Jews chose to establish other centres, in Babylonia and Egypt and eventually throughout the Greek world. They led the other nations of the world in moving away from land and state towards a supra-territorial existence in multi-ethnic communities.

dietary regulations

Rules concerning permitted and forbidden foods. Rules of this kind can be found in the Bible and the rabbinic literature, and are discussed in the HALACHA. They have become very complex over the years, and are observed more scrupulously in some households than in others. This is one of the key areas where KARAITE and RABBANITE laws differ, as much of the Rabbanite practice is based on rabbinic interpretation. Most of the rules concern meat and fish. Broadly speaking these can be divided into two groups, those determining which species of animal may or may not be eaten, and those concerned with the manner of death, preparation, cooking and serving.

The lists of forbidden and permitted animals are taken from the Torah (Leviticus 11 and Deuteronomy 14.3–21). There are three main classes of permitted animals: quadrupeds, birds and fish. Creatures which 'creep on the ground' are forbidden. KOSHER quadrupeds have to conform to two criteria: they must have cloven hooves and chew the cud. The only animal that has cloven hooves but does not chew the cud is the pig, which may be the reason why the pig has been viewed as the non-kosher animal par excellence. Cattle, sheep, goat and deer all come into the category of permitted animals. Horses, which have undivided hooves, as well as animals with paws such as rabbit and hare, are forbidden. As for birds, rather than provide general guidance the Torah lists the ones that are forbidden. As it happens, they seem to be birds that kill other animals or fish or that eat carrion. The implication is that all other birds are permitted, but since some doubt exists as to the identity of some of the birds on the list scrupulous Jews only eat domesticated birds that are known by tradition to be kosher, such as chicken, duck, goose, turkey and pigeon. Fish have to have fins and scales, a curious rule, since there do not seem to be any fish that have scales but not fins. By and large this rule causes no difficulties, but rabbis continue to argue over some doubtful cases, such as sturgeon, swordfish and turbot. All other animals are forbidden, except for certain kinds of locust that are specifically permitted.

Animals that are not kosher are called terefa (shortened by Ashkenazim to tref and by Sefardim to taref). Even a small quantity of terefa can contaminate a dish or foodstuff, and so scrupulous Jews are very attentive to the ingredients of prepared foods, such as biscuits that may be made with animal fat. If a pot or pan in which non-kosher food has been cooked is subsequently used for cooking kosher food it will render it terefa, but the utensil may first be cleansed in boiling water. (China and porcelain vessels cannot be cleansed.)

Animals that have been killed by other animals or that have died of their own accord are specifically forbidden (Exodus 22.30, Leviticus 11.39, Deuteronomy 14.21), as is the consumption of the blood of any animal (Leviticus 7.26–7, 17.10–14). This means that only those permitted animals and birds that have been properly slaughtered may be eaten. Elaborate rules have been developed for shechita (slaughter). The butcher (shochet) must be a person of moral integrity, and his knife must be extremely sharp and free from the slightest nick, so as to avoid inflicting pain on the animal. The animal's throat is cut with a single continuous movement, and the blood is immediately emptied out. An animal that has certain defects or diseases, even if properly slaughtered, is considered as terefa, so the butcher will examine the organs, particularly the lungs, with great care, and if necessary will consult a rabbi. Not all parts even of animals that have passed all these tests may be eaten. In particular, the sciatic nerve is not eaten, by very ancient custom (Genesis 32.33); since removing it (PORGING) is a difficult process, in some places, such as Britain, the meat of the hindquarters is not eaten at all by the scrupulous. Before the meat may be eaten the remaining blood is drawn out by salting. (Roasting or grilling over a naked flame is an alternative method.) Fish do not need to be killed in a special way or salted, as their blood is not considered to fall under the prohibition.

There is a further set of rules, based on a prohibition on eating 'a kid seethed in its mother's milk', which is repeated three times in the Torah (Exodus 23.19, 34.26; Deuteronomy 14.21). The rabbis understood this to mean that no kind of meat may be cooked in any kind of milk. As an extra precaution, they forbade the eating of meat and milk products at the same meal, even if they have not been cooked together. This rule in its turn has been extended, so that one has to wait a certain length of time after eating meat before eating dairy products; some people wait as much as six hours. More observant Jews keep separate sets of pots, dishes and cutlery for use with meat and dairy foods.

During the period of EMANCIPATION the rules were increasingly felt to be irrational and an intolerable burden on citizens trying to integrate themselves in modern society. Many Jews abandoned them partially or entirely. American Reform Judaism and Liberal Judaism in Britain categorized them as an anachronism and a barrier to true religiosity. In Orthodoxy they have been formally maintained; Conservative Judaism, in this as in so much else, occupies an intermediate position, rejecting alike the adherence to traditional norms which is characteristic of Orthodoxy and the radicalism of Reform. In theory there is nothing to prevent Conservative Jews from testing each of the regulations in relation to their own lives, to see whether it enhances or detracts from a meaningful religious existence. The result may well be a thoroughgoing adherence to the traditional halacha, but it may equally be a more selective approach, in which some rules (for example the prohibition on eating the flesh of certain animals) may be felt to be more important than others (for example the rigid separation of milk and meat products or the restrictions on food prepared by Gentiles).

One way round most of these demanding requirements is not to eat meat. Even vegetarians, however, must be on their guard against eating certain foods which transgress against one or other of the food laws, such as an egg with a blood spot, cheese made with animal rennet, or gelatin. There are also some restrictions on certain foods prepared or even handled by non-Jews.

During the festival of PASSOVER there are special, even more restrictive, dietary rules.

din ('law', 'lawsuit', 'judgment', 'justice') A word with many different meanings, all held together by the basic idea of justice. 'A din' or 'the din', means 'a law' or 'the law'. God's attribute of justice (middat ha-din) is balanced by his attribute of mercy (middat ha-rachamim). Din is the name of one of the ten SEFIROT, also known as GEVURA. A BEIT DIN is a place where lawsuits are heard and justice is dispensed. The word comes from the same root as DAYYAN.

dina de-malchuta dina (Aramaic, 'the law of the kingdom is the law') Legal device that has the effect of incorporating the law of the land into HALACHA, binding on Jews, provided it does not conflict with an existing prohibition in halacha.

dinei mamonot ('legal cases that can be resolved by monetary payment') In HALACHA, property cases, such as those arising from sales, loans and inheritances. The Mishnah (Sanhedrin 1.1) declares that they are to be heard by a panel of three judges. The term is extended to all types of cases that cannot lead to the death penalty (Sanhedrin 4.1).

dinei nefashot ('legal cases that can entail the death penalty') Capital cases. According to the Mishnah, they are heard by a lesser BEIT DIN of twenty-three judges (Sanhedrin 1.4).

dispersion Scattering abroad. In the Bible (Genesis 11.8) dispersion is a punishment visited upon an early generation of mankind who tried to build a tower that would reach up to the sky. According to the Mishnah (Sanhedrin 10.3) they have no share in the Coming Age (OLAM HA-BA). Its implications are thus inherently negative, although it is seen as an essential element in the human condition. Close study of the rabbinic literature reveals two different attitudes to dispersion, and there are traces of a dialectic between them. On the one hand, 'the dispersion of the ungodly is a benefit to them and a benefit to the world, but the dispersion of the righteous is a misfortune to them and a misfortune to the world'. On the other hand: 'Rabbi Eleazar said: God scattered Israel among the nations for the sole purpose that they should gain many proselytes. Rabbi Hoshaya said: God did Israel a favour in scattering them among the nations.' Dispersion has been a notable characteristic of the Jewish people for most of its history. Being concentrated in a particular place might seem to be necessary for the formation and preservation of a national identity, although there are several examples of other nations that are widely dispersed. In the case of the Jews, dispersal has come to seem almost an integral part of the people's experience, and it certainly bulks large in the way the Jewish people thinks of itself.
See also DIASPORA.

divorce Legal dissolution of marriage. The Jewish attitude to divorce is pragmatic: whatever the attitude may have been in earlier times, today it is seen as a matter for regret and is only practised as a last resort, when the marriage has irretrievably broken down. However, the sources speak of it in a matter-of-fact way, and no particular stigma attaches to a divorcee. As with the marriage, so with divorce, it is a matter for the couple themselves and not the state or the court. A rabbinic court is, however, invoked to ensure that the instrument of divorce (GET) is correctly drawn up and delivered, since any technical fault may render the divorce invalid and prevent a subsequent remarriage by the woman. Once the get has been duly delivered the parties are free to remarry, just as widows or widowers are.

Divrei ha-Yamim Alef, Divrei ha-Yamim Bet Hebrew names of the biblical books of 1 and 2 CHRONICLES, respectively.

dogma Authoritative formulation of doctrine. It is a moot point whether Judaism has dogmas. In the encounter with other faiths and philosophical movements Jewish thinkers have often felt challenged to define the distinctive and essential beliefs of Judaism (*see* CREEDS). However, in the absence of a central religious authority such statements have generally only had descriptive, not prescriptive force. For example, the resurrection of the dead would have been accepted as a dogma by many, and it is embodied in the liturgy, but probably only a minority of Jews would subscribe to it today. Even the existence of God, which might be thought a central and necessary belief for Jews, has been abandoned by many, probably a majority, of Jews today (*see* ATHEISM). All Jews would probably agree that Jewish identity is not defined by beliefs; consequently the role of dogmas in Judaism (whatever it may be) must be different from their place in Christianity. A deeply rooted emphasis on practice rather than theory also tends to limit the role of dogmas. However, those Jews who ascribe a central role to observance of HALACHA would probably also agree that one must believe that the halacha itself was revealed by God; this could be, therefore, an example of a dogma that has been widely accepted down the ages by many Jews. The early Reformers, in pejoratively naming the upholders of this view in its strong form 'Orthodox', implied that they were importing an alien, Christian, category into Judaism. The disagreements between Reform and Orthodox theorists thus tended to centre on beliefs, as those between Karaites and Rabbanites had done in the Middle Ages; in fact the term dogma is more likely to be used in the sense of 'false belief obstinately held to' than in that of 'true belief essential for salvation'.

Dönme (Turkish, 'convert', 'renegade') Muslim sect of Jewish origin, known among themselves less pejoratively as ma'aminim (believers). Before the population exchange between Turkey and Greece in 1922 they were strongly represented in Salonica; they are now mainly concentrated in Istanbul. The origin of the Dönme is in the Sabbatean movement of the 17th century. When SHABBETAI TSEVÍ accepted conversion to Islam in 1666 many of his devotees followed him, considering conversion as a step towards messianic redemption. Outwardly Muslim, they retained many of their beliefs and practices in secret.

Dov Ber of Mezhirich (d. 1772) Chasidic leader. Known as the MAGGID (either because he never had a rabbinic appointment or because the term occurs in the title of one of his books), he led the Chasidic movement after the death of the founder, the BAAL SHEM TOV, whom he met only a couple of years before the latter's death. He was an original and creative kabbalistic thinker and clearly had a charismatic personality.

dreidl Yiddish name for a small top used by Ashkenazi children in gambling games during CHANUKKA.

dress The Torah (Numbers 15.37–41, Deuteronomy 22.12) ordains a distinctive form of clothing for Israelites: they are to wear tassels on the corners of their clothes, marked with a purple thread. The purpose is said to be as a reminder of the commandments and a mark of holiness. Today this command is observed by men through the wearing of a special item of clothing (*see* TALLIT; TSITSIT). TEFILLIN could also be considered an example of distinctive clothing. The Torah also forbids cross-dressing (Deuteronomy 22.5). The only other biblical instruction concerning dress is a ban on clothes made from a mixture of fibres, specifically wool and flax (Deuteronomy 22.11) (*see* SHA'ATNEZ). On the whole Jews have not voluntarily worn distinctive clothing, although in some societies, because of conservatism, isolation, or for other reasons, they have ended up being recognizable by their dress. Rarely, distinctive marks have been imposed upon them, such as a special Jewish hat and a badge in the form of a wheel imposed in Catholic lands in the Middle Ages, a yellow star imposed by the Nazis, or a distinctive turban imposed under the Ottoman empire. Male Chasidim, exceptionally, have chosen to wear distinctive clothing; it is adapted from the dress worn by the Polish nobility. It consists of a long coat (kapóta), worn over breeches and hose, and a fur-trimmed hat (shtreímel). In accordance with the demands of modesty (tseni'ut), traditionalists cover the entire body, apart from the hands and face, in public. Such modesty is particularly enjoined by CHAREDIM on their womenfolk. On wigs see SHEÍTEL.

drunkenness Excess, like asceticism, is generally discouraged by legal codes and ethical treatises alike. This principle applies to the consumption of alcohol as well. However, on PURIM inebriation is encouraged, 'until one cannot distinguish between "Blessed be Mordecai" and "Cursed be Haman"'. Chasidim consider the consumption of alcohol conducive to spiritual joy, which led their opponents to accuse them of being drunkards. The involvement of many Jews in eastern Europe in the alcohol trade led to a particular sensitivity to the dangers of alcohol abuse.

dualism A view that seeks to explain the world, or some part or aspect of it, by the assumption of two independent principles. Both the Bible and later sources such as the Talmud and Midrash are pervaded by dualistic language, both in the realm of metaphysics (in a radical contrast between heaven and earth, God and the world, God and humankind) and in that of ethics (good and evil). Such language is used to make various kinds of points, for instance about the inability of humans to attain full knowledge of God, or the importance of doing good deeds and avoiding evil ones. Generally speaking, however, out-and-out dualism is avoided through an unchallengeable commitment to the essential unity of being. Unity is held to be inherently better than plurality or multiplicity. God is therefore one and has no rival or partner; God is also the source of the world's existence and is intimately concerned for its welfare. Since God is entirely good, the existence of evil in the world may seem to challenge the idea that everything in creation has its source in God; this is however what the rabbis asserted. Thus they stated that one is bound to bless God for bad things as for good ones (Mishnah, Berachot 9.5). However, the idea of God as the source of evil is treated with some delicacy; for example in the morning prayer (the YOTSER) the words of Isaiah 45.7, 'Forming light and creating darkness, making peace and creating evil' are revised to read: 'Forming light and creating darkness, making peace and creating all things'. This is the mainstream Jewish view, but radical dualism has been espoused more than once. It is found in the late Second-Temple period in two different forms, an antagonistic dualism, which sees the world as a battleground of opposing forces of good and evil not unlike the dualism associated with Zoroastrianism, and a kind of hierarchical dualism, in which a 'second God' who created the world is subordinated to the transcendent God. Certainly the second of these, and perhaps both, are firmly rejected and condemned by the rabbis, who speak of 'those who say there are two powers in Heaven'. Antagonistic dualism is found in kabbala (see SITRA ACHRA). As for human behaviour, the rabbinic conception of good and evil is saved from being dualistic by the idea of the two yétsers (see YÉTSER HA-RA): human beings are made with a potential to do good or evil built into their basic make-up, and the potential to choose evil is essential to the doctrine of free will. Both yétsers, however, originate in the one God. This concept has given rise to some difficulties for the philosophers, who ask how God can have knowledge of evil if he is all-good. Some are led to limit God's omniscience. For example Abraham IBN EZRA, commenting on the biblical verse 'The Lord knows the way of the righteous but the way of the wicked perishes' (Psalm 1.6), points out the implication: God does not know the way of the wicked as he knows the way of the righteous; what he does know is that the way of the wicked leads to perdition. A different kind of dualism based in an opposition between the material world and the world of ideas is characteristic of Platonism.

Dubnow, Simon (1860–1941) Russian Jewish historian. His great *World History of the Jewish People*, written in Russian, was first published in German in 1925–9; he also published a pioneering *History of Chasidism* (1930–32). Dubnow was a proponent of 'autonomism', calling for Jewish communal autonomy and minority rights to be recognized not only within a multinational Russian state but throughout the world. This, he felt, was the defining characteristic of Jewish life among the nations down the ages, from the time of the Talmudic rabbis in Roman Palestine and Babylonia through the Jewries of medieval Europe to the COUNCIL OF THE FOUR LANDS. As a convinced secularist he looked to the synagogues of Germany to convert themselves into secular national organizations, and hoped that a similar type of structure would emerge in America. Dubnow came to an original conception of Jewish national identity: the Jews, in uniquely maintaining a sense of nationhood while emancipating themselves from attachment to land or territory, represent the highest form of nation ever to have evolved. Born and raised in Russia, Dubnow lived in Berlin between 1922 and 1934; he was murdered by Nazis in Riga in 1941.

duchan Raised platform from which the priests officiated in the Temple. Today the term is applied to the raised platform in front of the ARK in synagogues, from which the priests perform the BIRKAT KOHANIM.

dúchenen (Yiddish) Ashkenazi name for the ceremony of BIRKAT KOHANIM, so called because the priests perform it from the DUCHAN.

Ecclesiastes *See* KOHÉLET.

echal (also hechal) Term used by Sefardim for the ARK in the synagogue. The term hechal was originally applied to the hall of the Temple.

ecology Originally a scientific term for the study of relationships between organisms and their environment, now applied loosely to human concern for the well-being of our planet. It has lately become a major concern on which all religions have been challenged to reflect, but it has to be said that the classical sources of Judaism, composed at times when the problems faced by human societies were very different, offer little guidance for theological reflection on ecological issues. Great weight has consequently been attached to a small number of texts thought to have some potential to contribute to contemporary debates. Prominent among these is the halachic concept BAL TASHCHIT, which was long ago interpreted as forbidding needless waste and destruction. This is one of the fastest-growing areas of Jewish theology, making use in innovative ways of general principles and specific insights of the classical sources, in conjunction with current ethical and practical considerations.

ecstasy In mysticism, state of intense exaltation achieved through meditation or worship, in which the self is transcended through a sense of the proximity of the Divine. In the Bible there are several accounts of prophets being seized by the divine power in a kind of momentary ecstasy for the purpose of teaching. This is different from the ecstatic states promoted in CHASIDISM, namely DEVEKUT (cleaving) and hitlahavut (enthusiasm). An early leader of CHABAD CHASIDISM, Dov Ber of Lubavitch (1773–1827), who was a firm believer in the value of ecstatic states, wrote a tract on ecstasy in which he distinguished between true ecstasy and various false forms of the experience pursued for cheap thrills.

Eda Charedit ('CHAREDI community') In Israel, collective term applied to charedim, embracing both Chasidim and Mitnaggedim. The community generally stands apart from the majority, ZIONIST sector of Israeli Jewry, and refuses to co-operate with Zionist or state institutions. They maintain their own separate educational system, in which the language of instruction is Yiddish, and have their own rabbis and rabbinical law courts.

Eden *See* GARDEN OF EDEN.

Edom 1 In the Torah, another name of ESAU (Genesis 36.1). The name is similar to the Hebrew word for 'red' (adom), and Esau at his birth is described as red (Genesis 25.25), which the rabbis in the Midrash interpret as a premonition of his penchant for hunting and bloodshed. Red is also the colour of the lentil stew with which Jacob purchases the birthright from Esau, and this is explicitly connected with the name Edom (Genesis 25.30). **2** In the rabbinic literature Edom is used as another name for the Roman empire, in part because Esau was the archetypal enemy of Jacob/Israel, and the rabbis (however implausibly) saw Jews and Romans as being locked in a struggle for world-domination, and in part because the two names Edom and Rome are very similar when written in the Hebrew alphabet, the letters D and R being easily mistaken for each other. Once Christianity became the official religion of the Roman empire, in the 4th century, Edom came gradually to be applied to Christendom in general.

education Talmudic Judaism placed a high value on study of Torah, which was regarded as a religious obligation binding on both boys and men. Elementary schooling was given in the beit séfer. Specialized rabbinic education was dispensed in the beit ha-Midrash, which was generally attached to a synagogue. As the rabbinic movement established itself in North Africa, Italy, Spain, Byzantium and elsewhere in the geonic period YESHIVOT were established there, primarily for the study of the Babylonian Talmud. The same system continued virtually unchanged for centuries. In eastern Europe the elementary school was known as CHÉDER; in the Ottoman empire the term CHABRA was used. The yeshiva education was dominated by the method of PILPUL until the reforms introduced by the VILNA GA'ON and his pupils (*see* CHAYYIM OF VOLOZHIN). The exclusively religious content of yeshiva education gave rise to conflict in the 19th century. In eastern Europe proposals to introduce a broader curriculum put forward by proponents of HASKALA were met with strong resistance by traditionalists. The post-emancipation opening up of state schools and universities to Jews gradually spelt the end of the older system for all but the most traditionalist Jews. S. R. HIRSCH, under the slogan TORA IM DÉRECH ÉRETS, made the combination of traditional Jewish and secular studies a key feature of modern Orthodoxy, provided the latter did not conflict with the former. Beginning in the middle of the century rabbinical SEMINARIES offered a modern approach to the Jewish sources coupled with the study of general subjects, with the aim of training rabbis who could preach in the vernacular and hold their own intellectually in conversation with the Christian clergy. At the same time, Jewish schools were opened to offer immigrant children, in particular, an opportunity to adapt to a new society without sacrificing their Jewish identity and values. Many Jews, however, while flourishing within the general educational system, grew up with little or no knowledge of Judaism, beyond perhaps what they could learn in a Sunday school supplemented for some with occasional evening classes. Recently there has been a strong revival in Jewish day schools, offering a full modern curriculum combined with Jewish education. There has also been a mushrooming of yeshivot and analogous institutions, particularly in Israel, where young Jews of both sexes from Western countries can study a traditional Jewish syllabus, often for a year or two between school and university.

Eduyyot ('testimonies') Tractate of the Mishnah and Tosefta, in order Nezikin, recording early rabbinic discussions on a variety of subjects.

Ehye A name of God, first found in the Bible (Exodus 3.14). In the ZOHAR it corresponds to the sefira Kéter (*see* SEFIROT).

Ehye Asher Ehye ('I am what I am') Self-designation of God in Exodus 3.14. In the story of the first meeting between God and Moses, at the burning bush, God introduces himself as 'your fathers' God, the God of Abraham, the God of Isaac, the God of Jacob' and gives Moses the task of leading the Israelites out of Egypt. Moses says: 'When I go to the Israelites and say to them, The God of your fathers has sent me to you, they will answer, What is his name? What shall I say to them?' God gives the mysterious reply: 'I am what I am [ehye asher ehye]. Tell the Israelites: I am has sent me to you' (Exodus 3.6–14). Both the translation and the interpretation of these words have caused many difficulties. RASHI explains: 'Just as I am with you in the present suffering [of slavery in Egypt], so I shall be with you in your servitude to the other nations.' For some philosophers this 'great tautology' is an ontological statement of God's unique and absolute being. Hermann COHEN is in this line of interpretation when he interprets the name as 'Being-as-such' or 'Unique Being'. Martin BUBER has a radically different interpretation, which has echoes of Rashi: 'I will be there such as I will be there' (first set out in *Königtum Gottes* (1932; *Kingship of God*, 1967)). The verb ehye here, as in the divine name YHVH, denotes not existence but presence. This interpretation, arising out of a long dialogue between Buber and Franz ROSENZWEIG, is central to Buber's theology.

Eicha Hebrew name of the biblical book of LAMENTATIONS.

Eighteen (benedictions), the *See* AMIDA.

Ein Kelohénu ('there is none like our God') Joyful hymn of praise sung at the end of the morning service (except among Ashkenazim, who sing it at the end of the additional service on Sabbaths and festivals). It is an ancient and very popular hymn that exists not only in Hebrew but in Judezmo, Arabic and other languages. The final verse, an urgent plea for redemption, is replaced in the Ashkenazi liturgy by a nostalgic reminiscence of the incense burnt in the Temple.

Ein Sof ('infinite', 'infinity') In kabbala, the ultimate, God. The term denotes the Godhead as it is in itself, the ground of all being, the source of all divine and earthly existence, as opposed to the various manifestations of God. In some kabbalistic systems it is outside the SEFIROT; in others, including that of the ZOHAR, it is equated with the first and highest sefira (Kéter). For most kabbalists it is totally unknowable and beyond the reach even of mystical contemplation. It is only made manifest through the Sefirot, and any study or worship must be addressed to them. *See also* LURIA, ISAAC; TSIMTSUM.

Ein Ya'akov ('Jacob's Well') Title of a comprehensive collection of aggadic portions of the Talmud, begun by Jacob Ibn Chabib of Salonica (c. 1450–1516) and completed by his son Levi Ibn Chabib of Jerusalem (c. 1484–1545). It includes annotations offering rational interpretations of the legendary material, and drawing out ethical teachings. First published in full in 1516, it has been reprinted more than a hundred times, and has proved immensely popular not only among Sefardim but even among Ashkenazim.

Einheitsgemeinde (German, 'integrated community') Term denoting the usual Jewish community structure in Germany and in countries influenced by German practice, in which members of different religious denominations (Orthodox, Liberal etc.) belong administratively to one community.

El A name of God, first found in the Bible, and often used in the form Eli, 'my God'. In the ZOHAR it corresponds to the sefira Chésed (*see* SEFIROT).

El Male Rachamim ('God, full of compassion') Prayer for the repose of the dead, chanted by Ashkenazim when a person observing YÓRTSAIT is called up to the Torah. It is also commonly recited after a burial, at a memorial service on the festivals, and on other occasions when the dead are commemorated. In its present form it is thought to date from the 17th century.

El Shaddai A name of God, found in the Torah (for example Genesis 17.1, Exodus 6.3). *See* SHADDAI.

Eleazar of Worms (c. 1165–1230) A leading figure of the CHASIDEI ASHKENAZ. A pupil of JUDAH THE CHASID, Eleazar was a prolific author in several genres. His best-known work is a halachic compilation entitled Roké'ach; he also composed commentaries on books of the Bible, the prayer book and PIYYUTIM, and several works of esoteric theology. He insists on the utter unknowability of the transcendent God: the link between this ultimate being and our world is the visible GLORY. Eleazar's wife and daughters were martyred by Christian crusaders.

election In theology, the doctrine that the people of Israel is particularly chosen by God. This idea is prominent in the Bible and in the liturgy. Among the many passages in the Torah expressing it are the following: 'If now you listen to my voice and keep my covenant, you shall be my treasured possession among all the peoples, because all the earth is mine, and you shall be mine, a kingdom of priests and a holy nation' (Exodus 19.5–6); 'Only in your forefathers did God take pleasure, to love them, and he chose their descendants, you, from among all peoples, as at the present time: so you must sensitize your hearts and no longer be obdurate, because the Lord your God is the God of Gods and the Lord of Lords …' (Deuteronomy 10.15–17). In the liturgy, a person called up to the Torah reading blesses God 'who has chosen us from all peoples and given us the Torah', and the special AMIDA for festivals contains the words 'You have chosen us from all peoples, you have loved us and taken pleasure in us, and exalted us above all tongues, you have sanctified us by your commandments, and brought us to your service, our king, and set your great and holy name upon us.' These sample quotations embody the key elements of election. Firstly, it is the universal God of the whole world who chooses Israel, not some local or tribal deity. Secondly, the purpose of the election is that Israel should be God's ministers and servants in the world. Thirdly, the election is set within the context of the COVENANT, and places obligations on the people, specifically to be attentive to God's voice and to obey his COMMANDMENTS. The precise interpretation of the election and its meaning varies greatly, even within the Bible. For the prophet Amos, for example, it is not an unmixed blessing: 'You only have I known out of all the families of the earth: therefore I shall punish you for all your iniquities' (3.2). The medieval philosophers do not pay much attention to the doctrine; Maimonides did not include it among his THIRTEEN PRINCIPLES and finds it totally incomprehensible (*Guide* 2.25). An exception is JUDAH HA-LEVI, who holds the extreme view that Jews are superior to other people as humans are superior to animals. An analogous sense of the cosmic uniqueness of Israel is found in the kabbala and consequently in Chasidism. It was the UNIVERSALISM of the Enlightenment that really challenged the particularism of election, and for most Reform thinkers it has become anathema.

Elijah Biblical prophet. He appears in the books of Kings (1 Kings 17–19 and 21; 2 Kings 12) as prophesying in the northern kingdom of Israel in the 9th century BCE. He is a model of zeal for God, and performs wonders such as restoring to life a dead child and calling fire down from heaven. At the end of his earthly life he does not die but is carried up to heaven in a whirlwind. Such a figure understandably left a strong impression on posterity. The prophecy of Malachi ends with a divine promise to send Elijah back before the 'great and terrible day of the Lord', and consequently he has been seen as the precursor of the Messiah, a role that is mentioned in prayers and songs, for example in the grace after meals and the HAVDALA. At the Passover SÉDER a cup of wine is poured for him and at one point the door is opened to welcome him. A chair is placed for him at circumcisions, and indeed 'Elijah's chair' is a regular part of the furniture in many synagogues.

Elijah of Vilna (Elijah ben Solomon Zalman) *See* VILNA GA'ON.

Elohim A name of God, found commonly in the Bible. Grammatically it is plural (from elóah, which is also found as a name of God, particularly in the book of Job), but as a name of God it is construed with a singular verb. In the liturgy God is often addressed as elohai, my God, or eloheínu, our God. In the ZOHAR it corresponds to the sefira Gevura (*see* SEFIROT).

Elul Twelfth month of the year counting from New Year; sixth counting from Passover. It is a period of preparation for the penitential days following (*see* NEW YEAR; TEN DAYS OF PENITENCE; ATONEMENT, DAY OF). It is customary to sound the SHOFAR every day throughout the month, and to recite SELICHOT. (Ashkenazim only recite them during the last week of the month.)

Elyon A name of God, first found in the Bible, where it is sometimes compounded with EL. Its meaning is 'most high'.

emanationism A key doctrine in NEOPLATONISM, relating God to the universe through a succession of emanations, each less pure than its predecessor. Medieval Jewish philosophers and mystics used the Hebrew term atsilut. In a distinctive Jewish development of the concept in kabbala all the emanations remain within the Godhead, and the emanations are thus a way of representing its complex structure and inner dynamics. Addressing themselves to the problem of the relationship between God and the visible world, the kabbalists agreed that the Divine in itself is beyond all human knowledge, even beyond mystical intuition. Between this utterly perfect and unknowable deity, generally called EIN SOF ('The Infinite'), and the created world the link is supplied by a series of emanations, beginning with the Divine Will and proceeding through a sequence of ten SEFIROT. The similarity of this system with that of the Neoplatonist philosophers is obvious, but it is also only superficial, since the kabbalistic emanations are all within the Godhead: even the lowest and most accessible of them is still beyond the physical world.

emancipation Liberation, originally of slaves. In Jewish historiography the term is applied specifically to the political process of the restoration of civil rights to the Jewish communities of Europe and European colonies overseas, beginning in the late 18th century in France and America, and in a more limited way in the Habsburg empire. The period of emancipation can be considered closed with the removal of special disabilities on Jews in Russia in 1917, provided one recalls that such disabilities still existed at that time in Spain and Portugal, and that they were reimposed by the Nazis in Germany and Austria and later in other European countries in the 1930s and 40s.

The early roots of the idea can be traced to the 17th century, but it really began to take off in the 18th-century ENLIGHTENMENT movement. In the modern nation-state, it was argued, all should share the same citizen rights, and all citizens should be equal before the law. Jews thus achieved civil equality at the same time as women and other religious and national minorities. It was a slow and arduous process, which met with enormous opposition from the forces of reaction.

Emancipation brought many opportunities for individuals, but posed a serious threat to the previously self-governing Jewish communities (kehillot). The power of the rabbis to impose a way of life dictated by a legal system (HALACHA) administered by them was removed once Jews became subject to the same laws as everyone else, and the role of rabbinic courts was reduced to matters of personal status and private arbitration. The CHÉREM lost its force. Many Jews converted to Christianity at this time, or abandoned Judaism without adopting another religion. The crisis provoked by this change led directly to a movement for internal religious reform (see MODERNISM). Emancipation favoured social integration, which had a profound effect on Jewish lifestyles and intellectual outlooks, and also influenced the worship of the synagogue. See also FAMILY; INDIVIDUAL, AUTONOMY OF.

emet Truth. A primary virtue, enjoined many times in the Bible and the rabbinic literature. According to the Talmud (Bavli, Shabbat 55a) it is the seal of God himself. The Hebrew word has the peculiarity that it begins and ends with the first and last letters of the alphabet respectively, while its middle letter is one of the two middle letters of the alphabet.

Emet ve-Emuna ('truth and firm belief', from the name of a prayer in the evening service) Statement issued in 1988 by a Commission on the Philosophy of the Conservative Movement. Arguing that Jews must hold certain beliefs, it concedes that historically the Jewish community never developed any one binding catechism, so that it is difficult if not impossible to pick out only one person's formal creed and hold it as binding. Instead, Emet ve-Emuna allows for a range of Jewish beliefs that Conservative rabbis believe are authentically Jewish and justifiable. The statement affirms belief in God and in the divine inspiration of the Torah; however it also affirms the legitimacy of multiple interpretations of these issues. Atheism, Trinitarian views of God and polytheism are all ruled out. Adopting an intermediate position between Reform and Orthodoxy, it explicitly rejects relativism and also literalism and fundamentalism.

emuna *See* FAITH.

Enlightenment Current in European thought characterized by belief in progress through reason. The Enlightenment gradually gained influence in the late 17th and the 18th century. In Judaism it is prefigured by SPINOZA and reaches its fullest flowering with MENDELSSOHN. Judaism was profoundly changed by Enlightenment, both from without and from within. From without, Enlightenment ideas about natural liberty and equality promoted discussion of religious toleration and of the place to be accorded to the Jews in society, which in turn led to a movement for Jewish EMANCIPATION. Internally, Jewish thinkers were influenced by the deistic beliefs arising from the Enlightenment. Deism, while adhering to the belief in a personal god, rejected religious doctrines that relied on revelation, and promoted the idea of rational religion, accessible to everyone through the exercise of reason. Moses Mendelssohn, an outstanding representative of Enlightenment philosophy, was committed to the wider diffusion of Enlightenment ideas. His book *Jerusalem* (1783) advocated religious tolerance on grounds of natural law, arguing that all religions, their diversity notwithstanding, agreed on the same basic, rationally demonstrable principles of morals and metaphysics. He developed a theory that distinguished between the eternal truths of natural religion, based on reason and therefore to be acknowledged by all, and the 'revealed legislation' that is the particular content of Judaism and binding on Jews alone. Mendelssohn's arguments contributed a theoretical underpinning for the idea of emancipation for enlightened Christians and Jews alike. Enlightenment ideas gained increasing influence within Judaism in the course of the 19th century, both in western and in eastern Europe (*see* HASKALA).

Érets Yisra'el Hebrew term for the Land of ISRAEL or PALESTINE. The term is attested in the Bible (Ezekiel 40.2, 47.18) and is common in the rabbinic literature, which distinguishes a category of 'commandments dependent on [being in] the Land' (Mishnah, Kiddushin 1.9), including eating the Passover lamb, bringing of first fruits to Jerusalem, and sanctification of the new moon. Special sanctity is held to attach to the Land, and it has been held to be meritorious to live in the Land, visit it on a pilgrimage, or at least be buried there. *See also* DIASPORA; EXILE AND RETURN.

érev ('evening') The day preceding the Sabbath or a festival. Thus one speaks of érev shabbat (Sabbth eve), érev pesach (Passover eve).

eruv ('mingling') Generic name for various legal devices aimed at easing the restrictive Sabbath laws. 1. Eruv techumin (mingling of boundaries) enables one to go beyond the normal Sabbath limit of 2,000 cubits, by previously placing enough food for two meals at the original limit; the distance is then doubled. 2. Eruv reshuyyot (mingling of properties) permits carrying on Sabbath within a space defined by a continuous wire supported on posts. This may be the space of an entire city. 3. Eruv chatserot (mingling of courtyards) allows carrying from all the houses opening into a single courtyard; it is achieved by placing some food from each house in the courtyard. 4. Eruv tavshilin (mingling of cooked food) makes it possible to cook for the Sabbath on a festival day immediately preceding it (when normally cooking ahead is forbidden), by symbolically beginning to cook for the Sabbath on the eve of the festival. Such legal fictions are only observed today by a minority of Jews who are particularly observant.

Eruvin ('minglings') Tractate of the Mishnah, Tosefta and both Talmuds, in order Mo'ed. It discusses the rules governing the various kinds of ERUV.

Esau (Esav) Son of Isaac and Rebekah; twin brother of Jacob. He is depicted as a hunter. Although he was born first, he sells his birthright to Jacob in exchange for a lentil stew (Genesis 25). Subsequently he is consumed with anger at Jacob, who flees from him; however, when the brothers meet again twenty years later they are amicably reconciled (Genesis 32). According to rabbinic commentators, the mysterious man who wrestled with Jacob by night at the crossing of the Jabbok just before this meeting, and who blessed him and gave him his name Israel, was Esau himself. The implication of this interpretation is that Jacob and Esau (Jews and Gentiles) have to wrestle with each other, but in the end the Gentiles are obliged to bless the Jews.

éshet cháyil ('woman of valour', or 'valiant wife') Alphabetical acrostic from the Bible (Proverbs 31.10–31), singing the praises of the ideal wife. 'Who can find a valiant wife? Her price is far above rubies. Her husband's heart trusts her; he has no shortage of booty. She repays him with good and not evil all the days of her life …' It has become customary for Ashkenazi husbands to chant it on Friday evenings in the presence of their wives, before eating dinner. Kabbalists also chant it; in fact the custom is thought to have originated with the kabbalists of SAFED, who identified the valiant wife with the SHECHINA. Describing a woman who takes all the labours, cares and financial management of the household on her shoulders while her husband 'sits with the elders of the land', it may be considered singularly inappropriate to real-life wives in the modern age, yet such is the power of tradition that it continues to be recited in many households today.

esnóga or **snóga** (from Portuguese senoga) Term used by Spanish and Portuguese Jews to refer to the synagogue. It is heard much less today than formerly, and seems to be going out of use. In the Ottoman empire it was sometimes applied to the women's section within the synagogue.

Esther (Ester) Biblical book, one of the FIVE SCROLLS. It is read at Purim, from a scroll (known as megillat Ester, scroll of Esther). The book is named for its heroine, a Jewish queen of Persia, who saves her people from attempted genocide at the hands of the chief minister, 'the wicked Haman'. *See also* MEGILLA.

eternity Boundless extent of time, or existence outside time. The Hebrew term is 'olam', which can also mean an extremely long time (*see* OLAM HA-BA); the words 'ad' and 'nétsach' are also used for an infinitely long future. According to the classic expositions of Jewish theology, God has no beginning or end. The doctrine is found in the Bible (e.g. Isaiah 44.6, Psalm 90.2) and reiterated in the liturgy (e.g. in ADON OLAM) and by the medieval philosophers (it is the fourth of Maimonides' THIRTEEN PRINCIPLES). However, the philosophers disagree about the detailed understanding of the relationship between God's eternity and time as we understand it. The ARISTO-TELIAN doctrine of the eternity of the universe posed a problem for Jewish philosophers who believed that the Bible describes CREATION from nothing. The idea of a promise of eternal life for humans is derived from that of the eternity of God; however, the details of this concept are not worked out. For some it is only available to the righteous; for others there is no life after death. The benediction after the reading of the Torah, which contains the words 'who has given us the Torah and implanted eternal life within us', implies a relationship between eternal life and the observance of the COMMANDMENTS of the Torah.

ethics

Body of doctrine concerning right and wrong behaviour. To be distinguished from law (HALACHA), which begins from revealed commandments. Ethics begins from the innate human sense of right and wrong. The whole of Jewish teaching is grounded in a passionate concern for justice and compassion in human relations, and in a fundamental belief not only in the perfectibility of humankind but in the obligation for all to strive to conduct their own lives on the highest possible ethical plane and to contribute as best they can to the betterment of society as a whole.

Judaism differs from the Greek ethical tradition in refusing to see human beings as the measure of all things or as the final arbiters of their own destiny, and in refusing to consider moral principles as having any independent existence which can be investigated through the scientific study of humanity and the world. Ethics, in the Jewish tradition, can only be, at best, a branch of religion, and is entirely dependent on religion. Consequently when we look at the ethical tradition in Judaism we need to think not only about the rules for leading a virtuous life and the emphasis they are given in relation to other elements in Judaism, but also about the ways in which they are related to ideas about the character of God and about understandings of God's relationship with humankind.

The foundations of the Jewish ethical tradition are firmly laid in the Bible, where such virtues as honesty, fairness and compassion are repeatedly commended to those who would obey God's will. Indeed, these are attributes of the biblical God, which humans are enjoined to imitate: this idea of imitatio Dei became one of the bases of ethical reflection in later Jewish thought. The virtuous person is called in biblical Hebrew 'tsaddik', a word which is related to the idea of justice. The biblical attitude is summed up in the celebrated utterance of the prophet Micah: 'He has told you, human being, what is good, and what the Lord demands of you; only to act justly and love mercy, and to walk humbly with your God' (6.8). The themes of personal righteousness and social justice which pervade the whole Bible emerge so strongly in the prophets that they can even find expression in the denunciation of religious observance when it has degenerated into an empty formalism. The biblical writers also interpret history in moral terms, so that national success or disaster is explained as reward or punishment by God: this attitude, too, was to have important repercussions in later Jewish thought.

The rabbinic literature, no less than the Bible, is a rich treasury of moral reflection and instruction, and some of the rabbis go so far as to see the real purpose of all the regulations of the Torah as being the improvement and perfection of humanity. The rabbis see each person as a battleground between two tendencies, the 'good inclination' and the 'inclination to evil' (*see* YÉTSER HA-RA). The rabbis were firmly opposed to dualism, and insisted that both 'inclinations' were implanted by God, and they further argued that the 'inclination to evil' should not be viewed only in a negative light: without it human life, with all its joys and misery, would be impossible. Nevertheless, Judaism demands that people should pursue virtue by mastering, so far as possible, the inclination to evil and subordinating it to the 'good inclination'. As for sinners, they are strongly exhorted to find their way back to God through TESHUVA, 'returning' or repentance, which is achieved by a recognition of one's error, and a sincere resolve not to repeat it in the future.

Underlying these rabbinic ideas is a deeply rooted belief in FREE WILL. People have to take responsibility for their actions; all good actions are rewarded and wrong actions punished. The system of rewards and punishments is a reflection of the justice of God, as indeed is all human justice. It would be a mistake, however, to assume on the basis of the theory of rewards and punishments that the primary motive for virtuous behaviour is expectation of reward or fear of punishment. 'Do not be like servants who serve their master so as to receive a wage, but let the fear of Heaven be upon you' (Mishnah, Avot 1.3). The fear which is mentioned in this ancient saying is not the fear of punishment but the FEAR OF GOD, which is not in contrast with the love of God but complementary to it. Both alike suggest an emotional relationship with God, which finds expression in virtuous action. In rabbinic thought actions are not right or wrong in the abstract, they derive their moral character from their motive. 'Do all your actions for the sake of Heaven', as one teacher puts it, and the rabbis set great store by the biblical maxim, 'In all your ways acknowledge him and he will direct your paths.'

In the ancient period there is very little ethical literature as such. We have some loosely arranged collections of practical moral maxims, such as are found in the biblical book of Proverbs or the Mishnah tractate Avot (which remains the most studied and best loved of all rabbinic texts); but there is no systematic codification of the rules for a moral life. It is only in the Middle Ages that the ethical tradition is channelled into a literature of its own and treated as a topic in its own right. The medieval philosophers, under the influence of Arabic and ultimately of Greek thought, pay considerable attention to ethics. A much discussed question is that of the autonomy of ethics: is an action good because it is commanded by God, or is it commanded by God because it is good? Implicit in this discussion is the belief, already found in the rabbinic writings, that certain fundamental ethical principles are binding on all humankind, Jews and non-Jews alike, as opposed to the detailed regulations of the halacha, which are binding on Jews alone. Solomon IBN GABIROL broke new ground in presenting an ethical system independent of halacha in his book *The Improvement of the Moral Qualities*, while Maimonides devoted an introductory section of his great code, the MISHNE TORAH, to a systematic discussion of the rules for an ethical life which gives considerable (some would say excessive) prominence to the Greek idea of the avoidance of excess.

In the history of the ethical tradition a special place is occupied by BACHYA IBN PAKUDA (late 11th century), whose *Book of Directions to the Duties of the Heart* became the classic exposition of Jewish ethical thought. Bachya's work is deeply influenced by Muslim mysticism, and the same somewhat mystical tendency found expression in other ethical treatises, such as the *Meditation of the Sad Soul* of ABRAHAM BAR CHIYYA. Not dissimilar in many ways, although deriving from a different strand in the Jewish mystical tradition, is the work of the CHASIDEI ASHKENAZ in the 13th century, such as JUDAH THE CHASID of Regensburg and his disciple ELEAZAR OF WORMS. Inner piety and meticulous morality with a strong ascetic tendency are the dominant characteristics of this remarkable movement, which is also associated with an unusual branch of the medieval ethical literature, the so-called 'ethical wills', in which scholars bequeathed to their children not worldly goods but moral advice. Similar testaments are known from antiquity; in the Middle Ages they constitute a distinctive tradition, and the will of Eleazar of Worms is a notable early example.

The medieval tradition, in its most extreme form, was sometimes liable to overstep the bounds of mainstream Judaism in its devotion to ASCETICISM, inwardness, and rigorous personal purity. In general, however, Judaism has always turned its back on inward-looking pietism, and insisted that Jewish life is to be lived in the family and the wider community. The attributes of saintliness are admired, but with severe reservations, and their attainment may not be within the reach of most ordinary mortals. The purpose of morality, according to this common view, is not so much the perfection of the individual as the improvement of society.

In the 19th century the Lithuanian MUSAR MOVEMENT, founded by Israel SALANTER, represents a remarkable renewal of the medieval spiritual and ethical tradition. The Musar movement did not discourage the academic study of the Talmud, but urged that it should be complemented by deep personal piety and by meditation on ethical texts, many of which were revived and republished as a result of this renewed interest. Study of these texts was a feature of the 'Musar houses', where both professional scholars and members of the wider public would retire for a period of self-scrutiny every day, and in academies which came under the influence of the movement they were chanted aloud to special tunes.

Meanwhile, in western Europe, the ENLIGHTENMENT brought about a revival of interest in the philosophical discussion of the place of ethics in Judaism. The description of Judaism as 'ethical monotheism', which became commonplace in the later 19th century, served the double purpose of underlining the affinity of Judaism with the 'RELIGION of reason' while stressing the ethical values which (insofar as they derive from the Bible) Judaism shared with Christianity. Such arguments served a useful apologetic purpose in their day, bolstering the respectability of Judaism in the eyes of rationalists and Christians alike. Thus the Enlightenment, while it challenged so much else in Judaism, actually had the effect of reinforcing ethics as being the most rational and universal ingredient in the Jewish tradition. For the 19th-century Jewish philosophers there was no argument about the nature of Jewish ethics or its importance in Judaism: the only problem was how to accommodate it within a particularistic religion.

The 19th-century reformers, with their radical critique of the halacha, eagerly promoted the idea of 'prophetic Judaism', and what they had in mind was not only the universal vision of the biblical prophets but also their appeal to moral values in challenging established power and practice and their championing of deprived and underprivileged members of society. It was only natural that they should stress the distinction between ceremonial and ethical commandments, and endorse the latter to the detriment of the former. Jewish secularists, too, especially the socialists among them, laid emphasis on the moral values which Judaism had given the world, and they too were inclined to recall the universalism of the prophets as an antidote to the particularism which they felt to be a bane of Jewish existence.

The major difference between reformers and secularists lay, as one would expect, in their attitude to religion. Reform Judaism remains within the paths mapped out by Jewish tradition in linking love of humanity with love of God, while secular Judaism is closer to the Greek ideal in placing human needs at the centre. Nevertheless, when it comes to a programme of action there is little difference between the two. The section on ethics in the COLUMBUS PLATFORM of 1937 encapsulates the Reform position. The first paragraph is a fair summary of traditional Jewish teachings, while the second, still entirely consonant with that tradition, could be accepted in its entirety by most secularists:

Ethics and Religion In Judaism religion and morality blend into one indissoluble unity. Seeking God means to strive after holiness; righteousness and goodness. The love of God is incomplete without the love of one's fellow men. Judaism emphasizes the kinship of the human race; the sanctity and worth of human life and personality and the right of the individual to freedom and the pursuit of his chosen vocation. Justice to all, irrespective of race, sect or class, is the inalienable right and the inescapable obligation of all. The state and organized government exist in order to further these ends.

Social Justice Judaism seeks the attainment of a just society by the application of its teachings to the economic order, to industry and commerce, and to national and international affairs. It aims at the elimination of man-made misery and suffering, of poverty and degradation, of tyranny and slavery, of social inequality and prejudice, of ill-will and strife. It advocates the promotion of harmonious relations between warring classes on the basis of equity and justice, and the creation of conditions under which human personality may flourish. It pleads for the safeguarding of childhood against exploitation. It champions the cause of all who work and of their right to an adequate standard of living, as prior to the riches of property. Judaism emphasizes the duty of charity, and strives for a social order which will protect men against the material disabilities of old age, sickness and unemployment.

Meanwhile, more conservative trends would insist on the link between ethics and halacha in its widest sense. Recent studies of contemporary ethical problems in such areas as sexual relations, business, and medicine have demonstrated how rich the halachic tradition is in moral insights which can still be applied fruitfully in today's very different situations. The results of such investigations, needless to say, are not always congruent with the most advanced views of Western secular thinkers, and liberal Jewish critics have pointed to certain traditional attitudes which they feel are no longer appropriate or helpful; but in general they reveal a compassionate concern for the rights of the individual, and particularly victims of exploitation and oppression, balanced by a view of the welfare of society as a whole, which is well within the broad trends of modern thinking, and which can make a genuine contribution to serious contemporary discussion.

etrog ('citron'; plural etrogim) A lemon-like fruit, one of the FOUR SPECIES carried and shaken at SUKKOT. Interpreted by ancient tradition as the 'fruit of a goodly tree' mentioned in the Bible in this context (Leviticus 23.40). For a very long time etrogim were grown in western Greece and exported from Corfu to Jewish communities around the world. At the end of the 19th century some eastern European rabbis began to cast doubt on the purity of the Corfiote etrogim, and at the same time the fruit began to be cultivated in the Land of Israel, so the Corfu etrog trade was suppressed, to the ruin of the local economy. Decorative containers, often made of silver, have been devised to store the fruit during Sukkot.

ets chayyim ('tree of life') Designation of the Torah (or more precisely of wisdom) in Proverbs 3.18. (This verse is sung in synagogue before the reading of the Torah.) The term is applied (with the plural atsei chayyim) to the two wooden rollers on which the Torah scroll is wound, since ets means wood as well as tree. They are sometimes carved or inlaid.

euthanasia The act or practice of putting painlessly to death. Euthanasia is considered to be murder, although some rabbis have argued that there is no obligation to keep someone alive mechanically who is not capable of independent life, particularly if the patient is in pain. It is also widely accepted, even among Orthodox

Jews, that pain-killing drugs may be administered even if they have the indirect effect of hastening death.

evil *See* DUALISM; YÉTSER HA-RA.

evil eye In folklore, power believed to be possessed by certain individuals that can damage the health or well-being of others. The Hebrew expression is áyin ha-ra, or more correctly ein ha-ra, literally 'the eye of the evil one'. A slightly different expression, áyin ra'a, meaning 'evil eye', is used by the rabbis in the sense of meanness or envy (cf. Proverbs 23.6).

excommunication Term borrowed from Christianity, where it refers to an ecclesiastical censure of exclusion from the 'communion of the faithful', and notably from administering or receiving the Sacraments. It is not properly applicable to Judaism, which lacks an equivalent to Christian holy communion. However, it is often applied to a range of rabbinic sanctions or punishments specified in the Talmud. The mildest of these, termed nezifa ('reprimand'), confined the offender to his home and cut him off from society for a single day in Babylonia or seven days in the Land of Israel. Niddúi ('banishment') was imposed for seven days in Babylonia, thirty in the Land of Israel, during which time the person concerned was only allowed contact with members of his immediate family. The third and most severe form of excommunication was CHÉREM, which was a total exclusion from the community accompanied with solemn ceremonies. It lasted for an indeterminate period. It was such a severe measure that generally the mere threat of it sufficed to ensure compliance to a communal ordinance. Like Christian excommunication, it was brought into disrepute through increasingly frequent use in the late 17th century (notably after the incident of SHABBETAI TSEVÍ), and gradually fell into disuse thereafter.

See also SPINOZA, BARUCH.

exilarch *See* BABYLONIA.

exile and return Theme of history that has conditioned a widespread and deeply rooted view of the destiny of the Jewish people. The foundations of this view of Jewish history were laid during and after the Babylonian exile (traditionally reckoned as 70 years, from the destruction of the First Temple in 586 BCE to its reopening in 516). Ezekiel, the prophet of the exile, repeatedly expresses the hope for the return from exile (e.g. 11.17: 'Thus says the Lord God: I shall gather you from the peoples and bring you together from the lands where you have been dispersed, and I shall give you the land [or soil] of Israel'). Ezekiel's vision of the resurrection of the dry bones (chapter 37) is a powerful image of national revival and return. As the first exile was strongly associated with the destruction of the Temple and its subsequent rebuilding, the second destruction by the Romans in 70 CE was interpreted as a new exile, even though in reality the DIASPORA was well established by this time. The language of exile and return permeated the synagogue liturgy, which also contains prayers for the rebuilding of Jerusalem and the Temple (*see* AMIDA; MIPNEI CHATA'EÍNU). The rabbis also developed the notion that the SHECHINA, which had formerly resided in the Temple, did not abandon Israel at the time of the destruction but accompanied them into exile. The medieval poets harp constantly on the theme of exile, none more vividly than JUDAH HA-LEVI in his so-called 'Hymns to Zion'. There is no doubt that the idea of a future return sustained Jews through centuries of isolation and oppression, and indeed renewed exiles, which were all too common in the Middle Ages. The banishment that left the strongest impression was the decree issued in Spain in 1492 which offered Jews a choice of baptism or exile. It was in the wake of this traumatic event that Isaac LURIA developed his distinctive interpretation of KABBALA in which the entire cosmos was seen as out of alignment and in need of repair (TIKKUN), and this doctrine in turn strongly influenced the teachings of SHABBETAI TSEVÍ. The EMANCIPATION was packaged as a homecoming: Jews need no longer feel themselves to be strangers in exile in the countries where they lived; henceforth they would be citizens, enjoying precisely the same rights and obligations as other citizens, and in exchange they must abandon any residual feeling of being a nation apart or yearning to be transported back to a lost homeland. It is in response to this ideology that the PITTSBURGH PLATFORM declares: 'We consider ourselves no longer a nation, but a religious community, and therefore expect neither a return to Palestine, nor a sacrificial worship under the sons of Aaron, nor the restoration of any of the laws concerning the Jewish state.' Not all religious Jews were prepared, however, to expunge the idea of exile (in Hebrew, galút) from their understanding of Judaism. Thus S. R. HIRSCH wrote: 'Israel's entire galut history is one vast altar upon which it sacrificed all that men desire and love for the sake of acknowledging God and Torah … I would be sorry if Israel had so little self-understanding … that it welcomed emancipation as the end of galut.' Meanwhile, in unemancipated Russia, the fundamentally secular CHIBBAT ZION and ZIONIST movements tapped into age-old spiritual yearning and theological discourse in promoting the idea of a this-worldly return to the Land of Israel. The Declaration of Independence of Israel (1948), using biblical language, proclaimed that 'the State of Israel will be open for Jewish immigration and for the Ingathering of Exiles'.

existentialism Modern philosophical movement promoting a return from abstract theorizing to an urgent concern for the real ground of human being. Within Judaism the fundamental insights of existentialism are most cogently expressed by Franz ROSENZWEIG in the opening of *The Star of Redemption*. All that is mortal lives in the fear of death. Philosophy, Rosenzweig argues, endeavours to persuade us that death is an illusion. But philosophy has failed: 'man's terror as he trembles before this sting ever condemns the compassionate lie of philosophy as cruel lying'. This premise is the starting point of a new way of thinking, which places human needs and feelings at the centre. Rosenzweig should thus be seen, along with the Protestant Karl Jaspers and others, as one of the founders of religious existentialism, to which the writings of Rosenzweig's close associate Martin BUBER have also made a significant contribution. Existentialism has left its mark on a good deal of modern Jewish religious thought.

Exodus (Shemót) Second book of the Torah, recounting the departure of the Israelites from Egyptian slavery. (The English title is derived from the Greek for 'departure'.) The term is also applied to this departure. The Hebrew name of the book is Shemot, '[These are the] names [of]', from its second word. The book describes the birth of Moses, his encounter with God at the burning bush and his mission to lead the Israelites to freedom, the TEN PLAGUES, the departure, the miraculous crossing of the Sea of Reeds, and the journey through the wilderness to Mount SINAI. The remainder of the book is taken up with an account of the giving of the TEN COMMANDMENTS and other laws and the story of the worship of the GOLDEN CALF, concluding with the construction of the TABERNACLE.

Ezekiel (Yehezkel) Biblical book, located among the Latter Prophets, presenting the utterances of the prophet of the same name, who is supposed to have lived during the Babylonian exile in the 6th century BCE. Its highlights are the vision of the divine chariot (merkava) (ch. 1) and the vision of the resurrection of the dry bones (ch. 37). The former is read in synagogues at SHAVUOT as it complements the THEOPHANY at Sinai, while the latter is read at Passover to complement the story of the exodus from Egypt.

Ezra Priest and scribe who, according to the biblical book bearing his name, instituted a series of reforms in the 5th century BCE after the return from the Babylonian exile. These included the dissolution of marriages between Jewish men and foreign wives, and a campaign for the observance of the Sabbath. The Talmud lists ten decrees promulgated by Ezra (Bavli, Megilla 31b), and goes so far as to declare that God would have given the Torah through him had Moses not preceded him (Bavli, Sanhedrin 21b).

Ezra-Nehemiah Biblical book, situated in the KETUVIM. Originally a single book named Ezra, it is now, following Christian usage, generally considered as two books, whose chapters are numbered separately. It falls into three main parts: Ezra 1–6, narrating the decree of the Persian King Cyrus permitting the Jewish exiles in Babylonia to return to Jerusalem and rebuild their Temple, and their subsequent return and successful completion of the building project under King Darius I; Ezra 7–10, describing Ezra's reforms, and Nehemiah (Nechemia), recounting the career of NEHEMIAH. Part of the book is written in Aramaic.

ezrat nashim ('women's courtyard') In the Temple, court beyond which women were not permitted to go. In the synagogue, section reserved for women, partitioned from the main men's section by a MECHITSA. Reform and Liberal, and most Conservative, synagogues have abandoned the separation of the sexes.

F

Fackenheim, Emil (1916–2003) Philosopher, particularly important for his contributions to HOLOCAUST THEOLOGY. Born in Germany, he emigrated to Britain in 1939 and eventually became Professor of Philosophy in the University of Toronto in Canada (1948–84). The positive lesson he drew from the Holocaust was that Jews live under an obligation to survive, thus 'depriving Hitler of a posthumous victory'. He went so far as to declare this a 614th commandment (referring to the 613 COMMANDMENTS of the Torah). *See also* TIKKUN.

faith Belief, trust or confidence. The corresponding Hebrew term, emuna, is related to the word AMEN. In the Bible and the rabbinic writings the meaning of emuna is confidence or trust: not 'belief that' but 'belief in'. It is a characteristic of the righteous (Habakkuk 2.4). The model of faith is the patriarch Abraham (Genesis 15.6), who had such faith that he could undertake to offer his own son as a sacrifice to God.

For the medieval philosophers, however, faith came to mean belief. So Maimonides' THIRTEEN PRINCIPLES were much later reformulated as a CREED, in which each clause begins with the words 'I believe with perfect faith', and in this form they even entered the prayer book. Modern thinkers have tended to reject this conception of faith, following in the footsteps of Moses MENDELSSOHN, who preferred to translate the opening words of Maimonides' 'creed' as 'I am firmly convinced', since he himself believed that Judaism had no dogmas, and therefore no creed.

One modern thinker who has written a good deal about faith is Ignaz MAYBAUM (1897–1976). While insisting that emuna means belief in the sense of confidence, he draws a distinction between belief and trust, which in Hebrew is bitachon. The Bible says, 'Blessed is the man who trusts in the Lord, and whose trust the Lord is' (Jeremiah 17.7). Unlike trust, belief implies unbelief. If I say 'I believe you', I may be hinting 'despite some doubts'. If I say 'I trust you', I have no doubts. Also, if I say 'I believe you', I am referring to a single statement; if I say, 'I trust you', I mean I shall believe your future statements too. That does not mean that trust has to be completely blind. 'Judaism is trust in God, and this trust in God is in our hearts without renouncing reason, common sense or everyday experience.' But trust means an attitude of complete confidence, like the trust a child has in caring parents. This trust is the faith of Abraham, Maybaum says, and it is also the characteristic of the true Jew.

Falasha *See* BETA ISRAEL.

family

A household, consisting wholly or mainly of people united by ties of blood.

Jewish society is built upon two main units, the family and the community. These are two very different spheres, and the rules and maxims of the Torah underline their difference (for example the festivals are observed differently in home and synagogue). No doubt some Jews find greater fulfilment in one or the other, and the balance may change in the course of an individual's life. But in the end both are equally necessary; to lose or minimize either is to sacrifice something essential and distort the character of Judaism.

The place of the family at the heart of Judaism reflects a human society in which most people are born into a family, grow up in the bosom of a family, and look forward to creating a family of their own, in which the family is the unit that underlies the legal and fiscal structures of society, and where the family home is the commonest building-block of the urban landscape. That kind of society is less familiar today than it was in past generations, and social change has profoundly affected the character of Jewish life. EMANCIPATION has also had an impact. Western civilization has tended to glamorize those whose individual fulfilment is crushed by the institution of the family or who pursue the claims of their destiny, very often in the service of the state or of the imagined good of the wider society, as soldiers or crusaders of various kinds. These ideals are totally at odds with those of traditional Judaism. Before the emancipation Jews were not called on to fight and die for the state, and had no reason to identify with its demands, which they generally experienced as hostile impositions. It was their private home life that gave them a sense of purpose and destiny, and that they did everything they could to protect and defend. During the age of emancipation, European and American Jews became assimilated to the ideals of the majority culture and subject to the same legal and political demands. They were conscripted or volunteered to serve in their countries' armies, and some had glorious military careers. Many Jews found that the only way to better their lot (or in many cases simply to survive in an increasingly industrialized job market) was to put family life behind them, for a while or for ever, and go off to the city or to the New World. Meanwhile, the Zionist movement summoned young Jews to leave their homes and become pioneers (*see* CHALUTS). These developments were as important in undermining traditional family values as were the pogroms and persecutions, the impact of war on powerless civilians, and the unprecedented waves of migration. Throughout all these dramatic changes, though, Jews tended to cultivate a glowing and no doubt romanticized image of what family life had been like before, in a more innocent age. Wherever and whenever they could they made an effort to rebuild the structures of family life, and the networks of friends and neighbours that would support it.

One fortunate sector of society, the wealthy Jewish bourgeoisie that grew up in the European cities after emancipation, were pleased to find that the values of their adopted class coincided perfectly, in this respect, with those of their ancestors: bourgeois life was founded on the family and glorified its virtues. Well-to-do

Jews in 19th-century Europe created a unique fusion of Jewish and bourgeois life, that was envied and imitated by less prosperous Jews. The atmosphere of a Jewish family gathering even today, a Passover SÉDER for example, owes as much to this 19th-century Jewish bourgeoisie as it does to the medieval ghetto or to Jewish life in the Greco-Roman period.

Karl Marx accurately observed this willing fusion of Jewish and bourgeois values: 'Judaism reaches its climax in the perfection of bourgeois society,' he wrote in his 1844 essay 'On the Jewish Problem'. Marx chose to focus on the negative aspects, as he saw them, of bourgeois life, and to overlook the positive ones. He had many Jewish followers, particularly among the majority of Jews who were pitifully poor. Jewish socialists were generally favourable to the Marxist aim of destroying the foundations of bourgeois life, including the family. This programme found its most extreme expression in the deliberate abolition of the family unit in the KIBBUTSIM of Palestine.

Meanwhile, contemporary Western civilization encourages individuals, particularly the young, to seek their own fulfilment at the expense of institutions such as the family that might thwart them. Young Jews are naturally receptive to this message. Jewish society favours upward economic mobility, and Jewish parents make sacrifices so that their children will do well. All too often that means that the children will leave home and adopt a very different lifestyle from that of their parents. Jewish singles have developed their own frameworks for Jewish growth and self-expression, such as the CHAVURA.

The Jewish family is extensive and has rather flexible boundaries. Family ties embrace not only those related to one another by blood, but also those related by marriage, including the marriage of other family members. (Those related by marriage are known as mechutanim.) In the past Jewish families were commonly very large, and a couple might find themselves living under one roof with not only their children but also their parents and even other family members who were single or who for some other reason had no home of their own. Nowadays this arrangement is less common, as family units generally have become smaller, and it is easier for lone individuals to fend for themselves, but a sense of the wider family remains strong, and it is still quite usual for members of the extended family to gather together for special occasions such as the Passover Séder.

In the traditional family precise and differentiated roles were attributed to men, women (married and unmarried) and children. Responsibility was distributed between men and women, the latter by and large taking more responsibility for the day-to-day running of the home (and in some cases the family business), while the overall and long-term responsibility fell upon men. Study of Torah was a religious obligation binding on men in particular, and it was considered meritorious (and still is in traditional circles) for a man to devote himself entirely to study and count on his wife to support the family. Children carried no formal responsibility, being under the legal age, but were expected to play their part within the family, obey their parents, and (particularly in the case of boys) commence their studies. Men, women and children also had distinct religious rituals allotted to them: for instance on Sabbath Eve the woman of the house lit the candles and her husband recited KIDDUSH, while at the Passover Séder the four questions (MA NISHTANA) were recited by the youngest child present.

Today inevitably for most Jews these ancient structures have become weakened, modified or demolished altogether. The 'new man' and the emancipated woman have made their appearance, and home life is more of an equal partnership with many of the roles being shared. Nevertheless, the ritual aspects of the old division, together with some social features, have proved remarkably resistant to change.

Fast of Esther Minor fast day observed on the 13th of Adar, the day before PURIM. It is first mentioned in the 8th century CE, and is associated with the fast ordered by Queen Esther (Esther 3.12), although this is explicitly dated in the text to the following month, Nisan. In ancient times the 13th of Adar was a joyful day known as Nicanor's Day, commemorating the victory of JUDAH THE MACCABEE over the Seleucid general Nicanor; as such it was a day on which fasting was forbidden. It is not clear why its character was changed so radically.

Fast of Gedaliah Minor fast day observed immediately after New Year, on the 3rd of Tishri. It commemorates the assassination of Gedaliah, the Jewish governor of Judaea appointed by the Babylonian King Nebuchadnezzar, at the hands of a member of the local ruling dynasty named Ishmael. Gedaliah had shared the view of the prophet Jeremiah that it was better to submit to the Babylonian occupiers than resist them. After his death, despite the pleas of the prophet to remain, Gedaliah's followers fled to Egypt, and Jewish self-government effectively came to an end. The fast is mentioned, with three others, in Zechariah 8.19.

Fast of the Firstborn Minor fast day observed by firstborn sons immediately before Passover, on the 14th of Nisan. It commemorates the saving of the Israelite firstborn when the Egyptian firstborn were killed (Exodus 12.29). It is first mentioned in the geonic period. Some avoid the fast by concluding the reading of a tractate of the Talmud on that day, and celebrating the achievement in the customary manner with a festive meal (see SIYYUM).

fasting Abstention from food and drink. Two Hebrew words are used, tsom, a word of Biblical origin, and TA'ANIT, literally 'affliction', based on the rabbinic interpretation of the biblical injunction 'you shall afflict yourselves' (Leviticus 23.27, see ATONEMENT, DAY OF). The Day of Atonement, the major fast of the Jewish year and the only one that is at all widely observed today, is the only fast explicitly mentioned in the Torah. It is also the only fast that can fall on a Sabbath; other fasts, if they would normally fall on a Sabbath, are postponed, usually to the following day, except those immediately preceding a festival, which are moved back to the preceding Thursday. Regular minor fast days, all commemorating biblical or historical occasions, are as follows: 3rd of Tishri (FAST OF GEDALIAH), 10th of Tevet (commemorating the beginning of the Babylonian siege of Jerusalem in 586 BCE), 13th of Adar

(FAST OF ESTHER), 14th of Nisan (FAST OF THE FIRSTBORN), 17th of Tammuz (the date of the breach in the walls of Jerusalem during the Roman siege of 70 CE) and 9th of Av (*see* TISH'A BE-AV). These are all observed only from sunrise to sunset, with the exception of the last, which runs from sunset to sunset. Several of these commemorate more than one occasion. In addition, there are various private and informal fasts.

fear of God In the biblical story of the testing of Abraham (AKEDA), Abraham, on the point of slaughtering his son, is told: 'Do not harm the child or hurt him, because now I know that you are a God-fearer' (Genesis 22.12). The fear of God is described as the beginning of knowledge (Proverbs 1.7), and the book of Kohélet concludes with these words: 'Finally, when everything has been heard, fear God and keep his commands, for this is the whole of the human condition: God judges every deed, even secret ones, to see if it is good or bad' (Kohélet 12.13–14).

The medieval philosophers, however, while agreeing that the fear of God is of central importance, are at pains to stress that it should not be founded on fear of punishment. They distinguish two kinds of fear, a lower type which is fear of pain, and a higher type which is what we would call reverence or awe: the feeling one has about someone who is incomparably more elevated than oneself.

Related to the fear of God is the fear of sin, which in rabbinic writings is often the equivalent of a moral sense: the person who fears sin naturally avoids it, not because of the fear of punishment, but, as the kabbalists in particular emphasize, out of reverence for God, because sin offends against God's grandeur and creates a barrier between the sinner and God.

Among modern writers on Judaism the great prophet of fear or reverence is Abraham Joshua HESCHEL. In his book *Man Is Not Alone* Heschel writes of the 'wonder or radical amazement' which he argues is the first step towards understanding the world and God.

'The beginning of faith,' he writes, 'is not a feeling for the mystery of living or a sense of awe, wonder or fear. The root of religion is the question what to do with the feeling for the mystery of living, what to do with awe, wonder or fear. Religion, the end of isolation, begins with a consciousness that something is asked of us. It is in that tense, eternal asking in which the soul is caught and in which man's answer is elicited.'

Heschel's philosophy of Judaism embraces and affirms the radical wonder or awe which has been a living stream within Judaism since the Psalmist's 'The heavens declare the glory of God'. By putting awe and mystery back into the heart of Judaism he touched a chord in Jews who felt alienated at the time from the rather arid rationalism associated with REFORM JUDAISM and the materialism of Jewish life in America, but who had no sympathy with the folkloric exoticism of NEO-CHASIDISM.

feasting Gathering for the consumption of special meals on joyful occasions. The occasions in question are of two kinds, regular religious FESTIVALS and special occasions such as weddings. Feasting on such occasions is not only encouraged but positively commanded. On festivals there are two meals (an evening meal and a midday meal), each with its own KIDDUSH. On Sabbaths a third meal (SE'UDA SHE-LISHIT) was added, on Saturday afternoon. It does not have a special kiddush, but among Chasidim it has taken on a ritual character. Some Jews celebrate a fourth Sabbath meal, known as the 'Meal of Rabbi Chidka'. On the Day of Atonement, as it is a fast, there are no meals, but it is considered meritorious to eat a substantial meal before and particularly after it. The special festive occasions which are marked by feasts are circumcision, bar or bat mitsva, betrothal and marriage, and also the completion of the study of a tractate of Talmud. More solemn and austere meals are prescribed for mourners returning from a funeral and before the fast of TISH'A BE-AV. Traditionally, eggs feature in both of these. *See also* CHEVRA KADISHA.

feasts *See* FESTIVALS.

Feinstein, Moshe (1895–1986) Traditionalist rabbi and halachic authority. Born in Belorussia, he emigrated to the United States in 1936 and was appointed to a position of ROSH YESHIVA in New York. He was closely involved in AGUDAT ISRAEL and was held in high esteem as one of their 'Torah Sages'. He published thousands of RESPONSA, as well as several volumes of CHIDDUSHIM and discourses. His influence on Ashkenazi traditionalism has been considerable.

feminism Movement dedicated to the eradication of inequality suffered by women in society. Jewish feminism began in earnest in the 1970s, as part of a campaign to draw attention to and to remedy the subordinate status of women within Judaism. Jewish feminists have not been united behind a single programme: while some have pressed for thoroughgoing reform of the religion so as to accord complete equality to women, others have embraced more limited aims of gaining religious and educational opportunities for women within Orthodoxy and the traditional wing of Conservative Judaism. Still others have called for a radical rethinking of Judaism, which is seen as inherently patriarchal. One major focus of feminists has been the representation of God in the liturgy in male language, as father, king and judge. As often happens in theology, once the basic questions were articulated it became clear that the problems were far deeper and wider than had been imagined, and the debate now concerns not only the gender of God but the whole of God's nature and activity when seen from a feminist perspective. It has taken a while to clear away some of the misleading undergrowth so as to lay bare some well-established theological points, such as the purely metaphorical and symbolic character of biblical and liturgical images (though they may be none the less hurtful for that), or the multiplicity of ways of relating to the one God. Feminists have reclaimed some long-established images of God as mother and nourisher, and have dwelt on the feminine gender of the SHECHINA.

festivals (also known as feasts) Days or periods of special sanctity in the calendar. These are generally joyful in character, but some are solemn or sad occasions. The Hebrew terms CHAG (plural chaggim), ZEMÁN (plural zemanim), MO'ED (plural mo'adim) and YÓMTOV (plural yomtévim) are used virtually synonymously, and are properly applied to the three pilgrim festivals (also called regalim) of SUKKOT, PASSOVER (Pésach) and SHAVUOT. SHEMINI ATSÉRET is considered by some as the last day of Sukkot and by others as a festival in its own right. All these are now observed for two days outside Israel, except by Reform Jews, who follow the biblical calendar. The other biblical festivals are the High Holydays (NEW YEAR and Day of ATONEMENT). On all these days work is forbidden (but *see* CHOL HA-MO'ED), and, with the exception of the Day of Atonement, FEASTING is ordained. SIMCHAT TORA is celebrated on the second day of Shemini Atséret (except by Reform Jews and in Israel). Minor festivals of post-biblical origin, on which work is permitted, are CHANUKKA, PURIM, TU BI-SHEVÁT and LAG BA-ÓMER, and the more obscure HOSHÁNA RABBA, PÉSACH SHENI and TU BE-AV. Two new Israeli celebrations of political events, Independence Day (YOM HA-ATSMA'UT), commemorating the declaration of independence in 1948, and Jerusalem Day (YOM YERUSHALÁYIM), commemorating the capture of the eastern part of Jerusalem in 1967, have been recognized as religious festivals by the local chief rabbinate.

See also FASTS.

finials Ornaments for the scroll of the Torah, generally made of silver, attached to the top ends of the rollers or staves (ETS CHAYYIM). They are first mentioned in the 12th century, but the earliest extant specimens are much later. They are commonly fitted with little BELLS, to make an attractive sound when the scrolls are processed around the synagogue. They are sometimes called rimmonim (pomegranates) or tapuchim (apples) because of their shape, but in fact they are made in a wide variety of forms.

finta A tax. In western Sefardi usage, synagogue dues assessed on each individual according to his means.

firstborn *See* FAST OF THE FIRSTBORN; PIDYON HA-BEN.

Five Scrolls (in Hebrew, chamesh megillot) Collective term for five short biblical books that are read publicly at certain festivals: Kohélet (Sabbath of Sukkot), Esther (Purim), Song of Songs (Sabbath of Passover), Ruth (Shavuot), Lamentations (Tish'a be-Av).

forgiveness Pardon of sin or harm. In the Bible, a prerogative of God. The sixth benediction of the AMIDA is a prayer for forgiveness, and such prayers form a dominant theme for the Day of ATONEMENT. According to the rabbis there are three prerequisites for forgiveness: confession, repentance, and a sincere resolve not to repeat the deed in question. In accordance with the principle of IMITATIO DEI, humans are also encouraged to forgive one another; the wrong must first be put right and the injured party must be appeased by the wrongdoer. The topic has become a subject of debate between Christians and Jews in connection with the Holocaust, and one which has given rise to misunderstandings rooted in the difference between Jewish and Christian understandings of forgiveness. Judaism knows nothing of vicarious forgiveness, in which one person forgives on behalf of another, nor can one forgive somebody other than the perpetrator of the offence. It follows that there is no forgiveness for murder, and that neither Holocaust survivors nor Jews in general can offer forgiveness, to perpetrators or their kin, for the wrongs done to those who perished.

Formstecher, Salomon (1808–89) Religious philosopher. His best-known work is *Die Religion des Geistes* (*The Religion of the Spirit*, 1841). The Jewish conception of God as a pure moral being, he argues, is revealed progressively to all humanity, gradually replacing the pagan 'religion of nature'. His book made an important contribution in its day to discussions of religious reform, and of Jewish particularism and universalism in the age of EMANCIPATION.

four cubits (in Hebrew, árba ammot) In halacha, the distance around a person in every direction that is considered to be under his direct and personal control.

four-letter name *See* INEFFABLE NAME.

four questions *See* MA NISHTANA.

Four Sons Passage of the Passover HAGGADA that enumerates four types of son mentioned in the Torah in connection with the commemoration of the exodus: wise, bad, simple, and incapable of putting questions. The Passover story is to be presented differently to each.

four species (in Hebrew, arba'a minim) Four different plants taken up and waved in synagogue during the morning service on SUKKOT. They are mentioned in Leviticus 23.40; together they constitute the LULAV. The plants in question are: a palm frond, three sprigs of myrtle, two sprigs of willow and a citron (ETROG).

Frank, Jacob (1726–91) Kabbalist and messianic figure. Born in Podolia, Poland, Frank claimed to be the reincarnation of all earlier prophets and messiahs, notably SHABBETAI TSEVÍ. He preached an original mystical form of Judaism incorporating some Christian elements. His opponents accused him and his followers of indulging in orgies. He eventually had himself baptized in a great public ceremony in Warsaw Cathedral, with the emperor as his godfather.

Frankel, Zacharias (1801–75) Rabbinical scholar. One of the outstanding figures of the WISSENSCHAFT DES JUDENTUMS movement, Frankel also made an important contribution through his scholarship and his authority to the religious reforms of his day. Born in Prague and educated there and in Budapest, in 1854 he was appointed principal of the newly created rabbinical seminary in Breslau, where he remained until his death. In 1851 he founded the *Monatsschrift für Geschichte und Wissenschaft des Judenthums*, the foremost learned journal in Jewish studies in his day. In his writings, notably *Darchei ha-Mishna* (*The Ways of the Mishnah*) and *Mevo ha-Yerushalmi* (*Introduction to the Palestinian Talmud*), he demonstrated that the so-called ORAL TORAH was a human creation that arose and developed in response to specific historical conditions. This view, which significantly influenced the Reform movement, earned him the outspoken hostility of Orthodox leaders such as S. R. HIRSCH. However, while arguing in favour of some liturgical and educational reforms, Frankel distanced himself from the proponents of radical change. In his view, even if the practices of Judaism had a human rather than a divine origin they should still be observed because they were sanctified by long and widespread usage. He surprised some of his admirers by dramatically walking out of a rabbinical synod in 1845 that voted to accept the principle of vernacular prayer. Frankel and those around him are sometimes referred to as the 'Breslau school', or as the 'Positive-Historical school'. Because of their open-minded investigation of the history of Jewish practice coupled with a rejection alike of the dogmatism (as they saw it) of Orthodoxy and the radicalism of Reform, they can be seen as the predecessors and in a sense the founders of CONSERVATIVE JUDAISM.

Frankists Followers of Jacob FRANK.

free will The idea that human beings are capable of genuine choice and are thus morally responsible for their actions. Strong biblical warrant for this belief was found in God's proclamation, 'I have set before you life and death, blessing and curse: therefore choose life ...' (Deuteronomy 30.19). In the context of Greek-inspired philosophical investigation the belief in free will gave rise to considerable difficulties when combined with the equally strong belief in divine providence, which could be interpreted to imply that our actions are predestined. Only very rarely, however, have Jewish thinkers limited the belief in human freedom on this account. On the contrary, so central has the belief in free will been considered that some thinkers have tended towards the other extreme, of circumscribing the scope of God's providence rather than suggesting that people are not fully responsible for their actions, for without this responsibility the whole basis of classical Jewish beliefs about morality would appear to be undermined. Chasdai CRESCAS was the only Jewish philosopher in the Middle Ages to deny free will so as to maintain the sovereignty of God. (*See* OMNISCIENCE.) In contemporary thought the belief is not much discussed except in the specific context of the problem of evil, highlighted by the Holocaust: how can a good God allow or tolerate evil? (*See* HOLOCAUST THEOLOGY.) The answer known as the free will defence maintains that the existence of evil is an inevitable consequence of the human power to choose. According to this view some people suffer as a result of others' free choice to do evil.

freedom *see* INDIVIDUAL, AUTONOMY OF.

fundamentalism Term of Christian origin but now extended to other religions, designating the disposition to interpret texts literally and treat them as infallible. Jewish fundamentalists maintain an unquestioning belief in the divine source and inerrancy not just of the biblical teachings but of the oral law as well (*see* TORA MIN HA-SHAMÁYIM). This belief is characteristic both of modern ORTHODOXY and of TRADITIONALISM. Fundamentalists typically turn their back on manifestations of modernism and secularism, and believe that the world can be saved from these dangers by the maintenance of an ancient faith of which they are the custodians; in reality, their leaders, who are generally invested with great authority, construct new religious identities and practices through reinterpretation of the past and the recreation of collective memory. More extreme fundamentalists feel bound to resist supposed oppression, sometimes by violent means. *See also* CHABAD CHASIDISM; CHAREDI; GUSH EMUNIM; YESHIVA.

G

gabbai Originally, a tax-collector; today, a synagogue warden. The Talmud, in common with other ancient writings, generally speaks of the office of tax farmer or tax gatherer and its holders with the greatest distaste, even declaring unclean a house which a gabbai has entered. An exception is made for those who collected and disbursed charitable contributions: these are mentioned with the greatest respect. In the Middle Ages the term was applied specifically to the administrators of communal welfare charities (of both sexes). In modern times it evolved further to designate a communal functionary: Chasidim applied it to the person who ran a REBBE'S court, and in contemporary synagogues a gabbai oversees the calling up of congregants to the reading of the Torah (*see* ALIYYA).

galut ('exile') A term signifying banishment. Its connotations are entirely negative. 'The term galut expresses the despair and helplessness felt in the presence of a great tragedy' (Solomon SCHECHTER). *See also* DIASPORA; EXILE AND RETURN.

gambling Playing games for money; betting. The HALACHA is ambivalent about gambling. The proceeds are distinguished from those of theft, since the intention to deprive someone of his property against his will is lacking, and thus they need not be returned; gambling debts, however, cannot be enforced. The Talmud makes a distinction between casual and professional gamblers; the latter (according to some, both categories) are disqualified as witnesses in a law court. On the other hand the SHULCHAN ARUCH permits gambling, and the 17th-century halachist J. H. Bacharach permitted raffles because of biblical precedents and because the winner can be assumed to have benefited from divine favour. Synagogues today often allow raffles and other games of chance if the proceeds benefit good causes, but this practice is frowned on by some rabbis. *See also* CHANUKKA.

Ganzfried, Solomon (1804–86) Halachic authority in Hungary. A leading spokesman for separatist Orthodoxy, he was the author of the popular halachic compendium the Kitsur Shulchan Aruch.

ga'on ('excellency'; plural ge'onim) Title of honour. It was accorded in Babylonia to the principals of the two main rabbinic academies, in Sura and Pumbedita, after the time of the completion of the Babylonian Talmud in the late 6th or early 7th and until the early 11th century. This period of Jewish religious history has come to be known as the geonic period; it was the time in which the teachings of the Babylonian

Talmud began to be developed and codified and to be spread around the Jewish world, reaching as far as Spain. Many RESPONSA of the Babylonian ge'onim have been preserved. Amram Ga'on in the 9th century is remembered as an early editor of the liturgy; Sherira Ga'on in the late 10th century as the author of a lengthy responsum setting out for the first time the history of the rabbinic literature. The most famous of all the Babylonian ge'onim is SA'ADYA GA'ON, one of the key figures in the history of rabbinic Judaism and the legitimate succession of rabbinic authority. There were also ge'onim in the Land of Israel, but they did not attain the renown and influence of their Babylonian counterparts and their history is obscure. The title was used elsewhere in the Middle East in the Middle Ages. In modern times the term has sometimes been applied to outstanding scholars (*see* VILNA GA'ON).

Garden of Eden (in Hebrew, Gan éden) Paradise, the abode of the righteous after death. According to the famous biblical story (Genesis 2–3) God planted a garden in Eden for ADAM AND EVE to live in. Various theories have been put forward about the location of this fabulous garden; what is clear is that it is described as being on earth. In later Jewish sources it is sometimes thought of as being outside our world, and some go so far as to distinguish two Edens, one on earth and one 'on high'. MAIMO-NIDES goes even further, and says that it is not a place but a state of being. In the rabbinic writings Eden is equated with the reward in store for the righteous.
See also GEHINNOM.

gártel (Yiddish) A girdle worn round the waist by Chasidic men when praying. It is said to serve the purpose of separating the pure upper part of the body from the impure lower part.

Gedaliah *See* FAST OF GEDALIAH.

gedolim *See* DÁ'AS TÓRA.

Gehinnom Hell, the place where the wicked are punished after death. The name is a corruption of Gei Bnei Hinnom (Valley of the Sons of Hinnom), the name of a valley just outside Jerusalem, where in ancient times children were burnt as an offering to the god Molech; it also served as a rubbish dump where refuse was burnt. It is the association with burning that presumably led to the use of the name for the place where in rabbinic thought the souls of the wicked are purged by torments. The Talmud specifies some categories of people who have suffered in this life and are therefore dispensed from Gehinnom: the poor, the sick, and some add henpecked husbands (Bavli, Eruvin 41b). The alternative name Gehenna is a Greek version of the name.
See also AFTERLIFE; GILGUL; OLAM HA-BA.

Geiger, Abraham (1810–74) Scholar and religious reformer. Born in Frankfurt, Geiger received both a traditional Jewish and a German university education. He held various rabbinic appointments, and for the last two years of his life he taught at the newly founded Liberal rabbinical seminary in Berlin, the Hochschule für die Wissenschaft des Judentums. Geiger was one of the outstanding scholars of the WISSENSCHAFT DES JUDENTUMS movement, and his published writings cover an astonishing range. His major work, *Urschrift und Übersetzungen der Bibel* (*The Original Text and Translations of the Bible*, 1857), is an early contribution to modern biblical criticism; he was also a pioneer of the study of the ORAL TORAH, of Jewish–Christian and Jewish–Muslim relations and of women's rights. It is as one of the founding fathers of REFORM JUDAISM, however, that Geiger is mainly remembered today. He laboured from an early age to revise Jewish thought and practice so as to make them better suited to the modern age and more attractive to young, educated Jews who were abandoning the synagogue in droves. He stressed the belief in progress: the Bible and Talmud represent an early, primitive stage in a revelation which is still continuing. Many traditional ceremonies (such as circumcision) are distressing to modern sensibility or incompatible with modern life. In any case, he argued, the law of God is essentially ethical, not ritual. Moreover, historical study shows that the rituals themselves have changed and developed, and there is evidence of this change in the Bible and Talmud themselves. Geiger became increasingly convinced of the need to 'dethrone the Talmud'. His theology was firmly universalistic and he saw Jews as having a mission to all humankind. In the synagogue, he favoured worship in the vernacular, and the elimination of particularistic prayers. He was an outspoken critic of the Orthodoxy of S. R. HIRSCH (a friend from student days); but he also opposed some radical reforms, such as moving the Sabbath to Sunday or abolishing circumcision.

Geiger–Tiktin affair Controversy that embodied and helped to define the emergence of Jewish MODERNISM in the early 19th century. In 1838 Abraham GEIGER was appointed to a junior rabbinic position in Breslau beside a strict traditionalist, Solomon Tiktin (1791–1843). The two clashed and denounced each other, and eventually Tiktin was forced out of office. In 1842 he published a pamphlet containing opinions solicited from various traditionalist rabbis in favour of his position. The council of the Breslau congregation responded by collecting replies from more progressive rabbis on the subject of 'the compatibility of free investigation with the exercise of rabbinic office', and they published these in two volumes in 1842 and 1843. Many of the leading rabbis of the day expressed their unequivocal support for development and change, and justified their view by reference to traditional sources, beginning with the Talmud, where divergent opinions are cited and laws are revised in the light of changing times. MAIMONIDES is cited as ruling, in his code, that 'every Bet Din must abrogate even Mosaic commands if this is necessary for the preservation of the religion in the light of the needs of the time', and the arch-traditionalist Moses ISSERLES is quoted as firmly supporting halachic change in the light of improved knowledge. The effect of the controversy was to bring the arguments in favour of progress into the open and to display the strength of the progressive rabbinate. It led directly to the rabbinic synods at Brunswick (1844), Frankfurt (1845) and Breslau (1846), and ultimately to the creation of the Breslau Seminary (1854), with Zacharias FRANKEL at its head.

gelila ('rolling') Act of rolling up and binding the Torah scroll after the public reading. In many Ashkenazi synagogues it is considered an honour to be called up to do this; in others it is delegated to boys below the age of BAR MITSVA.

gemár chatima tova ('conclusion of a good sealing') A greeting used before the Day of ATONEMENT. It is sometimes abbreviated to gemár tov (good conclusion). The idea underlying it is that (in the words of the liturgy) 'On the first day of the year it is inscribed, and on the Day of Atonement the decree is sealed, how many shall pass away and how many shall be born, who shall live and who shall die …'

gemara (Aramaic, 'study') Term applied to the major part of both the Palestinian and the Babylonian TALMUD, consisting of discussion and amplification of the MISH-NAH rather than the text of the Mishnah itself. In practice it can be used as a synonym of 'Talmud'.

gematria (from Greek geometria, 'geometry') Exegesis based on the numerical value of Hebrew words. Each Hebrew letter is also a number, and in gematria two words with the same numerical value can be substituted for each other. It is mentioned in the rabbinic literature, but really came into its own in the later kabbala, in Sabbatean circles and in Chasidism.

gemilut chasadim ('bestowing of kindness') Performing altruistic acts to others, particularly those less well off. It is declared in the Mishnah (Avot 1.2) to be one of the foundations of the world, and the Talmud (Bavli, Yevamot 79a) reckons it a distinguishing characteristic of the Jewish people. In the AMIDA it is proclaimed to be an attribute of God himself. *See* CHÉSED.

gender Division of humanity according to specific physical and/or psychological characteristics. Rabbinic law recognizes four genders or sexes: male, female, androgynos and tumtum. The androgynos (*see* ANDROGYNY) has the physical characteristics of both male and female, while the tumtum is a person of indeterminate sex. Carefully structured rules govern the behaviour of these various groups of people and their relations with each other (*see also* SEXUAL RELATIONS). For instance men and women are not allowed to dress in the manner considered appropriate for the other sex, and many laws, relating not only to marriage but to ritual purity, sacrifices, inheritance and other topics, affect the sexes differently. A man and a woman who are strangers are not usually permitted to be alone together (*see* YICHUD), while an androgynos is not to be left alone with either. While such rabbinic texts are sometimes invoked today in discussions of Jewish approaches to issues of sexual orientation and gender identity, it is doubtful to what extent it is legitimate to do so.

Genesis First book of the Torah, called in Hebrew Bereshit, after its first word. The book begins with the creation of the world (whence its English title, from a Greek word meaning 'coming into being'). After chapters describing the first people and their banishment from the Garden of Eden, Noah's flood and the tower of Babel comes the story of the three patriarchs, Abraham, Isaac and Jacob. Jacob and his twelve sons with their families are driven by famine from the Land of Canaan to Egypt; thus the scene is set for the next book, EXODUS. Great themes are laid out in the book, including the origins of the world and of the human race and its various peoples and languages, the beginning of monotheism, the COVENANT and the tribal origins of the people of Israel. On the moral plane there is a close engagement with the theme of good and evil and obedience to God. A motif running through the book is the tendency of brothers to quarrel, beginning with the murderous conflict of the first pair of brothers, Cain and Abel, continuing with Jacob and Esau, and ending with Joseph and his brothers, who are reconciled in Egypt near the end of the book. A related theme is that of older and younger brothers: Isaac and Jacob are both younger brothers who supplant their older siblings. All the stories of Genesis are elaborated in the AGGADA, notably in the rabbinic Midrash on Genesis (Bereshit Rabba).

geniza ('hiding away') Act of hiding away or a place where things (particularly written texts) are secreted. Two types of text in particular are hidden away: sacred texts, such as Torah scrolls and TEFILLIN, that are too worn out to be fit for use, and heretical books that are too dangerous to be allowed to circulate. In all cases, since they contain the name of God they cannot simply be destroyed or discarded. Consequently the custom grew up of burying them in a cemetery. While awaiting burial they were often stored in a specially designated room or container in the synagogue, known as the geniza. The grave in which they are buried is also marked with the same word. The Cairo Geniza is the name given to the manuscripts and printed papers, mostly very damaged, that were recovered from an old synagogue in Fustat (Old Cairo) towards the end of the 19th century. The majority were removed by Solomon SCHECHTER to Cambridge; others are found in various European and American libraries and in private collections. They number some 200,000 pieces, some over 1,000 years old, and together constitute the largest and most important haul of Jewish manuscripts ever discovered. Many of the manuscripts are documents (letters, legal deeds, etc.), that enable the everyday life of medieval communities and individuals to be reconstructed in extraordinary detail; others are long-lost literary works.

geonic period *See* GA'ON.

ge'onim *See* GA'ON.

ger ('temporary resident') Originally a term denoting a stranger or resident alien, it is now used for a PROSELYTE.

Gershom, Rabbenu (c. 960–1028) Ashkenazi Talmudist and halachic authority, known as the 'Light of the Exile' (Me'or ha-Gola). Gershom is one of the earliest scholars of Ashkenaz known to us by name, and little is known about him. He seems to have lived in Mainz, and headed a Talmudic school there. Among the writings attributed to him are commentaries on parts of the Talmud, RESPONSA and PIYYUTIM, but probably not all of these were actually his work: they seem to have been produced by his school over a considerable time. In a responsum, Gershom urged magnanimous treatment of those returning to Judaism after compulsory baptism. He is said to have convened a rabbinic synod which issued various decrees (takkanot) binding on Ashkenazim, notably one prohibiting POLYGYNY; others forbid a man to divorce his wife without her consent, or to open letters not addressed to him. These edicts, too, were not necessarily framed by Rabbenu Gershom, or even during his lifetime.

Gersonides (Levi ben Gershom) (1288–1344) One of the outstanding Jewish intellects of the Middle Ages, sometimes referred to by the acronym Ralbag. He lived in Provence. An extraordinary polymath, he was a brilliant mathematician and a considerable philosopher, and wrote commentaries to most of the books of the Bible. As a mathematician he invented a device to measure the angular distance between two stars, devised a camera obscura, and developed an original explanation of the movement of the stars. As a philosopher he was an uncompromising Aristotelian (*see* ARISTOTELIANISM), and a great admirer of Averroës, on several of whose works he wrote supercommentaries. His biblical commentaries favour the philosophical approach and allegory over the search for the plain meaning of the text; in fact in some of them he identifies the allegorical with the literal meaning. A distinctive feature of the commentaries is the provision for each unit of the text of the lessons that may be learned from it. His most famous work is *Milchamot Adonai* (*The Wars of the Lord*), completed in 1329, a treatise of religious philosophy which builds on MAIMONIDES but goes beyond him, and criticizes him on a number of points.

get A deed of divorce. The get does not simply record the divorce, but is the instrument by which the marriage is dissolved. Drawn up mainly in Aramaic, it is written by a qualified scribe and is delivered by the husband to the wife in the presence of two witnesses, who sign the document. Strict rules govern the writing of the get. *See also* GITTIN.

Gevura ('might') In kabbala, one of the SEFIROT.

gilgul ('rolling') Reincarnation or metempsychosis: the doctrine that souls migrate (or 'roll') from body to body. It is not a characteristic or widespread Jewish belief, and is not attested before the 10th century, when SA'ADYA GA'ON remarks that it is believed by some foolish Jews. It is only in kabbala that it is taken at all seriously. The ZOHAR explains that, to avoid being consigned to the punishment of hell (GEHINNOM), the soul migrates from one body to another, up to a maximum of three bodies. Later, three was held to be a minimum. If the soul of a sinner enters the body of a pious man it has an opportunity to be cleansed of its 'dross'; conversely, any sufferings endured by the pious man are seen as punishment not for his own sins but for those committed by his soul in a previous existence. Similarly, the prosperity of a sinner is due to the good deeds his soul has performed in a previous existence. (However by prospering in this life he consumes all his reward, so that he will be punished in the hereafter.) It was the LURIANIC KABBALA that gave a real boost to the idea of gilgul, by incorporating it within a well-developed theory. Every human soul endures an alienation or 'exile' from God, by virtue of its sins. These can cause it to be reincarnated in a lower form of life, and it continues its transmigration until it achieves TIKKUN. Such beliefs came to be widespread in eastern Europe, particularly among Chasidim; there are stories of Chasidic masters remembering their actions in a previous incarnation.

Ginsberg, Asher *See* ACHAD HA-AM.

Gittin ('deeds of divorce'; plural of GET) Tractate of the Mishnah, Tosefta and both

Talmuds, in order Nashim, dealing with the laws of divorce. The strict regulations governing the writing of the get and its delivery are set out in detail.

Giudesmo *See* JUDEZMO.

gizbar ('treasurer') Particularly in some Sefardi communities, term for a synagogue treasurer. The term can be traced back to the Bible (Ezra 1.8).

glory In theological and mystical thought, an attribute or a manifestation of God. In the Bible God's glory (kavod) is sometimes likened to a visible fire or light (Exodus 24.17, Ezekiel 1.28). The Hebrew term can be traced back to the earliest strands in the esoteric tradition. It is used as a name of God in the context of mystical speculation, and it can even be used to denote this type of speculation itself. SA'ADYA GA'ON introduced the term into his philosophical discussion of the unity of God. Stressing God's absolute unity and incorporeality, he insisted that the anthropomorphism of the Bible (that is, the description of God's activity in terms drawn from the human body) is purely metaphorical. As for the prophetic visions of God, Sa'adya argued that the prophets did not see God, but only the divine Glory, which was itself created by God. This theory of the 'created Glory' was to become an important part of the theology of the CHASIDEI ASHKENAZ. It allowed them to use intensely physical language in talking about the 'Glory', while maintaining the utter incorporeality of the hidden 'Creator'. *See also* AKDAMUT; ELEAZAR OF WORMS; HYMN OF GLORY.

God

The supreme being. It is impossible to sum up briefly the Jewish ideas about God, for several reasons, particularly the lack of an official creed and the great diversity of approaches that have been adopted. On the one hand, it is no doubt true that within the accepted canon of Jewish theological writing the existence of God is such a fundamental assumption that even to state it has sometimes been interpreted as too daring, because it somehow implies that the contrary is thinkable. And yet there are many Jews today for whom the non-existence of God is equally axiomatic. In the current age of unbelief many Jews who would like to believe in God feel betrayed and abandoned by him. This is certainly not the first period in history when this feeling has existed, but in the aftermath of the Holocaust it does seem to be particularly widespread and vocal. At the same time there are a large number of Jews, especially but not exclusively in Israel, who relegate all talk of God to an earlier, less scientific, more credulous period of history, and it is debatable on what grounds such voices can be dismissed as not really Jewish. Moreover, even some Orthodox rabbis would probably agree with the many Jewish thinkers down the centuries who have argued that God is essentially unknowable, and that any human statement about God is imperfect and open to question.

The knowability of God is debated particularly by the medieval philosophers. Joseph ALBO, in the 15th century, famously quoted a sage who said, 'If I knew God I would be God', and there is a general trend to insist that anything we say about God is liable to be false and misleading. All the qualities people attribute to him are extrapolated from human experience, which is by its nature fundamentally and categorically different from God. 'The secret of whose strength doth quite exceed / Our thought, as Thou transcendest our frail plane. / All might is thine, swathed in a mystic shawl, / The fundament of all: / Hid from philosophers thy name' (Solomon IBN GABIROL, *The Kingly Crown*, 1, tr. Raphael Loewe). Neoplatonist and Aristotelian philosophers agreed that we can neither know nor say anything about God's essence. Only his actions can be known, and even these, Maimonides insisted, only tell us what God is not like, not what he is like (*see* VIA NEGATIVA).

The philosophers, having established the impossibility of saying anything meaningful and true about God, somehow manage to end up saying a good deal about him. The kabbalists go even further along the negative way. They make an explicit separation between God as he can be known and God as he is in himself. The latter, termed the Infinite (EIN SOF), is utterly unknowable. Even the SEFIROT, which are contained, as it were, within God, do not have knowledge of the Ein Sof. The Ein Sof plays no part in creation or revelation, and is not an object of contemplation, study or prayer. These can only reach the Sefirot.

As to the existence of God, however, neither the philosophers nor the kabbalists entertained any doubts at all. Of course they lived in an age when God's existence was taken for granted by virtually everybody, Jew or non-Jew, with whom they came into contact. One wonders how they would have responded to the current situation, in which atheism and agnosticism are widespread, and when even religious Jews express serious doubts about God's power to act in the world.

In the rest of this entry I discuss the main sources about God in the Bible and the rabbinic writings, and then mention briefly some of the subsequent developments. For further discussion see the entries on individual authors, and the general entries HOLOCAUST THEOLOGY, KABBALA and THEOLOGY.

GOD IN THE BIBLE

The Bible does not present a single, coherent view of God, and there is very little that can be called theological discourse. Some generalizations are, however, possible. The biblical God may be superhuman, but he is definitely a person, an actor in a drama that encompasses the destiny of individuals and nations and indeed ultimately the whole of the universe. This personal God is often described in language that is so personal that it has proved an embarrassment to thinkers schooled in Greek thought. He is called a judge, a king, a shepherd, a man of war. He has emotions which are all too human: he is said to be jealous and angry, and he sometimes changes his mind and feels regret. Nor does biblical language hesitate to speak of God's activity as though he had a human body: he is described as sitting in the sky with his feet resting on the earth as on a footstool; his hand is raised up, his forearm is outstretched, his right arm is powerful; his mouth speaks, he roars aloud, and he has 'long nostrils' (meaning that he is patient and slow to lose his temper). No doubt this language can be explained as metaphorical or as poetic licence, but it is so common in the text that it inevitably colours the personality of the biblical God.

And yet at the same time the Bible is generally insistent that God is not visible. It is true that occasionally people see God (e.g. Exodus 24.9, Isaiah 6.1), but such passages are exceptional, and the general idea seems to be that normal, living people cannot see God. Even Moses was not allowed to see God, 'for no man can see me while living' (Exodus 33.20). The Israelites are reminded that 'when God spoke to you on Horeb out of the fire you saw no form; so take care not to relapse and make yourselves any idol in representational form, a carving whether male or female; a carving of any animal on the ground or of any winged bird that flies in the sky; a carving of anything that creeps on the ground or of any fish in the water underground; and not to look upwards to the sky and see the sun and moon and stars like an army in the sky, and abase yourselves and worship and serve them' (Deuteronomy 4.15–19, alluding to Exodus 20.3–5; cf. Deuteronomy 5.7–9). Worship of such images is acceptable for the other nations, but God's own people are forbidden to follow suit.

The polemic against worshipping God in a visible form is closely connected to the polemic against worshipping a multiplicity of gods. If there is any theological principle that is asserted repeatedly and consistently in the Bible it is the unity of God. The slogan 'the Lord is one' (Adonai echad), proclaimed in the first line of the SHEMÁ (Deuteronomy 6.4), is repeated by the prophet Zechariah in his vision of a day when 'the Lord shall be king of all the world, when the Lord shall be one and his name one' (Zechariah 14.9). This unity is understood as being not only numerical, meaning that God is singular and not, as some falsely claim, dual or plural; it also means that he is unique: because he is the one true God he is different in kind from all other gods men worship.

Another frequently stressed attribute of God is his eternity. He has always existed, and he always will exist; he is the First and the Last (Isaiah 44.6; cf. Psalms 90.2, 146.10). As we might say, he is outside time. He is also outside space. He is beyond the world and yet he is everywhere within it (cf. Psalm 139.7–10).

God in the Bible knows everything and can do anything he pleases: nothing is beyond his ability (Genesis 18.14; cf. Jeremiah 32.27). In other words from the Bible's often poetic language we gain an impression of someone whose vantage point is so high that he can see everything that happens on earth, however secret, including what has not yet happened, and whose strength is so great that nothing can thwart his will. But although he can be stern and a stickler for justice and fair play he is goodness personified and is loving and beneficent. Sometimes his patience is tried too far by human selfishness and rebelliousness, and then he can strike ruthlessly. But such events are rare and always justified. More often he is loving and forgiving.

The Bible tells a story, and in that human story God is intimately implicated from the very first moment. It was God who made the world out of chaos, and created the human race 'in his own image and form'. Later he chose Abraham, Isaac and Jacob and their descendants, the people of Israel, and made a covenant with them. When they became slaves of the Egyptians he rescued them, fed them in the desert, and at Mount Sinai gave them the Torah. Then he led them to the promised land and helped them to conquer it from its inhabitants, and eventually he took up residence in the Temple built by King Solomon in his capital city, Jerusalem. After Solomon the kingdom was divided into two, and as a punishment for bad behaviour the northern kingdom was destroyed by the Assyrians and the southern kingdom was later attacked by the king of Babylon, Nebuchadnezzar, who razed the Temple and led the people away as captives. After seventy years of exile the victorious Persian King Cyrus gave permission for them to return and rebuild the Temple. One day God will bring this cycle of history to an end with an ultimate intervention, which will leave Israel ruling the world from Jerusalem under God's kingship, and all the other nations acknowledging his rule.

GOD IN THE RABBINIC LITERATURE

The classical texts of rabbinic Judaism, the Talmud and Midrash, contain many observations about God, but they are not presented in a systematic way. Sometimes they reiterate biblical statements, sometimes they go beyond them, adapt them, or implicitly contradict them, but almost always the rabbis attach their remarks to a quotation from the Bible. This is the way of Midrash: to reread the Bible as a contemporary document.

We may illustrate this with some examples.

Psalm 65 begins with the obscure statement 'To you, God, silence is praise in Zion, and to you a vow will be repaid.' Often, though not always, it is such obscurities in the Bible that attract Midrashic interest. A rabbinic explanation connects this verse with the negative way of theology: no human language can do justice to the nature of God. 'It can be compared to a jewel without price: however high you appraise it, you still undervalue it '(Yerushalmi, Berachot 9.1, Midrash Psalms to Psalm 19.2).

' "May the Lord make his face to shine towards you" (Numbers 6.25): Rabbi Nathan says, This is the light of the Shechina, as it says (Isaiah 60.1): "Arise, shine, for your light has come, and the glory of the Lord has risen upon you" (Sifre Numbers, 41).' This interpretation, stressing the indwelling presence of God among his people, is offered to contradict another view, that the light in question is that of the Torah, implying a more remote and intellectual relationship between God and Israel.

' "I, even I, am He, and there is no god beside me; it is I who kill, and it is I who make alive; I wound and I heal" (Deuteronomy 32.39). This verse is a reply to [three categories of Jews]: those who say that there is no power in heaven, those who say there are two powers in heaven, and those who say there is no power who can make alive or kill, do evil or good' (Sifre Deuteronomy, 329).

In the absence of a systematic exposition of theological beliefs, we can gain a sense of rabbinic theology from the themes to which the rabbinic texts return again and again. The unity of God is one of these, evidently asserted in the face of a range of alternative theologies: not only pagan polytheism and philosophical scepticism, but also Christian Trinitarianism, Persian DUALISM, in which this world is a battleground between the forces of good and evil, and another kind of dualism in which the supreme God had an assistant, a sort of lesser god, in creating and administering the world. The rabbis insist adamantly that God is utterly alone and unique, and has no deputy or assistant. (He has an entourage of ministering ANGELS, but these are not divine beings.)

Building on biblical foundations, the rabbis continue to combine the idea of God's transcendence with that of his presence in the world, for which they have a special name, SHECHINA. The concept of Shechina preserves the idea of a loving personal God in the face of philosophical speculation that stresses his perfection and remoteness. The rabbis can even speak of the Shechina as sharing human suffering, or going into exile with the people of Israel. In the context of the strong insistence on divine unity, these two logically conflicting understandings of God are somehow superimposed, without the need for the inconsistencies to be analysed and resolved. It is rather similar with the twin images of God as ruthless judge and as loving parent. On the face of it these roles may seem irreconcilable, but in the rabbinic view of God they are held in balance:

> There was once a king who had some fragile goblets. He said, 'If I put hot water in them, they will shatter; if I put cold water in them, they will crack.' So the king mixed cold and hot water together and poured it in, and they were not damaged. Similarly God said, 'If I create the world with the attribute of mercy, sin will multiply; if I create it with the attribute of justice, how can it endure? I shall create it with both together, then it will endure.' (Genesis Rabba 12.15)

The method of the rabbinic argument may seem unsatisfying if one seeks the clarity of logical reasoning, but in the immediacy and intuitiveness of its apprehensions and the way it extracts multiple and often surprising answers from a close reading of texts it often seems remarkably modern.

LATER DEVELOPMENTS

The medieval Jewish intellectual tradition is dominated by ARISTOTELIAN philosophy (but *see also* NEOPLATONISM). The best known Jewish Aristotelian is MAIMONIDES, whose ideas about God are found not only in his philosophical masterwork, the *Guide of the Perplexed*, but scattered throughout his other writings such as his commentary on the Mishnah and his code of Jewish practice, the Mishne Torah. In fact the last-mentioned work opens with a classical statement of God's existence, combining and reconciling biblical and Aristotelian elements:

> It is the basis of all foundations and the pillar on which all wisdom rests to know that there is a Prime Being who brought into being everything that exists and that all creatures in heaven and earth and between them only enjoy existence by virtue of His existence. If it could be imagined that He did not exist, then nothing else could have existed. But if it could be imagined that all beings other than He did not exist, He alone would still exist and He would not suffer cessation in their cessation. For all things need Him but He, blessed be He, does not need a single one of

them. It follows that His true nature is unlike the nature of any of them. (Mishne Torah, Foundations of Torah, 1.1–3)

Of God's attributes little can be truly said, according to Maimonides, because of his utter otherness and the incapacity of human minds to grasp his nature. It is possible to describe his activity, as opposed to his essence, by analogy with human behaviour. When we say of his actions that they are good, we mean that we would have judged them good if they had been performed by humans. When on the other hand we say that he is one, we are not saying anything positive, but merely ruling out the opposite. This 'negative theology' has been influential, but has also had its critics, such as GERSONIDES, who denied that there was a difference of essence between divine and human attributes, or Chasdai CRESCAS, who insisted that the divine attributes really are to be understood positively.

A new era in Jewish conceptions of God begins with Baruch SPINOZA, who dismissed the whole medieval approach as intellectually unsatisfactory. According to his understanding of the relationship of cause and effect it was impossible that an immaterial, simple god should have made a material, complex world: an effect cannot be so different in nature from its cause. His conclusion, that God and nature are one and the same (*see* PANTHEISM), goes beyond what any other Jewish thinker, even among the Chasidim (*see* PANENTHEISM), has maintained, and indeed he did not himself put his views forward as representative of Judaism. But in setting out clear intellectual grounds for questioning the very foundations of medieval thinking about the relationship of God and the world he opened a door for other modern thinkers. The entire agenda for the discussion of God has been changed with the ENLIGHTENMENT. Under the influence of Immanuel Kant, much discussion has focused on God as the source of morality rather than as the creator of the natural world (although CREATION bulks large in the work of Franz ROSENZWEIG). This trend reaches an extreme point in the thought of Mordecai KAPLAN, who denies that God has an independent, personal existence, and prefers to see the word as a useful name for the source of human morality. A contrary tendency is represented by Martin BUBER, who insists on a personal God, although Buber would agree with the tradition that denies that anything can be known intellectually about God's attributes. The most challenging and original new impetus in thinking about God comes from FEMINISM, but it is too early to see exactly where this new way of thinking about old questions will lead.

See also DUALISM; FREE WILL; REVELATION; YÉTSER HA-RA.

gola ('exile') A term indicating the DIASPORA, and conveying a sense of alienation. *See* EXILE AND RETURN.

golden calf In the Torah, molten image made by the Israelites as they waited at the foot of Mount Sinai for Moses to return from the top of the mountain with the stone tablets containing God's TEN COMMANDMENTS (Exodus 32–3). In the scriptural account it is AARON who instructs the people to make the calf and supervises a feast in its presence. When Moses comes down and sees the calf and the people dancing, he breaks the tablets; then he burns the calf and grinds it to a powder, which he sprinkles on water, and makes the Israelites drink it. He orders the Levites to carry out a massacre, and they kill about 3,000 men. Later a plague breaks out because of the calf. There are several obscure features to this story. There is another golden calf story which echoes some details of the earlier one in 1 Kings 12.25–33: Jeroboam, after rebelling against the house of David, sets up two golden calves, one in Beth-el and the other in Dan. In post-biblical literature the story of the golden calf in Exodus becomes a byword for Israelite rebelliousness and idolatry. In the kabbala it plays a special role: death came into the world through the sin of ADAM; when Israel accepted the Torah this punishment was taken away, but with the sin of the calf immediately afterwards death was brought back. It will not be removed again until the coming of the MESSIAH.

golem An artificial man, produced by magic. In older Hebrew the word gólem means an unformed lump (Psalm 139.16), and by extension the rabbis use it of an uncultivated man. The Mishnah (Avot 5.7) lists seven differences between a golem and a wise man. The use of practical magic to create a man is mentioned in the Talmud (Bavli, Sanhedrin 65b), but it was only later that the term golem was applied to such a creature. The earliest source to use it in this way seems to be ELEAZAR OF WORMS, who gives a recipe for making a golem. The well-known story of the MAHARAL OF PRAGUE creating a golem is probably apocryphal. In this story, the rabbi found he was losing control of the golem, so he erased the divine name inscribed on its forehead and it reverted to dust.

Gomel ('bestows [favours]') Benediction, so called from its wording: 'Blessed are You, Lord our God, king of the universe, who bestows favours on the undeserving, for he has favoured me with such great good.' It is recited in synagogue by a person who is called up to the Torah after being in grave danger, during a journey or illness for example. The Gomel may also be said by a mother coming to the synagogue for the first time after giving birth.

Gordon, Aaron David (1856–1922) Ideologue and spiritual leader of the CHALUTS movement. Like Tolstoy, who influenced him deeply, Gordon produced an original synthesis of religious, social and political convictions, and acquired a considerable moral authority through the force of his personality and his unwavering commitments to the ideals he preached. He believed that physical labour on the land would bring about his personal redemption and also that of the Jewish people, and taught that pioneer work created an organic interrelationship between people, land and culture.

grace after meals Fixed sequence of benedictions to be recited after a meal including bread, called in Hebrew birkat ha-mazon (blessing of food). To say benedictions after food is regarded as a religious obligation, derived from Deuteronomy 8.10, 'When you have eaten and are full, you shall bless the Lord your God for the good land that he has given you'. The custom and indeed some of the wording goes back to the time of the ancient rabbis, who discuss it in the Talmud. There are four main parts: (1) blessing God for providing food for all; (2) thanksgiving for the Land of Israel; (3) prayer for the rebuilding of Jerusalem; (4) praise to God 'who is good and does good'. Various additions have been made over the centuries at the beginning and the end, and the form of words is varied for special occasions, such as Sabbaths and festivals, in a house of mourning or after a marriage. The full grace is rather long, and in emergencies a short form may be substituted. *See also* BENDIGAMOS; BENTSHN; MEZUMMAN.

Graetz, Heinrich (1817–91) Historian. Born in the province of Posen (Poznan), western Poland, he spent three years living in the home of S. R. HIRSCH as his pupil and amanuensis. He taught at the Breslau Rabbinical Seminary (*see* FRANKEL, ZACHAR-IAS) from its inauguration in 1854 until his death. His great work was his history of the Jews, *Geschichte der Juden* (11 vols, 1853–70; abridged English translation in 5 vols, 1891–2, repr. in 6 vols, 1967). This superseded all its predecessors and established itself as the authoritative history. Graetz insists that in Jewish history religion and politics are uniquely and inextricably intertwined. The focus in Judaism on national redemption rather than individual salvation enabled the Jews to survive the loss of their homeland; Jewish messianism looks forward to a return to this terrestrial homeland. Reform Judaism he saw as a betrayal of the fundamentally national character of Judaism. Graetz's work was naturally congenial to the proponents of ZIONISM.

gratitude Gratitude to God for his many favours is expressed in multifarious BENEDICTIONS (*see also* GRACE AFTER MEALS). In the Temple, individuals made thanksgiving offerings, and thanksgiving is the theme of several psalms that have been included in the liturgy (*see also* HALLEL). The eighteenth benediction of the AMIDA expresses gratitude to God '... for our lives, which are committed to your care, for our souls, which are entrusted to you, for your miracles, which are with us each day, and for your wonders and favours, which are with us at all times ...' Gratitude to one's fellow human beings is considered a great virtue, just as its opposite, ingratitude, is strongly condemned. (As the Bible puts it, 'Whoever repays good with evil, evil shall not depart from his house', Proverbs 17.13.)

Greek language Although Greek is spoken by only a small number of Jews today, in the Roman period it was the first or only language of a majority of the Jewish people, and it has left many traces in the vocabulary of Jews to this day, not only in English (in words such as Bible, phylacteries, prophet or synagogue) but in Hebrew words, such as apikóros, bima and piyyut. There are a small number of Greek loan-words in the Bible and they are abundant in the rabbinic writings. Rabbinic Hebrew reveals the influence of Greek in other ways as well, for example in the use of tenses or in the way words extend their semantic field. It was after the conquests of Alexander the Great in the latter part of the 4th century BCE that Jews, in common with other populations in the eastern Mediterranean region, came strongly under the influence of Greek culture. The Torah was translated into Greek: this translation, known as the Septuagint, still exists; nowadays it has no particular standing in Judaism, but it is clear that in antiquity it was read and studied as a sacred text.

The other books of the Hebrew Bible were eventually translated as well, and new works were composed by Jews in Greek, while new translations of the biblical books were made to accommodate changing needs. The most extensive Greek Jewish writings preserved today are those of the philosopher PHILO OF ALEXANDRIA and the historian JOSEPHUS. Almost all such Greek works that have survived, however, are preserved by Christian tradition; among Jews the use of Greek was gradually restricted to smaller and smaller numbers, as Hebrew (and to a lesser extent Aramaic) took over in the formerly Greek-speaking synagogues and Arabic and various Romance languages replaced spoken Greek. Very few traces of Greek remained in the prayer books of Greek-speaking Jews, for example a Greek translation of the book of Jonah that was read on the afternoon of the Day of Atonement until modern times in some synagogues.

Guide of the Perplexed *See* MAIMONIDES.

Gush Emunim ('bloc of faith') Irredentist Zionist movement founded in 1974 under the slogan 'The Land of Israel, for the people of Israel, according to the Torah of Israel'. The ideological roots of the movement are found in the teachings of Rabbi Abraham Isaac KOOK as interpreted by his son, Rabbi Tsvi Yehuda Kook. Historically its background is, firstly, the partition of Palestine in 1947–8 and, secondly, the Israeli victory in the 1967 Six-Day War, when the parts of Palestine allotted to the Arabs in 1947 (including the Temple Mount and other Jewish holy places) were occupied by Israel. Rabbi Kook and his followers interpreted the victory as a sign from God that the redemptive process was underway, and meanwhile the Israeli government began to plan and establish strategic settlements in the occupied territories. The 1973 Yom Kippur War, in which Israel snatched victory from the jaws of defeat, led directly the following year to the founding of Gush Emunim. The movement's mission was defined as follows: 'To bring about a major spiritual reawakening in the Jewish people for the sake of the full realization of the Zionist vision, in the knowledge that this vision's source and goal in the Jewish heritage and in Judaism's roots are the total redemption of both the Jewish people and the whole world.' Central to the movement's programme is the belief in a divine command to settle and control the entire biblical Land of Israel. Gush Emunim began to establish settlements throughout the occupied territories, and when the right-wing Likud party won control of the Israeli government in 1977 it supported this activity for political ends. Gush Emunim's message of practical messianism gradually became widely accepted, particularly as students of Merkaz Harav (the YESHIVA founded by Rabbi Kook) and similar yeshivot became teachers in the state religious school system. From non-violent beginnings the movement came to espouse more militaristic methods in combating the local Arab population and the presence of Islam, on the grounds that the state has failed to establish order and that therefore as guardians of the Land of Israel it is their duty to act so as to hasten the process of redemption. *See also* FUNDAMENTALISM.

ha-Kadosh baruch hu *See* KADOSH BARUCH HU.

ha lachma (Aramaic, 'this is the bread') Ancient Aramaic text that introduces the ritual of the Passover SÉDER. It is named after its opening words, 'This is the bread of affliction that our ancestors ate in the Land of Egypt'. It contains an invitation to all who are hungry to come and share the Passover meal, and looks forward to release from slavery and exile.

ha-Makom ('the Place') SUBSTITUTE NAME of God, used commonly in rabbinic texts. It is explained as follows: 'He is the place of the world but the world is not his place' (Genesis Rabba 68.9). It is rarely used today, but is preserved in a few phrases: for example mourners are traditionally comforted with the words 'May ha-Makom comfort you among the other mourners for Zion and Jerusalem'.

ha-motsi ('who brings forth') Benediction said before eating BREAD, thanking God 'who brings forth bread from the ground'. Traditionally the hands are first washed, then the benediction is said, preferably over a whole loaf, which is then broken and the pieces dipped in salt before being distributed to others at the table. The wording is based on Psalm 104.14.

ha-Shem ('the Name') SUBSTITUTE NAME of God, used commonly by Orthodox and traditionalist Jews today when not praying or saying a BENEDICTION. It is also common in medieval theological tracts, generally in the form ha-Shem yitbarach, 'the Name, may he [or it] be blessed'. In ancient Hebrew the word shem meant more than 'name': it indicated the character or essence of the person or thing named. The shem of God is sometimes referred to in the Bible as something as it were distinct from God himself and having a special sanctity. The same idea is found in the prayer book, sometimes citing these biblical verses. For example, in the morning prayers the ministering angels are described as singing praises to 'the Name of God, the great, mighty, awesome king, blessed be he'. On hearing the beginning of a benediction, 'Blessed are you, Lord', it is customary to respond 'Blessed be he and blessed be his Name!' After the first sentence of the SHEMÁ, proclaiming the unity of God, there is a response, 'Blessed be the name of his glorious kingdom for ever and ever!' (This could also be translated 'Blessed be his glorious majestic Name for ever and ever!') The ALÉYNU ends with a quotation from Zechariah 14.9: 'On that day [when God's kingdom is made manifest on earth] the Lord shall be one and his Name one.'

Habakkuk (Chavakkuk) Biblical book, eighth of the Twelve Minor Prophets. The prophet describes the ferocity of the conquering Babylonians, and looks forward to the ultimate triumph of good over evil.

Hadassi, Judah (12th century) Byzantine Karaite scholar and poet. His great work, entitled *Eshkol ha-Kófer* (*The Cluster of Henna*), is an encyclopaedic digest of Karaite theology and law.

Hafets Hayyim *See* CHAFETS CHAYYIM.

haftara (plural haftarot) The reading from the prophetic books that follows the reading from the TORAH in synagogue on Sabbaths and festival days. The precise meaning of the term is obscure; it is generally understood to mean conclusion or termination. Whereas the Torah is read in full in the course of a year, only excerpts are read from the prophetic books. The origins of this practice are lost in time; the choice of specific passages seems to have evolved in a relatively informal way – even today Ashkenazim and Sefardim read different haftarot on the same Sabbath. They are chosen because of their theological importance (many contain a message of consolation and hope) or because of some more or less obvious connection with the Torah reading. For example, on the first Sabbath of the yearly cycle, when the Torah reading is the account of the creation of the world followed by the moral degeneracy of the early generations of humans (Genesis 1.1–6.8), the haftara read by Sefardim is Isaiah 42.5–21, which opens with the creation of the world, continues with God's call to Israel to be a light to the nations and concludes, appropriately, with a verse about the Torah: 'The Lord was pleased, for his righteousness' sake, to make the Torah great and glorious'; Ashkenazim continue to 43.10 so as to conclude with another reference to the creation: 'Before me no god was made, and after me there shall be none'. On the second Sabbath the reading is about Noah's flood (Genesis 6.9–11.32); the haftara for Sefardim is Isaiah 54.1–10, which compares the Babylonian exile to the flood: 'For as I have sworn that the waters of Noah should no more go over the earth, so have I sworn that I would not be angry with you or rebuke you.' (Ashkenazim again read a longer haftara.) These links are typical of the relationship between Torah readings and haftarot. On festivals the haftara is connected with the theme of the festival. Certain other days have a special haftara, for example the four Sabbaths preceding Passover, the three Sabbaths preceding and four Sabbaths following TISH'A BE-AV, and a Sabbath which falls on New Moon or immediately precedes it. The person called to read the haftara is known as maftir (from the same root). It is considered an honour to be called up as maftir: a bar or bat mitzva is commonly chosen. (In Ashkenazi congregations boys below the age of BAR MITSVA are not eligible.) The maftir is first called up to the reading of a short passage from the Torah, usually a repetition of the last three verses of the regular reading. Then he (or she in egalitarian congregations) recites a special benediction, thanking God for choosing good prophets whose words are true and righteous. The haftara itself is usually read, unlike the Torah, from a printed text (manuscripts of the haftarot are occasionally used). It is generally chanted, using a traditional CANTILLATION that is different from that of the Torah; in Reform synagogues it is often read, in Hebrew or

English. After the haftara there are four benedictions: the first proclaims that all God's words are true and reliable; the second invokes God's compassion on Zion, 'which is the home of our life'; the third, with the seal 'Shield of David', prays for the coming of Elijah and the restoration of the dynasty of King David; the fourth speaks of the sanctity of the Sabbath, or the festival, as appropriate.

hagbaha ('elevation') The elevation of the Torah scroll in synagogue to show it to the congregation. In Sefardi congregations this is done before the reading of the Torah by an honorary officer or one of the LEVANTADORES. The Ashkenazi custom is to call a congregant up to perform hagbaha after the reading. On seeing the writing in the scroll the congregants chant 'This is the Torah that Moses placed before the Israelites' (Deuteronomy 4.44). Sefardim add 'The Torah that Moses commanded us is the inheritance of the congregation of Jacob' (Deuteronomy 33.4); Ashkenazim use instead words from Numbers 9.23: 'at the commandment of the Lord, by the hand of Moses'. British Reform synagogues follow the Sefardi custom.

Haggada ('narration') Prayer book for the home service for the eve of PASSOVER (*see also* SÉDER). The commandment to 'narrate' the exodus from Egypt is found in Exodus 13.8, and the core of the Haggada consists of rabbinic elaborations on the biblical exodus story. This part of the ritual goes back to early rabbinic times; other elements were added gradually, and early medieval Haggadot, recovered from the Cairo GENIZA, display a good deal of diversity. Today's printed Haggadot are more or less standardized, but there is a new trend to revise the text to suit the needs of different groups, such as Reform and Reconstructionist Jews, feminists or secular kibbutsim. Since every home has to have at least one copy, and some boast many, the Haggada is one of the commonest Jewish books. Large numbers of manuscripts exist, some of them lavishly illustrated, including some produced in the 18th century, long after the introduction of printing. The earliest extant printed Haggada was produced in Spain in 1485, but we cannot be sure this was the first time the text was printed. It is estimated that well over 5,000 different editions of the Haggada have been printed to date.

Haggai (Chaggai) Biblical book, the tenth of the Twelve Minor Prophets. It contains four prophecies delivered in the space of four months in the year 520 BCE, urging the returning exiles to rebuild the Temple.

Hagiographa *See* KETUVIM.

haham *See* CHACHAM.

hair The Bible has little to say about hair. Nazirites (*see* NAZIR) were forbidden to shave their hair (Numbers 6.5, 18; cf. Judges 16.17). It is a mark of mourning to leave one's hair dishevelled (Leviticus 10.6); shaving one's head as a mark of mourning is forbidden to Israelites in Deuteronomy 14.1 (JOB does it (Job 1.20), but there is nothing in the text to indicate that he was an Israelite). The Torah says: 'You shall not round the corners of your heads, nor shall you mar the corners of your beard' (Leviticus 19.27). It is further said of the priests: 'They shall not make baldness upon their head, neither shall they shave off the corners of their beard' (Leviticus

21.5). It is perhaps because of the vagueness and inconsistency of these texts that the halacha forbids in general the shaving of the BEARD or the sidelocks (PE'OT). Having one's hair cut is enjoined as part of the preparation for a festival; it is forbidden to mourners and during the counting of the ómer, except on LAG BA-ómer. On this day at the tombs of Rabbi Simeon bar Yochai and his son Eleazar in Meiron, in Galilee (*see* HILLULA), young boys have their hair cut for the first time, according to a custom that used to be widespread in the Middle East. The ritual is called halaka (from an Arabic word meaning shaving); the hair is thrown into a great fire, supposedly as a sacrificial offering. A young woman's long hair is said to be a sign of beauty (Song of Songs 4.1). Out of modesty, or to prevent them being a distraction to pious men, married women kept their hair covered in ancient times, and this practice is still observed by traditionalist and some Orthodox women today. Some Ashkenazi women go so far as to shave their heads on marriage, and wear a wig (called sheítel in Yiddish) or a headscarf. *See also* HEAD-COVERING.

Haketíya Form of Spanish spoken by Sefardi Jews in North Africa.

hakkafot ('circuits') Processional circuits of the synagogue, performed during SUKKOT and on SIMCHAT TORA. During Sukkot the FOUR SPECIES are carried and HOSHÁ-NOT are sung. On the last day, HOSHÁNA RABBA, there are seven hakkafot. On Simchat Tora at least seven hakkafot are performed, led by children carrying flags. The Torah scrolls are carried in the processions. Seven hakkafot are also performed at the dedication of a new synagogue. The name is also applied to the seven processions around a coffin performed by Sefardim prior to a burial, and to the seven circuits performed by some Ashkenazi bridegrooms around their brides. Hakkafot are also performed at the dedication of a new cemetery.

halacha

Law, legal study. The word halacha is commonly derived from the root halach, meaning 'walk', so that the word would mean something like the correct 'way' in which one should conduct oneself. This explanation has now been challenged in favour of a more formally legal etymology; indeed, halacha as it has traditionally been understood has certainly carried a sense of a higher obligation than that deriving merely from accepted or acceptable human conduct. Even halacha, however, does not mean exactly the same as 'law'. It includes within its scope both civil and criminal law and also religious regulations and precepts guiding human life in a less legal sense. The more developed halachic CODES OF LAW regulate minute details of personal, social and religious life as well as propounding general principles for human behaviour.

Halacha has attracted some of the finest Jewish minds over the centuries, and during the period of dominance of rabbinic Judaism, from the Talmudic period until early modern times halachic studies constituted the core of higher Jewish education. The halachic literature is enormous, and stretches in unbroken continuity from antiquity to the present. Each element in the halachic tradition, each legal judgment or responsum, is formulated in terms of the antecedent tradition. That is not to say, however, that halacha is constant and unchanging. On the contrary, like all legal traditions it is subject to a continuous process of adaptation to changing circumstances. The halacha is in a real sense a living tradition: it responds to the changing needs of real people, and in its turn it exerts an influence on their lives. It is true that the academic study of halacha covers a plethora of topics of little or no direct relevance to contemporary life, but the purpose of such study is to show how the original laws can be applied, ever more directly and minutely, in the lives of human beings striving to guide their actions according to the divine will as expressed in the Torah.

The first and most authoritative halachic texts outside the Bible are the Mishnah and the Talmud. These documents contain a great deal of AGGADA, but their halachic ingredient constitutes the foundation of all subsequent halacha. Neither document can be considered as a legal code. They both contain an enormous mass of legal material, some of which represents earlier attempts at codification, and all of which has been subjected to a complex process of editorial revision.

During the Middle Ages, halacha developed along somewhat different paths, in terms both of emphasis and of the types of literature produced. Three main types of halachic writing evolved. In the first place there are commentaries on the Talmud, of which the classic example is RASHI's commentary on the Babylonian Talmud. The commentaries are intended as a contribution to the study and teaching of the earlier texts. A related genre arising out of this study is that of the CHIDDUSHIM or novellae, refining points of halacha on which the sources are unclear or inconsistent. The second main type of writing consists of RESPONSA, replies by halachic experts to questions addressed to them by judges or communal leaders. The third, and in some respects the most novel, type of literature is the codes.

The need for a codification of the halacha arose from the enormous and unwieldy bulk of the traditional material, both within the Talmud itself and in the subsequent literature. To reach a decision on the basis of this traditional material demanded in each individual case an enormous effort, which could in any case only be attempted by a lawyer with a very thorough and competent training. The temptation to reduce the traditional decisions to a manageable compendium was naturally very strong. It was, however, strenuously resisted by many leading halachists at various times, who insisted on the danger of separating the halacha from its sources. Any decision needs to be made (they argued) on the basis of familiarity with the living tradition, and not by consulting a 'dead' codification. Consequently each of the great pioneering efforts of codification met with vigorous opposition, which effectively prevented the adoption of any standard and universally accepted code until virtually the end of the Middle Ages.

It was the SHULCHAN ARUCH of Joseph CARO that filled this role. Quickly disseminated through printing, it achieved enormous popularity, which was augmented when a Polish scholar, Moses ISSERLES, added notes on Ashkenazi practice (*see* MAPPA). The differences which had grown up between Ashkenazi and Sefardi practice are a reminder that in the Middle Ages halacha was still open to development, whether influenced from above, by authoritative interpreters, or from below, by popular custom. Isserles was a great believer in the validity of CUSTOM, and he criticized Caro for undervaluing it. In fact many practices which have become part of the fabric of Judaism originated in the Middle Ages. Through the halachic literature, especially the codes, such customs gradually acquired the force of law.

The Shulchan Aruch was the last great codification of halacha. Why the tradition of codification should have come to an end at this point is not clear, particularly since so much has changed in the intervening period that it is now palpably out of date. Perhaps its very success discouraged new initiative; perhaps the accelerated rate of change made a new code seem too vast an undertaking to contemplate. Halachic development is now embodied principally in responsa and in declarations by leading legal authorities and rabbinic committees. It is an unwieldy system, which demands enormous expertise and library resources, and places access to the full range of material beyond the reach of the general public and indeed of many rabbis (although this problem is currently being remedied by the use of computers). But in any case attitudes to the authority of the halacha and its place in Jewish life have undergone fundamental changes in the modern period.

For medieval Jews the halacha was divinely ordained and essentially unchanging, being revealed by God at Sinai once and for all time. There were even philosophers who argued that it would continue in force in the Coming Age (OLAM HA-BA). This was a disputed point, but all Jews agreed, against the Christians and Muslims, that God had never given and would never give any new revelation to supersede the Torah. As Maimonides put it in his celebrated THIRTEEN PRINCIPLES of Judaism: 'This Torah of Moses will not be abrogated, nor will another Torah come from God. Nothing may be added to it or removed from it, either from the written text or from the oral commentary.' Although there was a certain amount of discussion of the reasons behind the various commandments, there was no real questioning of the obligation to observe them. A good life was a life lived in obedience to God's will, and God's will was completely set out in the halacha. The rule of halacha was upheld by the rabbis, who exercised far-reaching jurisdiction under the system of judicial autonomy enjoyed by the Jews in the Middle Ages. They wielded powerful sanctions, including the ultimate sanction of exclusion from the community.

All this changed in the early modern period with political EMANCIPATION and the spread of the ideas of the ENLIGHTENMENT. Emancipation swept away Jewish judicial autonomy, except in certain limited areas of personal status. The rest of the halacha has, for practical purposes, fallen outside the scope of the courts. Even marriage, in most countries, is now subject in the first instance to the civil law of the land. As for sanctions, the halachic courts have lost most of the powers they formerly enjoyed, and they cannot even compel Jews to appear before them. Jews may still apply to the rabbinic court for a ruling on a religious question or for arbitration in a civil case, but this is now a matter of voluntary choice, and Jews commonly take their disputes to civil courts. The Jewish public no longer regards rabbis as primarily lawyers, and indeed many rabbis nowadays do not see themselves as lawyers at all.

Meanwhile modern religious philosophy and the science of biblical criticism have undermined the supernatural basis of the halacha. It is now possible for Jews to ask not only why God ordained certain commandments but whether God ordained them. Objections have been raised, on rational and moral grounds, to some of the commandments, and it has been objected that some of them are not merely anachronistic but downright unjust (*see* AGUNA; MAMZER for examples). These problems, and others like them, illustrate a particular difficulty in the operation of the halacha. It was long ago decided that a law can only be rescinded by a rabbinic assembly superior to that which decreed it. Since no contemporary assembly is deemed superior to the great SANHEDRINS of ancient times, no remedy seems to be available. Thus in cases where the halacha itself, even in its most liberal interpretation, provides no remedy, it would seem that nothing can be done by modern Orthodox authorities, short perhaps of convening a sort of ecumenical synod to undertake the reform of the law.

REFORM JUDAISM has adopted a completely different approach to halacha. The early theorists of Reform were united in their conviction of the need to reform the halacha, even if they were divided over the extent of the required changes or the appropriate theoretical justification for reform. Samuel HOLDHEIM, one of the leading early Reform rabbis, insisted that even the recognition of the divine origin of the law was no obstacle to its reform: 'The present age requires the clear enunciation of the principle that a law, even though divine, prevails only so long as the situations and conditions for which it was framed continue to exist: when these change the law too must be abrogated, even if its author is God.' His contemporary Abraham GEIGER advocated a thorough study of the tradition, with a view to deciding 'which rules of life are necessary, which institutions and religious practices may serve to improve the quality of religious life, which ones are moribund, and which are so at odds with our needs and circumstances as to offer no further helpful influence'.

Such views have persisted in Reform Judaism. The PITTSBURGH PLATFORM of 1885 frankly declared the Mosaic law to be obsolete and no longer valid: 'to-day we accept as binding only the moral laws and maintain only such ceremonies as elevate and sanctify our lives'. This 'pick and choose' approach is diametrically opposed to the divinely sanctioned halacha of the Middle Ages. Halacha is not a major concern of Reform Judaism today, and this is one of the main issues that distinguish it from CONSERVATIVE JUDAISM, where a non-fundamentalist theology does not prevent halachic issues from being of great concern. The real dividing line, though, is that separating Reform and Conservative Judaism on the one hand from Orthodoxy on the other; the key issue is the divine origin of the law (*see* TORA MIN HA-SHAMÁYIM).

One of the most celebrated Orthodox philosophers of halacha in recent times was Joseph Dov SOLOVEITCHIK. In his essay *Halachic Man* he explains and illustrates with examples some of the complexities and antitheses involved in living one's life according to halacha. He explains that halachic man has something in common with both the religious and the cognitive or scientific type, and yet is different from both. In particular, unlike the cognitive type of man he has a sense of the transcendent and longs for it, but unlike the religious man he does not aspire to ascend to it, but brings it down to earth into the FOUR CUBITS of the halacha.

Similar in some ways to the approach of Soloveitchik is that of Yeshayahu LEIBOWITZ, an Israeli scientist who wrote and lectured extensively on religious matters. However, Leibowitz goes further when he insists that the only purpose of obeying the commands is to serve God, and the only way to serve God is by obeying the commands. ' "You shall love your neighbour as yourself" without the continuation "I am God" is the great rule of the atheist Kant. So long as a person's religiosity expresses only his personal awareness, his conscience, his morality, or his values, the religious act is merely for himself and, as such, is an act of rebellion against the Kingdom of Heaven.'

This is an extreme view, and many observant Jews would have more sympathy with Soloveitchik's openness to the religious dimension, and would feel that if man's only role in the scheme of things is to obey blindly something is being missed both of the complexity of the human person and of the richness of the human sense of God.

The term is also used (with plural halachot) for an individual halachic teaching, and specifically one of the units of which the MISHNAH is composed.

halachic Midrashim Exegetical Midrashim on the books of the Torah (with the exception of Genesis). The best-known are the Mechilta (on Exodus), Sifra (on Leviticus), and Sifre (on Numbers and Deuteronomy). They are sometimes called Tannaitic Midrashim, because the rabbis they quote belong to the period of the Mishnah (*see* TANNA'IM). Unlike the Mishnah, however, they underline the relationship between scripture and HALACHA, that is between WRITTEN TORAH and ORAL TORAH.

Halachot Gedolot, Halachot Ketsuvot, Halachot Pesukot *See* CODES OF LAW; YEHUDA'I GA'ON.

halaka *See* HAIR.

Hallel ('praise') Term referring to biblical psalms of praise used liturgically. The term is applied in various ways. The most common use refers to Psalms 113–18, which are recited as a joyful celebration during the morning service on the three pilgrim festivals (SUKKOT, PASSOVER and SHAVUOT), ROSH CHÓDESH and CHANUKKA. The recitation is preceded by a benediction blessing God 'who has sanctified us by your commandments and has commanded us to recite the Hallel'. The formula usually suggests that there is a biblical commandment to perform the act; in this case the practice was instituted by the rabbis. (The same is true of the benediction over CANDLES on Sabbaths and festivals, and the reading of the scroll of Esther at PURIM.) After the recitation there is a benediction that concludes 'Blessed are you, Lord, king extolled with praises'. At Sukkot the FOUR SPECIES are held up and shaken during

Hallel. On some of the days enumerated above, namely the intermediate and concluding days of Passover and on Rosh Chódesh, an abbreviated Hallel is said. Hallel is included in the Passover SÉDER: it begins before the meal and continues after it. The Talmud discourages the recitation on any day when it has not been ordained. Nevertheless, in Israel the Chief Rabbinate has instituted the reading of Hallel on YOM HA-ATSMA'UT (Israel Independence Day) and YOM YERUSHALÁYIM (Jerusalem Day). The name Hallel is also given to Psalm 136 (the 'Great Hallel'). This is also recited during the Passover Séder. Finally, there is a 'daily Hallel', consisting of Psalms 145–50, which is recited as part of the morning service in synagogue.

halleluyah ('praise God!') A liturgical exclamation that is found twenty-three times in the book of Psalms, and is also used in the Jewish liturgy.

Hallevi, Yehuda *See* JUDAH HA-LEVI.

Hanukka *See* CHANUKKA.

hashkaba *See* ASHKABÁ.

Hashkivénu ('cause us to lie down') Evening prayer, so called from its opening words, 'Cause us to lie down, our father, in peace, and raise us up, our king, to a good and peaceful life'.

hasid, Hasidism *See* CHASIDISM.

Haskala A self-consciously Jewish offshoot of the ENLIGHTENMENT movement that spread eastward from Berlin during the 19th century, at first to Galicia (Austrian Poland, where it specially attacked CHASIDISM) and then throughout eastern Europe. The term, which literally means something like 'cultivation of the intellect', is an attempt to translate the German Aufklärung ('enlightenment') into Hebrew. Its devotees, known as maskilim, attacked and mocked the supposed obscurantism and superstition of the rabbis and their abuse of their powers, and advocated secular values and the replacement of the traditional education by modern, Western-style schools. They were strong proponents of the Hebrew language, and created a number of Hebrew scholarly periodicals. By the end of the 19th century the movement had run out of steam. Both secular Zionism and modern Hebrew literature have their roots in the Haskala.

Hasmonean revolt Jewish revolt against the Seleucid kingdom (a Greek kingdom based in Syria), which controlled much of the Middle East. The revolt, which broke out in 166 BCE, is described in the books of 1 and 2 Maccabees. (These books, of Jewish origin, are preserved in Christian tradition, having been abandoned by Jews.) It also figures in the Scroll of Antiochus, a much later Aramaic work created so as to be read at CHANUKKA, the festival that commemorates the revolt. (This work, too, however, fell out of use.) The revolt was marked by in-fighting between Jewish groups respectively committed and opposed to the introduction of a Greek-style constitution in Jerusalem and of a Greek lifestyle. The Hasmoneans were a priestly family prominently associated with the revolt, and with its success they advanced from being military leaders to being the ruling dynasty of a Jewish state and also high priests of the Temple. The period of Hasmonean rule (which eventually petered out in civil war and Roman conquest in the middle of the 1st century BCE) was a key one in the history of Judaism; although some of the details are a matter of scholarly controversy it seems that this was a time of rapid social, cultural and political change involving Hellenization (adaptation to Greek norms), conversion of some conquered populations to Judaism, the emergence of the factions of the Sadducees, Pharisees and Essenes, and the first appearance of such concepts as messianism, martyrdom and immortality.

hattarat hora'a *See* HÉTTER HORA'A.

havdala ('differentiation') Ceremony to mark the end of the Sabbath or a festival and the return to weekday life. It begins with a benediction over wine, and then comes the havdala benediction itself; it praises God 'who makes a distinction between holy and profane, between light and darkness, between Israel and the other peoples, between the seventh day and the six working days'. On Sabbaths there are two further benedictions, one over fragrant spices and the other over 'lamps of fire', said over a candle that is plaited so that it has several wicks. The special spice-boxes are often beautifully made according to fanciful designs. Afterwards it is customary to sing hymns in praise of ELIJAH, the harbinger of the Messiah. The term havdala can also be applied to these hymns.

head-covering The covering of the head while praying is not mentioned in the Bible (except that the high priest wore a mitre as part of his official vestments), and it seems that as late as the 13th century rabbis in France recited benedictions bareheaded. By that time, however, the Babylonian custom of covering the head to pray had gained wide acceptance, and many traditionalist and Orthodox Jewish men now keep their heads covered throughout the day, whether indoors or out. Other Jews cover the head only while in a Jewish home, and others again keep it covered while eating, particularly on Sabbaths and festivals. Reform Judaism was at first opposed to the custom of covering the head, but today many Reform and Liberal Jewish men cover the head to pray. Many women, too, now cover their heads to pray. *See also* HAIR; SKULLCAP.

heaven The sky; a name of God. In the Bible, the sky (shamáyim) is the abode of God (e.g. Psalm 115.16, Isaiah 66.1). During the Second Temple period the idea gradually developed that the righteous go to heaven after their death. The details of this heaven are nebulous. The rabbinic expression 'heavenly (or supernal) academy' (Aramaic metivta di-rekí'a, Hebrew yeshiva shel-má'ala) suggests that the souls of scholars are rewarded after death by admission to a higher institute of learning. Shamáyim (Heaven) is also a SUBSTITUTE NAME of God. It is found in Aramaic in Daniel 4.23 (26 in English versions) and in a work preserved only in Greek translation, the first book of Maccabees (e.g. 3.19). It is common in the Talmud, particularly in expressions like 'the fear of Heaven', 'the kingdom of Heaven'.

Hebrew (Ivri) A descendant of Eber, great-grandson of Shem (Genesis 10.24); a Jew. Thus ABRAHAM is described as a Hebrew (Genesis 14.13), and the prophet JONAH defines himself as a Hebrew (Jonah 1.19). The name has also been explained as meaning 'from the other side [of the Euphrates]', which is where Abraham came from.

Hebrew language A western Semitic language, related to ARAMAIC and ARABIC. Jews have used many languages, and some, such as JUDEZMO and YIDDISH, are closely associated with them, but the relationship of the Jews with Hebrew is unique. It is the original language of the Bible (apart from a few passages in Aramaic), and is the main language of Jewish prayer and of the halacha. Consequently it formed the basis of Jewish EDUCATION down the centuries. Many of the classic works of Judaism are written in Hebrew, including the MISHNAH, the MISHNE TORAH and the SHULCHAN ARUCH. The Jewish ENLIGHTENMENT (*see* BI'UR; MENDELSSOHN) and HASKALA movements promoted the use of Hebrew; its use as a spoken language in the Land of Israel was encouraged by the devoted efforts of the lexicographer Eliezer ben Yehuda (1858–1922), and in 1903 the Zionist schools adopted it as their language of instruction, thus ensuring that it would eventually become the main language of the state of Israel. This in its turn has encouraged a knowledge of the language among Jews world-wide, so that the trend towards vernacular prayer has been reversed. There are several different traditions of Hebrew pronunciation, most of which may be included under one of two main headings, Ashkenazi and Sefardi. While many of the differences between them are superficial and can be ascribed to the influence of Germanic and Slavic languages on the former and languages such as Spanish and Arabic on the latter, there are some very distinctive features that may go back to ancient dialects. In particular, one of the vowels pronounced 'a' by Sefardim is pronounced 'o' by Ashkenazim, and one of the consonants pronounced 's' by Ashkenazim is pronounced 't' by Sefardim. Additionally, Sefardim tend to stress words on the last syllable whereas in Ashkenazi pronunciation the stress tends to fall earlier in the word. (Thus Ashkenazim will say *kash*rus, *suk*ko, *suk*kos, *mat*so, whereas the Sefardi pronunciation followed in this book has kash*rut*, sukk*a*, sukk*ot*, mats*a*.) The Zionist movement adopted a modified Sefardi pronunciation, and this is the official pronunciation of Israel. For that reason it is tending to encroach on the Ashkenazi pronunciation in synagogues both in Israel and abroad.

Hebrew Union College American Reform rabbinical seminary, originally founded in Cincinnati, Ohio, in 1875, on the initiative of Isaac Mayer WISE. In 1950 it merged with the Jewish Institute of Religion, founded in 1922 in New York by Rabbi Stephen S. Wise. A third campus was opened in Los Angeles in 1954 to serve the growing Jewish community on the West Coast, and a fourth branch was established in Jerusalem in 1963. In addition to training rabbis and cantors for the Reform movement, HUC-JIR now offers a range of educational programmes.

Hebron Town south of Jerusalem, considered one of the HOLY CITIES of the Land of Israel. In the Bible the town is also called Kiryat Arba. In a cave here, called Machpela, according to the biblical narrative Abraham buried his wife Sarah and was later buried himself, together with other members of his family: Isaac, Rebecca, Jacob and Leah. (Rachel was buried near Bethlehem and Joseph in Shechem (Nablus).) The supposed site of the cave is now a holy place for Jews and Muslims. King David reigned from here before he moved his capital to Jerusalem. From 70 CE under the Romans until the Arab conquest in the 7th century Jews were forbidden to live in the town, and they were banned again when it was reoccupied by Christians from 1100 to 1248. With the arrival of Sefardi settlers after the completion of the Christian reconquest of Spain in 1492, Hebron became a noted centre of Jewish scholarship and piety; in the 19th century it also acquired a significant presence of CHABAD CHASIDIM; later a number of YESHIVOT were created here. Sadly, its recent history has been marred by appalling violence. Arab rioting in 1929 and 1936 led to the evacuation of the Jewish community; since the area was conquered by Israel from Jordan in 1967 it has been resettled, mainly by irredentist revivalists from America, and in addition to a presence in the historic centre they have created a nearby settlement under the old name Kiryat Arba (the settler movement GUSH EMUNIM mainly began here). The settlers have come under attack from local Arabs, and in 1980 six Jewish worshippers died in an attack at the Tombs of the Patriarchs. In 1994 29 Muslim worshippers were killed by a Jewish settler.

hechal *See* ECHAL.

hechalot ('shrines', 'palaces') Term designating a type of esoteric literature, and the associated spirituality, sometimes called merkava mysticism (*see* MA'ASE MERKAVA). A feature of this literature of the late Talmudic and geonic periods that was later taken up by the CHASIDEI ASHKENAZ is the subject's ascent to a succession of heavens, a journey attended by various dangers and rituals, until he reaches the heavenly throne. Some of the writing consists of hymns, often addressed to the throne-chariot (merkava).

héder *See* CHÉDER.

Heller, Yom Tov Lipmann (1579–1654) Central European halachist. He is best known for his Tosafot Yom Tov (1614–17), a commentary on the Mishnah. He also wrote a commentary on ASHER BEN YECHIEL's Piskei ha-Rosh, responsa, and some kabbalistic works. In his liturgical poems he laments the persecutions undergone by the Jews of Prague in 1618 and in the Ukraine in 1648.

hérem *See* CHÉREM.

heresy

Formal denial of any officially defined doctrine. This Christian term on the face of it is not directly applicable in Judaism, which lacks a central authority controlling DOGMA, but in reality the picture is more complicated. The term heresy is derived from the Greek word haíresis, 'choice', which was used in antiquity for any philosophical school. In this sense it is applied by the Jewish historian JOSEPHUS to three Jewish groups, the Sadducees, Pharisees and Essenes, that existed in his own day (*see* PLURALISM). He himself, he claims, had dabbled in all three, and he does not claim that any one of them had the truth while the others were false.

In Christian usage the term very quickly came to be applied to theological error, a development that accompanied the emergence of the Christian idea of 'orthodoxy'. We are poorly informed about any analogous developments in Judaism at the same period, but it appears that the rabbis, for all of their toleration of, and indeed fascination with, dissent, formally condemned certain beliefs, such as DUALISM, denial of resurrection, and denial of the divine origin of the Torah (see TORA MIN HA-SHAMÁYIM). A famous passage in the Mishnah (Sanhedrin 10.1) refuses a place in the Coming Age (OLAM HA-BA) to anyone who denies resurrection (or, according to some texts, that resurrection is mentioned in the Torah) or that the Torah comes from God, and to any Epicurean (APIKÓROS). Individual opinions are also cited condemning the reading of 'external books', healing by uttering incantations, or pronouncing the Tetragrammaton as it is written. Another rabbi cited in the Mishnah (Avot 3.12) denies a place in the Coming Age to one who 'profanes what is sacred, despises the festivals, shames his fellow in public, undoes the covenant of Abraham (i.e. circumcision), and reveals unauthorized interpretations of the Torah, even if he has a knowledge of Torah and good deeds to his credit'. Some commentators think this is intended as a condemnation of the Jewish Christians, but others disagree.

It is clear from such passages that, firstly, the rabbis at this time strongly attacked a number of beliefs or clusters of beliefs, and indeed actions, but, secondly, that they did not have the means to act against groups they condemned, for example by excluding them from the Jewish community or even apparently from their own gatherings. The legal instrument of CHÉREM (exclusion from the community) is not associated at this early period with doctrinal deviance.

The rabbis use a number of terms that are sometimes translated by 'heresy'. The commonest is minut, an abstract noun formed from min, plural minim, which originally means a type or category and is used to refer to various types of people who hold deviant beliefs and importune the rabbis with awkward questions. There has been a great deal of discussion about whether these can be identified with any particular group (such as the Jewish Christians), but it seems that the answer is negative: it is a generic term for individuals or groups holding different religious views from those promoted by the rabbis themselves.

In the course of the Middle Ages controversies on matters of faith and practice (notably those centring on KARAISM and on MAIMONIDES) sharpened a sense of orthodoxy and heresy, and in the modern period the messianic upheavals associated with SHABBETAI TSEVÍ and Jacob FRANK, and later the conflict surrounding the early spread of CHASIDISM, sensitized Jewish theologians still further to the notion of heresy. Jewish communities were sometimes torn apart by accusations and counter-accusations of heresy, and by the increasingly free use of the chérem.

Finally, the introduction of the Christian term 'orthodoxy' into Judaism in the early 19th century made explicit something that had not been formally recognized, namely an instinctive sense that certain doctrines were essential to Jewish faith and that to deny them was the mark of a heretic. The Karaite schism was sometimes invoked in this debate (see NEO-KARAISM). However, the real-life setting for the Orthodox–Liberal split was one of growing acceptance of pluralism, where old devices like the chérem had lost their sting. Today in effect religious Jews are divided by an article of faith, the divine origin of the Torah; this division runs very deep and gives rise on occasion to acrimonious accusations of heresy, particularly emanating from the more extreme FUNDAMENTALIST camp. Elsewhere in Jewry, however, such language is rarely heard.

Hertz, Joseph Herman (1872–1946) Rabbi. Born in Rebrin (Slovakia), he studied in New York, at Columbia University and the Jewish Theological Seminary. After serving as a rabbi in South Africa in 1913 he was appointed Chief Rabbi of the United Hebrew (i.e. Ashkenazi Orthodox) Congregations of the British Empire, an office he held with distinction until his death. He was a forthright and eloquent public speaker, an upholder of an enlightened ORTHODOXY in the face of LIBERAL JUDAISM and of ZIONISM in a generally unreceptive community. He reached a vast public through his writings, which include *A Book of Jewish Thoughts* (1917), a commentary on the Torah (5 vols, 1929–36; single-volume edition, 1938) and an edition with commentary of the authorized daily prayer book (3 vols, 1943–5).

Herzl, Theodor (1860–1904) Zionist leader. Herzl has come to be seen as the father of political Zionism. He came from a highly assimilated background, and it was probably the conviction of another assimilated Jew, the French officer Alfred Dreyfus, on a false charge of treason in 1895 (Herzl was covering the trial as a journalist) that suddenly made him question the whole process of EMANCIPATION. He at once set about writing the short text that was to become the foundation document of political Zionism, *Der Judenstaat*, known in English as *The Jewish State* (although *The State of the Jews* would be a better translation). In an age of nationalism, Herzl argued, the problem of Jewish identity and the related problem of antisemitism demanded a radical political solution: 'Let the sovereignty be granted us over a portion of the globe large enough to satisfy the rightful requirements of a nation; the rest we shall manage for ourselves.' Herzl worked out his plan in considerable detail, and presented it as a document for discussion and implementation. Among the Chovevei Tsiyon (*see* CHIBBAT ZION) in Russia, who were already well prepared for such a project, it met with an enthusiastic response, but the response in the West was more guarded. Nevertheless, Herzl felt sufficiently encouraged to convene an international congress to promote his plan. The First Zionist Congress met at Basle in Switzerland in August 1897. The Congress adopted the Basle programme, committed to the establishment of a national homeland for the Jews in Palestine, recognized by international law. The Congress also set up the World Zionist Organization, with Herzl as its president. Herzl devoted the remainder of his short life to building the WZO into an effective institution, and promoting his vision by every means possible. Herzl's efforts, although they did not meet with great success in his lifetime, contributed immensely to the Zionist movement, which eventually established the state of Israel in 1948.

Heschel, Abraham Joshua (1907–72) Religious philosopher. Born into a Chasidic dynasty in Poland, Heschel studied philosophy in Berlin, and for the last 26 years of his life he was professor of Jewish ethics and mysticism at the Jewish Theological Seminary in New York. In his writings he brings to the philosophy of religion something of the passion of the biblical prophets and the powerful Chasidic sense of the presence of God in the natural world. His influential book *Man Is Not Alone* begins with an encomium of what he calls 'wonder or radical amazement', which he argues is the first step towards understanding the world and God: knowledge begins not in doubt and rational argument but in wonder or reverence before the grandeur of the ultimate reality of the world we inhabit. Wonder goes beyond knowledge. Reverence is an innate human attitude. 'Reverence is one of man's answers to the presence of the mystery. The meaning of things we revere is overwhelming and beyond the grasp of our understanding. To the spirit of man his own spirit is a reliable witness that the mystery is not an absurdity, that, on the contrary, things known and perceptible are charged with its heart-stripping, galvanizing meaning.' The immediate and unquestionable feeling of awe that we feel before the grandeur of the stars in the sky or a dramatic sunset is the first step towards appreciating the reality of the transcendent and the demands that God makes of us.

Heschel's understanding of God is diametrically opposed to that of naturalists such as Mordecai KAPLAN. God is not merely a power or function, but a living reality, and it is a great shortcoming of religions to have lost the sense of immediacy and wonder at God's power and the sense of urgency about the demands he makes of human individuals and societies. Heschel's God, like that of the Bible and the rabbis, and unlike the God of the classical philosophers, has emotions and needs. God suffers together with his suffering creatures and is angry at their moral failures; and in particular he needs man as much as man needs him. Heschel was one of the outstanding Jewish religious philosophers of the 20th century, but was far from being a cloistered academic. He reached out to thousands in his books, he became famous as a political activist against the American war in Vietnam, and became something of an icon when photographed on a civil rights march in Selma, Alabama, arm in arm with Martin Luther King.

Heshvan *See* CHESHVAN.

Hess, Moses (1812–75) Early apostle of socialism, and precursor of ZIONISM. Born in Bonn, in 1848 he moved to Paris, where he spent the rest of his life. He was closely associated with Karl Marx (who called him 'the communist rabbi'), and espoused a utopian socialism that reflected his Jewish upbringing. His short book *Rom und Jerusalem* (*Rome and Jerusalem*, 1862) marked a progression from a cosmopolitan vision to a humanitarian Jewish nationalism. He called for the establishment of a Jewish nation in the Land of Israel, not so much as a response to antisemitism as because it represented the fulfilment of the genius of Judaism, which he identified with socialism. Dismissed or condemned by Jews in his day, he was retrospectively adopted by the Zionist movement. His remains were reinterred in Israel in 1961.

hester panim ('hiding of the face') Theological idea of the self-concealment of God. The phrase is borrowed from Isaiah 54.8: 'In a little wrath I hid my face from you for a moment, but with everlasting kindness will I have mercy on you, says the

Lord your redeemer.' It is cited by some theologians in an attempt to explain the apparent eclipse of God during the Holocaust. Thus Ignaz MAYBAUM writes: 'these catastrophes [the destruction of the First and Second Temple and the Holocaust] are "a small moment", "a little wrath", measured against the eternal love which God showers on his people'. Eliezer BERKOVITS goes further, and claims that in order for God to maintain his care for humanity as a whole he necessarily has to withdraw himself and allow even the most depraved of human beings to exercise their free will. (*See* HOLOCAUST THEOLOGY.)

hétter ('permission') Dispensation. There is no provision in Judaism for any human authority to grant dispensation from divine obligations, but halacha does allow a properly qualified rabbi (known as more hora'a, *see* next entry) to decide that the provisions of a rabbinic (not biblical) law or an established custom may be set aside in a specific case, for the sake of alleviating hardship. Such a rabbi may also annul a vow (with good reason): this is known as hétter nedarim. Hétter iska is a legal device to permit the lending and borrowing of money.

hétter hora'a or **hattarat hora'a** ('teaching permission') A rabbinical diploma, certifying that the holder has been examined and proved himself competent to rule on questions of ceremonial and civil law. The holder of such a certificate is known as more hora'a (literally 'teacher of teaching'). Notwithstanding the spread of the issuing of the hétter hora'a, particularly in Ashkenazi Jewry, many serving rabbis have not possessed it.

Hibbat Tsiyyon *See* CHIBBAT ZION.

hiddur mitsva ('adorning the commandment') Principle according to which religious objects should be made as beautiful as possible, beyond any formal requirements of the HALACHA.

High Holydays Term used to refer to the solemn festivals of NEW YEAR (Rosh ha-Shana) and the Day of ATONEMENT (Yom Kippur).

Hildesheimer, Ezriel (also Asriel, Israel) (1820–99) Orthodox rabbi and scholar. Born in Halberstadt, Hildesheimer played a leading part in the creation of modern ORTHODOXY. As rabbi in Eisenstadt (Kismarton) he founded the first YESHIVA to teach secular as well as traditional Jewish subjects and to use German and Hungarian as a medium of instruction, an initiative that earned him furious denunciation from the traditionalist rabbinate. In 1869 he moved to Berlin to lead the ADATH YISROEL congregation. Here he founded in 1873 the Berlin Rabbinical Seminary, which he directed until his death.

Hillel (late 1st century BCE–early 1st century CE) A teacher often quoted in the rabbinic literature and an important precursor of the rabbinic movement. He is described as a Babylonian who immigrated to the Land of Israel, although he seems to have known Greek well and resembles the type of the Greek sophist: a popular teacher who makes use of carefully constructed, enigmatic sayings to capture his hearers' minds. Many teachings are attributed to him and to his school (Beit

Hillel) in the Mishnah, including such well-known dicta as 'If I am not for myself who is for me? If I am only for myself what am I? And if not now when?' and 'Trust not in yourself until the day of your death'. The views of the school of Hillel are often contrasted with those of the school of SHAMMAI, and are usually preferred to them by the rabbis. Hillel was claimed by the dynasty of the patriarchs (*see* NASI) as their ancestor. Contrary to a common assumption, he is never given the title of rabbi in the sources; presumably it came into use after his time.

hillul ha-Shem *See* CHILLUL HA-SHEM.

hillula (Aramaic, 'wedding festivity') Commemoration of the death of a saintly rabbi, commonly accompanied by pilgrimage to his tomb. Closely associated to kabbalistic folklore, the hillula is a joyful occasion, resembling a wedding feast, as the soul of the departed rabbi is considered to have been reunited on his death with the SHECHINA in a mystical marriage. In Israel the best-known hillula is that of Rabbi Simeon Bar-Yochai on LAG BA-ÓMER, in honour of the second-century rabbi who is believed by kabbalists to be the author of the ZOHAR. Tens of thousands of people congregate annually at his supposed tomb at Meiron, in Galilee (*see also* HAIR). Other popular hillula celebrations are those of the 2nd-century TANNA Rabbi Meir the Miracle Worker at his supposed tomb near Tiberias on PÉSACH SHENI (14th of Iyyar), and of the BABA SALI (Israel Abu-Chatsera) at his tomb at Netivot in the Negev on the 4th of Shevát. Hillula pilgrimages are also held in Morocco, Tunisia, Egypt, Iran, and other countries. The hillula of the Ari (Isaac LURIA) is commemorated on the 5th of Av, and that of the Ben Ish Chai (YOSEF CHAYYIM) on the 13th of Elul. Hillula pilgrimages are mainly associated with Jews of the Muslim world, but the observance of hillula has also been adopted by the Chasidim; for example CHABAD CHASIDIM celebrate the hillula of their rebbes. *See also* MAIMUNA; PILGRIMAGE.

Hirsch, Emil Gustav (1851–1923) Reform rabbi. Born in Luxembourg, the son of Samuel HIRSCH, he emigrated to the United States in 1866 and from 1880 to his death was the spiritual leader of the Chicago Sinai Congregation. He also held a chair of rabbinical philosophy and literature at the University of Chicago. Hirsch was a prominent figure in American REFORM JUDAISM and a strong proponent of social justice.

Hirsch, Samson Raphael (1808–88) Orthodox rabbi. Born and brought up in Hamburg, he studied at Bonn university before taking up his first rabbinical appointment at Oldenburg, followed by others at Emden, Nikolsburg (Moravia) and Frankfurt. Like his fellow student at Bonn Abraham GEIGER, Hirsch early became convinced of the need to act to stem the drift of young Jews away from Judaism, and he espoused some radical reforms, such as the modern style of dress (including being clean shaven and wearing clerical robes), preaching in the vernacular, encouraging Bible study and marriage in synagogue, and even going so far as to abolish the KOL NIDREI service. He coined the slogan TORA IM DÉRECH ÉRETS, meaning that young Jews should study secular subjects side by side with Judaism. At the same time, unlike Geiger, he was firmly committed to the doctrine of the divine origin of the Torah (including rabbinic halacha as well as the Bible), and opposed the approach of the

HISTORICAL SCHOOL, which opened the door to far-reaching reforms. He is thus rightly seen as the father of modern ORTHODOXY.

In 1851 he became the rabbi of the Adass Yeshurun congregation in Frankfurt-am-Main, a position he held for 37 years, during which he transformed this small synagogue into the flagship of the new movement. However, whereas at the outset he claimed the support of the mass of German Jewry, over the years he was forced to recognize that the Orthodox were a shrinking minority, and, increasingly beleaguered, eventually he lent his support to the separation of the Orthodox from the united communities that had previously been the rule, and were increasingly dominated by reformers (*see* AUSTRITTSGEMEINDE). This was a very contentious issue that split German Orthodoxy; the impact of the controversy can still be felt today. Under the pseudonym 'Ben Uziel' Hirsch wrote a strong defence of traditional Judaism in *Neunzehn Briefe über Judenthum* (*Nineteen Letters on Judaism*, 1836). In 1838 he published *Choreb, oder Versuche über Jissroels Pflichten in der Zerstreuung* (*Horeb, or Israel's Duties in the Dispersion*), a modern interpretation of the 613 COMMANDMENTS. Hirsch also published an influential commentary on the Torah. *See also* ADATH YISROEL; EDUCATION; EXILE AND RETURN; MODERNISM.

Hirsch, Samuel (1815–89) Reform rabbi and religious philosopher. Born at Thalfang, near Trier, he served as chief rabbi of Luxembourg from 1843 until 1866, when he emigrated to the United States. Hirsch took part in the early rabbinical synods in Brunswick, Frankfurt and Breslau (1844–6) which laid out a programme of religious reforms, and he continued his dedicated advocacy of REFORM JUDAISM as rabbi in Philadelphia. He presided over an important rabbinical conference in Philadelphia in 1869, and was influential in the formulation of the PITTSBURGH PLATFORM of 1885. His best-known work is *Die Religionsphilosophie der Juden* (*The Religious Philosophy of the Jews*, 1842), in which he develops the view that Judaism and Christianity have equally valid but different roles in the world. He is also remembered for having proposed that the Sabbath should be moved to Sunday.

See also HIRSCH, EMIL GUSTAV.

Historical school Also called the Breslau school. Term applied to a 19th-century trend in MODERNISM that advocated moderate religious reforms based on the historical researches of the WISSENSCHAFT DES JUDENTUMS. The pioneer of this approach was Zacharias FRANKEL, who called it 'positive-historical', because, while rooted in historical study and thus rejecting the TRADITIONALIST view that halacha, in particular, being divinely revealed legislation, has no history, it also rejected the more radical reformist position that exploited the discovery of historical development to foist changes on a community that in some cases was not fully prepared for them. Just as change in the past had arisen gradually, in response to the demands of the hour, so further changes, in Frankel's view, had to arise naturally and in accord with Judaism's organic nature. (This conception played an important part later in the formulation by Solomon SCHECHTER of his conception of CATHOLIC ISRAEL.)

hitbodedut *See* NACHMAN OF BRATSLAV.

Hod ('splendour') In kabbala, one of the SEFIROT.

Hoffmann, David Zvi (1843–1921) Biblical and Talmudic scholar and halachist. Born in Verbo, Slovakia, Hoffmann, who in 1899 succeeded Ezriel HILDESHEIMER as principal of the Berlin Rabbinical Seminary, was an outspoken defender of ORTHODOXY and critic of REFORM JUDAISM, and at the same time was an able exponent of the HISTORICAL method in the study of rabbinic texts who was himself attacked by traditionalists. In the introduction to his collection of responsa, Melammed le-Ho'il, he deplores the dominant tendency of halachists to determine the law automatically on the side of CHUMRA.

hol ha-mo'ed *See* CHOL HA-MO'ED.

Holdheim, Samuel (1806–60) German rabbi. Born near Posen (Poznan) in western Poland, Samuel Holdheim came from a background relatively untouched by modern trends, and received a traditional Talmudic education, yet became one of the most uncompromising of reformers. He formulated the influential view that changing times demanded changes in the law, even if the law is agreed to be of divine origin. He went further, however, than most of his colleagues could follow him when he transferred the Sabbath services in his Berlin temple to Sunday, abolished several festivals, and officiated at marriages between Jews and Gentiles. Holdheim relied on the distinction between the religious and the national elements in Judaism: the latter (echoing SPINOZA) he declared to be obsolete since the loss of the Temple in Jerusalem. In practice he was willing to abandon many purely religious observances: what were important were the beliefs and ethics of Judaism. Holdheim's radical reforms went beyond what most German Jews would accept at the time, but they later found an echo in American Reform.

holiness

'Holy' in Hebrew is kadosh; 'holiness' is kedushah: the words combine the twin concepts of separation and dedication. The English word that most closely combines these two meanings is 'special': 'Now if you listen to my voice and keep to my covenant you will become my chosen possession out of all the peoples, because the whole world is mine. You shall be mine, a kingdom of priests and a holy nation' (Exodus 19.5–6). These words, spoken through Moses to the people Israel at Mount Sinai, indicate a key meaning of holiness: Israel are separated from the other peoples and dedicated to the service of God, just as priests are separated from other people and dedicated to his service. The 'sanctification' or dedication of the people is mentioned very often in the prayers.

At Sinai the holiness of Israel is linked to obedience to God's commands ('to listen' also means 'to obey') and loyalty to his COVENANT. Later it is linked to the holiness of God himself: 'You shall be holy as I the Lord your God am holy' (Leviticus 19.2). These words are followed by a series of regulations, beginning 'You shall each revere your mother and father, and keep my Sabbaths: I am the Lord your God.' And a little later it says: 'You shall keep my commands and carry them out: I am the Lord. You shall not profane my holy name, but I shall be made holy among the children of Israel: I am the Lord who makes you holy' (Leviticus 22.31–2). Profanity and profanation (CHOL, chillul) are the opposite of holiness and sanctification (kódesh, kiddush). By observing God's commands Israel preserve God's sanctity; by breaking them they profane it. 'Sanctification of the [divine] name' (KIDDUSH HA-SHEM) is the Hebrew equivalent of martyrdom, while its opposite, 'profanation of the name' (CHILLUL HA-SHEM), means blasphemy, bringing God's name into disrepute.

The holiness of God is a difficult concept to grasp. It hints at his uniqueness, his being absolutely separate and different from all other beings. The prophet Isaiah had a vision of the Lord sitting on an exalted throne, surrounded by winged seraphim who called to one another: 'Holy, holy, holy is the Lord of Armies: the whole world is full of his glory' (Isaiah 6.3). 'The holy God' is the conclusion of one of the benedictions of the AMIDA (*see also* KEDUSHA). The holiness of God is mentioned on several other occasions in the prayers, most notably in the KADDISH.

In the Bible the priests, the descendants of Aaron, were 'holy to the Lord', and these words were inscribed on the high priest's headdress, just above his forehead (Exodus 28.36). They ministered in the Temple, which was known as the sanctuary or holy place (mikdash). The inner shrine was the Holiest of Holies, but the whole city of Jerusalem where the Temple stood was called the holy city. The holiness of the Temple was unique; few hints of it remain today in the synagogue or in Jewish home life. A synagogue is not a sanctified building, and none of its contents or fittings is regarded as holy, although the ARK where the scrolls are kept is called aron ha-kódesh, 'holy ark'. Although there are still hereditary priests, they are people like everyone else: the last vestiges of their earlier status are that they may not come in contact with a corpse unless it is that of a close relation (Leviticus 21.1–4) or marry a divorcee (Leviticus 21.7). The Hebrew language is still sometimes referred to as 'the holy tongue' (or 'language of the sanctuary' – leshon ha-kódesh), because it was the language used in the Temple.

One area where the concept of sanctity is still very much alive is in the Sabbaths and festivals. The Bible speaks of the Sabbath as a day sanctified by God (e.g. Genesis 2.3, Exodus 20.8–11), and these verses are quoted (respectively in the evening and the morning) in the KIDDUSH.

The holiness of the Sabbath is linked to the holiness of Israel. This idea is made explicit in the Amida for Sabbaths: 'Lord our God, you did not give it to the other nations of the lands, nor did you make it the inheritance of idolaters, nor are the uncircumcised at home in its rest, but you have lovingly given it to your people Israel, to the descendants of Jacob whom you chose. The people who sanctify the seventh day will all receive ample sustenance and delight from your goodness. You took pleasure in the seventh day and made it holy, calling it the most desirable of days, a memorial of the story of Genesis.' (*See also* HAVDALA.)

Another area where the language of sanctification comes to the fore is in MARRIAGE, where the bridegroom betroths the bride with these words: 'See, you are sanctified to me by this ring according to the laws of Moses and Israel.' The married couple are separated from other people and dedicated to each other alone; adultery is a profanation of this solemn bond.

Judaism has generally remained close to the biblical concept of holiness as obedience to the divine commands, and it has not been greatly influenced by the Christian usage, in which the term carries a connotation of spiritual elevation.

Holocaust Term commonly applied to the ordeal of European Jewry under Nazi rule before and during World War II, and specifically to the attempt by the Nazis to exterminate the Jewish people. The word is derived from the Greek holókauston, which denotes something (usually a sacrifice) wholly consumed by fire. The related word holokaútoma was coined by the translators of the Torah into Greek as the equivalent of the Hebrew ola, a burnt offering. The word was applied after World War I to the terrible deaths of innumerable young soldiers in the trenches: it was thought suitable because it combined connotations of large numbers, death by fire, and the idea of sacrifice. After World War II there was for some time no recognized name for the experience of the Jews; by the mid-1960s 'Holocaust' had come into widespread use in the English-speaking world, and it is now established as the most usual term, although it has come to be criticized by some for its theological over-tones, and even in English the Israeli Hebrew term SHO'A is becoming increasingly familiar.

Holocaust theology

There is a large and fast-growing literature devoted to theological reflection on the Nazi Holocaust, much though not all of it focusing on the primarily philo-sophical problem of theodicy, namely how a God who is by definition all-good and all-powerful can cause or tolerate evil in the world that he commands. The basic issues raised by the Holocaust were hardly new ones. As a manifestation of the human capacity for evil it has many predecessors, the echoes of which can be traced in Jewish literature going right back to the Bible. The same can be said about the theological problems raised by the existence of evil in the world. In the area of the COVENANT, the idea of a special relationship between God and the Jewish people, one could cite the classical biblical challenge of the destruction of the Temple by the Babylonians, followed by the later destruction by the Romans and a whole series of events, culminating in the Russian pogroms, which were still in living memory at the time the Nazis came to power. The reasons are probably to be sought in other areas than theology: in the unprecedented enor-mity of the destruction and its extraordinary brutality, and in the traumatic betrayal of the aspirations of those who had put their faith in moral progress and in the values of German civilization. Nevertheless, the impact on theology has been profound, and after an initial phase of relative silence, from the 1960s on there has been a seemingly inexhaustible stream of publications addressing the issues raised for Jewish belief by the Holocaust.

Given the general eclipse of philosophical theology in the first part of the 20th century, it is surprising how many writers focused on the classic philosophical problem of theodicy, or justification of God: how can one reconcile such evil with the philosophers' portrait of a god who is both all-powerful and the embodiment of all goodness? However puzzling this crudely mechanical statement of the conundrum might be when applied to medieval philosophy, it hardly seems relevant to Jewish philosophy as it had developed in the 19th century and the early part of the 20th. In the thought of Hermann COHEN and Leo BAECK there is not much that humans can assert positively about God as ultimate reality, and there is little point in speculating about divine omnipotence and its possible limits: what we can talk about is human ethics and responsibility. In the more explicit naturalism of Mordecai KAPLAN there is even less reason to speculate about divine responsibility. Evil is not a philosophical problem for Kaplan, and insofar as he mentions it at all it is as an aspect of human behaviour.

The Bible appears to offer an answer: God is all-good, indeed he resembles a benevolent and patient ruler who is astonishingly forbearing, but ultimately he must act to punish wrongdoing. God does not shrink from inundating the world and drowning the whole human race, with the exception of a few individuals, on account of the evil that had infected society. Some traditionally minded writers attempted to apply this logic to the Holocaust, but the results were partial and unsatisfactory, and were received with nothing but outrage: how could one possibly claim that a million and a half babies and small children were brutally killed because of their sins, or indeed because of the sins of their parents? And how can one compare the possible sins of the Jewish victims with those of the non-Jewish perpetrators? Even the most biblical of post-Holocaust theologians, Ignaz MAYBAUM, who on one occasion went so far as to speak of God sending Hitler as his agent just as he sent the Babylonian King Nebuchadnezzar to destroy Jerusalem, drew the line at blaming the Holocaust on the sins of the victims.

Some theologians took refuge in silence, or in the shelter of divine inscrutability. HESCHEL, for example, rarely mentioned the subject of the Holocaust in his writing, even though his own life was disrupted by it and many members of his own family were among the victims. Other writers, like Eliezer BERKOVITS, appealed to the doctrine of HESTER PANIM: at certain times God removes himself from human affairs, so as to give mankind full opportunity to experience their own power to act, for good or ill. In part this is an application of the philosophical gambit known as the 'free-will defence': the gift of free will necessitates a voluntary limitation of divine power. It has not won wide favour from theists because it tends to harm the conception of divine providence: how can you say that God cares for us if he refuses to step in when we need him most? Even Martin BUBER, whose conception of God as 'everlasting You' had completely done away with earlier theology, since any discussion of God's attributes would transform him from a 'you' to an 'it', was forced to adapt his views: how could the God whose name is 'I shall be there' have been so notably absent? After the war he began to speak of an eclipse of God. Hard as it is for us to accept the absence of loving parents when we need them, it is even harder for us to accept the absence of God.

Our task is not to explain it but to learn to overcome it, to maintain our relationship with God despite what seems like a betrayal of that relationship.

Few have cared to go so far as the American Richard Rubenstein, who finds signs of an apocalyptic battle raging within God, ending with a definitive rupture of the covenant: God is no longer in control of Jewish history. Henceforth humans must turn to each other, and to nature, which is beyond history. Another American, Arthur COHEN, prefers to speak of a caesura. The Holocaust is unique: it cannot be considered an historical event like any other, but nor can it be removed from history and turned into a metaphysical object or an act of faith. He calls it a 'tremendum', the meaning of which will be made explicit only in REDEMPTION. Many Americans have chosen to link the catastrophe of Holocaust to the creation of the state of Israel. Irving Greenberg sees the Holocaust as annulling the partnership between Israel and God; in Israel the Jews voluntarily re-establish the covenant. For Berkovits, too, in Israel God's holy presence is proclaimed at the heart of his hiddenness. And for the Canadian Emil FACKENHEIM Israel embodies the 614th COMMANDMENT that sounds forth at Auschwitz: Thou shalt not hand Hitler posthumous victories. The power of the state of Israel defies the powerlessness to which the Nazis reduced their victims. Israel is the TIKKUN for the rupture of the Holocaust; outside Israel Jews can achieve tikkun through unconditional support for Israel.

New theological responses to the Holocaust continue to be elaborated. Some of the most interesting ones centre on rethinking the idea of covenant.

holy cities Term designating four towns in the Land of Israel, viz. HEBRON, JERUSALEM, TIBERIAS and SAFED. All are distinguished by the tombs of holy people.

Holy One, blessed be He *See* KADOSH BARUCH HU.

home *See* FAMILY.

homosexuality The concept of fixed sexual orientation in general is a modern one, and classical Jewish sources such as the Torah and Talmud offer little explicit guidance for those caught up in current, often fiercely waged, debates on such subjects as the recognition of same-sex unions and the ordination of gay and lesbian rabbis. Sexual relations between males, along with many other sexual practices, are condemned in the strongest terms in the Torah (Leviticus 18.12, 20.13) and in the Talmud (e.g. Bavli, Sanhedrin 53a–b, Yevamot 83b); moreover, the commandment to 'be fruitful and multiply' (Genesis 1.28) has always been taken very seriously and applied to all males without exception. Sexual acts between women are not explicitly mentioned in the Bible but are forbidden in the Talmud (Bavli, Shabbat 65a, Yevamot 76a). The halacha lays down very strict guidelines for what has been termed 'kosher sex', and does not countenance any sexual relations (and with some exceptions discourages social relations) except those between a man and woman who are married to one another. Consequently the idea of a committed, publicly accepted relationship of love between two people of the same sex is simply not entertained in the sources. So long as non-Jewish social mores and legislation coincided with this outlook the issue was very little discussed within Judaism, but with greater public toleration and eventually the legalization of homosexual acts and legal recognition of same-sex unions it has become a matter for debate among Jews too.

Generally speaking the various modernist religious movements have responded along predictable lines. The Reform rabbinate in the United States adopted a resolution as early as 1977 encouraging legislation to decriminalize homosexual acts between consenting adults and to prohibit discrimination against them as persons. In the 1980s the leading rabbinical seminaries on the left of the religious spectrum, Hebrew Union College and the Reconstructionist Rabbinical College in America and Leo Baeck College in Britain, all altered their policies to ordain openly lesbian and gay rabbis. However, it was not until 2000 that the American Reform movement decided to allow rabbis to officiate at same-sex commitment ceremonies; the British Liberal movement in 2003 agreed to the creation of a special liturgy for a commitment ceremony in synagogue, a step that at the time of writing the British Reform movement held back from taking. The Conservative movement in America moved more slowly. The rabbinic and synagogue arms of the movement declared themselves in favour of civil equality in 1991 and 1992 respectively; after years of heated debate, in December 2006 the movement's Committee on Jewish Law and Standards approved the ordination of openly homosexual rabbis, and commitment ceremonies for openly homosexual laity and rabbis, while maintaining the prohibition against penetrative sexual acts. However, a diametrically opposed responsum was also approved. The result is that individual synagogues, rabbis, and rabbinical schools have discretion to adopt either approach. Orthodoxy has continued to denounce homosexual acts and refused to condone same-sex unions, although individual Orthodox rabbis have recognized that there is a problem. The traditionalist wing has not gone even this far.

honey The only kosher food that comes from a non-kosher animal. Honey was barred from Temple sacrifices (Leviticus 2.11), no reason being given. The Talmud often discusses the use of honey, and also date-honey, which was used as a sweetening agent. On the eve of New Year it is customary to eat pieces of apple dipped in honey, in the hope of enjoying a good, sweet year. *See also* MAIMUNA.

Horayot ('instructions', 'legal decisions') Tractate of the Mishnah, Tosefta and both Talmuds, in order Nezikin, dealing with the legal situation when individuals or the majority of the people are led into transgression by a wrongful decision of a law court (based on Leviticus 4.1–21).

Hosea (Hoshé'a) Biblical book, the first and longest of the Twelve Minor Prophets. Hosea prophesied in the 8th century BCE. In the book he receives instructions to marry a prostitute – a symbol of Israel's unfaithfulness to God and God's unshakeable love.

Hoshána Rabba The seventh day of SUKKOT. Formally the last day of CHOL HA-MO'ED, it has a special character, going back to the days of the Temple, when worshippers processed seven times round the altar (whereas on the previous days of the festival they only processed once), waving the FOUR SPECIES and singing HOSHÁNOT, before beating willow sprigs on the ground, symbolically casting off their sins as they did so. A similar ceremony is still followed in the synagogue. During the Middle Ages the idea gained currency that on this day the penitential period beginning at New Year came to an end. (This aspect is particularly prominent in the Sefardi ritual.) A custom also arose of staying up on the night of Hoshána Rabba to read from the Torah. Among kabbalists a special order of service has evolved, including reading the entire books of Deuteronomy and Psalms and selections from the ZOHAR.

hoshánot (singular hoshána, 'O save [us]') Prayers or hymns chanted during the circuits of the synagogue (HAKKAFOT) during SUKKOT. 'Hoshána', a contracted form of the invocation hoshí'a-na (Psalm 118.25), forms the refrain. The hoshánot consist of a sequence of invocations, usually arranged alphabetically. The oldest are quite simple, but some very complex ones have survived from the early days of the PIYYUT (6th–7th century CE). These sometimes incorporate prayers for rain, and for agricultural prosperity.

The English word hosanna represents a Greek transcription of the Hebrew word hoshána.

Hoshé'a Hebrew name of the biblical book of Hosea.

hospitality A paramount virtue, of which the great model is ABRAHAM. The rabbinic literature contains many exhortations to hospitality, and advice on how to be a good host and a good guest.

human rights Jewish individuals and organizations, such as the WORLD JEWISH CONGRESS, were active supporters of the establishment of international human rights law in the years leading up to the creation of the UN Universal Declaration of Human Rights in 1948, and have continued to support subsequent initiatives. While persecution of Jews was the direct reason for such strong support, the view is often expressed that Jewish culture and human rights are mutually compatible or even intrinsically connected. In the first decades of international human rights law, rather superficially constructed links between Judaism and human rights were suggested. Such ideas are still voiced, but they are increasingly being replaced by more subtle views, a development which has been aided by research illuminating the complex relationship between human rights and Judaism with regard to fundamental principles as well as concrete areas such as fair trial, the death penalty and gender equality. The observation is often made that the focus of Judaism on working for JUSTICE in this world is well matched with the human rights regime. A long rabbinic tradition of aversion to the death penalty is a concrete example where Jewish law is viewed as compatible with human rights. With regard to some other fundamental principles the compatibility is less apparent and hence subject to more debate. For example, Jewish law, following biblical law, has tended to emphasize obligations rather than rights.

While widespread support of the underlying principles of human rights can be found in the different branches of Judaism, with regard to a number of specific issues Conservative and particularly Orthodox Judaism have encountered some difficulties. This applies in particular to religious freedom and women's rights.

Certain difficulties in the area of human rights have become apparent in the state of Israel. One such issue is family law, which in Israel is outside the secular legal system and subject to the rabbinic courts. In practice this works to the detriment of the rights of the individual. For example Jews can only marry Jews, as defined by the rabbinic authorities, and there is no civil marriage or divorce. A wife is unable to obtain a religious divorce if her husband refuses her a GET, and since civil divorce is not available the problem of the AGUNA is particularly severe in Israel. The organization Rabbis for Human Rights, founded in 1988 in response to what were seen as serious human rights abuses by the Israeli military authorities in the suppression of the Intifada (Arab uprising in the Occupied Territories), brings together Israeli rabbis of all denominations concerned to combat human rights abuses in the name of the Jewish tradition of humanity and moral responsibility. Among the issues it campaigns for are the status of women in Israel, the rights of foreign workers and the BETA ISRAEL, improvements in the Israeli health care system and an Israeli bill of rights.

Outside Israel the state has sometimes interfered in areas where HALACHA is considered to be in conflict with the human rights norms prevailing in society at large. For example in France for many years the civil courts have put pressure on a reluctant husband to grant his divorced wife a get by ordering him to pay her damages in respect of the damage caused by his refusal to do so. Jewish religious authorities sometimes work with the secular authorities to solve a problem embedded in Jewish law. In the United Kingdom, for example, Parliament passed the Divorce (Religious Marriages) Act in 2002 in an attempt to help the Orthodox Jewish authorities in solving the problem of the aguna.

Humanistic Judaism Movement founded in the 1960s that sees God and religion as human inventions and places humanity at the centre of its world view: Judaism is a cultural creation of the Jewish people. Seeing itself as an outgrowth of the ENLIGHTENMENT, it maintains that reason is the best key to truth and places a strong premium on ethics and cultural values. Humanistic Jews embrace Jewish history and cultural manifestations, and observe Jewish festivals and life-cycle events in a strictly secular fashion. Humanistic communities are led by guides, senior leaders and rabbis trained by an institute based in Detroit and Jerusalem. The International Federation of Secular Humanistic Jews (founded in 1985) serves as an umbrella organization for national associations in several countries.

humility A virtue that is frequently commended in the rabbinic literature. According to the Torah, Moses was the most humble man in the world (Numbers 12.3), and the Mishnah describes humility as one of the marks of a disciple of Abraham. Solomon IBN GABIROL wrote: 'I find humility a greater help than all my fellow men.' *See also* IBN SAHULA, ISAAC.

Hymn of Glory (Shir ha-Kavod) Medieval composition, also known as Anim Zmirot ('pleasant songs I sing'), from its opening words. The hymn originated in the circles of the CHASIDEI ASHKENAZ, and its author is commonly thought to be JUDAH THE CHASID. It is a passionate song of love to God, full of mystical terms and images. It still has an honoured place in the Ashkenazi liturgy: in many congregations it is sung before the open ark at the end of the Additional Service every Sabbath, the singing often being led (inappropriate as it may seem) by a young child.

Hymn of Unity (Shir ha-Yichud) Medieval composition divided into seven sections, one of which is read at the end of each morning service of the week by Ashkenazim. The hymn originated in the circles of the CHASIDEI ASHKENAZ, and its author is thought to be JUDAH THE CHASID or someone close to him. It combines mystical ideas (including the apparent PANENTHEISM of such expressions as 'You surround all and fill all and when all exists you are in all') with philosophical teachings originating with SA'ADYA GA'ON and Solomon IBN GABIROL.

Ibn Attar, Chayyim (1696–1743) Teacher and author. Born in Morocco, he had a Talmudic and kabbalistic upbringing, and felt called to contribute to the messianic redemption by settling in the Holy Land. On the way he stopped in Leghorn, where he established a YESHIVA. Eventually he arrived in Jerusalem, and founded another yeshiva for ascetic Talmudists, known as the Midrash Keneset Yisra'el. (The building is still extant, but the yeshiva ceased to function in 1866.) The most influential of his writings is his mystical commentary to the Torah, entitled *Or ha-Chayyim* (*Light of Life*, with a play on his name). This deeply personal and idiosyncratic work makes extensive use of allegory and interprets Torah in the light of KABBALA. In places the author describes his own mystical experiences. The work was very popular among CHASIDIM, who saw him as a forerunner; he was particularly admired by the BAAL SHEM TOV, who considered him a kindred spirit. Among Chasidim he is called the Holy Or Ha-chayyim.

Ibn Daud, Abraham (c. 1110–80) Aristotelian philosopher. Born in Cordova, he lived mainly in Toledo. In his book *The Exalted Faith* (written in Arabic but preserved only in Hebrew translation, under the title *Emuna Rama*) he argues that there is no conflict between faith and reason, and that the doctrines of Judaism are in harmony with those of ARISTOTELIANISM, except that he rejects the idea of the eternity of matter in favour of the doctrine of creation ex nihilo. His historical work *The Book of Tradition* (*Séfer ha-Kabbala*), written in Hebrew, traces the history of the chain of rabbinic tradition from the revelation at Sinai to his own day. It is an important source for Jewish history.

Ibn Ezra, Abraham (c. 1090–1164 or 1167) Biblical commentator, poet and philosopher. Born in Tudela, a border town of Muslim Spain, he spent some fifty years of his life in Spain. From 1140 on he lived a wandering life, travelling to Rome and other cities of Italy, then on to Provence and northern France and as far as London, where some think he died. He produced an enormous number of treatises on mathematics and astronomy, philosophy, language and many other subjects, which he wrote in Hebrew as the people among whom he lived did not understand Arabic. He also translated scientific works from Arabic into Hebrew. He has left a considerable body of sacred and secular Hebrew poetry, some of it humorous, some of it philosophical and some deeply religious. He is best known, however, for his biblical commentaries, which cover most books of the Bible. Ibn Ezra's commentaries have never achieved quite the same popularity as RASHI's, however, which is not surprising since they are much more demanding to read. Whereas Rashi's simple Hebrew can be followed by anyone with a modestly competent knowledge of the language, and his aim is to familiarize the reader with the traditional interpretation of the text, Ibn Ezra is an exact and exacting scholar, with a keen interest in philology and philosophy, who hardly lets slip an opportunity to expand on an unusual grammatical form or a philosophical idea. And whereas Rashi is content to follow Midrashic interpretations, Ibn Ezra does not hesitate to reject the traditional interpretation if it conflicts with his own scientific understanding of the text. At times he even permits himself obliquely worded comments which depart abruptly from traditional beliefs about the character of the Bible. He is evidently sceptical, for example, about the idea that the whole Torah was written by Moses, and he is also the first critic to suggest that the book of Isaiah was the work of more than one author. His commentary is one of the finest monuments of medieval Jewish scholarship, and both in its general method and its individual insights it anticipates more modern developments in biblical criticism.

Ibn Ezra, Moses (c. 1055–after 1138) Hebrew poet and philosopher. Considered by some the finest Hebrew poet of Muslim Spain, Ibn Ezra was born into a distinguished family in Granada, but ended his days an exile in the Christian north of the country. In addition to his poetry, he wrote two prose works in Arabic, a philosophical work of Neoplatonist inspiration on figurative language and a book about poetics. Several of his poems have entered the Sefardi liturgy, the best-loved being 'El nora alila' (or 'ngalila' in the Western Sefardi pronunciation), 'God, awesome in deeds, Grant us absolution at the hour of the closing of the gates', which is sung at the beginning of the NE'ILA service.

Ibn Gabirol, Solomon (1021 or 1022–c. 1070) Hebrew poet and philosopher in Muslim Spain. Born in Malaga, on the south coast, he spent most of his life in Saragossa.

Solomon Ibn Gabirol's major philosophical work, *The Fountain of Life*, which later came to exercise an important influence on Christian scholastic thought, is a work of pure metaphysics, divorced from any particular religious context. The same metaphysical ideas are expressed in religious terms in his long liturgical poem 'The Royal Crown', which in some rites has been incorporated in the prayers for the Day of Atonement. To the apparently intractable question how the imperfect world which we know can derive from God, who is a perfect, utterly spiritual being, Ibn Gabirol responds with a typically Neoplatonic theory of emanations: from the divine will (which is in a sense identical with God, yet distinct in its outward effects) there emanate the two basic principles of 'general matter' and 'general form', giving rise to a whole chain of emanations which ends with the present world, in which the divine will is still present. Man is a microcosm, partaking of both the intelligible and the corporeal worlds, and so able to grasp the spiritual, immaterial forms by his own powers. The details of this sophisticated system are far from clear, but the intention is obvious: to preserve the link between God and man while safeguarding the absolute perfection of God. He has left us a corpus of sacred and secular poetry of immense richness. Several of his poems besides 'The Royal Crown' have been incorporated in the Sefardi liturgy, as has his versified arrangement of the 613 commandments (AZHAROT).

Ibn Pakuda, Bachya *See* BACHYA IBN PAKUDA.

Ibn Sahula, Isaac (late 13th century) Kabbalist and fabulist. A member of a mystical circle in Guadalajara and a friend of the author of the ZOHAR, Isaac Ibn Sahula has left us a long and fascinating work in Hebrew rhymed prose entitled *Meshal ha-Kadmoni* (*An Ancient Fable*), a learned and serious-minded entertainment which takes the form of a debate between a cynic and a moralist on a number of key concepts (wisdom and knowledge, repentance, good counsel, humility and awe). It is the first work to mention the Zohar, but is largely free from mystical content or language; it is also the first literary work to sing the praises of MAIMONIDES. The author's expressed aim is to wean his readers away from foreign literature to Hebrew. The work is full of animal fables, some of which have been identified as describing cryptically intrigues at the court of King Alfonso X (Alfonso the Wise). It became very popular, and was the first Hebrew book to be printed with illustrations.

Ibn Tibbon, Judah (12th century) Translator. The founder of a dynasty of translators, Judah was born in Granada, in Muslim Spain, and settled in Lunel, in southern France. He conceived it as his mission to translate the great Arabic works of Jewish religious philosophy into Hebrew so that they would be accessible to Jews in Christian Europe. Among his many translations are SA'ADYA GA'ON's *Beliefs and Convictions*, BACHYA IBN PAKUDA's *Duties of the Heart* and JUDAH HA-LEVI's *The Khazar*.

Ibn Tibbon, Samuel (c. 1150–1230) Translator. Son of Judah Ibn Tibbon (*see* previous entry). His most famous translation is that of MAIMONIDES' *Guide of the Perplexed*. Samuel took immense pains to understand the often deliberately obscure language of the *Guide*, and corresponded with the author, asking for his advice on the translation of difficult passages. (The correspondence survives.) His primary aim was to be faithful to the original, and he took such care to cling closely to the word order of the Arabic that his translation strains the Hebrew language. For many readers down the centuries Ibn Tibbon's translation was the *Guide*, and its ingenious choices in rendering Arabic philosophical terminology have become standard in Hebrew. He also translated other works by Maimonides.

idolatry (in Hebrew, avoda zara, literally 'alien worship') The worship of images of the Divine. The Bible strongly condemns the worship by Israelites of any deity other than God, and the second of the TEN COMMANDMENTS forbids the making as well as the worship of any image or likeness (Exodus 20.4–5, Deuteronomy 5.8–9; *see* ART; GOLDEN CALF). It is one of the offences for which the death penalty is stipulated. In rabbinic Judaism idolatry is considered one of the three most heinous crimes (with sexual impropriety and bloodshed), which are not to be committed even at the cost of one's life (*see* MARTYRDOM; PIKÚ'ACH NÉFESH). An entire tractate of the Mishnah and the Talmud is devoted to the subject (*see* AVODA ZARA). The prohibition on idolatry is also one of the NOACHIAN COMMANDMENTS held to be binding on non-Jews.

ijma' (Arabic) In Karaite jurisprudence, CONSENSUS, agreement of scholars on the interpretation of law. The term is used in the same sense in Islamic jurisprudence.

illegitimacy See MAMZER.

imitatio Dei (Latin, 'imitation of God') The doctrine that humans should endeavour to take God as their model in conducting their lives. It may seem like a daring doctrine, given the fundamental difference in nature between God and humanity, but there is a clear warrant for it in the words of God in the Torah: 'You shall be holy for I, the Lord your God, am holy' (Leviticus 19.2). This same pattern of reasoning is applied by the rabbis and the medieval moralists to a wide range of human behaviour, often with great ingenuity. An early rabbinic comment on the expression 'to walk in his [God's] ways' (Deuteronomy 11.22) explains: 'Just as he is called Merciful, you should be merciful; just as he is called Compassionate, you should be compassionate'. Another comment, on Deuteronomy 12.5, 'You shall walk after the Lord your God', begins by remarking that it is impossible literally to 'walk after' God, who is called a 'devouring fire' in Deuteronomy 4.24, and continues: 'What the verse means is that you should walk after the qualities of the Holy One, blessed be He. As he clothes the naked [Genesis 3.21] you should clothe the naked. As he visits the sick [Genesis 18.1] you should visit the sick. As he comforts mourners [Genesis 25.11] so you should comfort mourners. As he buries the dead [Deuteronomy 34.6] so too you should bury the dead' (Bavli, Sota 14a). Maimonides, who denied that one could apply positive attributes to God (see VIA NEGATIVA), wrote that the only reason that the Torah ascribes to the Deity attributes such as 'long-suffering', 'abundant in mercy', 'righteous' and so forth is to teach us to cultivate similar qualities in ourselves by imitation. It is worth noting that the qualities in question are not those commanded in the halacha, such as honesty, respect for parents and elders, etc.; the doctrine of imitatio thus has the effect of providing a scriptural warrant for what are universally admitted to be desirable traits. The kabbalists invested the doctrine with a mystical meaning: to imitate God is to bring the various SEFIROT into play.

immersion (in Hebrew, tevila) Immersion in water of both individuals and utensils (for example in preparation for Passover) is practised as a means to ritual purification. See also BATHING.

immortality The idea that humans are composed of an immortal soul and a perishable body entered Judaism from Greek thought in the Hellenistic period. Despite the many philosophical problems associated with it, the doctrine has achieved enduring popularity. It is assumed at several points in the liturgy, as in this ancient prayer: 'My God, the soul you have given me is pure. You formed it and breathed it into me; you preserve it within me, and you will take it from me to life everlasting.' There is a clear allusion here to the biblical creation story (Genesis 2.7) – a fine example of the fusion of biblical and Greek elements in Judaism, which is already attested in Kohélet 12.7 (assumed to have been written under Greek influence): 'The dust shall return to the earth as it was, and the spirit shall return to God who gave it'. The Greek Jewish book called The Wisdom of Solomon (3.1–4) clearly embraces the doctrine of immortality: the righteous only appear to die; in reality their souls are in the hand of God. In the rabbinic literature the idea of the immortal soul is combined with that of the resurrection of the body and is generally subordinated to it (*see* AFTERLIFE), and this combination continues in the thought of some medieval writers such as SA'ADYA GA'ON. MAIMONIDES, however, gives more weight to immortality. Resurrection is only temporary, but the soul can achieve immortality through metaphysical contemplation – this is the ultimate purpose of human existence. (Maimonides asserts that this is what the ancient rabbis meant when they spoke of the 'world to come'.) In the modern age, as belief in bodily resurrection has been questioned, the idea of immortality has endured. Moses MENDELSSOHN's work *Phaedo* (1767) is a philosophical investigation of immortality, loosely based on Plato's dialogue of the same name. Immortality is affirmed in the early phase of American Reform in the PITTSBURGH PLATFORM, and is also strongly endorsed by some Orthodox authors. *See also* GILGUL.

impurity (in Hebrew, tuma) Ritual disqualification, to be distinguished from uncleanness. The taint of impurity, which disqualifies an individual from entering the sanctuary, eating sacred foods and touching sacred objects, is regulated in some detail in the Torah, particularly in the book of Leviticus. It can result from a wide range of causes, and is generally remedied by bathing. The subject occupies a whole order of the Mishnah and Tosefta (*see* TOHOROT), and the rabbis greatly extend the scope of the biblical regulations by introducing the concept of transmitted impurity, according to which someone who contracts impurity, for example by contact with a corpse, can transmit it to other people or objects. Only one tractate in this order, NIDDA, dealing with menstrual impurity, is taken up and commented on in the Talmud (both versions), presumably in line with a general belief that since the ending of the Temple cult most forms of biblical impurity no longer apply.

incense A mixture of aromatic substances burnt twice daily in the Temple. The recipe given in the Torah (Exodus 30.34) lists four ingredients (stacte, onycha, galbanum and frankincense), which are blended in equal quantities and seasoned with salt. The Talmud, however, records an ancient tradition mentioning eleven ingredients (Keritot 6a). This passage is still read in traditional synagogues today, even though there is no physical trace of incense in the worship of the synagogue. The practice may be associated with the kabbalistic idea that the smoke of the incense symbolizes the ascent of all creation to the SEFIROT, and that of the Sefirot themselves to the EIN SOF. According to the ZOHAR: 'Whoever reflects on the section on the incense and recites it daily will be saved from all evil … But it must be read with devotion.' The imagery of incense has entered several prayers in the liturgy.

incest The forbidden degrees of sexual relations with a close relative are listed in the Torah (Leviticus 18.6–18). These primary degrees were extended by the rabbis by the addition of several secondary degrees (Bavli, Yevamot 21a). The product of a union contravening one of the primary degrees is a MAMZER. Incest is mentioned in the Talmud (Bavli, Sanhedrin 74a) as one of three acts which one should not commit even if the alternative is certain death.

individual, autonomy of It is often said that Judaism, in contrast with

Christianity, is more concerned with the welfare, and ultimately the salvation, of the community than with that of the individual. This is true only up to a point. Both in the Bible and in the rabbinic literature the main emphasis is certainly on the whole Jewish people, or the whole of humankind, but in the Middle Ages a concern for the individual comes to the fore. MAIMONIDES, for example, interprets Judaism in such a way that it is not an end in itself but rather a means to the perfectibility of the individual. In the KABBALA, each human soul is a spark of Adam's soul, and each individual has a part to play in releasing the holy sparks, in accordance with his own soul-root. This idea becomes even more marked in CHASIDISM. In the modern period, with political EMANCIPATION, a tension became evident between individual and society, and also between the claims of two different conceptions of society. The idea of the nation requires that the needs of the individual should be subordinated to those of society as a whole. The rabbinate and the Jewish leadership found themselves fighting a rearguard action to retain the loyalty of their following. The tension is at its clearest in the celebrated words of Count Stanislas de Clermont-Tonnerre, a revolutionary and supporter of Jewish emancipation, to the French National Assembly during the debate on the eligibility of the Jews for Citizenship of France on 23 December 1789: 'As a nation, the Jews should be denied everything; as individuals, they should be granted everything.' In other words, the benefits of emancipation were only available to Jews as individuals, on condition they abandoned their claims for special treatment as a nation. Very many Jews over the following two centuries have succumbed to this temptation, despite the strenuous efforts of the rabbis and lay leaders of the community to retain their allegiance. This extreme example highlights the conflict between nation and individual in its most acute form, but there is always a certain tension between the individual's sense of his or her own needs and the state's requirement of obedience.

Plato attempted to harmonize the two by arguing that true freedom for the individual can only be found within the framework of the wise laws of the state, and his philosophy has exerted a strong influence on Judaism. Biblical law was seen by many to be a harsh burden imposed on the people of Israel (one ancient commentator goes so far as speaking of God picking up Mount Sinai, which symbolizes the divine legislation, and trapping the people underneath it), but a clever preacher explained that the text had been misread: the Torah does not say that the word of God was engraved (charut) on the tablets of stone, but that freedom (cherut) was on the tablets of stone (Exodus 32.16). Obedience to the law is real freedom: the law of God, as interpreted by rabbinic tradition, is not constraint but freedom, whereas what most people take for freedom is actually a kind of slavery. This view was very strong in rabbinic Judaism, but it had to face a keen challenge from KARAISM, which attached importance to communal CONSENSUS (ijma'), but also insisted on the judgment of the individual. Another outlet for individualism is found in personal devotion, which is attested in the Bible, particularly in the book of Psalms, and throughout the history of Judaism, being particularly prominent in the mystical tradition, in kabbalism and Chasidism.

ineffable name (in Hebrew, shem ha-meforash, 'explicit name') Holiest name of

God, only pronounced once a year in the Temple, and now never spoken aloud. The name in question is the TETRAGRAMMATON (YHWH or YHVH), which was only pronounced by the High Priest when he entered the inner shrine, the Holy of Holies, on the Day of ATONEMENT. A rabbinic tradition holds that the pronunciation was transmitted by the sages to their disciples once, or perhaps twice, in seven years (Bavli, Kiddushin 71a). Somehow, however, the knowledge died out. Nowadays it is pronounced ADONAI.

infertility The inability to have children is particularly associated in the Bible and the rabbinic literature with women, and is variously regarded as a misfortune, a curse, or a punishment for sins. Three of the four MATRIARCHS, Sarah, Rebecca/Rebekah and Rachel, all suffered from infertility and only managed to conceive after much prayer. The same is true of Hannah, the mother of the prophet Samuel, in the first book of Samuel. A wife's infertility is all the more worrying since procreation is regarded in the halacha as a divine command (Genesis 1.28); even though the command is addressed to men and women alike the rabbis rule that it is binding on men but not on women (Mishnah, Yevamot 6.6). They also say that a man 'should not abstain' even if his wife has been infertile for ten years. Supporting or teaching a child is described as tantamount to fulfilling the commandment of procreation (Bavli, Sanhedrin 19b).

ingathering *See* AMIDA; EXILE AND RETURN; MESSIAH; ZIONISM.

Isaac Second of the biblical patriarchs, son of Abraham and Sarah, husband of Rebekah (also written Rebecca) and father of Jacob and Esau (Genesis 21–35). The promises made to Abraham are renewed through Isaac rather than his older half-brother ISHMAEL. He is circumcised at the age of eight days (Genesis 21.4), thus setting the pattern for the CIRCUMCISION of Jewish boys to this day. He narrowly escapes being sacrificed by his father (*see* AKEDA) and his willingness to be sacrificed made him a model for martyrs in later times (*see* KIDDUSH HA-SHEM).

Isaiah (Yesháya) Biblical prophet and the book bearing his name. Isaiah son of Amoz is portrayed in his book as living in the latter part of the 8th century BCE, against the background of the conquest of the northern kingdom of Israel by the Assyrians (722–721) and the siege of Jerusalem by Sennacherib (701). However, references to the 6th-century Persian King Cyrus II and to the Babylonian exile and the return have led scholars (starting with Abraham IBN EZRA) to the conclusion that chapters 40–66 are the work of a later prophet (referred to as Second Isaiah or Deutero-Isaiah), an idea that is roundly repudiated by traditionalists and many Orthodox Jews. It is now widely held that there is a Third (or Trito-) Isaiah, who wrote chapters 56–66 in the late 6th or early 5th century BCE. The book of Isaiah is a source of many of the HAFTAROT, notably the seven 'haftarot of consolation' that are read on the Sabbaths between the 9th of Av and New Year.

Ishmael In the Torah, elder son of Abraham by his wife's maid, Hagar (Genesis 16–25). He is driven out with his mother at the request of Sarah, and becomes a bowman. His daughter marries Esau. In post-biblical usage, Ishmael stands for the Arabs, and later for the Muslim world.

Islam and Judaism Jews have lived and generally prospered within Muslim lands in Europe, North Africa and the Middle East until modern times. Together with Christians (and with Zoroastrians in Iran) they had the status of dhimmis (or zimmis) (protected persons). Dhimma status, according to Muslim law, guaranteed the subjects' life, property and religious practices in return for payment by each adult male of the poll tax (jizya). This mark of subjugation was probably more of a humiliation than a financial burden. Despite this guarantee, occasional periods of fanatical persecution are documented, but these have been exceptional. Islam has exercised a strong influence on both Rabbanite and Karaite thought, practice and general culture. In the modern age, as Jews in many Muslim lands acquired various rights and privileges that were at odds with the rules of dhimma, the ancient system was subverted, giving rise to hostility on the part of traditionally minded Muslims; this situation was greatly exacerbated by the arrival of ZIONISM, and the creation of a Jewish state in the heart of the Islamic Middle East. Meanwhile Jews have been disproportionately prominent in the scholarly study of Islam in Europe. An early example is Abraham GEIGER, whose 1833 doctoral dissertation was on the subject of Jewish influence on Muhammad and the Qur'an. Franz ROSENZWEIG reveals an interest in Islam (which he encountered in the Balkans in World War I) in *The Star of Redemption*: following JUDAH HA-LEVI, he accepts it as part of the monotheistic family, but claims that it is a civilization rather than a religion. Today there is a growing interest in Muslim–Jewish understanding and dialogue.

Israel (in Hebrew, Yisra'el) In the Torah, name given to JACOB, supposedly meaning 'exerting princely power with God and men' (Genesis 32.28). The descendants of Jacob are called the Benei Yisra'el or Israelites. In rabbinic and later usage, the name designates the whole Jewish community, or an individual Jew.

Israel, Land of (in Hebrew, ÉRETS YISRA'EL) Land considered since the time of the rabbis to possess a special sanctity as the territory promised to the descendants of Abraham in the Torah. In fact the borders of the land as defined by the rabbis do not coincide with those mentioned in the Torah (e.g. Genesis 15.18, Numbers 34), which are not consistent among themselves. As the rabbis are concerned with the purity of the land and the reciprocal COVENANT, they dwell on biblical agricultural laws (such as first fruits, seven-year rest and jubilee) regarded as binding only in the land, as opposed to those (like the Sabbath and DIETARY REGULATIONS) that are to be observed everywhere. The rabbis speak of the exile of the people from its land as a national calamity (*see* EXILE AND RETURN). This attitude is reflected in the liturgy, and has been influential in the mainly secular ideology of ZIONISM. *See also* GUSH EMUNIM; PALESTINE.

Israel, state of (in Hebrew, medinat Yisra'el) State in the Middle East created on the ending of the British Mandate in May 1948, with an overwhelmingly Jewish majority and a strongly Jewish identity. The creation of the state was the fulfilment of the dream of ZIONISM. Although the Zionist leadership was essentially secular, and in part anti-religious, there was a religious Zionist element (*see* MIZRACHI), and there was also a perceived need not to alienate the religious Jews locally and worldwide. The constitution of the state consequently represents a compromise between religious and SECULAR JUDAISM; conflicts related to this compromise have never been far in the background and have often broken out into civil commotion and even bloodshed. There is no separation of religion and state and no civil marriage. Religious observances such as the Sabbath and DIETARY REGULATIONS are obligatory in certain public sectors. Rabbinical courts are recognized by the state and integrated into the state's judicial system, and their rabbis and officials are state functionaries. On the other hand, Jewish law (HALACHA) is not the law of the land, although it has some influence on it. The religious establishment in Israel is largely Orthodox and moderately traditional; extreme traditionalists tend to keep aloof from its institutions (*see* CHAREDI; NETÚREI KÁRTA). It is only recently that Reform and Conservative Judaism have gained some hard-won and grudging concessions.

Israel Abu-Chatsera *See* BABA SALI.

Israel ben Eliezer *See* BAAL SHEM TOV.

ísru chag ('bind the festival [offering]', see Psalm 118.27) Day following each of the three major FESTIVALS, Sukkot, Passover and Shavuot. It is traditionally considered a joyful day, on which fasting is forbidden and funeral eulogies are not to be pronounced.

Isserles, Moses (c. 1525–72) Halachist. A prolific author, he is best remembered for his supplement to the SHULCHAN ARUCH, annotating the Sefardi work from an Ashkenazi halachic perspective. He also wrote an Ashkenazi commentary on the ARBA'A TURIM, entitled *Darchei Moshe* (*The Ways of Moses*). In this work he formulated the principle that CUSTOM has the force of law, thus ascribing enhanced authority to the ACHARONIM as against the RISHONIM. The effect of Isserles' work was to make the Sefardi codes, particularly the Shulchan Aruch, palatable in Ashkenaz. A man of versatile learning, he compiled various other halachic works, but he also wrote on kabbala, as well as compiling notes to MAIMONIDES' *Guide*. He lived in Cracow and is buried in the courtyard of the synagogue there that bears his name.

issur ('prohibition', 'prohibited object') Commonly encountered in the phrase issur ve-hétter ('prohibition and dispensation'; *see* HÉTTER), which denotes the area of ritual law, as opposed to civil and criminal law.

Iyov Hebrew name of the biblical book of Job.

Iyyar Eighth month of the year counting from New Year; second counting from Passover, roughly corresponding to May. LAG BA-ÓMER falls on the 18th of Iyyar.

Jacob (Ya'akov) In the Torah, son of Isaac and Rebekah (or Rebecca), also called Israel. He is considered as one of the three PATRIARCHS. The second half of the book of Genesis (25–50) is largely taken up with the narrative of his life: his struggles with his twin brother ESAU, his marriage to Leah and Rachel, two daughters of his cousin Laban, the birth of his twelve sons and one daughter to his two wives and two concubines, the family's emigration from the Land of Canaan to Egypt, Jacob's death in Egypt and his burial in the family tomb in Hebron.

Jacob ben Asher (c. 1270–1340) Halachist, also known as Baal ha-Turim (Master of the Turim), after his best-known work, the ARBA'A TURIM. A son of ASHER BEN YECHIEL, he was born in Germany and moved to Toledo in Spain with his father. In his book he aimed to bridge the gulf between Ashkenazi and Spanish approaches to halacha. He also wrote a commentary to the Torah.

Jacobs, Louis (1920–2006) English rabbi and theologian. An extraordinarily prolific writer on virtually every aspect of Judaism and a popular Orthodox rabbi, Jacobs became the focus of controversy (known subsequently as the Jacobs Affair) in 1961, when an invitation to become principal of the Orthodox rabbinical seminary, Jews College, was vetoed by the then CHIEF RABBI, on grounds of heresy, since (it was alleged) he had questioned the doctrine of TORA MIN HA-SHAMÁYIM in his book *We Have Reason to Believe* (1957). The controversy was intensified in 1964 when a rabbinic appointment to an Orthodox synagogue was again countermanded by the Chief Rabbi. His supporters established him in a synagogue of his own, where he enjoyed freedom from hierarchical interference. Eventually this synagogue became the flagship of the MASORTI movement in Britain.

Jamnia *See* YAVNE.

Jeremiah (Yirmíya) (d. after 582 BCE) Prophet whose prophecy is contained in the biblical book that bears his name, written during the collapse of the Assyrian empire and the rise of the neo-Babylonian, whose ruler Nebuchadnezzar destroyed the kingdom of Judah. Jeremiah interpreted these political events as God's will, and urged the people to submit to Babylon. According to the Talmud (Bavli, Bava Batra 15a) he is also the author of the books of Kings and Lamentations.

Jerusalem (Yerushaláyim) Capital of the kingdom of DAVID and now the capital of the state of ISRAEL. In Jewish law the city was invested with supreme sanctity, because of the presence of the Temple. It is referred to in the liturgy as the 'holy city', and the AMIDA is said facing towards Jerusalem. The restoration of Jerusalem at the end of time is the theme of several prayers, and the words 'Next year in Jerusalem' conclude the SÉDER and the Day of ATONEMENT service.

Jerusalem Day *See* YOM YERUSHALÁYIM.

Jew (in Hebrew, Yehudi; plural Yehudim) The term is derived ultimately from JUDAH, the name of a region in the Land of Israel centred on the city of Jerusalem. Under Persian rule (late 6th century to late 4th century BCE) this was organized as a province under the name Yahud. The Hebrew term derived from this name, Yehudi, occurs in the Bible, e.g. of Mordecai in the book of Esther (3.4, 9.31); in the same book (8.17) a related verb is used in the meaning 'to become a Jew', revealing the beginning of an evolution beyond simply a geographical origin. Today the term denotes someone of Jewish birth or religion, in accordance with the traditional halachic definition of a Jew as a person born to a Jewish mother or duly converted to JUDAISM. Attempts have been made, and continue, to modify or restrict the definition, e.g., on the liberal side, by admitting those born to a Jewish father and non-Jewish mother, by insisting on some Jewish upbringing, or on the traditional side by restricting conversion to Orthodox authorities.

Jewish Theological Seminary of America Conservative rabbinical college based in New York, with branches or affiliated institutions in Jerusalem, Buenos Aires and Los Angeles. Originally founded in 1886, it was refashioned under the presidency of Solomon SCHECHTER and became one of the foremost rabbinical seminaries and centres of Jewish learning in the world.

Jewishness The fact of being Jewish (generally by birth and allegiance rather than by religion).

Jewry 1 Jewish quarter of a town. **2** Collective term for Jews, as in 'world Jewry', 'Anglo-Jewry'.

Job (Iyov) Hero of the biblical book that bears his name. Job (who is not portrayed particularly as a Jew) is a man of exemplary righteousness whose faith in God is put to the test in the framework of a kind of wager between God and Satan. The bulk of the book consists of a long and skilfully crafted poetic meditation on the problem of evil. Job's historicity is debated in the Talmud (Bavli, Bava Batra 14b–15a): according to one view he was a contemporary of Abraham, while others maintained that the story is merely a parable and Job himself never existed. The book is read by Sefardim on the 9th of Av (TISH'A BE-AV).

Joel (Yo'el) Biblical book, second of the Twelve Minor Prophets. Nothing is known about Joel's life. His book is notable for its visions of the 'Day of the Lord', the future time when judgment will be passed on the wicked.

Jonah (Yona) Biblical book, fifth of the Twelve Minor Prophets. On the basis of a mention in 2 Kings 14.25 Jonah has been dated in the 8th century BCE, but his book can be (and often is) read as a fable about the value of repentance. For this reason the book has been designated as the prophetic reading for the afternoon of the Day of ATONEMENT. The book also teaches about the prophetic calling: Jonah is sent by God to preach repentance to the people of Nineveh, but tries to escape from his mission. God, however, calls him back; it seems there is no escape for a prophet from preaching God's word wherever he is sent.

Jonas, Hans (1903–93) Philosopher. Born in Germany, he lived at various times in England, Palestine/Israel and Canada before settling in 1955 in New York, where he taught philosophy at the New School for Social Research until his retirement in 1976. His best-known books are *The Phenomenology of Life* (1966) and *Das Prinzip Verantwortung* (*The Imperative of Responsibility*, 1984). In the latter he formulated the new ethical demand: 'Act so that the effects of your action are compatible with the permanence of genuine human life on Earth'. Jonas developed a distinctive line of thinking about the Holocaust: God was present at Auschwitz but incapable of intervening because he had renounced his mastery of history in favour of humanity. The posthumous collection of essays *Mortality and Morality: A Search for Good After Auschwitz* (ed. L. Vogel, 1996) is a good introduction to his thought, including his insistence on individual responsibility and on the place of the individual in the midst of the dialectic between reason and faith.

Joseph (Yosef) In the Torah, son of Jacob and Rachel. Sold into slavery by his brothers, he rises to become viceroy of Egypt through his remarkable capacity to interpret dreams. He is the only one of Jacob's sons not to give his name to a tribe; instead his two sons, Ephraim and Manasseh, are the ancestors of two half-tribes.

Josephus, Flavius (c. 38–c. 100) Historian and apologist. Born in the Land of Israel, Josephus participated in his youth in the Great Revolt against the Romans (66–73), and later settled in Rome, where he wrote, mainly in Greek, about Judaism. His most famous and most substantial books are his account of the revolt (*The Jewish War*) and a comprehensive presentation of Jewish history based in part on the Bible (*Jewish Antiquities or Jewish Archaeology*). He also wrote a defence of Judaism against various detractors (*Against Apion*), and a defence of his own conduct in the revolt (*Life*). All these works survive in Greek. They are an invaluable source, particularly for the Jewish history of his time, although naturally they cannot be read uncritically.

Joshua (Yehoshú'a) Biblical book, the first of the Former Prophets. It tells the story of Joshua, Moses' assistant and disciple, who leads the people of Israel into the promised land after the death of Moses, and supervises the division of the land among the tribes. According to the Mishnah (Avot 1.1) Joshua was an essential link in the chain of the transmission of the Torah: 'Moses received the Torah from Sinai and transmitted it to Joshua, who handed it on to the elders ...'

Judaeo-Spanish *See* HAKETÍYA; JUDEZMO; LADINO.

Judah (Yehudá) In the Torah, son of Jacob and Leah, who later gives his name to the largest of the tribes and eventually to the southern kingdom centred on JERUSALEM after the death of Solomon. He is an ancestor of King DAVID, and consequently of the Davidic MESSIAH. *See also* JEW.

Judah ha-Levi (c. 1075–c. 1141) Hebrew poet and religious thinker. Born in Spain, where he spent most of his life, Judah died in the Land of Israel, as we learn from letters in the Cairo GENIZA. Passionate yearning for Zion (an unusual subject for Hebrew poetry at the time) is a major theme in his verse, and it seems likely that he died on a pilgrimage to the Holy Land. His religious poetry is sublime, and several of his creations have earned a place in the liturgy, for example a hymn for the Day of ATONEMENT with the refrain 'Oh, that I might be a perfect slave of God my maker; though others drive me away, he always draws me near'. Besides his abundant corpus of poetry, Judah is also the author of an Arabic prose work, commonly known as *The Khazar* (the full title is *The Book of the Khazar: A Book of Argument and Demonstration in Defence of the Despised Faith*; it is sometimes referred to by its Hebrew title, *Kuzari*). It is an account of Judaism, setting out its merits in comparison to Christianity and Islam and to Aristotelian philosophy, and insisting on national experience and the continuity of Jewish tradition as outweighing the dogmatic claims of the other contenders.

Judah the Chasid (d. 1217) Ethical writer and pietist. One of the leading figures among the CHASIDEI ASHKENAZ, Judah was born in Speyer in the Rhineland and died in Regensburg. The SÉFER CHASIDIM used to be attributed to him; in fact it is the work of several hands.

Judah the Maccabee (d. 161 BCE) Military hero of the HASMONEAN REVOLT. He was one of the five sons of the priest MATTATHIAS of Modi'in, and assumed command of the rebel armies after his father's death. By 164 he had captured the Jerusalem Temple from the Seleucids and rededicated it to Jewish worship, the event that is commemorated at CHANUKKA. *See also* MACCABEES.

Judah the Nasi (d. c. 229) Scholar, communal leader, and supposed editor of the MISHNAH. Little is known of his life. He lived in Galilee, claimed descent from HILLEL, and was the hereditary ethnarch of the Jews (i.e. recognized by the Romans as the titular head of all the Jews in the empire). It is unclear how much of a hand he had in the compilation of the Mishnah. In the Talmud he is referred to simply as 'Rabbi'.

Judaism Term denoting the religious beliefs and practices of the Jews, so used by analogy with such words as Hellenism or Hinduism. Of Greek derivation, originally it denoted a JEWRY (1), but soon acquired the sense of adherence to the Jewish way of life, and eventually to Jewish religious beliefs. In Hebrew, an abstract noun, yahadut, denoting life lived in obedience to God, is first found in the Midrash on Esther.

Judenstern (German, 'Jewish star') Name given in Germany to a star-shaped hanging lamp used on the Sabbath.

Judezmo Name given in some communities of the former Ottoman empire to the form of Spanish spoken by Jews in these communities. The name, also written Giudesmo, is thought to derive from Judaizmo, 'Judaism'. The same language is referred to by other names, such as Espanyol, Franco-Espanyol, Judeo-Espanyol, Judyo (or Jidyo), LADINO, Romance or Zargon. The term is occasionally applied to the semi-cursive Hebrew script in which the language used to be written.

Judges (Shoftim) Biblical book, one of the Former Prophets. Its narrative continues that of the book of Joshua, and describes the varying fortunes of the people of Israel under the leadership of a succession of twelve military leaders called 'judges'. According to rabbinic tradition the author of the book was the prophet SAMUEL.

justice Divine attribute and human virtue. God is understood to be supremely just, yet at the same time his strict justice is tempered by his COMPASSION. Several Hebrew words convey the notion of divine justice: tsédek, mishpat, DIN. The biblical attitude is summed up in Abraham's rhetorical question, 'Shall the judge of the whole earth not do justice [mishpat]?' (Genesis 18.25). Human justice is a reflection of divine justice, and can be seen as the basis of the legislation of the Torah: 'Justice [tsédek], justice shall you pursue' (Deuteronomy 16.20); 'He has told you, O mortal, what is good, and what more does the Lord ask of you than to do justice [mishpat], love kindness, and walk humbly with your God?' (Micah 6.8). The pursuit of justice in the world has been a guiding imperative of Judaism throughout its history. *See also* HUMAN RIGHTS; RIGHTEOUSNESS.

K

kabbala

('received tradition') In the rabbinic and medieval sources the word denotes various kinds of tradition, but eventually it became a technical term to denote an esoteric theosophical system that developed in Provence and northern Spain in the course of the 12th and 13th centuries, culminating in the ZOHAR, and was reshaped and given a new lease of life in 16th-century Safed by Isaac LURIA.

The kabbalists draw a sharp distinction between God as he is in himself (the unknowable EIN SOF) and as he manifests himself, through a process of emanation, by means of ten SEFIROT, which are powers within the Godhead. Unlike the Neoplatonist theory of emanations, which constitute a graduated bridge between the totally abstract God and the totally concrete earth, the Sefirot are all within God; nevertheless they do function as a bridge between the perfection of the Ein Sof and the imperfection of our world, and they are an answer to the same intellectual problem. The human being, according to the kabbalists, is an image of the Divine, and through meditation on the Sefirot combined with virtuous deeds is able to ascend, as it were, and influence the Divine. Evil deeds, on the other hand, send up negative impulses that can disrupt the harmony of the Sefirot and impede the flow of divine grace.

In the Lurianic system man's task is to release the trapped holy sparks that are imprisoned among the 'husks' (KELIPPOT) that belong to the realm of the demonic (SITRA ACHRA). He is thus at the heart of a cosmic conflict between the holy and the demonic, and is enjoined to labour for the victory of the holy by fulfilling the COMMANDMENTS, and thus promoting harmony on high. This is the meaning of TIKKUN.

Kabbala became a more public and popular ideology after the time of Luria and his circle, and it enjoyed a tremendous resurgence in the form of CHASIDISM. Chasidism does not put forward a single theology; in fact it very soon became fragmented into a number of schools, all of which share a vivid sense of the presence of the divine energy within everything. This idea is pushed to its limit in the most intellectual branch of Chasidism, the Lithuanian or Chabad branch. TSIMTSUM, which in the Lurianic system preserves the Infinite from being directly implicated in the creation, does not really take place. Everything is in God, and from God's point of view the created universe does not really exist. This amounts to an extreme assertion of the unity of God, for all multiplicity is a kind of illusion. Such PANENTHEISM was strongly attacked by opponents of Chasidism, such as the VILNA GA'ON. His contemporary the great Prague Talmudist Ezekiel LANDAU was also deeply suspicious of kabbala, and it was partly under his influence that the Austrian emperors Joseph II and Franz Joseph II forbade the importation of kabbalistic literature into the empire. Jewish scholars, religious modernists and maskilim shared an antipathy to the mystical tradition, in keeping with the anti-obscurantist spirit of the Enlightenment.

The modern study of the subject was pioneered by Gershom SCHOLEM, who laboured untiringly on kabbalistic and other mystical texts, analysing the ideas they contain and tracing their history and their relationship with traditions outside Judaism. Scholem was not a kabbalist himself; on the contrary, he was a product and an adherent of German-Jewish rationalism. But his scholarly work had the effect of encouraging a renewed interest in the kabbalistic tradition. Unfortunately, genuine interest in recovering an authentic Jewish heritage has become confused with a modern quest for esoteric exotica and a spiritual 'quick fix' (*see* NEO-KABBALISM).

kabbalat shabbat ('welcoming the Sabbath') Prayers welcoming the Sabbath, prefaced to the regular evening service on Sabbath eve. The practice was introduced by the Safed kabbalists in the 16th century, and has achieved widespread popularity. The prayers include LECHA DODI.

Kaddish (Aramaic, 'sanctification') Aramaic prayer that begins 'Magnified and sanctified be his great name in the world which he created according to his will.' Its main themes are praise of God and prayer for the coming of his kingdom (*see* KINGDOM OF GOD). It is recited traditionally at the end of each section of every service, and on some other occasions. There are five forms of the Kaddish: the short or 'half' Kaddish (or Kaddish le'éla), which punctuates the service at certain fixed points; the full Kaddish (Kaddish titkabbal), said after major sections of the service; the rabbis' Kaddish (Kaddish de-rabbanan), said after the recitation or study of a passage of rabbinical literature; the mourners' Kaddish (Kaddish yehe shelama); and the great Kaddish (Kaddish de-etchadita), said at a funeral or on concluding the study of a Talmudic tractate. The wording has been varied in some modern liturgies. Although it is commonly considered a mourner's prayer, the Kaddish contains no mention of death or of grief, but is a glorification of God and a prayer for the coming of his reign on earth. The recitation of this prayer by mourners, both at the cemetery and subsequently, represents an act of submission to the divine will, and is popularly thought to bring merit to the soul of the departed.

Kadosh baruch hu ('The Holy One, blessed be He') SUBSTITUTE NAME of God, used when he is spoken of in the third person. In its Aramaic form, Kudsha berich hu, it is found in the KADDISH; this may well be the original form. In its Hebrew version it came at some unknown time to replace HA-MAKOM.

Kafach, Yichya *See* DARDA.

Kagan, Rabbi Israel Meir *See* CHAFETS CHAYYIM.

kal (from Hebrew kahal, 'congregation') A synagogue or congregation. The term is found particularly in Greece and neighbouring countries of the former Ottoman empire, often as the first element in the name of the congregation.

kal nidrei *See* KOL NIDREI.

kal vachómer ('light and weight') Form of argument commonly used in rabbinic exegesis. It is an argument from the smaller or lighter to the greater or weightier case. For example, if a particular act is forbidden on an ordinary festival, it is all the more to be avoided on the Day of Atonement, which is a uniquely solemn day. It is the first of the THIRTEEN HERMENEUTICAL RULES.

kalam (Arabic, 'speech') Method of dialectical argument on matters of theological speculation, originating in 8th-century Islam and defined as 'the science of the foundations of the faith and the intellectual proofs in support of the theological truths'. The aim of kalam, largely apologetic, was to justify religious beliefs by rational arguments, and Jewish thinkers, both Rabbanite and Karaite, shared its aims, with the difference that for the Jews the source of revealed truth was the Hebrew Bible, not the Qur'an. The outstanding figure of Jewish kalam is SA'ADYA GA'ON. The age of the Jewish kalam was short-lived, and it was soon superseded by a more fully fledged philosophical tradition which rested on Greek foundations, mediated through Arabic translations. *See also* AL-KIRKISANI, YA'AKUB; AL-KUMISI, DANIEL; MUKAMMIS, DAVID.

Kalischer, Zvi Hirsch (1795–1874) Rabbi in Posen (Poznan), western Poland. Kalischer was a traditionalist whose observation of early European nationalism suggested the possibility of a Jewish nationalism. 'The beginning of the Redemption', he wrote in 1836, 'will come through natural causes by human effort and by the will of the governments to gather the scattered of Israel into the Holy Land.' His most influential work was a pamphlet, 'Derishat Tsiyyon' ('Seeking Zion', 1862). His practical proposals for the ingathering of exiles, the restoration of sacrificial worship, and the revival of the agricultural laws regarded as binding only in the Holy Land give some historical perspective to the later blank rejection of these ideas in the PITTSBURGH PLATFORM. They were also opposed by other religious traditionalists, who maintained an old rabbinic prohibition on 'hastening the end', and insisted that redemption would come about in God's good time through his own supernatural intervention.

kalla 1 (Aramaic, 'academy') Month-long rabbinical conference, held twice yearly (in Adar and Elul) in Babylonia during the geonic period (*see* GA'ON). These gatherings were very widely attended, and were an opportunity for scholars to be examined on their work and for questions to be addressed to the Ga'on and other leading scholars. **2** ('bride') A bride. The term can also be applied to the Sabbath (*see* LECHA DODI).

kápel (Yiddish, 'little cap') A SKULLCAP.

Kaplan, Mordecai M. (1881–1983) Religious thinker, founder of RECONSTRUCTION-ISM. Born in Lithuania, Kaplan graduated from the Conservative Jewish Theological Seminary before serving as rabbi of an Orthodox congregation in New York. Gradually he became aware that he did not share the congregation's faith in a personal, supernatural god and he resigned his rabbinic position, despite reassurances that the congregation did not object to his beliefs provided he kept them to himself. He taught at the Seminary, and founded a new movement, Reconstructionism, which was intended to transcend the divisions between ORTHODOX, CONSERVATIVE and REFORM JUDAISM. Kaplan's view of Judaism is set out in his book *Judaism as a Civilization* (1934). Kaplan analyses Reform and what he calls neo-Orthodoxy (the modernist wing of Orthodoxy) and subjects both to withering criticism. Conservative Judaism he does not regard as an authentic third way but rather as an uneasy coalition between the centrist tendencies in the other two. He calls for a reorientation to the problem of religion, in the light of modern conditions and particularly the pluralism which has become a fundamental and permanent feature of Jewish existence. Study of Jewish history shows both the perennial and central importance of the 'God-idea' and the changing character of that idea in different times and places. What really matters is not how God is thought of, but how the idea is translated into action. Supernaturalism, Kaplan argues, has no place in modern religion; it is unproductive today to imagine God as a person or being outside and beyond the universe, and better to see it as our name for a power that makes for righteousness. Kaplan offers a programme for reinvigorating Jewish society and Jewish civilization, with the aim of helping each individual Jew to lead a more fulfilled life. The religious practices of Judaism are termed 'folkways', which roughly corresponds to the traditional idea of CUSTOM.

Over a very long career Kaplan evolved from advocating the retention of traditional observances but reinterpreting them in the light of new ideas to propounding the need to select 'from the Judaism of the past those beliefs and practices which, either in their original or in a reinterpreted form, are compatible with what we now recognize to be authentic'. Depending how one cares to look at it, Kaplan either put religion back into Jewish nationalism or cleansed Jewish religion of its outmoded supernaturalism. His distinction is to have wedded the best insights of the atheistic voices of Jewish peoplehood and civilization (of men like ACHAD HA-AM and Simon DUBNOW) to the synagogue-based society of the Diaspora. In fact Kaplan's conception of the synagogue as a kind of Jewish civic centre where secular and social activities have their place side by side with religious ones corresponds closely to the reality in Western countries. Although the movement he founded has remained relatively small, his views are probably shared by many Jews who do not belong to it, and who indeed may never have heard of it.

kapóta (Yiddish) A long outer garment reaching to the ankles, worn by Chasidim and other traditionalists of Polish origin.

kapparot ('atonements') Ceremony performed on the morning preceding Yom Kippur. A white fowl is taken, a cock for a man or a hen for a woman, and waved three times round the head, with the words: 'This is my substitute, this is my vicarious offering, this is my atonement. This fowl will go to its death, but may I enjoy a long, pleasant and peaceful life.' The bird is then slaughtered, and the meat is given to the poor, or it is eaten and its value given to the poor in money. Once widespread, this folk custom was vigorously opposed by Sefardi rabbis, because it seemed to them a superstitious, pagan custom, but it is still popular among some Sefardim as well as Ashkenazim to this day.

Karaism Branch of Judaism that denies the divine inspiration and halachic authority of the Talmud. The name is derived from the self-designation Benei Mikra, 'Scripturalists', because of the group's attachment to scripture and rejection of the rabbinic traditions. Now reduced to a numerically small sect, Karaism was once a very large and powerful movement that swept through the Jewish world, arousing strong feelings and outright condemnations. It began in Babylonia, Iran and Palestine in the 9th century, under Muslim influence, and claimed older roots going back to a time before the destruction of the Temple. Later it spread to the Byzantine empire, where it flourished from the 11th century until after the Ottoman conquest in the 15th century, to the Crimea, Lithuania and Egypt. Today the largest Karaite community, mainly of Egyptian origin, is found in Israel. Small communities also exist in Istanbul, the Crimea, Lithuania and elsewhere.

Karelitz, Abraham Isaiah *See* CHAZON ISH.

karet *See* KERITOT.

karpas (unknown origin) Salad greens dipped in salt water or vinegar during the Passover SÉDER.

kashrut ('fitness') Hebrew term for the DIETARY REGULATIONS. Ashkenazim commonly use the Yiddish pronunciation, káshrus.

kavod ('honour', 'glory') **1** Respect, particularly that owed to a parent or teacher, or to God. **2** GLORY.

kavvana ('intention'; plural kavvanot) Concentration or intention, particularly in connection with the performance of a commandment or the saying of prayers. The Talmud discusses whether a commandment observed without kavvana (that is, without the conscious intention to observe that specific commandment) has really been observed. The medieval codes remain divided on the question. The prayers are meant to be said with kavvana. As BACHYA IBN PAKUDA puts it, 'prayer without kavvana is like a body without a soul'. How to achieve proper kavvana is a matter of debate. It is said in the Mishnah that the pious men of old used to meditate for an hour, then pray for an hour, then meditate for another hour. The kabbalists understood kavvana as a concentration on the symbolic significance of the act. In the case of worship this approach soon led to a comprehensive meditative exercise, transforming worship from a public to an essentially private and personal activity. They developed a system of meditative kavvanot ('intentions') which focused on the secret meaning of each prayer, and helped the worshipper to use the canonical words of the prayer as stepping stones towards a perception of the NAMES OF GOD and the mysteries of the universe. The kavvanot, many of which were eventually formulated and incorporated in the published liturgy, were really different for each worshipper and for each moment, and it was held that no two prayers were ever alike. This was particularly stressed in the LURIANIC KABBALA: Isaac LURIA used to give his disciples meditative exercises based on combinations of letters in the divine name (TSERUFIM). The Chasidim put particular emphasis on kavvana, and the BAAL SHEM TOV taught that one should say to oneself before beginning to pray that one would be willing to die through powerful concentration on the prayers. The early Chasidim felt that a major obstacle to concentration on prayer was the requirement to pray at fixed times: they therefore did away with fixed times, and encouraged people to pray when they felt ready to do it with kavvana.

kedusha ('holiness') In general, the HOLINESS of God; in particular, name of a prayer declaring God's holiness, and recalling Isaiah's vision (Isaiah 6.3) of the angels declaring 'Holy, holy, holy is the Lord of Armies: the whole world is full of his glory'. The prayer exists in various forms and in different contexts in the liturgy. Its best-known occurrence is in the reader's repetition of the AMIDA on Sabbaths and festivals, where it replaces the third benediction.

kedushta (Aramaic, 'holiness') PIYYUT (type of KEROVA) composed to embellish the AMIDA on Sabbaths and festivals. The form of the kedushta became fixed in the early period of piyyut with a number of separate hymns, arranged in three groups corresponding to the three first benedictions of the AMIDA. Extraordinary ingenuity was displayed by the early authors of these poetic creations. Later, with the introduction of trained choirs into the synagogue, choral refrains were added to the old hymns and became a standard feature of new compositions. The Spanish poets remodelled the kedushta, introducing metrical hymns such as a PIZMON and a RESHÚT.

Kelim ('vessels') Tractate of the Mishnah and Tosefta, in the order Tohorot, dealing with degrees of ritual impurity.

kelippot ('husks', 'shells') Kabbalistic term for the powers of evil. The image goes back to an early text, the Sod ha-Egoz (Mystery of the Nut), which describes the divine chariot surrounded by four layers of husk, like the kernel of a nut in its shell. The image was taken up by the CHASIDEI ASHKENAZ and then by the early kabbalists, and with Isaac LURIA it became a very widespread metaphor for evil in general.

Keritot ('extirpations') Tractate of the Mishnah, Tosefta and Babylonian Talmud, in the order Kodashim, dealing with offences punishable by karet, literally 'cutting off', of which the Torah uses the formula 'that soul shall be cut off from its people'.

kerova (from Aramaic) Generic name for a hymn (PIYYUT) inserted in the AMIDA. It is thought to derive from Aramaic karova ('near'), a name given to the cantor as he approached the lectern to lead the congregation in prayer. The genre began in the early phase of piyyut in the Land of Israel. There are many types of kerova, the best-known ones being the KEDUSHTA, chanted prior to the KEDUSHA in the morning service for Sabbaths and festivals, and the SHIVATA, adorning the seven sections of the AMIDA of MUSAF (the additional service).

kéter ('crown') **1** (Kéter) In kabbala, the first and highest of the SEFIROT. It is the first impulse in the EIN SOF, the first motion, as it were, towards the other Sefirot. It is likened to a crown, placed above the body (the other Sefirot). Sometimes it is described in terms of pure white, sometimes of black, and sometimes it is said to be colourless, because it precedes colour. **2** Silver ornament placed on top of the Torah scroll, in the form of a crown. (In this sense sometimes kéter tora, 'crown of the Torah'.) **3** Term applied in the Muslim world to a precious Bible manuscript, such as the 10th-century Kéter Aram Tsova (also known as the Aleppo Codex).

Kéter Malchut ('royal crown') Devotional poem by Solomon IBN GABIROL. It is printed in Sefardi prayer books for the Day of ATONEMENT, and is still recited in part in the British Reform rite, which is based on the Sefardi tradition. In North African communities it is chanted around dawn, before the morning service begins. In some Ashkenazi prayer books it is included for private devotion. It is a magnificent meditation on the wonders of nature and the greatness of God, the frailty of human beings and their need for penitence, blending biblical Hebrew allusions with themes borrowed from Neoplatonist philosophy, and counts among the great Hebrew poems of all times.

ketubba ('written document') Legal document drawn up at the time of a marriage, and recording the undertakings made by the bridegroom, notably to provide a settlement for the bride if he divorces her. The term is also used for the amount of settlement specified. This settlement was intended as an obstacle to hasty divorce. The standard minimum sum was 200 zuz for a virgin or 100 zuz in other cases – a substantial sum in Talmudic times. The bridegroom could, and often did, add to this. The standard form of ketubba was originally drafted in Aramaic, the vernacular, and it has remained in Aramaic to this day, though now a translation is often supplied. It includes these words: 'I faithfully promise that I will be a true husband to you, I will honour and cherish you, I will work for you, I will protect and support you, and will provide everything that is necessary for your due sustenance, as it is fitting for a Jewish husband to do.' Today the ketubba is sometimes written by hand in the traditional manner, and sometimes filled in on a printed form. Either way it is drawn up just before the marriage (in some communities immediately afterwards) and read out at the beginning of the ceremony. It is signed by witnesses, and sometimes by the bridegroom as well. Reform Judaism has instituted an egalitarian ketubba in which the bride also has a voice. The ketubba, despite being a legal document anticipating the break-up of the marriage, has come to be regarded as a joyful symbol of the union, and has attracted ornamental embellishment, in exceptional cases of high artistic merit.

Ketubbot ('written documents'; plural of KETUBBA) Tractate of the Mishnah, Tosefta and both Talmuds, in the order Nashim, dealing with the rights and obligations of husband and wife in respect of each other.

Ketuvim ('scriptures') Third and last section of the Hebrew Bible. It is a miscellaneous compilation of historical, poetic and other works. The largest component is the book of Psalms (Tehillim), itself divided into five books on the model of the Torah.

These poems are used in private and public devotion. The Five Scrolls (Song of Songs, Ruth, Lamentations, Kohélet (Ecclesiastes) and Esther) are read publicly on specific annual occasions, and the book of Job, a profound meditation on the problem of suffering, is also read among Sefardim. The other books in this section are generally less studied and carry less authority than the rest of the scriptures.

kibbuts ('gathering') **1** Traditional term for the ingathering of exiles in the 'last days'. It is used in this sense in the Declaration of Independence of Israel. **2** One of the collective farms established by Zionist settlers in the Land of Israel. While a minority of the kibbutsim were set up by religious settlers and observed traditional Jewish practices, the great majority were secular, and self-consciously set out to divest themselves of anything smacking of religion. At the same time, being Zionist, they wished to assert a secular Jewish identity, and so created their own festivals derived from ancient observances tied to the land, such as a water-drawing festival, a sheep-shearing festival, an ÓMER-cutting ceremony, or a love festival on the 15th of Av (derived from TU BE-AV). These revivals did not stand the test of time, but other innovations, such as a secular SÉDER at Passover, proved more popular. The Sabbath has been retained as a day of rest. The first Reform kibbuts was founded in 1976, the first Conservative kibbuts in 1984.

kiddush ('sanctification') Ceremony and prayer declaring the holiness of the Sabbath or a festival. The ceremony is generally performed before the evening and midday meals, and normally consists of the usual benediction over wine, preceded by appropriate verses from the Torah, and a benediction for the sanctity of the day (kiddush ha-yom). The latter benediction runs as follows on Sabbath: 'Blessed are you, Lord our God, king of the universe, who has sanctified us by his commandments and taken pleasure in us, and has lovingly and willingly given us his holy Sabbath as an inheritance, a reminder of the story of Genesis. It is the first of the holy festivals, in memory of the exodus from Egypt. Out of all of the peoples you chose and sanctified us, and you have lovingly and willingly given us his holy Sabbath as an inheritance. Blessed are you, Lord, who makes the Sabbath holy.' On festivals the wording is varied as appropriate, and the SHEHECHEYÁNU is added. If the kiddush is immediately followed by a meal the blessing over bread is also said. It is customary to use a special silver goblet or beaker for the wine, known as a kiddush cup. The term has come to be used (like LE-CHAYYIM) for a gathering after the service when kiddush is said, often with the accompaniment of some light snacks.

kiddush ha-Shem ('sanctification of the name') Term for MARTYRDOM. Any worthy public act performed by a Jew is considered to reflect positively on God and thus to sanctify his name, as opposed to an act that brings him into discredit, which is a desecration of the name (CHILLUL HA-SHEM). The term kiddush ha-Shem, however, has come to be reserved for the ultimate act of sanctification, namely offering up one's life for God (in accordance with the command to 'love the Lord your God ... with all your soul', Deuteronomy 6.5).

Kiddushin ('sanctifications') Tractate of the Mishnah, Tosefta and both Talmuds, in the order Nashim, dealing with betrothal.

Kiláyim ('two kinds') Tractate of the Mishnah, Tosefta and Palestinian Talmud, in the order Zera'im, dealing with forbidden mixtures, called kiláyim in the Torah (Leviticus 19.19: 'You shall not mate your beasts kiláyim, you shall not sow your field kiláyim, and you shall not put on kiláyim clothes [SHA'ATNEZ].') There are thus three types of forbidden mixtures. It is forbidden to cross-breed two species of animal; it is further forbidden to yoke two species together (Deuteronomy 22.10). It is forbidden to sow or plant two crops in the same field. Finally, it is forbidden to wear clothes made from a mixture of linen and wool.

Kimchi, David (c. 1160–1235) Biblical commentator, also known by the acronym Radak. He lived in Narbonne, and was the son of a noted commentator and grammarian, Joseph Kimchi. His commentaries have a strong linguistic and philosophical bias, and he occasionally refutes Christian interpretations. He also wrote an important work of Hebrew grammar, entitled *Michlol*, and a treatise on textual criticism, *Et Sofer*.

kina ('lament'; plural kinot) A PIYYUT in the form of an elegy, often composed for TISH'A BE-AV. Such liturgical poems can be a vehicle for fervent national feelings and deep mourning for the loss of the Temple. Kinot also commemorate contemporary persecutions and catastrophes. The 'laments for Zion' of JUDAH HA-LEVI are kinot; they were imitated by poets in the Rhineland, who also wrote dirges on the massacres of local Jewish communities by crusaders and other Christian mobs in the period from the late 11th century to the mid-12th century. Kinot sometimes lament the fate of an individual.

kingdom of God Term found commonly in the rabbinic writings and the liturgy, and used in a number of ways which cannot easily be differentiated. Frequently it is contrasted with the earthly kingdom, which for the rabbis meant the Roman empire. Although it can suggest simply a personal submission to the rule of God, the contrast with Roman rule readily implies the age of redemption. This is the sense in which it is used in the KADDISH: 'May he establish his kingdom in your life and days, and in the lifetime of all the house of Israel, speedily and soon, and say Amen.' The idea is represented more elaborately in the second paragraph of the ALÉYNU:

> So we hope for you, Lord our God, that we may soon behold your splendid might, to remove idols from the world so that all false gods are eradicated, to perfect the world by the kingdom of the Almighty so that all mankind will call on your name, and to turn all evil-doers in the world towards yourself. All dwellers on earth will recognize and know that it is to you that every knee must bend and every tongue swear. Before you, Lord our God, they will bend and prostrate themselves, and to your glorious name ascribe honour; they will all accept the yoke of your kingdom, and you will reign over them soon for ever and ever. For kingship is yours, and for all ages you reign in glory, as it is written in your Torah: 'The Lord reigns for ever and ever.' And it is said: 'The Lord shall be king over all the world; in that day the Lord shall be one, and his name one.'

Implied here is the belief that earthly rulers are usurping a power which properly belongs to God alone, and that this denial of God's rule leads directly to the worship of false gods and material idols. The recognition of God's kingdom will thus bring all people to the worship of the One God.

Kings, book of (Melachim) Biblical book, divided into two parts, in the Former Prophets. It contains a historical narrative from the end of the reign of David to the destruction of the kingdoms of Israel and Judah. According to the Talmud (Bavli, Bava Batra 15a) the author was the prophet JEREMIAH.

Kinnim ('birds' nests') Tractate of the Mishnah, in the order Kodashim, dealing with the offerings of birds (turtle doves or young pigeons) prescribed in the Torah as offerings in expiation of certain offences or certain types of ritual impurity.

kippa ('dome') A SKULLCAP.

Kippur *See* ATONEMENT, DAY OF.

Kirkisani *See* AL-KIRKISANI.

Kiryat Arba *See* HEBRON.

Kislev Third month of the year counting from New Year; ninth counting from Passover, corresponding roughly to December. It is the month in which Chanukka begins.

Kitsur Shulchan Aruch Abridgement of the SHULCHAN ARUCH made by Solomon GANZFRIED (1804–86) in 1864. It has remained popular ever since.

kíttel (Yiddish) White robe of light linen that is part of the burial clothes (tachrichim – *see* BURIAL). It is worn by some on the TEN DAYS OF PENITENCE and at the Passover SÉDER, and by a small number of pietists on certain other occasions in the synagogue. Franz ROSENZWEIG has this commentary on the symbolism of wearing it on the Days of Penitence: 'Man is utterly alone on the day of his death, when he is clothed in his shroud, and in the prayers of these days he is also alone. They too set him, lonely and naked, straight before the throne of God.'

Klal Yisra'el ('community of Israel') The idea that the entire Jewish people constitutes a single indivisible unit with a common destiny. The term itself is attested rarely in the rabbinic literature, but the concept finds expression in a number of teachings, and nowhere more outspokenly than in the Talmudic statement that 'all Israel are responsible for one another' (Bavli, Shevuot 39a). It is in line with this idea that the later mystics introduced a short prayer to be said before performing any religious act, professing the speaker's readiness to act in the name of 'all Israel'. *See also* CATHOLIC ISRAEL.

kloyz *See* SYNAGOGUE.

kneeling Part of the prostration performed by priests and people in the Temple. It was a mark of submission strictly reserved to the worship of God, that could not be offered to any earthly ruler (see Esther 3.2). Since the destruction of the Temple it is no longer performed, except by some people during the Ashkenazi services for the TEN DAYS OF PENITENCE. 'Here he does what he refused to do before the king of Persia, and no power on earth can compel him to do, and what he need not do before God on any other day of the year, or in any other situation he may face during his lifetime ... He kneels only on beholding the immediate nearness of God' (Franz ROSENZWEIG).

knisa (Arabic) A SYNAGOGUE, particularly in Iran.

knowledge of God *See* BAECK, LEO; LOVE; MAIMONIDES, MOSES; MYSTICISM; REVELATION; VIA NEGATIVA.

Kodashim ('holy things') Fifth of the six orders of the Mishnah, dealing with sacrifices, ritual slaughter, and matters related to the Temple. Of the eleven tractates in the order, eight are represented in the Tosefta and seven in the Babylonian Talmud. The order is entirely lacking from the Palestinian Talmud.

Kohélet Hebrew name of the biblical book also known as Ecclesiastes. Mentioned in the opening words of the book, the word kohélet is of uncertain derivation and meaning. The name Ecclesiastes is taken from the Greek translation. One of the FIVE SCROLLS, the Kohélet is read in Ashkenazi synagogues on the Sabbath of Tabernacles (SUKKOT). It is a rather pessimistic, even fatalistic, reflection on the human condition, redeemed for some by the closing words: 'Fear God and obey his commands; there is no more to man than this. For God will bring every deed to judgment, for every hidden thing, whether it is good or evil.'

kohen (plural kohanim) A priest. Priesthood in Judaism has a very specific meaning: it is an inherited status, implying direct descent from AARON, the brother of Moses. A kohen traditionally enjoys certain privileges, a residue of the remote period when the priests were responsible for the administration of the sacrificial cult in the Temple, such as the right to be called up first to the reading of the Torah in synagogue and to pronounce the priestly blessing (Numbers 6.24–6) over the congregation, and he is subject to certain restrictions, for example he may not come into contact with a corpse, except that of a close relative, and he may not marry a divorcee. (In REFORM JUDAISM both the privileges and the restrictions have been abolished as having no significance and drawing unnecessary and inappropriate distinctions among Jews.) Priests exercise no authority by virtue of this hereditary status, and there is no connection whatever between the priesthood and the rabbinate: a priest may become a rabbi, in which case he is a rabbi like any other rabbi and a priest like any other priest.

Kohler, Kaufmann (1843–1926) Reform theologian. Born in Germany, Kohler emigrated to the United States, and after a series of rabbinical appointments became president of HEBREW UNION COLLEGE, where he taught theology (1903–21). Kohler convened the rabbinic conference that issued the PITTSBURGH PLATFORM, which was largely his work. He is the author of an influential book, *Jewish Theology* (1918). *See also* REFORM JUDAISM; THEOLOGY.

kol nidrei or **kal nidrei** (Aramaic, 'all the vows') Common name for the service for the eve of the Day of ATONEMENT, so called after a declaration of the same name with which the service opens. The declaration is an annulment of vows. It states, in the

Ashkenazi rite, that 'All the vows, bonds, promises, obligations, penalties and oaths wherewith we have vowed, sworn, devoted and bound ourselves, from this Day of Atonement until the next Day of Atonement ... shall be absolved, released, annulled, made void and of no effect.' In its original version, dating from the geonic period (*see* GA'ON) and still used in the Italian rite, the declaration referred to vows made during the preceding year. The Sefardi rite combines the two versions.

kolel ('inclusive') **1** Under the CHALUKKA system, a group of Jews in the Land of Israel maintained by charitable contributions from a particular Diaspora community with which they were particularly associated, and thereby enabled to devote their time to Talmudic studies. **2** Type of higher-level YESHIVA, originally founded by Rabbi Israel SALANTER in 1878. In Israel many of the students receive bursaries from public funds; elsewhere they are supported privately.

Kook, Abraham Isaac (1865–1935) Ashkenazi CHIEF RABBI of Palestine under British rule. Kook believed that the Jewish people and the Land of Israel were mystically bonded by the spirit of God. The Zionist movement, even at its most secular, was a divine instrument in bringing the redemption, which in his view was close at hand. He interpreted Zionism according to the kabbalistic notion of 'practical messianism', which links divine redemption to the actions of human beings. According to Rabbi Kook, the return to Zion and the establishment of a Jewish homeland in Israel will lead to redemption and the messianic era. *See also* GUSH EMUNIM.

kosher (Yiddish, from Hebrew kasher, 'fit') Term applied to food halachically fit for a Jew to eat or drink. *See* DIETARY REGULATIONS.

Krochmal, Nachman (1785–1840) Philosopher of history. Born in Brody, Galicia, Krochmal received a traditional Jewish education and later educated himself in German philosophy. He developed a Hegelian interpretation of Jewish history: like all peoples, he argued, the Jewish people has undergone phases of birth, growth and decline. However, in the unique case of the Jews, since the God worshipped in biblical religion is truly the Absolute Spirit that generates all finite particulars, the phase of decline was never final, but was always followed by national rebirth. There have been three such cycles: from the patriarchs to the Babylonian exile, from the return from Babylon to the destruction of the Second Temple, and the Middle Ages. Some scholars consider that he saw the ENLIGHTENMENT and the EMANCIPATION as heralding the start of a fourth cycle. Despite his traditional background and personal religious convictions, Krochmal was a firm believer in historical development in Judaism and specifically in the HALACHA. After his death his collected writings were sent to Leopold ZUNZ, who published them in 1851 under the title *More Nevuchei ha-Zemán* (*Guide for the Perplexed of the [Present] Time*). The book had a great influence on the HASKALA and on the WISSENSCHAFT DES JUDENTUMS movement, as well as, ultimately, impacting on the thinking of Reform and Conservative Judaism and Zionism.

Kudsha berich hu *See* KADOSH BARUCH HU.

Kumisi *See* AL-KUMISI.

Kuzari *See* JUDAH HA-LEVI.

L

Ladino A form of Spanish language that developed in the former Ottoman empire, also known as JUDEZMO. It is basically late-medieval Spanish, but displays a good deal of influence of Hebrew, Turkish and various local languages. Specialist scholars reserve the term Ladino for a specific form of the language used to translate the Bible: it combines Hebrew grammar with Spanish words.

Lag ba-Ómer ('33rd [day] of the Ómer') Also known, particularly among Western Sefardim, as Lag la-Ómer (identical meaning). Minor festival that falls on the 18th of Iyyar, the 33rd day of the counting of the ÓMER. Among Ashkenazim, the strict rules governing daily life during the Ómer period are lifted on this day: specifically, it is permitted to marry and to have one's hair cut. Among Sefardim, the restrictions are lifted from the following day until the end of the Ómer period. The origins of the festival are lost in time. Some traditions associate it with the BAR KOCHBA revolt. For kabbalists it is the date of the death of Rabbi Simeon bar Yochai (*see* HILLULA). According to a recently discovered document, on this date in 363 CE the Roman emperor Julian began a project to rebuild the Temple. In Israel today it is widely marked by lighting bonfires.

laity The ordinary people, as distinct from the clergy. If the term 'layman' has any sense in Judaism it ought to refer to the ordinary 'Israelites' who are neither priests nor Levites. In fact, however, this usage has never suggested itself, presumably because the distinction is such an unimportant one in practice. It is sometimes used to designate those who are not rabbis, presumably by analogy with the Christian use to denote those who do not belong to the clerical class, or the common use to denote those lacking some special (for instance medical) knowledge.

lamed-vavniks *See* THIRTY-SIX JUST MEN.

Lamentations (Eicha) Book of the biblical KETUVIM, one of the FIVE SCROLLS. It consists of four alphabetical acrostics bewailing the lot of the people of Judah during the siege and capture of Jerusalem by the Babylonians (587/6 BCE), followed by a poetic prayer for redemption. According to an old (and not very plausible) tradition, the author is the prophet JEREMIAH. The verse near the end, 'Turn us, O Lord, to you and we shall return; renew our days of old' (5.21) is now sung in synagogue when the ark is closed after the reading of the Torah. The entire book is read in synagogue on TISH'A BE-AV.

lamps *See* CANDLES; NER TAMID.

Land of Israel *See* ISRAEL, LAND OF.

Landau, Ezekiel (1713–93) Halachist. Born in Poland, Landau served as rabbi in Prague from 1755 to his death. He was strongly opposed to the study of KABBALA except by the most learned because of its place in the Sabbatean movement (*see* SHABBETAI TSEVÍ); he was suspicious of its contribution to CHASIDISM and criticized the usurpation of kabbala by the unlearned in that new movement. He was also outspokenly hostile to Jewish Enlightenment writers such as Moses MENDELSSOHN. A prolific writer on halachic subjects, he is principally remembered for his collection of RESPONSA, *Noda bi-Yehuda* (*Known in Judah*; 2 vols, 1776 and 1811), which is still regarded as an important authority by Orthodox rabbis.

lashon ha-ra *See* SLANDER.

lavadores (Spanish, 'washers') In Western Sefardi circles, name given to those who volunteer to constitute a society to perform the ritual washing of corpses (RECHITSA). *See also* CHEVRA KADISHA.

law *See* CODES OF LAW; DIN; HALACHA.

Lazarus, Moritz (1824–1903) Philosopher and psychologist. Born in Posen (Poznan), western Poland, Lazarus became a professor in Berne and subsequently in Berlin. He was a pioneer of the study of psychological characteristics of peoples. Within Judaism Lazarus is remembered for his book *Ethik des Judentums* (1898; *Ethics of Judaism*, 1901), in which he emphasized the universal rather than the particularistic aspects of Jewish morality.

le-chayyim ('to life') Toast uttered on drinking wine or other alcoholic drinks in company. The response is le-chayyim tovim u-le-shalom ('to a good life and to peace'). The expression le-chayyim has come to be applied to a light collation with wine or other drinks offered to the congregation at the end of the service on the Sabbath or other special days.

leap year A year that contains thirteen instead of the more usual twelve months. In each nineteen-year cycle the third, sixth, eighth, eleventh, fourteenth, seventeenth and nineteenth years are leap years. (The year 5768 AM (2007/8 CE) is the first year of such a cycle.) *See also* CALENDAR.

leaven, search for *See* CHAMETS; PASSOVER.

Lecha Dodi ('come, beloved') Mystical hymn welcoming the Sabbath bride and looking forward to the messianic redemption, composed by the Safed kabbalist Solomon Alkabets (1505–c. 1576). Alkabets belonged to a mystic brotherhood that had the custom of going out into the fields dressed in white towards sunset each Friday to greet the Sabbath, which they identified with the SHECHINA. The hymn is sung in the Friday evening KABBALAT SHABBAT service; as the last stanza is sung, congregants turn towards the entrance of the synagogue and bow to greet the Sabbath.

legal fiction A legal device to nullify the effect of an inconvenient law. *See* CHA-METS; ERUV; FAST OF THE FIRSTBORN.

lehning (from Yiddish) Term used by Ashkenazim for the reading of the Torah in synagogue.

Leibowitz, Yeshayahu (1903–94) Israeli scientist with a strong amateur interest in Jewish theology. Born in Riga, he became professor of organic and biological chemistry and neurophysiology at the Hebrew University in Jerusalem, but achieved considerable celebrity outside the scientific world for his outspoken views on religion and particularly for his attacks on certain widespread assumptions. These included the efficacy of prayer (prayer is a duty, not a device to exact favours from God), the attempt to explain the COMMANDMENTS (their observance is an end in itself and has no other purpose than to serve God), and mysticism (which he declared to be a form of idolatry). He was a stern critic of exaggerated and idolatrous adulation (as he saw it) of the state of Israel, and contemptuously dubbed efforts to ground Judaism in the Bible rather than the halacha as 'Protestant Judaism'.

levantadores (Spanish, 'those who raise up') Term applied by Western Sefardim to those entrusted with the honour of elevating the scroll of the Torah in the synagogue (*see* HAGBAHA).

levaya *See* BURIAL.

Levi, David (1742–1801) Theologian and translator. Born in London to modest immigrant parents, Levi earned his living first as a shoemaker and later as a hatter. He achieved fame as a writer, particularly as a vociferous apologist for Judaism and as a translator of the synagogue liturgy. In the former category he published *A Succinct Account of the Duties, Rites, and Ceremonies of the Jews* (1782) and *A Dissertation on the Prophecies of the Old Testament* (3 vols, 1793–1800). He translated the festival liturgies of both the Ashkenazi and the Spanish and Portuguese synagogues, setting the pattern for a long line of successors.

Levi ben Gershom *See* GERSONIDES.

Levi Yitzhak of Berdichev (d. 1810) Chasidic leader. A disciple of DOV BER OF MEZHIRICH, he was one of the few early Chasidim to serve as a town rabbi, in Berdichev. His commentary on the Torah and other books (entitled *Kedushat Levi, Holiness of Levi*) is regarded as a great Chasidic classic. He is remembered with admiration and affection far beyond Chasidic circles for his devotion to God and for pleading with him on behalf of the people of Israel.

leviathan Mythological sea monster mentioned in the Bible and the Talmud. It symbolizes the forces of chaos and evil, in conflict with the power of good. It is said that it will struggle with the wild ox at the end of time; both will be killed, and their flesh will be eaten by the righteous.

Levinas, Emmanuel (1905/6–95) Philosopher. Levinas was born in Kaunas

(Kovno), Lithuania (he was born on 12 January 1906 according to the Julian calendar then in use, 30 December 1905 according to the Gregorian calendar used in France). He moved to Strasbourg to study in 1923, and in 1928–9 he studied in Freiburg under Edmund Husserl and Martin Heidegger, both of whom influenced him deeply. Like them, he rejected the dominant philosophical concern with large metaphysical questions or with epistemology. He based his own philosophy on the moral responsibility of the human subject, which begins with the recognition of the legitimate needs of others. He differed from Martin BUBER in not envisaging a relationship of mutuality but insisting that one's responsibility to the Other is a one-way traffic. Levinas never forgot his Talmudic upbringing in Lithuania, and he published a number of 'Talmudic readings' (originally delivered at annual gatherings of French Jewish intellectuals), in which he drew out important lessons about the character of Judaism. For example he uses a rabbinic distinction between Jews and Greeks to highlight the contrast between Jewish and non-Jewish values today. In the course of a reflection on forgiveness he asks abruptly: 'One can forgive many Germans, but there are some Germans it is difficult to forgive. It is difficult to forgive Heidegger' (referring to his master's involvement with Nazism).

levirate marriage (from Latin levir, 'brother-in-law'; yibbum in Hebrew) Marriage of a widow to a brother of her late husband. Such a marriage is forbidden in Leviticus 18.16, but Deuteronomy 25.5–6 rules that where the dead husband has no children his brother has a duty to marry his widow: their first child is then considered the child of the dead man. If he is unwilling to undertake this duty he must perform CHALITSA. According to an old Karaite interpretation, the latter law cannot refer literally to a brother, as it would be in stark contradiction to the law in Leviticus; hence it must be taken to refer to a close relation. Rabbanites interpret the word 'brother' in Leviticus literally. The question whether or not levirate marriage is preferable to chalitsa is not answered clearly in the Talmud, but since the ban on POLYGYNY among Ashkenazim the former option is ruled out for a married brother, at least. Sefardi rabbis have tended to favour yibbum. In Israel the chief rabbinate has ruled against yibbum in all cases. The Talmudic tractate Yevamot is devoted to the subject.

Levites (Leviyyim) Descendants of the tribe of Levi, one of the sons of JACOB. Moses and Aaron belong to this tribe in the Bible. Descendants of Aaron are priests (*see* KOHEN); other descendants of Levi are known as Levites. In the Temple they were responsible for the music. Today they are called up second in the synagogue, after a priest, and they wash the priests' hands before the priestly blessing (BIRKAT KOHANIM). (Reform Judaism has abolished these vestiges of their special status.)

Leviticus *See* VAYIKRA.

lex talionis (Latin, 'law of like-for-like') Punishment of bodily injury by a like injury. The Torah states 'He who kills a man shall be put to death, and whoever kills an animal shall make it good, beast for beast. If a man injures another, as he has done so shall it be done to him: a fracture for a fracture, an eye for an eye, a tooth for a tooth, whatever injury he inflicted on the other shall be inflicted on him' (Leviticus

24.17–20; cf. Exodus 21.24–5). Another law states that a false witness is liable to be punished with the specific harm he planned to inflict on his victim: 'You shall show no pity, but exact a life for a life, an eye for an eye, a tooth for a tooth, a hand for a hand, a foot for a foot' (Deuteronomy 19.16–21). This harsh law is accepted in all its severity by most Karaite interpreters, but Rabbanites have interpreted it to mean that monetary compensation should be paid, except in the case of murder.

Liberal Judaism Name adopted by various Jewish movements and synagogue organizations in different European countries, all sharing a progressive attitude to Jewish belief and practice. The name first arose in Germany, where it replaced the earlier term REFORM JUDAISM towards the end of the 19th century. More recently, German Jews tended to define Liberal Judaism as being religiously less radical than Reform Judaism, but in fact a political consideration was central to the formation of Liberal Judaism, namely opposition to ZIONISM. The Association of Liberal Rabbis in Germany (Vereinigung der liberalen Rabbiner Deutschlands) was founded in 1898. In 1912 it issued 'Directives for a programme for Liberal Judaism', with a clearly anti-nationalist ideological orientation. The Liberal label was adopted by virtually all Reform synagogues. The lay organization Vereinigung für das liberale Judentum was established in 1908; it published a Liberal Jewish newspaper (*Jüdisch-Liberale Zeitung*). A substantial section of pre-War German Jewry was Liberal. The same was true in Austria and Czechoslovakia. German Liberalism has undergone a significant revival in recent years. In France the first Liberal synagogue (Union Libérale Israélite) was founded in Paris in 1907; in the Netherlands a synagogue was founded in The Hague in 1931, followed soon afterwards by another in Amsterdam. In both countries there are now several Liberal synagogues, representing a growing minority of Jews. On the continent of Europe Liberal Judaism has remained at the more conservative wing of Progressive Judaism. In Britain the contrary is true. The synagogues grouped together in the Union of Liberal and Progressive Synagogues (ULPS), whose origins lie in the Jewish Religious Union founded in London in 1902, are generally more radical, both in their theology and in their practice, than those of the British Reform movement.

lifnim mi-shurat ha-din ('within the line of the law') Term designating the application of higher ethical standards than those required by the law. The Talmud cites as an example of such behaviour the restoration of lost property to its owner when this is not required by the law (Bavli, Bava Metsi'a 24b). This attitude has been particularly associated with the pietistic strand in Judaism. According to the Mishnah (Avot 5.10) 'He who says "What is mine is yours and what is yours is also yours" is a pious man [chasid].' The CHASIDEI ASHKENAZ considered the application of such principles to be the essential quality of chasidism. There is, however, a problem here for those who see the law as a complete and divinely revealed guide to action: for an individual to apply what he considers to be higher standards in his life than those laid down in the law implies that he considers the divine commandments as less than perfect.

light *See* CANDLES; MENORA; NER TAMID.

Likkutei Amarim *See* TANYA.

Lilith Female demon mentioned once in the Bible (Isaiah 34.14). In the Talmud, because of an association with the Hebrew word for night (láyla), she is described as a creature of the night. In later legends she is the first wife of Adam, created, like him, from earth. She demands equality with him (which is why she has been adopted as a symbol by some feminists), and when he refuses she leaves him and attaches herself to the great demon, Samael. She figures in various stories in the ZOHAR, and is commonly referred to in folklore, particularly as a sexual temptress and as a threat to women in childbirth and babies.

liturgical reform *See* MODERNISM.

liturgy *See* PRAYER BOOKS.

Litvak (Yiddish) Term referring to Jews from Lithuania and adjacent regions.

loans Lending money to those in need is commended in the Torah (e.g. Leviticus 25.35); however, there are strict injunctions against using loans as a means of enriching oneself by charging interest (Exodus 22.24 (25 in some English translations), Leviticus 25.36).

love
(in Hebrew, ahava) There are three aspects to love: (1) love of God, (2) God's love of humanity and (3) love of people for one another.

(1) Love of God depends on knowledge of God (*see* BAECK, LEO; MAIMONIDES, MOSES; REVELATION; VIA NEGATIVA), since one can only love what one knows. (As has often been pointed out, the Bible uses the same verb for 'know' and 'love'). The love of God is described by the rabbis as the greatest of all the commandments. It is commanded in the SHEMÁ: 'You shall love the Lord your God with all your heart, soul and being' (Deuteronomy 6.5). The ancient rabbis explain that what is intended here is obedience to God's commands, although they admit that one can feel a deep emotional attachment to and longing for God, such as is spoken of in some of the Psalms and elsewhere in the Bible. The medieval authors, on the other hand, whether they are mystically or rationally inclined, tend to emphasize the emotional aspects. One of the main writers on the subject is BACHYA IBN PAKUDA, whose book *The Duties of the Heart* culminates in the love of God, defined as 'the soul's spontaneous longing for her Creator'. This is the ultimate aim of the religious person, when, emptying itself of the love for any material thing, the believer's heart is filled with the love of God. He has perfect faith and trust in God, and everything he does is in accordance with God's will. This love is completely disinterested and unselfish, and it occupies true lovers of God totally, to the exclusion of every other concern. Bachya represents a rare extreme among the thinkers of his day, though he has had some followers, particularly among the kabbalists and Chasidim. Even more sober philosophers like Maimonides, however, insist on the elevated status of the love of God, and he

uses the analogy of erotic passion (which is commonly employed also by the kabbalists) to indicate the intensity of the love of God. Still, knowledge is essential: Maimonides explains that the simple are taught to serve God out of fear; it is only when one comes to know God that one can begin to love God. 'Where there is little knowledge there is little love; where there is much knowledge there is much love.'

(2) The Psalms speak often of God's love for humankind, and the Song of Songs is understood as a dialogue of love between God and the Jewish people. The prayers of the liturgy often evoke this love, in particular in connection with the gift of the Sabbath and more broadly with all the commands of the Torah: in both cases the loving gift is associated with the choice of Israel as God's special people. So strong is the sense of God's love that we even find some sources explaining suffering, particularly the suffering of the righteous, as 'chastisements of love'. Just as a loving parent sometimes chastises a child, so God sometimes chastises those he loves (Proverbs 3.12). Others disagree with this view, which they feel conflicts with the idea of God's justice and with our sense of healthy behaviour for a lover. God's love is a key element in the thought of Franz ROSENZWEIG. God addresses man through speech, like a lover addressing his beloved. The words of the lover are not 'mere' words: they are a vehicle for his love. 'Death, the conqueror of all, and the netherworld that zealously imprisons all the deceased, collapse before the strength of love and the hardness of its zeal. Its glowing embers, its divine flames warm the stone-cold past from its rigor mortis. The living soul, loved by God, triumphs over all that is mortal, and that is all that can be said about it.' *See also* REVELATION.

(3) Among the commands of the Torah one of the most precious is 'You shall love your neighbour like yourself' (Leviticus 19.18). This has been variously explained as meaning you should love your neighbour 'as much as you love yourself' or 'because he is like yourself'. Maimonides adopts the first view: one must have as much regard for another's money or honour as one would for one's own. He goes so far as to comment: 'Anyone who gains honour for himself by bringing dishonour to his neighbour has no share in the Coming Age [OLAM HA-BA].' Others stress that the neighbour has the same feelings as you do, and before doing anything that might harm him you should put yourself in his place. The great teacher HILLEL summed up the whole Torah in the single maxim: 'Do not do to another what you would not wish him to do to you.' In recent times the love of one person for another has been put to good use by Martin BUBER in explaining his conception of the I–You relationship. The You does not have to be a fellow human – it can be an animal or even an inanimate object – but it is in the relationship of two humans that the relationship can be seen most clearly. The loving relationship between two people becomes a model for the relationship between people and God, for Buber and also for Franz Rosenzweig.

Löw, Judah *See* MAHARAL OF PRAGUE.

Lubavitch Belorussian town (commonly known as Lyubavichi) that served for over a century (until 1915) as headquarters of CHABAD CHASIDISM, with which for many Jews it has become virtually synonymous. The seventh and last REBBE of Lubavitch, Rabbi Menachem Mendel SCHNEERSON, interpreted the name of the town to mean 'city of love', and taught that the name symbolizes the warm, loving approach of the movement. Lubavitch Chasidim were active after the Russian Revolution in resisting attempts by the Soviet authorities to eliminate free expression of the Jewish religion, and since 1940, when the sixth rebbe, Rabbi Joseph Isaac Schneersohn (1880–1950), emigrated to the United States, Lubavitch has become a worldwide movement for the dissemination of Chabad teachings.

lulav 1 Branch or frond of a palm tree; one of the FOUR SPECIES waved ceremonially during SUKKOT. **2** By synecdoche, the four species taken all together. For example the benediction said on picking up the four species mentions only the lulav. It is a rabbinic, not a biblical, term. The lulav is waved during the HALLEL on each day of the festival, and it is carried during the HAKKAFOT. The lulav is commonly represented on tombstones, perhaps as a symbol of salvation, during the Roman period.

Luria, Isaac (1534–72) Kabbalist, also known as the Ari ('holy lion', and an acronym of 'the divine Rabbi Isaac'). Born in Jerusalem and brought up in Egypt, he settled in SAFED in 1570 and died there in an epidemic two years later. Little is known for certain about the last two years of his life, which had a truly revolutionary effect on Jewish mystical theology. His teachings were circulated orally and in writing by his disciples. Living as he did in the century following the epoch-making event of the completion of the Christian reconquest of Spain, when many Jews had been forced to become Christians and many others had become exiles, Luria was deeply troubled by the urgent need for messianic redemption. It seems that he considered himself to be the prophet Elijah, the harbinger of the Messiah, or the Messiah of the tribe of Joseph who would prepare the way for the Messiah, son of David. He devised a complex new kabbalistic theory to explain the fundamental defects in the world, and the same theory also pointed the way to redemption.

Lurianic kabbala System of KABBALA devised by Isaac LURIA. Unlike the earlier kabbala, this doctrine was not concerned only with the spiritual perfection of the individual but with that of the whole people of Israel and indeed of the entire world. Luria's explanation begins at the very beginning. Before the SEFIROT, and ultimately the universe, can be created, the EIN SOF must, as it were, make room by withdrawing into itself. This withdrawal (TSIMTSUM) leaves a kind of empty space into which a ray of divine light is projected in the form of the Primordial Man (ADAM KADMON), and from this the Sefirot emanated. The process of emanation is achieved through further streams of divine light which, pouring forth from the Primordial Man, produce the vessels into which the Sefirot will emerge. The Sefirot themselves are produced by a further radiation from the eyes of the Primordial Man. At this point an unplanned disaster takes place: the additional light is too powerful for the vessels of the lower Sefirot, and they collapse. Because of the breaking of the vessels (SHE-VIRA), nothing is quite as it should have been, so that the cosmos is flawed even before its creation. The Sefirot, now incapable of containing the divine light, are rearranged in 'configurations' (PARTSUFIM) in which they support and strengthen one another. In the Lurianic system there is a need for 'repair' (TIKKUN), in which humankind can play a part, by releasing and raising the sparks of divine light that are trapped in the power of evil (KELIPPOT). With the Lurianic doctrine of tikkun mysticism the quest for communion with God was given an important turn. A major active role in it is allotted to humankind, and specifically to Jews, who, by a life of mystical devotion to the divine law, have it in their power to release the imprisoned sparks and so bring about the redemption not only of the world but, so to speak, of the Divine itself. This release is achieved through meditation and 'intention' (KAVVANA). The purpose of the spiritual exercises of the Lurianic school is not just the blissful reunion of the individual soul with God, but the reparation of the whole cosmos. In this work the divine and human spheres are bound together by a closer bond than in Talmudic Judaism or even in the earlier kabbala represented by the ZOHAR: God and humankind need one other, and human actions can have an effect on God. The symbolism and language of the Lurianic kabbala had a great impact both on later kabbalists and on the Chasidim (*see* CHASIDISM).

Luzzatto, Moses Chayyim (1707–47) Kabbalist and Hebrew author, also known by the acronym Ramchal. Born and raised in Padua, he was banished to Amsterdam and ended his days in an epidemic in Acre. The cause of his banishment was his involvement in kabbalism. He wrote a number of kabbalistic works that he claimed were dictated to him by a MAGGID. A circle of disciples gathered round him, one of whom considered himself to be the Messiah of the house of David, while Luzzatto himself was seen as the reincarnation of Moses. The group was said to identify SHABBETAI TSEVÍ with the Messiah of the house of Joseph (*see* MESSIAH). It was particularly the accusation of Sabbateanism that led Luzzatto into trouble, and after his exile his books were burnt. Paradoxically, Luzzatto was not only a devotee of mystical messianism, he was also the author of a number of ethical works including one, *Mesillat Yesharim* (*The Path of the Righteous*, 1740), that is widely regarded as a masterpiece of the genre, and of allegorical dramas that rank among the first fruits of modern Hebrew literature.

Luzzatto, Samuel David (1800–65) Scholar, also known by the acronym Shadal. Born in Trieste, he taught at the rabbinical seminary in Padua from 1829 until his death. Considered one of the pioneers of WISSENSCHAFT DES JUDENTUMS, Luzzatto is a disconcerting mixture of open-mindedness and traditionalism. He was one of the first Jewish scholars to embrace historical and textual criticism of the Bible, yet in some respects he was quite conservative, for instance defending the single authorship of the book of ISAIAH. His attitude to religion was a romantic one, placing emphasis on sentiment and the moral instinct. On this basis he attacked both rationalism and mysticism. He identified two contrasting forces within civilization: Hellenism, or Atticism, promotes philosophy, reason and love of beauty, whereas Judaism promotes religion, morality and love of the good. He attacks Moses MAIMONIDES, Abraham IBN EZRA and Baruch SPINOZA for erring on the side of Hellenism. Kabbala he sees as alien to the Jewish spirit.

ma nishtana ('what is the difference … ?') Name given to a series of four questions asked, traditionally by the youngest person present, towards the beginning of the Passover SÉDER. The name comes from the opening words: 'What is the difference between this night and all other nights?' The specific questions relate to rituals observed at the Séder: the use of unleavened bread (MATSA) and bitter herbs (MAROR), the dipping of herbs and the practice of reclining rather than sitting. (The order of the questions differs in different rites.)

ma'amad ('station'; plural ma'amadot) **1** In antiquity, one of twenty-four divisions of the Land of Israel, which sent delegations (also called ma'amadot) to the Temple in Jerusalem to represent the community during the daily sacrifices. Those who remained at home gathered to read the creation story in Genesis and to fast (Mishnah, Ta'anit 4.2). Some scholars believe this may have been the origin of synagogue worship. **2** In the Babylonian and Spanish prayer rites, an evening of penitential prayer during the month of Elul and the TEN DAYS OF PENITENCE. **3** In the Spanish rite, a complete set of hymns for the entire Day of ATONEMENT. *See also* MAHAMAD.

ma'amin ('believer'; plural ma'aminim; Turkish plural maminler) Name applied by the DÖNME to themselves.

ma'ariv ('[God] who makes the evening') Evening service, so called from a key word of one of its benedictions, blessing God 'who makes the evening evening'. It is also known as arvit. Its nucleus consists of the SHEMÁ with its benedictions and the AMIDA. (The Talmud records a disagreement about whether the recitation of the evening Amida is obligatory or optional. Consequently it is customary for it to be said privately but not repeated by the reader.) The distinctive feature of the service liturgically is the recitation of HASHKIVÉNU. The term is also applied to a type of PIYYUT composed for the evening service.

ma'ase bereshit ('story of creation') The creation story, as told in the opening verses of the book of Genesis. The expression is first found in the Mishnah (Chagiga 2.1): 'The forbidden degrees [of sexual relations] may not be expounded before three persons, nor the story of creation before two, nor the story of the chariot (MA'ASE MERKAVA) before one, unless he is a sage who understands from his own knowledge.' In fact many interpretations of the cosmogony at the beginning of Genesis are found in exoteric (public) works such as the Midrash, but apparently it also attracted esoteric exegesis that was considered too difficult for the public at large and susceptible of leading people into heresy. The Babylonian Talmud explains the Mishnaic ruling as forbidding the public exposition of 'that which is below, above, before or after'. A number of works of this nature composed in the late Talmudic or early geonic period survive. In the Middle Ages rationalists such as Maimonides understood the term to mean the study of physics (as defined by Aristotle). The kabbalists applied it to the emanation of the SEFIROT.

ma'ase merkava ('story of the chariot') The account of the divine throne-chariot, in Ezekiel chapter 1. The Mishnah lists this and MA'ASE BERESHIT among the biblical passages that are not to be taught to all and sundry; similarly the Christian authors Origen and Jerome say that Jewish teachers teach the whole of the Bible (as well as the rabbinic traditions) to children except for four sections: the beginning of Genesis, the Song of Songs, and the beginning and end of Ezekiel. These may only be taught to students of mature years. Maimonides understood the term to mean the study of metaphysics; others applied it to mystical speculation. *See also* HECHALOT.

Ma'aser Sheni ('second tithe') Tractate of Mishnah, Tosefta and Palestinian Talmud, in the order Zera'im, dealing with the Second Tithe (Deuteronomy 14.22–7) and related topics. The Second Tithe is to be taken to Jerusalem in the form of produce and consumed there during the pilgrimage, or it may be sold and its cash equivalent must be spent in Jerusalem. In certain years this tax is replaced by the Poor Tithe (Deuteronomy 14.28–9).

Ma'aserot ('tithes') Tractate of Mishnah, Tosefta and Palestinian Talmud, in the order Zera'im, dealing with the subject of tithes, that is the First Tithe, which is due to the Levites (Numbers 18.21), and from which they pay a portion to the priests, the Second Tithe and the Poor Tithe (*see* MA'ASER SHENI).

Maccabees Name of four books that are not found in the Hebrew Bible but have been preserved in Greek in Christian tradition. All were written by Jews. 1 Maccabees was originally written in Hebrew, while 2 Maccabees claims to be an abbreviated version of a book written in Greek. Both were written in the late 2nd century BCE, and both recount the history of the HASMONEAN REVOLT, for which they are the main historical sources. 3 Maccabees was written in Greek a little later, and celebrates unsuccessful attempts by a Greek ruler of Egypt, Ptolemy Philopator, in the late 3rd century BCE, to desecrate the Temple and to destroy the Jewish communities of Alexandria and Egypt. 4 Maccabees, written in Greek at a still later date, is a philosophical sermon on the subject, dear to the Stoics, of the superiority of reason over the passions. It gives some examples, taken from 2 Maccabees, of fortitude and loyalty to the Torah in the face of terrible tortures. The title 'Maccabee' is obscure; it is thought to be derived from a Hebrew word for 'hammer'. It was bestowed on JUDAH THE MACCABEE for unknown reasons.

machlóket ('dissension') Term that is used by the rabbis to refer both to a reasonable difference of opinion, for example about the interpretation of a biblical passage or about a rabbinic law, and to a destructive division in a community. The Mishnah (Avot 5.17) explicitly recognizes the distinction, making the test whether or not the machlóket is 'for the sake of Heaven'.

Machshirin ('predisposers') Tractate of the Mishnah and Tosefta, in the order Tohorot, dealing with the role of liquids in conveying ritual impurity.

Machzikei Hadas ('upholders of the faith') An organization set up in 1879 in Galicia to support traditional values and combat modernism. It waged a vigorous campaign against Zionism in czarist Russia. There are several Machzikei Hadas congregations in North America and elsewhere. The form Machzikei Hadath is also used, e.g. for a congregation founded in London in 1891.

machzor ('cycle') In Ashkenazi usage, a prayer book for the festivals. The Machzor Vitry, compiled in the late 11th century by a pupil of RASHI, Simcha of Vitry, is a compendium including the prayers for the whole year according to the old French rite, but also a treatise on the calendar, the rules regulating the synagogue service and various RESPONSA and other items. Originally the term was applied to lists of special Torah readings and HAFTAROT, or to collections of PIYYUTIM arranged according to the cycle of the liturgical year.

maftir *See* HAFTARA.

Magen Avraham ('shield of Abraham') First benediction of the AMIDA.

Magen David ('shield of David') Designation of God at the end of the third benediction after the HAFTARA, a benediction that looks forward to the return of king DAVID as MESSIAH. The term is also applied to the six-pointed star or hexagram, often used today as a badge of Jewish identity. The origin of this practice is obscure. In antiquity and the Middle Ages it is found as an ornamental device or a magical sign. It is attested as a symbol in the 17th century, for example among the followers of SHABBETAI TSEVÍ, but it was in 19th-century Germany that it really became common as a symbol of Judaism, and it soon spread all over Europe and beyond. The ZIONIST movement adopted it as a badge at its first congress in 1897, and it was subsequently incorporated in the flag of the state of Israel. Franz ROSENZWEIG structured his great book, *The Star of Redemption*, around it: the book is in three parts, each containing three chapters; the first part is marked with a triangle with the apex at the top, the second part with a triangle with the apex at the bottom, and the third part with the two triangles superimposed in the form of a star. The Nazis adopted it as the form of the yellow badge that Jews were forced to wear as an identifying mark, but even this has not diminished its popularity, and today it is commonly worn as a pendant and incorporated in the design of synagogues and tombstones.

maggid ('one who speaks or tells') **1** A popular preacher. The institution of maggid has old roots in Ashkenaz, going back as far as the 11th century; by the 18th century it had become a characteristic feature of eastern European Judaism, where the town rabbi normally only preached twice a year, on the Great Sabbath before Passover and the Sabbath of Repentance before the Day of Atonement. The maggid was often an itinerant preacher, who was rewarded for his services by each community where he preached; some larger communities maintained a permanent maggid. **2** A heavenly messenger. By the 16th century it had become generally accepted that pious mystics could receive guidance or instruction direct from God through the internal voice of a spirit-guide. Joseph CARO and Moses Chayyim LUZZATTO were among the best known possessors of such a maggid.

magic The art of producing marvellous results by the use of natural or supernatural powers. The practice of magic is forbidden in the Bible, but folk belief in the efficacy of incantations, exorcisms, amulets and so forth made recourse to them very common at all times, until the present in some communities. The medieval thinkers discussed the question of whether magic really works or only appears to. Most maintained that it is effective, and that that is why it is banned; a minority, such as MAIMONIDES, dismissed it as mere superstition: any effect it has is due purely to psychological factors.

mahamad (from Hebrew ma'amad) In Western Sefardi usage, a synagogue council or governing body.

Maharal of Prague (d. 1609) Commentator, halachist and theologian. (Maharal is an acronym for Morenu Harav Rabbi Laib, Our Teacher Rabbi Löw.) Born in Posen (Poznan), western Poland, he served as rabbi in Moravia, Posen, and finally Prague, where his grave has become a tourist attraction. One of the most profound and prolific of Ashkenazi authors, the Maharal has left us a commentary on the Torah (*Gur Arye (The Lion's Whelp)*), another on parts of the Talmud, responsa, and an incomplete theological interpretation of the festivals. His theological system is nowhere set out in its entirety, but his expressed views taken together amount to a thoroughgoing and highly original account of Judaism for the age in which he lived. According to this, humanity's task is to bring to completion an imperfect world. The Torah, too, is incomplete, and it is up to the rabbis to draw out its meanings and apply them in the world. The new discoveries of science are not in conflict with the Bible and Talmud when these are properly understood. He was a harsh critic of the defects of the Jewish leadership of his day and the educational methods of the rabbinic schools, particularly PILPUL. *See also* GOLEM.

Maimon, Salomon (1754–1800) Philosopher. Born near Mir in Lithuania, he spent several periods of his life in Berlin, where he joined the circle of Moses MENDELSSOHN. Although largely self-taught, Maimon had an extraordinary philosophical mind, and is considered by some specialists to be among the outstanding philosophers of his time. (Kant described him as the sharpest of his critics.) Deeply impressed and influenced throughout his life by the strict rationalism of MAIMONIDES (whose name he borrowed as his own surname), Maimon devoted much of his writing to engaging with earlier Jewish thinkers, including Baruch SPINOZA, whose understanding of God he considered to have been fundamentally misinterpreted. Rejecting the character-ization of Spinoza's philosophy as atheism, Maimon suggested that it was really 'acosmism' (worldlessness), in that it denied objective reality to the world and maintained that only God was real. Spinoza was thus not an atheist but an unorthodox religious thinker. Maimon discerned traces of Spinoza's pantheism in the KABBALA. In addition to a series of philosophical books Maimon wrote an important autobiography (*Salomon Maimon's Lebengeschichte*, 1792; *Salomon Maimon: An Autobiography*, 1888). Several of his writings are still unpublished.

Maimonides, Moses (d. 1204) Philosopher, halachist and medical writer, also known by the acronym Rambam. He was born in Cordova, between 1136 and 1138, into a long line of rabbinic scholars. After a spell in Fez he settled while still in his twenties in Fustat (Old Cairo), where he served as a rabbinic judge and communal leader and also practised and taught medicine. Many of his writings survive, some of them in his own handwriting. They are extraordinarily varied, ranging from medical topics, such as asthma and haemorrhoids, through halachic writings and RESPONSA, to religious philosophy. His most famous and influential works are his halachic CODE OF LAW, the MISHNE TORAH, and his philosophical masterpiece, the *Guide of the Perplexed*.

Maimonides represents a peak in the history of Jewish religious philosophy. He gave Jewish rationalism its classical formulation, casting all his predecessors in the shade and pointing the way for all his successors, even for those who disagreed with his views. His achievement is perhaps less that of an original genius attempting a new departure than that of a brilliant, creative synthesizer. The dominant philosophy of his day, as developed by a succession of highly gifted Muslim thinkers, was a form of Aristotelianism deeply marked by Neoplatonist ideas. Its strength was its belief in the power of human reason to achieve knowledge and to organize this knowledge systematically. The religious tradition, on the other hand, was rooted in divine revelation embodied in the Bible. Maimonides gave full weight and validity to both revelation and reason, without trying to subordinate one to the other. He had a strong belief in the power of prophecy and revelation, and especially the revelation granted to Moses, the greatest of the prophets; but he had an equally strong belief in the power of reason, and in the exercise of reason as the supreme human task. In a vivid parable, he likened God to a king in his palace, whose subjects are wandering around in search of him. The majority of Jews, who simply carry out the commandments of the Torah, have not even set eyes on the palace. The students of the Talmud, who have no philosophical training and do not attempt to prove their faith by reason, have reached the palace but merely walk round the outside of it. Those who have embarked on a philosophical training have already entered the antechamber of the palace; when their studies are complete and they have learned the limit of what can be known and proved they will be inside the palace with the king. This devaluation of Talmudic study, commonly regarded as the crown of Jewish education, naturally provoked a bitterly hostile reaction in some circles. But Maimonides also insisted that there were strict limits on the extent that reason could serve as a guide. Beyond those limits, the only true guide is revelation, mediated by tradition. The most celebrated example of his limitation of the role of philosophical teaching is his endorsement of the biblical idea of the creation of the world, in the face of the Aristotelian doctrine of the eternity of the world, which he showed to be insufficiently established by rational proof.

It was Maimonides's synthesis between biblical religion and Aristotelian philosophy that won him his fame among subsequent thinkers, Jewish, Muslim and Christian, as the man who established faith on a sound philosophical basis. His carefully reasoned expositions also gave a boost to philosophical thought among a wider educated Jewish public. The *Guide of the Perplexed* came to be regarded as the philosophical exposition of Judaism par excellence, and his brief formulation of the THIRTEEN PRINCIPLES of the Jewish faith came to be regarded as a kind of creed, even being incorporated in simplified form in the synagogue liturgy. But the very success of the Maimonidean synthesis unleashed a violent reaction which shook Jewish intellectual life to its roots. Great as was the authority of Maimonides, several of his followers took him severely to task: thus GERSONIDES felt that he had compromised Aristotelian principles too far in the direction of Neoplatonism, while Chasdai CRESCAS put forward a penetrating philosophical critique of Aristotelianism itself. These differences among philosophers did not challenge the basic principle of free philosophical enquiry. In some circles, however, the whole basis of religious rationalism was attacked. In some cases this was a reaction against excessive rationalism and its strong appeal; others critics, such as the rabbis of northern France, who were solid in their condemnation of Maimonides, lived in a different cultural milieu, where Talmudic studies reigned supreme and the study of philosophy had never gained a foothold. Whatever the motives for the attacks, they were pursued with vigour and acrimony, and so heated did the controversy become that in 1232 the *Guide of the Perplexed* was publicly burnt in Montpellier by Christians, allegedly at the instigation of the anti-Maimonidean party. The anti-rationalist ferment unleashed by the Maimonidean controversy had an enduring effect on Jewish attitudes, and philosophical enquiry was effectively suppressed through much of the Jewish world for centuries.

Maimuna or **Mimuna** (origin uncertain) Home festivity at the close of Passover, observed by some Sefardim, particularly those from Morocco. It is considered a celebration of freedom, and also of the renewal of spring, and therefore of fertility. On the eve of Maimuna, families visit each other, and there is lavish hospitality. The table is traditionally decorated with wheat sheaves and a variety of symbolic foods, including milk for purity, eggs or bean pods for fertility, and dates or honey to symbolize a sweet year.

majority decision *See* CONSENSUS.

Makkot ('blows') Tractate of Mishnah, Tosefta and both Talmuds, in order Nezikin, originally part of the preceding tractate, Sanhedrin. It deals with the punishment of false witnesses, with the Cities of Refuge to which unintentional murderers may flee, and with the punishment of flogging.

Makom *See* HA-MAKOM.

Malachi Biblical book, the last of the Twelve Minor Prophets. 'Malachi' means 'my messenger', and it is unclear whether or not it is a proper name. The book begins with an affirmation of God's love of Israel and his hatred of Esau, and continues with vivid denunciations of various types of wrongdoing accompanied with visions of the 'Day of the Lord'.

Malchut ('sovereignty') In kabbala, one of the SEFIROT.

mamzer The offspring of an incestuous or adulterous union. A mamzer is severely limited in his choice of marriage partner: according to the Mishnah he may only marry another mamzer, a proselyte, or a freed slave. Liberally minded Orthodox authorities have tried to alleviate the problem by turning a blind eye to it, but they have not been able to abolish the category of mamzer or to mitigate its consequences.

mantle A textile covering to adorn and preserve the Torah scroll. In Hebrew the term me'il is often used. Mantles evolved gradually, from a simple sack-shaped cover placed over the closed scroll to a more elaborate structure with a flat rigid top on which the KÉTER could be placed. The Western Sefardi mantle consists of a rigid top, with two holes to allow the passage of the staves, to which a piece of cloth is attached so as to make a full skirt, open at the front (the side of the writing in the scroll), and with tassels along the lower hem. The material is generally a precious one, such as embroidered silk or silk brocade. The Ashkenazi mantle today also has a rigid top with two holes; two rectangles of cloth (often velvet) are attached to this and to each other, so as to make a straight-sided bag, often embroidered on the front with a design and perhaps the name of a donor. Eastern communities do not use mantles; they protect the scroll within a wooden case (tik) instead.

Ma'oz Tsur ('fortress, rock') Ashkenazi Chanukka hymn. An acrostic gives the author's name, Mordecai, but nothing more is known about him. The name comes from the opening words: 'Fortress, Rock of my salvation, it is pleasant to sing your praise. Restore my house of prayer, and there we shall offer thanksgiving …' The hymn recounts four past moments of salvation from troubles: the exodus from Egypt, the return from Babylonian captivity, the foiling of Haman's plot to exterminate the Jews of Persia, and finally the rededication of the Temple by the Hasmoneans. The vengeful tone of the words has given some offence (particularly an anticipation of 'the slaughter of the baying foe' that will precede the restoration of the Temple), and attempts have been made in Reform circles to revise it, but the popularity of the hymn itself seems unassailable. It is sung to a rousing tune adapted from an old German folk song.

mappa ('cloth') Term for various kinds of textile used in the synagogue. **1** A wrapper for the Torah scroll. (The term yeri'a is also used for this type of mappa.) Originally probably a square of fabric, it is now a long rectangle, the same height as the scroll, and as much as 3.5 to 4 metres wide. Some communities use a wrapper that is as long as the scroll itself, so that it forms a backing to the parchment that does not need to be adjusted every time the scroll is rolled on; this type is much easier to use but much more expensive and much heavier to carry. Ashkenazim do not use a wrapper. **2** A strip of fabric tied around the Torah scroll to secure it when it is rolled up. Both Ashkenazim and Sefardim use this; it is often tied with long ribbons. *See* *also* WÍMPEL. **3** A cover placed over the Torah scroll out of respect when it is open for the reading but is not actually being read (i.e. between the sections, when someone is being called up). **4** A cover for the reading desk on which the Torah is read. *See also* next entry.

Mappa ('cloth', i.e. tablecloth) Name given to the glosses added by Moses ISSERLES to the SHULCHAN ARUCH, specifying Ashkenazi practice where it differed from that laid down in Caro's great code. The Mappa is thus the 'tablecloth' spread on the 'Prepared Table' (the meaning of Shulchan Aruch). It was thanks to the Mappa that the Shulchan Aruch was enabled to become an authoritative halachic code for all Jews, Sefardi and Ashkenazi alike.

mara de-atra (Aramaic, 'master of the place') Term applied in rabbinic law to the authority of the local rabbi. If a question or dispute is referred to a local rabbi, his decision may not be undermined by appeal to rabbis elsewhere.

marbits tora ('propagator of Torah') Term used by Ashkenazi traditionalists to indicate someone who contributes to the propagation of knowledge of the Torah. Among Sefardim in the Ottoman empire it was a title given to a leading rabbi and teacher, and, latterly, to the head of a TALMUD TORA or YESHIVA.

Marcheshvan *See* CHESHVAN.

maror Bitter herb, eaten during the SÉDER ritual. In Mediterranean lands, lettuce or celery is traditionally used; Ashkenazim use horseradish.

marriage Traditionally, marriage has been regarded as the ideal state. It is considered a binding obligation to 'be fruitful and multiply', which is said to be the first commandment uttered by God to mankind (Genesis 1.28; cf. 9.1, 7), but marriage is also praised as conferring joy, love and harmony. Both the institution and its ceremonies have evolved considerably over the centuries. In the West, under Christian influence, there is a certain tendency for marriages to be performed in synagogue with a rabbi officiating and delivering an address, and with bridesmaids and a best man. Traditionally, however, the couple marry each other with no need of an officiant, and the ceremony may take place at home or even in the open air. It is performed under a canopy known as a chuppa, and the term chuppa has come to be used of the marriage itself. There are many variations in the details, but the following account, based on the Orthodox marriage ceremony, includes the most widely followed practices.

A marriage document or KETUBBA is first drawn up and witnessed, stating the date and place and recording the husband's acceptance of his obligations towards his wife, and the amount that he will pay her if he divorces her. Without a ketubba it is not strictly legal for husband and wife to live together.

Marriage is an occasion for rejoicing, but it is also a solemn moment for the bride and bridegroom, and they are supposed to fast from dawn until the end of the ceremony. Mindful of the serious responsibilities they are undertaking, when they say their prayers they include a confession of sins and some penitential passages. It used to be customary for the bridegroom to wear for the first time during the ceremony the KÍTTEL, a gift from his bride, serving as a reminder that 'in the midst of life we are near death'.

The bride and bridegroom are escorted to the chuppa by their parents, who stand under the chuppa with them, the bride and groom facing towards the east. The ensuing ceremony is in two parts, representing two stages which in ancient times were completely separate, the betrothal (erusin or kiddushin) and the marriage proper (nisu'in). After some opening songs and prayers, the officiant says the blessing over wine and then recites the benediction for betrothal. The bride and groom sip the wine, and the groom places a ring on the bride's right forefinger, saying: 'Behold, you are betrothed to me by this ring according to the law of Moses and Israel.' (In egalitarian marriages there is an exchange of rings.) The ketubba is then read out, and this concludes the first stage, the betrothal ceremony.

In the second stage seven benedictions are recited, linking the marriage on the one hand to the creation of mankind and on the other to the future redemption. The seventh benediction runs as follows: 'Blessed are you, Lord our God, king of the universe, who created joy and gladness, bridegroom and bride, mirth and song, jubilation and merriment, love and companionship, peace and friendship. Soon, Lord our God, may there be heard in the cities of Judah and in the streets of Jerusalem sounds of joy and gladness, the voices of bridegroom and bride, jubilant voices of bridegrooms from their bridal canopy and of young people feasting and singing. Blessed are you, Lord, who makes the bridegroom rejoice with the bride.' After another sip of wine the bridegroom breaks a glass, an ancient custom whose significance has been lost. It may have been intended originally to avert the forces of evil – or perhaps it is to remind the couple and their guests of the fragility of all happiness; it is often said to be a reminder of the destruction of the Temple. Technically the marriage is incomplete without being consummated by sexual union, symbolized by the bride and bridegroom spending some moments together after the ceremony. (This is known as yichud, 'unification'.) The marriage is also incomplete without feasting and dancing. (In very traditional circles the men and women dance separately.) The meal ends with a special grace, followed by a repetition of the seven blessings. *See also* LEVIRATE MARRIAGE.

martyrdom (in Hebrew, KIDDUSH HA-SHEM) Giving up one's life for one's faith. Martyrdom is not generally glorified in Judaism, but those who have died as martyrs are honoured as 'holy ones' (kedoshim). Complex legal discussions attend the question of whether voluntary martyrdom is ever demanded in the Torah, and if so under what conditions. From discussions in the Talmud it emerges that three commandments are regarded as so solemn that one should die rather than infringe them under external pressure: idolatry, incest and murder. However, where persecutors demand that a Jew infringe a lesser commandment as a symbolic gesture of disloyalty to the Torah the Jew should die rather than obey. Maimonides observes that to court martyrdom in other cases is tantamount to committing suicide, and therefore strictly forbidden. The TOSAFISTS, however, disagreed: they even argued that suicide and infanticide were legitimate when faced with the danger of APOSTASY. In taking this line they certainly had in mind the terrible massacres of entire Jewish communities by Christians during the First Crusade (1096). The Rhineland martyrs were remembered as having gone willingly to their deaths, even killing themselves and their children. Poems were sung in synagogue in their memory, and there are some other examples of laments in memory of martyrs. The additional service for the Day of ATONEMENT commemorates ten rabbis thought to have been martyred by the Romans for teaching the Torah at a time of persecution; in modern liturgies other martyrs, notably the victims of the Holocaust, are included in these prayers. Dirges for the martyrs have also been introduced into the services for TISH'A BE-AV and for certain Sabbaths.

mashgí'ach ('supervisor') Term normally used of a supervisor appointed by a rabbinic authority to oversee the KASHRUT of food products. It is also used of a tutor (mashgí'ach ruchani, 'spiritual overseer') who supervises the religious life of YESHIVA students (*see also* MUSAR MOVEMENT).

maskil ('intelligent'; plural maskilim) **1** Particularly in Sefardi usage, a title of honour for a learned man. **2** Since the 19th century, a devotee of the HASKALA.

masora ('tradition') An apparatus to the text of the Bible containing textual variants, conjectural emendations and notes on the way certain letters are to be written and on the number of letters, words and verses in each section. It was compiled by the MASORETES. Medieval manuscripts of the Bible often show two forms of the masora, the masora parva, indicated by abbreviated notes in the margins or between the columns, and the masora magna, a more detailed apparatus placed at the top and/or bottom of the page. At the beginning and end of the manuscripts, lists of masoretic notes are sometimes written in beautifully illuminated 'carpet pages'.

masóret ('tradition') Tradition plays a large part in rabbinic Judaism. According to the legendary Rabbi AKIBA, 'tradition is a fence around the Torah' (Mishnah, Avot 3.14). *See* TRADITIONALISM.

Masoretes Specialists in the textual study of the Bible, whose work culminated in the so-called Masoretic text, which is now the standard text of the Hebrew Bible. Research on ancient manuscripts from the Judaean Desert has shown that 2,000 years ago three main text types of the Torah co-existed. One of them was very similar to the consonantal form of what was to become the Masoretic text. (The others were closer to the Greek Septuagint and the Samaritan Pentateuch respectively.) The vowel signs and cantillation signs were added later, by the Masoretes.

The Masoretic text was given its present form by Aaron ben Asher in the Land of Israel in the 10th century, but the work of the Masoretes had extended over several centuries. The Masoretic text of the Bible consists of a traditional consonantal text, equipped with vowel signs to assist reading, and other signs that aid liturgical cantillation and phrasing, together with an apparatus, the MASORA. The various signs are followed in the public readings in synagogue, even though they are not written in scrolls of the Torah. Most readers, while making use of the vowel signs, pay only scant attention to the other features, but they respect Masoretic advice about certain preferred variants (termed kerí, 'reading') which are used in reading aloud even if a different form (called ketív, 'written'), sanctified by tradition, is written in the text. Modern research has brought about many advances in our knowledge of the history of the text and many emendations have been suggested, but so far as the religious use of the Bible is concerned, in public readings and preaching, Jews have remained ineradicably attached to the Masoretic text.

Masorti ('traditional') Modernist movement, closely related to CONSERVATIVE JUDA-ISM. In Britain, the term refers to a movement created under the spiritual and theological aegis of Louis JACOBS, and represented institutionally by the Assembly of Masorti Synagogues. In Israel the Masorti Movement was founded in 1979.

masturbation Rabbinic halacha is firmly opposed to all forms of 'wasting seed', although this prohibition is not entirely watertight, for example a man is allowed to have sexual relations with his wife even if he knows she is too old to conceive, and some authorities have permitted married couples to engage in forms of sexual activity that cannot result in conception. The kabbalists, however, tend to describe 'wasting seed' as the gravest of sins. For women masturbation is not prohibited, presumably because no 'waste of seed' is involved.

matriarchs (in Hebrew, immahot) The four wives of the PATRIARCHS, namely Sarah (wife of ABRAHAM), Rebekah/Rebecca (wife of ISAAC), and Rachel and Leah (wives of JACOB). They are thought to be buried in HEBRON, except for Rachel, whose grave is venerated near Bethlehem.

matsa Unleavened bread. All meal offerings in the Temple were of matsa, and it is a positive commandment to eat matsa on the first night of Passover. To intensify this observance it is customary to avoid eating matsa in the period before Passover. Strict rules govern the preparation of Passover matsa, so as to avoid any taint of leaven (CHAMETS). Matsa shemura or shemura matsa ('guarded matsa') is a special matsa used by the punctilious for the observance of the commandment on Passover eve: it is made from grain that has been watched from the time of harvesting to ensure that it is not in contact with moisture and therefore is unable to become chamets.

Mattathias (Mattityáhu) Priest who initiated the HASMONEAN REVOLT in 166 BCE. He was the father of JUDAH THE MACCABEE.

Maybaum, Ignaz (1897–1976) Theologian. Born in Vienna, Maybaum studied in Berlin and served as rabbi to several congregations in Germany before emigrating to Britain in 1939. Here he ministered to a Reform synagogue in Edgware (north-west London) and taught theology at Leo Baeck College, the rabbinical seminary that he helped to found together with other survivors from the Berlin Hochschule (see BAECK, LEO; GEIGER, ABRAHAM). Maybaum saw himself as a disciple of Franz ROSENZWEIG and self-consciously tried to transmit his thought to English speakers. However, his writing is dominated by reflection on the Holocaust (see HOLOCAUST THEOLOGY). Starting from the biblical belief that all Jewish history is the arena in which God manifests his paternal care for his people he arrives at the unusual and disturbing conclusion that, for reasons which may be hard for us to fathom, Hitler was doing

God's bidding. He was a pioneer of 'trialogue' (a word he seems to have invented) between Jews, Christians and Muslims.

mazal tov ('good luck') Greeting on an auspicious occasion. In antiquity mazal meant a constellation or sign of the zodiac, and so the term came to be used for the influence supposed to be exercised by the heavenly bodies on human affairs. Today it has no such connotations.

Me'am Lo'ez ('from a people of alien speech') Encyclopaedic commentary on the Bible, written in JUDEZMO. The title is borrowed from Psalm 114.1. The project was initiated by Jacob Chuli (d. 1732) in Constantinople. He published the first volume, on Genesis, in 1730, and the work was continued after his death by a long series of successors, partly on the basis of his notes. The commentary draws on a vast range of texts, including Talmud and Midrash, halacha and kabbala. It proved very popular, and has been reprinted many times.

meat *See* DIETARY REGULATIONS.

Mechilta *See* HALACHIC MIDRASHIM.

mechitsa ('partition') Physical division between male and female worshippers in Orthodox and traditionalist synagogues. It generally takes the form of a screen or curtain.

mechutanim People related by marriage. *See* FAMILY.

megilla ('scroll') **1** Common designation for the scroll of ESTHER, read in synagogue at PURIM. **2** (Megilla) Tractate of the Mishnah, Tosefta and both Talmuds, found in the order Mo'ed, dealing with the reading of the scroll of ESTHER, and other observances connected with PURIM.

megillot ('scrolls') *See* BIBLE.

me'il *See* MANTLE.

Me'ila ('misappropriation') Tractate of the Mishnah, Tosefta and Babylonian Talmud, found in the order Kodashim, dealing with the secular use of objects consecrated to the Temple.

Meir ben Isaac of Worms *See* AKDAMUT; AKEDA.

Meir of Rothenburg (d. 1293) German halachist. He was the last of the TOSAFISTS and the greatest of the Ashkenazi poskim (*see* POSEK) of the Middle Ages. He instituted a collection of all the RESPONSA of the Ashkenazi communities down to his time. Unlike his Ashkenazi contemporaries he took a positive line on the code of MAIMONIDES and tried to integrate it within his own work. He also composed PIYYU-TIM. Meir died in prison in Alsace, having refused an offer by the Jewish community to ransom him, as this would have constituted a dangerous precedent.

Meiri, Menachem (1249–c. 1316) Talmudist and theologian. Meiri, who lived in Perpignan, is mainly remembered as the author of commentaries on the tractates of the Talmud. As a Talmudic commentator he is held by many to be second only to RASHI. He is a thorough and systematic commentator with a strongly rationalistic turn of mind. He is notably independent and tolerant in his attitude to Christians and Muslims: although he considers their religious beliefs false, he maintains that since they submit their lives to the rules of religion they are in a separate category from pagans and in some respects are in the same category as Jews.

Melachim Alef, Melachim Bet Hebrew names of the biblical books of 1 and 2 Kings, respectively.

melammed ('teacher'; plural melammedim or melammedin) Term usually applied in former times to an elementary teacher, one who taught small children. Often of limited knowledge, they were generally poorly remunerated and their status in the community was relatively low.

melave malka ('accompanying the queen') Festive meal held at the close of the Sabbath, accompanied with songs in honour of the Sabbath queen and of the prophet Elijah.

meldado or **meldadura** (Judezmo, from modern Greek meletan, 'to study') Among Jews originating in the former Ottoman empire, a study session, for example a night of study held annually at SHEMINI ATSÉRET. Nowadays mainly reserved for a gathering for prayers and readings on the anniversary of a death, concluding with an ASHKABÁ.

memorial prayers For memorial services in synagogue see YIZKOR. *See also* ASHKABÁ; EL MALE RACHAMIM; KADDISH.

Menachot ('meal offerings') Tractate of the Mishnah, Tosefta and Babylonian Talmud, found in the order Kodashim, and dealing with the meal offerings made in the Temple.

Mendelssohn, Moses (1729–86) German philosopher. Born in Dessau, Mendelssohn moved to Berlin in 1743 and eventually joined the circle of the Berlin Enlightenment. He became a well-known figure in Berlin, and his writings, such as *Phaedon* (1767), gained him a Europe-wide reputation. Mendelssohn is rightly seen as the father of the Jewish Enlightenment. A champion of political emancipation of the Jews, he was often called upon to defend the teachings of Judaism from Christian attacks. In his book *Jerusalem* (1783) he distanced Judaism from Christianity by proclaiming that, whereas Christianity was a revealed religion, Judaism had no dogmas that were not accessible to the reasoning of any human being. Its only distinctive, divinely given heritage was its law. His German translation of the Torah, accompanied by a Hebrew commentary (BI'UR), introduced many German Jews to the ideas of the Enlightenment; no doubt for this reason, he was execrated by traditionalists. His last work, *Morgenstunden* (*Morning Hours*, 1786) is a demonstration of the existence of God.

menora The seven-branched lampstand of gold that stood in the tabernacle in the wilderness (Exodus 25.31–8, 37.17–24) and in the Temple. In the early centuries CE the image of the menora became a widespread symbol, perhaps as a symbol of the

Temple, or the seven planets (which, for the Ancients, included the sun and the moon), or of the light of the Torah spreading through the world. It is found on innumerable tombstones and figures prominently in the decoration of synagogues. Today it has come to be replaced as a Jewish symbol by the MAGEN DAVID, but can still be seen in synagogues, and has been adopted as an emblem by the state of Israel.

menstruation *See* NIDDA.

mercy *See* COMPASSION.

merit *See* ZECHÚT.

merkava *See* HECHALOT; MA'ASE MERKAVA.

meshummad An apostate; a Jew who has abandoned his people. The term is related to the word shemád, denoting religious persecution, enforced apostasy, and thus can be interpreted as implying a measure of coercion. Despite this, the connotations of the term are anything but sympathetic, perhaps because some of the best-known Christian persecutors of Jews in the Middle Ages and later were apostates from Judaism. *See* APOSTASY; MUMAR.

Messiah

Redeemer believed to be sent by God to usher in a new era of peace and harmony in which all humanity will worship the true God.

The doctrine of the Messiah is one of the most distinctive ideas of classical Judaism. Hermann COHEN called it 'the most significant and original product of the Jewish spirit'. The roots of the idea are found in the Bible, together with the term mashíach, which means 'anointed with oil' and can refer to any office holder, such as a king or high priest, who is anointed at his installation. The prophets look forward to a time when the people of Israel will be freed from subjection to other nations, and when justice and righteousness will be established in the world under the rule of God, and some of the prophets (Isaiah, Jeremiah, Micah, Zechariah) associate this transformation of history with an exceptionally exalted human leader. Others envisage a 'day of the Lord' when the dynasty of David will rule but there will be no special leader. These ideas are developed in the post-biblical literature, and the rabbinic writings are full of references to the idea of a Messiah who will rescue Israel from its historical predicament and inaugurate a golden age of peace and harmony. However, the concept is not developed with clarity, and many conflicting opinions are recorded. One rabbi, for example, states that it is vain to hope for a future Messiah, because the Messiah mentioned in the Bible came in the time of Hezekiah, at the beginning of the 7th century BCE. There is a widespread assumption that the messianic age is not a supernatural disturbance in history but rather, as the 3rd-century Babylonian teacher Samuel puts it, 'is no different from the present except that Israel will no longer be in subjection to the kingdoms of the world'

(Bavli, Berachot 34b). At the same time many rabbis insist that it is wrong to calculate when the redemption will come about, and still worse to take action to hasten it. Thus they were generally opposed to the occasional outbreaks of messianic fervour that arose particularly under Roman rule. Even this hostility, however, is not unanimous, and some rabbis, including the outstanding leader AKIBA, are said to have recognized the rebel BAR KOCHBA as the Messiah.

Several benedictions embodying rabbinic messianism have been included in the AMIDA, where they help to keep the ideas alive, with phrases such as: 'Sound the great horn for our liberation, and raise a banner to gather our scattered ones, and gather us together from the four corners of the earth'; 'Restore our judges as they were and our counsellors as at the beginning; remove from us sorrow and sighing and rule over us yourself alone'; 'Speedily uproot and crush, cast down and humble the rule of arrogance'; 'Return to your city, Jerusalem, in mercy, and make it your home as you have promised; rebuild it soon to last eternally, and set up the throne of David within it'; 'Cause the shoot of your servant David to sprout forth, and exalt his horn with your salvation, for we wait all day long for your salvation'; 'Restore the service to the shrine of your house, and willingly and lovingly accept the fire-offerings of Israel and their prayer'; 'May the remembrance of the Messiah, the son of your servant David and of Jerusalem your holy city, rise up before you'.

The early 7th century, a period of cataclysmic wars between Byzantium and Persia closely followed by the Arab conquest of the Middle East, witnessed a great intensification of messianic fervour. According to some there would be two Messiahs, a descendant of Joseph who would be slain in battle, and a descendant of David who would resurrect him and win the final victory over the Antimessiah (sometimes named as Armilos).

During the Middle Ages there is unanimity concerning the belief in a personal Messiah, but there is disagreement about whether the messianic age will be a natural or a supernatural event. Maimonides insists that it is wrong to imagine that the course of nature will change with the coming of the Messiah. The King Messiah will restore the kingdom of David to its former glory, restore the Temple and the sacrificial worship, and gather in the dispersed Israelites. He will be a wise ruler who will study the teachings of the Torah and compel all Israel to observe them. At the same time, he points out that the Talmudic rabbis had no detailed tradition on this subject, but tried to interpret the biblical teachings. The purpose of the messianic age, according to Maimonides, is not that the redeemed Israelites should lord it over the other nations, but simply that they should be free to study the Torah, so as to prepare themselves for the Coming Age or 'World to Come' (OLAM HA-BA).

Isaac LURIA gave a new direction to messianism by claiming that it is up to each individual either to impede or hasten the messianic redemption by performing good or evil deeds. In the LURIANIC KABBALA, after the breaking of the vessels sparks of divine light became trapped within broken fragments. Some sparks are imprisoned within the KELIPPOT (demonic forces). Human beings, by performing good actions and refraining from evil ones, can release the sparks. When all the sparks have been freed the Messiah will come.

SHABBETAI TSEVÍ was profoundly influenced by the ideas of the Lurianic kabbala, but he administered a new twist to them by teaching that the holy sparks may be released through the performance of sinful acts. Even when he eventually accepted conversion to Islam as the price of his life many of his adherents continued to believe in him, claiming that he had apostatized so as to release the holy sparks trapped in the domain of impurity. They continued secretly to perform 'holy sins' to bring his work to completion.

CHASIDISM, too, gives prominence to the idea of the holy sparks, and develops it still further. Sparks are trapped within food, drink and other mundane things, and therefore the Chasid must be fully involved with worldly matters in order to release them. In addition, each individual has the task of freeing not only his own sparks but those of others, which may in some cases be reached only after a long journey, and which only he and no one else can release.

There is no clear or unanimous understanding today about the Messiah or the messianic age. Orthodoxy maintains the belief in a personal Messiah who will come in God's good time to restore the sacrificial worship and lead all humanity back to God. Many of the 19th-century reformers wanted to do away with the whole idea of the Messiah, but eventually the concept of a messianic age was incorporated into Reform thought, not in the sense of the restoration of a Jewish state, which they rejected, but in the moral and political advances of the time. As the PITTSBURGH PLATFORM put it: 'We recognize in the modern era of universal culture of heart and intellect the approaching of the realization of Israel's great messianic hope for the establishment of the kingdom of truth, justice and peace among all men.'

This somewhat bland interpretation of a powerful doctrine has not satisfied everyone, and there has been a revival of interest recently in the kabbalistic and Chasidic approaches. Among neo-kabbalistic and neo-Chasidic groups the bringing of the Messiah occupies a high priority. Some are content with the straightforward idea of cultivating the good life and keeping the commandments of the halacha. An old saying is quoted with approval: If all Jews observed two successive Sabbaths properly the Messiah would come. Others pursue the liberation of the trapped sparks through meditation and by other means.

ZIONISM, although essentially a secular movement, makes use of some of the ideas and language of messianism. For example, the proclamation of the state of Israel in 1948 spoke of the ingathering of the dispersed and of the prophetic vision of liberty, justice and peace. The Zionist enterprise has united religious Jews with secular Jews, some of whom have been militantly anti-religious. The alliance has been an uneasy one, with the secularists prevailing both numerically and in terms of power and influence. The leading theoretician of religious Zionism, Abraham Isaac KOOK, maintained that, despite its secularist impetus, the Zionist movement represented 'the beginnings of the messianic age', quoting a Talmudic dictum that 'in the footsteps of the Messiah insolence will increase'. He was convinced that the holiness of the Land of Israel would penetrate the souls of the atheists, releasing their trapped sparks and bringing redemption in the very near future. Since the creation of the State, and particularly since the Six-Day War of 1967, some religious Zionists have taken to speaking of the creation of the state of Israel as the 'beginning of redemption', not as being itself the future restored kingdom, of which it lacks too many of the features, but at least an indication that the redemption is on its way. The GUSH EMUNIM movement has gone further, and seen the state itself as sharing in the character of the messianic kingdom, so that it is actually a first step towards the final goal of redemption. All Zionists are fond of a song that says: 'David King of Israel lives, lives and exists!'

There have been many examples of people, like Shabbetai Tseví, who either claimed to be the Messiah or had the claim advanced on their behalf by their followers. While there has been no outstanding claimant in recent times, some Jews have put forward particular political or spiritual leaders to be the Messiah. Leaving aside self-styled MESSIANIC JEWS, the most striking example was the Seventh Lubavitcher Rebbe, Menachem Mendel SCHNEERSON. Many of his followers hailed him as the Messiah, and gathered in public places singing 'We want Moshiach [the Messiah] now!' and even the Rebbe's death in 1994 did not put an end to their messianic enthusiasm.

Messianism seems to correspond to a deeply rooted yearning for redemption arising from a profound dissatisfaction with the real world when judged against religious teachings about the perfection and power of God. This perennial yearning, reinforced by the vivid words of the liturgy, has kept the messianic idea on the Jewish agenda.

messianic Jews Converts to Christianity who accept the Christian claims about Jesus and the Christian understanding of the Messiah as a supernatural, spiritual figure who is the son of God and part of a divine 'trinity'.

metivta Aramaic for YESHIVA. *See also* UNION FOR TRADITIONAL JUDAISM.

mezumman ('invited') Group of three or more who have eaten together (*see* ZIMMUN). According to the Mishnah (Berachot 7.2), women, slaves and minors are not to be counted in the mezumman, but the rule has not always been strictly observed: some authorities allow women to be counted, and there is a Sefardi custom that boys over the age of six may be included.

mezuza ('doorpost'; plural mezuzot) A handwritten parchment contained in an elongated case marked with the Hebrew letter shin (for SHADDAI), and fixed to the right doorpost of the house (as one enters). The first two paragraphs of the SHEMÁ (Deuteronomy 6.4–9 and 11.13–21) are written on the parchment by hand. Although these are sometimes described as amulets or talismans, and one may see pious Jews kissing them on entering or leaving a house, there is nothing magical about them: they are a reminder of the words of the Torah which are actually inscribed on them: 'You shall write them [the words of the Torah] on the doorposts of your house and upon your gates' (Deuteronomy 6.9, 11.20). The meaning is understood to be that everything that is done by Jews either inside or outside the home should be marked by an attentiveness to the Torah. The fixing of the mezuza on a new home is an occasion for rejoicing, accompanied by short religious service (CHANUKKAT HA-BÁYIT).

Mi she-Berach ('he who blessed') Prayer recited after a member of the congregation is called up to the Torah, so called because it opens with the formula 'May he who blessed our ancestors Abraham, Isaac and Jacob bless ...' (Egalitarian versions of the prayer also exist naming MATRIARCHS as well as PATRIARCHS. It is an old Sefardi custom to name the matriarchs instead of the patriarchs when blessings on women are invoked.) Such events as the birth of a child, a BAR MITSVA, a wedding, or even nowadays a silver or golden wedding or a seventieth or eightieth birthday, may be mentioned, and this is also a point in the service where prayers may be offered for someone who is ill. Charitable donations are customarily offered by the person called up, although some synagogues discourage the practice as confusing the material and the spiritual, and encouraging unseemly and invidious displays of wealth or generosity. A similar prayer calling down God's blessing on the entire congregation is said after the conclusion of the Torah reading and HAFTARA.

Miami Platform Declaration on ZIONISM issued by the CENTRAL CONFERENCE OF AMERICAN RABBIS on 24 June 1997, in anticipation of the first centenary of the First Zionist Congress. The Platform marks a formal reversal of a number of well-established principles of REFORM JUDAISM, notably on Zionism itself, on the status of the Hebrew language, and, in passing, on the authority of HALACHA. These new attitudes have emerged gradually over a long period, but this is the first time that they have received such clear and unambiguous expression. At the same time the Platform calls for significant changes in Israel itself, in line with the needs and ethos of Reform Judaism. It has six sections. The first affirms the unique character of the state of Israel, in line with the unique calling of the Jewish people. 'Its obligation is to strive towards the attainment of the Jewish people's highest moral ideals.' The second states (contradicting the 1885 PITTSBURGH PLATFORM) that Jews have never abandoned the hope for a national home in the Land of Israel; it supports the Jewish claim to national sovereignty, but urges 'that it be used to create the kind of society in which full civil, human, and religious rights exist for all its citizens'. The third declares that Israeli and Diaspora Jewry are interdependent. The fourth pledges political support and financial assistance to Israel and undertakes to promote the Hebrew language. It calls on Reform Jews to visit Israel and to settle there, in accordance with a halachic precept. Finally, it calls on Reform Jews to strengthen 'an indigenous Progressive Judaism' in Israel. The fifth section calls for equal legal rights for all religious interpretations of Judaism. The last section expresses the hope that the state of Israel will hasten 'the fulfilment of our messianic dream of universal peace under the sovereignty of God'.

Micah (Micha) Biblical book, sixth of the Twelve Minor Prophets. Micah seems to have lived in the 8th century BCE. His prophecy begins with a condemnation of political, social and religious abuses that if continued will bring about the downfall of the two states of Samaria and Judah, and continues with a vision of universal peace, with Jerusalem as the capital, under a ruler from Bethlehem. Replying to a questioner asking what sacrifices he should bring to God, offering thousands of rams or ten thousand rivers of oil, or even his eldest son, the prophet replies with the now famous words: 'He has told you, man, what is good, and what the Lord demands of you: only to act justly and love kindness, and walk modestly [or humbly] with your God' (6.8).

midde'orayeta (Aramaic, 'from the Torah') Technical term in HALACHA for COMMANDMENTS directly prescribed in the Torah, as opposed to those laid down by the rabbis.

Middot ('measurements') Tractate of the Mishnah, in the order Kodashim. It describes the layout of the Temple.

midrash ('investigation', 'interpretation', 'preaching'; plural midrashim). Term with a general and a specific application. The general application refers to interpretation or exposition of a text, usually from the Bible, in the fashion favoured by the rabbis: the main purpose is to draw out the various possible meanings and potential contemporary applications to be found in the text. This method is far removed from that used by historical and philological criticism, which aims to discover the conditions under which the text was first produced and to pin down the meaning intended by the author(s). In many ways it is closer to post-modernist readings, and consequently the term has come into widespread use in current literary criticism. In the specific application the term is often written with a capital M. It is the name given collectively to a mass of works compiled, mainly in the Land of Israel, between the 3rd and 11th centuries, preserving excerpts from sermons and lectures and other comments on the words of scripture, which are woven together into something resembling a commentary. In the 16th century the so-called Midrash Rabba was published, presenting originally independent Midrashim on each of the five books of the Torah and the FIVE SCROLLS, and so these ten Midrashim have acquired a kind of canonical status. However there are many more Midrashim surviving in whole or in part, and scholars have hardly begun to grapple with the complexities presented by this literature, which is one of the richest departments of the rabbinic tradition. While the Midrashic interpretations do not have explicit religious authority, they are read with interest and cited with affection, and they have exerted a strong influence on biblical commentary and preaching.

Unlike the Talmud, in which the material is organized according to subject matter, the Midrash is presented in terms of the biblical text itself. Some of the works take the form of a running commentary on a biblical book, while others present homilies on the texts selected for public reading on various Sabbaths and festivals. The overall effect in either case is similar: the Midrash is not a continuous and coherent commentary by a single author, but a compendium of expositions, some of which are attributed to named rabbis while others are anonymous. *See also* BEIT MIDRASH.

mikdash *See* HOLINESS; PILGRIMAGE; TABERNACLE.

mikra *See* BIBLE.

Mikva'ot ('ritual baths') Tractate of the Mishnah and Tosefta, in the order Tohorot. Its subject matter is ritual purification by BATHING. *See also* MIKVE.

mikve (plural mikva'ot) A ritual bath. The Hebrew word originally meant a 'gathering of water' (used of the sea in Genesis 1.10 and a pool fed by streams in Leviticus 11.36), but eventually it became a technical term for a cistern or pool suitable for ritual BATHING, and also for the ritual immersion of utensils. The word can also means 'hope'; for example the prophet Jeremiah (17.13) calls God the mikve of Israel. Rabbi AKIBA plays on the double meaning of this phrase in his famous saying: 'As the mikve cleanses the unclean, so does the Holy One, blessed be He, cleanse Israel' (Mishnah, Yoma 8.9). The use of the mikve has decreased dramatically in the past two centuries, although a certain revival has been observed among Orthodox Jews, particularly in the USA and France. Reform and Liberal Judaism do not on the whole consider it an indispensable element in Jewish life; except perhaps for proselytes, Karaite authorities now consider that purification can be effected just as well by a shower.

milk An animal product specially associated with the Land of Israel in the Torah's phrase 'a land flowing with milk and honey'. Milk from forbidden animals is itself forbidden, as is any combination of milk and meat products (*see* DIETARY REGULATIONS). Foods made from milk are specially associated with SHAVUOT, and also with MAIMUNA.

Mimuna *See* MAIMUNA.

mincha ('offering') The afternoon service. The service begins with some readings about sacrifices and incense (Ashkenazim omit these), and its core is the AMIDA, preceded and followed by psalms. It ends with ALÉYNU. On Sabbaths and fast days a short reading precedes the Amida, and on the Day of Atonement and (in some rites) other fast days a HAFTARA follows (*see* JONAH). Nowadays mincha is often said close to sunset (which is the latest time for the service), so that it may be closely followed by the evening service (MA'ARIV).

minhag 1 CUSTOM. **2** Prayer rite.

Minhag America *See* WISE, ISAAC MAYER.

Minhag Ari *See* PRAYER BOOKS.

minyan ('counting') A quorum required to make up a congregation for public worship. The old rule is that a minimum of ten adult male Jews are required for the recitation of certain prayers, particularly the Kaddish, the reader's repetition of the AMIDA and the Torah reading and HAFTARA. Conservative rabbis, seeking to remedy some of the more offensive distinctions between the sexes in the old halacha, allow adult women to be counted in the minyan. Of course in large communities the congregation is often far greater than a bare minyan: it may consist of hundreds or exceptionally even thousands of worshippers. But even in large gatherings the concept of minyan has its role to play. The worshippers do not all arrive simultaneously, and it is convenient to have a clear and incontrovertible definition of when enough people have arrived to allow public worship to begin. Traditionally it has been considered meritorious to be one of the minyan, that is to be among the first ten men to arrive at the synagogue. To make up a minyan is particularly important in small communities, where public prayer may have to be suspended if the crucial number of ten is not reached. Hence the old institution of the 'minyan man', a poor Jew who was paid to attend services and make up the numbers. Reform Judaism has abolished the whole concept of the minyan: prayers may be said with any number present, and services begin at advertised times. Apart from the regular worship of the synagogue a minyan may gather in any suitable place to say the public prayers. An obvious example of this is the minyan that gathers in a house of mourning. Another, more joyful, example is the recitation of the seven blessings at dinner on one of the seven days following a wedding. Even in the ordinary grace after food the presence of a minyan is marked by a special opening formula. But a group of people who happen to be together for whatever purpose, for example for a meeting, or because they work nearby, may decide to constitute a minyan to say their prayers together. This minyan may sometimes develop into a fixed gathering that becomes in a sense an alternative to the regular synagogue worship. It may grow in time into a fully fledged synagogue: many synagogues have begun in this way. But the members may well feel that 'small is beautiful', and foster the intimacy of a small minyan. The term is also applied to a system of counting, for example it is used in the wording of the KETUBBA for the method of counting the years.

Mipnei Chata'eínu ('because of our sins') Prayer recited at festivals and on the Day of ATONEMENT, so called because of its opening words, 'Because of our sins we have been exiled from our land'.

misheberach *See* MI SHE-BERACH.

mishkan *See* TABERNACLE.

Mishle ('parables [of]') Hebrew name of the biblical book of PROVERBS.

Mishna Berura Six-volume commentary on the first part of the SHULCHAN ARUCH, dealing with laws of everyday life, by the CHAFETS CHAYYIM, Israel Meir Kagan. It was published between 1894 and 1907, and has proved extraordinarily successful. It is popular among CHAREDI yeshiva students, and is regarded by many Orthodox Ashkenazim as an authoritative guide.

Mishnah Compendium of rabbinic teachings, mainly but not exclusively of a halachic nature, traditionally thought to have been compiled in the Land of Israel by Rabbi JUDAH THE NASI in the early 3rd century CE. It is the text around which both TALMUDS are organized. The title can mean 'study' in Hebrew, but it comes from the same root as the word mishne, meaning 'second' (*see also* MISHNE TORAH), so that while its obvious meaning is 'that which is studied' it may also imply that the work is a 'second Torah'. The subject matter of the Mishnah is arranged under six major headings called orders (sedarim, plural of séder), each subdivided into a number of tractates (massechtot, plural of masséchet or massechta; the former term is Hebrew and the latter Aramaic). There are sixty-three tractates in all. Each tractate is divided into chapters (perakim, plural of pérek), and each of these is divided in turn into smaller units to which the term mishna (plural mishnayyot) is applied (the term halacha, plural halachot, is also used). The first order, 'Seeds', is mainly concerned with agricultural laws, but it opens with a tractate devoted to prayers and blessings. Next comes 'Set Feasts', that is the regulations for Sabbaths, festivals and other special days. The third order, 'Women', contains tractates on marriage, divorce and other aspects of personal status. 'Damages', the fourth order, is concerned with the civil and criminal law, while the remaining orders, 'Holy Things' and 'Purity', deal respectively with temple sacrifices and the rules of ritual impurity (*see* table). These headings serve to define the interests of the Halacha in early rabbinic Judaism. The rabbis whose opinions are cited in the Mishnah are known as TANNA'IM. The Mishnah appears more interested in studying the halacha than in determining actual practice. It records innumerable disagreements without resolving them; it prefers representative cases rather than general principles of law; it discusses some laws that seem not to be of practical application. While there are many discussions of laws in the Torah the main focus is not directly on the Torah itself but on teaching, established practice, precedent and custom. The Mishnah is written in a type of Hebrew that is different from that of the Bible and presents many signs of Greek influence, including numerous Greek words. The text was first printed in Naples in 1492, with the commentary by MAIMONIDES. A corrected text was issued by Yom Tov Lipmann HELLER, together with his commentary (Prague, 1614–17). Current editions often include the commentary of Obadia Yare di BERTINORO. There is a very fine English translation by Herbert Danby (1933).

THE TRACTATES OF THE MISHNAH

FIRST ORDER: ZERA'IM/SEEDS	SECOND ORDER: MO'ED/SET FEASTS	THIRD ORDER: NASHIM/WOMEN
Berachot/Benedictions	Shabbat/Sabbath	Yevamot/Sisters-in-law
Pe'a/Gleanings	Eruvin/Fusion of Sabbath	Ketubbot/Marriage Deeds
Demái/Produce not	Limits	Nedarim/Vows
Certainly Tithed	Pesachim/Passover	Nazir/Nazirite Vow
Kiláyim/Mixtures	Shekalim/Shekel Dues	Sota/Suspected Adulteress
Shevi'it/The Seventh Year	Yoma/Day of Atonement	Gittin/Bills of Divorce
Terumot/Heave Offerings	Sukka/Tabernacles	Kiddushin/Betrothal
Ma'aserot/Tithes	Betsa or Yom Tov	
Ma'aser Sheni/Second Tithe	/Festival Days	
Challa/Dough Offering	Rosh ha-Shana/New Year	
Orla/Fruit of Young Trees	Ta'anit/Fast Days	
Bikkurim/First Fruits	Megilla/Scroll of Esther	
	Mo'ed Katan/Intermediate Days	
	Chagiga/Festal Offering	

FOURTH ORDER: NEZIKIN/DAMAGES	FIFTH ORDER: KODASHIM/HOLY THINGS	SIXTH ORDER: TOHOROT/PURITIES
Bava Kamma/First Gate	Zevachim/Animal	Kelim/Vessels
Bava Metsi'a/Middle Gate	Offerings	Oholot/Tents
Bava Batra/Last Gate	Menachot/Meal Offerings	Nega'im/Leprosy Signs
Sanhedrin/Law Courts	Chullin/Animals Killed for	Para/The Red Heifer
Makkot/Lashes	Food	Tohorot/Purities
Shevu'ot/Oaths	Bechorot/Firstlings	Mikva'ot/Ritual Baths
Eduyyot/Testimonies	Arachin/Vows for Valuation	Nidda/Menstrual Impurity
Avoda Zara/Idolatry	Temura/Substituted Offering	Machshirin/Rendering
Avot/Sayings of the Fathers	Keritot/Extirpation	Susceptible [to ritual
Horayot/Instructions	Me'ila/Sacrilege	impurity]
	Tamid/Daily Whole-offering	Zavim/Those Who Have a
	Middot/Dimensions	Discharge
	Kinnim/Bird Offerings	Tevúl Yom/He Who Has
		Bathed During the Day
		Yadá'im/Hands
		Uktsin/Stalks

Mishne Torah Code of rabbinic law compiled by Moses MAIMONIDES, and completed in 1177–8. It is also known as the Yad or Yad ha-Chazaka (Arm or Strong Arm), because it is arranged in fourteen books and the number fourteen when written in Hebrew letters forms the word yad. *See* CODES OF LAW.

mishpat *See* JUSTICE.

mitnaggedim ('opponents') Term applied to the opponents of CHASIDISM. Hostility to the new movement was at first considerable, particularly in Lithuania, where the VILNA GA'ON issued a ban against it in 1772. Gradually, with the success of Chasidism and the discovery of common threats in religious MODERNISM and secularism, the old hostility has become more muted, and Chasidim have sometimes made common cause with mitnaggedim (*see* CHAREDI).

mitsva ('commandment') **1** A law or COMMANDMENT. **2** In common parlance, a good deed.

mitsvot *See* COMMANDMENTS.

mizrach ('east') A plaque or other object placed on the east wall of a synagogue or private home (provided it is located to the west of Jerusalem) to indicate the direction of prayer.

Mizrachi Zionist political party founded in Vilna in 1902 by Rabbi Isaac Jacob Reines with the slogan 'The Land of Israel for the people of Israel according to the Torah of Israel'. Its object was to provide a voice for religious Zionists and to unite with secular Zionists in achieving a Jewish national home as an antidote to assimilation and antisemitism. The name was derived from that of Merkaz Ruchani ('spiritual centre'), an organization founded in 1893 by the early Zionist Rabbi Samuel Mohilever (1824–98) of Bialystok. The new party quickly gained a substantial international following (with an umbrella body named the World Mizrachi Organization) and became an influential element within the World Zionist Organization. In 1909 the foundations were laid for a network of schools in the Land of Israel where boys and girls were given a nationalist Jewish education in both secular and religious subjects. In 1922 a labour organization, Ha-Po'el ha-Mizrachi ('the Mizrachi worker'), was formed as a separate party under the slogan 'Torah and labour', with the aim of encouraging the integration of religious youth into the wider Zionist society, notably through the founding of co-operative and collective agricultural settlements. It created its own youth movement, Benei Akiva, with branches in the Diaspora, in 1929. In 1956 Ha-Po'el ha-Mizrachi merged with Mizrachi (while retaining its own identity as a labour movement) to form the National Religious Party (NRP, in Hebrew known by the acronym Mafdal). The NRP has been closely associated with the irredentist movement GUSH EMUNIM.

Mizrachim ('orientals') Term adopted by Ashkenazim in Israel to denote Jews whose family background is in North Africa and the Middle East (including India). The term originated in the 1950s and carries pejorative overtones. It is a misnomer, as many of the so-called 'Orientals' actually originate in the West, particularly in Morocco, which is called 'the West' (Maghrib) in Arabic. They are also often referred to as SEFARDIM, another misnomer as very many of them have no Sefardi background whatever. Both terms express and perpetuate unfortunate European racist and orientalist prejudices. Recently the term has come to be embraced by some 'Mizrachim' themselves as a political gesture.

mo'adim ('festivals') Sefardi name for a prayer book for the festivals.

mo'adim lesimcha ('festivals for joy') Greeting used on festivals, particularly by Sefardim. The traditional response is chagim u-zemanim le-sason ('feasts and solemn days for rejoicing'). Both phrases are borrowed from the festival AMIDA.

Modern Orthodoxy *See* ORTHODOXY.

---

modernism

Far-reaching reform that began in Hungary and Germany under the influence of the ENLIGHTENMENT and the movement for political EMANCIPATION. The new ideas manifested themselves at first in liturgical rather than in theological or legal reforms. In the early 19th century the issues which provoked debate included prayer in the vernacular, the introduction of sermons and music, the shortening of the service and the decorum of worshippers. It was only later that a theoretical basis was sought for the reforms with the help of theologians and historians.

The first truly reformed congregation was the New Israelite Temple Association, set up in Hamburg in 1817. The reforms included a strict insistence ondecorum, the introduction of choral and organ music, prayers in German and a German sermon. The liturgy was abbreviated, and the main emphasis was placed on the weekly Saturday morning service. The reforms were at once condemned by the BEIT DIN of Hamburg, but they were imitated elsewhere.

There was no agreement, however, about how far to proceed with the reformation of Judaism, and the modernizing movement was soon riven by acrimonious debates. The new ways found expression in a wide spectrum of formulations, ranging from the extreme theological conservatism of Samson Raphael HIRSCH to the extreme liberalism of Samuel HOLDHEIM and Abraham GEIGER. Characteristically, these three German rabbis had all enjoyed both a Talmudic and a secular university education, and much of the argument focused on how far it was permissible to allow the values of the surrounding culture to pervade Judaism.

The disagreements between Hirsch and Geiger and their respective followers found expression in polemics as bitter as those between modernists and traditionalists. For Hirsch belief in the inspiration and authority of the Bible, the Talmud and the whole corpus of rabbinic law became an article of faith. To budge from it even by an inch would open the door to unrestrained reform. Maybe that is why he was particularly firm in his opposition to Zacharias FRANKEL, a very conservative modernist who was himself an avowed enemy of what he termed 'negative reform leading to complete dissolution'. But the reformers argued that articles of faith are alien to the whole spirit of authentic Judaism, which proceeds through debate and consensus – or so they maintained – and they dubbed the new conservatism 'ORTHODOXY', a term borrowed from Christian theology, to highlight its dogmatic character. The name stuck.

Most of the main Jewish religious movements today owe their existence to the modernist movement, but Orthodoxy has come to align itself for most purposes with the traditionalist wing of Judaism, espousing FUNDAMENTALISM and considering the other modernist movements as a threat. The seeds of this attitude were sown by S. R. Hirsch himself and encouraged by some Orthodox leaders in the 20th century. Mass migration of traditionalists from eastern Europe to America, the Land of Israel and other countries has also nourished this realignment. Orthodox Jews today tend to consider themselves as upholders of the authentic Torah tradition, and see no essential religious difference between their own outlook and that of the traditionalist wing, which is often called ultra-Orthodoxy or extreme Orthodoxy.

modesty (in Hebrew, tseni'ut) A virtue, for both men and women. Biblical warrant for it can be found in Micah 6.8, which can be translated (in part) 'walk modestly with your God'. The term is particularly applied to women's dress, but it is equally applicable to every aspect of demeanour for both sexes.

mo'ed ('festival'; plural mo'adim) **1** A festival, as in the phrase CHOL HA-MO'ED, 'weekday of the festival'. **2** (Mo'ed) Second of the six orders of the Mishnah, dealing with regulations for the Sabbath and festivals.

Mo'ed Katan ('minor festival') Tractate of the Mishnah, in the order Mo'ed, with corresponding tractates in the Tosefta and both Talmuds. Its subject matter is the regulations for the intermediate days of the festivals of Sukkot and Passover (CHOL HA-MO'ED).

mohel someone who performs circumcisions. Although technically the duty to circumcise an infant son devolves upon the father, in practice the task is gratefully transferred to someone with experience and proven skill and expertise. According to the Talmud (Bavli, Chullin 9a) this is something (together with SHECHITA) that any rabbi ought to be able to do.

Molcho, Solomon (d. 1532) Kabbalist. Born Diogo Pires in Lisbon to a family forcibly converted to Christianity, he circumcised himself and devoted himself to kabbalistic studies, gained a reputation as a preacher, and even made an impression on the noted kabbalist and jurist Joseph CARO. After fantastic adventures in the course of which he spent thirty days praying and fasting in the guise of a Roman beggar in front of the papal palace (imitating a Talmudic description of the Messiah), was taken under the protection of the pope, gained a considerable following among Jews and Christians and endeavoured to curry favour with the emperor, Charles V, he was burnt at the stake in Mantua.

monogamy Marriage to one man or woman at a time. The Bible advocates monogamy for women but not for men; indeed, to have sexual relations with a married woman is a crime entailing the death penalty for both parties (Leviticus 20.10). Rabbinic law perpetuates the same distinction, but the so-called edict of Rabbenu GERSHOM makes monogamy the rule for Ashkenazim, motivated no doubt by the Christian environment rather than by an anachronistic concern for sexual equality. The sanctity of the exclusive bond between a wife and her husband is used in the Bible as an image for the relationship between Israel and God, particularly in the book of Hosea. The words spoken by God according to the prophet, 'I shall betroth you to me for ever, I shall betroth you to me with righteousness and justice, with love and mercy, I shall betroth you to me with faithfulness, and you shall know the Lord', are spoken by Ashkenazim as they wind the strap of the TEFILLIN around their middle finger like a wedding ring.

Montefiore, Claude J. G. (1858–1938) Theologian and founder of LIBERAL JUDAISM in England. After studying at Oxford University Montefiore enrolled at the Liberal rabbinic seminary in Berlin, where he met Solomon SCHECHTER, whom he brought to England as his personal tutor in rabbinics. His scholarly work was oriented towards the study of the New Testament, and, without in any way accepting the doctrinal claims of Christianity, he had a high regard for its ethical teachings. Together with an Orthodox scholar, Herbert Loewe, Montefiore published *A Rabbinic Anthology* (1938), in which the two editors conduct a lively discussion of the rabbinic excerpts from their respective positions. Montefiore was one of the founders of the Jewish Religious Union (1902), the forerunner of the Liberal Jewish Synagogue.

month *See* CALENDAR.

moral law *See* ETHICS.

Mordecai Uncle of Queen Esther in the biblical book of Esther. His refusal to bow down to the wicked Haman provokes the latter's plot to annihilate the Jews of the Persian empire. The Talmud discusses whether or not his intransigence was justified, given the extreme consequences. In the event the plot is frustrated, and the Jews' narrow escape is celebrated annually on PURIM. Mordecai is held up as the model of the proud Jew who refuses to bow down to any ruler but God.

morénu ('our teacher') Ashkenazi title indicating exceptional learning.

mori ('my teacher') Among Yemeni Jews, title of an elementary Bible teacher, to whom boys are sent at an early age to learn the rudiments of Hebrew and the Jewish religion.

Moriah Mountain and district where the AKEDA is described in the book of Genesis as taking place. Mount Moriah is identified with the Temple Mount in Jerusalem (2 Chronicles 3.1).

Moses (Moshé) Biblical hero, and the greatest of the prophets (Deuteronomy 34.10), who was chosen to lead the Israelites out of Egyptian slavery and to give them the Torah. The story of his life is told in the books of Exodus, Leviticus, Numbers and Deuteronomy. Notable moments are God's self-revelation to him at the burning bush, his song of victory after the crossing of the Sea of Reeds (Yam Suf, frequently mistranslated as the Red Sea), his forty days' stay on Mount Sinai, during which he neither ate nor drank, and where he received God's instructions to the people, the forty years in which he led the Israelites through the wilderness, and finally his death at the age of 120 before the crossing into the Promised Land. The rabbis call him 'Moses our rabbi', and evidently look to him as their own remote predecessor. The Midrash is full of legends and interpretations magnifying his personal qualities, and there is a special Midrash that describes his death: none of the angels is able to end Moses' life, so in the end God himself takes his soul away with a kiss. Nevertheless, neither the biblical nor the rabbinic writings elevate Moses to divine status: he remains an all-too-human figure. Moses MAIMONIDES, however, sees him as a superhuman person, and even incorporates this belief in his THIRTEEN PRINCIPLES. He writes: 'He comprehended more of God than any other man before or after him, in the past or the future, and we must believe that he attained a state of exaltedness beyond the human sphere, so that he reached the status of an angel.'

Moses ben Nachman *See* NACHMANIDES, MOSES.

Moses of Léon *See* ZOHAR.

mourning Grieving for the dead. Mourning is governed by very strict rules. The object of these rules is not to stifle or contain grief, but rather to provide support to the mourners and to help them over their time of trial and back into normal life. The definition of a mourner is a father, mother, son, daughter, brother, sister, husband or wife of the deceased. Children under BAR/BAT MITSVA age do not observe mourning, and there is no mourning or formal burial for an infant under thirty days old.

(Informal rites of grieving for stillborn babies and for infants are now being devised, because of a recognition that the parents need some means of channelling their grief.) Sons or daughters are distinguished from other mourners in a number of ways. For example, mourners have their clothes torn as a mark of grief: for sons and daughters this is done on the left, near the heart, while for other mourners it is done on the right side. (Nowadays, since people tend to object to expensive clothes being torn, the tearing is often done on a tie or a ribbon. Reform Judaism has abandoned the practice of tearing altogether.) The period of mourning extends to a year for one's parent; other mourners only mourn for a month.

Mourning proper only begins from the funeral. In the period between death and burial the mourner is known as an onen, and is not subjected to many particular rules, but, on the contrary, is relieved of religious obligations such as reciting prayers or saying the blessings before and after food. An onen is not supposed to drink wine, eat meat, indulge in luxuries or pleasures, or conduct business or professional activities. The main concern of the onen is to make arrangements for the funeral.

On returning home from the cemetery the mourner (who is now known as an avel) is offered a plate of food, which generally includes hard-boiled eggs and other round foods. It is customary to light a candle which will burn for the next seven days. Some people cover the mirrors in the house of mourning, or turn them to face the wall.

Mourning comes in three stages. The first, and most intense, lasts for seven days, and is known as shiva ('seven'). In fact, since the day of the funeral counts as the first day and shiva ends one hour into the seventh day, it actually lasts rather less than six days; moreover, on the Sabbath no outward signs of mourning are observed. If a festival falls during the period the shiva ceases and is not resumed. During shiva the mourners remain at home and sit on low stools (whence the popular expression 'to sit shiva'). They are not supposed to work or attend to their business affairs, have sexual intercourse, bathe, use cosmetics or creams, shave or have their hair cut. It is customary not to study Torah. After three days the rules are relaxed a little, and those who must go back to work may do so. Prayers are held in the house of mourning, and friends gather, to offer condolences, show solidarity, and provide a MINYAN so that the KADDISH may be said. The mourners are not expected to act as hosts: friends often bring food, and take it on themselves to serve it, and to underline this reversal of the norms there is a tradition, still observed by some, that a mourner receives greetings but does not initiate them.

The next period, sheloshim ('thirty'), continues until the morning of the thirtieth day after the funeral. During this phase mourners continue to refrain from shaving and having their hair cut, they do not listen to music and do not attend weddings or parties. (The restrictions on shaving and hair-cutting are often ignored today, and even Orthodox Jews sometimes cease to observe them after the shiva.) At the end of the sheloshim mourning is at an end, except for children of the deceased who continue until twelve months after the death.

The date of death is commemorated each year by lighting a memorial candle and by reciting Kaddish (*see* ASHKABÁ; YÓRTSAIT).

Mukammis, David (Daud al-Mukammas) (9th–10th century) Iraqi philosopher who is credited with having introduced the KALAM into Jewish thought. His Arabic work *Twenty Chapters* consists primarily of proofs of the existence of God.

mumar Term applied to a Jew who openly repudiates Jewish teachings and practices. In practice it is a synonym of MESHUMMAD. *See also* APOSTASY.

musaf ('additional') Additional service on Sabbaths and festivals, recited immediately after the morning service (shacharit). It consists essentially of an AMIDA and concluding prayers. On New Year it contains a sequence of SHOFAR blasts accompanied with appropriate readings. On the Day of Atonement it includes the AVODA. Prayers for dew are inserted at Passover and prayers for rain at SHEMINI ATSÉRET.

Musar movement 19th-century movement for the renewal of the medieval spiritual and ethical tradition. It was founded in Lithuania by Israel SALANTER (1810–83). Musar ('ethics') is the name given to a type of literature beginning in the Middle Ages which went beyond the letter of the law in promoting religiously sensitive behaviour. The Musar movement collected and studied these texts. Unlike Chasidism, of which it was in some sense a rival, the Musar movement did not discourage the academic study of the Talmud, but urged that it should be complemented by deep personal piety and by meditation on ethical texts, many of which were revived and republished as a result of this renewed interest. Study of these texts was a feature of the 'Musar houses', where both professional scholars and members of the wider public would retire for a period of self-scrutiny every day, and they were chanted aloud to special tunes so as to fix them in people's minds. The enduring legacy of the movement is to be found in the Lithuanian-style YESHIVOT, in which instruction in Talmud and halacha is combined with inculcation of the FEAR OF GOD. A feature of these yeshivot is the appointment of a MASHGÍ'ACH ruchani, a spiritual overseer who, in addition to offering moral guidance to students, delivers regular Musar discourses.

music Music was an issue dividing traditionalists and modernizers in the 19th century. Instrumental music was not used in the medieval synagogue, and the prayers and hymns were usually chanted to traditional melodies. The reading of the Torah and the HAFTARA had their own traditions of cantillation. A greater emphasis on beautiful music is discernible from the 16th century on, the first known composer of synagogue music being Salamone Rossi (c. 1570–1628) of Mantua. Meanwhile the Lurianic kabbalists of Safed sang melodies to beautify the prayers and to help them concentrate on their mystical meanings. Later the Chasidim composed their own melodies or adapted current folk songs, and cultivated music enthusiastically in their quest for ecstasy. A distinctive Chasidic contribution is the wordless melody (niggun). As Jews became acquainted with the music of the world around them the synagogue cantors (*see* CHAZZAN) became more self-conscious and ambitious. In central and western Europe of the emancipation era a great deal of synagogue music was composed, particularly for Reform temples with their organ and choir. The best-known composers of the time, such as Salomon Sulzer (1804–90) of Vienna, Samuel Naumbourg (1815–80) of Paris and Louis Lewandowski (1821–94) of Berlin, successfully blended traditional eastern-European Jewish elements with the dominant musical styles of their day. The 19th-century heritage still dominates synagogue music today, although modern composers have added their contributions, and many congregations have deliberately chosen to move away from art music towards more traditional styles of cantorial or congregational singing.

mysticism

When we speak of 'Jewish mysticism' we mean not so much the individual's private quest for union with God as a quest for knowledge of the Divine pursued by groups, who committed their ideas to writing. The modern study of the subject was pioneered by Gershom SCHOLEM, who laboured untiringly on kabbalistic and other texts, analysing the ideas they contain and tracing their history and their relationship with traditions outside Judaism. What these texts testify to is really a gnosis, in the sense of esoteric knowledge reserved for the members of a group, by means of which they believed they had direct access to knowledge of God not available to those who toiled in the mainstream texts such as the Talmud. It is a learned tradition, which tends to take on the outward form of classical Jewish scholarship (for example the ZOHAR is made to look like a rabbinic MIDRASH). Many of the authors were scholars with a reputation in another field (*see* CARO, JOSEPH; LUZZATTO, MOSES CHAYYIM).

In the wake of Scholem's work there has been a good deal of scholarly interest in the various mystical schools, such as the Descenders of the Chariot (Yordei Merkava, *see* MA'ASE MERKAVA) and the CHASIDEI ASHKENAZ, as well as the classical kabbalists of the Middle Ages and the SAFED school of the 16th century.

The three main elements within the mystical tradition are knowledge of God (*see* REVELATION), LOVE of God, and communion with God (DEVEKUT). The knowledge of God tends to take the form among mystics of esoteric knowledge which is transmitted from teacher to pupil and generally guarded from dissemination among the public at large. The origin of the esoteric tradition was sometimes associated with figures in the very remote past, such as Abraham or even Adam, with the implication that it is independent of the revelation at Sinai. However it can as easily take the form of an allegorical or symbolic interpretation of the Torah, in which the Hebrew words are held to be keys to hidden truths. These esoteric interpretations were often represented as going back to the early rabbis. The mystic does not receive a new revelation, but rediscovers the meaning of Torah, which speaks with a living voice to anyone who approaches it with an open heart.

The mystical knowledge of God is also fed by external sources, in which a significant part is played by Neoplatonist philosophy, with its insistence on the unknowability of the ultimate One, which is linked to the world by a series of emanations (*see* EMANATIONISM). The prolific literature of KABBALA bulks large in the history of Jewish exploration of the nature of God, but it is an exploration conducted far from the beaten paths of rational enquiry.

In a sense the theosophy of the kabbala can be seen as a reaction against the remoteness and abstraction of the God of the philosophers. But the VIA NEGATIVA of the philosophers, the denial of the possibility of ascribing any positive attributes to God as the biblical writings appear to do, can also be seen as opening the door to mysticism. The mystic responds to the challenge of God's unknowability not by denying it or turning his back on it, but by reaching out passionately towards it. This response can be observed even in people who are normally thought of as philosophers rather than mystics. Thus Solomon IBN GABIROL'S poetry expresses a powerful personal yearning for knowledge of God, and even Maimonides sometimes appears to describe the quest for knowledge of God in mystical terms. In fact it is not easy to draw the line between religious philosophy and mysticism, just as it is not always easy to draw the line between biblical exegesis and mystical allegory. The fascination of the Chasidei Ashkenaz and the kabbalists with the idea of God's essential unknowability is attested in their efforts to safeguard it by distinguishing between the ultimate God, who is beyond all possible human knowledge, and the various divine powers or manifestations, which can legitimately be contemplated and explored. Of course this distinction can easily lead to DUALISM, or even to polytheism, and the Jewish mystics were careful to guard against any imputation of a denial of the essential unity of God.

The mystical tradition in its most intense forms has virtually disappeared, killed off by the destruction and dispersal of the old communities where it was once a vital force, in Morocco, the Middle East, and eastern Europe, and by the spirit of rationalism and materialism which now prevails in the main centres of contemporary Jewry. There are some communities of kabbalists and Chasidim, but they are isolated from the main streams of Jewish life. After a period of suspicion and outright hostility in the 19th century, Jewish scholarship has turned its attention to the mystical literature, and some very serious scientific studies have emerged. But scholarly investigation of mysticism is a very different thing from mysticism itself, and these studies only serve to underline the difference between the mystical and the scientific mind.

There have been a few attempts to integrate kabbalistic or Chasidic ideas within a modern philosophy of Judaism, of which the most original is the mystical Zionism of Abraham Isaac KOOK. The influential modern religious thinkers Martin BUBER and Abraham Joshua HESCHEL were deeply marked by their encounters with Chasidism, and they both published a number of studies of the subject. Buber, in particular, can be credited for a remarkable renewal of interest in the potential Chasidic contribution to modern spirituality, and although it has been questioned how far his portrait of Chasidism is an accurate one he has certainly succeeded in making the spirit of Jewish mysticism speak with a living voice to people reared in the Western rationalist tradition. Recent years have seen a growing interest in the mystical tradition (*see* NEO-CHASIDISM; NEO-KABBALISM). But the enduring influence of Jewish mysticism is to be found, if anywhere, in the liturgy of the synagogue, where despite all the modern reforms the prayers of the Merkava mystics, the hymns of the Chasidei Ashkenaz and the kabbalists and the soulful tunes of the Polish Chasidim still live on.

N

Nachman of Bratslav (1772–1810) Chasidic master and religious thinker. A great-grandson of the BAAL SHEM TOV, he rejected the worldliness and superficiality, as he saw it, of the Chasidism of his day. He developed a conception of Judaism, rooted in the LURIANIC KABBALA, in which God is, in a sense, absent from the world, so that religious doubts are inevitable and all rational attempts to understand God are doomed to failure. He gathered around himself a close-knit circle of devotees over whom he exerted an extraordinary influence. He demanded a high degree of dedication, self-discipline and loyalty, and insisted that they should spend at least an hour each day in hitbodedut ('seclusion'), that is in a passionate outpouring of feelings in personal conversation with God. After his death they determined not to appoint a successor, but continued to pay their devotion to their dead master. His followers are consequently known as the 'dead Chasidim'. Their centre is in Jerusalem, where their master's throne is placed next to the holy ark in their synagogue. His grave in Uman (Ukraine) is now a place of PILGRIMAGE.

Nachmanides, Moses (1194–1270) Scholar, kabbalist and communal leader. Also known as Moses ben Nachman, Ramban (an acronym), and Bonastruc ça Porta (his Catalan name). He was born and lived in Girona, and had close connections with Barcelona, where he took part in an important public disputation with a representative of Christianity. In 1267 he settled in the Land of Israel, where he died. Nachmanides was a prolific author; more than fifty of his works survive, most of them concerned with HALACHA. Of enduring importance is his commentary on the Torah, which is the main source for his kabbalistic ideas (although in principle he was opposed to the writing down of kabbala). In a commentary on Job he explains the suffering of the individual with the doctrine of metempsychosis (GILGUL).

Nachum Hebrew name of the prophet NAHUM.

nagid (Hebrew or Aramaic, 'prince') Honorific title bestowed on the leaders of the medieval community in Muslim Spain and Egypt. The most famous holder of the title is Samuel the Nagid (Samuel Ibn Nagrela) (993–1056), who held the office of vizier to the king of Granada and was one of the finest Hebrew poets of all time and a rabbinic scholar of note.

Nahawendi or **Nihawandi, Benjamin** (9th century) Commentator and legal writer. He lived in Iran or Iraq. Considered one of the founders of KARAISM, he was a prolific author, but little remains of his writings. He is known to have written a number of commentaries on biblical books. His main surviving work is a *Book of Laws*, on civil and criminal law.

Nahum (Nachum) Biblical book, seventh of the Twelve Minor Prophets. The 7th-century BCE prophet gives us a vivid description of the fall of Nineveh, the capital of the Assyrian empire. The disaster is a punishment from God.

names and naming Traditionally Jews are named with patronyms (N son or daughter – in Hebrew ben or bat – of M) rather than surnames. This form is still used in the synagogue and in other religious contexts. Today the mother's name is sometimes added. Use of the mother's name alone is sometimes found among kabbalists and Chasidim. Traditionally a boy is named at his circumcision, a girl when her father is called up to the Torah soon after the birth. A more egalitarian system, introduced in Reform Judaism, is for babies of both sexes to be named at a blessing ceremony in synagogue. Proselytes take the patronym Avraham Avínu (Abraham our Father). Various assumptions govern the choice of names. Today biblical names are favoured, but this has not always been the case (very few of the ancient rabbis had biblical names). On the whole, names of the 'villains' of the Bible (Cain, Esau, Ahab and so forth) are avoided. Most names of Talmudic rabbis are acceptable, as are some names that entered the culture of rabbinic Judaism later (such as the Greek name Kalonymos and its Hebrew equivalent Shemtov). Among Ashkenazim there is a repertoire of Yiddish names (such as Kalman, Mendel or Hirsh). Ashkenazim sometimes pair a Yiddish name with a Hebrew one that is thought of as its equivalent, as in Menachem Mendel, Naftali Hirsh, Dov Ber, Judah Löw or Leib. It is common to name a baby after a family member, and it is usual in many families for a first son to be named after his paternal grandfather, a second son after his maternal grandfather, a first daughter after her paternal grandmother, and a second daughter after her maternal grandmother. Ashkenazim, however, have a deeply rooted taboo against naming any child after a living relative. In the Ottoman empire it was customary to use names indicating good fortune or hinting at some family history of misfortune, such as Simantob, Mazaltob, Chayyim, Rachamim, Nissim, or for a girl Fortuna. There is an old custom of changing the name of someone who is gravely ill (to baffle the angel of death, it is sometimes said). Sometimes a name such as Chayyim ('life'), Raphael ('God the healer') or Vida ('life' in Spanish) is used. Hereditary priests and Levites carry the additional name ha-Kohen or ha-Levi; these may be considered the oldest extant Jewish surnames. Variants have established themselves as surnames, such as Katz (acronym of kohen tsédek, righteous priest) or Segal (for segan levi, deputy Levite). Other surnames grew up in the course of the Middle Ages, and in the course of the 19th century, thanks to legislation in the various countries where Jews lived, the adoption of surnames became almost universal.

names of God By far the commonest designations of the Deity in the Bible are the Tetragrammaton (usually pronounced ADONAI) and ELOHIM. There is an observed tendency for the former to be used when God's special relation with Israel is in view, the latter in connection with the world and humanity at large (as in the creation story at the beginning of Genesis). The rabbis associate the Tetragrammaton with the divine attribute of mercy and Elohim with the attribute of strict justice. Other biblical names include Ehye or EHYE ASHER EHYE, YAH, EL, SHADDAI, TSEVA'OT and ELYON, as well as many designations which are properly understood as attributes or titles rather than proper names, for example 'The Rock', 'The Holy One of Israel'. JACOB BEN ASHER lists seventy divine names found in the Bible: he reaches this total by including many attributes. In the rabbinic literature a number of new names are used, presumably so as to avoid making over-frequent use of the holy biblical names, in obedience to the third of the TEN COMMANDMENTS: 'You shall not make vain use of the name of Adonai your God'. These include HA-MAKOM (The Place), (ha-)KADOSH BARUCH HU (The Holy One, blessed be He), Shamáyim (HEAVEN), Ribbono shel-Olam (Lord of the Universe). New names appear again in the Middle Ages, of which the most common is Ha-Shem yitbarach (The Name, may it be blessed). The medieval philosophers use designations taken from Greek philosophy, such as Prime Being, First Cause, Beginning of Beginnings. According to MAIMONIDES, all the names, with the exception of the Tetragrammaton, are not proper names at all but descriptions of God's actions. The kabbalists have a vast array of names, all laden with layers of esoteric explanations. Indeed NACHMANIDES holds that the entire Torah is made up of permutations of divine names. The biblical names are identified by the kabbalists with the various SEFIROT, and a new name, EIN SOF, is used for the ultimate, unknowable God.

Nashim ('women') Third of the six orders of the Mishnah, Tosefta and both Talmuds. Its tractates deal with issues of personal status, such as marriage and divorce.

nasi Title that has had different connotations at different periods. In the Bible it is used of the tribal chiefs and later on of kings; it can have messianic overtones, and it may be in this sense that BAR KOCHBA referred to himself as 'the Nasi of Israel' on documents and coins. In the rabbinic literature it is applied to the hereditary ethnarchs or patriarchs of the house of HILLEL who were recognized by the Romans as representing the Jews of the empire (*see* JUDAH THE NASI). This office came to an end in 425 with the failure of the direct succession. It is unclear to what extent the title was used with messianic connotations and how far it was seen simply as a title of honour. The rabbis also projected the title back into pre-rabbinic times, using it of figures from the 2nd century BCE to the 1st century CE whom they regarded as predecessors of their own school who wielded outstanding authority. In the Middle Ages the title was accorded to leaders of the community by both Karaites and Rabbanites. Nasi was the surname of a distinguished Portuguese family, of whom the most outstanding member was Don Joseph Nasi, Duke of Naxos under the Ottomans (d. 1579), who rebuilt the city of Tiberias and encouraged Jewish settlement in the Holy Land. In modern Israel the title has been revived as that of the president of the state.

nationalism *See* BUND; CHIBBAT ZION; UNIVERSALISM; ZIONISM.

Nazir ('Nazarite') Tractate of the Mishnah, Tosefta and both Talmuds, found in the order Nashim. The tractate deals with the rules pertaining to the vow and status of the Nazirite or Nazarite (Numbers 6.1–21). A man or woman who has taken such a vow is not allowed to consume wine or any other grape product, to contract ritual defilement through contact with a corpse, or to cut their hair.

Nedarim ('vows') Tractate of the Mishnah, Tosefta and both Talmuds, found in the order Nashim. The tractate deals with vows and oaths and the means of annulling them.

Nega'im ('contagions') Tractate of the Mishnah and Tosefta, found in the order Tohorot. The tractate deals with the infection described in Leviticus 13–14 (usually translated, inaccurately, 'leprosy'), as it affects people, clothes and buildings.

negative theology *See* VIA NEGATIVA.

Nehemiah (Nechemia) Biblical book, one of the Latter Prophets. *See* EZRA-NEHEMIAH.

ne'ila ('locking') The concluding service of the Day of ATONEMENT, so called because it is held at the time when the gates were locked in the Temple. As the sun begins to go down the mood of the prayers changes, and a tone of confidence and hope enters the words and melodies. In the Sefardi liturgy the service begins with a beautiful hymn by Moses IBN EZRA, 'El nora alila'. As this is the last opportunity to pray for forgiveness before the divine judgment is sealed, the wording of the AMIDA is altered from 'inscribe us in the book of life' to 'seal us in the book of life'. It also contains the poignant words: 'Open a gate for us, at the time of the locking of the gate, for the daylight is fading; as the daylight fades and the sun sets and fades, we approach your gates.' The ending of the service is dramatic. After the singing of AVÍNU MALKEÍNU for the last time, the reader proclaims the opening words of the SHEMÁ, 'Hear, O Israel, the Lord is our God, the Lord is one!' This is repeated by the congregations and then the response 'Blessed be his glorious, majestic name for ever and ever' is repeated three times. 'The Lord – he is God!' is then said seven times, and finally a single, very long blast is sounded on the SHOFAR, signalling the termination of the fast.

neo-Chasidism Name given to an observed revival of the values and ethos of Chasidism in American Jewry, beginning in the 1960s, both within the various modernist denominations and outside them. A key figure in the early spread of the movement was Shlomo Carlebach (d. 1994), 'the singing rabbi', whose musical compositions enjoyed widespread popularity. He founded several synagogues with a welcoming atmosphere of spirituality, and groups of 'Carlebach minyanim' (*see* MINYAN) mushroomed in the United States and in Israel. Another important figure, who, like Carlebach, had a background in Chabad Chasidism was Zalman Schachter-Shalomi, founder of the P'nai Or Religious Fellowship. An offshoot of this is ALEPH (*see* RENEWAL).

neo-kabbalism Name given to a contemporary revival of interest in the KABBALA among Jews with no previous acquaintance with mystical Judaism, and indeed proving attractive to some non-Jews.

neo-Karaism Name sometimes applied to various forms of Judaism thought to attribute excessive authority to the Bible and to undervalue the 'oral Torah' (*see*

KARAISM). The term has been applied (particularly in London) to 18th-century Jews from families that had lived as Christians in Portugal, and to 19th-century Reform Jews. The phenomenon itself is complex, and has not been fully investigated. It certainly derives, at least in large measure and not necessarily consciously, from Christian, and specifically Protestant, influence. Zionist culture is not immune to it: Yeshayahu LEIBOWITZ complained of the 'Protestantization' of Judaism, by which he meant a tendency in Israel to refer to the Bible as if it were the only source of authority in Jewish tradition.

neo-Orthodoxy *See* ORTHODOXY.

Neolog Modernist religious movement that arose in Hungarian-speaking parts of the Habsburg empire in the late 18th century. A founding figure of the movement was Aaron CHORIN. Neolog synagogues embraced some of the liturgical reforms introduced in Germany in the early 19th century and gradually became the numerically dominant movement in Hungary. On the emancipation of Hungarian Jewry in 1868 separate Neolog and Orthodox organizations were recognized by the state. (At this time Neolog Jews also came to be known as Congress Jews.) Today it is affiliated to the worldwide network of CONSERVATIVE JUDAISM.

Neoplatonism Philosophical movement with roots in late antiquity that had a considerable impact on Jewish thinkers in the Middle Ages, an impact that was dwarfed, however, by that of ARISTOTELIANISM. The first significant Jewish Neoplatonist was Isaac Israeli (9th–10th century); the outstanding work of Jewish Neoplatonist philosophy was the *Fountain of Life* by Solomon IBN GABIROL. His long devotional poem KÉTER MALCHUT is also based on the Neoplatonist system. BACHYA IBN PAKUDA, JUDAH HA-LEVI and Abraham IBN EZRA are also influenced by Neoplatonism. *See also* EMANATIONISM.

ner tamid ('perpetual lamp') In the tabernacle in the wilderness, and later in the Temple, a lamp to be kept alight constantly (Exodus 27.20–21, Leviticus 24.2–3). It is customary to have such a lamp in the synagogue too. It is suspended in front of the ARK, and nowadays is often powered by electricity.

nesi'at kappáyim *See* BIRKAT KOHANIM.

Nétsach ('victory') In kabbala, one of the SEFIROT.

Netúrei Kárta (Aramaic, 'Guardians of the City') Anti-Zionist CHAREDI organization in Jerusalem that broke away from the AGUDAT ISRAEL in the 1930s because of the latter's willingness to co-operate with the Zionists. They refuse to co-operate in any way with Zionist or state institutions; they do not recognize the state of Israel and refuse to pay taxes or take any financial support from it. They are mainly concentrated in the quarter of Me'a She'arim.

Nevi'im ('prophets') Second of the three divisions of the Hebrew Bible. It contains eight books, two of which are divided into two parts each, while another (the so-called Minor Prophets) consists of twelve short works. These eight books tell the story of the people from the entry into the Land of Canaan under Joshua to the

Babylonian exile, and contain the teachings of individual prophets. The authority of the Nevi'im is secondary to that of the Torah. Only short selections are read out in synagogues, chosen to accompany the readings from the Torah (*see* HAFTARA).

New Moon *See* ROSH CHÓDESH.

New Year (in Hebrew, Rosh ha-Shana) Autumn festival, marking the beginning of the TEN DAYS OF PENITENCE. In the Torah it is not called 'New Year' (on the contrary, it is designated as the first day of the seventh month, because the Torah counts the months from Nisan). In fact it has no particular name in the Bible: it is simply called 'a memorial of blowing the shofar' (Leviticus 23.24; see also Numbers 29.1). It is also known sometimes as Yom ha-Din, 'Day of Judgment': it is taught that at this time all Jews are judged in relation to their actions during the preceding year, and that on the Day of ATONEMENT, nine days later, their fate is sealed. New Year is consequently a time of serious reflection and self-examination. In synagogue the SHOFAR is blown, and the prayers contain references to judgment and forgiveness (*see* AVÍNU MALKEÍNU). Ashkenazim tend to dress in white for the services, and during the ALÉYNU prayer they kneel and prostrate themselves. Yet in the home something of the sweetness of the festival comes out, in the festive family meals, and particularly in the custom of dipping the bread at the beginning of the meal into honey rather than salt, and then eating apple dipped in honey, accompanied with the wish to be granted 'a good, sweet year'. The joyful theme yields to a more sombre mood of repentance in the folk ceremony of TASHLICH.

nezifa *See* EXCOMMUNICATION.

Nezikin ('damages') Fourth of the six orders of the Mishnah, Tosefta and both Talmuds. Its tractates deal mainly with matters of civil and criminal law.

nidda ('impurity') **1** A menstruating woman. **2** Menstrual impurity. The biblical laws on the subject (Leviticus 15.19–30) became a matter of intense interest to the rabbis. **3** (Nidda) Tractate of the Mishnah, Tosefta and both Talmuds, found in the order Tohorot. The tractate deals with questions related to menstrual impurity. It is the only Mishnaic tractate in this order to have been deemed worthy of discussion in the Talmud.

niddúi *See* EXCOMMUNICATION.

Nieto, David (1654–1728) Rabbi and theologian. Born in Venice, he ministered to the Sefardi congregation in London from 1701. A strong defender of traditional beliefs, he attacked neo-Karaite, fundamentalist and Sabbatean tendencies in his flock. In a sermon he delivered in 1703 he attacked the view known as Deism, which sees Nature as, essentially, a self-contained system that, once created, works independently of God according to its own rules. Nieto pointed out that 'Nature' was a modern invention unknown to the Bible or the Talmud, and he declared that there was no distinction between God and Nature. This laid him open to accusations of PANTHEISM. He clarified his views in his book *De la divina providencia* (*On Divine Providence*, 1715).

niggun ('tune') A melody, for example one associated with a particular prayer or hymn. Today the term is largely applied to wordless melodies favoured by the Chasidim, which they find particularly inspiring. *See also* MUSIC.

Nihawandi, Benjamin See NAHAWENDI, BENJAMIN.

nikkur *See* PORGING.

Ninth of Av *See* TISH'A BE-AV.

Nisan Seventh month of the year counting from New Year, corresponding to late March and early April. It is the month in which Passover falls. In the Torah, where it is also called Aviv ('spring'), it is declared to be the first month of the year (Exodus 12.2). It is regarded traditionally as a festive period when public mourning is to be avoided.

Noachian commandments Commandments considered binding on all human-kind. There are only seven of these: to refrain from (1) idolatry, (2) blasphemy, (3) incest, (4) murder, (5) robbery and (6) eating meat from a living animal, and (7) to establish courts of justice. They are mentioned in the Talmud (Bavli, Sanhedrin 56a; a longer list is found in Bavli, Chullin 92a). There is no evidence that the list was known earlier than late antiquity, although some scholars have tried to argue that it has an earlier origin. According to Maimonides, a Gentile who acknowledged the divine origin of these laws might qualify as a truly pious man. The whole concept has been of merely theoretical import, although the LUBAVITCH Chasidim have tried to convert Gentiles to their observance.

Noah (Nóach) Hero of a section of the book of GENESIS (6.9–10.32). Much of this section is taken up with the story of the great flood, in which the whole human race is drowned as a punishment for bad behaviour except for Noah, his three sons and their wives. After the flood God blesses Noah and his sons but warns them not to shed (or indeed consume) blood: 'Whoever sheds a man's blood, by a man shall his blood be shed, for in the image of God made he man' (9.6). God undertakes solemnly never to send another flood, and makes the rainbow a symbol of this pact. Noah becomes a farmer and plants a vineyard, but he becomes drunk with his own wine; in an enigmatic story his son Ham sees him drunk and naked, and another son, Shem, receives his blessing. The section ends with a genealogical table showing how the various nations and language groups descend from Noah's three sons. Noah is described as 'a righteous man, perfect in his generations' (6.9; see also Ezekiel 14.14); the Talmud points out that this could imply a limited or relative perfection (Bavli, Sanhedrin 108a).

notarikon (Greek, 'shorthand') A type of shorthand in which words and phrases are represented by their initial or key letters; more usually, an exegetical device that treats biblical words as if they were acronyms. The device is relatively common in the rabbinic writings, and is also used by the kabbalists.

novellae *See* CHIDDUSH.

Numbers (Bemidbar, 'in the wilderness [of Sinai]') Fourth book of the Torah. The narrative continues from the preceding book, Leviticus; it is interspersed with some laws and regulations. The book begins with a census of the people, whence its English name (the Hebrew name comes from the first distinctive word in the book). This census is in preparation for the journey through the wilderness to the Promised Land. Twelve chosen men are sent to spy out the land; their report (only two of their number dissenting) is that the land itself is fertile, but that the inhabitants are big and strong and have walled cities, and cannot be defeated. The people, discouraged, want to return to Egypt. In a terrible utterance, God punishes them by decreeing that the whole generation will die in the wilderness (13–14). Other graphic moments in the narrative are the rebellion of Korach and his followers and their unnatural fate (16), the death of Miriam and Aaron and the prediction that Moses himself will die before the people enters the Promised Land (20), the prophecies of Balaam, who is hired to curse the Israelites but blesses them instead (22–4), the violent action of Phinehas, the prototype of all religious zealots (25), and the protest of the daughters of Zelophehad, who manage to get the laws of inheritance amended so that daughters may inherit in the absence of a son (27). Much of the narrative is taken up with the journeys through the wilderness and the problems attendant on such a journey, such as the shortage of water and the people's faint-heartedness and fickleness.

The threefold priestly blessing (6.22–7) has found a permanent place in the liturgy of the synagogue.

numerology The study of the supposed symbolic value of numbers. In the Bible certain numbers (notably seven, ten, twelve and forty) are repeated in different contexts and seem to have some special significance, but this is not spelt out and it is not suggested that there is some kind of numerical system underlying the world. PHILO OF ALEXANDRIA built elaborate symbolic interpretations on the biblical numbers. The rabbis sometimes express an interest in this type of numerology, but more commonly they focus on the numerical value of Hebrew words (*see* GEMATRIA). The kabbalists were particularly fond of this type of symbolism.

nusach 1 A prayer rite (as in nusach sefarad, the Sefardi rite). **2** The traditional manner of chanting the various prayers. **3** In textual studies, a variant reading.

O

Obadiah (Ovadia) Biblical book, fourth of the Twelve Minor Prophets. The shortest book in the Bible, it has only one chapter; it is dated in the 6th century BCE.

obedience

Traditionally a key virtue. The Bible encourages obedience to parents, to righteous leaders, and particularly to God; indeed this last is the ideal attitude of the individual and the community. The archetype of obedience in the Torah is ABRAHAM. In the story of the AKEDA he is told to offer his son to God as a burnt sacrifice. He unhesitatingly obeys; fortunately it turns out to be only a test. The outcome: 'All the nations of the world will be blessed by your descendants because you listened to my voice' (Genesis 22.18).

In Hebrew the same verb means to listen and to obey, so that Abraham was rewarded for his obedience as well as his attentiveness. Similarly, the opening words of the SHEMÁ, 'Listen, Israel' (Deuteronomy 6.4), could be translated 'Jew – be obedient'. When Moses tells the people the laws he has received from God at Sinai they respond: 'Everything that the Lord has said we will do and obey (or be attentive)' (Exodus 24.7).

The reward of obedience is spelt out in Deuteronomy 11.13–15:

> If you are truly obedient to the commands I am giving you today, to love the Lord your God, and to serve him with all your hearts and souls, I shall send the rain of your land at the right time, early rain and late rain, you shall gather in your corn, new wine and oil, I shall put grass in your meadows for your cattle, and you shall eat your fill.

This passage forms part of the Shemá; like many other passages in the Torah it draws a very close connection between obedience and prosperity. The reward for obeying the commands is a long life, and the punishment for disobedience is death. Nowhere is this stated more clearly than in Deuteronomy 30.15–18:

> See: I am setting before you today life and good and death and evil, in that I am commanding you today to love the Lord your God, to walk in his paths and to keep his commands and rules and laws; so that you will live and be numerous, and the Lord your God will bless you in the land which you are entering to take possession

of it. But if your heart is diverted and you are disobedient, and you let yourself be distracted and worship other gods and serve them, I tell you today that you will perish, you will not live a long life on the land you are crossing the Jordan to take possession of.

This whole structure of obedience to commands, rewarded by health and prosperity, is built on the foundation of an anthropomorphic conception of God (*see* ANTHROPOMORPHISM). God as supreme authority is modelled on a human ruler or father, who gives orders and demands obedience. Later tradition, particularly in its more philosophical strands, expresses unhappiness about this conception, which seems inappropriately concrete. Can the divine spirit inspire humans in such a way as to command a certain way of life or course of action? And in that case can we be certain that the command has been correctly understood? Does it not all boil down effectively to individual humans usurping the role of God and telling other humans what they must or must not do?

Such speculation, however, was confined to an intellectual elite until the 19th century, when it became widespread among the Jewish leadership, starting in the German-speaking countries. Until then, rabbinic Judaism had taught that the commands of the Torah (as interpreted and modified by the rabbis) had to be observed scrupulously because they were the word of God. Since the growth of critical biblical study this approach has become difficult to sustain intellectually, but it should be noted that it is still maintained by ORTHODOXY as a matter of faith. Concern was also expressed about another aspect of the structure: REWARDS AND PUNISHMENTS.

Despite these various criticisms, the idea of obedience to the divine command is still accepted by virtually the whole of the traditional and Orthodox sectors of Jewry, and receives limited assent from others.

Oholot ('tents') Tractate of the Mishnah and Tosefta, in the order Tohorot, dealing with the rules concerning ritual impurity imparted by contact with a corpse. This contact need not be direct, and can be transmitted in several degrees.

olam ha-ba

('the coming age', sometimes translated 'world to come') Rabbinic doctrine of a Coming Age, after the end of the current era (in Hebrew, olam ha-ze). There is considerable ambiguity and even contradiction about this doctrine in the sources. The Coming Age is distinguished from the days of the MESSIAH: the days of the Messiah are imagined as essentially this-worldly, whereas the Coming Age probably involves a fundamental change in the order of creation. As one rabbi put it, 'The days of the Messiah do not differ at all from the present except that Israel will no longer be in bondage to the kingdoms of the world.' But if some information can be gleaned, however dimly, about the days of the Messiah from the visions of the prophets, when it comes to the Coming Age we are completely in the dark. To quote another rabbi, 'Every prophet prophesied only for the days of the Messiah;

but as for the Coming Age, no eye has seen what God has prepared for those who wait for him.' This does not prevent the rabbis, however, from placing a strong emphasis on the Coming Age in their teaching, and even speculating about its character. 'In the Coming Age there is no eating or drinking, no reproduction or business, no jealousy or hatred or competition, but the virtuous sit with crowns on their heads feasting on the brightness of the Shechina' (Talmud Bavli, Berachot 17a). In other words, all those features of human life which derive from our animal nature and the influence of the YÉTSER HA-RA will be removed, and humans will be like angels, living eternally in a kind of sublime impassivity. The rabbis sometimes contrast the future age with the present one in a way which almost implies that this life is to be preferred: at least it offers certain experiences which we will be denied in the Coming Age. So one teacher declares, 'Better is one hour of repentance and good deeds in this age than all the life of the Coming Age' (Mishnah, Avot 4.17), while another states that we shall have to give an account on Judgment Day of every good thing which we might have enjoyed and did not (Talmud Yerushalmi, Kiddushin 4.12). Three things, according to the Talmud (Bavli, Berachot 57b), give us a foretaste of the Coming Age: the Sabbath, sexual intercourse, and a sunny day. Despite some discussion (Tosefta, Sanhedrin 13.2), it is considered that righteous Gentiles as well as Jews have a share in the Coming Age.

An attempt to condense the rabbinic views about the hereafter into a coherent summary (which is not easy) might go something like this: After death the souls of the virtuous are dispatched to the GARDEN OF EDEN, while those of the wicked undergo a period of punishment in GEHINNOM. The coming of the Messiah will be preceded by social and economic crises; then the prophet Elijah will return, a great trumpet will sound and the exiles will be gathered in; there will follow a cataclysmic war, known as the war of Gog and Magog, and after that the world will be renewed in the messianic era, which will be an era of peace and harmony on earth. Eventually the dead will be resurrected and judged together with the living, and those who survive the judgment will live eternally in the Coming Age.

Later Jewish thought continues in general to regard the Coming Age as an other-worldly state of being. The attitude of the medieval philosophers is determined to a large extent by their view of the RESURRECTION. At one extreme, MAIMONIDES, who has difficulty fitting resurrection into his system, virtually identifies the Coming Age with the IMMORTALITY of the soul. He could not conceive of an eternal body. NACHMANIDES, on the other hand, who takes a strong line on resurrection, has no difficulty imagining the Coming Age as denoting the world as it will be after the resurrection. The body will be reunited with the soul, and will itself become transformed and, as it were, soul-like.

While thinkers in the Middle Ages were happy to discuss the hereafter in all its details, today there is less interest in the subject. Modernist versions of Judaism tend to place less emphasis on the Coming Age than on the immortal soul, and in the case of Reform on the messianic age seen naturalistically as a time of peace and justice on earth. Many Orthodox Jews, however, feel bound to follow the traditional doctrines of the resurrection and the Coming Age. *See also* AFTERLIFE.

olam ha-ze *See* OLAM HA-BA.

ómer ('sheaf') In the Torah, a harvest offering of a newly cut sheaf of barley made during the festival of Passover (Leviticus 23.9–14). The period of seven weeks between Passover and Shavuot is known as the 'Counting of the Ómer'. For reasons which remain unclear the counting of the ómer became a period of sadness, during which weddings do not take place. Traditional and Orthodox Jews do not shave or have their hair cut. The thirty-third day (known as Lag Ba-Ómer) is, however, a joyful day, when marriages are permitted. The precise date on which the counting begins has been a matter of dispute, first between Sadducees and Pharisees and later between Karaites and Rabbanites. The former in each case followed literally the biblical instruction to count 'from the day after the Sabbath' (Leviticus 23.15), the latter interpreting this to refer to the first day of the festival.

omnipotence Unbounded power: an attribute of God. According to classical theology going back to the Bible, nothing is too hard for God to do. However, there are certain things we would not normally even imagine God trying to do. Logically impossible things fall under this heading. This subject is investigated further by the medieval philosophers.

omniscience Unlimited knowledge: an attribute of God. The basis of this doctrine is in biblical texts such as 1 Samuel 16.7 or Psalm 33.13–15. In its more developed form, the doctrine states that God knows everything, hidden and revealed, past present and future. The question then arises whether this doctrine is compatible with that of FREE WILL. How can I have genuine choice if God already knows what I will choose to do? This is a genuine conundrum, to which there is no satisfactory answer. GERSO-NIDES went so far as to argue that God's knowledge is limited to universals and does not extend to particulars: thus he knows the possible choices open to an individual, but not which way the individual will choose to act. Abraham IBN EZRA takes a similar line, observing that since God cannot know what it is like to be wicked his knowledge of the wicked individual is inevitably limited. MAIMONIDES, however, insists strenuously that divine knowledge is unlimited and yet human freedom is real. Most have chosen to follow this intellectually difficult yet religiously satisfying middle path.

óneg Shabbat ('Sabbath delight') Phrase used by the rabbis to refer to the special character of the Sabbath day and everything conducive to enhancing a sense of joy and well-being on this day. The origin of the phrase is in Isaiah 58.13–14, 'If you call the Sabbath a delight … then you will receive delight from the Lord'. According to the Sabbath prayers, 'Those who keep the Sabbath and call it a delight shall rejoice in your kingdom'. The rabbis recommend that even the poorest Jews should light lamps in their homes and eat well on the Sabbath, and óneg Shabbat is marked, for example, by using the best table linen and silverware for the Sabbath meals. Special candlesticks, often of silver, are used for lighting the Sabbath candles. The practice of lighting lamps or candles on the Sabbath has its origin entirely in the doctrine of óneg Shabbat. As Maimonides says: 'Even if one has no food, and has to go begging for money to pay for the oil required for the lighting, it is his duty to do so, for this is part of óneg Shabbat.' The Zionist poet Bialik, who was concerned that Zionist society should not lose its continuity with the Jewish past, instituted Sabbath afternoon gatherings in Tel Aviv under the name 'óneg Shabbat' in the 1920s. Refreshments were served, and the proceedings included Bible study, a lecture, and the singing of Sabbath songs. The custom spread throughout the Land of Israel and further afield. In America, the term is often applied to a similar gathering in synagogues and temples after the Friday evening service.

onen *See* MOURNING.

oral Torah Rabbinic doctrine, sometimes called oral law, having the effect of investing the teachings of the Talmud with equal authority to that of the written Torah. The precise relationship between the material in the Torah and the Talmud is a subject which has been much discussed since early times, as has the relative authority attaching to each class of material. Although historically the Talmud is of a much later date than the Torah, the tradition itself regards both as complementary components in a single whole. The underlying idea is not so much that the teachings of the Talmud, after being formulated by the rabbis, were handed down for a time in unwritten form (although this idea is certainly often discussed), but rather that Moses received both parts at Sinai, one part to be written down and the rest to be transmitted orally, until in due course this part too was committed to writing. Oral Torah is, however, not a finite body of teachings but something like a process, in which later and even future interpretations play their part. *See also* RABBANISM; TORA MIN HA-SHAMÁYIM.

ordination *See* HÉTTER HORA'A; RABBI; SEMICHA.

organ Musical instrument. Rabbinic sources refer to a kind of hydraulic organ that existed in the Temple, but after the destruction of the Temple no equivalent was used in synagogue worship, and instrumental music was absent from Jewish worship until the modern pipe organ was introduced in the early stages of the MODERNIST movement, not without considerable controversy. In Germany organs were installed experimentally in Seesen in 1810 and Berlin in 1815, and more permanently in Hamburg in 1818 (with a non-Jewish organist); the first synagogue organ in North America was introduced in the Reform temple in Charleston, South Carolina, in 1841. The traditionalist opponents of the organ argued that its use on the Sabbath (even if played by a Gentile), far from contributing to ÓNEG SHABBAT, would infringe the halachic restrictions relating to the Sabbath; that all music, except at weddings, is forbidden as a token of mourning for the Temple; and that in general the organ constituted an aping of Christian custom. Despite such opposition, the organ soon became a regular feature of modernist, particularly Liberal, synagogues in central and western Europe and in Reform temples in the USA. Notable organs can be seen in the great 19th-century synagogue buildings, such as the (Neolog) Great synagogue in Budapest, the (Orthodox) Great Synagogue (Synagogue des Victoires) in Paris, and the (British Reform) West London Synagogue. Against the general trend in European Orthodoxy, the French rabbinate decreed in 1856 that the use of the organ, as long as it was played by a non-Jew, was permissible even on Sabbaths and festivals. The debate over the organ was renewed in American Conservative Judaism; organs are now often found in Conservative synagogues. However, the appeal of the organ is not what it once was.

Orla ('foreskin') Tractate of the Mishnah, Tosefta and Palestinian Talmud, in the order Zera'im. It deals with rules concerning the fruit of young trees. According to the Torah (Leviticus 19.23–4), in their first three years their fruit is to be considered as 'uncircumcised'; in the following year it is 'holy'; from the fifth year on it may be freely eaten. This is one of the few agrarian laws that are considered to apply even outside the Land of Israel.

Orthodox Union *See* UNION OF ORTHODOX JEWISH CONGREGATIONS OF AMERICA.

Orthodoxy

Term applied originally in the 19th century to the conservative wing of MODERN-ISM; today it is often used indiscriminately for the entire fundamentalist wing of Judaism (*see* FUNDAMENTALISM; TRADITIONALISM). The term Modern Orthodoxy is a label claimed by those attempting to adhere to the ideals of the original Orthodox movement, which is also sometimes referred to as neo-Orthodoxy. Samson Raphael HIRSCH can be considered as the founder of Orthodoxy, and his books, such as the *Nineteen Letters on Judaism* and *Choreb*, are among the movement's classics. The young Hirsch had had a vision of the best values in Judaism marching forward arm in arm with those of the German universities. The rapid growth of more radical Reform hardened his resistance to change, and his Orthodoxy became increasingly defensive and reactionary. In 1853, in response to the announcement that a new-style rabbinical seminary was to be established in Breslau (*see* FRANKEL, ZACHARIAS), Hirsch published an open letter to the leaders of the seminary which was a tirade against the historical study of the Bible and the Talmud, which he rightly perceived was undermining the fundamental belief that God had revealed the Torah to Moses on Mount Sinai. This commitment to a rigid and inflexible doctrine of revelation, increasingly difficult to maintain rationally, ultimately undermined Hirsch's conception of a fruitful marriage between Jewish and secular studies (TORA IM DÉRECH ÉRETS), and stifled the radical elements in Orthodoxy that had made it so exciting in its early days.

For Orthodox Judaism today the Torah – meaning all the teachings of the Bible and the Talmud and subsequent canonical literature, and especially the practices codified in the SHULCHAN ARUCH and other halachic sources – is divinely revealed and immutable. There is little or no room in this view for open-minded biblical criticism or for historical analysis of the Talmud. Orthodoxy likes to claim that it is doing no more nor less than continue the main stream of authentic Judaism as it has flowed down from ancient times. It has been suggested that this claim makes it difficult for the leadership of Orthodox Judaism to guide the movement into new paths or even to present a coherent and interesting statement of its aims, the more so as Orthodox rabbis often seem fearful of being criticized by their own followers and colleagues. Recently some leading Orthodox rabbis in the

United States and in Israel have found a distinctive voice, but they have difficulty making it heard in a movement that is dominated by neo-traditionalist tendencies, largely attributable to the enormous dominance of Jews of eastern European origins, who have little understanding of or sympathy for the cultural matrix from which the movement arose.

In the 19th century Orthodoxy steered a delicate middle course between Reform and traditionalism and earned the suspicion and hostility of both. Its social base and intellectual foundations, however, placed it firmly in the modernist camp. Subsequent developments sharpened the polemic between Orthodoxy and the more progressive wing of religious Jewry, while gradually eliminating the border that divided it from the more traditional elements. Today Orthodoxy, while remaining a substantial and vocal presence within world Jewry, is in considerable disarray, very largely because of uncertainty as to whether it is essentially a conservative modernizing movement or a progressive traditionalist one. Orthodoxy still seems outwardly strong in Western countries, particularly in those (such as Britain or France) where it enjoys a position of institutionalized supremacy, but as a modernist movement it occupies an uncomfortable – some would say an impossible – position, vulnerable to attack both from the anti-modernist right and from the anti-dogmatic left. Orthodoxy appears to be uncomfortably straddling the fence between traditionalism and modernism, allying itself openly with the traditionalists (who have come to be termed, misleadingly, 'ultra-Orthodox', as if they were a branch of Orthodoxy) yet conscious of competing for members with the more progressive movements.

Ovadia Hebrew name of the biblical book of Obadiah.

P

Pale of Settlement Historical territory, mainly on the western fringes of Russia, to which Jews were confined under Czarist rule. The origins of the Pale lie in the successive partitions of Poland among its neighbours, Russia, Austria and Prussia, at the end of the 18th century. Before the first partition, in 1772, very few Jews lived in the Russian empire. The annexation of part of Poland brought substantial Jewish populations under Russian rule, and the decision was taken to retain the former frontier as a line of demarcation east of which Jews were generally forbidden to reside. Further territories were added in the second and third partitions (1793 and 1795), and the principle of the Pale was extended to other areas at various times – for example Bessarabia was included in 1818, and Astrakhan and Caucasus were subjected to the same rules from 1804 to 1835. Jews were allowed into the Russian interior on a temporary basis for a specific purpose, on business, or to study or learn a trade, and permanent residence rights were granted to a small minority of prosperous merchants, skilled artisans and those with a higher degree, such as doctors, but the large mass of Jews were confined within the Pale, where in many places they constituted the majority of the population, and where they were deprived of economic and other opportunities. The Pale in the 19th and early 20th centuries became an extraordinary hothouse for developments in Judaism, ranging from the essentially secular HASKALA and CHIBBAT ZION movements and the associated revival of the Hebrew language, as well as the renewal of Yiddish literature and the growth of diverse Jewish socialist movements, through new trends in religious education and scholarship and the ethical MUSAR MOVEMENT, to politico-religious innovations such as MIZRACHI and AGUDAT ISRAEL.

Palestine Name given at various times to a region, variously defined, adjoining the southern part of the eastern shore of the Mediterranean Sea, and broadly corresponding to the historic Land of Israel (*see* ISRAEL, LAND OF). The name was first used by the Roman government, replacing the earlier name Judaea, after the crushing of the BAR KOCHBA revolt; it was based on the name of the Philistines, an ancient enemy of the Jews at the time of King David, and was no doubt intended to indicate that this was no longer to be considered in any way the land of the Jews. In modern times it was at first a purely geographical designation with no particular political reference, but it began to acquire political overtones again towards the end of World War I. While a British army under General Allenby was advancing towards Ottoman-held

Jerusalem, the British government issued a statement of policy now known as the Balfour Declaration (2 November 1917), viewing with favour 'the establishment in Palestine of a National Home for the Jewish people'. The term was also used by the Arab leader Emir Feisal in a memorandum submitted to the Paris Peace Conference, and in an agreement he signed in January 1919 with the Zionist leader Chaim Weizmann. Following representations by the Zionist Organization, plans were laid for Palestine to be provisionally recognized as an independent state under a Mandate accorded by the League of Nations to Great Britain, which would be responsible for implementing the 1917 Declaration. (The Declaration was held, to the disappointment of the Zionists, not to apply to the parts of Palestine lying east of the Jordan River.) The Mandate came into effect on 29 September 1923 and ended with the British withdrawal and the simultaneous declaration of an independent state of Israel in May 1948. During this period the name Palestine was freely used by Jews, side by side with the Hebrew name Érets Yisra'el (Land of Israel), and various Jewish institutions and companies carried the name Palestinian or Palestine, as some continue to do. After 1948, however, the name came to be used less by Jews, and it has now been adopted by the Arabs of the region and consequently is viewed with disfavour by Jews.

panentheism The doctrine that the world as a whole is embraced by God. In panentheism, as in classical Jewish monotheism, God is both transcendent (beyond the universe) and immanent (present within it). There are elements of panentheism in KABBALA, for instance the ZOHAR speaks of God 'filling all worlds' and 'surrounding all worlds', and the idea of the world being within God is made more explicit by some kabbalists. The doctrine is particularly prominent in CHASIDISM, especially in CHABAD CHASIDISM, although the term as such is not used. The saying 'The whole world is full of [God's] glory' (Isaiah 6.3) is understood to mean that God is literally in the world. In the Chabad version of TSIMTSUM, only God enjoys real existence, and the created world only appears to exist from the point of view of the creatures. The Chasidic understanding of the relationship of God and the world was strongly attacked by the MITNAGGEDIM, on the grounds that it undermines any distinction between holy and unholy, good and evil, and hence brings into question the laws of the Torah.

pantheism The doctrine that the world as a whole is identical with God. Pantheism takes various forms, all of them incompatible with the belief in a transcendent divine being. Baruch SPINOZA, with his maxim Deus siue natura ('God, or nature'), appears to espouse pantheism.

Para ('cow', 'heifer') Tractate of the Mishnah and Tosefta, in the order Tohorot, dealing with purification from ritual impurity by means of the ashes of a red heifer (Numbers 19).

parasha or **perasha** ('division', 'section') In the reading of the Torah, a division of the SIDRA. In the scroll of the Torah, it may be either PETUCHA or SETUMA. The term is also used (confusingly) by Sefardim as a synonym of sidra.

pardes (of Persian origin, 'orchard') A term sometimes associated with mysticism, but particularly employed in the theory of biblical exegesis, as an acronym standing for the four types of interpretation, peshát ('plain meaning'), rémez ('allusion'), derásh ('homiletical exposition') and sod ('mystical reading'). This fourfold system is first attested in 13th-century Spain, and has been compared to current Christian theories of exegesis.

párev or **párve** (Yiddish) Term applied by Ashkenazim to foods classified as neither milk nor meat; they can therefore be eaten with either.

parnas (plural parnasim) Title of honour applied to communal leaders. The term is of uncertain origin; its original meaning may be 'one who sustains', which would suggest that it may once have indicated some kind of financial official. The Talmud states that a parnas is to be chosen by the rabbis, but that their choice is to be ratified by public approbation (Bavli, Berachot 55a). In modern times parnas is a title of honour for a communal dignitary, in both Ashkenazi and Sefardi usage. The heads of the COUNCIL OF THE FOUR LANDS were called parnasim. In Western Sefardi congregations they constitute a governing board, chaired by the parnas presidente.

paróchet ('curtain') In Ashkenazi usage, a curtain that hangs before the ARK in the synagogue. The term is derived from the curtain mentioned in the account of the tabernacle in the Torah, that divided the holy space from the most holy (Exodus 26.31–3).

particularism A doctrine that would limit moral or spiritual concerns to a particular group; the opposite of UNIVERSALISM. In Judaism the most obvious type of particularism is the doctrine of ELECTION or chosenness, which envisages God's love as being either limited to the Jews or bestowed on them in greater measure than on non-Jews. The related conception of the HALACHA as a law given exclusively to Jews and binding on them alone is also particularistic. The Mishnaic dictum that 'All Israel have a share in the Coming Age' (Sanhedrin 10.1) has sometimes been interpreted to mean that non-Jews will be excluded; however this is not the generally accepted understanding.

partsufim (of Greek origin, 'faces') In LURIANIC KABBALA, configurations of SEFIROT, enabling them to contain the divine light after the breaking of the vessels (SHEVIRA).

Passover (Pésach) Spring festival commemorating the exodus from Egypt. It begins at the full moon of Nisan and continues for seven days (eight days outside Israel, except among Reform Jews). The Hebrew name Pésach refers in the Torah to the lamb sacrificed on the eve of the exodus (Exodus 12.3–13); it is traditionally understood to mean 'pass-over', because in the story God 'passes over' the homes of the Israelites when he smites the Egyptians with the killing of the firstborn. (An alternative translation is 'protection'.)

Passover requires thorough preparation of the home. According to the Torah, 'no CHAMETS is to be seen within your limits' (Exodus 13.7; cf. 12.15, 19). The home, and particularly the kitchen, is therefore subjected to a very thorough spring cleaning. Old food is thrown out and fresh food is brought in, and bread is replaced by unleavened bread (MATSA) for the period of the festival. Pots and pans, plates and dishes, knives and forks must all be specially treated, discarded or withdrawn from use, and some households keep a special set of kitchen utensils and tableware to be used only at Passover. According to old custom a 'chamets-hunt' takes place the evening before the festival commences, with a few crumbs being left deliberately to be found and ceremoniously swept up, to be burnt the next morning (*see* BITTUL CHAMETS; BI'UR CHAMETS). Firstborn sons are supposed to fast on the day leading up to the SÉDER, in remembrance of the killing of the Egyptian firstborn (Exodus 12.29) (*see* FAST OF THE FIRSTBORN). On the morning preceding the festival the preparations intensify. The last chamets is burnt, and after mid-morning no more chamets may be eaten. The evening meal (Séder) is a feast, and for many Jewish homes this is the largest and most festive dinner of the year.

Those families that observe the festivals for two days will have a second Séder the following night; the rest have only one Séder. In the synagogue service for the first day a prayer for dew marks the transition from winter to summer. On the Sabbath the HAFTARA is EZEKIEL'S vision of the resurrection of the dry bones, an allegory of renewal and redemption. Some Ashkenazim read the SONG OF SONGS, which sings of the spring and is understood allegorically as containing allusions to redemption, on this day. The intermediate days of the festival are CHOL HA-MO'ED, an in-between time that shares in the sanctity of the festival but during which work, at least of the more essential kind, is permitted. The special food laws continue to be observed, and only unleavened bread may be eaten. The seventh day (or seventh and eighth days) is a full festival.

In the liturgy Passover is called 'the festival of our freedom' or 'liberation', and this is the dominant theme of the whole festival. The story of the exodus from Egypt is read not just as an historical commemoration but as a type of all liberation, both personal and national, within history. It also looks forward to the final redemption, which is why a cup of wine is poured at the Séder for Elijah, the harbinger of the Messiah, and why the Séder finishes with the cry: Next year in Jerusalem!

patience A divine and a human virtue. God's patience or forbearance is referred to in the Torah under the quaint anthropomorphism 'long nostrils', notably in the THIRTEEN ATTRIBUTES (Exodus 34.6), where it is understood to mean that he does not immediately punish sinners, but gives them an opportunity to turn from their wicked ways. On the principle of IMITATIO DEI humans, too, are encouraged to display patience.

patriarch (in Hebrew, av; plural avot) A powerful father-figure. There are considered to be three biblical patriarchs, ABRAHAM, ISAAC and JACOB. Their graves are venerated in the cave of Machpelah in HEBRON. The term was also applied by the Romans in the late 3rd and early 4th centuries to the hereditary rulers of the Jews (*see* NASI). *See also* MATRIARCHS.

patronymic *See* NAMES AND NAMING.

payyetan (from Greek) A composer of PIYYUT.

Pe'a ('corner') Tractate of the Mishnah, Tosefta and Palestinian Talmud, in the order Zera'im, dealing with gifts to the poor. The source of the title is the corner of the field mentioned in Leviticus 19.9 and 23.22 (see also Deuteronomy 24.19–24): during harvest the crops in the corners of the field must be left for the poor to gather, and the gleanings must also be left uncollected. The tractate also discusses the Poor Tithe (Deuteronomy 14.28–9).

peace (in Hebrew, shalom) Term indicating both the absence of war and, frequently in the liturgy and in rabbinic thought, fulfilment and well-being in the widest sense, comparable to the Greek philosophical idea of happiness. The ending of conflict among nations is a prominent constituent of the prophetic vision of the messianic times (Isaiah 2.4), and the rabbis list peacemaking among the virtuous deeds, even sanctioning white lies for the purpose. Many rabbinic sermons extol the benefits of peace, of which the following are some typical specimens. Rabbi Simeon bar Yohai said: 'Great is peace, for all blessings are contained in it, as it says, "The Lord will bless his people with peace" (Psalm 29.11). 'Bar Kappara said: 'Great is peace, for if it is needed by the beings above, who know neither jealousy nor hatred nor contention nor wrangling nor quarrelling nor strife nor envy, as it says, "He who makes peace among his high places" (Job 25.2), how much more is it needed by those below.' Rabbi Yudan ben Rabbi Yose said: 'Great is peace, for God's name is peace, as it says, "And he called the Lord Peace" (Judges 6.24).' The verse 'He who makes peace among his high places', which has acquired a fixed place in the liturgy at the end of the Kaddish ('May he who makes peace among his high places make peace for us and for all Israel'), is interpreted in one rabbinic homily as meaning that God makes peace one of the highest virtues. It is as a great gift from God that peace is mentioned frequently in the prayer book; in fact each of the main prayers (AMIDA, KADDISH, GRACE AFTER MEALS) ends with a prayer for this gift. The reference to peace for Israel in these prayers should not be understood in too narrow a sense. The sources make it plain that peace is indivisible, and cannot be confined to one people alone. It is in line with this thought that some reformed liturgies have amended the words of the prayers, removing the word Israel or replacing it by 'all the world' or 'all humankind'. The wish for peace is also a greeting, in the form 'shalom aleichem' (may peace be with you); the reply is 've-aleichem shalom' (and may peace be with you). This is often abbreviated simply to shalom. On Sabbath the greeting is 'Shabbat shalom' (peaceful Sabbath). *See also* AARON.

Pentecost (Greek, 'fiftieth') Name sometimes given in English to the festival of SHAVUOT, because it falls on the fiftieth day after Passover.

pe'ot ('corners') Sidelocks. According to Leviticus 19.27, it is forbidden to 'round the corners of the head', which is understood by the rabbis in the Talmud (Bavli, Makkot 20b) as forbidding the shaving of the temples. The custom arose in the Habsburg empire of letting the sidelocks grow completely uncut. A similar custom arose in Yemen.

See also HAIR.

perasha *See* PARASHA.

Pésach *See* PASSOVER.

Pésach Sheni ('second Passover') A second opportunity to eat the Passover lamb, a month after the first Passover, afforded in the Torah to those who were ritually unclean or absent on a journey (Numbers 9.9–25). The practice is no longer observed, but some mark the date by eating some MATSA. *See also* HILLULA.

Pesachim ('Passover offerings') Tractate of the Mishnah, Tosefta and both Talmuds, in the order Mo'ed, dealing with the observance of PASSOVER.

peshát ('simple') In biblical exegesis, the plain or straightforward meaning of the text. It is commonly contrasted with DERÁSH (but for a more complex distinction *see* PARDES). The pursuit of the plain meaning became an important issue in the Middle Ages, RASHI and Abraham IBN EZRA being among the main proponents of peshát.

pesukei de-zimra *See* ZEMIROT.

peticha ('opening') **1** Formula opening a BENEDICTION. It takes the form 'Blessed are you, Lord our God, king of the universe ...' (*See also* CHATIMA.) **2** Opening of the ARK in synagogue. **3** Name given to various types of PIYYUT. It can be the equivalent of RESHÚT. **4** In some MIDRASHIM, an opening section (sometimes called 'proem') that discusses a verse from the KETUVIM, before moving on to the verse of the weekly or festival reading.

petucha ('open') Technical term for a PARASHA that in a SÉFER TORA begins on a new line (*contrast* SETUMA). In a printed text this is indicated by a Hebrew letter p, repeated three times if it is the first parasha of a SIDRA.

Pharisees Religious and political party that began in the early 1st century BCE and disappears from the historical record at the time of the destruction of the Temple in 70 CE. Rabbinic Judaism views them as its own predecessors, who were punctilious in observing the rules of impurity and tithing and in some sense extended the rules of priestly purity to ordinary Jews. The movement seems to have gained great popularity. The name (in Hebrew, Perushim) may indicate separation (from the wider society) or scriptural interpretation, or perhaps a combination of the two. Some of their opponents explained it as 'elitists'.

Philo of Alexandria (d. after 40 CE) The first Jewish philosopher whose works have survived. He was a prolific author, writing in Greek, yet it appears that he had little or no impact on the living Jewish tradition, and his writings have only survived because they were copied by Christian scribes. The impetus to write PHILOSOPHY seems to have come to Philo from the encounter that took place within the Judaism of his day between biblically based Judaism and Greek thought based mainly on Plato. Many of his books try to reconcile the two by interpreting the Bible as a kind of textbook of Platonism.

philosophy

The pursuit of truth through the exercise of reason. The place of philosophy within Judaism has been the subject of much, sometimes acrimonious, debate down the ages, with some authorities insisting that since the source of all true knowledge is divine revelation there is little or no scope for the independent exercise of human reasoning, except perhaps in the interest of strengthening faith. Nevertheless, there has been an important succession of Jewish philosophers committed to the view that reason is a God-given faculty that can genuinely help us to a better understanding of the human condition, the world we inhabit, and even the nature of the Divine. These thinkers have always operated under the direct influence of the dominant philosophies of their day, and their concern has been to expound the essence of Judaism in the current philosophical idiom, or to use the insights of philosophy to achieve a new interpretation of Judaism. The lonely figure of Baruch SPINOZA is exceptional in combining a genuinely independent philosophical quest having universal ramifications with a certain engagement with the traditional teachings of the Bible and Jewish tradition. Hermann COHEN, on the other hand, pursued a professional career detached from Jewish dimensions until the end of his life, when he turned to the philosophical study of Judaism. Since his time many individual Jews have been philosophers, without coveting or deserving the title of 'Jewish philosophers'.

The story of Jewish philosophy begins with Platonism, and specifically with PHILO, who endeavoured to weave together biblical and Platonist ideas. Curiously, although there are many signs of the influence of Plato and other Greek thinkers in the rabbinic literature, and although we know of Jewish members of the Platonist school, Philo stands alone within the historical record: we do not know what other Jews before or after him (if any) pursued the same project of synthesis.

ARISTOTELIANISM dominates the medieval Jewish intellectual tradition, but there is also an important NEOPLATONIST strand, of which the prime representative was Solomon IBN GABIROL. The dominant influence in this period is Greek thought mediated through Arabic translations and interpretations.

If the medieval Jewish philosophers worked against the background of Arabic thought, the thinkers of the ENLIGHTENMENT period were writing in a German milieu, and under pressures imposed by emancipation. A Jew like Moses MAIMONIDES was certain of his place in society, with fewer privileges than a Muslim, but enjoying a stable and clearly defined status, and able to engage confidently on that basis with Muslim thinkers, whose intellectual background he shared and who had no desire to convert him to Islam. If no similar Jewish philosophy emerged in medieval Christendom, no doubt it was because it offered no such basis for a confident Jewish participation in intellectual life. As late as the end of the 19th century brilliant young thinkers such as Edmund Husserl and Henri Bergson, who might have made a great contribution to Jewish religious thought, succumbed to the pressure to convert to Christianity. Others turned their backs on religious philosophy and engaged in 'neutral' currents of thought opened up by the Enlightenment, where their Jewish identity would be no handicap. And those Jewish thinkers who remained faithful to Judaism felt the need to engage in apologetics, justifying Jewish values in the face of Christian or German ones.

Moses MENDELSSOHN, a contemporary of Kant and friend of Lessing, represents these dilemmas in an acute form. Mendelssohn embraced the principles of the Enlightenment wholeheartedly while remaining faithful, as he saw it, to Judaism. In his book *Jerusalem* he drew a sharp distinction between universal reason and particularist, 'revealed' law. This dichotomy between the Enlightenment man and the traditional Jew determined in a sense the destiny of Jewish religious philosophy throughout the 19th century. On the one hand, a succession of idealists (such as Salomon FORMSTECHER, Salomon Ludwig STEINHEIM and Samuel HIRSCH) pursued the theme of the religion of reason, describing Judaism in terms drawn from contemporary German philosophy; on the other, the partisans of 'divine legislation' (Samuel David LUZZATTO, Samson Raphael HIRSCH, Elia BENAMOZEGH and others) focused on the realm of practice.

Hermann Cohen, straddling the threshold of the 20th century, marks a new beginning in Jewish religious philosophy. A distinguished academic philosopher, founder of the Marburg neo-Kantian school, Cohen stands in the line of German Jewish idealists, and in his 19th-century writings God serves only as an idea that supports the structure of his philosophy of ethics. In the last part of his life, however, Cohen began seriously to address the God of faith. Rejecting Kant's view that Judaism was obsolete, Cohen declared it to be true religion, and in his book *Religion of Reason out of the Sources of Judaism* he completed, as it were, the project initiated by Mendelssohn.

The rise of EXISTENTIALISM marks a new and important turn in Jewish thought, with such outstanding figures as Franz ROSENZWEIG, Martin BUBER, Abraham HESCHEL and Emmanuel LEVINAS. Their influence is felt strongly today.

Taking the Jewish philosophical tradition as a whole, we must admit that its impact has been enormous, both within Judaism and outside it (both Philo and Maimonides had an influence on Christian philosophy). And yet this impact has not been at all straightforward. Philo was a dead end within the Jewish tradition. Maimonides met opposition during his lifetime and after his death his books were burnt, as his detractors considered that philosophy was inimical to faith. Since the Enlightenment, as Jews have gradually been drawn into the mainstream of Western academic activity, many Jewish philosophers have felt free to ignore the kinds of questions that their predecessors felt called to respond to out of the sources of Judaism.

phylacteries *See* TEFILLIN.

pidyon ha-ben ('redemption of the son') Ceremony performed thirty days after the birth of a firstborn son, in response to the instruction in the Torah: 'Dedicate to me every firstborn, the first fruit of every womb among the Israelites, whether of human or beast: it is mine' (Exodus 13.2). This instruction is understood to apply only to male children: a daughter does not have the status of a firstborn. The child is ceremonially purchased back (the original meaning of 'redemption') from a priest (KOHEN) who is invited to share in a festive meal. The priest asks the father whether he prefers to hand over his son or five pieces of silver. The father hands over five coins, and various blessings are recited.

piercing The Torah forbids cutting into the body in the context of mourning the dead (Leviticus 19.28, Deuteronomy 14.1), and commentators tend to explain this as a pagan religious ritual (see also 1 Kings 18.28). The halacha discourages any self-disfigurement, because the human body, as the work of God, should be treated with respect.

pikú'ach néfesh ('watchful concern for life') Principle of HALACHA, laying down that the duty of saving of a human life overrides all other commandments, with the exception of the prohibitions on idolatry, incest and bloodshed. The verse of the Torah often cited in this context is Leviticus 18.5, which says of the laws that one 'should live by them', interpreted as meaning that one should not die for them. Even if there is doubt as to whether the danger is life-threatening, everything should be done to save a life, even if it involves working on the Sabbath (Mishnah, Yoma 8.6).

pilgrimage

Travel to a sacred shrine. The Temple in Jerusalem, while it stood, was a great centre of pilgrimage not only for Jews living in the Land of Israel but for the Diaspora as well. Pilgrimage was a legal obligation stipulated three times in the Torah: 'Three times a year all your males shall appear before the Lord your God' (Exodus 23.17, 34.23; Deuteronomy 16.16). These three festive pilgrimages (regalim, singular régel) beat the cyclical rhythm of the Jewish year. The autumn festival, falling immediately after the most solemn moment of the Temple's year, the Day of Atonement, came to be considered the most significant, and it was often known simply as 'the festival' (chag). Although for male Jews the duty to make the pilgrimage three times each year had, strictly speaking, the status of a divine commandment, in practice it was regarded as a non-obligatory but highly meritorious act. While many Jews living within relatively easy reach of Jerusalem made the pilgrimage only occasionally, sources from the early Roman period describe the holy city as being thronged at each of the festivals with countless pilgrims (numbering over a million according to some accounts), many of whom had come from as far away as Iran, Ethiopia and Rome. Clearly for these Jews the pilgrimage represented a very special occasion, perhaps a once-in-a-lifetime journey, necessitating long and costly preparations. The pilgrims (who included women, even though the strict duty was laid only on men), brought with them financial contributions as well as animal and vegetable offerings. They thus made an important material contribution to the Temple and the holy city. The pilgrimage to Jerusalem also fulfilled a vital function in binding together the worldwide Jewish community, symbolizing the unity of the scattered people and favouring the dissemination of new ideas throughout the Jewish world.

This phase came to an abrupt end in 70 CE, when the Temple was destroyed.

Henceforth pilgrims to the site of the destroyed Temple, their joy alloyed with bitterness, recited the words of the prophet Isaiah (64.10): 'Our holy and splendid temple, where our ancestors praised you, has been burnt down, and our most precious possession is now a ruin.' The dominant mood of these pilgrims was one of grief and mourning. Even more bitterly humiliating was the fact that access to the holy city was not freely available: under pagan and Christian rulers the Jews were sometimes completely excluded from Jerusalem; even when they were allowed access the journey was difficult and dangerous, and there were heavy taxes to pay. Yet apparently, despite all the hardships and humiliations, Jewish pilgrims kept on coming. After the Arab conquest in 638 conditions became much easier, and it seems that the numbers of pilgrims increased; some came to settle in Jerusalem, others just to visit. Those who were able brought gold for the maintenance of the Jewish community, for the relief of poverty and the upkeep of the scholars. As in Temple times, the preferred time of the year for pilgrimage was the autumn festival, and pilgrims came not only from the Land of Israel but from far and wide. Some of them went in fulfilment of a vow made at a time of distress. They prayed particularly on the Mount of Olives, outside the city to the east and facing the site of the Temple; they also prayed at the gates of the city: access to the Temple Mount itself posed problems because it had become a Muslim shrine. At the end of the Festival of Tabernacles a great gathering was held on the Mount of Olives.

Jerusalem retained its sanctity throughout the centuries; and it received many famous visitors. A notable pilgrimage was that of the early Chasidic master NACH-MAN OF BRATSLAV in 1798–9; after his return to Poland he would declare: 'Wherever I go, I am still in the Land of Israel.' Another distinguished visitor was the English philanthropist Sir Moses Montefiore, who made the journey to Jerusalem six times between 1827 and 1875 (on the last occasion he was over ninety years old). Montefiore contributed generously to the upkeep of the Jewish community of the city, and the buildings he built for them outside the walls of the Old City, including a striking windmill, can still be seen. They are a reminder that the pilgrims' visits to the city can have mixed motives and effects. It was under Ottoman rule that the spot which is especially venerated today, the 'Wailing Wall', or western retaining wall of the Temple precinct, acquired its status. The wall itself is ancient, but according to tradition it was one of the early Ottoman sultans who cleared the area and allowed the Jews to pray and lament there. Though no formal rituals of pilgrimage are associated with it, this relic of the Temple still attracts Jews both young and old, traditionalist and more secularized: families come to celebrate the BAR MITSVA, and those in anxiety or distress thrust little notes into crevices in the wall. (Between 1948 and 1967, when access to the Wailing Wall was barred to Jews by the Jordanian authorities, many went instead to the traditional tomb of King David on Mount Zion, from which they could view the Old City.)

Apart from the pilgrimage to Jerusalem, which is the only one officially sanctioned and observed by Jews worldwide, in some countries there is a custom, going back to the Middle Ages, of visiting the tombs of individuals reputed for their piety or learning as a sign of respect or to offer up prayers. This custom is particularly well established in Morocco and other parts of North Africa, where it is not confined to Jews: in fact Jews, Muslims and Christians visit each other's shrines. In Poland the Chasidim developed the custom of visiting the tombs of their rebbes on the anniversary of their deaths. In the Middle East, particularly in Israel, Iraq and Iran, the tombs of biblical patriarchs and prophets attract pilgrims, and the kabbalists of Safed identified tombs of famous ancient rabbis all over Galilee. All these sites are visited by pilgrims, particularly kabbalists and Chasidim. Such observances, however, are completely unknown in the West.

There are innumerable such shrines, some of the most important of which are described below, beginning in the Land of Israel.

Not far south of Jerusalem is the traditional site of the tombs of Abraham and his family at HEBRON, which is also a Muslim shrine. Legend holds that four couples are buried here: Abraham and Sarah, Isaac and Rebecca, Jacob and Leah, and also the first human couple, Adam and Eve. Pilgrims to Jerusalem have tended to include the holy city of Hebron on their itinerary. Jerusalem pilgrims also adopted the custom of visiting the supposed tomb of the prophet Samuel (Nebi Samwil), where an annual festivity was formerly held.

The north of Israel, particularly around the holy cities of Tiberias and Safed, is dotted with tombs bearing the names of the great rabbis of the Talmud. Tiberias boasts the burial places of the ancient rabbis AKIBA, Chiyya bar Abba and Huna, Rab Kahana and Jeremiah, as well as that of Moses MAIMONIDES; the holiest shrine here is that of Rabbi Meir the Miracle Worker, where Ashkenazim and Sefardim maintain rival sanctuaries. Further north, at Meron, the tomb of another Rabbi, Simeon bar Yohai, the reputed author of the ZOHAR, attracts tens of thousands of pilgrims at LAG BA-ÓMER (*see* HILLULA). They gather on the afternoon preceding the holy day in Safed, and process joyfully through the narrow streets of the old town bearing Torah scrolls decked with flags. Before nightfall they reassemble within the shrine at Meron. They dance in the courtyard to the sound of antique musical instruments and sing hymns to the holy master. Thousands of candles cover the two tombs of Simeon and his son Eleazar, while on the roof oil-soaked rags blaze all night in two great copper vessels. The next day small children are brought into the shrine, where their hair is cut for the first time; the hair is thrown into the fire as an offering. The pilgrims also visit other tombs and holy sites in the vicinity, such as the tombs of HILLEL and Shammai, and that of Rabbi Yochanan the Shoemaker.

Of the many Jewish shrines of the Middle East, some of which are undoubtedly of very great antiquity, the most famous were traditionally the supposed tombs of the prophet Ezekiel at el-Kafal and of Ezra the Scribe at Kurna, both in Babylonia (modern Iraq). These used to attract pilgrims from all over the Middle East, including Iran, but Arab–Zionist tension, ongoing since the 1950s, has effectively eradicated this ancient custom. The Jews of Iran also have their own shrines, many of which also carry associations with biblical heroes, notably the tombs of Esther and Mordecai and the prophet Zechariah at Hamadan, and of the prophet

Habakkuk nearby at Tuserkan. The Jews of Yezd in response to dreams and vows attend the shrine of the prophet Elijah at Nasrabad; other old shrines, such as the tombs of Daniel at Shushtar, Isaiah at Isfahan and Zippora near Qum, and of Abraham IBN EZRA near Meshed, are no longer practicable for Jewish pilgrimage. The most popular site for Jewish pilgrimage in Iran is the shrine of Serach, daughter of Asher (one of the sons of Jacob), at Lenjan, some thirty kilometres west of Isfahan. According to local legend this otherwise obscure saint appeared miraculously in Iran and rescued the Jews from persecution, notably at the time of the Safavid Shah Abbas II (c. 1666). The ziyyarat or pilgrimage, generally undertaken to fulfil a vow, for example on the occasion of the birth of a son, consists of crawling into a grotto inside which can be seen the tunnel through which Serach travelled from the holy Land. Not far away is the shrine complex, known as chele khune, 'the house of forty', on account of the old practice of coming here at the beginning of the summer month of Elul and staying until the end of the Day of Atonement, forty days later. Here is located the Synagogue (knisa) of the patriarch Jacob, where it is meritorious to worship thrice daily.

Egypt once had many sites of local pilgrimage. By far the most popular sanctuary (mikdash) was that of Dammuh, an abandoned site on the western bank of the Nile south of Cairo. (Recent research has shown that this was the last surviving synagogue of the ancient royal capital of Memphis.) Many GENIZA documents refer to the pilgrimage (ziyyara) to the 'synagogue of Moses' at Dammuh. The most popular time for mass pilgrimage was the summer festival of Shavuot, commemorating the giving of the Torah at Sinai; a lesser observance was on the 7th of Adar, the supposed date of the birth and death of Moses. Pilgrims might stay for several days, and there are indications of riotous feasting and merrymaking, which tends to be a feature of mass pilgrimage everywhere.

In Tunisia the venerable al-Ghriba synagogue on the island of Djerba attracts back expatriates for the long-established annual pilgrimage.

In Morocco, veneration of saints is a very marked feature both of Judaism and of Islam. Their shrines are dispersed all over the country, mainly in the Atlas mountains but also along the coastal plain and in the eastern regions. A recent study managed to gather information about no fewer than 571 Moroccan Jewish saints (of whom twenty-one were women). Many of the sites are traditionally visited by both Jewish and Muslim pilgrims. With the resettlement of large numbers of Moroccan Jews in Israel, new shrines have sprung up there to satisfy the religious needs and customs of the immigrants.

In Europe, whatever may have been the situation in earlier times (and pilgrimage never seems to have been an established custom here outside the areas that have been under Muslim influence), it is now almost non-existent, and most European Jews, or Jews of European origin, would not instinctively associate it with Judaism as it has existed since the destruction of the Temple in Jerusalem. However, there are regular visits to a few shrines, such as the tomb of Nachman of Bratslav in Uman in Ukraine. *See also* ALIYYA; BETA ISRAEL; CHAGIGA.

pilpul A method of study consisting of sharp-witted argument. The origin of the term is obscure: it has been connected with the Hebrew word pilpel, 'pepper'. It is generally applied to topics in HALACHA, rather than AGGADA. Pilpul is mentioned with approval by the rabbis as a means of acquiring knowledge of Torah (Mishnah, Avot 6.6), and no doubt it is an excellent mental discipline as well as a way of teasing out the possible meanings of a text. In time, however, it came to be pursued almost as an end in itself, and was severely criticized. The term is sometimes used pejoratively, in the sense of 'hair-splitting'.

Pirkei Avot ('chapters of Avot') Name popularly given to the Mishnah tractate AVOT.

Pittsburgh Platform Declaration of principles for Reform Judaism in the United States, issued by a rabbinic gathering convened by Kaufmann KOHLER at Pittsburgh, Pennsylvania, from 16 to 19 November 1885, in the spirit of synods held in Germany in the 1840s. Isaac Mayer WISE presided. The Platform, while expressing respect for all religions, asserts that Judaism 'presents the highest conception of the God-idea'. The Bible reflects 'the primitive ideas of its own age'; modern advances in science, morality and social behaviour must take precedence over its demands, and the Bible's ceremonial regulations concerning diet, purity and dress are abandoned, as is any hope for a return to Palestine. 'We recognize in Judaism a progressive religion, ever striving to be in accord with the postulates of reason.' The Platform ends with a statement accepting the immortality of the soul, and rejecting bodily resurrection, and another on the duty to solve the injustices in society. The document was adopted by the CENTRAL CONFERENCE OF AMERICAN RABBIS in 1889. *See also* COLUMBUS PLATFORM; MIAMI PLATFORM; PITTSBURGH STATEMENT.

Pittsburgh Statement Declaration of principles adopted in May 1999 at the Pittsburgh Convention of the (Reform) CENTRAL CONFERENCE OF AMERICAN RABBIS. According to the preamble, the Statement 'affirms the central tenets of Judaism – God, Torah and Israel – even as it acknowledges the diversity of Reform Jewish beliefs and practices'. Under the heading 'God' it describes prayer, study and the performance of the COMMANDMENTS (mitsvot) as a response to God (while leaving open the vexed question of the divine or human origin of the commandments). Torah is described as 'the foundation of Jewish life' and 'God's ongoing revelation to our people and the record of our people's ongoing relationship with God', which, again, could be interpreted as falling short of declaring the commandments of the Torah to be divinely ordained, although it is certainly susceptible of such an interpretation. The statement makes a commitment to the study of all the commandments and 'the fulfilment of those that address us as individuals and as a community', some of which, it admits, have not previously received attention from Reform Jews. As for Israel, the statement seeks to open doors to Jewish life to people of all ages, to varied kinds of families, to all regardless of their sexual orientation, to converts to Judaism, and to all individuals and families, including the intermarried, who strive to create a Jewish home; it further calls for active encouragement of 'those who are seeking a spiritual home to find it in Judaism'. The remaining clauses essentially reiterate previous Reform statements or express uncontroversial beliefs.

piyyut (from Greek) A liturgical hymn, or the genre in general. The word is thought to be derived from post-classical Greek pi-i-tís, a poet, or pí-i-ma, a poem. The piyyutim constitute the richest and most inventive corpus of Hebrew poetry, and among their composers (known as payyetanim) are many of the best-known Hebrew poets. The origins of piyyut are obscure; it seems to have originated in the Land of Israel in late antiquity, perhaps in association with the beginnings of a fixed synagogue liturgy in Hebrew. The works of the early payyetanim, from the 5th to the 7th century, reveal an extraordinary linguistic, poetic and exegetical inventiveness. After the Arab conquest of the region in the 630s for some reason the main centre of creativity shifted from the Land of Israel to the Babylonian Diaspora, the most skilful payyetan here being the multi-talented SA'ADYA GA'ON. A new phase began in Muslim Spain in the 10th century (*see* IBN GABIROL, SOLOMON), and with the Christian reconquest and a decline in conditions in the south poets including Abraham IBN EZRA, Moses IBN EZRA and JUDAH HA-LEVI in the 12th century migrated to the Christian north, where new indigenous styles of piyyut emerged, one of the noted authors being the well-known kabbalist NACHMANIDES. Meanwhile the taste for embellishing the synagogue service with poetic compositions spread to Byzantium and Italy, and to Ashkenaz, including England. There was hardly a region where the art was not practised, by RABBANITES and KARAITES alike. The names of literally thousands of payyetanim are known, and tens of thousands of their creations survive. These constitute an important subject of research. Throughout the Middle Ages voices were raised against the use of piyyutim; Maimonides, for instance, found in their recitation 'the major cause for the lack of devotion of the masses'. Similar considerations led the 19th-century reformers to excise most of the piyyutim from the liturgy: they were found to be obscure, theologically dubious, and an impediment to concentration on the prayers. All modernist prayer books, however, contain some piyyutim today, even if it is only in the Eastern traditions that congregants really take pleasure in chanting cycles of hymns (*see* BAKKASHA). *See also* the major genres: AVODA; AZHARA; hoshána at HOSHÁNOT; KEDUSHTA; KEROVA; KINA; MA'ARIV; RESHÚT; selicha at SELICHOT; SHIVATA; YOTSER.

pizmon (from Greek) A song, particularly: **1** a choral refrain to a PIYYUT, such as a KEDUSHTA; **2** a type of selicha (*see* SELICHOT).

plagues of Egypt *See* TEN PLAGUES (OF EGYPT).

pluralism

A situation, and by implication general acceptance of a situation, in which no single group is dominant or lays exclusive claim to power or truth. The structure of authority in Judaism, in which there is no single central power, means that it is inherently tolerant of dissent, even though such tolerance has often been curtailed or challenged by individuals or (more usually) groups that felt they possessed a unique and exclusive authority.

A good example of pluralism is provided by JOSEPHUS. Writing about Israel in the time of the Hasmonean wars of the 2nd century BCE, he divides the Jews of the time into three 'philosophical schools', and sums up their differences as follows:

> At that time there were three schools among the Jews: the Pharisees, the Sadducees and the Essenes, and they all held different views about human behaviour. The Pharisees hold that some, but not all, events are the work of Fate: in some cases it is for us to decide whether they should happen or not. The Essenes claim that Fate is mistress of everything, and nothing befalls people except by its decision. Meanwhile the Sadducees rule Fate out altogether, considering that it counts for nothing and has no effect on human actions, but that everything is up to us: we ourselves are responsible for the good things that happen to us, while the bad things happen because of our poor planning. (Josephus, *Jewish Antiquities* 13.171–3; see also his *Jewish War*, 2.162–5. *See also* HERESY.)

We can only dimly apprehend the various versions of Judaism that existed side by side after the destruction of the Temple, because most of our information comes from a single strand, that represented by the rabbis. It is clear, however, that a number of rival interpretations co-existed, and we also know that big cities tended to have several synagogues, as indeed they do today. The rabbinic movement, over a long period, gradually gained the upper hand, but it did not go unchallenged. Much of the dissent eventually crystallized around KARAISM, a reforming movement that was strong between the 9th and 11th centuries in the Middle East, and thereafter in the Byzantine empire. So acute was the rift between the Karaites and their Talmudically oriented opponents, the Rabbanites, that they formed separate communities in the same towns, which in at least one place (Constantinople) had to be separated by a wall so as to keep the peace.

Later, after the expulsion from Spain, separate communities of different origin were set up, purely for historical rather than theological reasons, in the cities of the Ottoman empire. Salonica in its heyday had synagogues which bore such names as Castilla, Catalan, Aragon, Calabria and Puglia (Apulia). Congregations of Sefardim and Ashkenazim existed side by side in western European cities such as Amsterdam, Hamburg and London. In this way the ground was prepared for the pluralism that exists today. The distinctions were, however, more social than religious, and membership of a community was determined by descent rather than free choice. As for pluralism of belief, the early modern period saw increasing use of the threat of EXCOMMUNICATION and accusations of heresy. With EMANCIPATION, however, the rabbinate in Europe gradually lost the power to impose its views by force, and today there are no limits on pluralism, as expressed concretely in synagogues of the different modernist movements standing almost shoulder to shoulder in the streets of central London or New York.

Although the prevalence of atheism coupled with a habit of questioning all received orthodoxy makes the present age different from earlier periods, it would be wrong to imagine that the radical nature of contemporary disagreements is totally novel. The debate about the extent of God's interference in human affairs, described by Josephus two millennia ago, has a strangely modern ring, particularly reminiscent of arguments in Israel today. While it would not be entirely accurate to liken contemporary secularists to the ancient Sadducees, who did not deny the existence of God but, on the contrary, were concerned to distance him from any contact with evil, there is something similar between their views in practice. The Essene position on this issue is close to the view of those who refuse to recognize Israel as a Jewish state, arguing that God will send the redemption when he wills it, and that it is wrong for humans to try to 'hasten the end' (*see* AGUDAT ISRAEL; NETÚREI KÁRTA). Moderate religious opinion would correspond, then, to the standpoint of the Pharisees, that all choices involve both God and man.

P'nai Or *See* NEO-CHASIDISM.

polygamy Marriage to more than one person at a time. While Jewish law tolerates POLYGYNY, at least in theory, it is deeply opposed to the notion of one woman having sexual relations with several men, except in the framework of successive marriages (*see* MONOGAMY).

polygyny The taking by one man of a plurality of wives. The Bible seems to find the practice completely unexceptional, although it does not particularly promote it as an ideal. Of the king it says 'he shall not multiply wives to himself, so that his heart turn not away' (Deuteronomy 17.17). In the extreme case of King Solomon, his seven hundred wives and three hundred concubines are indeed said to have turned away his heart (1 Kings 11.3) – explained in the previous verse as seducing him to false religion. Of the patriarchs, Abraham had a wife and a concubine, Isaac one wife and Jacob two wives and two concubines; the Torah makes no comment on these various family configurations, although it records the poor relations between Abraham's wife and concubine as quite normal (Genesis 16). The Talmud does not explicitly discourage polygyny, although it discusses some of the issues (a husband must pay due attention to a clause in his wife's KETUBBA prohibiting him from taking additional wives, and if he does take more wives he must be able to fulfil his marital obligations towards all of them). The so-called TAKKANA of Rabbenu GERSHOM prohibits Ashkenazim from taking more than one wife; this is generally understood to arise from the situation of living as a minority within a Christian environment, rather than from any deeper moral considerations. It does not change the fundamental acceptance of polygyny within halacha, which is the source of the perceived inequality of the sexes in the case of the AGUNA.

pomegranate In the Torah colourful pomegranate-shaped balls adorn the hem of the High Priest's robe (Exodus 28.33). Today the distinctive shape of the pomegranate is sometimes evoked in the carving of FINIALS. Pomegranates figure several times in the erotic poetry of the Song of Songs; they are often interpreted allegorically as denoting the Torah. *See also* RIMMONIM.

Porat Yosef *See* TRADITIONALISM.

porging (in Hebrew, nikkur) Removal of forbidden fats and nerves from meat. This is a highly skilled activity, and many kosher butchers feel unable to porge correctly, so simply discard cuts such as the hindquarters. This is the part of the animal that contains the sciatic nerve, which according to the Torah must not be eaten by Israelites (Genesis 32.33).

posek ('a decider'; plural poskim) A rabbi who enjoys authority to decide questions of HALACHA. This authority derives from communal consensus, and is not formally bestowed.

Positive-Historical school *See* HISTORICAL SCHOOL.

post-Zionism A term applied to various critical positions that challenge the Zionist narrative of Jewish history in the Land of Israel. Founded on post-modern understandings of history, it attempts to reclaim alternative voices from the past that have (it argues) been suppressed. Its proponents employ scholarship in the interests of righting historic wrongs and reshaping Israel's collective memory and identity in the furtherance of justice. They tend to portray Zionism as a pernicious ideology grounded on immoral premises, which in addition to perpetrating intolerable injustices on the local Arab populations, misrepresents the Jewish historical experience, notably the relationship between Israel and the Diaspora and the position of the Jews of Muslim countries.

prayer (in Hebrew, tefilla) Whereas the Bible reports the prayers of individuals, the Talmud places the focus of prayer very firmly in the public domain of the synagogue. Jews are encouraged to pray with the community in preference to praying alone. MAIMONIDES argues as follows: 'Communal prayer is always hearkened to and even if there are sinners among them the Holy One, blessed be He, does not reject the prayers of the many. Consequently, a man should associate himself with the community and he should not recite prayers in private when he is able to recite them together with the community' (Code, Rules of Prayer 8.1). Although the rabbis were sensitive to the view that prayer should not be something fixed, but rather a sincere and spontaneous outpouring of pleas for mercy and supplications before God (Mishnah, Avot 2.13), they also formulated detailed regulations about when, where and how to pray. Prayer is regarded as a duty (there is disagreement as to whether the obligation derives from the Torah or the rabbis). When the rabbis speak of 'the prayer' they mean the AMIDA (Eighteen Benedictions).

prayer books The early history of the codification of Jewish liturgy is obscure. The earliest influential codifications are the Séder Rav Amram Ga'on and the SIDDUR of SA'ADYA GA'ON, compiled in Babylonia in the 9th and 10th centuries respectively, and the Machzor Vitry, made in northern France in the 11th. Many other documentary sources survive from this period, testifying to the diversity of local rites. Over time the Babylonian rite gradually replaced the Palestinian and other rites virtually everywhere (just as the Babylonian Talmud replaced the Palestinian Talmud). The Land of Israel resumed a central role, however, in the 16th century, with the kabbalistic school of Isaac LURIA in SAFED. Luria's distinctive prayer book, the Minhag Ari, based on the Spanish rite but incorporating distinctive Lurianic beliefs, was widely diffused and became particularly popular among the CHASIDIM. Although the introduction of printing led to the disappearance of many individual rites, there is still great diversity in prayer books, which has increased to some extent in the past century. In Britain an important milestone in the standardization of worship was the publication in 1890 of the *Authorized Daily Prayer Book of the United Hebrew Congregations of the British Empire*, commonly known as Singer's Prayer Book after its editor, Simeon Singer. Singer's Prayer Book has been issued in a succession of revised editions, and is still very widely used in British Orthodox synagogues and found in many homes. Meanwhile the Sefardi, Reform and Liberal congregations have issued their own prayer books, as have the Conservative, Reform and Reconstructionist movements in America. The American ArtScroll editions are becoming increasingly popular; they adopt a traditionalist approach to the service, and are equipped with helpful notes and explanations.

Whereas the earliest manuscript prayer books tended to encompass prayers for every occasion, nowadays a clear distinction is drawn between the SIDDUR, which contains daily and Sabbath prayers, and the MACHZOR, containing festival prayers, often with separate volumes for the various festivals. Prayer books are provided in synagogues, but are also commonly found in Jewish homes. Most homes also possess the prayer book for the home celebration of Passover, the HAGGADA.

The prayer book has two faces: it is a repository of religious beliefs that have accumulated down the ages, and it is an important textbook. In the absence of definitive creeds or catechetical education, it constitutes the only induction many Jews ever receive into the theological beliefs of their faith. Its influence is thus considerable, and the various modernist movements have not been slow to realize this and revise the books in line with the message they wish to put across. While traditional liturgies evolved over a long period by a kind of sedimentary process without the active intervention of an editor, modern liturgies are edited by individuals, or more often by panels of rabbis, concerned to purge the text of theological ideas that have been discarded and to incorporate others that have been adopted. Among the distinctive features of modern liturgies are the abandonment of many passages deemed too obscure or antiquated for contemporary worshippers (especially when translated into the vernacular), the introduction of some modern prayers and meditations, and in some books anthologies of passages for study or discussion. Gender-inclusive language has been adopted, some formulae that could be deemed offensive to non-Jews have been removed, and contentious religious beliefs such as bodily RESURRECTION have been amended. In such ways the liturgy has been brought up to date, and made more suitable for worship in the modern age.

precepts *See* COMMANDMENTS.

priest *See* KOHEN.

Principles, Thirteen *See* THIRTEEN PRINCIPLES.

profanation *See* CHILLUL HA-SHEM; HOLINESS.

Progressive Judaism 1 In Britain, a synonym of LIBERAL JUDAISM, preferred as a title by some congregations. **2** More generally, a collective term for the Reform, Liberal, Progressive and Reconstructionist movements. *See* WORLD UNION FOR PROGRESSIVE JUDAISM.

prophecy Moral and spiritual leadership, under divine inspiration. Commonly misunderstood as denoting prediction of the future, the word comes from a Greek root meaning to speak forth or proclaim. The line of biblical prophets is considered by the rabbis to have come to an end in the 5th century with Haggai, Zechariah and Malachi. There are indications, however, of a belief in the Middle Ages that prophecy would soon be renewed, as a prelude to the messianic age. The medieval thinkers disagreed about the nature of prophecy. MAIMONIDES, in the sixth of his THIRTEEN PRINCIPLES, sees it as a combination of exceptional human aptitude and divine grace. 'There are human beings with very intellectual natures who have great perfection: their souls are predisposed to receive the form of the intellect. This human intellect joins itself to the active intellect, and a supernal emanation is cast upon them. These are the prophets.' JUDAH HA-LEVI adopts a different perspective, and sees prophecy as entirely a divine gift. He further specifies that it is limited to Jews living in the Land of Israel. In his view, Jews are by nature superior to non-Jews; CRESCAS, who agrees that prophecy is limited to Jews, explains that this is because only a rigorous training grounded in the Torah can prepare a man to become a prophet.

prophet (in Hebrew, navi) An inspired leader. In the Torah ABRAHAM is called a prophet (Genesis 20.7), but the greatest of all the prophets is Moses: 'No prophet has arisen in Israel like Moses, whom the Lord knew face to face' (Deuteronomy 34.10). MAIMONIDES incorporates this belief in the seventh of his THIRTEEN PRINCIPLES (no doubt in part at least as a way of distancing Judaism from the Muslim belief in Muhammad as the last and greatest of the prophets). After Moses there is a gap in the succession of prophets (although the judge Deborah is called a prophet, Judges 4.4), until the time of Samuel, at the beginning of the period of the monarchy, with which the stories of the various prophets as told in the books of Samuel and Kings are intimately associated. The kings of Israel were anointed to office by prophets, who occasionally spoke out against the immorality of royal actions. The 'literary' prophets whose words are embodied in the books bearing their names, from Hosea and Amos in the 8th century BCE to Malachi in the 5th (some parts of the prophetic books may be even later than this), represent the acme of biblical prophecy, notable for the insistent demands both for social morality and for justice for the disadvantaged members of society, such as widows and orphans.

prophetic books *See* BIBLE; HAFTARA.

Prophetic Judaism Title sometimes claimed by REFORM JUDAISM. It is meant to imply a greater emphasis on the prophetic writings of the Bible than on the Torah, and particularly on the prophetic message of social justice and morality.

proselyte (in Hebrew, ger) A convert to Judaism. The word 'proselyte' is Greek in origin, and means an immigrant or resident alien. It is first used in the Greek translation of the Torah (the Septuagint) at Exodus 12.48, 'If an immigrant immigrates among you to make the Passover for the Lord, you shall circumcise any male one, and then he shall immigrate to do it.' The verb translated 'immigrate' here clearly means to join a community; it translates a Hebrew verb (gur) meaning 'to sojourn', 'to live somewhere on a temporary basis'. The related Hebrew noun ger is generally translated as 'proselyte' on the basis of the Greek translation. The rabbis distinguish two kinds of ger, a ger toshav or 'resident ger', who undertakes to observe the seven NOACHIAN COMMANDMENTS, and a ger tsédek or 'righteous ger', who accepts all the rules of Judaism. The thirteenth benediction of the AMIDA prays for God's compassion to be stirred towards the righteous proselytes. The Talmud lays down rules for their acceptance into Judaism: they must have sincere, disinterested motives, they must be given some instruction in the commandments of the Torah, they must be baptized, males must be circumcised, and they must offer a sacrifice on acceptance. All these procedures are still followed, except for the sacrifice, which is not operable in the absence of a temple. There is considerable disagreement among the various modernist movements both about the desirability of admitting converts and about the procedures.

proselytism The active pursuit of prospective converts. The American Reform rabbinate's PITTSBURGH STATEMENT declares: 'We believe that we must not only open doors for those ready to enter our faith, but also to actively encourage those who are seeking a spiritual home to find it in Judaism.' Such statements are rare in contemporary Judaism, and there is no doubt that the position of Jews living an often precarious minority existence has historically inhibited the development of any such movement. In earlier times, however, before the Jews became subject to Christian and Muslim legislation that punished proselytism with death, there are signs that it was actively pursued. In the Roman empire Judaism spread widely, particularly among women, apparently. There are recorded cases of entire populations being converted, for example the Idumeans (Edomites) under the Hasmonean king John Hyrcanus (late 2nd century BCE), or the Khazars in southern Russia in the 8th century CE.

Protestrabbiner (German, protest-rabbis) Group of Liberal and Orthodox rabbis in Germany who protested against the holding of the first Zionist Congress on German soil (in Munich) in 1897. This was a rare example of Liberal–Orthodox co-operation. The congress was moved to Basle in Switzerland.

Proverbs (Mishle) Biblical book, in the third division (Ketuvim), consisting of collections of aphorisms, often of a practical nature. Its author claims to be King Solomon, but this claim is not taken seriously (even in the Talmud, where the book is said to have been compiled in the court of King Hezekiah in the late 8th century BCE, Bavli, Bava Batra 15a). *See also* ÉSHET CHÁYIL.

providence (in Hebrew, hashgacha) Power that is believed to govern the world and guide all things. The idea that God oversees the world and cares for his creatures is found in many places in the Bible, and although different views were taken in the last centuries of the Temple (*see* PLURALISM) the rabbis continued the Pharisaic and

Stoic belief that God's providence extends over even the tiniest details of creation. 'No one so much as hurts his finger here below unless it has been ordained above' (Bavli, Chullin 7b). The rabbis do not discuss the operation of providence in detail, however; this task was left to the medieval philosophers. These distinguish two types of providence, general and special. The latter refers to God's care for individuals, and it turned out to be a problematical concept. MAIMONIDES and GERSONIDES limit it to humans, and indeed to those humans who merit divine attention because of their intellectual acumen and piety. CRESCAS argues that it extends to all human beings. All these thinkers would deny that God decides whether, say, a particular cow will live or die or a particular spider will catch a particular fly. This, however, is what the CHASIDIM maintained. As one early master put it, 'One ought to believe that even a piece of straw that lies on the ground does so at the behest of God, who decrees that it should lie there with one end facing one way and the other end the other way.'

Psalms (Tehillim) First and longest book of the third division of the Bible (Ketuvim). It consists of 150 poems, on a variety of themes and in various styles, divided informally into five books. An old view holds that they were written, or at least collected, by King David; many of them have headings stating that they are by him or even associating them with particular moments in his life. Others, however, have headings attributing them to other authors. Several seem to have been used liturgically in the Temple, and the psalms figure prominently in the worship of the synagogue. The book of Psalms is not read in its entirety in the services, although some pious Jews do read the whole book privately each week, or even each day. Instead, particular psalms or sequences of psalms are read at specific points in the service or on special occasions. For example, Psalms 100 and 145–50 are said in the daily morning service, Psalms 19, 34, 90, 91, 135, 136, 33, 92, 93 and 145–50 (in that order) on Sabbath and festival mornings, and in the conclusion of the morning service the 'psalm of the day' is recited, prefaced with the words 'this is the day of the week, on which the Levites in the Temple used to say'. On Friday evening the Sabbath is welcomed with Psalms 95–9 and 29, a custom introduced by the SAFED kabbalists. Psalms 145 and 24 (on weekdays) or 29 (on Sabbaths) are sung when the scroll of the Torah is returned to the ARK. A special liturgy of psalms (HALLEL) is sung on festival days: it consists of Psalms 113–18, preceded and followed by a special blessing. Associations for the saying of psalms were formed in many places; they are rare today.

Pseudo-Jonathan *See* TARGUMIM.

Pumbedita Town on the Euphrates in northern BABYLONIA remembered for its famous rabbinic academy, founded in the 3rd century CE, where much of the groundwork for the Babylonian Talmud was laid. Its name is inseparable from that of its rival at SURA. The academy was moved to Baghdad (retaining its name) in the late 9th century, giving it a distinct edge over Sura, and closed in the mid-11th century.

Purim Minor festival with a major theme: deliverance from persecution. It is held on the 14th of Adar (Second Adar in leap years), and is not a holiday from work. The main (and only official) ceremony is the reading of the scroll of ESTHER, which tells the story of the deliverance of the Jews of the Persian empire from extermination at the hands of the wicked Haman. Tradition lays down various other observances, such as a fast on the preceding day and a feast on the day itself, making charitable gifts, and taking food to friends or neighbours, but the most striking features of the home celebration are the licence, indeed encouragement, to drink to the point of oblivion, and a riotous carnival atmosphere, with the wearing of masks and fancy dress (even cross-dressing, forbidden in the Torah, is tolerated). Children act out the story of Queen Esther, and three-cornered pastries filled with poppy seeds, known as 'Haman's ears' or 'Haman's pockets', are traditionally eaten.

Q

Qirqisani *See* AL-KIRKISANI.

Qumisi *See* AL-KUMISI.

R

Rabban (Aramaic, 'our master') Title of honour applied in the period of the Mishnah to a few outstanding rabbis, such as YOCHANAN BEN ZAKKAI.

Rabbanism Term applied to the movement defending the authority of the ORAL TORAH in the Middle Ages, in contradistinction to KARAISM which denied it. The adherents of the movement are known as Rabbanites.

Rabbenu Gershom *See* GERSHOM, RABBENU.

rabbi

A scholar, teacher and judge. The title is derived from the Hebrew word rav ('great'), and according to some it began as a form of address, meaning 'my master'; others believe the ending has no possessive force (*see* RIBBI). The title seems to have originated in the 1st century CE, to denote someone distinguished for his scholarship and powers of leadership, within the movement that we nowadays call 'rabbinic Judaism' which is the ancestor of virtually all the forms of Judaism current today. The title was only used in the Land of Israel (*see* RAV (2)). The RABBIS retrospectively bestowed the rabbinic title on Moses, calling him Moshe Rabbénu, 'Moses our rabbi', presumably because they considered him to embody in a very high degree the qualities associated with a rabbi.

Originally there seems to have been a formal recognition or ordination of new rabbis, symbolized by a laying on of hands (SEMICHA). Only those who had been ordained in this way were able to use the rabbinic title. In the 4th century the practice of ordination ceased and the title was bestowed as a mark of honour on any teacher of Torah. Much later, in the Middle Ages, a new form of ordination was instituted among the Ashkenazim, in which a prominent scholar examined a candidate in his competence in Jewish law, and if satisfied issued him with a licence to issue decisions (HÉTTER HORA'A). It was suggested by Isaac ABRAVANEL that this system was borrowed from the nascent universities, from which Jews were excluded. Contemporary rabbinic ordination derives in part from this institution, and, particularly in the more traditional wing of Judaism, the sources of rabbinic law still play a large part in the rabbi's education. In the 19th century rabbinic SEMINARIES began to be established, at first in Europe and later in the United States, which aimed to impart a much broader education in Jewish history and thought, and to train rabbis for their new role as preachers and spiritual leaders. These modern rabbis were also encouraged to obtain a university education in addition to their study at the seminary.

In the meantime an important change had occurred affecting the basic character of the rabbinate. Originally, Torah study had been an end in itself and an obligation on all Jews, and it was felt to be wrong to earn one's livelihood from it. Great rabbis like MAIMONIDES earned their living as physicians or from some trade. From the 16th century, however, it became commoner for a community to employ a rabbi as its legal authority and religious leader, and in this way the rabbinate became a profession. After the EMANCIPATION in Europe the rabbinate became assimilated more and more to the model of the Christian ministry, and we even find a hierarchical system growing up, in which CHIEF RABBIS are recognized by the state as the spiritual heads of the Jewish community, and come to exert authority over other rabbis, a development which has no basis in Jewish law or tradition. Many rabbis are employed by synagogues to offer religious leadership and provide a wide range of services to the community. Some of those who hold rabbinic appointments, however, do not hold a rabbinic qualification, just as some of those who are qualified as rabbis have no communal rabbinic appointment.

Until recently, in keeping with the general character of Judaism at the time, the rabbinate was reserved to men. Since the early 20th century women have played an increasingly prominent role in religious leadership (beginning in the British Liberal movement). The Reform seminary in Berlin ordained a woman as rabbi in the 1930s, but she was killed by the Nazis; after the war the impetus was lost, and it was some time before the issue came to the forefront of discussion again. With the growth of Jewish feminism in the late 1960s pressure began for the ordination of women as rabbis, at first in the Reconstructionist and American Reform movements. In 1972 the Reform movement in America ordained its first woman rabbi; the British Reform movement and the American Conservative movement followed suit in 1975 and 1985 respectively. In these Progressive movements the rabbinical seminaries now have more or less equal numbers of male and female students. Orthodoxy has yet to take the plunge, although the subject is under discussion at the more liberal fringe of the movement.

A synagogue service does not need to be led by a rabbi. Any congregant may lead the prayers (although Orthodoxy does not permit women to lead men in prayer). In keeping with the trend to transform the rabbi into a minister of religion, conducting services has come to be part of the function of a modern rabbi, at least at the more Progressive end of the spectrum. In some larger synagogues this role belongs to the CHAZZAN or cantor.

See also CHACHAM; REBBE.

Rabbi *See* JUDAH THE NASI.

rabbinic Judaism Term applied to the form of Judaism devised by the rabbis of the Mishnah and Talmud and maintained throughout the Middle Ages and the early modern period. Its main characteristics are the belief in the ORAL as well as the WRIT-TEN TORAH and the authority of the rabbis as teachers and judges.

Rabbinical Assembly The rabbinical body of CONSERVATIVE JUDAISM in America. Founded originally in 1901 in Philadelphia, it adopted its present name in 1918. The first female member was admitted in 1985. Its committee on Jewish Law and Standards deliberates and offers guidance on contemporary halachic issues, often in the form of RESPONSA.

Rabbinical Council of America Rabbinical body serving the ORTHODOX rabbinate in the United States and also Canada, Israel and elsewhere. The council was founded in 1936 in New York. It maintains a committee (Vá'ad Halacha) that formulates halachic positions on a range of contemporary issues.

rabbinism Term sometimes used for RABBINIC JUDAISM.

rabbis, the Expression commonly applied collectively to the rabbis of the Mishnah and Talmud.

rachamim *See* COMPASSION.

Radak *See* KIMCHI, DAVID.

Rambam *See* MAIMONIDES, MOSES.

Ramban *See* NACHMANIDES, MOSES.

Ramchal *See* LUZZATTO, MOSES CHAYYIM.

Rapoport, Solomon Judah (Leib) (1790–1867) Scholar, rabbi of Prague from 1840, and one of the founders of the WISSENSCHAFT DES JUDENTUMS, also known by the acronym Shir. A rationalist, who admired earlier rationalists such as Moses MAIMONIDES and Abraham IBN EZRA and strongly opposed KABBALA and CHASIDISM, Rapoport seems with hindsight a strangely ambiguous figure. While embracing the principles of historical research and even of biblical criticism and supporting HASKALA and the diffusion of secular knowledge among Jews, he never gives any hint in his writings of a critical attitude to the ORAL TORAH, and he never seems to have contemplated applying reason to the adjustment of Judaism to new conditions, as was done by the religious reformers. His whole attitude to REFORM JUDAISM was extremely negative and hostile.

Rashi (1040–1105) Acronym of Rabbi Solomon Yitschaki, a scholar and commentator whose academy at Troyes in Champagne attracted students from far and wide. Rashi's commentary on the Bible draws freely on the Midrash, but his approach is entirely different. In simple style he comments on each verse in turn, concentrating on explaining difficulties and obscurities rather than reading extraneous ideas into the text. His work acquired enormous popularity, partly because it could be used for teaching children. It was widely copied and studied, and was in due course one of the first Hebrew works to be printed; it became itself the object of numerous commentaries, and is often found printed in editions of the Hebrew Bible alongside the biblical text. His commentary to the Babylonian Talmud opened up that obscure and difficult text to generations of readers. He has also left sòme RESPONSA. *See also* TOSAFISTS.

rationalism The view that reason is the ultimate foundation of knowledge. The Bible and the Talmud, while they contain much rational argument, never put reason forward as superior to faith. With the rise of KALAM a tension between the two sources of knowledge became explicit, and as philosophical enquiry took hold some thinkers came close to asserting that reason is the only true source. The ENLIGHTENMENT, often called the Age of Reason, gave rise to the view that the doctrines of Judaism are entirely consistent with the universal 'religion of reason'. (*See* MENDELSSOHN, MOSES; COHEN, HERMANN.)

Rav 1 The first Babylonian AMORA. According to the Talmud (our only source of information about his life), he studied in the Land of Israel under JUDAH THE NASI, returning to Babylonia in 219. He is considered as the founder of the famous academy of SURA. **2** ('great') Title used in BABYLONIA in the Talmudic period as the equivalent of 'rabbi'. It is used today by some Hebrew speakers (sometimes with the definite article, ha-rav).

Rav, The *See* SOLOVEITCHIK, JOSEPH DOV.

reading of the Torah *See* TORAH READING.

rebbe (Yiddish, 'rabbi') Title used by CHASIDIM for their religious leaders, also known as tsaddikim. Theirs was a new type of leadership, which was different from the rabbinate in not being based on halachic expertise. Some rebbes also served as town rabbis, but they exercised a charismatic leadership over a following that was often widely scattered, in distinction to the rabbis, whose authority was strictly local. The Chasidim established a principle of hereditary succession for rebbes, which has sometimes been imitated in non-Chasidic circles. The tsaddik or rebbe demanded complete submission from his followers, and his authority was based not on his learning but on his spiritual stature, which could sometimes border on the supernatural. Some were even said to work miracles, and holiness was thought to attach to the food they had blessed or their cast-off clothes. They are believed to have the power to intercede for their followers after their death, and some followers of the late Lubavitcher Rebbe became convinced that he was the MESSIAH and would return after his death. This is all far removed from the authority of the rabbi, although the uninstructed observer may easily confuse a Chasidic rebbe with a rabbi.

rechitsa ('washing') Ceremonial washing of a corpse, performed by members of the CHEVRA KADISHA (*see also* LAVADORES). Special rules and customs govern this ritual, which is always carried out by people of the same sex as the deceased. Rechitsa gedola (major washing), a specially elaborate form of washing, which can last several hours, is performed on the bodies of rabbis who in their life were DAYYANIM or were distinguished as spiritual leaders.

Reconstructionism An American-based movement that views Judaism as a progressively evolving civilization, based on the ideas of Mordecai KAPLAN. It originated as a radical offshoot of CONSERVATIVE JUDAISM. As a leading figure at the JEWISH THEOLOGICAL SEMINARY OF AMERICA for many years (he joined the teaching staff in 1909), Kaplan pressed for liturgical reform and innovations in ritual practice from inside the framework of Conservative Judaism. Frustrated by the dominance of more traditionalist voices at the Seminary, he and his followers decided that the ideas of Reconstructionism would be better served through the creation of a separate denomination. The split became formalized in 1968 with the establishment of the Reconstructionist Rabbinical College.

The key element in Kaplan's thought is a naturalistic theology that has been compared to the thinking of John Dewey (1859–1952). Kaplan maintained that God is not a person, but that language about God is a means of focusing our aspirations to improve human life and make the world a better place to live in.

As there is no room in this theology for HALACHA as revealed law, Reconstructionism tends to classify all of halacha as 'folkways' rather than COMMANDMENTS. It promotes many traditional Jewish practices, while holding that where there is a conflict with contemporary Western secular morality the latter takes precedence.

A Platform on Reconstructionism, issued in 1986, makes the following points: Judaism is the result of natural human development; there is no such thing as divine intervention. Zionism and ALIYYA are encouraged. Reconstructionist Judaism is based on a democratic community where the laity can make decisions, not just rabbis. The Torah was not inspired by God; it only comes from the social and historical development of Jewish people. The classical view of God is rejected; God is redefined as the sum of natural powers or processes that allows mankind to gain self-fulfilment and moral improvement. The idea that God chose the Jewish people for any purpose, in any way, is morally untenable, because anyone who has such beliefs 'implies the superiority of the elect community and the rejection of others'. Reconstructionism, while formally the smallest of the American Jewish denominations, gives expression to attitudes that are widespread throughout American Jewry; it has been termed 'the civic religion of American Jews'.

red heifer *See* PARA.

redeemer (in Hebrew, go'el) One who brings about REDEMPTION. The English word is derived from a Latin verb meaning 'to buy back'; this conveys well the sense of the Hebrew equivalent. In the Bible the word go'el is used of a next of kin who exercises certain functions, such as ransoming a kinsman who has sold himself into slavery, or buying back alienated family property (Ruth 4.4). This is the role that God is poetically described as playing in texts such as Isaiah 59.20 and Jeremiah 31.11. These verses are used in the liturgy, where God's role as redeemer of his people is specifically mentioned in the benediction following the SHEMÁ and in the seventh benediction of the weekday AMIDA. The liturgy addresses God using various Hebrew synonyms of go'el, as in the following: 'Besides you we have no king, redeemer [go'el], rescuer [pode] or deliverer [matsil]'. Despite this insistence that God is the only redeemer (which may be intended to distance Judaism from Christianity), the liturgy also uses the term go'el of the MESSIAH, as in the first benediction of the

Amida: ' ... who remembers the pious deeds of the patriarchs, and who in love will bring a redeemer to their children's children for his name's sake'. This apparent contradiction can be explained by arguing that it is God who is the true redeemer, and the Messiah will only be doing his bidding.

redemption 1 (in Hebrew, pidyon) Buying back, for example ransoming captives, or the firstborn son (*see* PIDYON HA-BEN). **2** (in Hebrew, ge'ulla). Action of freeing from oppression or captivity. It is applied particularly to God's part in the Exodus from Egypt, and to the future cosmic transformation, in the time of the MESSIAH, that will free the world from conflict, oppression, and in general from the dominion of evil forces. In the KABBALA, God himself is, as it were, redeemed, when the SHECHINA is restored from exile (*see* TIKKUN). In secular Zionist parlance, the term refers to the buying of land in the Land of Israel by Jews. Religious Zionists speak of the creation of the state of Israel as the 'beginning of redemption' (in Aramaic, atchalta di-ge'ula); this concept of an intermediate step on the way to redemption has no foundation in earlier Jewish thought.

Reform Judaism

General term designating the more radical wing of religious MODERNISM. Its broad characteristics are openness to change, and a willingness to subordinate values and practices derived from tradition to the perceived needs of changing times. Its roots are in 19th-century Germany, and in the deep radicalism of men like Abraham GEIGER and Samuel HOLDHEIM, prepared to do away with any heritage from the past that stood in the way of the spiritual and moral regeneration of Judaism. Key elements of Reform Judaism as it developed in Europe were the 'normalization' of Jewish life and the breaking down of barriers between Jews and Gentiles, including the abolition of laws and customs that stood in the way of this process, a strong sense of the common ground between the Jewish and Christian religions and the mission of the Jews to bring the moral values of the Bible to the world in conjunction with the younger faith, and a strong commitment to the ideals of social justice identified with the biblical prophets and brought up to date to embrace such principles as the equal status of men and women within Judaism. The movement was consolidated and disseminated through a new-style rabbinate, trained in modern rabbinical seminaries to be familiar with the critical study of the sources and to be able to preach attractively in the vernacular. The reform of the religion was advanced through a series of rabbinical synods, whose decisions were taken back by the rabbis to their congregations. The term is used as the official title of synagogue organizations in various countries; for Reform Judaism in the United States and in Britain see below.

REFORM JUDAISM IN AMERICA

Reform Judaism claims to be the largest Jewish movement in North America, with more than 900 congregations affiliated to the UNION FOR REFORM JUDAISM and some one and a half million individual members.

Radical though European Reform was, its progress was hampered to a large extent by structures of society and state that were generally resistant to change and favourable to tradition and stability. America, on the other hand, to which increasing numbers of central and western European Jews were emigrating in the course of the 19th century, provided an ideal breeding ground for Reform. There was no presumption in favour of tradition; on the contrary, there was a strong feeling that the past must be left behind and transcended. Individualism and initiative were encouraged, and a spirit of common fraternity encouraged Jews who had never been allowed to feel entirely German to consider themselves American in every sense of the word, even while remaining committed to their own religion. The small numbers of Jews and the lack of rabbinic authorities in the pioneering days meant that an emphasis on traditional observance was lacking.

The first Reform congregation on American soil was set up in Charleston, South Carolina, in 1825, at a time when there were only some 5,000 Jews in America. By 1875 the number had swollen to a quarter of a million, and the majority of the newcomers were from German-speaking lands. In 1842 a group of immigrants founded a Reform congregation in Baltimore, but a more momentous event took place three years later, with the creation of Congregation Emanu-El in New York. Within a decade this congregation had a synagogue seating 1,000 congregants, in which men and women sat together (a practice not yet established in Europe) and the decorous worship was accompanied by a mixed choir; it also had its own prayer book, devised by its rabbi and spiritual leader, Leo Merzbacher, who ironically had come from Europe with a certificate of Talmudic competence signed by the great opponent of modernism, Moses SOFER.

The man who may be considered the architect of American Reform was Isaac Mayer WISE. Although in many ways he was a conservative, who never abandoned his belief that the Torah was revealed by God and written down by Moses, Wise was thoroughly in tune with America and the opportunities it offered to Jews to combine loyalty to their country and their religion. Indeed in some ways he saw American democracy as a natural outgrowth of Judaism. Wise was appointed in 1854 to a congregation in Cincinnati, Ohio, a rapidly growing centre which, under Wise's tutelage, was to become the powerhouse of American Reform Judaism. In 1873 a convention in Cincinnati set up the Union of American Hebrew Congregations, and soon afterwards a rabbinical seminary, the HEBREW UNION COLLEGE, was established.

A conference of rabbis in Pittsburgh in 1885 formally adopted a kind of creed, known now as the PITTSBURGH PLATFORM. Its chief architect was Kaufmann KOHLER, a leading progressive theologian of the movement. The purpose was to mark Reform Judaism off clearly from Orthodoxy and the nascent Conservative movement, on the one hand, and on the other from more radical movements like the Society for Ethical Culture, founded in New York in 1876/7, which rejected any claim to Jewish particularism or a special mission.

By 1937 the Pittsburgh Platform no longer seemed to represent the aspirations and beliefs of the movement, and a new statement, the COLUMBUS PLATFORM, was drawn up by Samuel Cohon. This adopted a more positive approach to ceremonial and observance and to the Jewish people and Palestine. Further statements are to be found in the CENTENARY PERSPECTIVE (1976), the MIAMI PLATFORM (1997), and the PITTSBURGH STATEMENT (1999)

American Reform is associated with Progressive Jewish organizations in other countries in the WORLD UNION FOR PROGRESSIVE JUDAISM.

Reform is by far the most radical of the three main movements in American Judaism. Some of its attitudes have stirred up controversy, for example in revising the definition of Jewish identity to include the offspring of a non-Jewish mother and a Jewish father brought up as Jewish, and permitting the ordination of gays and lesbians as rabbis.

REFORM JUDAISM IN BRITAIN

Reform Judaism in the UK represents a moderately progressive position (intermediate between LIBERAL and MASORTI Judaism). Its synagogue organization has the title Movement for Reform Judaism (until June 2005, Reform Synagogues of Great Britain). The movement began in a pragmatic, non-ideological way, with moves in the 1830s of Sefardi and Ashkenazi Jews living in the West End of London to found a local synagogue, against the wishes of the existing synagogues, which were in the East End. The West London Synagogue of British Jews was founded in 1840, and some modest liturgical reforms were gradually introduced. The foundation of a Reform synagogue in Manchester in 1856 was also due to local factors. Other synagogues followed, but there was no attempt to set up any form of national organization until the 1940s. By this time the movement had been greatly strengthened by immigrant rabbis from Germany, Austria and Czechoslovakia in the 1930s. It was under their impetus that a rabbinical seminary (Leo Baeck College) was established in 1956, mainly by graduates of the Berlin Hochschule (*see* GEIGER, ABRAHAM; MAYBAUM, IGNAZ). The title Reform Synagogues of Great Britain was adopted in 1958. The movement enjoys good relations with the Liberal Jewish movement (which has co-sponsored the College since 1964) and the Masorti movement.

régel (plural regalim) One of the three pilgrim FESTIVALS.

reincarnation *See* GILGUL.

religion System of rituals and beliefs. Neither the Bible nor the Talmud has any word corresponding to religion. The nearest equivalent is perhaps TORAH, in the sense of the totality of teachings. In the Middle Ages, when philosophers began to consider the differences between Judaism, Christianity and Islam, they adapted the Hebrew word dat (plural datot), which previously meant 'law', to designate the abstract concept of a religion. This choice indicates the sense that the essence of Judaism is to be found in practice and its study rather than in theoretical doctrine. Since the ENLIGHTENMENT Judaism has increasingly come to be studied as a religion, analogous to other religions. At the same time, Jews themselves have come to be divided into those who think of themselves as religious and those who see themselves as non-religious (*see* SECULAR JUDAISM), or even anti-religious. Consequently Judaism is now studied in the context of the academic discipline of Religious Studies, but only a part, perhaps a minority, of the Jewish people subscribe to the beliefs and lifestyle studied in this context.

renewal Term applied since the 1970s to various programmes to revitalize Jewish communal and religious life. The roots of this activity can probably be traced to CHASIDISM in the 18th century and to the modernist reforms of the 19th, both of which attempted to remedy what they saw as the moribund and stultifying nature of contemporary Judaism. The language of renewal is found explicitly in Moritz LAZARUS's book *Die Erneuerung des Judentums* (*The Renewal of Judaism*, 1909). Writers such as ACHAD HA-AM, Martin BUBER, A. J. HESCHEL, Mordecai KAPLAN and Franz ROSENZWEIG also spoke of renewal. It was in the late 1960s, however, particularly in America, that 'Jewish renewal' really got going; a first manifestation of it was the CHAVURA movement. It was not limited to any one organized religious movement: in fact some manifestations of it are secular (such as Project Renewal, an American initiative aimed at regenerating impoverished communities in Israel); from America it soon spread to Israel and to other countries. Renewal appealed to individuals in search of a heightened spirituality that could be expressed in Jewish terms (*see* NEO-CHASIDISM; NEO-KABBALISM), or concerned to express Jewish values in political and social action. The Vietnam War, the 1967 Six-Day War and the civil rights movement all played their part in creating the atmosphere out of which renewal was born. ALEPH – Alliance for Jewish Renewal – is an American organization dedicated (in its own words) 'to the Jewish people's sacred purpose of partnership with the Divine in the inseparable tasks of healing the world and healing our hearts' (*see* TIKKUN).

Renouveau Juif Movement of Jewish renewal in France created in the 1970s, partly in response to a perception of anti-Jewish and anti-Israel prejudice in French life and particularly among the dominant political class, and partly out of dissatisfaction with what were seen as the empty formalism and materialism of the Jewish establishment organizations. Tapping into feelings that had been fermenting since the 1967 war (closely followed by the student revolt of 1968), the movement mobilized a surprisingly large following (bringing tens of thousands of Jews out onto the streets in a demonstration in 1980, after a bomb attack on a Paris synagogue), and has been credited by some commentators with contributing to the election of the Socialist president François Mitterrand in 1981. Originally representing a counter-culture, Renouveau Juif came to dominate the establishment organizations and has fostered considerable debate about the future of Jewish identity in France.

repentance *See* TESHUVA.

reshút ('permission'; plural reshuyyot) A type of PIYYUT, introducing the poet to the congregation, or introducing the prayer that he is about to chant. The genre was first developed by the synagogue poets of Spain from the 11th century on; their poems are often intensely personal and spiritual. It was borrowed from the Spaniards by the poets of Ashkenaz, who developed the form with some ingenuity, and sometimes wrote reshuyyot in Aramaic.

responsa (in Hebrew, teshuvot) Answers to questions of Jewish law and observance submitted to halachic authorities. There are estimated to be some 300,000 medieval responsa, and they constitute the case law of the medieval HALACHA, exercising a vital formative influence on the evolution of the law.

resurrection The belief in resurrection of the dead at the end of time can be found in a few places in the Bible, and had become widespread among Jews by the time of the destruction of the Temple. It was an article of faith, apparently, for the PHARISEES and the rabbis, and is mentioned in the liturgy, notably in the second benediction of the AMIDA. Some medieval thinkers, however, had problems with it and preferred to define the AFTERLIFE rather in terms of immortality of the soul. That is also probably the position of most Jews today who retain a belief in the afterlife. Orthodox liturgies generally preserve the original wording of the second benediction. For example Singer's PRAYER BOOK (1992 edition) translates it as follows:

> You, O Lord, are mighty for ever; You revive the dead; You have the power to save. You sustain the living with loving kindness, You revive the dead with great mercy. You support the falling, heal the sick, set free the bound, and keep faith with those that sleep in the dust. Who is like You, O Master of mighty deeds? Who resembles You – a King who puts to death and restores to life, and causes salvation to flourish? And You are sure to revive the dead. Blessed are You – the Lord, who revives the dead.

Reformed liturgies, on the other hand, generally revise the Hebrew or the translation, or both. The British Reform prayer book *Forms of Prayer* (1977) renders the same benediction:

> You, O Lord, are the endless power that renews life beyond death; You are the greatness that saves. You care for the living with love. You renew life beyond death with unending mercy. You support the falling and heal the sick. You free prisoners, and keep faith with those who sleep in the dust. Who can perform such mighty deeds, and who can compare with You – a king who brings death and life, and renews salvation. You are faithful to renew life beyond death. Blessed are You Lord, who renews life beyond death.

These carefully chosen words, while not specifically ruling out resurrection, leave open other possibilities. *See also* EXILE AND RETURN; OLAM HA-BA.

revelation God's self-revelation to humans. The Bible, which often speaks of revelation, lacks a specific term for it. God is said to 'appear' to the patriarchs and prophets, and he often 'speaks' to them. The language of such communication proved uncomfortably concrete to later readers. This is why at Exodus 19.18, 20, when God is said to 'descend' on Mount SINAI, the Aramaic TARGUM of Onkelos translates the verb by 'revealed himself' (itgaley). In fact the Bible itself occasionally indicates resistance to the idea of a visible God, most clearly in God's words to Moses: 'No human can see me and live' (Exodus 33.20). The Talmud (Bavli, Yevamot 49b) contrasts this with the prophet Isaiah's claim to have seen God sitting on an exalted throne (Isaiah 6.1). Isaiah, say the rabbis, saw 'through a glass, darkly'. In general, revelation is associated with prophecy. Moses, the greatest of the prophets, received the highest type of revelation, and in particular it was through him that the Torah was revealed (*see* TORA MIN HA-SHAMÁYIM); other prophets received lesser kinds of revelation. The medieval philosophers tended to see the prophetic gift as essentially the perfection of the human intellect. (JUDAH HA-LEVI stands out in maintaining that revealed knowledge is essentially different from and superior to rational knowledge). For the philosophers, as for the kabbalists, human knowledge of God is limited, God-in-himself being totally unknowable (*see* EIN SOF). Moses MENDELSSOHN, building on foundations laid by Moses MAIMONIDES, insists that Judaism does not claim any knowledge about God that comes purely from revelation and is not accessible to human intellect; only the laws of the Torah are 'revealed'. Even this dimension of revelation was soon questioned under the influence of the ENLIGHTENMENT, however. Developments in theology and biblical studies made it increasingly difficult to believe that God descended into the world and literally gave the Torah to humans. (This belief was, however, made into a dogma in ORTHODOXY.) Progressive Judaism preferred to speak of a 'progressive revelation': God did not reveal himself once and for all at Sinai but continues to reveal aspects of himself day by day. Franz ROSENZWEIG put the doctrine of revelation firmly back at the heart of Judaism; in fact he saw it as the starting point of any theology. He made revelation one of the key elements of his book *The Star of Redemption*, together with CREATION and REDEMPTION: these are the three moments when God, as it were, breaks into the world. His understanding of revelation is grounded in a theory of divine LOVE. *See also* CHABAD CHASIDISM; GLORY; GOD; SHECHINA.

revivalism Worship and practice centring on religious fervour, prayer and preaching. The best-known example of Jewish revivalism is CHASIDISM.

rewards and punishments Theological shorthand for the belief that God rewards those who keep his commandments and punishes those who do not. Experience does not consistently bear out the validity of the assurance that obedience will be rewarded with long life and freedom from want and anxiety (see Leviticus 26, Deuteronomy 28). Indeed, the problem is recognized in the Bible itself, for it is a major theme of the books of Job and Kohélet (Ecclesiastes). The ancient rabbis are also aware of the problem, but they conclude that it is beyond human comprehension: 'It is not in our power to explain the prosperity of the wicked or the suffering of the righteous' (Mishnah, Avot 4.15). The GRACE AFTER MEALS includes this quotation from King Solomon: 'I was young and now I am old, and I have never seen a righteous man abandoned or his descendants begging for bread.' In some homes these words are not said aloud, for fear of giving offence to a poor guest, or simply because they are contrary to experience. The idea of reward and punishment in the AFTERLIFE emerged in the Hasmonean period as an attempt to overcome these objections, and became a key doctrine in the Middle Ages, but carries problems of its own.

ribbi Sefardi spelling of the title 'rabbi'.

Rif *See* ALFASI, ISAAC.

righteousness

(in Hebrew, tsédek or tsedaka) A key virtue in the Torah and subsequent Jewish teaching. The people of Israel are commanded to pursue righteousness (Deuteronomy 16.20). A word which can be a synonym of justice, righteousness goes beyond strict justice in connoting a concern for the well-being of all members of society, including those who are disadvantaged but who have no particular claim to justice. The demand for righteousness in this sense is an important element in the commands of the Torah (Exodus 22.21–7, Leviticus 19.9–18, Deuteronomy 24.10–15). It is even more important in the prophets, because it is set against a hypocritical façade of false justice and religiosity:

> Tell my people their transgression and the House of Jacob their sins:
> They consult me every day and seek to know my ways,
> Like a nation that acts righteously and has not rejected the justice of its God,
> They ask me for righteous laws, seeking to be close to God.
> 'Why have you not seen our fasting, or noticed our self-affliction?'
> Is this what you call a fast, a day acceptable to the Lord?
> This is the fast of my choosing:
> To loosen the fetters of injustice, to untie the knots of the yoke,
> To set free the downtrodden and snap every yoke,
> To share your bread with the hungry and take the poor and homeless into your house,
> To cover anyone you see naked, and not ignore your own flesh and blood.
>
> (Isaiah 58.2–7)

Passages like this one appealed to the 19th-century reformers. The Zionists, too, quoted them with approval, and the declaration of the state of Israel in 1948 says that the state 'will be based on the precepts of liberty, justice and peace taught by the Hebrew prophets'.

Of particular interest in this context is the MUSAR MOVEMENT, founded in Lithuania by Israel SALANTER. Salanter addressed himself at first particularly to businessmen: he explained that some Jews who observed the ritual requirements of Judaism meticulously could still be unscrupulous in their business dealings or their treatment of their employees. Consequently it was essential not only to study halacha but to delve deeply into the ethical literature, such as BACHYA IBN PAKUDA's *Duties of the Heart* or Moses Chayyim LUZZATTO's *Mesillat Yesharim*.

The Chasidim gave their own interpretation to righteousness when they applied the term tsaddik, 'righteous one', to their own charismatic leaders (*see* REBBE). The qualities of the tsaddik are extraordinary saintliness and almost superhuman gifts. While such a figure has some antecedents in classical Judaism, for example in biblical wonder-working prophets like Elijah or Elisha, in its Chasidic form it is a new development, and has little to do with the traditional concept of righteousness.

The relationship between righteousness and the halacha is a delicate one, because while traditional Judaism insists that the halacha embodies God's will for the Jewish people and therefore by definition represents the highest standards of morality, the idea of righteousness implies that there is a higher standard. The halacha itself acknowledges a category of actions which fall 'inside the [strict] line of the law' (LIFNIM MI-SHURAT HA-DIN). An example of such behaviour which is actually quoted in the Talmud is restoring lost property to its owner even in circumstances where the law does not require it. Most people would instinctively feel that such an action was meritorious.

In current use the term TSEDAKA has only one meaning: almsgiving.

rimmonim ('pomegranates') Name given to FINIALS, which sometimes have the shape of a pomegranate.

Rishon le-Tsiyon ('first in Zion') Title of the Sefardi CHIEF RABBI of Israel, in use at least since the 17th century.

rishonim ('earlier [authorities]') Term applied in halachic discussion to older authorities, as opposed to ACHARONIM ('later [authorities]'). The chronological definition of the rishonim is not fixed. The term tends to be applied to halachists from the 10th to the 15th or 16th century. Their writings consist mainly of commentaries on Talmudic tractates and on ALFASI's code, and CHIDDUSHIM.

Romaniots or **Romaniotes** Jews following the Byzantine prayer rite and traditions. The name derives from Romania, the name given to the territories of the Byzantine empire by western Europeans in the Middle Ages; the name was adopted by Byzantine Jews, who referred to themselves as 'the communities of Romania'. Their prayer book has come to be known as 'Machzor Romania'. Their spoken language was mainly Greek. After the Ottoman conquest in the 15th century, and the subsequent arrival of large numbers of Sefardim and Italian Jews, the Romaniot traditions were gradually edged out. Today there are only two functioning Romaniot communities in Greece (Ioannina in the west and Halkidha on the island of Evvia). Other originally Romaniot synagogues do not now generally follow the Romaniot rite. A Romaniot community, Kehila Kedosha Janina, was founded in New York in 1906; its synagogue, built in 1927, is still in use.

Rosenzweig, Franz (1886–1929) German religious philosopher and educator. Born in Cassel into an assimilated Jewish family, he seriously contemplated conversion to Christianity, out of a sense that Judaism no longer had anything to offer. Realizing, however, that his knowledge of Judaism was insufficient for such a move, and after a religious experience during a Day of Atonement service in Berlin, he devoted himself instead to discovering more about Judaism and to educating the wider German Jewish public in it. He also wrote one of the key works of modern Jewish thought: *Der Stern der Erlösung* (1921; *The Star of Redemption*, 1970).

This book, begun on army postcards sent home to his mother from military service in World War I, has come to be recognized as one of the most important Jewish texts of modern times. Rosenzweig begins from real human experience, and more precisely from the fear of death. Since philosophy cannot cure us of this fear, philosophy is false, and so is its pretension to reduce everything to a single principle. A new way of thinking is needed, which will give full weight to our own needs, and to the natural perception of God, humanity and the world as three separate entities. He examines each in turn, proceeding by way of negation to assertion, and then considers the relationship of each element with the others. The triad God–humankind–world leads in this way to the triad creation (seen in the relation of God to the world)–revelation (seen in the relation of God to humanity)–redemption (seen in the relation of humanity to the world). Rosenzweig symbolizes the conjunction of these two triads in the six-pointed star, a symbol of Judaism and the source of the book's title (*see* MAGEN DAVID). Within this simple structure there is contained a vast wealth of suggestive insights, developed through personal experience rather than traditional doctrines or logical arguments, and couched in a deliberately oblique and poetic language. Language as a means of communication plays a cardinal role in Rosenzweig's thought, as does love, which is fundamental to the relationship between God and humanity. *The Star of Redemption* is not a description or analysis of Judaism – it is much more wide-ranging than that, and much more personal – but it contains within itself a novel and creative reappraisal of the spirit of Judaism as exemplified in its beliefs and practices. Rosenzweig opens the door to a new, existentialist philosophy of religion.

Rosenzweig died in 1929, at the age of 43, of amyotrophic lateral sclerosis, a muscular disease which had left him almost totally paralysed for several years. Yet his short life was extraordinarily productive. Once he had realized how little German Jews of his generation really knew about Judaism he opened an adult study centre in Frankfurt (the Freies Jüdisches Lehrhaus) where others could join him in the quest for an authentic Judaism, mediated by what he called 'the new thinking'. Martin BUBER became one of the lecturers at the Lehrhaus, and he and Rosenzweig collaborated on a new German translation of the Bible, which Buber completed after Rosenzweig's death.

Rosh, the *See* ASHER BEN YECHIEL.

Rosh Chódesh Day or days of the new moon. In ancient times the day of the new moon was important enough to be compared to the Sabbath (2 Kings 4.23, Isaiah 1.13); nowadays it is a minor observance. Work is permitted, although there is an old tradition that women have a holiday, and there is a tendency now to see Rosh Chódesh as a women's festival. Beginning in the United States in the early 1970s, Orthodox women's prayer groups are held on Rosh Chódesh, and groups of women gather to perform rituals celebrating rebirth and renewal. *See also* HALLEL.

Rosh ha-Shana ('new year') Tractate of the Mishnah, Tosefta and both Talmuds, in the order Mo'ed, dealing with rules concerning ROSH CHÓDESH and NEW YEAR.

Rosh Yeshiva ('head of yeshiva') Principal of a YESHIVA. The office arose, as a new type of religious leader, in eastern Europe with the proliferation of yeshivot attracting students from far and wide. The Rosh Yeshiva was often a scholar renowned for his academic knowledge of the law. Even within modern Orthodoxy, former yeshiva students may consider their Rosh Yeshiva to be their true spiritual guide, while recognizing the practical authority of their local rabbi. A certain rivalry sometimes arises between yeshiva heads and rabbis, or even CHIEF RABBIS.

Ruth (Rut) Biblical book, one of the FIVE SCROLLS. It tells the story of Ruth, a Moabite widow who follows her mother-in-law, Naomi, back to her homeland in the territory of Judah, and marries a kinsman of Naomi's. Their son, Obed, is regarded as Naomi's child; he is the grandfather of King DAVID. According to the Talmud (Bavli, Bava Batra 14b) the book was written by the prophet Samuel; it is currently dated much later. It is read in synagogue at SHAVUOT.

Sa'adya Ga'on (882–942) Scholar, translator and poet. Born Sa'adya ben Joseph in the Fayyum region of Egypt (hence another name, al-Fayyumi), he moved to the Land of Israel and eventually to Babylonia, where in 928 he was appointed principal of the academy of SURA. Sa'adya was one of the most talented and versatile Jewish scholars of the Middle Ages, and his arrival in Sura brought a breath of fresh air to the Babylonian schools, previously concerned almost exclusively with the transmission of the Babylonian Talmud and with halacha derived from it. Not only did he introduce the Palestinian Talmud into the Babylonian schools, as well as other rabbinic works from the Land of Israel, he also set to work writing in an extraordinary range of genres, from legal treatises on specific topics (written in Arabic) to Arabic translations of the Torah and other biblical books (the TAFSIR), Hebrew hymns (PIYYUTIM), an edition of the prayer book (SIDDUR) with relevant rules and customs, and various grammars, dictionaries, commentaries and polemical writings. His most important work is generally considered to be the Arabic *Kitab al-Amanat wal-I'tikadat* (*Book of Beliefs and Convictions*, 933), which reached a wider Jewish audience when it was translated into Hebrew by Judah IBN TIBBON. This was the first classical exposition of Jewish religious philosophy. Grounded in KALAM, it sees no conflict between the content of revelation and what can be known by reason. It would be possible for unaided reason to reach the truth without the help of revelation, but revelation has two advantages: it makes the truth accessible to all, whatever their intellectual aptitude, and it protects philosophers against falsehood by setting out the goal of their reasoning before they embark on their intellectual journey. Despite the superficial resemblance between this viewpoint and that of Moses MENDELSSOHN, Sa'adya has no doubt that Judaism is the only true religion: the others are all human creations, and only Judaism is divine. His book can be seen as the starting point for all future Jewish religious philosophy.

Sabaoth *See* TSEVA'OT.

Sabbateanism *See* SHABBETAI TSEVÍ.

Sabbath

(in Hebrew, Shabbat) Sacred day of rest, observed from sunset on Friday until dusk on Saturday. In the synagogue it is marked especially by a reading from the Torah scroll, followed by a HAFTARA, at the morning service (SHACHARIT), and by an additional service (MUSAF) which follows. Shorter readings from the Torah scroll occur on Sabbath afternoon (MINCHA). In the home there are rituals of welcome for the Sabbath, with special meals, and there is a custom of singing ZEMIROT at the table. The sacred character of the Sabbath day demands that it be formally separated from the days that precede and follow: it is inaugurated by the lighting of CANDLES or oil lamps, and its departure is marked by a ceremony known as HAVDALA.

The primary reason given for the observance of the Sabbath in the Torah is as a commemoration of the creation of the world, when God is described poetically as resting on the seventh day. 'For in six days the Lord made heaven and earth and the sea, and everything that is in them, and rested on the seventh day; therefore the Lord blessed the Sabbath day and declared it holy' (Exodus 20.11; see also Genesis 2.2–3). The Bible singles out the seventh day as a day of rest from all work, and the HALACHA enumerates various categories of work which are forbidden on this day. Thirty-nine such categories are listed in the Mishnah, and each category has several sub-categories. The prohibitions extend not only to the various kinds of manual work and trade, but also to lighting a flame, travel, writing and handling money. Like the DIETARY REGULATIONS, the rules of Sabbath observance have always been considered among the most important features of the distinctively Jewish way of life. Besides the negative rules about work, there is also a positive teaching that the Sabbath should be a day of joy, traditionally expressed in various forms of physical self-indulgence as well as the avoidance of fasting and mourning. Sabbath joy is more than the spontaneous relief of hard-working people who are enjoying a break from their labours. It is has something of a religious character, and is known in Hebrew as ÓNEG SHABBAT, in allusion to a passage of the Prophet Isaiah (58.13–14). The arrival of the Sabbath is likened to the entry of a bride or a queen. Some sources speak of a Jew possessing an 'additional soul' on the Sabbath, and of the angels that enter the home at this time. The kabbalists, in welcoming the Sabbath as a bride, imagine that they are welcoming the SHECHINA, the presence of God. On this day, they claim, the male and female elements in the Godhead are united, hence the souls that enter children conceived on the Sabbath are particularly sublime.

The CHASIDIM take the rejoicing on the Sabbath particularly seriously. Before the beginning of the holy day they purify themselves by immersion in the MIKVE, and they dress in special clothes. Setting aside an old prohibition, they are fond of dancing on the Sabbath, and they experience the holiness of the day with great intensity. When they eat the Sabbath meals in the presence of their leader, the tsaddik, he passes around to his followers food from the dishes he has tasted. Chasidim are particularly aware of the mystical dimension of the Sabbath at the third meal, in the afternoon. As the light fades they listen to the teaching of the tsaddik, communicated to him by the Shechina. They also have an additional meal after the departure of the Sabbath, to escort it on its way. (*See* FEASTING.)

Orthodox Judaism maintains the full rigour of the traditional halacha, and insofar as new questions are posed it tends to respond strictly so as to avoid any risk of infringing the prohibition on work. For example the use of electricity has been subsumed under the heading of fire, and so one may not switch on an electric light manually. On the other hand, in keeping with a constructive approach to the application of technological progress to halachic questions, the use of time switches and other automatic devices is permitted. The Orthodox Sabbath is not only a 'day off work', it is a period of time out of time, which is hedged around with minute regulations which exclude not only cooking and most other household chores but even many recreational activities. Driving in a car is ruled out; so are gardening, playing musical instruments, and anything involving the use of money.

Reform Judaism, no less than Orthodoxy, lays stress on the observance of the Sabbath as a day set apart from other days. In accordance with its guiding principles, however, it has abandoned the detailed traditional prohibitions. It is ultimately up to individual Reform Jews to decide how to celebrate the Sabbath.

Conservative Judaism, committed to the principle of revitalizing the halacha in keeping with the demands of the times, has tended to focus attention on positive practices associated with Sabbath observance (lighting candles on Sabbath eve, serving special Sabbath meals, attending synagogue services) rather than on the various prohibitions. It has also consciously cultivated the traditional idea of 'beautification of the commandment' (HIDDUR MITSVA), in this case by promoting a warm and pleasant Sabbath atmosphere in the home and encouraging the use of attractive equipment (candlesticks, wine-cups, bread covers and so on). The specific relaxation of the prohibitions has been a subject of some controversy, and it has proved hard to reach agreement on definitive changes in the halacha. The Law Committee of the RABBINICAL ASSEMBLY has, however, sanctioned the use of electricity and, more radically, it has also permitted travel on the Sabbath for the specific purpose of attending services.

The strictest rules for observance of the Sabbath are those of the KARAITES. Originally these not only forbade the kindling of a fire but even insisted that any flames lit before the Sabbath should be extinguished. This made the Sabbath a very austere affair, and a particular hardship in cold climates, such as in Crimea, where the prohibition on fire was maintained until relatively recent times. Elsewhere it was gradually abandoned, by the end of the 15th century in Lithuania and perhaps a little later in Egypt.

See also AMIDA; BAKKASHA; BATHING; BREAD; CHALLA (1); ERUV; HOLINESS; JUDENSTERN; KABBALAT SHABBAT; KIBBUTS; KIDDUSH; LECHA DODI; MELAVE MALKA; ORGAN; PIKÚ'ACH NÉFESH; SAMBATYON; SE'UDA SHELISHIT; SHAVUOT.

sacrament In Christian usage, a concrete sign of a sacred thing. An example from Judaism would be CIRCUMCISION, the outward sign of the COVENANT. However the category of 'sacrament' in this sense is not known in Judaism. The literal meaning of 'sacrament' is 'making holy', which corresponds to the Hebrew KIDDUSH. See also KIDDUSH HA-SHEM.

sacrifice Offering to God. Ancient Jewish worship, until the destruction of the Temple in Jerusalem, was based on sacrifices of animals and of flour mixed with oil. In addition to public sacrifices laid down for weekdays, Sabbaths and festivals, private sacrifices were required of individuals on certain occasions; individuals could also choose to bring free-will offerings. The Bible contains hints of a view that there was more to religious life than animal sacrifices, and after the destruction of the Temple some rabbis described it retrospectively as an obstacle to true religion. Nevertheless, the official stance of rabbinic Judaism was that the destruction had made the sacrificial system temporarily inoperative. The Mishnah records details of the Temple ritual for posterity, and the liturgy includes prayers for the restoration of the Temple and of sacrificial worship. Modern liturgies have tended to omit such prayers, or at least to print them in smaller type. Sacrifice of animals does figure in the AVODA service on the Day of ATONEMENT, but some reformed liturgies represent this as an outmoded rite. There is a widespread view that prayer has replaced sacrifices.

Sadducees Ancient sect. Their origin is obscure: they seem to have come to prominence as political opponents of the PHARISEES in the Hasmonean period, and to have more or less disappeared after the destruction of the Temple. This may reflect their close connection with the Temple priesthood. Their name is thought to derive from that of the high priest Zadok (2 Samuel 8.17). Some scholars have detected some similarities between the practices of the KARAITES and those of the Sadducees, but no clear conclusions can be drawn from these. All our information about them comes from non-Sadducee sources that are generally unsympathetic to them, so that it is hard to reconstruct their beliefs. It seems that they rejected the ORAL TORAH and the belief in RESURRECTION. *See also* AFTERLIFE; HERESY; ÓMER; PLURALISM.

Safed (Tsefát) Town in Galilee, considered one of the HOLY CITIES of the Land of Israel. In the 16th century, with the arrival of refugee scholars from Spain, it became the site of remarkable kabbalistic activity and rabbinic scholarship. Among the famous scholars of Safed were Joseph CARO and Isaac LURIA.

salamátia (unknown origin) In Greece, dinner held the night before a circumcision, and attended by the rabbi, relatives and friends. *See also* VIOLA.

Salanter, Israel (1810–83) Scholar and ethicist, founder of the MUSAR MOVEMENT. Born in Lithuania (his surname Salanter was chosen to indicate that he spent his student years in the town of Salant), he had a great influence on the local YESHIVOT, with his insistence that it was not enough to study the Talmud and perform the commandments, one had to work on one's deeper personality to learn the habit of sensitivity to the ethical demands of Torah. Later in his life he travelled to Germany and to Paris, to lecture to university students on Judaism; he died in Königsberg.

salt In antiquity, salt was rare and precious. In the Temple, all the sacrifices and cereal offerings were salted. In recollection of this, when the benediction HA-MOTSI is said at the beginning of a meal the bread is dipped in salt. According to the DIETARY REGULATIONS, meat must be salted and left to stand for an hour to drain the blood before cooking.

salvation Deliverance from oppression or other sufferings (*see also* REDEMPTION). 'Salvation' is used as the translation of the Hebrew terms yeshu'a and teshu'a, which are found in the Bible and the liturgy. It generally refers to concrete situations, occasionally to the messianic deliverance, but there is no equivalent in Judaism to the Christian concept of salvation from the taint of original sin.

Samaritans Religious and ethnic community, now numbering only a few hundred, mostly settled around Nablus, in the ancient territory of Samaria, and in Cholon, near Jaffa. They claim descent from the ancient Israelites, have a hereditary high priesthood, and their own text of the Torah (known as the Samaritan Pentateuch), which is written in the old Hebrew (palaeo-Hebrew) ALPHABET, and differs from the Masoretic text, notably in prescribing sacrifices on Mount Gerizim, near Nablus (where the Passover lamb is still sacrificed). Samaritans have no other biblical books, and maintain a number of distinctive beliefs. Since ancient times their relations with Jews (or Judaeans) have been fraught. The rabbis regard them as Jews in some respects, and as Gentiles in others (for example for purposes of marriage, although their own laws allow a Samaritan man to marry a Jewish woman, provided she agrees to observe the Samaritan way of life).

Sambatyon A legendary river of stones that was said to flow only on weekdays, resting on the Sabbath.

Samuel (Shemu'el) Biblical book, one of the Former Prophets, named after its central character, the prophet Samuel. Following Christian usage, the book is commonly divided into two, but originally it was one book and remained so in Hebrew Bibles until the 15th century. The book describes the transition from the rule of the judges to the monarchy. The first book begins with the story of the birth of Samuel, who later anoints Saul as king and, after Saul loses God's favour, anoints David as king in his place. The second book describes the reign of David, the expansion of his kingdom, his moral failure and the subsequent troubles afflicting his family. According to the Talmud (Bavli, Bava Batra 15a), Samuel himself was the author of the first part of the book, up to his death; it was then completed by others.

sanctification *See* HOLINESS; KIDDUSH.

sandek (of Greek origin) The person who holds the child on his lap during the CIRCUMCISION ceremony. It is regarded as a great honour to be invited to discharge this role.

Sanhedrin (from Greek synhedrion, 'council') **1** Name of an ancient Jerusalem law court that functioned in the centuries leading up to the final destruction of the Temple. Rabbinic sources portray it, unhistorically, as an assembly of rabbis, which is the form it took once rabbinic Judaism became established, in Yavne and later in Galilee. It seems to have died out in the early period of Christian rule, in the 5th century, since when there has been no central Jewish legal authority. Attempts have been made from time to time to revive the institution. In the 1530s Jacob Berab of SAFED, an exile from Spain, reinstituted the long-defunct rabbinic ordination and canvassed the idea of restoring the Sanhedrin, as a visible expression of rabbinic autonomy in the Land of Israel and in preparation for the coming of the Messiah. The idea was strongly opposed by the chief rabbi in Jerusalem and nothing came of it. A very different plan was that of Napoleon I at the beginning of the 19th century. As part of his plan of integrating minorities like the Jews into the new French state he convened an assembly of Jewish notables in 1806, followed the next year by the convocation of a Great Sanhedrin. It consisted, like the ancient Great Sanhedrin, of seventy-one members (only forty-six of whom, however, were rabbis), and effectively ratified the emperor's project of integrating the Jews into the state by stripping the rabbis of all their powers in civil matters. A proposal soon after the creation of the state of Israel in 1948 to revive the Sanhedrin, with a view to introducing new legislation, met with strong opposition and was abandoned. *See also* BEIT DIN.

2 Tractate of the Mishnah, Tosefta and both Talmuds, in order Nezikin, dealing with rules and procedures of law courts, and related matters, mainly of civil and criminal law. Chapter 10 in the Mishnah begins with a discussion of categories of people who 'have no share in the Coming Age [OLAM HA-BA]'; this passage has become a key text for the study of rabbinic dogma and eschatology.

Satan ('adversary') Malign ANGEL, supernatural tempter, embodiment of evil. Satan does not play much of a role in Jewish thought. In the Bible there are a couple of references to an angel who is called 'the adversary' (Zechariah 3.1–2, Job 2.1); only once is the term used as a proper name (1 Chronicles 21.1). Rabbinic sources from the Land of Israel rarely mention him, but in Babylonian sources there are numerous references. One of these (Bavli, Bava Batra 16a) identifies him with the YÉTSER HA-RA and with the angel of death. There are many superstitious beliefs about him in Jewish folklore.

Satmar Chasidic dynasty, originating in Satu Mare, Romania, where their founder, Joel Teitelbaum (1888–1979), was the Chasidic rebbe from 1929. After World War II he established a new community in Williamsburg (Brooklyn, New York); it became one of the largest Chasidic groups in the United States, and it also runs the largest YESHIVA in the world. The Satmar philosophy was shaped to a high degree by their charismatic founder; it is distinguished by uncompromising hostility to ZIONISM, in the belief that the existence of the state of ISRAEL violates HALACHA and delays the coming of the MESSIAH.

savora'im (Hebrew plural of Aramaic savora, 'expositor') Collective name given to a shadowy group of Babylonian rabbis who filled the gap between the last AMORA'IM and the first ge'onim (*see* GA'ON). Very few names of individual savora'im are known. They are thought to have edited the Babylonian Talmud from materials compiled by the Amora'im, but the precise extent of their contribution is a subject of scholarly disagreement.

Schachter-Shalomi, Zalman *See* NEO-CHASIDISM.

Schechter, Solomon (1847–1915) Scholar and theologian. Born at Foscani in Romania, he was Reader in Talmudic and Rabbinic Literature at Cambridge from 1892 to 1902, and president of the JEWISH THEOLOGICAL SEMINARY in New York from

1902 until his death. His greatest contribution to scholarship was to realize the importance of the manuscripts found in the Cairo GENIZA and to transport them to Cambridge. He began studying and publishing them immediately. As a theologian he laid the foundations for CONSERVATIVE JUDAISM as a new movement based on the outlook of Zacharias FRANKEL and the HISTORICAL SCHOOL and adapted for American Jewish life. He is specifically associated with the idea of CATHOLIC ISRAEL. From slow beginnings Schechter and others built the Seminary into an outstanding centre of education and research, training a new type of rabbi, and set up the United Synagogue of America, now the UNITED SYNAGOGUE OF CONSERVATIVE JUDAISM.

Schneerson, Menachem Mendel (1902–94) Seventh and last of the dynasty of LUBAVITCH rebbes. Born in Nikolaev, Ukraine, he settled in New York in 1941, and ten years later he succeeded his father-in-law, Joseph Isaac Schneersohn (1880–1950), the sixth Rebbe, upon the latter's death. Under his leadership Lubavich Chasidism grew from a small remnant into a successful worldwide movement, largely because of his gifts as an organizer, educator and communicator. Towards the end of his life he came to the view that the messianic age was at hand, and many of his followers identified him as the Messiah.

Scholem, Gershom (Gerhard) (1897–1982) Scholar. Born and brought up in Berlin, he became a Zionist and moved to Jerusalem in 1923. After working as a librarian and lecturer, in 1933 he became the first professor of MYSTICISM at the Hebrew University. Scholem made the study of the mystical tradition of Judaism his life's work, and thanks to him, after being consigned to limbo by the rationalists of the WISSENSCHAFT DES JUDENTUMS movement, it was restored to the mainstream of academic Jewish studies. Scholem felt that 19th-century scholarship had taken the soul out of Judaism and had treated it as a dead object of scrutiny.

scrolls Books written on continuous bands of parchment (generally made up from sheets stitched together). This was the older way of writing books, before the codex (the book with separate pages) was invented. Thus the biblical books and other ancient literature were originally written on scrolls. The Dead Sea Scrolls, discovered in the Judaean Desert since 1947, give a vivid idea of what such scrolls were like. In Jewish worship the Torah is traditionally read from a handwritten parchment scroll (SÉFER TORA), as is the book of ESTHER. In some communities the HAFTARA is read from a scroll. The text of the MEZUZA and TEFILLIN is also written in this way. ACHAD HA-AM held up this continued use of the scroll as a key example of the power of tradition in religion.

secular Judaism Name given to the modern phenomenon of Jews who identify with Judaism but reject its religious dimension. This tendency, whose roots are in the 19th-century Russian HASKALA, has become an established feature of contemporary Jewry. It has developed no coherent ideology, and has no specific institutional base (although it commonly finds expression in various kinds of cultural and political associations). People who describe themselves as secular Jews often have a strong attachment to traditional features of Judaism, including what are normally considered to be religious rituals (emptied, of course, of their religious meaning). An obvious example of this is the observance in the non-religious kibbutsim in Israel of the Sabbath and Jewish festivals, which are given a naturalistic interpretation that manages to preserve a good deal of their traditional character. *See* ATHEISM; HUMANISTIC JUDAISM.

Séder ('order', 'arrangement') Term applied to various 'orders', for example an order of service, a collection of laws or customs, or a division of the MISHNAH, but most commonly applied to the home service for the eve of Passover (two successive evenings in the Diaspora, except for Reform Jews), or for the whole evening gathering, including the festive meal. The basic rules of the celebration are found in the Torah (Exodus 12–13), but they were considerably elaborated in the Greco-Roman period, and the meal as celebrated today retains noticeable elements from a Roman banquet. These include the custom of reclining on a cushion, and of dipping herbs in salt water or sweet paste (CHARÓSET). Symbolic foods adorn the table: three sheets of unleavened bread (MATSA), serving as a reminder that the Israelites left Egypt in such haste that there was no time to let the dough rise; MAROR or bitter herbs, because the Egyptians embittered the lives of the slaves; a roasted shank bone of lamb, a reminder of the Passover offering of a lamb, appointed in the Torah to be eaten as the meal of the day (nowadays lamb is avoided for the actual meal). A roasted egg is another reminder of the sacrifices. There are also green leaves (KARPAS), because this is springtime, salt water for the tears of the afflicted, and a sweet reddish-brown paste, charóset, which is said to evoke the mortar used by the slaves in construction work. Each of these foods has its place in the ritual.

Wine plays a special part in the Séder. Each participant is supposed to drink at least four glasses, and an extra goblet is placed on the table for the prophet Elijah, who according to folk belief will come again to herald the Messiah.

The participants in the Séder dress as they would for a formal dinner or special occasion. In some Ashkenazi families it is still the custom that the head of the household, who will lead the ceremonies, wears a KÍTTEL. The book containing the Bible readings and prayers, and often useful reminders about the conduct of the Séder, is known as the HAGGADA.

The rituals of the Séder are strictly laid down by tradition and followed in due order. The first of the four glasses of wine is for the KIDDUSH of the festival, which opens the proceedings. Those present then wash their hands (a ewer and basin are passed round the table for this purpose). Then the leader dips some parsley or another salad vegetable in salt water and passes it around to everyone. He takes the middle matsa of the three, breaks it in half, and sets one half aside. This is the AFIKOMAN, the symbolism of which is now shrouded in obscurity. The narration proper then commences, in response to four questions (MA NISHTANA), usually asked by the youngest child present.

The reply begins: 'We were Pharaoh's slaves in Egypt. The Lord our God brought us out from there by power and force. And if the Holy One, blessed be He, had not brought our ancestors out of Egypt, then we, our children, and our grandchildren would continue to be enslaved to Pharaoh in Egypt. That is why, however wise or clever or old we are, however knowledgeable in Torah, we must obey the command to talk about the Exodus from Egypt. The more one talks about it, the more praise-worthy it is.'

There follows a lengthy series of comments on the biblical account of the Exodus, and in some homes, not content with reciting the traditional texts, the participants add their own explanations, and their own comments on the theme of liberation, because the theme of Passover is not only the historical exodus but everything it symbolizes, including the contemporary political implications of freedom as well as its moral and spiritual dimensions, and also the future redemption. The three main symbols, the roast lamb, unleavened bread and bitter herbs, are each singled out and explained, and then the HALLEL is recited, consisting of Psalms 113 to 118, followed on this occasion by the 'Great Hallel', Psalm 136.

The Hallel is interrupted by the meal. (Originally the meal was eaten at the begin-ning, before the four questions, which are evidently a response to it.) There is a series of blessings before the meal, on wine (the second glass), hand washing, bread and matsa (of course matsa is used for both of these, since leavened bread is strictly forbidden), and maror (bitter herbs). The maror is first dipped in the charóset, and then it is eaten in the form of a sandwich between two pieces of matsa. After the meal, when the afikoman has been bought back from the children, it is broken in pieces which are either eaten or kept until the next Passover. Then GRACE AFTER MEALS is sung, followed by the drinking of the third glass of wine.

After the end of the Hallel there are some prayers, and then the fourth glass of wine is drunk, at which point the proceedings are technically over, and the following concluding hymn is sung:

The Passover Séder is concluded
According to custom and ordinance.
As we have been found worthy to celebrate it
So may we be found worthy to celebrate it again.
Pure One, dwelling in Your habitation,
Raise up the countless congregation.
Take and lead the saplings of Your stock –
Redeemed with joyous song – to Zion.

The theme of redemption, which runs through the whole Séder, is expressed one more time in the final exclamation:

Next year in Jerusalem!

The evening does not end here, however, but a cheerful sing-song ensues, a reward for the children who have stayed awake this long.

Sefardim Jews who consider their family origins to lie in Spain or Portugal. The name is derived from the biblical place name Sefarad (Obadiah 20), which is iden-tified by the medieval commentators with Spain. Jews generally flourished under Muslim rule in Spain, although there were periods of intolerance that led some (such as MAIMONIDES) to emigrate. As the Christian reconquest advanced conditions for Jews became more difficult. In 1391 there was an outbreak of violent attacks that caused a wave of emigration which lasted through the next century, until in 1492, with the capture of the last Muslim city (Granada), the remaining Jews were given a choice of emigration or baptism. Many Jews left for North Africa and the Ottoman empire. The Jews of Portugal were confronted with a similar choice in 1497, but here there were few opportunities for escape, and many were forced to adopt the Christian faith. In both Spain and Portugal the converts and their families were watched carefully by the Inquisition, but many still kept up their Jewish identity and some beliefs and practices in secret (*see* CONVERSION; XUETAS), and when the opportunity arose they left for other parts of western Europe and the Americas. Eventually many of these returned to the open practice of Judaism. In this way 'Eastern' Sefardi communities grew up in Salonica, Constantinople, and elsewhere in the Ottoman empire (*see also* SAFED), while 'Western' Sefardi communities (also called 'Spanish and Portuguese') developed a little later in Amsterdam, Hamburg, London, and eventually New York, with a distinctive ethos of their own. Some of the Spanish exiles settled for a while in parts of Italy, but they were expelled again in the 16th century along with the local Jews, many of whom settled in the new Sefardi colonies in the East and eventually became integrated in them. The Iberian émigrés preserved their own prayer rite (which is closer to the old Babylonian rite than the ASHKENAZI one is). In the Ottoman empire they spoke Spanish, which gradually developed into a dialect of its own (*see* JUDEZMO; LADINO); in the West they tended to use Portuguese. The Sefardi pronunciation of Hebrew, strikingly different from that of the Ashkenazim, also has eastern and western variants. In Israel the term 'Sefardim' is applied generally to non-Ashkenazim (*see* MIZRACHIM). The official Israeli pronunciation of Hebrew is based on the Eastern Sefardi pronunciation, with some modifications.

Séfer Chasidim ('book of the pious') Work of pietism and ethics, originating among the CHASIDEI ASHKENAZ and attributed to JUDAH THE CHASID (d. 1217). It exists today in two versions (a short and a long recension), neither of which is likely to represent the original book. It is a collection of homilies, anecdotes and moral and practical teachings that sheds considerable light on life in Ashkenaz in the 12th century.

Séfer ha-Bahir ('the bright book') The earliest work of KABBALA, written in the late 12th century in northern Spain or Provence. It is the first work we have that discusses the SEFIROT and the female aspects of the Godhead that are both such distinctive features of the kabbala. It influenced the ZOHAR, written about a century later. Like the Zohar, it is presented in the form of a MIDRASH. The discovery that this was an early and important work of kabbala is due to Gershom SCHOLEM, who wrote his doctoral dissertation on it. Many questions remain about the composition of the book and the sources of its ideas.

séfer tora ('scroll [or book] of Torah') Scroll containing the five books of the TORAH, used for the public reading in synagogue. Strict rules govern the writing of a séfer tora. The parchment on which it is written must come from a kosher animal, and the sheets are sewn together using tendons from a kosher animal. It is written by a SOFER, using a quill pen and black ink. The letters are written with great care, in a special type of writing in which thirteen of the letters of the alphabet are decorated with 'crowns'. The letters and words are spaced out, never run together, and tradition also dictates the amount of space to be left at the end of each section (*see* PETUCHA; SETUMA) and at the end of each book. Even the number of lines in a column is governed by traditional rules. When the scroll is completed a celebration (SIYYUM) is held; those present take part in writing the last letters, following guidelines from the sofer. In this way they are considered symbolically to have each written a scroll of their own, which is considered a religious obligation. The completed scroll is attached to wooden rollers (*see* ETS CHAYYIM), and either placed in a TIK or covered with a MANTLE. (*See also* FINIALS; TAS; YAD.) The scrolls are kept inside the ARK, and taken out to be read, or at certain other fixed times in the service. They are always treated with the utmost care and indeed reverence. The congregation stands as they are brought out and processed, and again as they are displayed before or after the reading, and when they are taken back to the ark. It is customary to bow towards the scroll as it is processed, and to touch it with the TALLIT and kiss the tallit as it is carried past, or when one is called up to read. Some authorities object to any gesture that makes it appear that the scroll itself is being venerated.

sefira ('counting') Counting of the days of the ÓMER, from the second day of PASS-OVER, when a symbolic sheaf of the new barley crop was offered in the Temple, until SHAVUOT. It is customary to count the days and weeks aloud, and some families have an 'ómer board' which helps them to keep count. Maimonides remarks that there is an atmosphere of expectancy about the counting of the days from the exodus to the revelation at Sinai: it is like someone who expects a visit from his closest friend, and counts the days until he sees him. *See also* SEFIROT.

Sefirot (plural of SEFIRA, probably from Greek) In KABBALA, the ten powers or eman-ations within the Godhead. The origin of the term is obscure; some scholars asso-ciate it with a Hebrew homonym meaning 'counting' (*see* previous entry); more plausible is the explanation that it derives from the Greek sphéra, 'sphere'.

The ten sefirot are:

Kéter	Crown
Chochma	Wisdom
Bina	Understanding
Chésed	Love
Gevura	Might
Tiféret	Beauty
Nétsach	Victory
Hod	Splendour
Yesód	Foundation
Malchut	Sovereignty

According to this system, the Infinite, EIN SOF, which is totally unknowable, becomes manifest through the emanation of ten powers or potencies, which are the source of all cosmic energy. It is in this way that the kabbalists bridge the seemingly uncros-sable chasm between the infinite Godhead and the finite world. It must be stressed,

however, that unlike the NEOPLATONIST theory of EMANATIONISM, in which the emanations reach into the world, in kabbala all the Sefirot are within God. The three
highest Sefirot are beyond all human understanding. Kéter, 'Crown', the first emanation from the Ein Sof, represents the first inchoate stirring of a will to create the
universe, but as yet it is a preliminary stage, which only becomes, as it were, a will to
create in Chochma, 'Wisdom', in which all the creative processes are potentially
contained, to be understood in their details in Bina, 'Understanding'. Chésed,
'Love', and Gevura, 'Might', are a pair: Chésed represents unadulterated love,
which would enfold and overwhelm the world if it were not held in check by Gevura,
representing judgment, which is in turn softened by love. It is Tiféret, 'Beauty',
which holds the two in balance. Beauty in turn is supported by another pair, Nétsach, 'Victory' and Hod, 'Splendour', and all these eight merge in Yesód, 'Foundation', which brings the power of the other Sefirot into Malchut, 'Sovereignty', which
represents God's rule over the created world and is identified with the SHECHINA.

The Sefirot are sometimes represented in the form of a human body. The Crown is
above the head. Wisdom is the brain and Understanding the heart. Love and Might
are the right and left arms, Beauty the torso and Victory and Splendour the right and
left legs. Foundation, the generative principle, is the sexual organ, and Sovereignty is
the mouth. The body in question is a male body, but the Sefirot themselves are
divided into male and female. Those on the right are male and represent divine love,
while those on the left are female and represent divine judgment. The ones in the
middle represent the harmonization of the two opposing principles. Beauty, known
as 'Holy One, blessed be He', is male, but sovereignty, the Shechina, is female. In
addition to these holy Sefirot there are Sefirot belonging to the SITRA ACHRA.

selichot ('forgivenesses'; singular selicha) Penitential hymns. The genre is among
the oldest of liturgical hymns (*see* PIYYUT). Selichot express regret for sins, and invoke
divine forgiveness (hence the name). Whole services of selichot were instituted in
Babylonia for the nights during the penitential month of Elul and the TEN DAYS OF
PENITENCE; they lasted from midnight to dawn. This custom was imitated elsewhere,
and a rich poetic repertoire was evolved. In Ashkenaz themes from the sufferings of
the Rhineland communities at the hands of Christians were introduced into the
selichot, sometimes in the form of meditations on the story of the AKEDA, a subject
that the Rhineland Jews made peculiarly their own, and also in a sub-genre known as
gezerot, '[harsh] decrees', recording the bitter fate of the Jews at the hands of the
Crusaders. Today selichot are still recited daily by Sefardim for the whole month of
Elul and the first ten days of Tishri, to the Day of Atonement, while Ashkenazim
begin reciting them from the beginning of the week in which New Year falls. They
are also recited on fast days, and on Mondays and Thursdays (unless these happen to
be festive days).

semicha ('laying on [of hands]') Rabbinic ordination. The term was originally used
of a ritual of laying one's hand on a sacrificial victim before it was slaughtered. Later
it was applied to the ceremony in which a teacher recognized his pupil as being a fit
person to teach and to decide questions of law. The rabbis ruled that semicha could
only be performed in the Land of Israel, not in the Diaspora. The practice seems to

have died out in the 4th or 5th century, and since only someone who had himself received semicha could transmit it, it could not be restored. In 1538 in Safed a Spanish exile, Jacob Berab, attempted to reintroduce it, but the rabbi of Jerusalem, Levi Ibn Chabib, objected to not having been consulted, and raised sufficient opposition for the plan to be abandoned. Rabbinic ordination as currently practised is not strictly speaking semicha, but HÉTTER HORA'A; nevertheless it is commonly referred to as semicha.

seminary An institution for the training of rabbis combining study of traditional sources with modern methods of study and professional training. It is a recent device in Judaism, associated with MODERNISM and used self-consciously as a means of propagating it. The oldest extant rabbinical seminary is probably the Collegio Rabbinico Italiano, founded in Padua in 1821, although it has moved several times, and was closed from 1871 to 1887 and again under the Fascists. The opening of the Breslau Seminary in 1854 was a momentous event in the history of modernism, not least because of the centrist position it took, which upset Orthodox and Liberals alike (*see* FRANKEL, ZACHARIAS; HISTORICAL SCHOOL; ORTHODOXY). Seminaries were opened soon afterwards in London (Jews' College, 1855) and Paris (Séminaire Israélite de France, 1859). Other important 19th-century European seminaries were those in Budapest (1877), Berlin (Liberal 1872, Orthodox 1873) and (Vienna (1893). In the United States the HEBREW UNION COLLEGE in Cincinnati was founded in 1875 and the JEWISH THEOLOGICAL SEMINARY in New York in 1886 (it was fundamentally reshaped by Solomon SCHECHTER in 1902). The Orthodox Rabbi Isaac Elchanan Theological Seminary was founded in New York in 1896; it grew into what is now YESHIVA UNIVERSITY. Among the many seminaries founded more recently and functioning today are Leo Baeck College, London (1956), Seminario Rabínico Latinoamericano, Buenos Aires (1962) and the Reconstructionist Rabbinical College, Philadelphia (1968).

Sephardim *See* SEFARDIM.

sermon An address, generally based on a text or a topic of concern, delivered in the context of a religious service. Preaching in German and other vernacular languages was an important element in the MODERNIST reforms of the 19th century (*see* VERNACULAR PRAYER), although it was not as much of an innovation as its detractors claimed. In fact the practice had a long history, both in the Ashkenazi and in the Sefardi world. What was new was the prominence the reformers gave to the sermon within their worship, and eventually the emphasis on the training of rabbis able to preach impressively in the vernacular. Leopold ZUNZ, in his important work *Die Gottesdienstliche Vorträge der Juden* (*Devotional Sermons of the Jews*, 1832), traced the history of the sermon back to antiquity to demonstrate its deep roots in Jewish religious life.

setuma ('closed') Technical term for a PARASHA that in a SÉFER TORA begins after a blank space, but not on a new line (*contrast* PETUCHA). In a printed text this is indicated by a Hebrew letter s (sámech), repeated three times if it is the first parasha of a SIDRA.

se'uda shelishit ('third meal') Festive meal eaten on Sabbath afternoon, in obedience to a Talmudic injunction to honour the Sabbath day by eating three meals on it rather than the usual two. The kabbalists attached special significance to this meal, and the CHASIDIM made it a prominent part of their communal religious life, gathering at the tsaddik's table, listening to their master's words, and singing songs or wordless melodies. Such gatherings can continue for several hours, long after the official end of the Sabbath.

sex *See* GENDER.

sexual relations

Social and intimate relations between women and men is a topic that occupies many pages in the halachic and ethical sources, and it is not without its inconsistencies and even contradictions. Generally speaking, the rabbinic writings reflect a society in which men and women lived largely separate lives and were considered to have different roles in society. Many of the rules of the halacha in this area have as their aim the preservation of this system. (For instance the Mishnah, Ketubbot 5.5, stipulates the work a woman must do for her husband: 'grinding flour, baking bread, washing clothes, cooking food, suckling her child, making his bed, and working wool'.) When it comes to sexual acts, the rabbis acknowledge the power of the sexual urge and generally regard it as a positive element in human life (*see* ASCETICISM), but they place severe restrictions on sexual activity. The first and greatest restriction concerns who may legitimately have sexual intercourse with whom. In practice this excludes all relations except for those between married couples, and thus incest, group sex and under-age sex are all ruled out by definition. Sexual acts between males are also forbidden, on the basis of a biblical prohibition (Leviticus 18.22, 20.13), while lesbian sex, which is not mentioned in the Bible, is forbidden by the codifiers under the rather vague heading of 'Egyptian acts' (Leviticus 18.3) (*see* HOMOSEXUALITY). Solitary sexual activity is forbidden for males, who are also encouraged to avoid anything that might lead to it. (The ZOHAR describes it as the most defiling of all sins.) Since this ban is based on a biblical prohibition on 'wasting seed', many authorities hold that it does not apply to women.

Even within marriage sexual activity is closely regulated by the rule-books. It is forbidden during the wife's menstrual period and for the seven following days, when she is in a state of ritual impurity according to biblical law (Leviticus 18.19; cf. 15.19–31). She is similarly 'impure' after giving birth (Leviticus 12). During these periods the woman is termed a NIDDA, and the whole subject of nidda impurity and the consequent prohibitions is discussed with almost obsessive interest in the halacha. The main restriction is to refrain from sexual intercourse, and at the end of the period the wife is to immerse herself in a ritual bath (MIKVE). After that, normal sexual relations may resume until the next menstrual period.

'Normal sexual relations' are also governed by various rules, specifying for instance that they must be conducted with sobriety and modesty, in darkness, and with the husband uppermost. They are not permitted if the wife is unwilling, or if she is too eager. On the other hand, the husband is to have regard to the wife's pleasure, and he is not allowed to deny her sexual intercourse altogether. The Mishnah (Ketubbot 5.6) goes so far as to lay down the 'duty of marriage' (Exodus 21.10), that is to say the minimum intervals for sexual activity, ranging from every day for the unemployed to once every six months for sailors.

The recognition that the woman's sexuality places demands on the man is a noteworthy and constant feature of the rabbinic outlook. The rabbinic consensus agrees that a wife may make sexual demands of her husband, and he may not reasonably refuse. At the same time, the husband is encouraged to have a rich and full sexual relationship with his wife. He may kiss any part of her body and have intercourse in any way he likes, even if this involves 'spilling of seed', provided he does not make a habit of this. And on the other hand, he is not allowed to think of another woman while making love to his wife, or have intercourse with her if it is his intention to divorce her.

Today Jewish attitudes to relations between the sexes tend to be broadly in line with those of the surrounding society. CHAREDIM, however, particularly in Israel, attempt to impose the traditional rules very strictly, even to the extent of insisting on segregation in public buses.

Sforno, Obadiah (c. 1475–1550) Italian scholar. Born in Cesena, he studied medicine at Rome and acquired a reputation as a Hebraist and jurist. His best-known work is his commentary on the Torah, in which he pursues the plain meaning (PESHÁT) and avoids the kabbalistic interpretations that were prevalent in his day. He also wrote commentaries on other biblical books, and a treatise (*Light of the Nations*) in which he combats various ARISTOTELIAN doctrines using arguments drawn from scripture.

sha'atnez Cloth made of a mixture of wool and linen. The word occurs only twice in the Torah and its origin and meaning are unknown; the interpretation just given is derived from the context in Deuteronomy 22.11, 'You shall not wear sha'atnez, wool and linen together'. (The other reference is Leviticus 19.19.) Curiously, the priests wore vestments made of this precise mixture. The prohibition is still observed by traditionalist and many Orthodox Jews, and it is possible to buy cloth and clothing certified free from sha'atnez.

Shabbat 1 Tractate of the Mishnah, Tosefta and both Talmuds, in order Mo'ed. It discusses the various kinds of work that are prohibited on the Sabbeth, as well as various observances specific to the Sabbath day. **2** *See* SABBATH.

Shabbat shalom ('a peaceful Sabbath') Greeting offered on the SABBATH.

Shabbetai Tseví (1626–76) The most famous and (for a time) successful among a series of messianic pretenders. Born in Smyrna, he gathered an enormous following at a time of intense millenarian expectation among Jews and Christians. He publicly proclaimed himself the Messiah in Smyrna in December 1665, and the waves of messianic fervour spread as far afield as Amsterdam and London. When he went to Constantinople in 1666 to confront the Sultan he was arrested and imprisoned, but he went on holding court in captivity and the enthusiasm of his followers did not diminish. Offered a choice between death or conversion to Islam he chose life. Some of his adherents converted with him (*see* DÖNME; MA'AMIN). Others remained Jews but maintained their faith in him in secret. Some believed that he would return in glory to usher in the messianic age. Some of his ideas remained extraordinarily influential among kabbalists for a long time, and this provoked an anti-kabbalistic reaction. It has been claimed that CHASIDISM was influenced by Sabbatean ideas; certainly the MITNAGGEDIM often accused the movement of Sabbatean tendencies. *See also* FRANK, JACOB.

shacharit (from Hebrew sháchar, 'dawn') The morning service.

Shadal *See* LUZZATTO, SAMUEL DAVID.

shádchen (Yiddish, from Hebrew, a matchmaker) A professional (or unofficial) matchmaker, especially in the SHTETL.

Shaddai A NAME OF GOD, found in the Torah, often in the combined form EL SHADDAI. Shaddai on its own is found in Job 5.17. It is also an element in various personal names, such as Tsurishaddai ('Shaddai is my rock'). The origin and meaning of the name are unknown. (A rabbinic interpretation, 'Who [says to the world] enough!' meaning that God imposes limits and controls on his creation (Bavli, Chagiga 12a), has no basis in philology.) In the ZOHAR Shaddai corresponds to the sefira Yesód (*see* SEFIROT). *See also* MEZUZA.

shalom *See* PEACE.

shamáyim *See* HEAVEN.

Shammai (late 1st century BCE–early 1st century CE) A teacher often quoted in the rabbinic literature, who is paired and contrasted with HILLEL. For example, he was said, unlike Hillel, to be of a stern, unfriendly disposition; however one of his few recorded apophthegms states 'Receive every man with a cheerful expression on your face' (Mishnah, Avot 1.15). Many disagreements on HALACHA are recorded between the School of Shammai and the School of Hillel.

shammash ('servant') The beadle of a synagogue. In the Middle Ages his role was sometimes extended to include that of town crier. The term was also used of the beadle or usher of a BEIT DIN. By extension, it is applied to the additional (ninth) light that is used to light the other lamps or candles at CHANUKKA.

Shas 1 ACRONYM (from Hebrew, **sh**isha **s**idrei mishna, 'six orders of the Mishnah') for the TALMUD. **2** TRADITIONALIST religious political party in Israel.

shaving *See* BEARD; HAIR; MOURNING.

Shavuot ('weeks') Summer festival, held on the 6th of Sivan (and on the following day in the Diaspora, except among Reform Jews). It is called 'the festival of weeks'

(Exodus 34.22, Deuteronomy 16.16) because it falls seven weeks after Passover, or to be more precise: 'You shall count from the day after the Sabbath, from the day when you offer the sheaf [ÓMER] of the waving, seven whole sabbaths, until the day after the seventh sabbath you shall count fifty days' (Leviticus 23.15–16). Conventionally, the word 'sabbath' here is understood in the sense of 'week', except on its first occurrence, when it is understood by the rabbis to refer to the first day of Passover. The KARAITES took it to mean the Sabbath of the week of Passover, so that they always celebrate Shavuot on a Sunday. In this they follow, consciously or unconsciously, the interpretation of the SADDUCEES and the SAMARITANS. (The BETA ISRAEL have a different interpretation: they understand it to mean the entire Passover week, and so they celebrate Shavuot on the 12th of Sivan.) From this passage of the Torah, and particularly from the fact that the festival is not named here and its mention does not begin a new section of the text, the rabbis do not call it Shavuot but Atséret (a term that they understand to mean 'completion' or 'ending'), because they see it as concluding the Passover rather than being a new festival in its own right. The rabbis further calculated that the date of Shavuot is the date of the giving of the Torah at Sinai. Exodus and Torah, redemption and revelation, are thus intimately connected: the exodus was not an end in itself but a necessary step towards the giving of the Torah. In the liturgy Shavuot is called 'the festival of the giving of our Torah'. This was a radical reinterpretation of a festival that in the Torah is designated simply as a harvest festival (Exodus 23.16) for offering first fruits of the wheat harvest (Exodus 34.22, Numbers 28.26). In synagogue the Torah reading includes the TEN COMMANDMENTS, and the book of RUTH is read, presumably because it mentions the barley and wheat harvests. It is customary to decorate the synagogue with plants and flowers; it is also customary to eat dairy products. Shavuot is considered, because of its association with Torah, a propitious time to hold CONFIRMATION services. *See also* AKDAMUT; AZHARA; EZEKIEL; PENTECOST; TIKKUN LEIL SHAVUOT.

Shechina ('indwelling') The divine presence in the world, specifically among the people of Israel. It was considered to be specially present in the Jerusalem Temple. The CHASIDEI ASHKENAZ, following SA'ADYA GA'ON, equated it with the created Glory. The kabbalists identified it with the lowest of the SEFIROT, also called Malchut (Sovereignty). This is a female principle in the Godhead, and the kabbalists use highly charged erotic language in describing its union with the male principle, represented by the sefira Tiféret (Beauty) and the divine name 'the Holy One, blessed be He'. The human sexual act is described as mirroring this union. The SAFED kabbalists introduced the practice of preceding the performance of any COMMANDMENT with a declaration of the intention to perform it 'for the sake of the unification of the Holy One, blessed be He and his Shechina'. The formula has found its way into many traditionalist prayer books and is therefore recited by people who have little sense of its origin and deeper meaning. As the rabbis speak of the Shechina going into exile with the people of Israel, so the kabbalists envisage that in our unredeemed world part of God is, as it were, exiled from the rest of God. This is a daring image, and they insist that it should not be understood in a literal sense. The Shechina has been embraced by the feminist movement as a way of underlining that God has not been understood as exclusively masculine in the Jewish tradition and as providing the means to phrase prayers and benedictions in the feminine gender.

shechita Ritually proper slaughter of animals. *See* DIETARY REGULATIONS.

shehecheyánu ('who has caused us to live') Name of a benediction recited at festivals and whenever something is enjoyed for the first time. It takes its name from its first key word. The wording is 'Blessed are you ... who has caused us to live, preserved us, and permitted us to reach this time'.

sheítel (Yiddish) A wig, made of natural or artificial HAIR, worn by some married Ashkenazi women as a mark of modesty.

Shekalim ('shekels') Tractate of the Mishnah, Tosefta and Palestinian Talmud, in order Mo'ed, dealing with regulations concerning the half-shekel tax that was used for buying communal offerings for the Temple. It contains interesting information about the Temple's financial management.

shelíach tsibbur ('communal delegate') Title for the person who leads the prayers in a synagogue.

sheloshim *See* MOURNING.

Shem *See* HA-SHEM.

Shemá ('listen') Sequence of passages from the Torah, recited evening and morning. The passages in question are Deuteronomy 6.4–9 and 11.13–21, and Numbers 15.37–41. The name Shemá comes from the opening word of the first passage, which begins, 'Listen, Israel: the Lord is our God, the Lord is One'. These words have come to be regarded as the basic affirmation of Jewish faith. The following sections speak of love of God, the need to study, teach and discuss the words of the Torah, agricultural prosperity as a reward for obedience to the commandments, and the wearing of tassels (TSITSIT) as a reminder of God's commandments. The opening of the Shemá is among the first prayers that a Jewish child learns, and generations of Jews have striven to die with its words on their lips (*see* DEATH). Two of the three passages are copied on the MEZUZA, and they also figure among the passages of Torah which are contained in the TEFILLIN.

shemád *See* MESHUMMAD.

Shemini Atséret The eighth day of the festival of SUKKOT, falling on the 22nd of Tishri (and also the following day in the Diaspora, except in Reform congregations). The name (based on Numbers 29.35) is generally translated 'eighth day of solemn assembly'; however, it could also mean 'eighth day of conclusion' (*see* SHAVUOT), in other words simply the last day of Sukkot, and this is the way it is understood by the rabbis. This day is chosen to mark the liturgical transition from summer to winter, and in the additional service (MUSAF) prayers for rain are recited before the open ARK. The concluding words of the prayer, 'causing the wind to blow and the rain to fall', are added to every AMIDA from now until Passover. *See also* SIMCHAT TORA.

shemitta ('letting rest') Term applied to the seventh or sabbatical year, in which according to the Torah the land must lie fallow (Exodus 23.10–11, Leviticus 25.1–22) and all debts are to be cancelled (Deuteronomy 15.1–3). The laws of shemitta are discussed by the rabbis in tractate SHEVI'IT. The precise succession of sabbatical years has been lost, but agreement has been reached on the designation of the seventh year in Israel today (for example 2007/8 and 2014/5 are considered sabbatical years), and various legal fictions are employed to allow those who still observe the law to lead a normal life at this time.

Shemone Esre *See* AMIDA.

Shemót ('names [of]') Hebrew name of the biblical book of Exodus, of which it is the second word.

Shemu'el Alef, Shemu'el Bet Hebrew names of the biblical books of 1 and 2 Samuel, respectively.

shemura ('keeping', 'observing') Term applied to MATSA made from flour that is supervised from the time the grain is harvested, to ensure it does not come into contact with any moisture, which would render it CHAMETS. Such matsa is used by the particularly scrupulous on the first night of Passover.

shevarim Sequence of three broken notes on the SHOFAR. The Hebrew term has been explained as meaning 'broken'. The sound is said to suggest sobbing.

Shevát Fifth month of the year counting from New Year; eleventh counting from Passover. The 15th day (TU BI-SHEVÁT) is the New Year for trees.

Shevi'it ('seventh [year]') Tractate of the Mishnah, Tosefta and Palestinian Talmud, in order Zera'im, dealing with the laws of SHEMITTA.

shevira ('breaking') 'Breaking of the vessels', in LURIANIC KABBALA, is the name given to a cosmic catastrophe that is supposed to have taken place before the universe came into being. It is a central element in the Lurianic system, resulting in the scattering of the sparks of divine light. With its doctrine of shevira the Lurianic kabbala introduced a new dimension into Jewish messianism. According to this theory, as the creative light of God was pouring into inchoate Creation, some of the vessels or channels containing it collapsed under the strain and broke. The fragments scattered and fell, together with the sparks of divine light trapped in them, giving birth to base matter and to the SITRA ACHRA (the domain of evil). More than this, the whole well-ordered scheme of the universe was dislocated by the collapse, and nothing remained in its allotted place. The 'breaking of the vessels' is a disaster of unimaginable magnitude, as a result of which the whole cosmos, and not just mankind or the material world, is in urgent need of salvation or reparation (TIKKUN). It is the Jews' task to complete this reparation by performing mitsvot (COMMANDMENTS) with the correct mystical intention, so as to release the trapped sparks and restore them to their divine source. When this process is complete, redemption will come not only to humankind but also to the whole cosmos and, in a sense, to God himself.

Shevu'ot ('oaths') Tractate of the Mishnah, Tosefta and both Talmuds, in order Nezikin, dealing with various kinds of oaths.

Shir *See* RAPOPORT, SOLOMON JUDAH.

Shir ha-Kavod *See* HYMN OF GLORY.

Shir ha-Shirim ('the song of songs') Hebrew name of the biblical book The Song of Songs.

shisha ('six') Celebration held by Iraqi Jews on the sixth night after the birth of a child. Daughters are named on this occasion.

shiva *See* MOURNING.

Shiva-asar be-Tammuz *See* TAMMUZ.

shivata (Aramaic, 'seven') PIYYUT (type of KEROVA) composed to embellish the AMIDA of the additional service (MUSAF) on Sabbaths and festivals, so called because it has seven sections.

Shneur Zalman of Lyady (1745–1813) Founder of CHABAD CHASIDISM, also known as the Alter Rebbe ('the Old REBBE'). Born in Liozno, near Vitebsk in Belarus, he studied Talmud and then went to learn about prayer from the great Chasidic master DOV BER OF MEZHIRICH and his son, Abraham 'the Angel'. At Dov Ber's suggestion, he produced at the young age of 25 a revised version of the SHULCHAN ARUCH; it is still held in high regard by Chasidim and non-Chasidim alike. Imprisoned by the Russian authorities in 1798 on charges of sedition originating with MITNAGGEDIM, he was released on the 19th of Kislev, a date that is still celebrated as a joyful day by Chabad Chasidim. After his release he settled in Lyady. His most enduring work is the TANYA, a systematic treatment of Chasidic beliefs from a Chabad viewpoint.

Sho'a ('catastrophe') Term used, at first in Israel and now also more widely, for the attempt by the Nazis and their allies to exterminate the Jewish people during World War II (*see also* HOLOCAUST; YOM HA-SHO'A).

shochet Someone qualified to perform ritually fit slaughter of animals (SHECHITA). *See* DIETARY REGULATIONS.

shofar Horn sounded at New Year. Although a horn from any KOSHER animal may be used, preference is given to a ram's horn because of the symbolism of the ram that was sacrificed in place of Isaac in Genesis 22, which is one of the readings for the festival. (The rabbis rule out a cow's horn, however, because it is reminiscent of the sin of the GOLDEN CALF.) There is no prescribed size or shape for the shofar: some are short and crescent-shaped, some are long and straight with an upward turn at the end, while others spiral exuberantly. It takes a certain amount of skill to produce a fluent sound, but apart from this skill there is no special qualification to blow the shofar in synagogue. The rabbis laid down an elaborate sequence of blasts, made up of various combinations of three types of call, TEKI'A, TERU'A and SHEVARIM. These are played during the MUSAF service at New Year, ending with a long call known as a great teki'a (teki'a gedola). A single long blast concludes the service for the Day of Atonement. The shofar is not sounded on the first day of New Year if it falls on a Sabbath (except by Reform Jews).

Different reasons are given for the blowing of the shofar, some of which are alluded to in the liturgy, which cites a series of biblical verses referring to the shofar. Maimonides offers a striking explanation in his Code:

> It seems to say: Awake, you sleepers, you who have fallen asleep in life, and reflect upon your deeds. Remember your Creator. Do not be among those who miss reality and pursue shadows instead, who waste their years seeking after vain things that neither benefit nor save them. Look well to your souls, and improve your deeds. Forsake every one of you your evil ways and thoughts.

This view is well suited to the mood of the liturgy for the festival, which lays a strong emphasis on repentance and self-improvement.

Shoftim ('judges') Hebrew name of the biblical book of Judges.

shomer ('guardian' or 'observer'; plural shomrim) **1** In halacha, a custodian of property or bailee, that is a person to whom property is entrusted on the understanding that it will be returned (see Exodus 22.6–14 (7–15 in some English translations)). Four types of shomer are recognized, and their responsibilities in case of loss of the property or damage to it are different. **2** A supervisor, for example one who oversees the KASHRUT of food in a slaughterhouse, processing plant or kitchen. **3** A watcher, someone who sits with a corpse. **4** Observant, particularly in the compound phrase shomer Shabbat, used of one who keeps all the rules of Sabbath.

shtadlan In the Middle Ages, a prominent Jew who represented the Jewish community to the ruling power.

shtar A document. An antiquated English word, starr, meaning a bond, is derived from this term.

shtetl (Yiddish, 'little town'; plural shtétlach) **1** A Jewish community in pre-war eastern Europe (see PALE OF SETTLEMENT). **2** General term for the Jewish presence in eastern Europe. Nostalgia is often expressed among descendants of émigrés from the Pale in the United States and elsewhere, particularly in popular fiction, about the 'lost world of the shtetl'.

shtibl (Yiddish, 'little room'; plural shtíblach) A prayer room, as distinct from a SYNAGOGUE. The habit of praying in private rooms was cultivated by the CHASIDIM, as they were often barred from leading prayers in synagogues owing to their liturgical innovations.

shtreímel (Yiddish) A fur-trimmed hat worn by traditionalists of Polish origin, particularly CHASIDIM.

shul (Yiddish) Ashkenazi term for a SYNAGOGUE.

Shulchan Aruch ('spread table') The latest and most widely accepted of the authoritative codes of halacha. First published in 1565, the Shulchan Aruch was compiled by Joseph CARO, an exile from Spain who settled in SAFED. It is a digest of Caro's larger work, the Beit Yosef ('house of Joseph'), which in turn was based on an earlier compilation, the ARBA'A TURIM ('four rows') of JACOB BEN ASHER. The Shulchan Aruch was compiled with the needs of Caro's fellow Sefardim in mind, but an Ashkenazi contemporary, Moses ISSERLES, appended his MAPPA ('tablecloth'), providing Ashkenazi rules and customs where these differed.

Following the pattern introduced by Jacob ben Asher, Caro divides the laws under four headings. The first section, Órach Chayyim ('path of life'), deals with the ritual obligations of daily life, including worship and prayer and the observance of Sabbath and holy days. Yore De'a ('teacher of knowledge'), the second section, contains ritual and dietary regulations. Éven ha-Ézer ('stone of help') concerns itself with rules of personal status, marriage and divorce. Finally, Chóshen Mishpat ('breastplate of judgment') covers civil law.

Although it is now more than 400 years old, and in the intervening period many changes have taken place in Jewish life and many developments have been introduced in halacha, the Shulchan Aruch has never been superseded as a basic reference work. There are innumerable commentaries on it, dating almost from the time of its publication. A whole school of commentators existed in Vilna in the 17th century, and the commentary by the VILNA GA'ON, relating the laws to their source in the Talmud, helped to spread the influence of the work still further. Indeed, although he was a notorious opponent of the young Chasidic movement, it was probably under the Ga'on's influence that the founder of the Chabad branch of Chasidism, SHNEUR ZALMAN OF LYADY, compiled his own reworking of the Shulchan Aruch, thus ensuring that his followers would be brought under the discipline of the great halachic code and respect its authority.

The Shulchan Aruch is still viewed with affection and respect by Orthodox Jewish laymen. It is available in abridged and translated form, and new commentaries continue to be written. The most important and influential of the modern commentaries, both on the first section, the Órach Chayyim, are the MISHNA BERURA of Israel Meir Kagan (the CHAFETS CHAYYIM), and the CHAZON ISH of Abraham Isaiah Karelitz. Each of these authors was among the great leaders of traditional Judaism in his own day, and both alike succeeded, by focusing on the exhortation to moral and spiritual perfection, in breathing life into the dry bones of the halacha, and making the code into a guide to religious living instead of merely a list of dos and don'ts.

siddur ('setting in order'; plural siddurim) A prayer book, usually containing orders of daily and Sabbath prayers. It is customary for siddurim to include additional material such as halachic rules for prayer, passages for study and private devotion, prayers for special occasions and table songs (ZEMIROT). For festival prayer books *see* MACHZOR.

sidra (Aramaic, 'arrangement') One of the fifty-four divisions of the Torah. According to the annual cycle of readings now current, one sidra (occasionally two joined together) is read in synagogue each Sabbath, beginning on the Sabbath following

SIMCHAT TORA. The opening section is also read on Sabbath afternoon and on Monday and Thursday morning. Each sidra is known by one of its opening words.

Sifra *See* HALACHIC MIDRASHIM.

Sifre *See* HALACHIC MIDRASHIM.

Sigd *See* BETA ISRAEL.

simchat bat ('rejoicing for a daughter') Ceremony, of recent date, devised among modernist Ashkenazi Jews to celebrate the birth of a daughter and give her her name. For a comparable, long-established Sefardi ceremony *see* ZÉBED HA-BAT.

Simchat Tora ('rejoicing in the Torah') The last of the sequence of autumn festivals. In Israel and in Reform synagogues this coincides with SHEMINI ATSÉRET; in other Diaspora congregations it is celebrated on the second day of Shemini Atséret. This is the day when the annual reading of the Torah is concluded and resumes again immediately at the beginning. It is a time of joyful celebration, heightened by the fact that it marks the end of a very long period of solemnities and festivities. All the scrolls are taken out of the ARK and processed around the synagogue seven times, accompanied by singing and dancing (*see* HAKKAFOT). Members of the congregation are honoured by being called up to be the 'bridegroom of the Torah' (chatan tora) and the 'bridegroom of Bereshit [Genesis]' (chatan Bereshit), but in some synagogues all the congregants are called up, and it is also customary to call up the children, the only day in the year when they are called up to the Torah. The children are given sweets and apples, and they process behind the Torah waving appropriately decorated flags. The two 'bridegrooms' (who in Progressive congregations may be 'brides') make a party for the whole congregation.

From a historical point of view the most interesting thing is that this popular festival does not have old roots. It is not mentioned in the Torah or the Talmud, nor is it named during the liturgy for the day, which speaks only of Shemini Atséret. JACOB BEN ASHER mentions in his 14th-century code the custom of recommencing the sequence of Torah readings as soon as it is completed on this day, 'so that Satan has no opportunity to accuse the Jews of making an end of the Torah'. The various other practices associated with the festival grew up gradually, and spread from one part of the Jewish world to the rest, even as far as India.

Simeon bar Yochai (late 1st–early 2nd century) One of the best-known of the TANNA'IM. According to the rabbinic writings (our only source for his life) he was a pupil of AKIBA and a teacher of JUDAH THE NASI. Some rabbinic texts purport to come from his school. Legend has it that he went into hiding in a cave for fear of the Romans, and remained there for twelve or thirteen years. According to the kabbalists, during this period of seclusion the mystical doctrines contained in the ZOHAR were revealed to him. They celebrate his HILLULA at LAG BA-ÓMER, the supposed date of his death.

sin Hebrew has many words that can be translated as 'sin'. The commonest are chet (originally 'missing a target') and avera ('transgression', 'overstepping a mark'). In rabbinic thought, sin is not an inherent part of human nature, it is the result of the YÉTSER HA-RA getting the better of the yétser tov. The liturgy for the Day of Atonement enumerates several general categories and numerous specific types of sin (*see* AL CHET; ASHÁMNU; VIDDUI). The rabbis teach that forgiveness is available for all sins (as ALBO put it, 'Human power to sin cannot be greater than the divine power to forgive'). *See also* ATONEMENT; FEAR OF GOD; FORGIVENESS.

Sinai Name of the mountain where the Torah is believed to have been revealed; figuratively, it denotes the event of this REVELATION. The doctrine of 'Sinai', meaning the divine source of the laws of the HALACHA, is often invoked in the rabbinic writings in the form 'from Sinai'. For example certain laws that are not mentioned in the written Torah but are considered to have the same status as if they were are called 'laws of Moses from Sinai'. The Mishnah tractate Avot begins with a 'chain of trad-ition', linking the rabbis through an unbroken line of tradition to Sinai; it opens with the words: 'Moses received Torah from Sinai and passed it on to Joshua …' According to some rabbinic texts Moses received at Sinai not only all the laws of the written Torah (including some that according to the Torah itself were given later) but the entire ORAL TORAH, and even the answer that will be given in the future to a question from an intelligent student.

Singer's Prayer Book *See* PRAYER BOOKS.

sitra achra (Aramaic, 'the other side') In kabbala, the realm of evil. The term seems to have been invented by the author of the ZOHAR, and is used in subsequent kab-balistic literature. The 'other side' is the demonic or left side, which is constantly striving to seduce the SHECHINA away from her husband, the right side, called the side of holiness (sitra di-kedushta). The kabbalists repeatedly try to deflect the obvious charge of DUALISM.

Sivan Ninth month of the year counting from New Year; third counting from Passover, and corresponding approximately to June. The festival of SHAVUOT falls on the 6th of the month (6th and 7th in the Diaspora).

six hundred and thirteen commandments *See* COMMANDMENTS.

siyyum ('completion') **1** Celebration held on finishing the study of a tractate of the Talmud. It is accompanied by a meal, a discourse on the halachic lessons of the tractate, and prayers. *See also* FAST OF THE FIRSTBORN. **2** Celebration of the completion of the writing of a SÉFER TORA.

skullcap (in Hebrew, kippa; in Yiddish, kápel or yármulka) Form of HEAD-COVERING currently favoured by Jewish men. The practice is attested among Ashkenazim from the early 18th century (it has been suggested that it is borrowed from the higher Roman Catholic clergy, who wear a skullcap during the Mass). It has now become very widespread, particularly indoors. There are two basic types of Jewish skullcap, the larger 'Orthodox' skullcap, usually made of black satin or velvet, and the smaller, more colourful 'Zionist' skullcap, usually crocheted, and sometimes incorporating the wearer's name. Various other types exist, sometimes implying an association with a specific group. CHAREDIM often wear a big black skullcap under their hat. The practice of wearing a 'Zionist' skullcap out of doors became common, particularly among students, after the 1967 Israel–Arab war. The FEMINIST movement has encouraged the wearing of skullcaps by women, particularly during prayer.

slander Gossip spread with the intention of damaging another's reputation is forbidden in the Torah (Exodus 23.1) and severely condemned by the rabbis, whether the information in question is true or false. The Hebrew expression lashon ha-ra (evil tongue) strictly applies when the information is true. The rabbis do not limit their condemnation to rumour spread with the intention of causing harm. An exception is made in the case of testimonials and other character references, where failure to disclose unbecoming facts may be detrimental to a third party. *See also* CHAFETS CHAYYIM.

snóga *See* ESNÓGA.

Society for Ethical Culture *See* REFORM JUDAISM (IN AMERICA).

sofer ('scribe', plural sofrim) **1** In the Bible, title of a high administrative official. **2** In the rabbinic literature, term used, in the plural, to designate a class of learned men, precursors of the rabbis themselves, responsible for transmitting laws and the text of the Torah. **3** In later Talmudic passages, an elementary teacher. **4** One trained to write a SÉFER TORA, TEFILLIN and MEZUZA (in this sense, sometimes called sofer stam, the second word being an ACRONYM).

Sofer, Moses (1762–1839) Leading opponent of MODERNISM in all its forms (including political emancipation and Enlightenment ideas, as well as religious reforms), also known as the Chatam Sofer. Born in Frankfurt, he was appointed rabbi of Pressburg (Bratislava) in 1806. His outlook is encapsulated in the slogan 'innovation is forbidden in the Torah' (in Hebrew, chadash asur min ha-tora). He spread his ideas through his teaching (he founded a very large YESHIVA where many rabbis were trained) and through his RESPONSA.

Soloveitchik, Joseph Dov or **Joseph Ber** (1903–93) Orthodox theologian and educator, known to his followers as 'the Rav'. Born in Pruzana (Pruzhany), Belarus, he studied in Warsaw and Berlin and in 1932 emigrated to the United States. In 1941 he succeeded his father as head of the rabbinical school at YESHIVA UNIVERSITY. In the 1950s he emerged as the leading light of American Orthodoxy, and greatly contributed to the strengthening of the movement's presence in North American Jewry through his personal teaching and his writings. In his books *Ish ha-Halacha* (1979; *Halachic Man*, 1983), *The Halachic Mind* (1986) and *The Lonely Man of Faith* (1992) he placed the existential commitment to HALACHA firmly at the centre of the life of the Jewish man. Soloveitchik firmly maintained the Orthodox insistence on combining Talmudic with secular learning, and engaging fully with Western thought.

Song of Songs (Shir ha-Shirim) Biblical book in the KETUVIM, one of the FIVE SCROLLS. It consists of love lyrics woven together, and has been interpreted at least since the beginning of the 2nd century CE (when AKIBA is said to have strongly defended its holy status) as an allegory of the love between Israel and God. It is read in synagogue by Sefardim on Friday evening and by Ashkenazim at Passover.

Sota ('woman suspected of adultery') Tractate of the Mishnah, Tosefta and both Talmuds, in the order Nashim, dealing with the case of a woman suspected of adultery (Numbers 5.11–31).

soul *See* AFTERLIFE; DEVEKUT; GILGUL; IMMORTALITY; LOVE; OLAM HA-BA; TIKKUN.

Spanish and Portuguese Jews *See* SEFARDIM.

sparks, trapped *See* KELIPPOT; LURIANIC KABBALA; MESSIAH; SHEVIRA; TIKKUN.

spices *See* HAVDALA.

Spinoza, Baruch (1632–77) Philosopher. Born in Amsterdam to Portuguese parents, he was placed under a CHÉREM because of his 'evil opinions and acts' in 1656; he ended his days in The Hague. Spinoza's understanding of God – which as generally understood is pantheistic, that is to say there is no difference between God and nature – stands outside any authoritative Jewish theology, and, to be fair, Spinoza himself did not claim to be representing a Jewish perspective on God. Spinoza conducts a thoroughgoing attack on the very foundations of religion, and rejects any attempt to derive the material world from a transcendent God. Although Spinoza retains the word 'God', and indeed gives it a central part in the exposition of his ideas, his God is far removed from the God of traditional Judaism, who is a personal agent distinct from the created world. Spinoza's God is an impersonal and infinite substance, and everything derives its being from God's existence and is subject to strict laws of necessity. Thus although superficially it may appear to preserve the classical beliefs in a single, unique God on whom everything depends, in reality Spinoza's thought is totally at odds with theistic belief. Nevertheless, his Jewish upbringing is apparent in his writings, for example in his *Tractatus* he bases his argument that the Torah was not written by Moses but by Ezra on some arguments originally put forward by Abraham IBN EZRA. Echoes of the thought of the SAFED kabbalists have also been found in his thought. Spinoza's works are not addressed specifically to Jews, but to European thinkers at large, and they take their place within the wider history of modern philosophy. It was only after Jewish thinkers had begun to participate in that wider history that the influence of Spinoza began to be felt in Jewish thought. For example, Moses MENDELSSOHN expressed a deep interest in, and sympathy for, his ideas. *See also* MAIMON, SALOMON.

spiritualism System of beliefs and practices of which the purpose is to enter into communication with the dead. Necromancy, together with other forms of divination, is forbidden in the Torah (Deuteronomy 18.10–12). On the other hand, in 1 Samuel 28 King Saul, after approaching a necromancer, holds a conversation with the dead prophet Samuel. The rabbinic attitude to such matters is not straightforward, and some medieval halachists seem to have no problem in permitting attempts to contact the spirits of the dead. The SHULCHAN ARUCH (Yore De'a 179.14) sums up the halacha as follows: 'It is permitted to make a dying person swear to return after his death so as to convey some information that he will be asked for. Some permit an attempt to do this even after the person has died, provided one does not conjure up the actual corpse but only the dead man's ghost.' As for participating in spiritualist séances and the like, some halachic authorities forbid it on general grounds but there is no real agreement on the subject.

Star of David *See* MAGEN DAVID.

Statement of Principles for Reform Judaism *See* PITTSBURGH STATEMENT.

Status Quo Loose grouping of synagogues in Hungary that refused to be labelled either NEOLOG or ORTHODOX following the official recognition granted to these two larger movements following the emancipation of Hungarian Jewry in 1868. Various motives determined the choice of the various constituents not to ally themselves to one or other of the big groupings. Some simply wished to maintain their own identity, which they felt was compromised; some had instituted moderate reforms that marked them off from the Orthodox but found Neolog Judaism too radical; some adhered to versions of Orthodoxy that were less extreme than the one that dominated the Orthodox organization; still others followed various Chasidic rebbes and did not want to be dictated to by non-Chasidim. With the passage of time the Status Quo sector managed to retain its identity, tending towards modernist Orthodoxy as the Chasidim eventually realigned themselves with the Orthodox. However they have never constituted more than a tiny proportion of Hungarian Jewry.

Steinberg, Milton (1903–50) A disciple of Mordecai KAPLAN who became one of the pillars of the RECONSTRUCTIONIST movement. Like Kaplan he was a rationalist deeply concerned with the dilemmas of Jewish survival and open to current intellectual trends. However, he diverged radically from his teacher in refusing to relegate God to an aspect of nature or a figment of the human mind. He wanted Jews to take God seriously, and shortly before his early death he launched a demand for a return to Jewish theology. While fully aware of the limitations of the medieval philosophers, Steinberg expressed confidence in the power of reason to address questions of faith, and in the power of faith to transcend facile intellectualization. He wrote: 'Religious faith is a hypothesis interpreting reality and posited on the same grounds as any valid hypothesis.'

Steinheim, Salomon Ludwig (1789–1866) Philosopher. Born in Bruchhausen, Westphalia, he worked as a doctor in Altona before settling permanently in Rome. Steinheim was a profound and independent-minded thinker who challenged many received ideas. His fame as a thinker rests on his four-volume *Die Offenbarung nach dem Lehrbegriffe der Synagoge* (*Revelation According to the Doctrine of the Synagogue*, 1835–65). In it he attacks the rationalism of Moses MENDELSSOHN and his school. Where Mendelssohn denied the revelation of doctrines not accessible independently by human reason, Steinheim maintains that revelation makes manifest truths that human reason could not have constructed on its own, although it is capable of testing and accepting them. Steinheim's arguments made him unpopular both among reformers and among upholders of traditional belief, but he raised serious questions, some of which are still of value today. He has been claimed as a forerunner of EXISTENTIALISM and of the modern study of religion.

Steinschneider, Moritz (1816–1907) Bibliographer. It is hardly an exaggeration to say that, in an age of outstanding scholars of Judaism, Steinschneider placed the twin sciences of manuscript research and bibliography on a sound footing virtually single-handed. His contribution to Jewish studies (WISSENSCHAFT DES JUDENTUMS) is immeasurable. Born in Prossnitz, Moravia, he settled in Berlin in 1845. (He had previously been a student there, and received encouragement from Leopold ZUNZ and Abraham GEIGER.) His enormous output (his own bibliography runs to some 1,400 items) includes catalogues of Hebrew printed books in Oxford and Hebrew manuscripts in Leiden, Munich, Hamburg and Berlin, as well as comprehensive bibliographic surveys such as his vast study of Jewish translations, *Die hebräischen Übersetzungen des Mittelalters und die Juden als Dolmetscher* (*The Hebrew Translations of the Middle Ages and the Jews as Interpreters*, 1893).

substitute name A name used to avoid another, specifically a way of naming God avoiding names that are considered too holy for non-sacred use. Examples are (ha-) KADOSH BARUCH HU, HA-MAKOM, HA-SHEM and Shamáyim (*see* HEAVEN). English, too, has substitute names, such as the Almighty, the Eternal, the Holy One, blessed be He. Recently a habit has grown up among English-speaking traditionalists of writing G-d instead of God. JUDEZMO has its own substitute names, including El Criador (the Creator), El que no es a nombrar (He who is not to be named), El tavan (He who is above, from Turkish tavan, 'ceiling').

suffering *See* ATONEMENT; LOVE.

Sufism A form of Islamic mysticism. Sufism nourished various streams of Jewish mysticism, notably through the Duties of the Heart of BACHYA IBN PAKUDA. Its influence is also felt strongly in Egypt, where the title 'Chasid' (pious one) was applied to a number of rabbis who adopted the path of introspection and self-discipline, and where the son (Abraham) and grandson (Obadiah) of MAIMONIDES composed Sufi works and attracted a certain following. The long-term influence of Sufism on Judaism is mainly felt in Chasidism, particularly in such ideals as equanimity and self-annihilation (BITTUL HA-YESH), and in the CHABAD idea that the world has no real existence independent of God.

sukka ('hut'; plural sukkot) **1** A simple, impermanent structure roofed with greenery thin enough to allow the stars to be glimpsed, part of the observance of the festival of SUKKOT. It must be built out of doors, so as to be exposed to the elements, but it is permissible to build it on a roof or an open balcony. It is made in obedience to the Torah, where God states (Leviticus 23.42–3): 'You shall live in huts for seven days; all native-born Israelites shall live in huts, so that future generations may know that I made the Israelites live in huts when I brought them out of the Land of Egypt.' Theoretically, therefore, one should take all one's meals in the sukka and even sleep in it for the seven days of the festival. (There is no obligation to do either if the rain is coming in.) In accordance with the principle of 'adorning the commandments'

(HIDDUR MITSVA) it is customary to decorate the sukka with flowers and fruit, and it is also customary to invite guests to share the joy of the sukka. There are also invisible holy guests (USHPIZIN). **2** (Sukka) Tractate of the Mishnah, Tosefta and both Talmuds, in the order Mo'ed, dealing with laws concerning the festival of SUKKOT.

Sukkot ('huts') Autumn festival, also known as Tabernacles, beginning on the 15th of Tishri and lasting for seven days; the eighth day is SHEMINI ATSÉRET. The rabbis sometimes refer to it as 'the Festival' (chag), with no further description, as though it were the high point of the religious year, or at least of the autumn pilgrimage period that began before New Year. In the liturgy it is called 'the season of our rejoicing' (zemán simchaténu), and this element of rejoicing is specifically mentioned in the Torah (Deuteronomy 16.13–15). The rejoicing is related in this passage to the harvest, 'when you have gathered in your corn and your wine ... because the Lord your God shall bless you in all your increase, and in all your manual labour, therefore you are bound to rejoice'. The festival is also mentioned as a harvest festival in Exodus 23.16 and Leviticus 23.39. The latter text is part of a longer context in which the festival is described in different ways. In 23.33–8 it is described in language resembling the description of the Day of ATONEMENT that immediately precedes it: it is to be a solemn gathering on which no work is to be done and various sacrifices are to be offered. In 23.40 the instruction is given 'You shall take on the first day the fruit of goodly trees, branches of palm trees, boughs of thick trees, and willows of the brook, and you shall rejoice before the Lord your God for seven days'. And then in 23.41–3 it is explained differently: it is to be observed by living in huts for seven days, in memory of the exodus and the wandering through the wilderness (*see* SUKKA). The festival is thus observed through the symbol of wandering, the sukka, and through the 'taking' of the FOUR SPECIES, identified as citron (etrog), palm, myrtle and willow. 'Taking' is understood literally as picking them up. A palm frond, three sprigs of myrtle and two of willow are bound together and held in the right hand, the lemon-like fruit of the citron is taken in the left, and they are waved up, down, and to the four points of the compass after the recitation of an appropriate blessing. The four species are also carried in procession around the synagogue, accompanied by the singing of 'Hosannas' (HOSHÁNOT). On the seventh day of the festival seven circuits are made, which is why this day is known as the Great Hoshána (HOSHÁNA RABBA). Some Jews still observe the custom of beating a bunch of willow sprigs on this day until the leaves come off.

Sura Town in southern BABYLONIA made famous by its rabbinic academy, founded in the early 3rd century CE, where much of the groundwork for the Babylonian Talmud was laid. It is said to have had a student enrolment of around a thousand in its early days, and, like other Babylonian academies, was funded by communal taxes and private donations, of which Sura received the lion's share. Its name is inseparable from that of its rival at PUMBEDITA, over which it maintained a certain pre-eminence in the early geonic period. The academy was moved to Baghdad (retaining its name) in the 10th century, and was given a new lease of life after a period of decline by the appointment of SA'ADYA GA'ON at its head in 928. It faded away, with the gaonate itself, from the mid-11th century.

synagogue

A meeting place, particularly for the purpose of worship; a Jewish community. The word comes from Greek synagogé, 'assembly'. The Hebrew term is beit kené-set, 'house of assembly'. Many Ashkenazi Jews refer to it by the Yiddish term shul, meaning a school. This may reflect the fact that the synagogue sometimes doubled as a house of study, although that is strictly a separate institution, called in Hebrew beit midrash. The word kloyz (related to 'cloister' in English) was formerly used in central and eastern Europe for a synagogue, or for a house of study that doubled as a synagogue. Some Jewish communities use the term 'temple' in preference to 'synagogue'. This usage originated in 18th-century Europe, probably under the influence of French Protestantism; it gained currency in the 19th-century Reform movement, which was attracted by its allusion to the ancient Temple in Jerusalem. American Reform has retained the term, and it has been adopted by some Conservative congregations.

The synagogue is the visible side of the Jewish community. The community in turn is made up of a number of families and individuals. The word 'synagogue', in fact, can be used to refer to the community rather than the building. Despite what is sometimes said to the contrary, this is not a modern development aping the Christian use of the word 'church', but goes right back to the origins of the word 'synagogue'. In Greek Jewish texts from the ancient world (especially outside the Land of Israel) 'synagogue' usually means the community of the Jews.

Each synagogue is autonomous, since Judaism acknowledges no central human spiritual authority, and no overarching organization. There may well be two or more synagogues in a single town, many more in a big city, representing different quarters of the town, or different origins of the members, or different religious ideologies (*see* PLURALISM). Sometimes one synagogue is technically a branch of another. In some cities or countries some or all of the synagogues may be brought together under a single communal structure. For example in London many of the Orthodox Ashkenazi synagogues share a common organization, the UNITED SYNAGOGUE. In Paris both Ashkenazi and Sefardi synagogues belong to the CONSISTOIRE. Whatever the relationship between the synagogues, however, members are free to transfer their membership from one synagogue to another, to belong to more than one at the same time, or to worship occasionally or even regularly in a synagogue they do not formally belong to. It may even happen that members of the same family belong to different synagogues.

It is considered meritorious to help to found or run a synagogue, to attend its services and to contribute generously to its charitable funds. A special prayer is said after the reading of the Torah calling down God's blessing on 'those who unite to form synagogues for prayer, and those who gather in them to pray; also those who provide lamps for lighting and wine for kiddush and havdala, food for wayfarers and alms for the poor, and all who occupy themselves loyally with the needs of the community'.

A synagogue is generally administered by a council and by honorary officers (chairman or president, secretary, treasurer and so forth), who are members, elected by the membership. (Traditionally, this is a male preserve. The right of women to vote or hold office is a subject currently under debate in Orthodoxy.) There may also be wardens (*see* GABBAI), who supervise the smooth running of the services. It is conventional to refer to these persons collectively as the lay leadership, to distinguish them from the rabbi and his or her assistants, but there is no foundation in Judaism for this distinction (*see* LAITY).

Synagogues come in all shapes and sizes, and there are no particular architectural requirements. They tend to reflect local architectural trends, sometimes flirting with church or mosque architecture and sometimes deliberately avoiding it. In the medieval period they were often small and discreetly located, so as not to attract attention to themselves. The Chasidim in Poland, barred from the synagogues, chose to worship intimately in a little room (SHTIBL). In the course of the 19th century grand 'cathedral' synagogues were built in the large cities of Europe and America, reflecting the size, wealth and self-assurance of the post-EMANCIPATION communities. The favoured styles belonged to the classic European repertoire, but Gothic was deliberately avoided (presumably it was regarded as too 'churchy'), Romanesque and the vaguely exotic Byzantine and unambiguously oriental Moorish idioms being preferred. The 20th century is marked by a more adventurous approach, and some very interesting and unusual synagogues have been built, such as Frank Lloyd Wright's synagogue at Elkins Park, near Philadelphia, or Heinz Rau's white dome for the Hebrew University in Jerusalem.

Synagogues frequently identify themselves on the outside by means of a Hebrew inscription or some Jewish symbol such as a six-pointed star of David (MAGEN DAVID) or a seven-branched candelabrum (MENORA). Internally, the dominant feature is the holy ARK, which normally occupies the middle of the wall closest to Jerusalem. The ark usually has the form of a tall cupboard with double doors opening outwards. Above it hangs a lamp known as the eternal light (NER TAMID), and in Ashkenazi synagogues a curtain (PARÓCHET) hangs in front of the ark. The only other prominent item of furniture is a flat or sloping desk on which the scroll of the Torah is placed when it is opened for the reading. This stands on a raised dais (BIMA, ALMÉMAR, TEBA), reached by steps and often partly enclosed by railings or a balustrade.

The need to accommodate the ark, placed against one wall, and the reading desk, often located in the centre of the synagogue, imposes awkward constraints on the design, particularly in terms of the seating. Traditional synagogues often have wooden pews arranged in the long axis of the hall, facing the reading desk which takes up a large part of the centre. This arrangement suits the reading of the Torah, but means that congregants must make a ninety-degree turn when the ark is opened or when they face Jerusalem to recite the AMIDA. An alternative arrangement, pioneered by the Reform movement but now found in other kinds of synagogue too, combines the ark and reading desk on a single platform at one end of the building, leaving the rest of the hall free for seating and obviating the need to turn. Traditional and Orthodox synagogues have separate seating for men and women; often the women are relegated to a gallery or separated from the men by a screen or other physical barrier (MECHITSA), but in extreme cases they are placed in a separate room where they are completely hidden from male worshippers.

The style of worship in a synagogue is very variable. It can be very grand and formal, with wardens in top hats and tailcoats, strict decorum and sublime ORGAN and CHORAL MUSIC, or at the other end of the spectrum, as in a Chasidic shtibl, it can be intimate and homespun, do-it-yourself and raucous, with congregants arriving at intervals throughout the service and chatting uninhibitedly to one another. Most services fall somewhere between the two.

Although the prayers may be led by a rabbi, they do not have to be, and often are not. In a smaller traditional synagogue the male congregants may well take it in turn to serve as SHELÍACH TSIBBUR. In larger synagogues there is often a salaried reader or cantor (CHAZZAN).

Synagogue Council of America An umbrella organization, founded in 1926 and dissolved in 1994, bringing together the synagogue and rabbinic associations of the Orthodox, Conservative and Reform movements.

Ta'anit ('fast') Tractate of the Mishnah, Tosefta and both Talmuds, in the order Mo'ed, dealing with laws and practices related to various types of fast, primarily fasts undertaken to avert droughts.

tabernacle Portable shrine erected by the Israelites in the wilderness, according to the Torah. In Hebrew it is called mishkan (abode [of God]), mikdash (sanctuary, the name later used for the Jerusalem Temple) and óhel mo'ed (tent of meeting). Detailed instructions for its construction and furnishings are recorded in Exodus 25–31, and the construction itself is narrated in Exodus 35–40. The tabernacle was set within a rectangular outer courtyard, screened off by curtains. In this courtyard stood the sacrificial altar, where the main sacrificial rituals were performed. The tabernacle itself is described as a rectangular structure, three sides of which were rigid, being made of upright planks; the eastern side was made of woven textiles and formed the entrance. Textiles and skins of animals draped over the top gave the sanctuary the appearance of a tent. Its inner space was divided into two parts. The larger part, nearer the entrance, was called the Holy (Kódesh). Only priests could enter into it; it contained a gold lampstand (MENORA), a gold table, and a gold altar for burning incense. The smaller, western part, the Holy of Holies (Kódesh ha-Kodashim) was only entered by the High Priest, once a year, on the Day of Atonement. In many details the tabernacle prefigures the Temple.

Tabernacles *See* SUKKOT.

tachanun ('supplication') Part of the daily liturgy (omitted on Sabbaths, festivals and certain other specified occasions). It consists of prayers, a psalm and a hymn; the actual details vary in different prayer rites. On Mondays and Thursdays a longer version of tachanun is recited.

tachrichim *See* BURIAL.

tafsir (Arabic, 'commentary') Name given to various Arabic and Persian biblical commentaries, but particularly applied to the Arabic translation of the Torah by SA'ADYA GA'ON. This translation has been very widely known and studied, and even read out in synagogue with the Hebrew, so that its influence on the culture of Arabic-speaking Jews has been enormous.

tahara *See* BURIAL.

takkana ('device', 'regulation'; plural takkanot) A regulation or decree, usually issued to revise the HALACHA for the public good. The Talmud mentions various takkanot supposedly instituted at various historical periods going right back to Moses. Post-Talmudic takkanot are only considered binding on communities under the jurisdiction of the authority promoting them. Among the best known are the takkanot attributed to Rabbenu GERSHOM, such as that prohibiting POLYGYNY. The term is also applied to local bye-laws.

tallit or **tallet** A prayer shawl having fringes at the hems and tassels in the four corners. Sefardim prefer the form tallet; Ashkenazim always say tallit. It is sometimes called tallit gadol (greater tallit), to distinguish it from the tallit katan (lesser tallit, or TSITSIT). It is worn in obedience to a commandment in the Torah (Numbers 15.37–40, Deuteronomy 22.12) to wear a tsitsit (fringe) on one's clothes, as a reminder of God's laws. The tallit is worn by men (it is an eastern European custom for unmarried men not to wear it; other Ashkenazim generally consider it should be worn from the age of BAR MITSVA). Women are traditionally exempted from wearing the tallit, but in recent years it has become increasingly common for Progressive women to wear it. It is worn daily during morning prayers (and at the additional service if there is one). At the afternoon and evening services in the synagogue only the SHELÍACH TSIBBUR wears it. On the Day of ATONEMENT it is worn at all five services; on TISH'A BE-AV it is worn in the afternoon instead of the morning.

See also BURIAL.

talmid A pupil or disciple.

talmid chacham ('disciple of a sage'; plural talmidei chachamim) A learned person. This is not a title bestowed by the community or the academy, but a generic term for men exerting an authority based on public recognition of their learning and their high moral standing.

talmid chaver *See* CHAVER.

Talmud

('study') The foundation text of rabbinic Judaism. There are actually two Talmuds, the Palestinian Talmud (often called the Yerushalmi) and the Babylonian Talmud (or Bavli). Both record the debates of the AMORA'IM. The Yerushalmi quotes no Amora later than around 400 CE, and consequently is thought to have been edited a little later than this date; some scholars consider it to have been composed in a hurry, and to show signs of being unfinished. The Bavli was clearly composed much later, because it quotes Babylonian Amora'im of the 6th century. Both contain a mixture of HALACHA and AGGADA. Although the two Talmuds differ considerably in content, there is a great deal of material which is common to both, and the basic organization of the two is the same. Each is set out in the form of a commentary (known as GEMARA) on the text of the Mishnah: typically a passage of the Mishnah is quoted, and a detailed discussion (which may actually wander far from the content of the Mishnaic passage) follows. In a sense neither Talmud is complete, since they both lack a gemara on long passages of Mishnah, extending to whole tractates. The Babylonian Talmud is much longer than the Palestinian, but the Palestinian Talmud contains a gemara on several tractates of the Mishnah which have none in the Babylonian Talmud. With the decline of the rabbinical schools of the Land of Israel and the rise of those in Babylonia, the Babylonian Talmud came to enjoy far greater authority than the Palestinian, but both have been copied and studied continuously since late antiquity; with the revival of rabbinic studies in Israel in recent times there has been renewed interest in the teachings of the Palestinian Talmud. It is convenient to refer to the whole of this literature as 'Talmud', even though the rabbinic scholar is well aware of the differences between the Mishnah, the Palestinian Talmud, and the Babylonian Talmud.

The subject matter of the Talmud is arranged under the same orders and tractates as the Mishnah. It is interesting to note that the last two orders (Kodashim and Toharot) are virtually ignored in the Gemara, with the exception of the food laws and the rules concerning menstrual impurity, while the agricultural laws, which were only regarded as binding in the Land of Israel, are not dealt with systematically in the Gemara of the Babylonian Talmud. The implication is that the Amora'im, despite their strong academic interests, were concerned primarily to elucidate the law in those areas which were of continuing practical significance. And indeed, although they frequently discuss biblical commandments and their hypothetical ramifications, they also often cite actual cases, arising out of the experience of the law courts or questions addressed to the rabbis in their capacity as academic lawyers. Moreover, the rabbis display a deep sensitivity to actual custom, MINHAG.

The Talmud is a huge work which occupies many volumes; moreover, it is written in a mixture of Hebrew and Aramaic, in a distinctive and difficult style, and even people who have learned to read biblical Hebrew fluently are unable to read the Talmud without extensive further training. It is therefore the domain of rabbis and scholars, and is not really accessible to the wider Jewish public. Nevertheless, its authority in traditional rabbinic Judaism is enormous, even outstripping that of the Bible in some respects. Its claim to authority has not gone unchallenged, however. In the Middle Ages the adherents of KARAISM impugned it, and demanded a return to scripture alone, and in the early 19th century the reformer Abraham GEIGER declared that it was an 'ungainly colossus' that must be toppled if there were to be any true religious or political progress for the Jews. His contemporary Samuel HOLDHEIM wrote boldly: 'The Talmud spoke with the ideology of its own time, and for that time it was right. I speak for the higher ideology of my own time, and for this age I am right.' The Reform movement has accepted that the Talmud, like the Bible if not more so, is not a divine text but a human creation.

Study of the Talmud does, however, figure on the syllabuses of contemporary Reform rabbinical colleges, even if the laws and regulations which make up a large part of its subject matter are not considered binding. It is seen as an important historical document, and a source of many inspiring teachings. The criticisms to which the Talmud has been subject in the modern period have served to heighten the authority which has been invested in it by Orthodoxy.

Many commentaries have been written on the Bavli in whole or part, of which the most famous is that of RASHI. Three of Rashi's grandsons were among the TOSAFISTS, who lived in France and Germany in the 12th and 13th centuries and supplemented Rashi's pioneering work.

Current editions of the Babylonian Talmud are based on the text published by the Romm publishing house in Vilna in 1880–86, which in turn was based on the first printed edition, published by Daniel Bomberg in Venice in 1520–23. In these editions the text is accompanied by Rashi's commentary and by the Tosafot. An English translation of the whole Bavli was published by the Soncino publishing house in London in 35 volumes in 1935–52 (reprinted in 18 volumes in 1961), and a bilingual edition with helpful notes is being produced under the direction of the Israeli rabbi Adin Steinsaltz (New York, 1989–). The Yerushalmi has not been so well served, either by commentators or by translators.

talmud tora ('study of the Torah') Study is a religious obligation. 'It is a fine thing to combine talmud tora with a worldly occupation,' says a rabbinic maxim (Mishnah, Avot 2.2), 'because the combined labour involved leaves no time for sin.' Talmud tora can also mean a school where Torah is studied.

Tamid ('perpetual burnt offering') Tractate of the Mishnah, with partial GEMARA in the Babylonian Talmud, in the order Kodashim, describing the daily Temple service, and in particular the sacrifice that was offered twice daily.

Tammuz Tenth month of the year counting from New Year; fourth counting from Passover, corresponding roughly to July. The 17th (Shiva-asar be-Tammuz) is a fast day, thought to commemorate the breaching of the walls of Jerusalem by the Romans in 70 CE, and other sad events of the remote past. This day inaugurates a period of three weeks of sadness, until the 9th of Av (*see* TISH'A BE-AV), during which pious Jews abstain from any kind of celebration.

Tanach Hebrew designation of the BIBLE. It is an acronym of the names of its three parts: Torah ('instruction'), Nevi'im ('prophets') and Ketuvim ('writings'). This threefold division, which differs from the usual Christian arrangement of the books, is very old, and is thought to reflect the stages in which the text was codified. It still influences the way in which the sections are regarded, and the use which is made of them. The first section, the Torah, is regarded as the most sacred and authoritative: in synagogue it is read in a series of continuous lections from texts written by hand on specially prepared parchment scrolls. The lections from Nevi'im are only selected excerpts, read from printed texts, while the books of Ketuvim, with a few notable exceptions (such as the Psalms and the FIVE SCROLLS), do not figure in the public readings.

Tanna'im ('those who repeat or teach'; from Aramaic 'tanna' with Hebrew plural ending) Term used specifically of the rabbis cited as authorities in the MISHNAH. The rabbis of this period (late 1st to early 3rd century CE) are collectively designated 'the Tanna'im', and the period itself is referred to as the 'Tannaitic period'.

Tanya (Aramaic, 'it was taught') The fundamental text of CHABAD spirituality. The name Tanya comes from its opening word. Also known as Likkutei Amarim, it was composed by SHNEUR ZALMAN OF LYADY and first published in 1796, and in its complete form in 1814. It has enjoyed enormous popularity, and has been published in innumerable editions. The Tanya is a systematic treatment of kabbalistic and Chasidic themes from a distinctive point of view. The first part deals with the theology of the religious life; the second part addresses mystical theology. The book is treated by LUBAVITCH Chasidism with a respect that seems to verge on veneration.

tapuchim ('apples') Term applied to FINIALS, which sometimes have the form of the fruit.

Targumim ('translations') Name applied to various translations of biblical books into ARAMAIC. Their origin is thought to be in synagogal practice, when a vernacular translation was given in conjunction with the Hebrew reading to help the public understand the Hebrew words. Some of the Targumim adhere very closely to the actual words of the Hebrew and to what might be called their plain meaning, while others import a greater or lesser amount of explanatory material and even mini-sermons, but all of them represent an interpretation of what the Hebrew text means. The best-known Targum of the Torah is the one attributed to Onkelos (a shadowy figure of whom nothing is known). A straightforward, relatively unadorned rendering of the Hebrew, this became the favourite Targum for Babylonian Jews, and is still printed in many Bibles facing the Hebrew text. Jews in the West (Land of Israel and associated areas) used a variety of translations of the Torah, the best-known being the Targum Yerushalmi (Jerusalem Targum), often called Pseudo-Jonathan. A translation of the prophetic books is also named after Jonathan (of whom, again, nothing is known for certain). The various Targumim from the Land of Israel paraphrase the Hebrew and add explanations and even snippets of sermons. All the Targumim are based on a Hebrew text resembling the Masoretic text (*see* MASORETES), and show signs of rabbinic exegesis.

tas ('plate', 'tray') Silver shield or breastplate suspended on a chain from the staves of a closed Torah scroll, over the MANTLE.

tashlich ('you will throw') Folk ceremony, performed on the afternoon of NEW YEAR, when Jews go to water, preferably to a river or the sea where there are fish, and shake their clothes as if to cast off every trace of sin, while reciting appropriate biblical verses, such as Micah 7.18–20, which contains the words 'and you shall throw [tashlich] into the depths of the sea all their sins'. The origin of this practice is unknown, and there is no mention of it before the 15th century: it may represent a Jewish adaptation of a pagan ritual.

tattooing The practice of tattooing is understood as being forbidden in the Torah, at Leviticus 19.28: 'you shall not incise any marks upon yourselves'. The interpretation of the verse is unclear, because in the Hebrew a key word (ka'aka) is not found anywhere else and is of unknown meaning, and also because there is a reference to an inscription (ketóvet). The Mishnah (Makkot 3.6) insists that the prohibition only applies to writing that is pricked into the skin with some permanent dye. One rabbi goes so far as to insist that what is forbidden is the tattooing of the name of a pagan deity, because the verse of Leviticus ends 'I am the Lord'. Despite this, the halacha is considered to forbid tattooing in general, as a disfigurement of the body.

teba ('chest') Name preferred by Sefardi and oriental Jews for the raised reading desk in the synagogue. (Ashkenazim call it almémar or bima.)

tefilla *See* AMIDA.

tefillin (Aramaic) Phylacteries: leather boxes attached to the forehead and upper arm (near the heart) with leather straps during weekday morning prayers. The boxes contain handwritten parchment scrolls with four texts from the Torah: Exodus 13.1–10, 13.11–16; Deuteronomy 6.4–9, 11.13–21. These verses all speak of 'a sign on your arm and frontlets between your eyes'.

Tehillim ('psalms') Hebrew name of the biblical book of Psalms. Pronounced Tíllim by some Ashkenazim.

Teitelbaum, Joel *See* SATMAR.

teki'a Blast on the SHOFAR. The Hebrew term comes from a verb used in the Bible for sounding the shofar. It is thought to have a triumphant tone. In the sequences of shofar blasts laid down for NEW YEAR each short sequence begins and ends with a teki'a. The entire sequence ends with a 'great teki'a' (teki'a gedola). The same long-drawn-out sound ends the last service for the Day of ATONEMENT.

temple Building devoted to worship. The Bible mentions Israelite temples in various places, but by far the most important temple was the one built in Jerusalem (on the so-called Temple Mount) by King Solomon in the 10th century BCE and rebuilt some seventy years after being destroyed by the Babylonians in 586 BCE. This Second Temple was looted and desecrated by the Seleucid (Syrian Greek) army in 167 BCE and rededicated by JUDAH THE MACCABEE in 165. King Herod the Great rebuilt it in the style of his own day. It was destroyed by the Roman army in 70 CE, and was never rebuilt, although it is possible that sacrifices were held on the site during the BAR KOCHBA revolt and again after the Persian conquest in the early 7th century. An attempt by the Roman emperor Julian to rebuild it was thwarted by an earthquake in 363. After the Arab conquest a Muslim shrine (the Dome of the Rock) was built on the site. Jewish prayers and hymns contain many references to the hope for the rebuilding of the Temple and the restoration of sacrificial worship, and in the AMIDA God is blessed as 'the rebuilder of Jerusalem'. (Such hopes are generally omitted from modern Reform liturgies.) The Mishnah (particularly in tractate Middot) contains descriptions of the layout and ritual of the Temple, perhaps collected from surviving priests; these are preserved either out of sacred nostalgia or in the hope that some day the rituals may be restored. At some time the custom arose of praying at the Herodian retaining wall of the Temple Mount (the Western Wall, sometimes called the Wailing Wall), and Jews have retained the custom of facing towards the site of the Temple when praying, wherever in the world they may be.

Outside Jerusalem the only recorded attempt to build a temple and offer sacrifices since biblical times was at Leontopolis in Egypt, where émigré priests established a temple in Ptolemaic times; it was closed down by the Romans some three years after the destruction of the Jerusalem Temple. The term temple was re-introduced in Reform Judaism, beginning with the Hamburg Temple (founded 1817, dedicated 1818); this Continental European practice was followed in America, where it has been taken up by some Conservative congregations. It never caught on in Britain. *See also* PILGRIMAGE.

Temura ('exchange') Tractate of the Mishnah, Tosefta and Babylonian Talmud, in the order Kodashim, dealing with the transfer of sanctity from a sacrificial animal to an unsanctified animal.

Ten Commandments Precepts revealed by God to Moses at Sinai and engraved on two tables of stone. The text is preserved twice in the Torah, with different wording (Exodus 20.1–17, Deuteronomy 5.6–21). The expression 'ten commandments' is not found in the Torah, but we do find the phrase 'ten words' (Exodus 34.28), applied to a different (and according to some scholars an older) list (see also Deuteronomy 10.4). It is this phrase that has entered standard Jewish usage. The Ten Commandments are not considered by the commentators to be a self-contained legislation or a summary of the 613 COMMANDMENTS of the Torah. It is perhaps for fear that they might be understood as more important than the other commandments or as the only valid ones that the practice of reading them out in the liturgy was discontinued in the early Middle Ages. The Reform movement reinstituted the practice in modern times.

Ten Days of Penitence (in Hebrew, yamim nora'im, 'awesome days') The ten first days of the month of Tishri, beginning with NEW YEAR and ending on the Day of ATONEMENT. This is the last opportunity to make amends for sins of commission or omission in the hope of obtaining a favourable judgment before the heavenly ledgers are finally closed. Some rise early to recite penitential prayers, and read improving tracts. It is recommended to seek forgiveness from all those one may have wronged during the year just elapsed, so as to be able to concentrate one's efforts on atoning for sins against God. The synagogue liturgy of the Days of Penitence contains allusions to God's majesty and all-seeing justice.

ten plagues (of Egypt) (in Hebrew, éser makkot) Afflictions brought on the Egyptians by God in the Torah so as to induce Pharaoh to let the Israelites go (Exodus 3–12). They are, in order, the changing of the water of the Nile to blood, swarms of frogs, lice, wild beasts, an infection of the Egyptian livestock, an epidemic of boils, hail, locusts, darkness, and finally the killing of all the Egyptian firstborn. At the Passover SÉDER they are enumerated, and it is customary to spill a drop of wine, or wine mixed with water, as each one is mentioned.

Tenth of Tevet *See* TEVET.

terefa *See* DIETARY REGULATIONS.

teru'a ('blowing the shofar') Series of short notes on the SHOFAR, part of the sequence sounded at NEW YEAR. The festival is described in the Torah as a day of teru'a (Leviticus 23.24, Numbers 29.1).

Terumot ('heave offerings') Tractate of the Mishnah, Tosefta and Talmud Yerushalmi, in the order Zera'im, dealing with the rules concerning the heave offering that had to be given by Israelites to the priests out of the produce of the harvest, and by priests according to the Torah (Numbers 18.8–14, 25–32).

teshuva ('returning') Repentance. As the name suggests, teshuva is understood as a return to God, and it is a necessary preliminary to ATONEMENT. Biblical verses about returning therefore figure in the liturgy for the Day of Atonement, for example Hosea 14.2: 'Take with you words and return to the Lord', and Ezekiel 33.11: 'I have no pleasure in the death of the wicked, but that the wicked turn from his evil way and live.' *See also* BÁ'AL TESHUVA.

teshuvot *See* RESPONSA.

Tetragrammaton *See* INEFFABLE NAME.

Tevet Fourth month of the year counting from New Year; tenth counting from Passover, roughly corresponding to January. The month begins during CHANUKKA. The 10th of the month is a fast day, commemorating the beginning of the Babylonian siege of Jerusalem (see 2 Kings 25.1). According to tradition the 9th is the anniversary of the death of EZRA and the 20th that of MAIMONIDES.

tevila *See* IMMERSION.

Tevul Yom ('one who was immersed that day') Tractate of the Mishnah and Tosefta, in the order Tohorot, dealing with various laws of ritual impurity. The title of the tractate refers to the individual who, having incurred any impurity for which the Torah says 'he shall be unclean until evening', has undergone ritual immersion for the purpose of cleansing himself but must still wait for evening before being totally clean.

theodicy *See* HOLOCAUST THEOLOGY.

---

theology

Systematic study of belief in God and what it entails. The subject-matter of Jewish theology embraces the Jewish conception of God, how it has changed over the centuries, and what kinds of understanding of God are possible today. It is sometimes claimed that Judaism does not have a theology. This is demonstrably untrue if it is taken to mean that there is no theology within Jewish traditional texts. The classical texts – the Bible and the Talmud – are full of theological statements and reflections on God's nature and activities, even if these are not expressed in systematic form. Sources influenced by Greek-style philosophical thinking, however, do address theological issues in a systematic manner (see GOD; PHILOSOPHY). Perhaps what is meant by those who deny the place of theology in Judaism is not its existence but its centrality: unlike Christianity, Judaism is not constructed around theological claims (see DOGMA), and other issues, notably HALACHA, have tended to occupy a more central place within Jewish education.

The sources for the study of Jewish theology are diverse. First and foremost among the sources is the Bible, for several reasons. Even if many Jews can no longer accept that the Bible is literally revealed or inspired by God, it is held in such a high regard by most Jews that no other written text can approach it. Reference to biblical quotations provides, in effect, common ground to Jews who might disagree on virtually everything else. The rabbinic writings, although rich in theological materials, are less well known, particularly among Reform Jews. The classic works of medieval Jewish religious philosophy, such as the writings of SA'ADYA GA'ON, BACHYA IBN PAKUDA, MAIMONIDES, GERSONIDES, CRESCAS and ALBO, represent serious attempts to construct Jewish theological arguments, often in contradistinction to Islamic or Christian formulations. Often, however, they seem remote from contemporary concerns; the same is true of the kabbalistic and Chasidic writings such as the ZOHAR or the TANYA.

Perhaps the most influential source of theological beliefs today is the liturgy. The reason is obvious. A Jew does not need to make the effort to decide on a course of reading and carry it through, or need to decide between different approaches or schools. The liturgy is ready-made and very widely accepted, and it is sufficient to attend the synagogue week by week to absorb, almost without being aware of it, a large dose of theology. It is necessary to draw a distinction, though, between traditional liturgies, which have grown up over a very long period by a kind of sedimentary process without the active intervention of an editor, and modern liturgies, edited by individuals or more often by panels of rabbis, concerned to purge the text of theological ideas that have been discarded and to incorporate others that have been adopted. The traditional liturgies do not reject the biblical view of God. On the contrary, they take it very seriously and frequently quote from the Bible. They are fond of quoting from the three parts of the Bible – the Torah, Prophets and Writings – as though to stress their underlying unity. But they modify and even subvert the biblical view by juxtaposing with it beliefs from other sources, often of a philosophical or mystical character. Sometimes the result is faithful to the Bible, but at other times it is rather different from the image of God derived from a simple reading of the Bible (for an example see YOTSER).

This change is evidence of a sensitivity to theological issues, and a similar concern is found throughout the liturgy. The main beliefs identified by the philosophers are all put forward in the form of prayers and hymns (for an example see YIGDAL), combined in various ways and adorned with biblical allusions and proof texts, so that the worshipper comes to learn the principles themselves but also to think about them in depth.

Among modern thinkers, it is hard to say that rationalists, like MENDELSSOHN, FORMSTECHER, STEINHEIM or Samuel HIRSCH, made a permanent contribution to Jewish theology. Hermann COHEN, on the other hand, introduces a new era in Jewish reflection on God. He seems to draw a line under a period that was rich in publications but ultimately sterile, because its main concern was to demonstrate the congruence of Jewish with German culture. In Cohen's late writings we can witness, as it were, the Jew breaking through and demanding to be heard. One feature of Cohen's writing about God points clearly towards Jewish theology as it was to develop in the 20th century: his principle of correlation. God cannot be properly thought of without man, and man cannot properly be thought of without God. Consequently, despite the huge gulf that divides them, man and God are related to each other. God creates, and man is created; God reveals, and man receives the revelation; God redeems, man is redeemed. None of these events has any meaning if one of the two terms is removed.

Cohen served as a model and an inspiration to a younger generation of German Jews, and notably the leading German Jewish theologians of the 20th century, Leo BAECK, Franz ROSENZWEIG and Martin BUBER. There is a strong apologetic tendency in all three, as they try to demonstrate that Judaism is not either the monster or the ghost that it was often portrayed as by Christian authors. Unlike their 19th-century predecessors, they are not content to defend, but carry the war, as it were, into the enemy's camp. At the same time they introduced a strong element of encounter into discourse about God.

Buber was once asked if he believed in God. After a slight hesitation he said he did. Later he wondered if he had been truthful, and he drew this distinction: 'If belief in God means being able to speak of him in the third person, I do not believe in God. If belief in him means being able to speak to him, I do believe in God.' Nothing could encapsulate more succinctly the gap that separates Buber from his 19th-century forebears.

With Buber we seem to leap across the centuries of philosophizing to the biblical God who is not studied but encountered, albeit anthropomorphically. For most modern theologians the crucial point about God, in the Bible, throughout Jewish history, and in the lives of men and women today, is not that he exists in the abstract but that he is present in the life of the individual and the people.

Meanwhile, ideas that had been matured in Germany were translated into the language of America by men like Solomon SCHECHTER, who has been dubbed 'the theologian of the HISTORICAL SCHOOL', and the giants of American Reform Judaism, Kaufmann KOHLER and Emil G. HIRSCH. While Kohler, who in his youth had been a pupil of the German Orthodox leader Samson Raphael HIRSCH, retained an attachment to the ideals and rituals of Jewish tradition, his brother-in-law Emil Hirsch, whose father was the Liberal German thinker Samuel Hirsch, was an out-and-out rationalist. The Pittsburgh Conference of Reform Rabbis (1885) was dominated by Kohler, and the statement it issued, the celebrated PITTSBURGH PLATFORM, begins with a statement about what it calls, in unashamedly philosophical jargon, the 'God-idea':

We recognize in every religion an attempt to grasp the Infinite, and in every mode, source or book of revelation, held sacred in any religious system, the consciousness of the indwelling of God in man. We hold that Judaism presents the highest conception of the God-idea as taught in our Holy Scriptures and developed and spiritualized by the Jewish teachers, in accordance with the moral and philosophical progress of their respective ages. We maintain that Judaism preserved and defended, midst continual struggles and trials and under enforced isolation, this God-idea as the central religious truth for the human race.

While this statement is more concerned with asserting the place of Judaism alongside the other religions in a pluralistic society, it does also convey a certain position about the God of the Jews, which is intended to distance the Reform movement from two opposing extremes, ethical humanism on the one hand and Jewish PARTICULARISM on the other. At the same time it contains a strong hint that God is not so much a real if supernatural being as an idea that all sensitive humans share and to which Jews are open to an outstandingly high degree. Universalism rubs shoulders with pride in the Jewish heritage; philosophical theism marks a compromise between full-blooded faith and secularism tending to atheism.

In this approach can be seen the seeds of the fully formed naturalistic theology of Mordecai KAPLAN. The influential writings of Abraham Joshua HESCHEL, on the other hand, mark a return towards the theology of encounter associated with the generation of Buber and Baeck.

The Nazi Holocaust (*see* HOLOCAUST THEOLOGY) put paid to the confident belief in moral progress and universal human brotherhood characteristic of the Pittsburgh Platform and its age. It also raised again in an acute form and on a massive scale the most intractable conundrum in classical theology: how can a good and all-powerful God preside over a world in which such evil acts are committed? The enormity of the evil blocks attempts to think about it. As Arthur COHEN has put it: 'The death camps are a reality which, by their very nature, obliterate thought and the human programme of thinking.' It is not that the Holocaust put an end to belief in God for those who lived through it. On the contrary, an investigation conducted among survivors revealed not only that many had come through with their faith in God unimpaired, but that for some their faith was strengthened, while a significant minority who had previously been atheists found God in the camps. However, survivors and theologians alike have found it impossible to solve the riddle 'How could a God who is good and omnipotent let the Holocaust happen?' It has been pointed out that there is nothing inherently unique about the Nazi Holocaust: the same questions about God are raised by every single case of suffering. The biblical book of Job deals precisely with this issue. Nevertheless, whether because of the hugeness of its scale or for some other reason, the Holocaust seems to have cut short a very fertile period of Jewish theologizing that began in the early 19th century in Germany.

In the absence of real progress on the central issues of Jewish theology, there are many developments currently among special interest groups; some of these developments are attracting a great deal of interest, and will eventually feed into the mainstream. This has already begun to happen with FEMINISM. ECOLOGY is another area that has attracted interest latterly, exposing to the limelight older materials that had been forgotten or treated as marginal. The idea of God as creator and sustainer of the world is, of course, fundamental to classical theology, and there are many Talmudic and later rabbinic teachings on the subject of the proper human treatment of nature, but it is only recently that they have been brought together into a coherent argument in the framework of wider ecological concerns.

It would be misleading to end with the impression that theological discussion is at all widespread among Jews at the present time. The reasons for this neglect are manifold, and include not only the apparent predominance of secular and materialistic values and the continuing bewilderment resulting from the Holocaust, but also uncertainty arising from the PLURALISM which has become such a pronounced feature of contemporary Jewry. It is hard for the diverse religious denominations to find a common basis on which to begin to air their theological disagreements in a constructive spirit, and even harder for religious and secular Jews to approach each other in sophisticated debate about the place of God in Jewish life. If this analysis is correct, it is not the lack of topics for discussion that is the obstacle, but the lack of a common language.

theophany An appearance of God in visible form. God's self-revelation at SINAI is sometimes referred to as a theophany, but that is not quite accurate, as according to the Torah the Israelites heard a divine voice but saw no form. On the other hand, immediately afterwards God is said to have shown himself to Moses, Aaron, Aaron's sons Nadab and Abihu, and seventy of the elders of Israel: 'And they saw the God of Israel; under his feet there was, as it were, a sapphire pavement as pure as the sky itself' (Exodus 24.10). Yet a little later, when Moses asks to be allowed to see God's glory, he is told: 'You cannot see my face, for no human being can see me and live' (Exodus 33.20). Moses is allowed to see God's back (a theophany of sorts), but not his face (33.23). Other theophanies in the Bible are those of Isaiah ('I saw the Lord sitting on an exalted throne', 6.1) and Ezekiel ('upon the image of the throne was an image like that of a man above it … this was a vision of the image of the glory of the Lord', 1.26–8). The TARGUMIM and commentaries are keen to stress that none of these visions was an actual vision of the appearance of God. *See also* REVELATION.

Thirteen Attributes Characteristics of God mentioned in Exodus 34.6–7: The Lord, the Lord, God, merciful and gracious, long suffering, and abounding in kindness and truth; extending kindness to the thousandth generation, forgiving iniquity and transgression and sin, and clearing [the guilty]. (By the omission of two words at the end, the last attribute is turned from a negative into a positive one.) They are recited in the liturgy, particularly before the open ARK on festivals, and during the SELICHOT.

thirteen hermeneutical rules List of exegetical principles, attributed to Rabbi Ishmael (2nd century CE). An earlier list of seven rules is attributed to HILLEL, a century and a half earlier, and a later one of thirty-two rules to Rabbi Eliezer the son of Rabbi Yose the Galilean, in the generation after Ishmael. Ishmael's list has been incorporated in the morning service, and can be found in many prayer books.

Thirteen Principles List of fundamental Jewish beliefs compiled by MAIMONIDES and included in his commentary to Mishnah, Sanhedrin. They are (1) the existence of God, the creator of all things; (2) his absolute unity; (3) his incorporeality; (4) his eternity; (5) that he is the only object of worship; (6) the authenticity of prophecy; (7) that Moses is the greatest of the prophets; (8) that the Torah was revealed to Moses; (9) the immutability of the Torah; (10) God's omniscience and foreknowledge; (11) rewards and punishments; (12) the Messiah; (13) the resurrection of the dead. These principles are incorporated in prayer books in two forms, once as a 'creed', in which each article begins 'I believe with perfect faith', and once as a hymn (YIGDAL).

thirty-six just men Legendary group of righteous men whose virtue sustains the world. They are sometimes called lamed-vavniks, because the Hebrew letters lamed and vav stand for the number thirty-six. The basis of the idea is in a Talmudic saying that there are at least thirty-six truly righteous men at any time who are permitted to see God. According to the legend the thirty-six are people of humble background who do not know each other. In times of crisis they reveal themselves and save their people.

Tiberias (Teverya) Town on the western shore of the Sea of Galilee, considered one of the HOLY CITIES of the Land of Israel. It was an important centre of rabbinic scholarship from the 3rd century CE well into the Middle Ages. The Talmud Yerushalmi (*see* TALMUD) was edited there, as was the Masoretic text of the Bible. Moses MAIMONIDES was buried in Tiberias, and his tomb is still visited. The supposed tomb of YOCHANAN BEN ZAKKAI is nearby. At the hot springs a couple of miles to the south is the supposed tomb of Rabbi Meir the Miracle Worker (*see* HILLULA). In the 16th century the Ottoman sultan granted the town to a Jewish courtier, Don Joseph NASI, the Duke of Naxos, and many Jews settled there. A group of Chasidim arrived in the 1770s.

Tiféret ('beauty') In kabbala, one of the SEFIROT.

tik ('case') Cylindrical or polygonal hinged case of wood or metal in which the Torah scroll is kept and read in oriental communities.

---

tikkun

('repair') Healing or reparation of the imperfect world. In the LURIANIC KABBALA the term is applied to the reparation of the disruption caused by the breaking of the vessels (SHEVIRA). Reparation is achieved through the partsufim or configurations, which are different arrangements of the ten SEFIROT. The same process has to be applied within a series of four interlinked worlds, the World of Emanation, the World of Creation, the World of Formation, and the World of Action. The original breaking of the vessels was a cosmic event occurring, as it were, within the

Godhead long before the creation of our world, and Adam, the father of the whole human race, was intended to achieve the reclamation of the holy sparks and so restore the world to harmony. However, Adam by his disobedience not only failed to fulfil this task but precipitated a further disaster, a second breaking of the vessels. Adam's soul shattered, and a spark of it is trapped within each of his descendants. A third catastrophe occurred during the giving of the Torah at Mount Sinai, which was potentially a further opportunity to set the realm of the Sefirot to rights, when the people rebelliously worshipped a golden calf (Exodus 32–3). After this new disruption there is no other opportunity to restore harmony in a single act, but tikkun is a matter of piecemeal, step-by-step restoration which will only be completed in the messianic age.

Every individual Jew now has the personal duty to share in the task of restoring cosmic harmony by avoiding evil and doing good and thereby releasing the holy sparks from the demonic realm of the 'husks' (KELIPPOT) and enabling them to fly upwards to share in the reparation of the Sefirotic realm. In addition, since the second disaster, each human being has its own soul, a fragment of the soul of Adam, which needs to be perfected and reclaimed. A burden of active responsibility thus falls upon the individual.

The early Chasidim seized on the Lurianic concept of tikkun and made it even more the responsibility of the individual by shifting the focus from the cosmos to the soul of each person. 'Breaking' and 'repair' can become psychological concepts, and in the thought of some Chasidic masters the repair is considered so valuable that it is possible to say that the breaking only happened for the sake of the repair. CHASIDISM attaches a very high value to ethical and pious behaviour, through which the Chasid can raise up his own sparks, and achieve closeness to God. There is also, however, a strong tendency in Chasidism for individuals to attempt to improve themselves not so much through study and knowledge as through contact with, and imitation of, a charismatic leader, the tsaddik or REBBE, without whose mediation they are unable to lift up the sparks. Chasidism thus represents a radical and unique development of the concepts of the Lurianic kabbala, which, in their revised form, reached a huge new Jewish public and are still influential in some circles today.

The philosopher Emil FACKENHEIM projects a different, this-worldly, image of tikkun in his book *To Mend the World* (1982). The Holocaust disrupts and challenges our understanding of God and of history, yet somehow demands what may seem impossible: 'A Tikkun, here and now, is mandatory for a Tikkun, there and then, was actual. It is true that because a Tikkun of that rupture is impossible we cannot live, after the Holocaust, as men and women have lived before. However, if the impossible Tikkun were not also necessary, and hence possible, we could not live at all.' Fackenheim rejects the possibility of applying the kabbalistic concept of repair by means of obedience to the mitsvot to the post-Holocaust world. The Nazis killed the kabbalists, and their tikkun died with them. After the Holocaust a new point of departure is needed, and Fackenheim finds it in the state of Israel, a miraculous rebirth which offers new hope in the midst of total chaos.

There is little if anything left of the transcendent element in Fackenheim's version of tikkun.

The same is true of the sense in which the term tikkun is commonly used in Jewish youth and renewal movements today, where it refers to concrete ecological objectives, recycling, planting trees, using renewable forms of energy, as well as working for social justice. This is a purely this-worldly vision of tikkun which totally ignores its kabbalistic history. Both ecological and social reformers, in taking action to repair real damage, seem to be embodying a certain religious ideal in a practical way that can be attractive to young Jews to whom talk of the realms of the Sefirot and ADAM KADMON might seem mere mumbo jumbo.

The term tikkun is also applied to an anthology of readings for nocturnal vigils preceding certain festivals (see next entries).

tikkun chatsot ('midnight preparation') Midnight prayers, instituted by the kabbalists of SAFED in the 16th century. They are intended to commemorate the destruction of the Temple, and include certain psalms, as well as petitions and lamentations.

tikkun leil Hoshána Rabba ('preparation for the night of Hoshána Rabba') Cycle of texts recited by very pious Jews on the night of HOSHÁNA RABBA. They include the entire biblical books of Deuteronomy and Psalms.

tikkun leil Shavuot ('preparation for the night of Shavuot') Cycle of texts recited by very pious Jews on the first night of SHAVUOT. They include the enumeration of the 613 COMMANDMENTS as well as the Song of Songs.

tikkun soferím ('correction of the scribes') **1** One of a number of corrections of the Hebrew text of the Bible believed by the rabbis to have been introduced by the ancient scribes (see SOFER). **2** An unvocalized copy of the Torah, often a facsimile of the Torah scroll printed in book form, used to practise the Torah reading.

Tiktin, Solomon *See* GEIGER–TIKTIN AFFAIR.

Tíllim *See* TEHILLIM.

tish (Yiddish, 'table') **1** A Chasidic gathering at the table of the REBBE, usually on Friday or Saturday evening. The rebbe generally delivers a discourse and blesses people, and may distribute portions of his food. **2** The 'groom's table' preceding a wedding. It is a custom among some Ashkenazim for men to gather around a table while the bridegroom says some words of Torah, often interrupted with jokes, toasts and singing.

Tish'a be-Av ('9th of Av') Day of mourning for the destruction of the First and Second TEMPLES. According to the Talmud (Bavli, Ta'anit 29a) both were destroyed on this date. Various other calamities are said to have taken place on this date. The day is observed with a twenty-four-hour fast, from sunset to sunset. In synagogue the book of LAMENTATIONS is read (in some communities the book of Job as well), and kinot (see KINA) are recited. According to an old legend, the MESSIAH was born on the day the Temple was destroyed. SHABBETAI TSEVÍ is believed to have been born on the 9th of Av, and his followers observe it as a feast day. Karaites observe the fast on the 10th, the actual date of the burning of the Second Temple, and the date of the destruction of the First Temple according to Jeremiah 52.12.

Tishri or **Tishrei** First month of the year counting from New Year; seventh counting from Passover. It corresponds roughly to October. The New Moon of Tishri is NEW YEAR, and the first ten days are known as the TEN DAYS OF PENITENCE, concluding with the Day of ATONEMENT on the 10th. The festival of SUKKOT begins on the 15th, and SHEMINI ATSÉRET falls on the 22nd. *See also* FAST OF GEDALIAH; SIMCHAT TORA.

tithes Tenth part of one's annual income, set apart for a particular purpose. The system of tithing is laid down in the Torah and discussed in the Talmud, but is no longer in use. It was considered obligatory only in the Land of Israel, where a symbolic and voluntary equivalent has been instituted in the traditionalist community. *See* DEMAI; MA'ASER SHENI; MA'ASEROT; PE'A; TERUMOT.

tizku le-shanim rabbot ('may you be found worthy to [enjoy] many years') Greeting used by Sefardim at New Year and other festivals.

Tohorot ('purities') **1** Sixth order of the Mishnah and Tosefta, dealing with laws of ritual impurity and purification rituals. Tractate NIDDA has a GEMARA in both Talmuds, otherwise Talmudic discussion is lacking in this order. **2** Tractate of the Mishnah and Tosefta, in the order Tohorot, dealing with the susceptibility of foods to ritual impurity.

Tora im dérech érets ('Torah with the way of the world') Slogan of modern ORTHODOXY, encouraging the study of Judaism together with general studies. The origin of the phrase is in Mishnah Avot 2.2, where it is understood to mean 'study of Torah combined with gainful employment'. Samson Raphael HIRSCH employed it in a different sense: in an age in which young Jews felt faced with a stark choice between Jewish education in a YESHIVA and enrolling in a university, he encouraged them to combine the two, as he himself had done. The phrase became a shibboleth of Orthodoxy.

Tora le-Moshe mi-Sinai ('Torah [given] to Moses from [God at] Sinai) Term applied in rabbinic tradition to laws not stated explicitly in scripture but considered to have the status of biblical law.

Tora lishmah ('Torah for its own sake') Pursuit of Torah-study for no ulterior purpose. Disinterested study is highly praised by the rabbis. 'He who occupies himself in the study of Torah for its own sake merits many things – in fact he deserves the whole world' (Mishnah, Avot 6.1). The Talmud comments that if one studies Torah for its own sake it becomes an elixir of life, but if one studies it for some other purpose it becomes a deadly poison (Bavli, Ta'anit 7a). The possibility is envisaged, however, that one may begin by studying from some other motive and end up doing it for its own sake (Bavli, Pesachim 50b).

Tora min ha-Shamáyim ('Torah from Heaven [i.e. from God]') Phrase denoting the doctrine that God's will is revealed in the Torah. Based in the REVELATION at SINAI, the doctrine embraces not only the words of the written Torah but the ORAL TORAH as well. The doctrine is formulated as follows by MAIMONIDES in his THIRTEEN PRINCIPLES: 'The eighth principle of faith: that the Torah has been revealed from Heaven. This denotes our belief that the whole of the Torah in our possession today is the one that was transmitted to Moses and that it is all of divine origin ...' This view has come under heavy attack in modern times. Biblical criticism undermined the traditional view of the unity of the written Torah and showed that it was made up of elements produced at different times and from different points of view. The scholars of the HISTORICAL SCHOOL demonstrated that the oral Torah had a historical development, and indeed that the doctrine of Tora min ha-Shamáyim itself came at the end of a long process of evolution.

See also HERESY.

Torah ('teaching') Collective term for the teachings, used in a spectrum of specific meanings, ranging from the most concrete and narrow (the first five books of the BIBLE) to the widest and most abstract, in which it is virtually synonymous with the content of Judaism as a whole. In its narrower meanings Torah is sometimes translated as 'law', a translation based on Christian usage and ultimately on the ancient Greek translation of the Torah. This is, however, a misleading translation since Torah includes a great deal of non-legal material (*see* AGGADA).

Rabbinic Judaism includes both the WRITTEN TORAH and the ORAL TORAH under the heading of Torah. The Torah is seen as the most precious gift given by God to Israel as a seal of the COVENANT. There are many references to it in the liturgy of the synagogue. Yet, while Jews are enjoined to love the Torah, it is never an object of worship. Two of the THIRTEEN PRINCIPLES of the Jewish faith formulated by MAIMONIDES refer to the Torah. The eighth asserts that it comes from God (*see* TORA MIN HA-SHAMÁYIM); the ninth that it is immutable: 'The ninth principle: the abrogation of the Torah. This means that the Torah will not be abrogated and that no other Torah will come from God. Nothing is to be added to it or taken away from it, either of the written or of the oral Torah, as it is said [Deuteronomy 13.1]: You shall not add to it or subtract from it.' Maimonides' main concern here is to rebut the claims of Christianity and Islam to have received a new revelation supplanting the older one. Both these principles are difficult for many modern Jews to subscribe to if taken literally.

See also CHUMMASH; REVELATION; SÉFER TORA; TORAH READING.

Torah reading (in Hebrew, keriat ha-tora) Reading from the Torah scroll, in the presence of a MINYAN, in the synagogue. The Torah is divided up into sections (each known as a parasha among Sefardim or among Ashkenazim as a sidra), and one of them is read each week at the Sabbath morning service, so that the whole Torah is read in the space of a year. Some additional readings are inserted on special occasions. In addition the beginning of the reading for the following Sabbath is read on Sabbath afternoon, Monday and Thursday. Special readings are prescribed for festivals, ROSH CHÓDESH, fast days, CHANUKKA and PURIM. The ark is opened and a SÉFER TORA (or two, exceptionally three, depending on the number of readings prescribed for the day) is removed. The scroll is carried in procession round the synagogue, and taken to the reading desk, where its ornaments and covering are removed. It is then unrolled a little and held up so that the congregation can see the written words. (The Sefardi custom is to display it before the reading; Ashkenazim do it afterwards instead.) Members of the congregation are 'called up' by their Hebrew names, beginning with a priest and a LEVITE if any are present. It is considered an honour to be called up. Each section is divided into shorter readings according to the number of people to be called up (see PARASHA). The person called up recites a blessing before and after the reading. In Reform and Liberal synagogues only a short portion of each sidra is read. After the conclusion of the Torah reading the scroll is rolled up and 'dressed'. A short portion from the prophetic books (HAFTARA) is then read. Special prayers are then said, for the congregation, for the state and its government, for the state of Israel, and before each new month for blessings during the coming month. The scroll is then processed once more round the synagogue and replaced in the ARK. See also ALIYYA.

Tortosa Disputation See ALBO, JOSEPH.

tosafists Authors of the TOSAFOT. The first tosafists are thought to have been the grandsons of RASHI, whose commentary on the Talmud is often the starting point for their comments. Some scholars claim to have detected the influence of contemporary Christian scholarship on their aims and methods. See also MEIR OF ROTHENBURG.

tosafot ('additions') Annotations (CHIDDUSHIM) to the Babylonian Talmud written in northern France and Germany between the 12th and 14th centuries. They are printed in standard editions of the Talmud, together with RASHI'S commentary, which they complement.

Tosefta (Aramaic, 'addition') Compilation of Tannaitic teachings (see TANNA'IM), closely related to the MISHNAH. Some specialists believe that the name should be read as Tosefata (additions, in the plural); in places the work reads like a supplement to the Mishnah, expanding or commenting on it. Opinions as to the dating of the work vary widely; some believe it was compiled soon after the Mishnah, others that it was made up to three or four centuries later.

---

traditionalism

Trend (sometimes called, misleadingly, 'ultra-Orthodoxy') characterized by the attempt to exclude new external influences on Judaism, and to preserve, so far as possible, the values and practices which prevailed in the late medieval period. The emphasis is on practice, and on the study of the Talmud and the great legal codes. The importance of tradition is not so much that it confers authority in itself, but rather that it guarantees the authentic transmission of the divine revelation. Traditionalists commonly describe themselves as 'Torah-true', meaning that they are the true custodians of the divinely given commandments. Traditionalism tends to be deeply suspicious of any knowledge or belief explicitly originating outside the tradition, and this suspicion may extend to long-established elements such as medieval Jewish philosophy. Modern philosophical and political ideas are particularly suspect.

The Jewish communities of the Middle Ages were essentially self-governing entities, with relatively little social, cultural or religious contact with their environment; the various communities were attached to each other in a far-flung network. The rabbis were the guardians of the religious norms and traditions, and they issued rulings on questions affecting individuals or the community as a whole. In determining points of law the chief authority was the Babylonian Talmud, as interpreted and made more relevant in a large and constantly growing body of halachic literature. The leaders of the community enjoyed various sanctions, and in the last resort could expel those who flouted their authority from the community (see CHÉREM). In these circumstances tradition was universally respected, change was slow, the ultimate objective of education was to train worthy rabbis, and the profession of rabbi was honoured.

In eastern Europe in the 18th century a major shock was delivered to the old system by CHASIDISM, which challenged not only the authority of the rabbis, but their whole system of values. However, as a successful Chasidic movement found itself in the position of the Jewish establishment all over Poland and even further afield, and as its leaders themselves confronted the challenge of the HASKALA, it became less radical in its stance, and from ridiculing Talmudic casuistry it began to concern itself with punctilious observance of the halacha. In the late 19th century, Chasidim were strong supporters of the MACHZIKEI HADAS, who are nowadays considered to be among the most staunchly traditionalist of Jews, and today Chasidim consider themselves and are considered by others to belong firmly in the traditionalist, CHAREDI camp, together with MITNAGGEDIM. (See also AGUDAT ISRAEL.)

The massive emigration of Jews from eastern Europe since 1880, coupled with the Nazi genocide in Europe, have had the dual effect of destroying the old centres of traditional Judaism and of spreading it to new places, particularly in the United States and Israel, which are by far the largest centres of Jewish population today. Those immigrants who were most resolutely attached to the traditional style of Jewish life created their own communities where they could live in self-imposed isolation from the threats posed by the modern world, while others joined existing communities, on which they gradually came to exert a marked influence. The characteristic and most important institution of traditionalist Judaism is the YESHIVA, with its focus on study of the Talmud read as an authoritative guide to Jewish living today.

Charedi traditionalism is a product of the Ashkenazi, specifically the eastern European, world. (In central and western Europe various forms of MODERNISM became dominant.) The history of the Sefardi communities of North Africa and the Middle East in their encounter with the modern world was completely different. While many Sefardi intellectuals, and even rabbis, were fascinated by the new ideas coming in from France, Italy and elsewhere, there was not the same polarization and conflict that divided the Ashkenazim. The Sefardi world was never divided into opposing camps like conflicting adherents of Haskala and religion, Chasidim and Mitnaggedim, modernists and traditionalists. On the contrary, successive waves of foreign influence have tended to enrich the tradition rather than challenge and unsettle it.

In Israel, however, the unique position of the Sefardi community has gradually led it to adopt its own form of neo-traditionalism, to some extent modelled on and influenced by its Ashkenazi counterpart but also nourished by elements of the Sefardi tradition such as a strong attachment to the mystical sources of Judaism, which among Ashkenazim is more or less confined to the Chasidim. Up to the end of World War I, under Ottoman rule, Sefardim constituted the backbone of the Jewish presence in the Land of Israel. Deeply pious and traditional, they clustered around the holy places of Jerusalem, Hebron and Galilee, of which they considered themselves the custodians. They were not immune to the influence of outside ideas, however, and a yeshiva named Porat Yosef was set up in Jerusalem, providing a new style of intellectual religious leadership for Sefardim not only in Israel but in the Diaspora as well. Under British rule immigration from Europe dramatically altered the numerical balance of Ashkenazim and Sefardim, but after independence in 1948 mass immigration from Arab countries brought in large numbers of Jews who were relatively untouched by the encounter with religious and secular Zionism and with Western ideas. They were also socially disadvantaged, and after a difficult period of adjustment they began to clamour for recognition of their own cultural identity, a demand that found vigorous expression in the 'Black Panther' movement of the 1960s and 70s. The waves of social and spiritual renewal converged in political activism under the leadership of rabbis and former yeshiva students, of which the most visible manifestation is the religious political party named Shas.

Traditionalism, in the sense just discussed, is different from traditional Judaism, meaning a practice unselfconsciously continued from generation to generation, such as one can still find in parts of North Africa, for example. It is of the essence of traditionalism that it consciously cultivates tradition, in the face of perceived threats from the forces of modernity, and even on occasion reinvents it.

transmigration of souls *See* GILGUL.

Tresar (Aramaic, 'twelve') Collective designation of the TWELVE MINOR PROPHETS.

trust *See* FAITH.

tsaddik *See* REBBE.

tsedaka ('righteousness') In the Bible, a term referring to any kind of righteous behaviour; in rabbinic and medieval Hebrew it is limited to almsgiving. The etymology is a reminder that the relief of poverty is not a choice but an obligation binding on those better off (see Deuteronomy 15.9–11). MAIMONIDES, in his code, insists that anyone who can afford to do so must give to the poor according to their needs, beginning with members of one's own family, then to one's townspeople, and finally to those from other towns. Charity should be given cheerfully and willingly; anyone who gives grudgingly, with a surly face, nullifies the merit of his giving. He distinguishes eight degrees of charitable giving, the highest being that aimed at making the recipient self-supporting, so that he is no longer reliant on charity.

tsédek *See* RIGHTEOUSNESS.

Tsefania Hebrew name of the biblical book of ZEPHANIAH.

Tsefát *See* SAFED.

tseni'ut *See* MODESTY.

tserufim ('combinations') System of kabbalistic meditation on letter-combinations. It derives from an earlier tradition associated particularly with Abraham ABULAFIA, whose 'prophetic kabbala' offered various techniques to aid the ascent of the soul.

Tseva'ot NAME OF GOD. It is derived from the biblical expression Adonai Tseva'ot, often translated 'Lord of Hosts' (in the sense 'Lord of Armies'), and perhaps referring to God's supremacy over the stars and the powers of heaven. The phrase can also be understood as a name, the Lord Tseva'ot. It is listed in the Talmud as one of seven divine names that are so holy they must not be erased (Bavli, Shevu'ot 35a).

tsimtsum ('contraction') A key component in LURIANIC KABBALA. Whereas in earlier kabbala everything proceeds from the EIN SOF in a relatively orderly and consistent process of emanation and creation, the Lurianic system introduces a number of complications and changes of course, of which the most important are conveyed through the images of tsimtsum and SHEVIRA. The idea of tsimtsum arises from the difficulty that the very infinity of the Ein Sof appears to allow no room for creation. Accordingly in the Lurianic system the very first event is a contraction of the Godhead into itself, as it were, leaving a kind of vacuum in which the world can come into being. This drastic revision of earlier theory, important though it is within the content of kabbala, remains in the domain of the speculative, and its main effect is to remove the taint of PANTHEISM, which in many people's minds attached to kabbala, by establishing a clear division between the infinite God and the finite world.

tsitsit ('fringe') Fringes or tassels attached to the four corners of garments. The Torah commands that such fringes be worn on the hems (Numbers 15.38) or corners (Deuteronomy 22.12) of garments. Today this commandment is observed in two ways, in the TALLIT or tallet, worn during prayer, and the arba'a kanfot (four corners) or tallit katan (lesser tallit) worn all day. This is a four-cornered garment resembling a small scapular, with a hole for the head, worn by men and boys usually beneath the outer clothing. They often contrive to make the tsitsit visible; some go so far as to wear the whole garment outside the outer clothing so as to leave no doubt that they are fulfilling the commandment. Most Jews seem to have abandoned this traditional practice, whereas the wearing of the tallit is gaining ground.

Tu be-Av ('15th of Av') Ancient festive day, when according to the Talmud young women danced in the vineyards wearing white robes, in the hope of finding a husband. Sadly, this practice has fallen into abeyance. Today the day is marked only by the minor liturgical detail of omitting TACHANUN. In Israel there has been an attempt by secular Zionists to celebrate it as an equivalent of St Valentine's Day.

Tu bi-Shevát ('15th of Shevát') A joyful day of uncertain origin. TACHANUN is not said on this day, which according to the opinion of the school of HILLEL was once the 'birthday' of trees, for the purpose of tithing and 'uncircumcision' (*see* ORLA). In the 17th century, under the influence of the kabbalists of SAFED, it became customary to eat different kinds of fruit, particularly those mentioned in the Bible as growing in the Land of Israel. In 1753 an elaborate ritual for eating these fruits was published in Salonica, and its rules are followed by Jews originating in the former Ottoman empire. The Zionists took advantage of these various associations to make the day a time for schoolchildren to plant trees.

Tudesco (from Spanish Tedesco, 'German') In Western Sefardi usage, an ASHKENAZI.

tuma *See* IMPURITY.

tumtum *See* GENDER.

Twelve Minor Prophets Twelve biblical books (Hosea, Joel, Amos, Obadiah, Jonah, Micah, Nahum, Habakkuk, Zephaniah, Haggai, Zechariah, Malachi) included among the Latter Prophets. The term 'minor' does not refer to their importance but simply to their length. These twelve short books were gathered together into a single scroll in order to ensure their preservation. They are known collectively as 'The Twelve' (Tresar). (*See table*, 'The Books of the Bible', p. 37.)

two powers *See* DUALISM.

U-netánne tókef ('we evoke the solemn holiness of this day') Hymn recited in the Ashkenazi and Italian rites during the additional service of the Day of ATONEMENT. It was composed under the Byzantine empire, although legend associates it with a martyr rabbi named Amnon of Mainz, who, after being tortured during the Crusades, was carried dying into the synagogue and expired while reciting this prayer. It is a graphic and haunting evocation of divine judgment:

> We evoke the solemn holiness of this day, for it is a day of awe and terror. On it your dominion is exalted, your throne is established with love, and you sit upon it with truth. Truly you are the only judge, arbiter and all-knowing witness, you inscribe and seal, you enumerate and reckon, you recall all that is forgotten, you open the book of memorial and it recites itself, and the seal of every human hand is upon it. A great shofar is sounded, a still small voice is heard, the angels are dismayed, seized with fear and trembling, and they say, 'This is the Day of Judgment: the army of heaven is to be inspected and judged.' For even they cannot be justified in your judgment. As for dwellers on earth, you pass them all before you in their ranks. As a shepherd inspects his flock, passing them beneath his crook, so do you pass and count and reckon, inspecting every living soul, determining the measure of every created being, and writing down their decreed sentence. On New Year it is inscribed, and on the fast of the Day of Atonement it is sealed: how many shall pass away and how many shall be created; who shall live and who shall die, who at his appointed time, and who before it, who by fire and who by water, who by the sword and who by the wild beast, who by hunger and who by thirst, who by earthquake and who by plague, who by strangling and who by stoning, who shall have rest and who shall roam, who shall be calm and who shall be tormented, who shall be tranquil and who shall be afflicted, who shall become poor and who shall become rich, who shall be brought low and who shall be raised up. But penitence, prayer and charity may avert the severity of the sentence.

Uktsin ('stalks') Tractate of the Mishnah and Tosefta, in the order Tohorot, dealing mainly with the transmission of ritual impurity from impure parts of a plant to the rest of the plant.

ultra-Orthodoxy *See* TRADITIONALISM.

Union for Reform Judaism Association of Reform congregations, founded in 1873 by Isaac Mayer WISE as the Union of American Hebrew Congregations (UAHC). The name was changed in 2003, partly in recognition of the failure of Wise's ambition of creating a non-denominational association, and partly to acknowledge that some member-congregations were outside the United States. The UAHC created and has a continuing care for the HEBREW UNION COLLEGE, and has a broad concern with Jewish education. Rabbis of member organizations of URJ belong to the CENTRAL CONFERENCE OF AMERICAN RABBIS.

Union for Traditional Judaism Religious movement that broke away from the American Conservative movement in 1990, following the latter's decision to train women for the rabbinate. It sees itself as non-denominational, and as working to encourage traditional observance among all Jews. The UTJ accepts critical methods in the study of sacred texts, but rejects CONSERVATIVE JUDAISM's belief that its rabbinate has authority to reinterpret or even set aside traditional HALACHA in the light of contemporary circumstances. The Metivta, its rabbinical school, does not ordain women as rabbis, but offers study programmes for men and women that do not lead to ordination.

Union of American Hebrew Congregations *See* UNION FOR REFORM JUDAISM.

Union of Orthodox Jewish Congregations of America Association of Orthodox synagogues in the United States and Canada, also known as the Orthodox Union (OU). It was founded in 1898 during a period of mass immigration from eastern Europe, by leaders of the JEWISH THEOLOGICAL SEMINARY OF AMERICA. It grew slowly until the 1950s, when membership began to increase substantially. Today it plays an important role in certifying KOSHER food products.

Union of Orthodox Rabbis of the United States and Canada Union of traditionalist (CHAREDI) rabbis, also known as Agudas Harabbonim, founded in 1902.

Union of Sephardic Congregations Organization founded in New York in 1929 to promote the religious interests of SEFARDIM.

union with God *See* DEVEKUT.

United Synagogue London association of Orthodox synagogues, with affiliates elsewhere in Britain, constituted by Act of Parliament in 1870.

United Synagogue of Conservative Judaism American congregational association, formerly known as the United Synagogue of America, founded in 1913 by Solomon SCHECHTER.

universalism
Outlook that values the human race as a whole above any single one of its components, including the Jewish people. It is opposed to PARTICULARISM or nationalism. The fact that the Bible begins with the creation of the world and humanity instead of the beginnings of the people of Israel appears to lend support to the universalist position. A rabbinic teaching cited in the Mishnah (Sanhedrin 4.5) says: 'The fact that [in the Bible] one man was created [rather than separate

founders of each nation] teaches us that none of us can say to another: 'My father was greater than your father.' The Bible is full of reminders to the Jews that their God is the God of all the nations. '"You Israelites, are you not just like the Ethiopians to me?" says the Lord. "Just as I brought Israel out of Egypt, did I not bring the Philistines out of Caphtor and the Arameans out of Kir?"' (Amos 9.7). The biblical book that expresses this universal vision most powerfully is Isaiah. There is only one God for all humankind, and even if they do not recognize him now they will at a future time:

> I am the Lord, there is no other;
> there is no god besides me.
> I will strengthen you, although you have not known me,
> so that men from the rising and the setting sun
> may know that there is none but me. (45.6)

The same idea is expressed in the prayers. In the Ashkenazi liturgy the strongly particularistic ALÉYNU prayer is immediately followed and, so to speak, neutralized, by a more universal vision. The first prayer says: 'It is our duty to praise the Lord of all things, to magnify the Author of creation, who has not made us like the nations of the lands, nor placed us like the families of the world, who has not made our portion like theirs nor our destiny like that of their multitude.' And the second: 'Therefore we hope in you, Lord our God, that we may soon behold your glorious might, when you remove paganism from the earth and idolatry is uprooted, when the world is set to rights under the kingdom of Shaddai and all mankind call on your name, and all the wicked of the earth are turned towards you. All the inhabitants of the world shall realize and know that it is to you that every knee must bend and every tongue swear loyalty.'

In this vision, God is the Lord of all humankind, even if his rule cannot be said to be established until all people acknowledge him as God. This is a rather different idea from the one found in many sources, that the universal God chose the Jews to be his special people, and gave them the commands contained in the Torah, but that he gave the non-Jews a simplified law code with only seven laws in it. A Gentile who obeys all of these NOACHIAN COMMANDMENTS is as 'good' as a Jew who obeys all 613 COMMANDMENTS of the Torah.

The ENLIGHTENMENT led to deep embarrassment or impatience with Jewish particularism, and at that time the universalistic side of Judaism was seen as a useful counterbalance to it. For Moses MENDELSSOHN, for example, Judaism has always consisted of three elements: general truths, historical truths and commandments. The second and third categories belong to the Jews as a nation, but the general truths are not revealed by God to the Jews alone, but to all rational beings: 'Their effect is as universal as the salutary influence of the sun'.

Mendelssohn and other Enlightenment thinkers insisted that Judaism does not teach that only Jews can be saved. A later German philosopher, Hermann COHEN, quoted with approval MAIMONIDES' statement that the righteous from among the nations have a share in the Coming Age (OLAM HA-BA). Cohen agreed with Mendelssohn in seeing no contradiction between Judaism and the universal religion of reason. He believed that humanity, in the modern era of the nation-state, was being drawn ever closer together and developing towards overcoming national differences, and he identified this universal vision with that of the biblical prophets. He did not define the Jews as a 'nation' (a term he reserved for the citizens of a nation-state) but a 'nationality', a purely ethnic group held together by its religion. The Jews long ago abandoned their statehood, thus pointing toward the supranational future of mankind. As a Jew, Cohen felt at home in the culture of modern Germany, which he saw as being close to the outlook of the prophets.

We may compare the statement of the so-called 'Protest Rabbis' (PROTESTRABBI-NER) who united in 1897 to oppose the holding of the first Zionist Congress on German soil: 'We comprise a separate community solely in respect of religion. With regard to nationality, we feel totally at one with our fellow Germans, and therefore we strive towards the realization of the spiritual and moral goals of our dear fatherland with an enthusiasm equalling theirs. History made its decision eighteen hundred years ago about Jewish nationhood through the dissolution of the Jewish state and the destruction of the Temple.'

In other words, although the universal vision of the prophets is perfectly compatible with the idea of the national destiny of the Jews, once this national destiny came to be identified in the modern period as a political one, culminating later in the creation of a specifically Jewish nation-state, some universalists came to see the two as standing in opposition to each other. This attitude is often associated with LIBERAL JUDAISM, although it is not confined to it. The 'Protest Rabbis' included both Liberal and ORTHODOX rabbis. The father of German Orthodoxy, Samson Raphael HIRSCH, was opposed to expressions of Jewish nationalism, and declared that 'the more the Jew is a Jew, the more universalist will his views and aspirations be, the more joyfully will he seize every opportunity to give proof of his mission as a Jew, the task of his Judaism, on new and untrodden ground, the more joyfully will he devote himself to all true progress in civilization and culture.'

In America the REFORM rabbis in 1885 firmly rejected the claims of nationalism in the PITTSBURGH PLATFORM: 'We recognize in the modern era of universal culture of heart and intellect the approach of the realization of Israel's great messianic hope for the establishment of the kingdom of truth, justice and peace among all men. We consider ourselves no longer a nation but a religious community, and therefore expect neither a return to Palestine, nor a sacrificial worship under the administration of the sons of Aaron, nor the restoration of any of the laws concerning the Jewish state.'

This is an explicit rejection of ZIONISM, as well as a rebuttal of any imputation of dual loyalties. Both Reform and Orthodox Judaism were associated for a long time with anti-Zionism, which was very widespread among middle-class Jews in the West. Since the Holocaust this is no longer the case, and declared anti-Zionism is relatively rare (but *see* POST-ZIONISM).

Universalist opposition to Jewish nationalism took a different form at the same period among Jewish socialists. In its most extreme form, it asserted a strong faith in the brotherhood of all people. Rosa Luxemburg, for example, wrote to a friend: 'I have no separate corner in my heart for the ghetto: I feel at home in the entire world wherever there are clouds and birds and human tears.' Others found it harder to abandon the idea of the nation entirely. Especially in Russia, where anti-Jewish feelings were strong even among socialists, many Jewish socialists felt that it was essential to combine the maintenance of the idea of Jewish nationality with the pursuit of socialist goals. In fact, Jewish universalism has always maintained a sense of the distinctive existence of the Jewish people.

ushpizin (Aramaic, from Latin hospites, 'guests') The biblical heroes Abraham, Isaac, Jacob, Joseph, Moses, Aaron and David, whose presence is welcomed into the SUKKA on successive evenings of the festival of SUKKOT with elaborate greetings composed by Isaac LURIA.

V

váchnacht (Yiddish, 'night vigil') Among Ashkenazim, name given to the night before a circumcision. Relatives gather to recite psalms, and in some communities it is customary to hold a festive meal.

Vayikra ('and he called') Hebrew name of the biblical book of Leviticus, of which it is the first word.

Verein für Kultur und Wissenschaft der Juden *See* WISSENSCHAFT DES JUDENTUMS.

vernacular prayer The language of prayer has been a hotly debated issue. The Talmud allows prayers to be said in any language, but throughout the Middle Ages it was universally accepted that the only language suitable for most public prayer was Hebrew. Some German Reformers at the beginning of the 19th century promoted prayer in German, seeing in the Hebrew language an obstacle to understanding and therefore to true spirituality, and also a barrier between Jew and Gentile. Even Orthodox modernists favoured a greater understanding of the prayers, and printed the prayer book with a facing translation. The leading reformer Abraham GEIGER was ambivalent. He referred to Hebrew as a 'foreign dead language', and maintained that most German Jews were more affected by German prayers than by Hebrew ones; yet he had a deep love for the Hebrew language, and used it in his synagogue. The important rabbinical conference at Frankfurt in 1845, under Geiger's influence, declared that while there was no objective legal necessity for retaining Hebrew in the service, yet it was subjectively necessary to do so. In a further vote it became clear that a slight majority were in favour of eventually replacing Hebrew by German or using the two languages side by side. This was not acceptable to Zacharias FRANKEL, the leader of the most conservative wing, and he withdrew from the conference; ever since, the attitude to Hebrew in the synagogue has been one of the issues dividing Reform from Conservative Jews. But even within the Reform movement the attitude has been by no means unambiguous or unanimous. British Reform, for example, has tended to favour a half-and-half mix, and has retained the tradition of printing its bilingual prayer books starting from the right, like Hebrew books, while Liberal Judaism in Britain at first virtually eliminated Hebrew, and its prayer books opened from the left like English books. When Isaac Mayer WISE, the great pioneer of Reform in America, issued his new prayer book, *Minhag America*, in 1857, it contained a totally Hebrew text opening from the right, and a separate English or German translation opening at the left. Those congregations that wished to do so could pray entirely or mainly in the vernacular, and this became increasingly common in Reform congregations. In the 20th century, however, there was a notable return to the use of Hebrew: the COLUMBUS PLATFORM of 1937 included the use of Hebrew among the elements of tradition it proclaimed were required by a Jewish way of life, and the later emergence of a symbiosis between Reform and Zionism, with its strong espousal of the Hebrew language, further strengthened the place of Hebrew in Reform Judaism. (*See also* MIAMI PLATFORM.)

via negativa (Latin, 'negative way') Theology of negation, based on the belief that since God is beyond human comprehension we can only say what he is not, not what he is. This approach is rarely found in Jewish sources before the Middle Ages, but there are traces of it. For example the Talmud (Yerushalmi, Berachot 9.1) explains the words of Psalm 65.2, 'Praise is silence for you, God', as meaning that the ultimate praise of God is silence. Both BACHYA IBN PAKUDA and Moses MAIMONIDES among medieval Jewish thinkers develop the idea of negative attributes. For Maimonides to say that God is one is to deny that he is plural – what his unity is like we really have no idea. Again, to say that God exists means that his non-existence is impossible. If we cannot say anything positive about God, what is the purpose of negative attributes? It is to 'conduct the mind towards what must be believed concerning God', which is the realization of the utter inadequacy of our language when it comes to describing God. 'Only God can apprehend what he is.' Hence Maimonides agrees with the Talmud that, for God (and only for God), silence is praise.

viddui ('confession') Litany of public confession, as a means to expiation and ATONEMENT. The Great Confession or Viddui Rabba (AL CHET) and Lesser Confession or Viddui Zuta (ASHÁMNU) are prominent elements in the liturgy for the Day of ATONEMENT.

Vilna Ga'on (Elijah ben Solomon Zalman, 1720–97) Talmudist, halachist and commentator. His immense erudition alone would suffice to make Elijah of Vilna one of the outstanding figures in the history of Jewish scholarship, but in addition, despite his extreme reticence and ascetic habits, he was called to exercise leadership in his period, a time of powerful and conflicting intellectual and religious currents, notably the ENLIGHTENMENT (he was a contemporary of MENDELSSOHN) and CHASIDISM (he was a younger contemporary of the BAAL SHEM TOV). He was opposed to both. Despite being a scholar with a keen critical mind, who believed that it was essential to have a sound knowledge of secular subjects such as mathematics and natural science, he did not think that such subjects should be pursued for their own sakes but only as a necessary aid to the study of Torah. Far from being wedded to rationalism, he was a kabbalist himself, and he criticizes Maimonides for being so led astray by 'accursed philosophy' as to reject belief in demons, incantations and amulets. On the other hand he became the leader of the opposition to Chasidism (*see* MITNAGGEDIM), convinced as he was that they were under the influence of Sabbateanism, that their emphasis on personal piety would oust the Talmud from its pre-eminent position, and that their doctrine of PANENTHEISM was heretical. He was an extraordinarily prolific author. Among his writings are commentaries or annotations on the Torah, both Talmuds, and the SHULCHAN ARUCH. *See also* CHAYYIM OF VOLOZHIN; EDUCATION.

viola (Spanish, 'eve') Eve of the circumcision. In Salonica and other places, it was formerly customary for friends to gather in the house where a circumcision was to take place for a festive meal. After a short sermon from the rabbi, a children's choir would sing songs mentioning the prophet Elijah. The child's maternal grandmother traditionally sat up all night watching over mother and child.

Vital, Chayyim (1542–1620) Kabbalist of SAFED. He was the closest disciple of Isaac LURIA, and wrote down his teachings. Convinced that he himself was the Messiah, he kept a diary that would establish his messianic claims, full of dreams and visions. His major work, *Ets Chayyim* (*Tree of Life*, punning on his name), is an extensive compendium of Luria's teachings.

W

Wailing Wall *See* WESTERN WALL.

washing Hand washing is mandatory or customary in various circumstances, such as on getting up in the morning, before eating bread, after sexual intercourse and after visiting a cemetery. A small pitcher with two handles is customarily used for pouring water over the hands, since water straight from the tap is not adequate for ritual washing. A benediction is said. (Exceptionally, it is said after the act, so that it may be pronounced in a state of purity.) In the Temple the priests washed their feet as well as their hands. Today they still have their hands (but not their feet) washed before blessing the people (BIRKAT KOHANIM). *See also* BATHING.

Weeks, Festival of *See* SHAVUOT.

Western Wall (Kótel Ma'aravi) Also known as the Wailing Wall. Part of the retaining wall of the Temple Mount in Jerusalem, constructed by King Herod towards the end of the 1st century BCE. After the destruction of the TEMPLE in 70 CE Jews adopted the practice of visiting Jerusalem to lament the loss of the shrine. Since the 16th century the wall has been a place of prayer for Jewish residents and visitors, and in the late 19th century it also entered the wider Jewish consciousness in literature and art. In the early 20th century worshippers began to light candles there and to thrust written petitions addressed to God into cracks between the stones. Between 1948 and 1967 the wall was under Jordanian control and closed to Israeli visitors; when Israel captured the area during the 1967 war it became a focus for national sentiment, and the nearby buildings were demolished to make a spacious plaza to accommodate crowds of worshippers, including BAR MITSVA celebrations and military swearing-in ceremonies. The Israeli rabbinate insisted on segregation of the sexes.

wig *See* CHAREDI; SHEÍTEL.

wímpel (German, 'strip of cloth') In Germany and Alsace, a Torah binding (*see* MAPPA) often made from a baby's swaddling clothes. These are stitched together in such a way as to form a band of cloth on which appropriate wording and pictorial designs are embroidered or painted.

wine Alcoholic drink made from fermented grape juice. Wine occupies a unique place in Judaism among all food and drink. It has a benediction of its own (… bore peri ha-géfen, 'creator of the fruit of the vine'), and occupies a prominent place in central rituals such as KIDDUSH, HAVDALA, SÉDER, MARRIAGE and CIRCUMCISION. Drinking is encouraged on PURIM and SIMCHAT TORA, and required at PASSOVER. The wine used on all these occasions is a sweet red wine. The HALACHA forbids the use by Jews of 'libation wine' (yein nésech), that is wine that may have been used by Gentiles in their religious rituals, and traditionalists and some Orthodox Jews extend this ban to all wine made or handled by Gentiles.

Wise, Isaac Mayer (1819–1900) Reform rabbi. Wise may be justly considered the father of American REFORM JUDAISM, although his major vision of a single united American Judaism was never realized. He received a traditional Jewish education in his native Bohemia, and emigrated to America in 1846. After a period spent as a rabbi in Albany, New York, when he came into conflict with his congregants by introducing reforms they found unacceptable, he was appointed in 1854 to a congregation in Cincinnati, Ohio, where he stayed for the rest of his life. Through his vision and dedication and the force of his stubborn personality this fast-growing Midwestern city became the powerhouse of Reform in America. But Wise was not a believer in what has been called the 'Judaism of labels'. In conditions of anarchic diversity his ambition was to establish a single form of the religion that would suit all American Jews, and in 1857 he published a prayer book entitled *Minhag America* (*American Rite*), which he hoped would gain general acceptance beyond denominational boundaries. He believed that the fundamental ideals of Judaism were those of America (indeed, at one point he predicted that in fifty years Judaism would have overtaken Christianity to become the religion of America as a whole).

Wise was the type of the moderate reformer: convinced of the need to modernize Judaism, for example by shortening services and introducing VERNACULAR PRAYER, he was also committed to the Talmud and opposed to textual criticism of the Torah. Inevitably he was attacked from both flanks. But despite constant conflict he achieved an enormous amount. The creation of the UNION OF AMERICAN HEBREW CONGREGATIONS, the HEBREW UNION COLLEGE and the CENTRAL CONFERENCE OF AMERICAN RABBIS can be ascribed to his initiative (and all three titles testify to his faith in a united, non-denominational Judaism).

Wissenschaft des Judentums (German, 'scholarly study of Judaism') A trend in the study of Jewish history and literature that arose in early 19th-century Germany, nourished by the methods of modern scholarship and closely associated with the aims of religious MODERNISM. Wissenschaft is the German for 'science' (here in the sense of scholarship in general), and the leading figures of this school wanted to apply to the study of the Jewish past the most rigorous standards of scholarship as practised in the German universities, in the face of ignorance and indifference within the Jewish community, as well as a deeply ingrained habit of uncritical study in the YESHIVOT, and prejudice outside in the form of Christian evangelism and political opposition to Jewish EMANCIPATION. The origins of the movement have been traced to the Verein für Kultur und Wissenschaft der Juden (Society for Jewish Culture and Scholarship), created in 1819. Leopold ZUNZ was one of the founders of the Verein; he was to become one of the outstanding figures of the Wissenschaft movement, whose numbers also included the historians Isaak Jost and Heinrich

Graetz and students of religious sources such as Abraham GEIGER and Zacharias FRAN-KEL. The movement was not limited to Germany; it was a Europe-wide movement involving figures such as Samuel David LUZZATTO in Italy and Nachman KROCHMAL and Solomon Judah RAPOPORT in Galicia. The creation of rabbinical SEMINARIES, beginning in Breslau in 1854, although motivated largely by religious needs (to train rabbis for post-emancipation Europe), would be inconceivable without the Wissenschaft movement, which provided the intellectual and methodological basis for the seminaries, which, in turn, provided an academic base for scholars who were still barred from holding university chairs. They published their research in the flagship learned journal of the movement, the *Monatsschrift für Geschichte und Wissenschaft des Judenthums* (created 1851), and in other similar journals that sprang up in its footsteps. Their studies opened a new era in the knowledge and understanding of the Jewish past. Their aim was to demonstrate how Jewish religion, literature and thought had developed in response to the different cultural and intellectual environments in which Jews had lived. Bibliography and manuscript studies, together with linguistic accuracy, were the bedrock on which Wissenschaft was built. Texts were edited critically, and studied within their original historical context. The scholars of the Wissenschaft movement laid the foundations for all subsequent Jewish scholarship, which still relies on their publications and broadly follows their aims and methods.

World Jewish Congress Representative and campaigning body, with headquarters in New York. Founded in Geneva in 1936 to mobilize opinion and action against the anti-Jewish policies of the German Nazi government, the WJC continues to campaign against perceived threats to Jews everywhere. It describes itself as 'the permanent address of the Jewish people'.

World Sephardi Federation Zionist organization founded in 1925 with the aim of encouraging the emigration of Sefardim to Palestine.

World to Come *See* OLAM HA-BA.

World Union for Progressive Judaism The international umbrella organization of the REFORM, LIBERAL, PROGRESSIVE and RECONSTRUCTIONIST movements, originally established in London in 1926, with the aims of uniting permanently the various Progressive Jewish movements already in existence in various countries of the world, and of establishing a presence wherever there were Jewish communities prepared and committed to undertake such a challenge. Since 1973 its headquarters have been located in Jerusalem.

written Torah In RABBINIC Judaism, term used in contradistinction to the ORAL TORAH, and denoting either the five books of Moses or the Bible as a whole.

Xuetas (Catalan, origin obscure, possibly from a word for pork; pronounced shwé-tas) In Majorca, Christians descended from Jews who were forcibly converted in the early 15th century. Some of them have recently recovered an attachment to Judaism.

yad ('hand') Pointer used in the reading of the Torah, to indicate the place and to avoid touching the parchment. It is generally made of silver, and shaped at the end in the form of a hand with a pointing finger. When not in use it is suspended from the staves on a chain.

Yad or **Yad ha-Chazaka** *See* MISHNE TORAH.

Yadá'im ('hands') Tractate of the Mishnah and Tosefta, in the order Tohorot, dealing with issues concerning ritual impurity acquired or transmitted by the hands. The topics discussed include WASHING of the hands, and their paradoxical impurity conveyed by handling sacred texts.

Yah A NAME OF GOD, first found in the Bible (for example Exodus 15.2). It appears to be a shortened form of the INEFFABLE NAME, and is found as an element in personal names (such as Isaiah, 'Yah my salvation', or Uzziah, 'Yah my strength'). (*See also* HALLELUYAH.) In the ZOHAR it corresponds to the sefira Chochma (*see* SEFIROT).

yáhrzeit *See* YÓRTSAIT.

yamim nora'im *See* TEN DAYS OF PENITENCE.

yármulka *See* SKULLCAP.

Yavne Town in the coastal plain of Israel, just north of Ashdod and a short distance from the sea, known to the Romans as Jamnia. It was here that the first rabbinic academy was founded, by YOCHANAN BEN ZAKKAI, supposedly during the siege of Jerusalem, around 68 CE. The academy, the centre of the rabbinic movement, remained here until the BAR KOCHBA revolt, when it moved briefly to Lydda and then to Usha in Galilee. During the early days at Yavne important decisions were taken affecting the future direction of rabbinic Judaism and its role in the renewal and reorganization of Judaism in the Land of Israel and the Diaspora after the catastrophe of the destruction of the Temple.

year *See* AM; BCE; CALENDAR; CE.

Yefet ben Eli (late 10th century) Karaite biblical scholar and polemicist. Probably born in Basra, Yefet settled in Jerusalem and joined the Mourners of Zion (*see* AL-KUMISI). Yefet's real claim to fame is as a biblical exegete. He devoted a large part of his life to the composition of commentaries in Arabic on the entire Bible. These deliberately incorporated the work of his Karaite predecessors as well as his own ideas, so as to constitute a repository of Karaite exegesis; they were later used by Rabbanites (such as Abraham IBN EZRA) as well as by Karaites. In these commentaries he often attacks the leading exponent of Rabbanism, SA'ADYA GA'ON, against whom he also wrote a polemical work, now lost. He also engaged in polemics against Islam and Christianity.

Yehezkel Hebrew name of the biblical book of Ezekiel.

yehidim (from Hebrew yechidim, 'individuals') In Western Sefardi usage, full members of the congregation.

Yehoshú'a Hebrew name of the biblical book of Joshua.

Yehuda'i Ga'on (8th century) Head of the academy of SURA in Babylonia from 757 to 760. He is remembered as a key figure in the history of the codification of HALACHA, and several dozen of his RESPONSA have been preserved. Little else is known about him. He was considered to be the author of the early attempts to codify halacha, the Halachot Pesukot, Halachot Gedolot and Halachot Ketsuvot, but these attributions, particularly the last two, are highly questionable.

yeri'a *See* MAPPA (1).

Yerushalmi The Palestinian TALMUD.

Yesháya Hebrew name of the biblical book of Isaiah. Also known as Yeshayáhu.

yeshiva ('sitting') Traditional Talmudic academy. The term originates in ancient rabbinism, in which sitting was specifically associated with study, as well as judging legal cases – two activities that were closely related for the rabbis. (The posture associated with eating was reclining; only mourners sat to eat.) So characteristic an institution did the yeshiva become in rabbinism that the Talmud imagines biblical figures such as Jacob studying in a yeshiva and they even speak of a 'yeshiva on high', presided over by God himself, where the souls of departed scholars discuss Torah with him (and even dare to disagree with him). In the geonic period (*see* GA'ON) the two great Babylonian yeshivot of SURA and PUMBEDITA played a key role in the development of rabbinic culture. The institution came to be widely imitated, at first throughout the Arab world, in the Middle East, North Africa and Spain, and later also in Ashkenaz. By the 17th century eastern Europe was the greatest centre of yeshivot (although they could be found throughout the Sefardi and Ashkenazi dispersions). At this time they were still small institutions under the care of the local rabbi and with no organized programme of study. This situation changed with the creation of the famous Volozhin yeshiva in 1803 (*see* CHAYYIM OF VOLOZHIN). This was an independent academy, with its own principal (the ROSH YESHIVA), buildings and administrative staff. This model was copied throughout eastern and central Europe, particularly in Lithuania (but not in Poland, where the Chasidim evinced little interest in this type of education). The teaching in these yeshivot was focused on detailed but largely theoretical study of Talmudic texts. After the destruction of the European yeshivot during World War II some of them were re-established in the United States and Israel. Many new yeshivot have been opened, mostly based on the Lithuanian model, although there are now some Chasidic and Orthodox institutions. Traditionally yeshiva education is reserved for men, but there are now some yeshivot catering to women. Yeshivot have proliferated in recent decades in Israel, thanks to a law exempting their students from military service, and although this has inevitably led to a lowering of standards, the best yeshivot are highly regarded and attract students from around the world. Many of these are ba'alei teshuva or 'penitents', young Jews who have been brought up without much religious education, and are attracted by traditional values and the rigour of the yeshiva method of study. The BÁ'AL TESHUVA movement has been assisted by, and has in turn contributed to, the introduction of new ways of teaching traditional Judaism in some yeshivot, and the yeshiva model has come to be imitated in some less traditional circles. *See also* BENEÍ TÓRA; EDUCATION; GUSH EMUNIM; KOLEL; MUSAR MOVEMENT; TRADITIONALISM.

Yeshiva University Orthodox educational institution in New York. Founded in 1886, it has grown from a boys' school into a fully fledged university, with an affiliated theological SEMINARY.

Yeshurun Biblical name meaning 'just' or 'honest', and used as a synonym for Israel (for example Isaiah 44.2). *See also* ADATH YISROEL.

Yesód ('foundation') In kabbala, one of the SEFIROT.

yétser ha-ra ('formation for evil') In rabbinic thought, the urge to sin, considered to have been implanted in human nature from the creation of the human race. According to the Torah, 'the formation of the human mind is evil from youth on' (Genesis 8.21). The word translated 'formation', yétser, has also been translated as 'imagination' or 'inclination', although it comes from the Hebrew verb used in the story of the creation: 'The Lord God formed the man of dust from the ground' (Genesis 2.7). A peculiarity in the way this verb is written in the Masoretic text led the rabbis to suggest that the man was formed with a dual inclination, to do good and to do evil. Retaining the vocabulary of 'forming' they called the former yétser tov (good formation or inclination) and the latter yétser ha-ra (formation or inclination for evil). This is the basis of the doctrine of FREE WILL: humans are completely free to choose to do good or evil. The theological cost is the perennial puzzle of how an all-good God can have by implication created something evil. The rabbis attempt to get round this by arguing that the inclination for evil is not itself evil, because without it human life as we know it could not exist. As the rabbis put it, without it a man would never get a job, have children or build a house. (As this remark suggests, they tended to identify the inclination for evil with the sexual urge.) They saw human life as a constant battle between the yétser tov and the yétser ha-ra, but there is no suggestion that it is possible to overcome the urge to do evil permanently. The truly valiant warrior is 'he who conquers his own yétser, as it is written [Proverbs 16.32]: He who is slow to anger is better than a mighty warrior, and he who rules his own spirit than one who captures a city' (Mishnah, Avot 4.1). They do suggest, though, that the Torah with its commandments has been given as an aid in fighting the yétser. This idea is expressed even more strongly in the ZOHAR: 'The good inclination desires the joy of the Torah but the inclination for evil desires the joy of wine, fornication and pride. Therefore one should always be in dread of the great day, the day of judgment, the day of reckoning, when nothing can act as your shield except the good deeds you have performed in this world.'

A novel voice is that of SHNEUR ZALMAN OF LYADY, who declares in the opening section of the TANYA that the righteous man or tsaddik has killed his yétser through fasting, and so belongs in the ranks of the saints, who are no longer subject to temptation. Chasidism in general ascribes to the tsaddik (*see* REBBE) the power, together with Torah and joy in the service of God, to help the Chasid to free himself from the shackles of the yétser.

Yevamot ('sisters-in-law') Tractate of the Mishnah, Tosefta and both Talmuds, in the order Nashim, dealing with the laws of LEVIRATE MARRIAGE.

YHVH, YHWH *See* INEFFABLE NAME.

yichud ('unification'; plural yichudim) **1** Seclusion for sexual purposes (*see* GENDER; MARRIAGE). **2** Meditation on the various possible combinations of the INEFFABLE NAME, originating in SAFED in the circle of Isaac LURIA. Luria offered his followers different yichudim to be performed by different people and at different times. They were supposed to have an effect on the elevation of the mystic's soul and on the upper worlds. Some yichudim are printed in kabbalistic prayer books, but the more esoteric yichudim (which are thought to carry spiritual and even bodily risks) seem to have died out.

Yiddish A form of German language, with strong influence from Hebrew and other languages, particularly Slavonic. It is historically the spoken language of Ashkenazi Jewry, and its spread reflects that of the Ashkenazi Jews. It began in the Rhineland, spread eastwards to Poland from the 13th century, and eventually moved back to central and western Europe in the 18th and 19th centuries, and on to North and South America and South Africa. In modern times it has suffered as the language of Ashkenazim from linguistic assimilation, from the competition of Hebrew, and from the Holocaust, which took a devastating toll of eastern European Jewry. Today it is viewed with great nostalgia by Ashkenazim, but younger speakers tend either to be enthusiasts who have made a special effort to learn the language, or to belong to socially and culturally isolated communities of religious traditionalists. Because of the dominance of Hebrew as the main written language of Jews in the Middle Ages and early modern period such Yiddish literature as survives is addressed to a readership of women and other less educated people. Modern Yiddish literature is mainly secular and anti-religious in orientation.

Yigdal ('he is great') Hymn attributed to the 14th-century Roman poet Daniel ben Judah. It is a versified rendering of the THIRTEEN PRINCIPLES of Maimonides, and is sung at the end of the evening service on Sabbaths and festivals. It may be translated:

Great is the living God and to be praised: existing and unlimited by time.
Unique in his uniqueness he is One, concealed in his infinite unity.

He has no body, no substance or form, no image can define his holiness.
Preceding all created things, the First, with no beginning to his primacy.
Eternal Lord is he, and all the world declares his greatness and his majesty.
To men he chose to glorify his name he gave abundant gifts of prophecy.
No prophet has there been in Israel like Moses, who beheld him face to face.
Through him, the prophet 'faithful in his house', God gave his people the one true
   Torah.
Nor will he ever abrogate his law or substitute another in its place.
He sees into the secrets of our hearts and knows the end of all things in advance.
For all good deeds he grants a due reward, but punishes the sinner for his sin.
Finally our Anointed will he send to save those who await the glorious end.
The dead our loving God to life will raise: for ever be his name adored with praise!

There are slight differences in wording between the Ashkenazi and Sefardi versions
of the hymn, and Sefardim often add a fourteenth line, 'These are the thirteen
principles, the foundation of God's religion and his Torah', or ' ... the foundation
of Moses' Torah and his prophecy', or words to that effect. Isaac LURIA was opposed to
the singing of the hymn, and following him the Chasidim do not use it. Some
reformed liturgies alter the last line to remove the reference to resurrection.

Yirmíya Hebrew name of the biblical book of Jeremiah. Also known as Yirmiyáhu.

Yitschaki, Rabbi Solomon *See* RASHI.

yizkor ('may he [God] remember') Service in memory of the dead, normally held by
Ashkenazim on the last days of the festivals and on the Day of ATONEMENT.

Yochanan ben Zakkai (1st century) One of the leading TANNA'IM of the first
generation, who is remembered as the founder of rabbinic Judaism after the destruction of the Temple. According to a probably unhistorical legend he had himself
carried out of the besieged city of Jerusalem and asked the Roman general to let him
found a school in YAVNE.

Yo'el Hebrew name of the biblical book of Joel.

Yom ha-Atsma'ut (modern Hebrew, Independence Day) Anniversary of the independence of the state of Israel in 1948. Among religious Zionists it is celebrated, as
decreed by the rabbinate of Israel, on the 5th of Iyyar (or on the preceding Thursday
if the anniversary falls on a Friday or Saturday) by a special service. This religious
dimension is not observed by the AGUDAT ISRAEL, while the NETÚREI KÁRTA have proclaimed the day one of communal mourning.

Yom ha-Kippurim *See* ATONEMENT, DAY OF.

Yom ha-Sho'a (modern Hebrew, 'Holocaust Day') Israeli commemoration of the
victims of the Holocaust, held symbolically one week before YOM HA-ATSMA'UT. While
this is not strictly a religious commemoration some synagogues hold special services
on the day.

Yom Kippur *See* ATONEMENT, DAY OF.

Yom Tov *See* BETSA; YÓMTOV.

Yom Yerushaláyim ('Jerusalem Day') Israeli secular celebration of the conquest of eastern Jerusalem (including the Old City) during the Six-Day War in June 1967, and the subsequent administrative unification of the city. It is celebrated on the 28th of Iyyar. During the days preceding the celebration, Israeli schools highlight the importance of Jerusalem in Jewish thought down the ages, and the day is marked by 'pilgrimage' to Jerusalem. The Chief Rabbinate of Israel has decided that it should be marked with the recital of HALLEL.

Yoma (Aramaic, 'the day') Tractate of the Mishnah, Tosefta and both Talmuds, in the order Mo'ed, dealing with the observance of the Day of ATONEMENT, and focusing particularly on the rituals observed in the TEMPLE on this day.

yómtov (Yiddish, from Hebrew, 'good day') Ashkenazi word for a festival, often pronounced yúntif. The greeting is 'gut yómtov', or, in English, '(a) good yómtov'.

Yona Hebrew name of the biblical book of Jonah.

yórtsait or **yáhrzeit** (Yiddish, 'year-time') Among Ashkenazim, the anniversary of a death. It is marked by lighting a candle and by saying KADDISH in synagogue.

Yosef Chayyim (1832–1909) Iraqi scholar, also known as Ben Ish Chai ('son of a valiant man', 2 Samuel 23.20), after one of his best-known works. A popular preacher in Baghdad, he was the author of some seventy books. His collection of homilies *Ben Ish Chai* (1898) is still regarded as a valuable halachic compendium; each homily on the weekly PARASHA begins with a mystical interpretation and concludes with halachic rulings. His other works include RESPONSA and other halachic writings, and many PIYYUTIM.

yotse ('coming out') Compliant with a COMMANDMENT. It is short for yotse yedeí chovato, literally 'coming out of [i.e. fulfilling] one's obligation'.

Yotser ('forming') **1** Morning prayer, in which God is praised for making the sun and moon. The prayer makes use of the words of God in Isaiah 45.7: 'Forming light and creating darkness, making peace and creating evil, I the Lord am the maker of all these'. The theological idea behind these words is God's uniqueness: those who claim that there is one source of light and good and another of darkness and evil are mistaken, because there is only one God. However, the statement that God is the creator of evil must have seemed too direct and shocking at some point, because in all liturgies the prayer reads: 'Forming light and creating darkness, making peace and creating all things.'

2 A type of PIYYUT made up of a cycle of five poems adorning the blessings preceding and following the SHEMÁ. The term is narrowly applied to the first of these, also called guf ha-yotser ('yotser itself').

Zavim ('people with a discharge') Tractate of the Mishnah and Tosefta, in the order Tohorot, dealing with rules concerning impurity related to emission of bodily fluids.

zébed ha-bat Among Sefardim, naming ceremony for a daughter.

Zechariah (Zecharia) Biblical book, eleventh of the Twelve Minor Prophets. In the first eight chapters the prophet (who is considered by the rabbis as one of the last of the prophets, living in the late 6th century BCE, at the time of the rebuilding of the Temple) assures the people, through a series of visions, that God will restore Israel to its former glory. The last six chapters, considered by scholars to be an addition by a different author, are strongly eschatological and are interpreted as referring to the messianic age. The words 'And the Lord shall be king over all the earth; in that day shall the Lord be one, and his name one' (14.9) have been chosen to conclude the ALÉYNU.

zechút ('merit') In rabbinic thought, merit acquired through the observance of a COMMANDMENT. Such merit leads to divine favour which benefits not only the individual but others as well. A ramification of this idea is the doctrine of zechút avot (merit of the PATRIARCHS), according to which the goodness of the patriarchs was so great that benefit accrues on account of them to many generations of their descendants. It is mentioned liturgically in the first benediction of the AMIDA.

zemán ('time', 'occasion'; plural zemanim) One of several terms denoting a FESTIVAL.

zemirot (usual singular zémer) Table songs sung during the Sabbath meals and at HAVDALA. The practice is attested by the beginning of the 12th century in Ashkenaz, and was further popularized by the SAFED kabbalists in the 16th century. Zemirot were composed in their hundreds; a small selection is printed in prayer books (or special booklets) today. The term is also applied to biblical songs recited daily at the beginning of the morning service. Ashkenazim call these pesukei de-zimra (Aramaic, 'verses of song').

Zephaniah (Tsefania) Biblical book, ninth of the Twelve Minor Prophets. The prophet Zephaniah lived in the second half of the 7th century BCE. He castigates the people of Jerusalem for their IDOLATRY, and prophesies doom if the people do not repent. The book ends, however, with a message of consolation: God will gather in the exiles and restore the fortunes of the people in the eyes of all the other nations.

Zera'im ('seeds') First of the six orders of the Mishnah, mainly dealing with agricultural subjects. The exception is the first of its tractates, Berachot, which is concerned with prayers and benedictions.

Zevachim ('animal sacrifices') Tractate of the Mishnah, Tosefta and Babylonian Talmud, in the order Kodashim, dealing with sacrifices of animals and birds.

zimmun ('invitation') Formula recited before GRACE AFTER MEALS when three or more people have eaten together, inviting the company to 'bless Him of whose [gifts] we have partaken'. The formula is varied if there are ten or more present (*see* MINYAN). *See also* MEZUMMAN.

Zion Name of a hill in Jerusalem. The precise location of the Mount Zion mentioned in the Bible is a matter of scholarly disagreement; some identify it with the Temple Mount. There is agreement that the hill currently bearing the name, southwest of the present city walls, on which the tomb of King David is shown to visitors, is not the original Mount Zion. In biblical poetry, particularly in the Psalms, Zion is used as a synonym of Jerusalem, and is charged with intense symbolic value. The liturgy develops this biblical language, and speaks often of Zion (sometimes personified as a female figure) in the context of EXILE AND RETURN.

Zionism Modern political movement of national liberation, aimed at bringing about the settlement of the Jews in a land of their own. The term was coined by one of the leaders of CHIBBAT ZION, Nathan Birnbaum (1864–1937), but the man who is considered the founder of political Zionism is the Austrian Theodor HERZL. As a secular movement, it was opposed by most religious Jews, although there were always some who supported it (*see* MIZRACHI). Religious opposition to Zionism was basically of two kinds: traditionalists maintained that it was wrong to force God's hand, and that he would send REDEMPTION in his own good time, and modernist exponents of UNIVERSALISM objected to any form of PARTICULARISM. Since the Holocaust and the creation of the state of ISRAEL anti-Zionism has become weaker (but *see* AGUDAT ISRAEL; CHAREDI; CHAZON ISH; DIASPORA; EDA CHAREDIT; POST-ZIONISM; SATMAR), and most of the modernist movements now endorse it. For its part, Zionism has had an uneasy relationship with Judaism, tending to portray it as an outmoded relic of life in the Diaspora, yet careful not to alienate religious supporters, particularly in the Diaspora. In Israel, it has instigated some public rituals of a quasi-religious character, and has encouraged religious Jews to find a place in the religious calendar for important events in Zionist history (*see* YOM HA-ATSMA'UT; YOM YERUSHALÁYIM). *See also* ACHAD HA-AM; ATHEISM; BUBER, MARTIN; HESS, MOSES; KOOK, ABRAHAM ISAAC; MESSIAH; MIAMI PLATFORM.

zivvug ('copulation') In LURIANIC KABBALA, coupling of the PARTSUFIM in order to strengthen the SEFIROT.

ziyyara, ziyyarat (Arabic) A PILGRIMAGE to a shrine or cemetery (particularly in the Middle East).

Zohar ('splendour') The classic text of KABBALA. Mostly written in an artificial Aramaic, the book has the form of a commentary on the Torah, outwardly resembling the MIDRASH and purporting to go back to the time of the TANNA'IM. It is made up of a number of parts, not all by the same author. The main author is known to be Moses of León (d. 1305), but kabbalists maintain an old belief that the true author is a Tanna, SIMEON BAR YOCHAI, who is often mentioned in the work. The Zohar is a vehicle for the theosophical ideas of the kabbala, centring on the doctrine of the ten SEFIROT, produced by emanation from the ultimate and unknowable EIN SOF. It spread from Spain around the Mediterranean, and after it was printed in Italy in the late 1550s it became even more widely accessible. It was regarded by many as a sacred book, and some North African synagogues contain two holy ARKS, one for the Torah and another for the Zohar. The book became enormously influential in CHASIDISM, and it is said that the BAAL SHEM TOV always carried a copy around with him. The opponents of the Chasidim (MITNAGGEDIM), led by the VILNA GA'ON, also accepted the sanctity of the Zohar, but this sanctity never became a matter of dogma. Nineteenth-century rationalism was strongly opposed to the reverence paid to the Zohar.

Zunz, Leopold (1794–1886) German scholar. Zunz was a pioneer of the application of the methods of modern critical research to Jewish history and literature, and he is rightly seen as the father of WISSENSCHAFT DES JUDENTUMS. He established the foundations of serious study of the religious history of the Jews in a series of monumental studies, on the sermon (1832), synagogue poetry (PIYYUT) (1855 and 1865), and the liturgy (1859). His personal religiosity is ambiguous. Ordained a rabbi by the reformer Aaron CHORIN, he never practised as a rabbi, and tried to keep out of public debates about religious reform; yet while speaking up against some extreme reforms he lent unambiguous support to major liturgical reforms through his historical researches and attributed resistance to change to 'prejudice and ignorance rather than true insight'. In his contradictions he was not untypical of the scholars of the Wissenschaft movement; his position stands closest to that of the HISTORICAL SCHOOL.

Maps

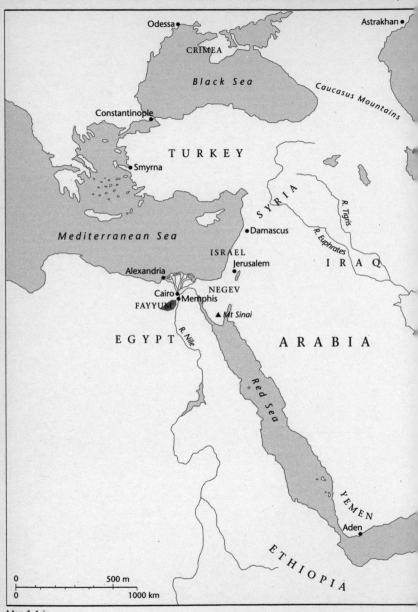

Map 1 Asia

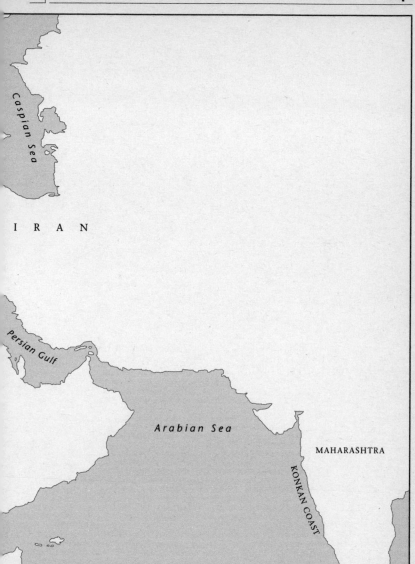

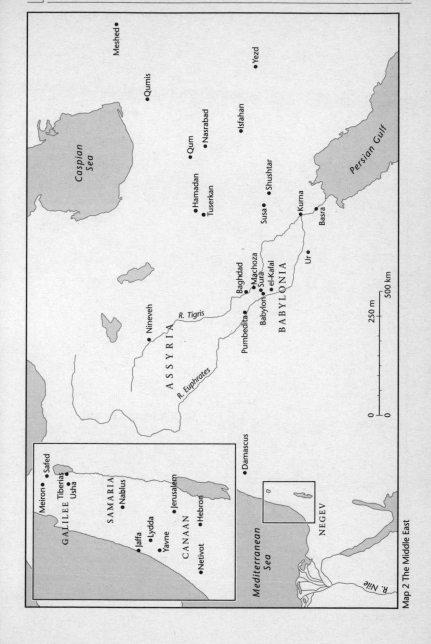

Map 2 The Middle East

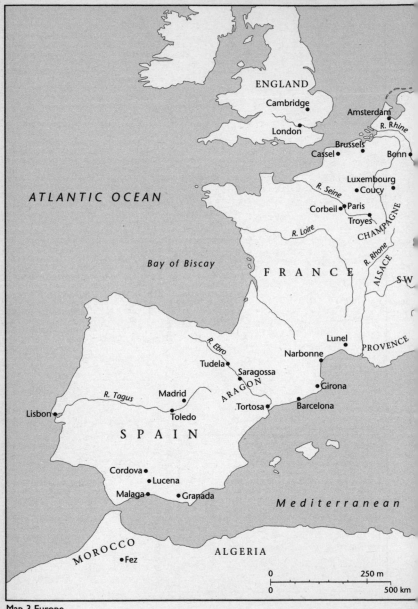

Map 3 Europe

LITHUANIA

• Königsberg

RUSSIA

• Freiburg • Hamburg
Oldenburg • Altona

WESTPHALIA

POSEN

R. Vistula

• Brunswick Berlin
• Halberstadt • Posen

GERMANY

• Warsaw

POLAND

• Leipzig

Marburg

Theresienstadt
Frankfurt am Main • Prague

R. Oder

• Auschwitz
• Cracow

CZECHOSLOVAKIA

• Worms
• Speyer
• Strasbourg

Regensburg

MORAVIA

• Rebrin

R. Danube

Nikolsburg • Prossnitz

• Verbo

R. Rhine

AUSTRIA Vienna •
• Pressburg

Eisenstadt • Budapest

• Berne

ITZ.

HUNGARY

• Arad

TRANSYLVANIA

Soncino Padua Trieste
• Venice
Mantua

R. Danube

• Cesena

• Leghorn

ITALY

Rome •

Adrianople
•

Salonica
•

• Naples

• Ioannina

GREECE

• Halkidha

Sea

TUNISIA

• DJERBA

Map 4 Eastern Europe

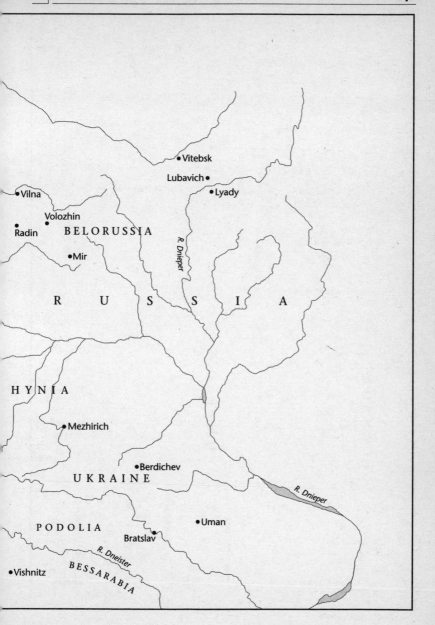

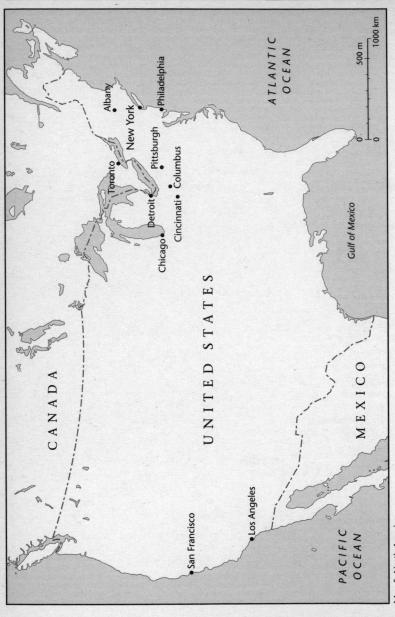

Map 5 North America

Gazetteer

Place name	Alternative name	Map
Aden		1
Adrianople	Edirne	3
Albany		5
Alexandria		1
Alsace		3
Altona		3
Amsterdam		3
Arad		3
Aragon		3
Astrakhan		1
Auschwitz	Oswiecim	3
Babylon		2
Baghdad		2
Barcelona		3
Basra		2
Belz		4
Berdichev		4
Berlin		3
Berne	Bern	3
Bessarabia		4
Bobov		4
Bonn		3
Bratslav		4
Breslau	Wroclaw	4
Brody		4
Brunswick	Braunschweig	3
Budapest		3
Cairo		1
Cambridge		3
Cassel		3
Cesena		3

Place name	Alternative name	Map
Champagne		3
Chicago		5
Cincinnati		5
Columbus		5
Constantinople	Istanbul	1
Corbeil		3
Cordova		3
Coucy		3
Cracow	Kraków	3, 4
Damascus		1, 2
Detroit		5
Djerba		3
Eisenstadt	Kismarton	3
Fez		3
Frankfurt am Main		3
Freiburg		3
Galicia		4
Ger	Góra Kalwaria	4
Girona	Gerona	3
Granada		3
Halberstadt		3
Halkidha	Chalcis	3
Hamadan		2
Hamburg		3
Hebron		2
Ioannina		3
Isfahan	Esfahan	2
Jaffa	Yafo	2
Jaroslaw		4
Jerusalem	Yerushaláim	1, 2
el-Kafal		2
Kattowitz	Katowice	4
Königsberg	Kaliningrad	3, 4
Kovno	Kaunas	4
Kurna		2
Leghorn	Livorno	3
Leipzig		3
Lemberg	Lviv	4
Lisbon		3
London		3
Los Angeles		5
Lubavich	Lyubavichi	4
Lublin		4

Place name	Alternative name	Map
Lucena		3
Lunel		3
Luxembourg		3
Lyady		4
Lydda	Lod	2
Machoza		2
Malaga		3
Mantua		3
Marburg		3
Meiron		2
Memphis		1
Meshed		2
Mezhirich	Mezhirech	4
Mir		4
Nablus		2
Naples		3
Narbonne		3
Nasrabad		2
Netivot		2
New York		5
Nikolaev		4
Nikolsburg	Mikulov	3
Nineveh		2
Odessa		1
Oldenburg		3
Padua		3
Paris		3
Philadelphia		5
Pittsburgh		5
Podolia		4
Posen	Poznan	3
Prague		3
Pressburg	Bratislava	3
Prossnitz	Prostejov	3
Pruzana		4
Pumbedita		2
Qum	Qom	2
Qumis		2
Radin		4
Rebrin		3
Regensburg	Ratisbonne	3
Riga		4
Rome		3

Place name	Alternative name	Map
Safed	Tsfat	2
Salonica	Thessaloniki	3
San Francisco		5
Saragossa	Zaragoza	3
Satmar	Satu Mare	4
Shushtar		2
Smyrna	Izmir	1
Soncino		3
Speyer		3
Strasbourg		3
Sura		2
Susa	Shoosha	2
Tarnow		4
Theresienstadt	Terezín	3
Tiberias	Tveria	2
Toledo		3
Toronto		5
Tortosa		3
Transylvania		3
Trieste		3
Troyes		3
Tudela		3
Tuserkan		2
Uman		4
Ur		2
Usha		2
Venice		3
Verbo		3
Vienna		3
Vilna	Vilnius	4
Vishnitz		4
Vitebsk		4
Volhynia		4
Volozhin		4
Warsaw		4
Westphalia		3
Worms		3
Yavne	Jamnia	2
Yezd	Yazd	2

The Hebrew Alphabet

This is a simplified table, which is not intended to be used for specialized purposes. In particular, it shows only the consonants and omits the vowel signs. The pronunciation of some letters varies according to their place in the word or phrase, or according to the origin of the speaker; no attempt has been made here to indicate these complex distinctions. For explanation of the various columns *see* the entry ALPHABET, HEBREW in the dictionary.

name	square form	final form	trans-literation used in this book	other current trans-literations	semi-cursive ('Rashi') form	Israeli cursive form	Palaeo-Hebrew form	numerical value
álef	א		none	'				1
bet, vet	ב		b, v					2
gímel	ג		g					3
dáled	ד		d					4
he	ה		h					5
vav	ו		v	w				6
záyin	ז		z					7
chet	ח		ch	ḥ				8
tet	ט		t	ṭ				9
yod	י		y, i					10
kaf	כ	ך	k	kh				20

name	square form	final form	transliteration used in this book	other current transliterations	semi-cursive ('Rashi') form	Israeli cursive form	Palaeo-Hebrew form	numerical value
lámed	ל		l					30
mem	מ	ם	m					40
nun	נ	ן	n					50
sámech	ס		s					60
áyin	ע		none	', ng				70
pe	פ	ף	p, f	ph				80
tsáde	צ	ץ	ts	tz, ṣ				90
kof	ק		k	q				100
resh	ר		r					200
sin, shin	ש		s, sh	ś, š				300
tav	ת		t	th, s				400

The Jewish Calendar

	Tishri		Cheshvan		Kislev		Tevet		Shevát		Adar
1	New Year (Rosh ha-Shana)	1		1		1	🕎🕎🕎🕎🕎🕎🕎🕎	1		1	
2		2		2		2	🕎🕎🕎🕎🕎🕎🕎🕎	2		2	
3	Fast of Gedaliah	3		3		3		3		3	
4		4		4		4		4		4	
5		5		5		5		5		5	
6		6		6		6		6		6	
7		7		7		7		7		7	
8		8		8		8		8		8	
9		9		9		9		9		9	
10	Day of Atonement	10		10		10	Fast	10		10	
11		11		11		11		11		11	
12		12		12		12		12		12	
13		13		13		13		13		13	Fast of Esther
14		14		14		14		14		14	Purim
15	Tabernacles (Sukkot)	15		15		15		15	Tu bi-Shevát	15	
16		16		16		16		16		16	
17		17		17		17		17		17	
18		18		18		18		18		18	
19		19		19		19		19		19	
20		20		20		20		20		20	
21		21		21		21		21		21	
22	Shemini Atséret	22		22		22		22		22	
23	Simchat Tora*	23		23		23		23		23	
24		24		24		24		24		24	
25		25		25	Chanukka 🕎	25		25		25	
26		26		26	🕎🕎	26		26		26	
27		27		27	🕎🕎🕎	27		27		27	
28		28		28	🕎🕎🕎🕎	28		28		28	
29		29		29	🕎🕎🕎🕎🕎	29		29		29	
30				30	🕎🕎🕎🕎🕎🕎			30			

■ High holy days　　■ Pilgrim festivals　　□ Other festive days　　□ Minor fasts and solemn periods

* Extra day of festival not observed in Israel or by Reform communities

	Nisan		Iyyar		Sivan		Tammuz		Av		Elul
1		1		1		1		1		1	
2		2		2		2		2		2	
3		3		3		3		3		3	
4		4	Yom ha-Atsma'ut	4		4		4		4	
5		5		5		5		5		5	
6		6		6	Shavuot	6		6		6	
7		7		7		7		7		7	
8		8		8		8		8		8	
9		9		9		9		9	Tisha be-Av	9	
10		10		10		10		10		10	
11		11		11		11		11		11	
12		12		12		12		12		12	
13		13		13		13		13		13	
14	Fast of the first-born	14		14		14		14		14	
15	Passover (Pésach)	15		15		15		15	Tu be-Av	15	
16		16		16		16		16		16	
17		17		17		17	Shiva-asar be-Tammuz	17		17	
18		18	Lag ba-Ómer	18		18		18		18	
19		19		19		19		19		19	
20		20		20		20		20		20	
21		21		21		21		21		21	
22		22		22		22		22		22	
23		23		23		23		23		23	
24		24		24		24		24		24	
25		25		25		25		25		25	
26		26		26		26		26		26	
27	Yom ha-Sho'a	27		27		27		27		27	
28		28	Yom Yerushaláyim	28		28		28		28	
29		29		29		29		29		29	
30				30				30			

PENGUIN REFERENCE LIBRARY

THE PENGUIN DICTIONARY OF INTERNATIONAL RELATIONS

EDITED BY GRAHAM EVANS & JEFFREY NEWNHAM

'Cogently argued and lucidly expressed. The scholarship is impeccable'
Professor J. E. Spence

It's the twenty-first century, and the political landscape has never been so explosive. Will history repeat itself, or are we entering a new phase of governmental relations? No one can say for sure, but *The Penguin Dictionary of International Relations* provides the clues. A must for any student or teacher of politics, this exceptional text is the only guide on the market to this complex and constantly shifting subject. The entries are lucid, wide-ranging and lengthy, offering detailed explanation of the *Arab–Israeli conflict*, *weapons of mass destruction* and much more.

- Covers major events, from the *Cold War* to *Hiroshima*

- Includes substantial articles on fundamental political and philosophical concepts, such as *intervention*, *nationalism* and *just war*

- Describes key organizations in detail, from the *ANC* to *UNO*

- Explains specialist terms, from *agent-structure* to *zero-sum*

ONLY PENGUIN GIVES YOU MORE

PENGUIN REFERENCE LIBRARY

**THE PENGUIN DICTIONARY OF LITERARY TERMS
& LITERARY THEORY**

EDITED BY J. A. CUDDON

'Scholarly, succinct, comprehensive and entertaining ... an indispensable work of reference' *The Times Literary Supplement*

Now over thirty years old, J. A. Cuddon's *The Penguin Dictionary of Literary Terms and Literary Theory* is a reference classic, a stunning survey of literature and theory that stands as the first port of call for any reader or student of literature. Consistently updated since, Cuddon's work illuminates the history and complexity of literature's movements, terms and major figures in relaxed, accessible prose. From *existentialism* to *caesura* to *doggerel*, the text ranges authoritatively over both high and low literary culture and theory, and is the primary reference source for anyone interested in writing or reading.

- Gives definitions of technical terms (*hamartia, iamb, zeugma*) and critical jargon (*aporia, binary opposition, intertextuality*)

- Explores literary movements (*neoclassicism, romanticism, vorticism*) and schools of literary theory (*feminist criticism, new historicism, structuralism*)

- Covers genres (*elegy, fabliau, pastoral*) and literary forms (*haiku, ottava rima, sonnet*)

ONLY PENGUIN GIVES YOU MORE

PENGUIN REFERENCE LIBRARY

THE PENGUIN HANDBOOK OF LIVING RELIGIONS

EDITED BY JOHN R HINNELLS

'Excellent ... This whole book is a joy to read'
The Times Higher Education Supplement

Religion is more relevant than ever. From Islam to fundamentalism to the Kabbalah, faith is never far from the headlines, making our understanding of it utterly crucial. *The Penguin Handbook of Living Religions* is designed with this in mind. Crammed with charts, maps and diagrams, it comprises lengthy enlightening chapters on all of today's major religions, from Hinduism to Christianity to Baha'ism, as well as additional essays on cross-cultural areas, such as gender and spirituality. Each chapter represents a book's worth of information on all twenty-first century religions, featuring detailed discussion of the history, culture and practices of each. Comprehensive, informative and compiled by a team of leading international scholars, it includes discussion of modern developments and recent scholarship.

- Explains the sources and history of the world's religions, from Buddhism, Christianity, Hinduism, Islam, Sikhism and Zoroastrianism to regional groups in Africa, China and Japan

- Describes different doctrines, practices and teachings, including rites of passage and specific rituals

- Explores the role of gender and diaspora in modern religion

ONLY PENGUIN GIVES YOU MORE

PENGUIN REFERENCE LIBRARY

THE PENGUIN DICTIONARY OF GEOGRAPHY

EDITED BY AUDREY N. CLARKE

Winner of the Association of College and Research Libraries Choice Award

Global warming, ethnic cleansing, plate tectonics: our world is changing fast, and geography is at the core of it all. *The Penguin Dictionary of Geography* is the leading guide to the subject, giving clear, concise definitions of key concepts in physical and human geography, from the *shadow effect* to *eluviation* to *cladistics*. This award-winning text is targeted at students and teachers from GCSE upwards, and also takes account of new developments in this fast-changing subject.

* Ideal for any student from GCSE to undergraduate

* Includes clear, easy-to-read diagrams and illustrations for entries such as *cliff formation*, *plate tectonics* and *population pyramids*

* Explains terms used in human geography, from *sociology* to *psychology*, *population studies* to *economics*

* Covers terms connected with all aspects of the natural environment, from *geology* to *economy*, *climatology* to *soil science*

* Discusses recent developments in such areas as *feminist geography*, *sustainability* and *globalization*

* Ranges from core vocabulary to specialist terms and concepts

ONLY PENGUIN GIVES YOU MORE

PENGUIN REFERENCE LIBRARY

THE PENGUIN DICTIONARY OF GEOLOGY

EDITED BY PHILIP KEAREY

'User friendly ... concise but informative'
The Times Higher Education Supplement

Siderophile, interfluve, charnockite: these are the terms that define the earth that
we live on. The study of earth sciences is a complex one, full of specialist terms,
making an authoritative dictionary a crucial purchase. *The Penguin Dictionary of
Geology* is the most extensive and authoritative guide to earth sciences available.
Covering over 7,700 key terms in meticulous detail, it explains not only the core
vocabulary of 'the study of the solid earth' but also incorporates the related
disciplines of astronomy, biology, environmental geoscience, chemistry and
physics. The result is an up-to-date dictionary that will be a must-buy for student,
researcher or keen amateur geologist.

- Gives comprehensive coverage of the core subject areas in sharp, concise
  definitions, from *labile* to *birnessite* to *ventifact*

- Provides helpful tables showing geological ages of the earth and SI conversion
  units

- Includes an extensive easy-to-use topic-based bibliography for further reference

ONLY PENGUIN GIVES YOU MORE

PENGUIN REFERENCE LIBRARY

THE PENGUIN BOOK OF FACTS

EDITED BY DAVID CRYSTAL

'One of the greatest reference books ever published' *Independent on Sunday*

Funafuti is the capital of which south Pacific island? Which dog-toting film star's real name is Frances Gumm? How far is Brussels from Paris? *The Penguin Book of Facts* is the most comprehensive and authoritative general factbook available. Calling upon his famously encyclopaedic knowledge, David Crystal has compiled this international information bible with meticulous precision, layering fact upon fact in a logical order, from the beginnings of the universe to the World Water Skiing Union. It is not only the authoritative and infinite breadth of knowledge that sets this dictionary apart; Crystal has added an invaluable and comprehensive index that makes finding that elusive fact all the easier.

- Contains more facts than any other book of its kind and is illustrated throughout

- Includes contributions from over 250 experts

- This is the updated edition of *The New Penguin Factfinder*

ONLY PENGUIN GIVES YOU MORE

PENGUIN REFERENCE LIBRARY

THE PENGUIN DICTIONARY OF CLASSICAL MYTHOLOGY

EDITED BY PIERRE GRIMAL

'An essential source' *Library Journal*

Who bore children by a bear and was transformed into a bird as punishment? Why exactly did Zeus turn his lover into a cow? Classical myth is a vibrant and entertaining world, and Pierre Grimal's seminal text *The Penguin Dictionary of Classical Mythology* is indisputably the finest guide available. Meticulously researched and thoroughly cross-referenced, the text is accessible and informative, sweeping in its breadth and comprehensive in its detail. You will find the no less than *four* versions of the beautiful *Helen*'s birth, as well as lengthy explanations of all the major figures and events – from *Odysseus* to *Heracles* to *Troy* to the *Jason* and the *Argonauts*.

- Discusses all the heroes and heroines of Homer, Sophocles, Aeschylus and Euripides (amongst many others), from *Venus* to *Pandora* via *Apollo* and *Aphrodite*

- Demonstrates how and where classical mythology has resurfaced and influenced the works of later painters and writers, from Freud to James Joyce

- Includes comprehensive cross-referencing and genealogical tables to show the complex links between different characters and myths

ONLY PENGUIN GIVES YOU MORE

PENGUIN REFERENCE LIBRARY

THE PENGUIN DICTIONARY OF CRITICAL THEORY

EDITED BY DAVID MACEY

'Lucid, spirited entries…Controversial territory, bravely surveyed'
Marina Warner

'Remarkable…It is certainly a reference book I will want to have on my own shelves' David Lodge

The twentieth century contributed a multitude of influential ideas, but where do you start deciphering them? *The Penguin Dictionary of Critical Theory* is the perfect first step into this complex world. Highly acclaimed, this dictionary collates all the major ideas, thinkers and movements that arose or influenced the last century, from *film noir* to *Derrida* and *Freud* to *postmodernism*. This is a book of a thousand introductions and a vital handbook for any student or other philosophically-minded person.

- Includes incisive overviews of the work of key figures, from *Arendt* and *Bataille* to *Orwell* and *Nietzsche*

- Offers powerful summaries of areas such as *deconstruction* and *desire*, *object relations* and *Orientalism*, *postcolonial theory* and *structuralism*

- Gives clear explanations of the links and the disagreements between different thinkers and schools

ONLY PENGUIN GIVES YOU MORE

PENGUIN REFERENCE LIBRARY

THE PENGUIN DICTIONARY OF ART AND ARTISTS

EDITED BY PETER AND LINDA MURRAY

'A vast amount of information intelligently presented, carefully detailed, abreast of current thought and scholarship and easy to read'
The Times Literary Supplement

Why exactly did Van Gogh cut off his ear? Was Warhol an original, or was he just a copyist? The answers to all this and more are found in *The Penguin Dictionary of Art and Artists*, the essential guide to over 700 years of creative endeavour. A brilliant, updated seventh edition of an essential reference work, it charts the lives of over 1200 painters, as well as a wide range of periods, ideas, processes and movements. Any artist or student of the arts will not be able to survive without one. Each entry features extensive cross-referencing and listings of galleries where the artist's work can be seen.

- Short, incisive biographies on every notable (and not so notable) artist of the past seven centuries, from *Caravaggio* to *Picasso* to *Zoffany*, citing their location in the world's museums

- Descriptions of artistic techniques (*collage*), styles (*nocturne*) and materials (*stump*)

- Definitions of artistic movements, from *Cubism* to *Impressionism* to *Dada*

ONLY PENGUIN GIVES YOU MORE

PENGUIN POCKET REFERENCE

THE PENGUIN POCKET DICTIONARY OF QUOTATIONS
EDITED BY DAVID CRYSTAL

The Penguin Pocket Dictionary of Quotations is essential reading for
anyone searching for the perfect quotation – whether you need a
snappy one-liner for a speech or a remark of brilliant insight for your
written work. With this pithy and provocative selection of wit and
wisdom, you will never be lost for words again.

– Includes quotations from a vast range of people, from film stars to
  politicians
– Arranged alphabetically by name of person quoted, with the original
  source for each quotation given
– Provides a full index of key words to help you find each quotation
  quickly and easily

---

www.penguin.com

PENGUIN POCKET REFERENCE

THE PENGUIN POCKET SPELLING DICTIONARY
EDITED BY DAVID CRYSTAL

The Penguin Pocket Spelling Dictionary is indispensable for anyone
who wishes to check a spelling quickly and easily. It shows how to
spell virtually all the words you are likely to encounter on a daily basis
and highlights areas where mistakes are commonly made.

- Includes over 70,000 entries

- Gives capsule definitions for unusual and frequently confused words,
  and panels discussing points of interest

- Provides British and American spellings

PENGUIN POCKET REFERENCE

POCKET ROGET'S® THESAURUS
GEORGE DAVIDSON

Roget's Thesaurus is the world's most trusted wordfinder and a writer's best friend, and this Pocket edition is ideal for helping you to find the exact words you need for all your written work. It will help improve your knowledge and use of the English language, build up your vocabulary and provide the key to stimulating and creative writing.

- Contains over 880 sections, covering objects, activities and abstract words and phrases
- Includes formal English, technical language, slang and jargon
- Provides full cross-referencing

'The indispensable guide to the English language' *Daily Express*

www.penguin.com